Exploitation,
Conservation,
Preservation

Exploitation, Conservation, Preservation

A GEOGRAPHIC PERSPECTIVE
ON NATURAL RESOURCE USE

by
SUSAN L. CUTTER
HILARY LAMBERT RENWICK
WILLIAM H. RENWICK

Rutgers University

ROWMAN & ALLANHELD
PUBLISHERS

ROWMAN & ALLANHELD

Published in the United States of America in 1985
by Rowman & Allanheld, Publishers
(A division of Littlefield, Adams & Company)
81 Adams Drive, Totowa, New Jersey 07512

Library of Congress Cataloging in Publication Data

Cutter, Susan L.
  Exploitation, conservation, preservation.

  Includes index.
  1. Natural resources. 2. Environmental policy.
I. Renwick, Hilary Lambert. II. Renwick, William H.
III. Title
HC21.C96 1985   333.7′2   84-18298
ISBN 0-86598-129-9

Cover and text design by Herb Fink.

85 86 87 / 10 9 8 7 6 5 4 3 2 1

Printed in the United States of America

Contents

4   The Ecological Bases of Natural Resources

5   Population: The Human System

6   Agriculture and the Soil Resource

7 Rangelands: Food Resources for Animals

8 Forests: A Multiple Use Resource

14   Minerals: Finite or Infinite?

15   Energy: The Universal Resource

16   Predicting the Future: Global Modeling

Epilogue

Tables and Figures

Tables

Figures

Preface

Natural resource conservation has been an important college level course for several decades, and many good texts have been written on the subject. In the fifteen years since the first Earth Day, students' interest in environmental issues has been high. The textbooks most used in these years have reflected the ideals of the recent environmental movement, with a concern for natural environmental processes, pollution control, the population explosion, and depletion of mineral and other resources.

The environmental movement of the 1960s and 1970s was one of idealism. Today those ideals have been incorporated into many aspects of government policy, business practice, and the everyday concerns of the general population. Since natural resource issues are now an integral part of our economic, political, and social lives, we as concerned citizens must examine the many facets of these issues.

In this book, we have integrated physical, economic, social, and political considerations in our examination of the major natural resource issues facing the world today. We take the view that none of these factors alone determines the suitability of a resource for any particular use at any particular time. Rather a dynamic interplay causes continuing changes in methods and rates of resource exploitation. The title, *Exploitation, Conservation, Preservation,* includes three value-laden and politically charged words that have been at the heart of the natural resources debate over the last century. The subtitle, *A Geographic Perspective on Natural Resource Use,* reflects the tradition in the geographic discipline of integrating studies of physical and human phenomena in understanding human use of the earth.

Although we share this approach to the subject, we come from diverse scientific, philosophical, and political backgrounds. Accordingly, with the exception of the epilogue we have avoided, as much as possible, taking any one point of view. Instead, we have attempted to include a wide range of opinions and interpretations of natural resource issues, in the hope that this will provide both a balanced review and a basis for discussion.

A glossary has been included for students' use. The definitions given are not universal but rather they are specific to usage in this text.

In the early stages of preparing the manuscript, various chapters were the primary responsibility of one or two of us. In its final form, however, each of us has written at least part of each chapter. We have shared these responsibilities equally, and our names are listed alphabetically.

During the preparation of the manuscript, many people aided us by providing reference materials, illustrations, critical reviews, and moral support for our efforts. Our thanks for their hard work go to Jacquelyn Beyer, Robert Dahl, David

Greenland, Elizabeth Hobbs, Susanna Leers, Ned Lipman, Robert Ostergren, Joanna Regulska, and Robert Roundy. In addition, for their heroic efforts we thank the staff of the Rutgers Cartography Laboratory, notably Gina Bedoya, Paul Fasano, Ken Klothe, William McMullen, Michelle Pronio, and Michael Siegel. The Rutgers Cartography Laboratory or we as authors produced figures and photographs not otherwise credited. To Langdon S. Warner, we extend warm thanks for help with the chapter on oceans. We also greatly appreciate the efforts of our editor, Paul Lee, who knew when to be in touch and when to stay away. We would also like to thank the production staff including managing editor Toby Dicker Hopstone for their assistance during the final stages of the project. And of course, we thank Penelope, Barbara, Donna, and Margaret. All of you have helped us during this arduous and challenging period. The three of us accept all responsibility for any errors and share credit with everyone who helped us for any praise this book may receive.

S.L.C.
H.L.R.
W.H.R.

CHAPTER ONE

Natural Resources: Thoughts, Words, and Deeds

INTRODUCTION

Have you ever wondered what went into the manufacture of the pencil you are now using? A seed germinated and consumed soil nutrients, sprouted and was warmed by the sun, breathed the air, was watered by the rain, and grew into a beautiful straight tree. The tree was cut down. It rode a river's current, was stacked in a lumber yard, and was sawed into small pieces. This wood was transported to a factory where it was dried, polished, cut, drilled, inserted with graphite (which is made from coal), and painted. Then consider how the pencil made its way to you. It has been packaged attractively with appealing letters painted down its side, shipped via truck, and stored in a warehouse. Your pencil's active life will not end with you, as it may be used by many other hands and minds, if you lose or discard it.

Where are the natural resources in that description? *Resources* are things that have utility. *Natural resources* are resources that are derived from the earth system and exist independently of human activity. The seed, the tree, the soil, air, rainwater, sun, river, and graphite are all natural resources. They are out there, despite whether human beings choose to use them. They are the "neutral stuff" (Zimmerman, 1951) that makes up the world, but they become resources when we find utility in them.

Now, consider the role of human effort in the creation, sale, and use of that pencil. What motivates people to select and use some portions of the neutral stuff? It is here that we are able to isolate the subject matter of this book. That is, geographers examine the interactions between human beings and the neutral stuff—the earth and its working parts. When we focus on natural resources, we are asking, What portions of the earth's whole have people found of value? Why? How do these values arise? How do conflicts arise? How are they resolved? Even though neutral stuff may exist outside of our use, it becomes a resource within the context of politics, culture, and economics. Let us begin, then, to try to understand how and why resources emerge and are used and fought over.

RESOURCE COGNITION AND VALUE

A resource does not exist without someone to use it. Resources are by their very nature human-centered. To complicate the picture, different groups of people value resources differently. Let's look at the role of environmental cognition in the emergence of resource use.

Environmental cognition is the mental process of making sense out of the environment that surrounds us. To cognize, or think about the environment, leads to the formation of images and attitudes about the environment and its parts. Because we constantly think and react to the environment, our cognition of it is constantly changing on some levels. Nevertheless, certain elements of environmental cognition will remain stable throughout our lives. There are a number of factors that influence our cognition of resources and thus how they will be used. These can be grouped into five broad categories: (1) cultural background, (2) view of nature, (3) social change, (4) scarcity, and (5) technological and economic factors (see Figure 1.1).

There are many different cultures in the world, and each has a different system of values. What is valued as a resource in one may not be valued in another. In fact, what has value and meaning in one culture may be regarded as a nuisance in another. The mesquite, a deep-rooted dry-lands shrub, is a good example. Ranchers in West Texas feel the need to fight the thirsty mesquite because they perceive that it dictates what will flourish and what will wither and die in the semiarid environment. Range grasses are shallow-rooted and do not compete well with mesquite, and without these grasses, range animals are deprived of a source of food. According to a recent article, "The rancher enjoys with his mesquite the same relationship that Wile E. Coyote maintains with the Roadrunner in the children's cartoon; the rancher will try anything short of nuclear weapons to conquer mesquite" (*Time*, 1982). Yet, not too long ago, the Indians of the American Southwest lived quite harmoniously with the now pesky mesquite. The

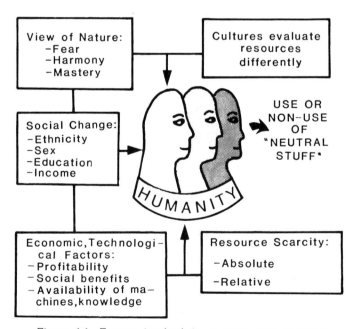

Figure 1.1 Factors involved in resource use cognition include cultural evaluation, view of nature, social change, economic and technological factors, and resource scarcity.

mesquite was used for fuel and shade, while the bush's annual crop of high food-value beans was a staple resource. Even diapers were fashioned from the bark. Recently, mesquite became popular as a fuel for gourmet barbeques.

A society's view of itself relative to its natural environment is the second indicator of how it will ultimately use natural resources. On an idealized spectrum, different world views range from fear of or domination by nature through trying to live in harmony with nature to a desire to have control of nature (Kluckhohn et al., 1961) (see Figures 1.2 and 1.3). Of course, there is variation within any one group; not all members will agree on their view of nature.

Social change also influences the value and use of resources. The composition of societies is constantly changing. People grow older, richer, and poorer, and the cultural makeup of societies changes. All of these factors, particularly ethnicity, sex or gender, education, and income, influence how societies cognize and use resources. For example, higher income households in the U.S. use more water than do lower income households. Lobsters in colonial New England were fed to indentured servants as a cheap food resource. It was not until in the late 19th century and the influx of southern European immigrants, who regarded the lobster highly, that it became a valuable culinary delicacy.

Cognition of future resources is colored by historical and current use. Cognitions also change over time. Because of this, planning for natural resource use in the future must take account of these changes. Economists, politicians, and industrialists find it difficult to forecast accurately future resource uses (see Chapter 16). As a result, we may overlook today a resource that will become invaluable in twenty years.

Figure 1.2 A Japanese garden. Such formal gardens express love for nature's forms but require rigid control over their arrangement and appearance.

Figure 1.3 Formal European gardens of the 16th century, such as this one at Schönnbrunn Palace in Vienna, expressed a view of nature as beautiful when wholly under human control.

The fourth factor influencing natural resource cognition and use is resource scarcity. As a natural resource becomes scarce or is cognized as becoming scarce, its value may increase. This scarcity may be of two different types. *Absolute scarcity* occurs when the supplies of that resource are insufficient to meet present and future demand. The exhaustibility of all supplies and known reserves of some resources is possible, if improbable. The dwindling supply of some of our land resources such as wilderness could conceivably lead to an absolute scarcity of these. *Relative scarcity* occurs when there are imbalances in the distribution of a resource rather than the insufficiency of the total supply. This can be either short or long term. Climatic fluctuations resulting in floods, droughts, or frost routinely cause relative shortages of fresh produce. Open space was not considered a resource until it became relatively scarce in urban areas. Then it became something to be valued, protected, and incorporated into urban redevelopment plans. Relative scarcity also results from one group being able to control the ownership or distribution of resources at the expense of another group. In the energy crisis of the mid-1970s, Americans were told by both environmental and industry experts that the supply of oil and gas was dwindling—and that it would be impossible to meet future demand due to absolute scarcity of the resource. Yet, ten years later, we see higher prices and a more than adequate supply, suggesting that relative scarcity was in fact the cause of the energy crisis.

Finally, the fifth set of factors that influence resource cognition and use are technological and economic, both basic to understanding the role of scarcity. Technological factors relate to our knowledge and skills in exploiting resources.

Groundwater is not a resource until it is made available by drilling a well and installing pumps or other means to bring it to the surface. Desert lands have little agricultural value unless we possess the technical capability to collect and distribute irrigation water, at which time they become very valuable. Deuterium in the oceans is not presently a resource, except for its use in weapons. However, if we learn how to control the fusion reaction for energy production in the future, it will become a resource.

Economic factors combine technology and cognition, as reflected in our pricing system. That is, the value or price of a commodity is determined by its physical characteristics plus our ability and desire to exploit those characteristics. In a capitalist economic system a commodity will not be exploited unless this can be done at a profit. Therefore, as prices change, things become (or cease to be) resources. A deposit of oil in a remote location may be too expensive to exploit today, but if prices rise substantially it may become profitable to exploit and sell that oil; at that time it becomes a resource.

Rarely is the status of a resource determined by technological, cognitive, or economic factors alone; usually it is a combination of these. The nuclear power industry is a good example. The development of fission reactors and related technology was necessary for uranium to become a valuable energy resource. But rapid expansion of nuclear generating capacity depends on this energy source being economically competitive with other sources, such as coal and oil. Coal has become costly to use, in part because of concerns about the negative environmental effects of air pollution. This high cost of coal-generated electricity helped make nuclear power competitive. But the belief that nuclear power is unsafe, along with related environmental concerns, has necessitated modifications in plants that have driven up the cost of nuclear power to the point that it is less economically attractive today than in the early 1970s. In addition, many people, citing environmental and health fears, reject nuclear energy at any price. The interplay of these forces will continue to affect the choice of nuclear power relative to other energy sources for some time.

KINDS OF RESOURCES

Classifying Resources: How Useful a Task?

There are various ways to classify resources. We can ask, How renewable are they? and Who benefits from them? *Perpetual resources* (Figure 1.4) are resources that will always exist in relatively constant supply regardless of how or whether we exploit them. Solar energy is a good example of a perpetual resource; it will continue to arrive at the earth at a reasonably constant rate for the forseeable future. In the past the atmosphere and precipitation were regarded as perpetual resources. Recently, however, their quality and the absolute supply of rainfall in some locations have been questioned.

Resources that can be depleted in the short run but that replace themselves in the long run are called *renewable* or *flow resources.* Forests, most groundwater, and fisheries are good examples. Although they can be depleted by harvesting in excess of the replacement rate, if given sufficient time and the right conditions, natural processes will replace them. The key to maintaining the availability of

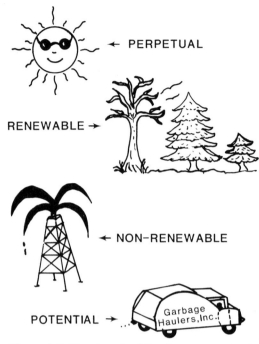

Figure 1.4 The four traditional resource classifications. In reality, a resource can shift from one
category to another.

renewable resources is keeping our rate of use at or below the rate of natural
replacement.

Nonrenewable or *stock resources* exist in finite supply and are not generated
at a significant rate in comparison to our use of them. Once they are used up,
that is the end of them. Most geologic resources, such as fossil fuels and mineral
ores, are of this type.

Finally, *potential resources* are not resources at present but may become
resources in the future depending on cognitive, technological, and economic
developments (see Chapter 13). Their potential depends in part on decisions
made about them today. Should we make decisions that eliminate them from
consideration (e.g., allowing a plant or animal species to become extinct), then
there is no chance of our discovering a resource value in them.

Although it may seem that these definitions are relatively clear, to a large
extent the status of any resource as perpetual, renewable, or nonrenewable
depends on the time scale we view it in and on how we manage the resource.
Even though rainfall on the global level is reasonably constant from year to year,
in many areas the quality of that water has been changed by industrial and
auto emissions producing acid rain. In a longer time scale, there is some evidence
that we may be causing climatic changes that would become evident in the next
century, causing increases or decreases in rainfall at the regional level if not
worldwide. Generally regarded as a renewable resource, soil will restore some
degree of its natural fertility if left in grassland for a few years. But, if accelerated
erosion removes a substantial portion of the soil profile, the ability of that soil
to support plants that restore nutrients and organic matter may be impaired. It

may be centuries before the soil is again productive. That time period is probably too long to consider the soil renewable in human terms. Similarly groundwater is generally considered a renewable resource, but in many areas, particularly desert areas where it is so important, the natural rate of recharge is *very low,* and in some cases there is presently little or no recharge. In these cases the groundwater is effectively a stock resource; once it is used, it is lost forever (see Chapter 9). For these reasons traditional definitions of resources tell us little about the true nature of particular resources. In fact, they may be harmful, leading us to think that a renewable resource will always be available regardless of how we exploit it. These classifications illustrate, however, that not all resources are equal to the demands put on them. They also indicate the importance of examining the detailed characteristics of resources and their ability to meet our needs under varying conditions.

Conserving Resources: What Does It Mean?

Certainly, few politicians would ever admit to being against the conservation of natural resources, but just as certainly people disagree on what that phrase means. Some believe that it means limited or no use of certain resources. A person with this point of view might maintain that no air pollution is acceptable and that wilderness cannot be wilderness if there are any people in it. Others feel that conservation means efficient use. They argue that a resource should be used to produce the greatest possible human good. Resources are beneficial, but only if they are used; disuse is seen as waste. Some of the history of the development of these two viewpoints in the U.S. is discussed in Chapter 3.

The disagreement, however, is even more complex than this. There are many definitions of the meaning of efficient, because few agree on what is truly beneficial. Is profit the highest benefit? Or is spiritual renewal the best use? If a beautiful valley is filled with four houses to the acre, each resident has a home and a quarter-acre of land. Is this a more efficient and beneficial use than making the valley into a park, so that thousands can enjoy it, albeit less often?

Also, how much time should be considered for use of a resource? Should its beneficial use be spread over many years, in small amounts? Or should we gain all the benefits we can now and use other resources in the future? In some cases these questions can be answered in rational terms, but much of the time they are philosophical or political in nature. As suggested by the title, this book presents many viewpoints regarding resource use along a spectrum from those who advocate full use (or exploitation), through those who would conserve (or balance use with protection) to those who would preserve (or remove from use those resources in need of full protection).

THE SYSTEMS APPROACH

In the 4th century B.C., the Greek philosopher Aristotle stated that the whole is greater than the sum of its parts. This view, more fully developed over the centuries, argues that we should understand the entire world by examining all of it at once, rather than looking at each of its constituent parts and then adding them up. During the 20th century this holistic view has gained acceptance in many fields of study. As a rebellion against traditionally narrow scientific viewpoints, it advocates a comprehensive, integrated view of the world instead of a limited, reductionist one.

This line of thinking was formalized in the scientific community in the 1950s under the heading of *general systems theory* (Bertalanffy, 1950). Systems thinking is a way of viewing the world. The systems approach encourages understanding of complex systems and provides an array of systems-management alternatives. The focus is on the comprehensive treatment of a whole by a simultaneous treatment of all parts. A systems approach not only examines the parts individually but also looks at how they interact both with each other and as part of the entire system. The systems approach embodies two perspectives, a qualitative and a quantitative framework. The qualitative framework provides the philosophy, that is, the way of looking at issues and understanding them. The quantitative framework provides the methodology and techniques for measuring systems and assisting in exploring decision-making alternatives. The development of techniques of measurement, advances in statistics, and use of computers aided the rapid acceptance of systems thinking since the 1960s. Systems thinking, then, provides us with a way of analyzing systems or problems and helps us anticipate potential outcomes to recognized problems. Geographers use the systems approach to make sense of both natural and human systems and to better understand why the two types interact as they do.

What Is a System?

A *system* is a set of interrelated components or parts that form a whole. These components have relationships with each other. In examining a system the researcher emphasizes not only the specific attributes of each component but the interactions between components. There are a number of general properties of systems that will aid our understanding of them. First, not only are all systems part of larger systems, but they also contain smaller systems (see Figure 1.5). For example, a river is only a part of the larger hydrologic cycle; a river also contains smaller systems such as floodplains or ecological zones within tributaries. Second, all systems interact with each other. Third, there is an infinite number of systems in the world or, for that matter, the universe.

There are three major kinds of systems: isolated, closed, and open. An *isolated system* exists apart from all interactions with other systems. Neither energy nor matter flows across its boundaries. Can you think of an example? Probably not, for the isolated system exists only in theory. In a *closed system*, energy flows across its boundaries but matter does not. With the exception of the occasional meteor and spacecraft, the earth can be thought of as a closed system. On earth we find *open systems*, across whose boundaries both energy and matter flow. These are the physical and cultural systems that interact to form the world as we know it.

Complexities in Systems

There are many challenges in studying systems. One of these includes the definition of system boundaries. Should the boundary be defined spatially to cover a specific geographic area like a drainage basin? Or should it be defined

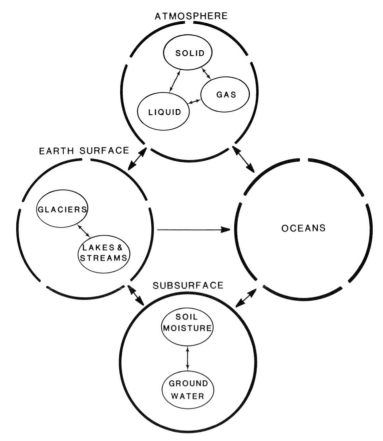

Figure 1.5 Interacting hydrologic systems. Each of the four major systems is made up of component systems.

temporally by looking at a single unit of time? The research question must be well defined, so that appropriate boundaries can be chosen.

Problems also arise because of a need to delimit the effects of systems. Internal effects are those impacts of the system's activity that are felt by the system itself. External effects are those impacts that are felt outside that system. For example, community A discharges wastewater from its sewage treatment plant, causing external effects on the downriver community B, which uses the river as a source of drinking water. In economic terms, these are referred to as externalities (see Chapter 2). Community A may discharge wastewater into the river, only to have its own drinking water supply contaminated if the intake point is below the discharge point. Here, the effects are internal to that community and system.

Knowledge of the short- and long-term effects of systems activity is another complexity. How can we predict with any confidence the effects of today's activities on tomorrow's world? This problem is particularly acute in toxic substances management where the impacts of chemicals on the environment do not and will not emerge for many years. Along the same line, there are differences between separate impacts and synergistic impacts. *Separate impacts* are measured sequentially. The impact of solid waste disposal on a community or the decrease in air quality in the same community are examples of separate impacts. A *synergistic impact* is not only cumulative but also produces an impact greater than the sum of its parts. In the case of water, effluents may actually interact with each other to produce more serious or hazardous forms of pollution.

Lastly, system change is complex. If a system does not change over time it is termed *static*. A *dynamic* system is constantly changing in response to new environmental conditions or to changes in its energy, matter, or information components. A dynamic system may reach equilibrium, where the inputs and outputs are equal. This condition is referred to as a *steady-state system.* Systems in disequilibrium either have more inputs than outputs or more outputs than inputs. In either case, the system is not balanced and is in a constant state of disarray. In a dynamic equilibrium system, outputs become inputs back into the system, which minimizes the external effects of the system's activity. This is often called a *closed-loop system.*

SYSTEMS THINKING AND NATURAL RESOURCES

As we saw with the example of the pencil, natural resource use involves elements of both human and physical systems. The natural systems include the forest ecosystem and the hydrologic cycle; the human systems include technological, economic, and social systems. For improved resource management it is helpful to understand as much as possible about how these systems operate. However, we cannot always know the full details of how a system works. In such a case, does it mean that a systems analysis is meaningless? Not necessarily. It is here that the notion of the "black box" is helpful. Because systems components react to their inputs and in turn produce outputs, we do not necessarily need to have complete information about the system's components or of their precise operations. We can infer a great deal, as long as we know something about what is going in and what is coming out and are able to monitor any changes. The more we know about the system's components, the more we are able to predict the impacts of changes in the system. However, the black box syndrome need not block understanding. A basic unit in the study of the workings of the natural world is a special form of system, called the *ecosystem*. It is a manageable portion of the environment, in which most of the significant energy, matter, and information flows can be measured with some confidence (see Chapter 4).

GENERAL OUTLINE OF THE BOOK

In this book the analysis of natural resources and management policies has both physical and human foci. We stress the interrelationship among the physical attributes of resources, their role in economic systems, and the political and social factors that govern decision-making about their use. We take the view that, even though resources can be classified as perpetual, renewable, nonrenewable, or potential at any given time, they are dynamic and subject to modification or redefinition. Human activity has as much effect on the nature of resources as do natural processes.

Part I focuses on the human and natural components of resource use. Chapter 2 provides an overview of the economics of natural resource use, including pricing systems, demand elasticities, externalities, and the relationship between economic growth and resource use. In Chapter 3 the decision-making process governing resource use and the historical origins of current conservation philosophies in the U.S. are discussed. Chapter 4 provides a review of the ecological bases of natural resources, while Chapter 5 examines the human population system.

Part II deals with specific resource issues. These include agriculture (Chapter 6), grazing (Chapter 7), forests (Chapter 8), water quantity and quality (Chapters 9 and 10), air resources (Chapter 11), oceans (Chapter 12), potential and amenity resources (Chapter 13), minerals (Chapter 14), and finally energy resources (Chapter 15).

Part III examines resource policy for the future and speculates on future resource systems. This includes a critique of models of the future including doomsday predictions (Chapter 16) followed by an epilogue presenting each author's view of the future.

REFERENCES AND ADDITIONAL READING

Bertalanffy, L. von. 1950. An outline of general systems theory. *British J. Phil. Sci.* 1.2, 134–65.

Kluckhohn, F.R., et al. 1961. *Variations in value orientations.* Evanston, Illinois: Row, Peterson & Co.

Time. 1982. Mesquite. March 1.

Zimmerman, E.W. 1951. *World resources and industries.* New York: Harper & Brothers.

TERMS TO KNOW

absolute scarcity
black box
closed-loop system
closed system
cognition
flow resource
general systems theory
internal and external effects
isolated system
natural resources
neutral stuff

nonrenewable resource
open system
perpetual resource
potential resource
relative scarcity
renewable resource
resource
steady-state system
stock resource
system

STUDY QUESTIONS

1. What is a natural resource?
2. What are the five categories of factors that influence resource cognition?
3. Is the list of resources unchanging through time? Why or why not?
4. What are the four major categories of resources?
5. How is it that soil can be both a renewable and a nonrenewable resource?
6. What is meant by the statement "the whole is greater than the sum of its parts"?
7. What are the qualitative and quantitative aspects of systems theory?

CHAPTER TWO

Economics of
Natural Resources

INTRODUCTION

Decisions on the exploitation, management, and protection of natural resources must be made within the social context of a particular culture. No matter what the political ideology or social system, a mechanism must exist for the exchange of goods and services. In most societies this mechanism is price—the *utility* or value society places on an item. The price of a good or service is usually represented by its monetary equivalent. In some cases, however, the price of a good or service can include less tangible values. For example, even though many in the U.S. consider clean water and free-flowing streams valuable, it is often difficult, if not impossible, to place a specific monetary value on such a resource.

As we saw in Chapter 1, natural resources are defined by a society's cognition of that resource and its technical ability to extract the resource. Thus, the value, and therefore price, of the resource can change over time. Since the cognition of a resource can also vary from person to person, the value and price can also change. To further complicate matters, the resource value held by some user groups will be dictated by easily defined market forces, whereas others will have a more intangible system of determining price. A forester, for example, will determine the value of a woodlot based on prevailing market prices for lumber. A hunter, however, will be reluctant to use the supermarket price of meat or poultry to estimate the value of the same woodlot as a game habitat.

The study of natural resource economics requires an understanding of how cognition of natural resources is reflected in the world's various economic systems. No matter what the political system, any study of natural resource economics must first address the relationship between resources that have a monetary value or price and those that do not.

This chapter reviews the role of economics in natural resource management in the U.S. It asks, first, how do we place a value on a natural resource? To operate within an economic system, a value or price of a resource must be determined. Yet, there are many values of a resource that may not be reflected in price. Determination of resource value is, therefore, a key issue in understanding how economic forces influence both the use and the management of a resource. Second, how do these economic forces shape our use and management of resources? Natural resources are cognized mainly as commodities allocated by supply and demand as reflected in price. Many natural resources, however, have unique characteristics (exhaustibility, scarcity, renewability) that alter the economic forces that normally dictate how the economic system controls our use of resources. In addition, an individual's view of how a resource is to be used complicates efforts to apply conventional economic principles to natural resources. For example, short-term pricing mechanisms dictate the use and management of a resource quite differently than would pricing systems based on long-term social needs.

BUILDING BLOCKS OF ECONOMIC SYSTEMS

Characteristics of Natural Resources

In most societies, natural resources are the basic building blocks of the economic system. As raw or unaltered materials, their value is not enhanced by human inputs such as labor. Natural resources thus often have a lower monetary value than the commodities manufactured from them. The value of a standing forest is less than when the trees are cut. Once trees are cut, milled, and dried, value is added to the timber and its price increases. By the time the wood is made into a house or a piece of furniture, the original price of the standing tree accounts for a fraction of the value of the finished product. There are instances where natural resources have a high value "in the ground," but it is the consumer that drives the price up in such cases. If demand is greater than the amount of the resource available, demand, not extraction costs, will determine price.

A second characteristic of natural resources is that supply is relatively inelastic over short periods of time; that is, supply does not change much in response to sudden changes in demand. This is especially true with mineral resources. Suppose, for example, the demand for a particular metal increases significantly. Existing mines can increase production to a certain extent by hiring more miners and purchasing more equipment. To meet the large demand, however, a large increase in production is needed. Building new mines requires geologic exploration, new roads, and other infrastructure before ore extraction actually begins. These changes take time, generally years, so that the supply cannot keep up with increased demand in the short run. This inelastic nature of many resources can encourage wide fluctuations in price. Sudden changes in demand can cause a dramatic rise or fall in price, yet there is little that the producers can do in the short term to ensure a steady long-term trend.

Another characteristic of natural resources is a relatively high degree of substitutability among raw materials with similar properties. Not only can one metal be substituted for another in an automobile, but recently plastics, fiberglass, carbon fibers, and other synthetic materials have begun to replace metals for many purposes. Beet sugar can be substituted for cane sugar, and coal, natural gas, petroleum, and hydropower can be substituted for one another to produce electricity. While this substitutability contributes to stability for the makers of finished products, it often leads to considerable volatility in natural resource markets. The endless pattern of boom and bust cycles in one-employer mining towns is one of the sadder human consequences of this volatility (see Issue 14-1 in Chapter 14).

Finally, for some natural resources, particularly minerals, supply is theoretically infinite, assuming the buyer can pay the price. This is a fourth characteristic of natural resources. Most metals exist in the earth's crust in much greater total quantities than we currently need. The problem is that in only a limited number of locations are they found in high enough concentrations or close enough to the surface to allow extraction at a profit (see Chapter 14). As long as industry is willing to pay a little more to obtain them, miners can dig a little deeper or refine less concentrated ores or go to more remote sites like ocean basins and still obtain the desired commodity. At some point, the users will find that it is ultimately cheaper to recycle used metals than to mine new ores. At that point demand will be met by recycling (see Chapter 14). When we also consider that most minerals can be substituted, then it seems unlikely that a situation will arise in which the world runs out of raw materials. On the other hand, the theoretical supply of energy may or may not be infinite, depending on which technologies are available. Activities such as mining and recycling may very well be limited by shortages of energy rather than shortages of raw minerals.

Pricing Systems

Natural resources are commodities; we desire them for their ability to provide the basic needs of life—food, clothing, shelter, happiness. As commodities, they must somehow be allocated among individuals, groups, and nations either by bartering (exchange of one good for another) or through some type of market exchange involving currency and a pricing system. In most cases the price of the resource is dictated by a determination of its value based upon supply of and demand for the product. Allocation of the resource is not necessarily dictated by price. The economic system, within which resource values are determined, can shape decisions on resource allocation as much as can price. Let's examine the concept of price and the major economic systems in more detail.

Economic Systems

There are three major types of economic systems worldwide: subsistence, commercial, and centrally-planned (Berry, Conkling, and Ray, 1976). In subsistence economies, there is no surplus production of goods. Resources are consumed by those who produce them to meet their basic needs for food, shelter, and clothing. Hunter-gatherer societies such as those found in the tropics or nomadic herding societies are good examples of this type of economic system, but they are not a dominant pattern today.

In a commercial economy, there is a surplus of goods produced, which are exchanged between producers and consumers in the market place. Commercial economies have three primary distinguishing characteristics—profit, specialization, and interdependence. Producers are motivated by a desire for profit, involving pressure to produce goods at a low cost. This usually leads to specialization (producing one good rather than many) and interdependence (reliance on others to provide raw materials or market goods), both of which increase the efficiency of production. This leads to increased production and a lowering of the per unit cost. Profit and efficiency are dictated by these free market forces, where supply and demand govern the price and the quantity of goods exchanged. In a commercial economy, then, the use and allocation of natural resources is governed by many factors, most notably market competition and profit maximization.

These are usually reflected in the price of the commodity. The United States is a good example of a commercial economy.

In centrally-planned economies, the central government controls and allocates resources. The notion of a free market does not exist. Producers market goods and services to the central government, which in turn controls both the supply and price. The allocation of resources by the central government is a function of clearly defined goals and objectives ranging from strict monetary gain to social, economic, and regional parity. The Soviet Union and some Eastern European nations are good examples of centrally-planned economies. In any system, however, some value or price is placed on a resource, permitting its exchange and use by society.

Prices thus can be determined in a variety of ways. For example, the price of a good can be determined by the amount of labor required to produce it or by how much a consumer is willing to pay. Another approach says that in a free market system different producers will compete by reducing prices until they equal the cost of production. Finally, some argue that the price of goods should be a function of the energy required to produce them (Cottrell, 1978).

Even though each of these address at least one aspect of determining the value of resources, in the final analysis in commercial economies, it is the interaction between supply and demand that determines both the price of a good and the quantity sold at that price. This is also true in international markets involving countries with centrally-planned and commercial economies.

Supply, Demand, and Price

The law of supply and demand says that both the amount of a good demanded by consumers and the amount the producers are willing to supply vary as a function of price. As price increases, the quantity consumers are willing to buy decreases and vice versa. On the other hand, as price increases, the quantity that producers are willing to sell increases and conversely. The two curves are plotted together in Figure 2.1; their intersection determines the equilibrium price and quantity sold. If there is a change in prevailing market conditions (e.g.,

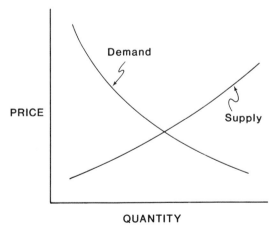

Figure 2.1 Supply and demand curves. Quantities supplied and demanded vary with price.

increasing scarcity of a commodity), then it will cost producers more to supply that commodity. Now they will either require a higher price to produce the same amount, or they will supply less at the same price. Similarly, a change in the value consumers place on a commodity will alter demand with resulting changes in price and quantity sold. Supply and demand operate in the manner described above to determine price only when there is perfect competition. Perfect competition exists when no individual consumer or producer exerts influence on the market, when all producers and consumers have equal access to the market, and when the government does not intervene in the market.

These assumptions about the relationship between supply, demand, price, and perfect markets are constantly violated particularly with the development of monopolies or near-monopolies. A *monopoly* exists when a single buyer or seller dominates the market. *Monopolistic* or *oligopolistic competition* describes the process whereby only a few buyers or sellers are present and either (1) follow a price leader in fixing the price of the commodity or (2) engage in discriminatory practices to set prices so as to maximize their own profits. At such times, the government may intervene in the market either to increase competition or to regulate the market directly. The relationship between supply and demand can also change due to imperfect markets. Because of the volatility of markets like minerals, there are many monopolies involved in the exploitation of natural resources. The size of the investment required to develop resources also limits competition in this area.

There are many resource oligopolies in the world today; they are often referred to somewhat inaccurately, as cartels. A *cartel* is a consortium of commercial producers whose purpose is to limit competition among other producers of the same resource to keep prices artificially high. Similar industries, such as refineries or resource-rich exporting countries, have banded together in attempts to fix world prices of their commodity. The Organization of Petroleum Exporting Countries (OPEC) is a good example of a true cartel. It consists of thirteen member nations who supply a little more than half of the non-communist world's supply of crude oil. Although there are many other resource oligopolies (e.g., the copper, cocoa, bauxite and diamond industries) that would like to have the economic clout of cartels, only the diamond industry retains a truly cartel-like control over its market and prices.

RESOURCE VALUE:
QUANTIFYING THE INTANGIBLES

Not all resources have a value that can be expressed in monetary terms. Consider, for example, the price of clean air or the price we should pay for an unobstructed view of the ocean. Nevertheless, most people do place a subjective value on these resources, and this value should be taken into consideration when choosing among resource management alternatives.

The techniques most widely used by resource decision-makers in assessing resource options are benefit–cost analysis and cost–effectiveness analysis. *Benefit–cost analysis* is used to decide whether or not a project should be undertaken. Federal, state, and local government frequently use benefit–cost analysis to decide whether a particular resource project or regulatory program should be adopted. Such social benefit–cost analysis can be very different from the analysis conducted by a private firm. Instead of simply calculating the present value of expected future monetary costs and benefits, a social benefit–cost analysis requires quantification of items without obvious monetary value, such as the benefits of clean water or the costs of reduced wildlife habitat (see Chapter 13). The U.S. Bureau of Reclamation and the U.S. Army Corps of Engineers have used benefit–cost analyses for decades as justification of their resource development projects.

Cost-effectiveness analysis is used to decide the most effective means of carrying out a project after it has been approved. It involves summing all the costs and monetary returns of each alternative to find the most efficient way to achieve the desired objective. Cost-effectiveness thus aids a governmental agency or firm in determining the least costly and most efficient approach to implementing a development project or regulatory program. Benefit–cost analysis is a tool for helping society make choices on the allocation of resources, whereas cost–effectiveness analysis aids the individual firm or agency in implementing those allocation choices.

Benefit–Cost Analysis

Because this technique is often used as a rationale for certain programs, we will discuss it in more detail. When you go to the supermarket, you are constantly making choices over what and how much to buy. How long will that small jar of peanut butter last? Is it worthwhile to buy a larger jar just to save a few cents? Should I settle for hamburger even though I want prime rib? Economic theory tells us that individuals making such decisions often balance the perceived costs and benefits of each and purchase those items whose benefits appear to outweigh costs by the greatest margin.

The same judgment process in the supermarket can also be found in natural resource decisions. Judgments on whether to build a dam, invest in new timberland, or clean up a polluted river usually involve some type of formal or informal benefit–cost analysis. The analysis itself can range from the elaborate accounting used to justify large governmental water projects (see Chapter 9), to the judgments made by individual farmers, foresters, or fisherfolk. In any case, a value is placed on the expected costs and benefits of a specific project or regulatory program and then these are compared over a given time period (five, ten, or more years). Since there are many variables involved, the most expedient means to compare these costs to benefits is to place a price on each of them. This includes pricing the resource in question, placing a price on the improvements that accrue from the project, and pricing the costs of not completing the project.

This calculation must frequently take into account non-monetary variables (good health, clean air, peace and quiet), if it is properly done. Determining these non-monetary values can have a major impact on the outcome of the credit–debit accounting. Often, the organization conducting the benefit–cost analysis has a vested interest in some particular outcome, leading it to bias its estimates of resource benefits to favor that outcome. In other words, the benefits are inflated to cover the costs resulting in a favorable B:C ratio. This is easy to do since the value determinations of non-monetary variables are highly subjective and open to many interpretations. One common approach to applying the result of a cost–effectiveness analysis is to develop a cost–benefit ratio by separately summing the costs and benefits over time, then dividing benefits by costs. A B:C ratio greater than 1 indicates that benefits are greater than costs and the project should go forward. A B:C ratio can be very misleading when the cost–benefit analysis includes potential environmental impacts. Any project will presumably have some environmental impacts, regardless of the benefits and costs. These impacts should be applied to either the calculation of costs (by addition) or the calculation of benefits (by subtraction) and should be used consistently. Another problem is that the present value of future costs or benefits depends on the interest rate or discount rate used in the calculations. Small changes in interest rates can result in very large differences in project costs. Despite these problems, B:C ratios are frequently used to justify many public works projects (see Issue 2.1).

Quantifying Price

When faced with a decision, for example, on whether to permit lumbering in a national forest, a resource manager seeks various types of information to place into the benefit–cost calculation. Some of this information, such as the value of

---

ISSUE 2.1: The Economics of Sand Dollars

Proponents of commercial economic systems often view themselves as cold, hard realists willing to let the vagaries of the marketplace dictate supply, demand, and price. Does such an approach work in the world of politics as well? An examination of the actions of proponents of recent national legislation protecting barrier islands along the East and Gulf coasts of the U.S. illustrates how economic realities influence a political decision.

Two-thirds of the population of the U.S. live within 100 miles of either the Atlantic or Pacific Oceans or the Great Lakes. The demand for shorefront recreational property, therefore, is high, and access to beaches is a major issue in coastal areas. For over thirty years, environmental groups have been trying to preserve the barrier islands of the East and Gulf coasts from development. The barrier islands, located just off shore, are narrow strips of sand that protect the mainland from coastal storms, enclose highly productive estuaries, and provide habitat for migratory birds and recreation for millions of people. There are over 300 barrier islands, spits, and beaches stretching in a chain from Maine to Texas. Approximately one-

third are fully developed; one-third are at least partially protected by inclusion in National Seashores, parks, and wildlife refuges; while the remaining third are only partially developed but remain in private ownership (U.S. Department of the Interior, 1983).

Barrier islands are inherently unstable as they move and change shape in response to sea level rise, tides, storms, and the longshore transport of sand. Despite the expenditure of billions of dollars in erosion control, neither the U.S. Army Corps of Engineers nor any other governmental agency or private concern has been able to stem the erosion of barrier island beaches. The combination of increasing pressure for development and escalating erosion control costs led to a political impasse by the mid-1970s.

Real estate developers and environmentalists continued to battle over the fate of individual islands, winning some and losing some, while the federal government started to question its own policies. In 1977 the U.S. Department of the Interior conducted a study of the impact of federal policies on the development of barrier islands. By 1980, the Department concluded that the actions

standing timber or the cost of replanting trees after harvest, can be expressed in monetary terms. Other information, such as the value of lost wildlife habitat or the value of lost recreational areas, cannot be readily translated into a monetary value or price. These so-called incommensurables and intangibles can frustrate and often invalidate any benefit–cost analysis.

Incommensurables are effects (both benefits and costs) that can, though not easily or with a great amount of precision, have some monetary value or price attached to them. *Intangibles,* on the other hand, cannot be measured at all, even though economists constantly try. The trick in benefit–cost analysis is to separate the incommensurable effects from the intangible effects. Again, it is imperative to define clearly the limitations of such methods for quantifying these incommensurables.

Economists employ a broad range of techniques to establish the monetary value of incommensurable effects for their benefit–cost calculations. Three of the most commonly used techniques are willingness to pay, proxy value, and replacement cost.

Willingness to pay is a method whereby potential users of a resource are asked how much they are willing to pay for access to the resource, or, conversely, how much society would have to pay the individual not to use the resource. An

of several federal agencies were unintentionally subsidizing development on the flood- and storm-prone islands. Federally insured flood insurance, for example, permitted the building and rebuilding of houses in high-risk areas. Sewage treatment plants funded by the Environmental Protection Agency (EPA) were also encouraging development. Disaster assistance and erosion control also contributed to the problem by increasing development, instead of limiting it. This 1980 study examined several alternative courses of action, which were translated into a matrix of benefits and costs.

The quantification of the benefits and costs of federal actions on barrier islands led to a curious political alliance. By 1980, the federal government, Congress, and environmental groups agreed that something had to be done to prevent the "New Jerseyization" of the remaining less-developed barrier islands but disagreed on how to do it. Despite an intense battle between environmental groups and the Reagan Administration's first Interior Secretary, James Watt, two pieces of legislation were created. The 1981 Omnibus Budget Reconciliation Act prohibited issuance of federal flood insurance

to anyone building on an undeveloped barrier island. The Coastal Barrier Island Resources Act of 1982 then created a 186-unit system of protected areas within which federal subsidy of development is severely limited.

The U.S. Department of the Interior's initial quantification of costs and benefits of various alternatives, ranging from complete protection to doing nothing, became the final cost–effectiveness analysis, because the decision to protect barrier islands had already been made before the impact statement was finished. By examining the costs of various alternatives, it helped decision-makers implement policy. The risk of development on barrier islands is now placed squarely on the individual property owners who derive the benefits of living in these dynamic environments. The federal government and indirectly the individual taxpayer no longer subsidize developers and property owners. The savings to the American taxpayer as a result of this policy amounts to more than $5.4 billion per year (U.S. Department of the Interior, 1983).

example, is a survey of beach users to determine how much they are willing to pay to use the beach or how much they would have to be paid not to go to the beach. The value of the latter could be used to estimate recreational losses resulting from an oil spill that washes ashore. The former could be used to justify beach nourishment projects, importing sand to maintain the beach.

Another technique is determination of the substitute or *proxy value* of a resource, a price assigned to a commodity in the absence of a market value. Here, the value of a day's hunting, for example, is estimated by summarizing the hunter's investment in supplies, time, and travel and dividing this figure by the number of days of hunting. This becomes the estimated value that would have resulted if the project or exploitation did not occur in the first place. Estimating the decline in commercial fish harvest resulting from the destruction of their habitat by an oil spill is another example.

The last technique is called *replacement cost.* This is simply the determination of the cost of replacing the resource that is being used, such as the substitution of clean sand for sand polluted by an offshore oil spill.

The accuracy of these and other methods of estimating the price of incommensurable resources varies (Conservation Foundation, 1980). It is important to recognize the limitations of such techniques as well as their ability to provide the necessary data for benefit–cost calculations. They are useful in placing a comparable value (price) on those resources that normally do not have one, but only within the limitations discussed above.

MANAGEMENT AND ALLOCATION OF RESOURCES

Economic forces shape the value and price of a resource and also enhance or constrain the allocation and management of the resource. The influence of economics on management decisions can best be classified into three categories: ownership, social and environmental costs, and the economics of the individual company or firm.

Ownership

Many natural resources are held in communal, rather than private, ownership. This is true both for government-owned resources such as national forests and offshore mineral rights and for resources for which no formal ownership is designated such as air or oceans. Even though these resources are theoretically owned by everyone, they are, nevertheless, exploited by private individuals and corporations for individual profit. We call these resources *common property resources.* This discrepancy between ownership and management responsibility causes problems in the allocation and management of resources.

The conflict was described by Garrett Hardin (1968) in an article entitled "The Tragedy of the Commons." He showed that if a common property resource is used by a group of individuals, then as long as those individuals are motivated by the desire for personal rather than group profit they will eventually overexploit the resource. The reasoning behind this argument is quite simple. To the user, common property resources offer unlimited opportunities for exploitation that are available equally among all users. It is always in the individual's own best interest to increase use even to the point of overuse and degradation of the resource, as the benefits to the individual will always exceed his or her costs. Hardin concludes that there must be some institutional arrangement that prohibits overuse and encourages conservation. Often, unfortunately, these arrangements will benefit some resource users and hurt others. Hardin's ideal can be reached only if someone loses. The following example should clarify the issue. If a group of people all dump sewage into the same water body, everyone suffers, but for just one person not to dump sewage would be foolish. This one person would still suffer from everyone else's pollution and would not gain only a small benefit from the reduction. The consequence is that some governing body must step in, and through that body all must agree to regulate their use of the resource for mutual benefit.

The importance of the management of common property resources is that it is best to limit the rate of exploitation so that all users benefit. There are, however, no means by which to enforce these limits because access to the resource is unlimited. As a result, some form of intervention is needed, or mismanagement and overuse of the resource will occur. This intervention can be in the form of federal regulations such as the Clean Air and Water Acts or international treaties like the recently negotiated Law of the Sea Treaty. Some of the problems of managing such common property resources as air, water, and oceans are discussed subsequently (see Chapters 9, 10, 11, and 12).

Social Costs

In commercial economies both the producer and the consumer bear the costs of production. These production systems are considered efficient if they maximize output (finished goods or services) at any level of production. Recently economists and others have recognized that not all production systems are efficient. There are certain spillover effects from production that enter the environment and affect consumers disproportionately. These spillover effects are called *externalities* and include pollutants from modern industrial plants, which are routinely discharged into one of the many common-property resources (air, water, public land, oceans).

The problem with externalities is that the private- or government-operated producer wants to minimize costs and maximize profits, forcing the local community to absorb the externality (Seneca and Taussig, 1974). For example, industry XEQ is located upstream from Farmer Brown. XEQ routinely discharges chemicals into the same stream Brown uses to irrigate his crops. Eventually, there is damage to the crops as a result of the contaminated water. Any costs that are attributed to these spillover effects are termed external costs (hence the term externalities). XEQ does not incur any cost for polluting the stream, yet Farmer Brown pays the price in the form of either a reduced harvest because of the pollution or increased costs for a new source of water. Externalities are not borne by the firm in the course of production but are simply imposed on neighbors like Farmer Brown or on society as a whole. Such costs are outside the market system and are not reflected in the price of the manufactured good. *Social cost* is a general term used to connote the costs of initially producing a good plus any external costs.

External costs can be found in any form of production in both commercial and centrally-planned economic systems. In most cases, the pricing structure that dictates the allocation of natural resources does not fully embrace external costs in the price paid for the resource. We are thus left with the problem of managing and coping with these externalities. There have been a number of techniques developed for dealing with them. Most often, these involve some type of economic pricing mechanism or governmental intervention in the form of pollution regulations. Externalities are also called residuals, and residuals management has become a major focus of natural resource economics.

Residuals management describes and quantifies the inputs and outputs of a production system including the residuals (Kneese, Ayres, and d'Arge, 1971). Residuals management advocates a steady-state production system where inputs and outputs are balanced. It recognizes that inputs are not totally consumed in production and eventually end up as waste products (residuals) that then have a cost or price affixed to them.

Specific techniques have been developed to manage residuals. The residuals tax or effluent charge, which was first proposed by Kneese and Bower (1971), would have producers of goods, not consumers, pay for the residuals they have discharged. Under this "polluter pays" principle, taxes are levied against firms in relation to how much pollution they release into the environment. A residuals tax forces the polluter to bear the true social costs of production and contamination of common property resources by internalizing the externalities. It encourages the polluter to reduce the quantity of residuals, since the tax is in direct proportion to the amount discharged. The assessed fee is used either to clean up the environment or to compensate those consumers who are adversely affected by the pollution.

Another technique of residuals management is the throughput tax or disposal charge. Producers of goods are charged a materials fee that reflects the social costs of disposal of the residuals. This tax would, of course, be passed on to the consumer in the form of increased prices for the commodity. While a throughput tax might provide an incentive to recycle and make products last longer, many of the disposal charges currently used, such as deposits on beverage containers, are quite controversial. Both of these taxing mechanisms influence the price of a commodity beyond the simple demand and supply accounting.

Today, most pollution control regulations involve considerable costs, which are borne by the government or by the polluting industries. In the former case, it is the taxpayers who actually bear the cost; in the latter, it is the purchasers of a polluting company's products. Those who pay for pollution control may or may not be those persons who benefit from elimination of pollution. However, the government finds this method of paying for pollution control easier to implement than some of the other methods discussed above.

Economics of the Individual Firm

Thus far our discussion has focused almost entirely on the economics of large governmental agencies and how they manage and allocate natural resources. Private firms are equally important when discussing natural resource economics.

Microeconomics refers to the economics of the individual firm or company. In a commercial system, resource exploitation is undertaken by the firm rather than by society as a whole, so that it is worth examining some microeconomic phenomena that affect natural resource decisions.

The primary goal of a private firm is to earn money for its owners. This is done by investing money in the physical plant (land, machinery, equipment) and in other production inputs (labor, energy) to produce goods that can be sold for more money than was invested. The owner's costs in producing a given good can be divided into two categories, fixed and variable costs.

Fixed costs are bills that must be paid regardless of how much of the product is made in a given time. Fixed costs are primarily the costs of owning the means of production (the physical plant). If the money needed to set up a plant was borrowed, then the fixed costs are the interest payments on the loan; if the money was not borrowed, then they are the cost of not investing the money somewhere else. In general, fixed costs consist mainly of the interest on the value of the physical plant, and costs of maintaining the plant.

Variable costs consist of labor, energy, transportation, and similar inputs in the production process itself, and these vary according to the rate of production. Variable costs are a relatively constant percentage of the selling price of the goods produced, although there are some levels of output that are more efficient than others. Let us assume there is a given investment required to open a particular mine. Afterward, the variable costs are in direct proportion to the rate of extraction of minerals. The faster the minerals are extracted, the greater the profit, since the fixed costs need to be borne for a shorter period of time.

The optimal rate of production is determined by a combination of fixed and variable costs. Fixed costs always have the effect of making the optimal rate of production higher. As interest rates go up, the need to recover the initial investment in a short time increases; hence, rates of production or resource exploitation need to be increased. As a result, there are economic pressures on the firm to maximize the rate of production, regardless of its conservation policy in the long run. This generalization applies only to a single facility, such as a single mine or a single forest unit. A large corporation owning many mines will vary its total output not by varying output at every mine simultaneously but by closing or opening mines. That is how it keeps its fixed costs as low as possible. In most cases there will be pressure on the mining firm to maximize the rate of extraction to recover fixed costs, often at the expense of other environmental considerations.

Another important aspect of the firm relative to natural resources is the degree of liquidity of its assets, or how easily the firm can sell out if it needs to. Remember, the goal of any company is to turn a monetary investment into monetary return, and production of a particular commodity is simply a means to that end. An oil company consists of a group of people who have particular expertise in finding, extracting, and selling oil and who also own the equipment needed to do those things. If that oil company has an opportunity to invest its capital in a housing development or a soft drink bottling plant and receive a greater return on investment than it would in drilling for oil, then it will do so. Only the existing investment in oil-related equipment and experience prevent an oil company from taking its money elsewhere if the financial opportunities are more attractive in some other business.

One significant trend in business in the last two decades, but particularly in the late 1970s and early 1980s, has been toward the *diversification* of large corporations. Tobacco companies buy soap companies; oil companies buy electronics companies; and steel companies buy oil companies. This diversification serves to, among other things, protect large companies from unfavorable market conditions in particular sectors of the economy. It also serves to weaken the commitment of a company to the long-term stability of a particular enterprise or resource. For example, over the last several years some companies have been purchasing farmland as rapidly rising land prices have appealed to some speculative investors. In certain areas of the U.S., large diversified corporations have become major holders of agricultural land. If they carry on a policy of maximizing return on investment in relatively short periods of time (ten to twenty years), then they may very well be driven to practices that lead to excessive soil erosion over longer time periods. In this instance the best interests of the firm are not the best interests of society as a whole.

The large forest-product (lumber, paper) companies are an exception to this tendency of corporations to be interested only in short-term returns. Although many of them are diversified, they also own large tracts of land that require decades to produce harvestable trees. As a result they maintain a long-term commitment to those lands and their ability to produce trees.

Another important trend of the last few decades has been the formation and growth of multinational corporations. These companies operate in several countries or own or collaborate with companies in several countries. They have the ability to shift resources, production, and marketing activities from one country to another depending on where potential profits are greatest. They are generally large enough to have major control over markets in individual nations, if not at the world level. Their ability to move money and commodities internationally greatly limits the controls that individual governments have over them, making it more difficult to force consideration of social costs in decision-making. Recently, new controls have been established on the disposal of hazardous wastes in the U.S. and other wealthy nations. Many Third World nations, however, have either chosen not to restrict this activity or lack the ability to do so. As a result, hazardous wastes are now exported and disposed of in other countries, often improperly, rather than being properly handled in the country of origin.

During the mid-1980s, the People's Republic of China offered to accept, on a paying basis, the developed world's nuclear and other radioactive waste for long-term storage in the remote and unpopulated Gobi Desert. This suggests that some nations are so desperate for foreign exchange that they are willing to take on dreadful environmental risks. Skeptics, on the other hand, suspect that China will attempt to reprocess wastes for use in building the nation's nuclear arsenal. Capital also moves internationally, and this movement is not always in the best interests of all countries. One of the factors in the decline in domestic oil exploration in the U.S., that preceded the energy crises of the 1970s, was the movement of American exploration and production activities overseas, particularly to the Middle East.

Multinational corporations have also greatly increased the degree of worldwide economic integration. Markets for resources are controlled by world supply and demand rather than at the national level. A shortage or scarcity of a commodity in one country causes increases in prices in other countries.

CONCLUSIONS

The business of natural resource use is fundamentally no different from any other business. It is governed by the same desire to turn investment into profit as quickly as possible and is subject to the same vagaries of economics caused by fluctuating interest rates, inflation, and the ups and downs of business cycles. While we often blame our government, big corporations, foreign governments, or natural calamities for problems related to natural resource supply or prices, in almost all instances the real causes can be traced to the economic constraints on the business involved and the simple desire of companies to make as much profit as possible.

Natural resources, however, differ from other commodities in that they are fundamentally important to us all, and many are commonly owned. Decisions involving natural resources are, therefore, very likely to have external costs and social effects that businesses do not normally consider. Government intervention is necessary to modify the management process, so that intangible resources, long-term needs, and social costs can be managed along with the commodities that move through the economic system.

REFERENCES AND ADDITIONAL READING

Berry, B.J.L., E.C. Conkling, and D.M. Ray. 1976. *The geography of economic systems.* Englewood Cliffs, New Jersey: Prentice-Hall.

Conservation Foundation. 1980. "Cost-benefit analysis: a tricky game." *Conservation Foundation Letter.* December:1–8.

Cottrell, A. 1978. *Environmental economics.* New York: Wiley, Halsted Press.

Hardin, G. 1968. The tragedy of the commons. *Science* 162:1243–48.

————. 1972. *Exploring new ethics for survival: the voyage of the spaceship Beagle.* New York: Viking.

Kneese, A.V., R.V. Ayres, and R.C. d'Arge.

1971. *Economics and the environment: a materials balance approach.* Baltimore: Johns Hopkins University Press.

Kneese, A.V., and B.T. Bower, eds. 1971. *Environmental quality analysis: theory and method in the social sciences.* Baltimore: Johns Hopkins University Press.

Seneca, J.J., and M.K. Taussig. 1974. *Environmental economics.* Englewood Cliffs, New Jersey: Prentice-Hall.

U.S. Department of the Interior. 1983. *Final environmental statement: undeveloped coastal barriers.* Washington, D.C.: Government Printing Office.

TERMS TO KNOW

cartel
common property resources
diversification
externalities
fixed costs
free-market forces
incommensurables
inelastic
interdependence
microeconomics
monopoly

multinational corporations
oligopolistic competition
perfect competition
profit
residuals management
residuals tax
social cost
specialization
throughput tax
variable costs

STUDY QUESTIONS

1. What are the four characteristics of natural resources?
2. What are the three major economic systems?
3. Do the laws of supply and demand work perfectly? Why or why not?
4. What is the difference between benefit–cost analysis and cost–effectiveness analysis? Between incommensurables and intangibles?
5. What are the three ways in which economic considerations influence natural resource management decisions?
6. How are residuals managed?

CHAPTER THREE

Environmental Ideology and the Decision-Making Process

INTRODUCTION

Government policy is a fundamental determinant of how natural resources are exploited and conserved. In the United States, the policies that control natural resource use have been developed over three centuries by both governmental and private actions. Governmental policy is a product of the political process, constrained by history and precedent. The political process, in turn, is essentially one of confrontation and compromise among many disparate interests, both economic and ideologic. This chapter begins with a brief overview of human impact on the environment worldwide. This sets the stage for discussing the historical development of natural resource policy in the U.S. and the laws and institutions that have evolved since European settlement. A section on decision-making and resource management summarizes the models developed to explain why U.S. resource decision-makers proceeded as they have. In addition, this chapter examines the various ideological and economic interest groups that are the major forces in the national political arena today and how the political process establishes and modifies natural resource policy.

NATURAL RESOURCE USE: A HISTORICAL PERSPECTIVE

Conservationist Max Nicholson sees human history as a process of increasing our ability to manipulate and alter usable aspects of the physical environment. He suggests (1970) that in the early stages of human evolution, at least 2 million years ago, the natural environment was largely unaffected by humans. Small numbers of proto-humans in their hunting bands, with simple technology (bone, stone, and wood tools and hunting pits), were generally capable of competing with animal species. Like animals, proto-humans were also at the mercy of climate and topography. Early humans did not have the technological skills to master the earth's more difficult climates. Thus they were best able to use the food and shelter resources of open and coastal lands, locations that were far more vulnerable to natural hazards such as floods than to any alteration by people.

Nicholson and others agree that the first human tool to have a major environmental impact was fire. Early humans used it to drive animals into traps; when agriculture was developed between 10,000 and 7,000 B.C., fire was used to clear land for crops and to create grazing areas for livestock. Fire is the only case in which the capacity of modern technology to alter the environment is matched by that of the pretechnological humans. The deliberate use of fire affected the environment in three ways: (1) it affected a large area, since it was widespread; (2) it was a repetitive process and could cover the same areas at frequent intervals; (3) it was highly selective in its effects on animal and plant species, having a negative effect on some, while encouraging those with rapid powers of recovery or resistance to fire (Nicholson, 1970). The environmental result was to improve the yield of certain species for human use and to modify the vegetation cover. These early effects were confined largely to tropical, subtropical, and temperate forests and grasslands, as well as to some wetlands.

At least 10,000 years ago the human race had spread to all continents except Antarctica. With the shift from hunting and gathering to agriculture, human culture developed more sophisticated food production tools for harvesting, transporting, and planting. Also, in drier areas in the Middle East and later elsewhere, large-scale irrigation works were built. The sedentary life of the agriculturalist went hand-in-hand with the development of cities. Agriculture and urbanization led for the first time to a substantial change in land use, from natural to human-made forms of productivity, in the form of fields, streets, homes, and irrigation ditches. The development of cities led to large-scale environmental disruption and change, because of the concentration of large populations and the wide areas in which land was cultivated, grazed, cleared of trees, and subjected to erosion to support the urban population. Also, through the domestication of plants and animals, people were able to direct the energy and nutrients of an ecosystem to produce more of certain foods than the environment would naturally. This, in turn, permitted the growth of human populations beyond the limits set by their preagricultural patterns. Thus, agriculture raised the capacity of the earth to support human beings.

Since about 1000 B.C., humans began to move freely around the world, and rulers began to dominate large regions from a distance. Settlements and their impacts were no longer necessarily small in scale or localized in effect.

Beginning in the 15th century, colonialism placed European hands firmly on the environments and resources of far-distant lands. These colonial powers were interested in removing and using resources, with little regard for environmental consequences, either abroad or close to home. Hand-in-hand with this process, industrialization led to a global-scale use of fuel and mineral resources, altering or destroying local and regional ecosystems and perhaps ultimately affecting global climate and other environmental patterns. Nicholson (1970) suggests that until recent centuries, human influences on the environment were direct and concrete. It is only in modern times that indirect impacts have also been significant.

He contrasts positive indirect influences, such as the conservation movement and regional planning, against expanding multipurpose demands on the land, the rapid spread of human occupance, and the growing range of environmental "nuisances" such as pollution.

In summary, the last three millennia, and particularly the last 500 years, have seen a transformation in the kinds and scales of natural resource use in the world. Early societies depended primarily on locally available resources with relatively little trade, whereas now most of the goods we consume come from quite far away. Resource use systems have become complex, with a wide variety of goods used in everyday life. This increasing complexity has isolated us somewhat from the basic raw materials provided by the environment and made us more dependent on human systems of resource manipulation and distribution. There clearly are innumerable ways of making a living in the world today. No single commodity or geographical area is indispensable, and resource management has become a task of selecting which resource utilization techniques are most appropriate for our needs at any given time.

DEVELOPMENT OF U.S. NATURAL RESOURCE POLICY

The history of natural-resource policy in the U.S. from the 17th century to the present can be organized into six phases. In most cases these do not have distinct beginning and ending dates and overlap considerably. However, approximate dates are indicated since they are useful in distinguishing important historical trends. The discussion here is not intended to be exhaustive but rather a summary of some of the major actions and events that form the basis of much of current U.S. conservation philosophy and policy.

Phase I: Exploitation and Expansion (1600–1870)

When the early European settlers arrived in North America, they found a vast continent full of natural resources in apparently limitless supply, particularly in comparison to urbanized and developed Europe. Their purpose was to establish stable and profitable colonies. To accomplish this, the European landholders who controlled settlement promoted population growth and resource extraction to maximize their security and prosperity. The colonial economy was, by design, based on exporting raw materials to industrial Europe, with agriculture for domestic food production. The enormous land area of North America then was the primary resource for this economic development, and exploitation of its natural resources was the means to the desired end.

The forests that covered most of the eastern third of the continent were seen partly as a resource and partly as nuisance. Even though wood was needed for fuel and construction, there was a vast amount of forest land compared to productive agricultural land, which placed a lower value on forest land use. The forests, then, were cleared as rapidly as possible to make room for agriculture. In addition, the prevailing aesthetic attitudes toward forests were different from today. Forests were seen as unproductive, undesirable, and dangerous, whereas agricultural land was productive, attractive, and secure (Figure 3.1). Except in a very few instances, regulations limiting the clearing of forests were unknown,

Figure 3.1   Canoeing on the Pine River in Michigan. Americans today enjoy the wilderness but in previous centuries it was a place to be feared.

as was the notion of natural resource conservation. This exploitative attitude toward the land prevailed for about the first 250 years of European occupation of North America, until the mid- or late-1800s. The growth of an industrial economy in the 19th century had little effect on this, except perhaps to increase the demands of urban populations for food, timber, and later, coal. Forests were first culled of the most valuable trees; later, the remaining timber was generally clear-cut and often burned. Agriculture in many areas consisted mainly of a very few crops grown for sale, and, except for liming soils in some areas, little was done to maintain, let alone enhance, soil fertility. As a result soil erosion was rapid and declines in fertility forced abandonment of land after only a few years, particularly in the southeastern U.S.

As the nation expanded westward, political as well as economic goals required rapid settlement and development of the Great Plains. With each major territorial expansion from the Louisiana Purchase to the Alaska Purchase (the annexation of Texas excepted), the federal government acquired possession of vast acreages. In the early 19th century, much government land was sold to provide income to the fledgling republic as well as promote settlement. Several laws were passed in the mid-1800s to promote settlement, largely by transferring government-owned lands to private ownership either for free or at a nominal cost. The most notable among these laws were the Homestead Act of 1862, the railroad acts of the 1850s and 1860s, the Timber Culture Act of 1873, and the Mining Act of 1872.

The Homestead Act and the railroad acts were specifically designed to encourage settlement, especially in the Great Plains. The Homestead Act allowed any qualified settler 160 acres free of charge, and the railroad acts granted huge rights of way to the railroad companies to finance construction of transcontinental and other rail lines that would further accelerate settlement of the West. Most of the land granted to the railroads was sold to other private interests, but substantial acreages remain in railroad ownership today, particularly in California. The Timber Culture Act and the Mining Act granted free access to forests and minerals to anyone willing to exploit them. There were widespread abuses of these privileges, which resulted in land companies and speculators acquiring vast acreages at nominal expense. Even though these laws were successful in stimulating settlement and economic development, they also encouraged excessive exploitation by artificially depressing the price of resources. Environmental degradation usually followed, as was true with the forests of the upper Midwest (Michigan, Wisconsin, and Minnesota). Here much timber was lost to wasteful logging practices and fires, and soil was lost to accelerated erosion.

In the late 19th and 20th centuries the practice of promoting exploitation of resources for economic growth was limited somewhat by the growth of the conservation movement. Exploitative policies continued into the 20th century, however, with legislation such as the Reclamation Act of 1902, which provided for development of water at public expense for crop irrigation in the arid west. Today, natural resource exploitation for economic prosperity is still the basis of government management of mineral resources such as coal and oil. It is also an important consideration in the government's management of such other areas as water and rangelands.

Phase II: Early Warnings (1840–1870)

During the time when settlement was rapidly advancing westward with the stimulation and encouragement of the government, a few individuals were suggesting that the exploitation of resources was too rapid and too destructive. In general these persons were intellectuals and academics who did not enjoy popular audiences for their criticisms, thus the effects of their writings were limited. Eventually, though, their warnings were heard by decision-makers in government, which led to a new concern for conserving and preserving resources.

Among the early American writers advocating wilderness preservation were Ralph Waldo Emerson and Henry David Thoreau, who argued on philosophical grounds against continued destruction of natural areas by logging and similar activities in the 1840s and 1850s. However, George Perkins Marsh, in his book *Man and Nature, or Physical Geography as Modified by Human Action,* published in 1864, was perhaps more influential in the conservation versus exploitation debate. Marsh was both a public servant and a scientist, and this combination led him to advocate government action to protect natural resources. Although a native of Vermont, Marsh traveled widely in the Mediterranean, an area long damaged by overgrazing. He saw a parallel between the Mediterranean situation and the damage done by sheep grazing in the Green Mountains in his home state. In *Man and Nature,* Marsh argued that humans should attempt to live in harmony rather than in competition with nature (Figure 3.2). More importantly, Marsh argued that natural resources were far from inexhaustible. The book was widely read and had considerable influence on Carl Schurz, who later became Secretary of the Interior under Rutherford Hayes in 1877.

Figure 3.2 A seawall on Massachusetts' Cape Cod. This is an example of living in spite of—not in harmony with—nature.

Phase III: Establishing a Conservation Ethic (1870–1910)

This phase included a series of developments in the late 19th century, when many of the federal government's basic doctrines of natural resource conservation were established. The primary tenet was that land resources should be managed for long-term, rather than short-term, benefits to the general population. This phase, dominated by concern for forest resources and to a lesser extent wilderness preservation, began in the 1870s and was marked by the first significant government action aimed at restricting exploitation of natural resources.

By the late 19th century, the forests of much of the eastern U.S. were either entirely cut over or were rapidly becoming so. It is not surprising that the forest resource was the first focus of the emerging conservation efforts in the 1870s. Carl Schurz launched an attack on corrupt and wasteful practices in timber harvesting on federal lands, bringing the extent of the problem to the public eye. In 1872, the New York Forest Commission halted the sale of state forest lands, an action that eventually led to the creation of the Adirondack Forest Preserve (now Adirondack State Park). The most significant development during this period was the passage of a rider on a public lands bill in 1891. This gave the President the authority to set aside, by proclamation, forested lands, thus reserving them from timber cutting. President Benjamin Harrison quickly began withdrawing land from timber cutting, and in 1897 additional reservations by Grover Cleveland brought the the total forest reserves to about 16 million hectares (40 million acres). Although the federal government thus had established what would later become the National Forest System, it had no real management policy for these lands. In 1898, Gifford Pinchot was appointed as the first Chief Forester. Pinchot was trained as a forester in Europe, where the field had been well established for some time. He brought with him a knowledge of the scientific basis for land management, in particular the notion of *sustained yield* forestry. The principle of sustained yield management of renewable resources states that harvests should not exceed levels that can be maintained indefinitely. It has since been firmly incorporated into all aspects of official federal policy, although there is some debate as to whether the principle is truly followed in practice.

In 1901, Theodore Roosevelt became president, and his administration represented the culmination of this phase of American natural resource history. Roosevelt was an adventurer and an outdoorsman and, as such, had a personal appreciation for the values of undeveloped land, particularly the still untouched wilderness areas of the western U.S. Pinchot was one of his key advisors, and with the forester's advice, Roosevelt added large acreages to the national forest reserves. By the end of his administration, these reserves totaled 70 million hectares (172 million acres). Later, large acreages were added to the national forests in the eastern U.S. after the passage of the Weeks Act in 1911, which provided for federal acquisition of tax-delinquent cutover lands.

Theodore Roosevelt was also instrumental in expanding what would later become the National Park System. Yellowstone was reserved as a national park in 1872, and several other parks were created in this period. Roosevelt reserved the Grand Canyon from development by invoking the Antiquities Act. Passed in 1906, this act was primarily intended to allow the President to preserve national historic sites such as buildings and battlefields. Roosevelt, however, used it to create the Grand Canyon National Monument, which later became a national park. Some seventy-eight years later, Jimmy Carter used this same act to temporarily preserve hundreds of millions of acres in Alaska while Congress debated the Alaska Lands Bill. Finally, near the end of his presidency, Roosevelt sponsored the first White House Conference on Conservation, further bringing the issue to public attention and concern.

Another important figure during this period was John Muir, who founded the Sierra Club in 1892. Muir was a naturalist and wilderness advocate, whose primary area of interest was the Sierra Nevada Range of California. The Yosemite region was one of his favorite spots, and he led the battle to protect the area from damage by sheep grazing, by establishing what would later become Yosemite National Park.

One of the more significant battles of his life was fought over the preservation of the Hetch–Hetchy Valley. This valley is adjacent to the Yosemite Valley and was similar in scenic beauty. Hetch–Hetchy was, however, a convenient source of water for the growing city of San Francisco and an excellent dam site. Muir fought hard to prevent the damming of the Tuolumne River but eventually lost, in a battle with a former ally in the conservation movement, Gifford Pinchot. Pinchot was, of course, a conservationist, but he believed in conservation for maintenance of the productive capacity of natural resources. To prevent development was contrary to the notion that resources could be used for general benefit of the population, and Pinchot opposed Muir in the debate over Hetch–Hetchy. In the end, the development interests prevailed, and today the valley is a reservoir providing water and electricity to the cities of northern California.

The Hetch–Hetchy controversy made clear the distinction between *conservation,* encouraging careful husbanding of resources yet not condemning their use, and *preservation,* stopping all use or development on the basis that some areas and resources are too valuable to be used. During this third phase major achievements in resource conservation were made. The principles of sustained yield management and of preservation of outstanding natural features for future generations were established and some of the major ideological "camps" emerged. The preservationists and the conservationists can be seen in the debates over natural resources even today.

Phase IV: Conservation for Economic Recovery (1932–1941)

The Great Depression of 1929–1941 and Franklin Roosevelt's New Deal of the 1930s had more impact on all aspects of modern domestic policy than in any other period in American history, and natural resource use was no exception. The Depression provided the impetus for massive programs aimed at relief, recovery, and prevention of future problems of the type then encountered. Most of the major programs of this period were aimed at combatting the problems of the Depression, either directly or indirectly. The Civilian Conservation Corps, for example, did not represent a major new policy. Instead, it was a make-work program that put many of the unemployed to work on conservation projects, principally planting trees and maintaining or constructing park facilities. In contrast, two major agencies established by the New Deal, the Tennessee Valley Authority (TVA) and the Soil Conservation Service (SCS), were aimed at correcting problems that, if not major contributors to the Depression, were very much worsened by it.

The Appalachian region of the Southeast had long been economically depressed and was among the areas hardest hit by the Great Depression. The forests were largely cut over, farms were not competitive with those in the Midwest, soil erosion and flooding were particularly severe, and significant industrial employment was not available. The TVA was the first major effort to address this wide range of problems in an integrated, regional, resource-management and economic-development program. The program took a twofold attack. Dams were constructed to generate hydroelectric power and control floods. The power generated was used to support new industries, particularly fertilizers but later munitions. Forests were replanted to control erosion, and many other smaller erosion control measures were instituted, in part to protect the newly created reservoirs from sedimentation. The TVA today is mostly an electric power generating authority, but its important legacy in natural resources is that it represents the recognition that good natural resource management and economic vitality are interdependent, and both must be undertaken together for long-term economic stability.

In addition to dam construction in the Tennessee Valley, many large dams were completed in the arid western states, including the Hoover Dam on the Colorado River and several dams in the Columbia River basin (Figure 3.3). These were seen as important government investments in agriculture and electric power generation and were to help revitalize agriculture and provide new sources of energy for industry.

The agricultural expansion in the Midwest and Plains during the late 19th

Figure 3.3 Grand Coulee Dam in eastern Washington. This is one of the major hydroelectric/ irrigation/recreation reservoirs built by the federal government in the Columbia River system.

and early 20th centuries took advantage of the naturally fertile soils of that region, and farming was successful without significant inputs of fertilizers or other means to maintain soil fertility. Severe soil erosion was widespread, but it took the economic collapse of the 1930s and the ensuing Dust Bowl conditions in portions of the Midwest and Plains to focus attention on the problem. Several dry years on land marginal for farming, combined with economic hardship brought by low farm prices led to severe wind erosion in Oklahoma, Colorado, and nearby areas, forcing thousands off the land.

The Soil Erosion Service, created in 1933, was established in response to these problems. Hugh Hammond Bennett became the first director of the newly renamed Soil Conservation Service in 1935. He led an extensive research effort to determine the causes of soil erosion and devise means to prevent it. This effort resulted in the development and implementation of many important soil conservation techniques, with dramatic reductions in soil erosion in much of the nation. The Agricultural Adjustment Administration, forerunner to the present Agricultural Stabilization and Conservation Service, was established to provide payments to farmers who reduced crop acreage. This not only reduced farm surpluses but also helped support prices and reduced the rate of soil erosion.

Another significant piece of legislation of this period is the Taylor Grazing Act of 1934, which established a system of fees charged for grazing on federal lands, with limitations on the numbers of animals that could be grazed. This was a partial response to widespread accelerated erosion caused by overgrazing. The act also closed most of the public lands to homesteading, effectively ending the large-scale transfer of public lands to private ownership begun in 1862. Today, these public lands are administered by the U.S. Bureau of Land Management. The Natural Resources Planning Board was another milestone of resource management during the term of Franklin Roosevelt. It was a major step toward establishing long-term comprehensive natural resources planning.

In summary, the F.D.R. years saw great increases in federal resource management and conservation activities. Most of the new programs were conceived as a result of the Depression and were designed to alleviate the problems of the time as well as prevent future mismanagement of resources. The need for careful management of renewable resources, particularly soil and water, was recognized, and the close relationship between economic and resource problems became clear.

Phase V: The Environmental Movement (1962–1976)

The years 1940 to 1960 saw relatively few new developments in conservation policy. The 1940s were dominated by war, and the economic recovery and ensuing prosperity of the 1950s placed little attention on natural resources. There was, however, considerable progress in soil, water, and forest conservation, expanding on the achievements made under Franklin Roosevelt. The major federal actions of this period were largely in the area of recreational activities, with the expansion of the national parks and similar recreational areas in response to increased use by the American public.

By the 1960s, attention was being focused on the quality of life available to Americans and the notion of natural resources became more broadly defined. Two significant books published in 1962 and 1963 called attention to this broader view of natural resources and signaled the beginning of a new era of attention to environmental pollution as a major threat to natural resources and the quality of life.

One of these was *The Quiet Crisis,* by Stewart Udall, Secretary of the Interior under John F. Kennedy. In this book Udall related much of the history of natural resource use in the U.S., particularly focusing on the destruction of natural environments and wildlife. He called for renewed attention to the human effects on the environment, echoing many of the sentiments of G.P. Marsh 100 years earlier. The second book was Rachel Carson's *Silent Spring,* which described the effects of pesticides on the ecosystem and predicted drastic environmental consequences of continued pollution.

Throughout the 1960s, a popular movement for pollution control grew, led largely by scientists, student activists, and a few government officials such as Stewart Udall. Many influential authors argued that the environment had already been severely damaged and that urgent action was needed to restore health and prevent further damage to both natural and managed ecosystems. A major focus of the movement was the disparity between a limited resource base on "Spaceship Earth" and a rapidly growing world population that already faced severe shortages of food and raw materials. The result was a long list of laws passed in the late 1960s and early 1970s aimed at reducing pollution, preserving wilderness and endangered species, and promoting ecological considerations in resource development. Some of the more important of these are the Wilderness Act of 1964, the Clean Air Act of 1963 and its amendments of 1970 and 1977, the Federal

Water Pollution Control Act of 1964 and its amendments of 1972, the Coastal Zone Management Act of 1972, and the National Environmental Policy Act of 1970 (NEPA). The laws relating to specific resource problems such as air and water pollution have been the most important in terms of improving environmental quality. They are discussed in more detail later in this and other chapters.

The *National Environmental Policy Act* (NEPA) represents the first comprehensive statement of the U.S.A.'s environmental policy and illustrates the character of this phase of American natural resources history. Section 101 of NEPA contains a statement of the federal government's environmental responsibilities. These are to:

1. fulfill the responsibilities of each generation as trustee of the environment for succeeding generations;
2. assure for all Americans safe, healthful, productive, and esthetically and culturally pleasing surroundings;
3. attain the widest range of beneficial uses of the environment without degradation, risk to health or safety or other undesirable and unintended consequences;
4. preserve important historic, cultural, and natural aspects of our national heritage, and maintain, wherever possible, an environment which supports diversity and variety of individual choice;
5. achieve a balance between population and resource use which will permit high standards of living and a wide sharing of life's amenities; and
6. enhance the quality of renewable resources and approach the maximum attainable recycling of depletable resources. (Council on Environmental Quality, 1980:426–427)

These are lofty goals, but they reflect the idealism of the time as well as the far-reaching concerns of the environmental movement. They emphasize quality of life, preservation or maintenance rather than exploitation, and the concern with a limited and finite resource base supporting a rapidly growing population. NEPA also established the requirement for environmental impact statements to ensure compliance with its policies.

Phase VI: Pragmatism and Reassessment (1976–Present)

By the late 1970s a complex set of laws, regulations, and procedures was in place along with a bureaucracy to administer them. The mass of environmental legislation generated in the preceding decade was being translated into everyday action (Figure 3.4). The energy crises of the mid-1970s emphasized the need for resource conservation. Substantial improvements in environmental quality were being made, particularly in the areas of air and water pollution. With an upsurge of concern on the part of the general public about the effects of pollution on health, the Toxic Substances Control Act and the Resource Conservation and Recovery Act were signed into law in 1975 and 1976, respectively.

At the same time, public debate shifted away from the rather abstract issues of ecological stability and environmental quality and began focusing more on economic problems. With a downturn in the national and world economic situation, the costs of improving environmental quality began to be seen by some as contributing to economic problems; others saw the costs as greater than the benefits derived. When President Reagan took office in 1980, he rode

Figure 3.4   A poster for Earth Day 1980. This occasion celebrated a decade of environmental concern and activism.

a tide of political conservatism that turned away from the idealism of the 1960s and focused more on stimulating economic development. Public lands policy shifted from federal management and conservation to state or private control of resources and exploitation to improve supplies of raw materials, especially energy. Federally owned coal, which had not been sold during earlier administrations because of an oversupply of minable coal, was once again made available to the industry. In its rush to divest the federal government of its holdings, the Department of the Interior sold coal leasing rights in many areas at below-market value. Pollution abatement efforts by the federal government were reduced in favor of state and local control over these policies. Attention was also turned toward reducing the costs of pollution control to industry. Clearly resource conservation had entered a new phase that considered the economic aspects of resource decisions along with the ecological goals established in the 1960s and 1970s.

CURRENT NATURAL RESOURCE POLICY

The history of policy development for natural resource use reviewed in the previous section shows that many important goals have motivated government decision-making at one time or another. Many of these are embodied in policy today. There are four general goals: to promote economic development, to conserve resources for the future, to protect public health, and to preserve important natural features.

Clearly the most frequent motivation for government actions with respect to natural resources has been to promote economic development. This began with the land divestitures of the 18th and 19th centuries and continues today in the management of our national forests, offshore oil resources, rivers, and grazing land. The construction of major dams and reservoirs on rivers for hydroelectric-power generation, irrigation, or flood control addresses this goal. It is vividly seen in the recent increases in federal mineral-lease sales, where development rights were sold at below market value to stimulate production. It is also the primary justification for one of the basic tenets of public-land management policy, that of multiple use. The concept of *multiple use* holds that public lands should be used for several different purposes simultaneously. It was elaborated in the Multiple Use and Sustained Yield Act of 1960 and restated in NEPA, but it originated much earlier.

In encouraging economic development, the companion to the multiple-use concept is the idea of sustained yield, which aids in achieving the second goal, to conserve resources for future generations. This, of course, is the fundamental principle of renewable-resource management established by Pinchot in forest management, but it applies equally to the mission of the Soil Conservation Service and indeed to every agency managing renewable natural resources.

The third goal, to promote public health, is the basis for most pollution control legislation. Many of the early laws regulating potential health hazards in the environment were enacted at the state level, and major federal actions in this area did not appear until the late 19th and early 20th centuries. Today most of the water and air quality standards established by the government are based on health criteria (see Chapters 10 and 11).

The fourth major goal of natural resource policy is to preserve significant natural features that are valuable for aesthetic or scientific reasons, if not for economic ones. This is the aim of the extensive legislation enacted regarding wilderness preservation and protection of endangered species, and it is the principal mission of the National Park Service. This goal also forms the basis of some water quality criteria and is considered one of the uses of public lands incorporated in multiple-use planning.

Many natural resource policies combine these different goals. Water pollution control, for example, not only protects the public health but also provides recreational, aesthetic, and economic benefits to fisheries. All of the agencies involved in resource management address these multiple goals in devising management strategies, and this combination of purposes also plays an important role in creating political coalitions to enact new laws. Together they form the basis of sound resource management.

HOW RESOURCE DECISIONS ARE MADE

Several different groups are involved in any decision over the use of natural resources: resource managers, social agents, and interest groups. Membership in these groups is not constant; any individual may shift from one role to another as the decision-making process unfolds (Figure 3.5).

A *resource manager* is the individual or agency in physical contact with the resource and has a direct stake in how that resource is used or misused. Resource managers include an individual farmer concerned with soil erosion, a

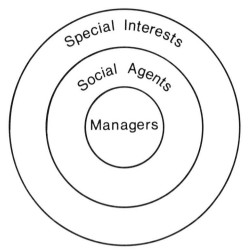

Figure 3.5 Participants in the resource-use decision-making process. Individuals may shift roles, depending on the resource issue under consideration.

forest ranger charged with managing a particular National Forest, or the Secretary of the Interior who manages the resources under his or her jurisdiction—parks, public lands, and the like.

Resource managers are subject to outside influences, or social agents. These range from the agricultural extension agents, to forest rangers' superiors in the U.S. Department of Agriculture to the President of the United States who oversees the Secretary of the Interior. These social agents provide technical expertise and direction to the individual managers in the field. The goals, objectives, and responsibilities of the social agents are broader than those of the resource manager. Social agents are thus influenced by interest groups who have a stake in how a resource is eventually used. Special interests range from timber companies seeking access to a national forest to supermarket chains who buy farm produce to environmental groups seeking to preserve a piece of nature.

Conflicts between participants inevitably lead to disagreement over management policies (Figure 3.6). These disagreements are further complicated by goal-oriented and mitigation-oriented management strategies. That is, there are governmental bodies charged with the management of a resource who are *goal-oriented,* and those charged with regulation and protection of environmental quality, who are *mitigation-oriented.* Often there are conflicts between the two bodies, even when they are in the same agency. Decision-making then becomes very difficult and usually involves conflict, cooperation, and compromise between the resource manager, social agents, and interest groups (Issue 3.1).

The Politics of Environmental Legislation

At the national level, the fundamental decision-making process is, of course, the congressional legislative process. Laws are initially drafted by individual legislators, or more commonly groups of legislators and their staffs. They are discussed

Figure 3.6 Western forest lands in the Front Range, just outside Colorado Springs, Colorado. These lands have many sometimes conflicting uses, and management decisions concerning them are often controversial.

ISSUE 3.1: A Symbol of the Environmental Movement

In late 1982 a new environmental center was opened in New Jersey. It is to be the centerpiece of a new park, DeKorte State Park. The park will be built in an area called the Hackensack Meadowlands, a vast area of tidal marshes in northeastern New Jersey, about five miles from Manhattan. DeKorte State Park will encompass some 810 hectares (2000 acres). The New Jersey Turnpike and several other transportation arteries pass through the site. It is surrounded by Newark Airport, the Meadowlands Sports Complex (Giants stadium, horse racing track, indoor arena), and numerous industrial and warehousing facilities. The park will include about 486 hectares (1200 acres) of wetlands, 253 hectares (624 acres) of sanitary landfills, and 71 hectares (176 acres) of roads and other rights of way. The landfills will be covered with soil and vegetated. A winter

sports facility, a camping area, picnic areas, and a scenic overlook will be built on them. The environmental center itself is built on the edge of an active landfill and includes a visitor's center overlooking the marsh, a museum, laboratories, and an auditorium. Does this sound strange? How did it come to be that the State of New Jersey chose to locate this new showpiece of environmentalism amid garbage dumps?

New Jersey is the most densely populated state in the U.S. It lies between the New York and Philadelphia metropolitan areas, right in the middle of Megalopolis. New Jersey has long served this urban region as a vegetable garden, industrial park, suburb, transportation route, port facility, and waste-disposal site. Not surprisingly, it has more than its share of pollution, and open space for recreation is at a premium. At the same

before the various congressional committees that have responsibility for particular areas of government policy. These committees modify the proposals, and if approved, forward them to the full Senate or House of Representatives for amendment and approval. When, usually after much debate and revision, they are passed by both houses of Congress, they are forwarded to the President to be signed. At each stage of the process, resource managers, social agents, and interest groups make their feelings known, and their opinions may either be incorporated or ignored in the proposed legislation.

Each law is unique, and each one is subject to different forces depending on the course the process takes from initial proposal to final enactment. A good example of the politics of environmental legislation is the Alaska National Interest Lands Conservation Act passed in 1980. This act, better known as the Alaska Lands Bill, is a good example because the battles over it were particularly intense and involved many different actors. Few environmental laws in recent decades have been as controversial.

Alaska has an area of about 148 million hectares (375 million acres), and virtually all of this was owned by the federal government when Alaska became a state in 1959. The terms of the Statehood Act required, however, that 42 million hectares (104 million acres) eventually be turned over to the state. In 1971, Congress passed the Alaska Native Claims Act, which paved the way for construction of the Alaska Pipeline by providing a settlement of the land claims of the native peoples. This act called for 18 million hectares (44 million acres) to be turned over to the natives. But before these lands could be transferred, it was necessary for the federal government to decide, by the end of 1978, which

time, it has suffered many of the ills of other eastern urban areas in the last few decades, seeing loss of industries and jobs to other areas, decay in inner cities, and race riots. The communities surrounding the Hackensack Meadowlands suffered as much as any others. The Meadowlands themselves are too low and wet to be used as residential or commercial property and, until recently, consisted primarily of marsh, transportation and utility conduits, storage facilities, junkyards, and garbage dumps.

In the 1960s, the Meadowlands began to be seen as a resource to stimulate new economic growth in this depressed region and to increase the tax rolls of the surrounding communities. A plan gradually emerged, wherein the state would establish a development authority that would have power to levy taxes, make land-use deci-sions, and develop the land. The authority would oversee planning and construction of new offices, shopping centers, housing, and industry, which would presumably replace the less desirable economic activities predominating at the time. As this plan was evolving, the environmental movement was also gathering steam.

Being a densely populated state, there is a relatively high degree of awareness and concern over environmental issues in New Jersey, and the politicians recognize this. The Hackensack Meadowlands are, of course, wetlands, which have recently become recognized as ecologically valuable in such tasks as maintaining primary production in estuaries, improving water quality, and providing wildlife habitat (see Chapter 12). And so in addition to creating new industrial, commercial, and residential facilities in this

lands it would retain ownership of and of these lands which would be preserved as wilderness and which would be open to development. The Alaska lands issue was thus a classic battle of preservation versus development, and the stakes were high: spectacular and unique natural areas containing potentially very valuable mineral and timber resources. The battle took much longer than was expected. To prevent development of some areas while Congress debated, President Carter proclaimed about 17 million hectares (44 million acres) as national monuments.

In 1977 the House of Representatives was the first to take up the Alaska lands issue. Morris Udall, a leading environmentalist in Congress, introduced a bill that would have placed nearly 69 million hectares (170 million acres) in the "four systems"—the national parks, wildlife refuges, forests, and wild and scenic rivers. In contrast, a proposal introduced by Alaska Representative Don Young would have placed 10 million hectares (25 million acres) in the four systems, and another 23 million hectares (57 million acres) in a joint state–federal management area, managed for multiple uses. The battle lines were drawn, and the special interests went to work. One of the most effective of these was the Alaska Coalition, a group of conservation organizations that banded together to press for a preservation-oriented bill. On the other side were the State of Alaska, which wanted as much development potential as possible, and industry groups like the American Mining Congress and the Western Oil and Gas Association. In the process of these negotiations, the various proposals were modified and eventually narrowed to two: the Udall bill and another that would have preserved much less land. Public sentiment for preservation was mobilized by the Alaska Coalition, which produced and distributed literature and films depicting the spectacular wilderness. In the end this sentiment was very important, and the Udall bill passed by a wide margin.

Once the House had passed its bill, the Senate began deliberations on its own versions of the bill. In general the Senate was less conservation-minded than the House, though there was a powerful group supporting a bill very similar

---

new plan for the Meadowlands, it became necessary to include such things as wildlife refuges and parks. The new environmental concern also spurred the state to commit itself to ending all garbage dumping in the Meadowlands eventually. What better place to build the new park than on old garbage dumps? They settle as the garbage decays and is compacted, and so they are unsuitable for buildings or roads. In addition, wells can be drilled in them to extract methane gas— recycling! The dumps themselves can become symbols of the new resolve to protect our environment, to preserve wetlands, and to plan new developments carefully to avoid the environmental disasters of the past.

Politics is a game of compromise, not agreement. Not all the parties to a decision will be likely to agree on all issues, but if all parties achieve at least some of their goals, then a consensus can be reached and action can be taken. In the Meadowlands everybody got a piece of the pie. The real estate developers got access to valuable property, the municipalities got new developments broadening their tax bases, the sports promoters got the sports complex, and the environmentalists got an end to garbage dumping and recognition of the value of wetlands, all of which is why the environmental center was built on a garbage dump.

to the House-passed bill. But the bill that finally emerged from committee in the Senate was different, with substantial reductions in areas designated as wilderness and more access for development in other areas. This was far from acceptable to the two Alaskan Senators, Ted Stevens and Mike Gravel, who vowed to filibuster to prevent passage of a bill that restricted the state's control over its lands. The debate was a heated one, and at one point the Senate went into closed session after a shouting match between Stevens and Gary Hart of Colorado. Eventually Stevens and Gravel's attempts at a filibuster failed as the Senate voted to cut off the debate. The Senate version, as finally passed, placed 42 million hectares (104 million acres) in the four systems, substantially less than the 51 million hectares (127 million acres) in the House bill. Wilderness designation was made for 27 million hectares (67 million acres) in the House bill, but only 23 million hectares (57 million acres) in the Senate version, which also permitted mineral exploration in some wildlife refuges.

After Senate passage of its bill, the House again took up the issue under threats of a filibuster if it failed to agree to the Senate version. It did accept the Senate version of the bill, and finally in late 1980 President Carter signed the bill. It was most certainly a compromise but not an entirely happy one. Morris Udall said he got most of what he wanted even though there were still some unacceptable provisions, which he hoped would be modified in the next Congress. And Don Young was pleased that the bill did allow for more mineral exploration than the original House bill, but he too said he wanted to change things in the next Congress to allow for even more exploration and development.

Throughout the debate on the Alaska lands, the changing strengths and fortunes of the actors could be seen. Conservationists were buoyed by support from the Carter Administration, particularly Secretary of the Interior, Cecil Andrus. In the midst of the debate, the Alaska legislature was repealing income taxes and rebating millions of dollars to its citizens as a result of accumulating oil revenues, actions that earned no extra sympathy for their demands for resource development. Carter and most environmental groups hailed the bill as the most significant environmental achievement of the Carter Administration. Mike Gravel was defeated in a primary election during the height of the debate, and one of the major issues was his inability to force the Senate to recognize Alaska's interests. But at the same time, industry won some crucial battles, and most of the valuable mineral and timber resources were opened to development.

The congressional process is one of compromise, and the most effective means for compromise is to make sure everyone is satisfied. Each actor, each interest group, is given at least token recognition of its interests, in an attempt to gain support for the final outcome. The particular characteristics of that outcome—which interest group gets more of what it wants and which gets less—depends on the strengths of the various power bases. In the case of the Alaska Lands Bill, the environmentalists had much more popular support than their opponents, which resulted in a bill generally regarded as a significant achievement for conservation.

Organizational Decision Making

The legislative process is not the only way in which environmental law is decided. There are over fifty federal entities involved in natural resources policy and decision-making (Table 3.1). Many times overlapping jurisdictions, different goals,

Table 3.1 Federal agencies with major responsibility for environmental policy or management

Department of Interior
National Park Service
Bureau of Land Management
Fisheries and Wildlife Service
Geological Survey
Mineral Management Service
Bureau of Reclamation
Office of Surface Mining
Bureau of Mines

Department of Agriculture
Forest Service
Soil Conservation Service
Agricultural Conservation and Stabilization Service

Department of Commerce
National Oceanographic and Atmospheric Administration

Department of Energy
Federal Energy Regulatory Commission
National Center for Appropriate Technology
Nuclear Waste Policy Act Project Office

Department of Defense
Army Corps of Engineers
Departments of Army, Navy, Air Force, Marines

Executive Office of the President
Council on Environmental Quality

Independent Agencies
Environmental Protection Agency
Tennessee Valley Authority
Bonneville Power Commission
Water Resources Council
National Science Foundation/National Research Council
Nuclear Regulatory Commission
Great Lakes Basin Commission
Synthetic Fuels Corporation
Federal Emergency Management Agency

and antagonistic staffs result in interagency squabbling over the management of specific resources. There are also intra-agency conflicts between the temporary political appointees, who head the agencies, and their professional civil servant staffs. How these agencies go about making decisions and implementing policy is crucial to our understanding of natural resources management in the U.S.

There are very few differences between how organizations make decisions and how individuals do. The difference is one of scale and complexity. In the types of decisions that are made and how they are made, governmental and other public organizations are similar in at least four ways. Publicly-oriented decisions usually respond to human need and require government efforts for implementation. Second, government agencies are influenced by the opinions of others such as lobby groups or political action committees. In addition, these decisions can be influenced by the motivations or political philosophies that underlie the decision-makers' choices (Issue 3.2). Finally, decisions will often be avoided because they are painful in terms of conflict between the governmental entity and the other groups or individuals. This results in nondecisions, which are, in fact, a form of decision-making. Non-decision-making is more pervasive in the U.S. than most people realize (O'Riordan, 1976). For example, Environmental Protection Agency administrators under Ronald Reagan in the early 1980s were often directed to avoid making environmentally oriented decisions that would be harmful to business interests.

There are several ideal procedures that if followed would assure good decision-making (Janis and Mann, 1977). The decision-makers should thoroughly investigate a wide range of alternative courses of action and objectives to be filled. All available information should be gathered, including expert opinions. The positive and negative aspects of each alternative should also be considered before taking any action.

In theory, good quality, objective decisions are possible, but in practice many factors bias decision-makers as well as their conclusions, resulting in less than perfect decisions. One of these is the constraint imposed by organizational tradition—we've always done things this way, there is a tradition to maintain. Also, there are constraints imposed by bureaucratic procedures, such as the endless arguments between regional and home offices or between divisions of the same organization. There are also constraints on decisions that are imposed by the demands of the executive role. A decision-maker may feel that he or she cannot show friendliness to subordinates since it might be construed as a sign of weakness and would hamper negotiations with a lobbyist or other interest groups. Perhaps one of the most important constraints is the lack of objective standards for assessing alternative outcomes. This forces the decision-maker to be sympathetic to social and political pressures and special interests. Decision-makers often rely on stereotypes such as believing the information of uneducated people to always be unreliable, which result in biased decisions. Bias can be introduced by an individual decision-maker's cognition of his or her role and intuitive assessment of the likelihood of the success or failure of the chosen course of action. And, of course, decisions are often made with insufficient or imperfect information, particularly in the case of environmental management.

Strategies in Natural Resource Decision-Making

Given that we live in an imperfect world with many complexities, it is surprising that we have been able to make sound environmental decisions at all. Decision-making in natural resources management is divided into three general categories: satisficing, incrementalism, and stress management. *Satisficing* is the consideration of two policy alternatives, which are examined sequentially and compared to one another. The best choice is then selected from these two. The goal of satisficing is to look for the course of action or alternative that is just good enough and meets a minimal set of requirements. This type of approach is cost-effective because the full range of alternatives is not researched, being too costly in time and money. Thus, the collective resources of the decision-maker or agency are used more efficiently. A negative aspect of this strategy is the limited range of alternatives from which to select the best choice. Satisficing is an appealing approach to managers because it is simple and can be used in many other areas besides resource use decision-making.

Incrementalism is used when the problem or resource issue is not clearly defined or when there are conflicting goals, values, or objectives (Mitchell, 1979). Incremental decisions are made by muddling through as they come across an administrator's desk. He or she may not know what is wanted but does know what should be avoided. As a result, incrementalism is not used to set broad policy guidelines such as the satisficing strategy, but rather to alleviate the shortcomings in the present policy in its day-to-day administration. This sequential approach is regularly used to cope with the bureaucratic politics that often result in compromising and shifting coalitions. Incrementally made decisions are often disjointed, seemingly contradictory, and reflect minute changes in policy.

The third strategy, *stress management,* is the approach most commonly used in government. Stress management is the response to an issue once it becomes a critical problem. This is a seat-of-the-pants planning effort to come to grips with the looming impact of the problem. Policy is then determined on a piecemeal basis to deal with the immediate problem at hand. There may be

---

ISSUE 3.2: Ideologies of Natural Resource Management

Most political debates are defined by the ideological viewpoints of the participants, and natural resource decision-making is no exception. Ideology generally refers to adherence to broad, comprehensive bodies of thought such as capitalism or Marxism. Ideology thus affects opinions on issues by determining the information used in decision-making as well as the ways in which problems are defined. If the same body of information on some particular topic is put before people with differing ideologies, their interpretations of the information will differ, as will their recommendations for appropriate action. However, in an open political system there can be as many ideological variations as there are participants, and two people may agree on most issues yet be worlds apart on some specific topic. It is, therefore, impossible to describe all the viewpoints that enter into the natural resources debate, but sketches are provided of a few common viewpoints to give an idea of the ideological frameworks that people adhere to today.

For example, there is a fairly well-defined body of data that is used to estimate how much recoverable petroleum remains in the United States. One might think that experts would have little trouble in agreeing on a procedure for analyzing those data and, hence,

on the conclusion that is reached. But, in fact, reasonable estimates made by competent analysts vary by as much as a factor of ten. The key word here is "recoverable." The choice of which method to use to calculate recoverable petroleum resources is affected by ideological outlook. A capitalist would tend to think in terms of economic recoverability and conclude that because oil will become too expensive to extract, it will be replaced by other energy sources. Hence, oil companies will, in fact, only be able to recover a portion of what is in the ground. A socialist, on the other hand, would be more inclined to think in terms of technical recoverability and conclude that there is a lot of recoverable oil, using the drilling and pumping technology likely to be available over the next few decades. If the recovery is worth the labor, we will get it.

Recently, many environmental experts have presented their viewpoints on the issue of the major causes of the present environmental crises. From these, we have constructed a few examples of important ideological approaches. Each includes an example of how an adherent to the viewpoint would answer the question, What are the major causes of the environmental crisis? (This question shows the ideological bias of the inquirer, since not all persons would agree

little consideration of long-term effects in the rush to get something done quickly. For example, when it was realized that certain industries contributed to local air pollution, regulations were put into effect in the 1970s that required higher smokestacks so that the pollutants would not afflict nearby communities. In the long run, however, this stress management decision may have a larger negative impact, since these airborne pollutants are contributing to the acid rain problem that may lead to major deforestation and water pollution problems hundreds of miles from the smokestacks. Thus with stress management choices, there is no time for a discussion of larger policy questions. All decisions must be made immediately and implemented as quickly as possible (Kasperson, 1969). There is very little time to discuss all the alternatives or the implications of new rules and regulations. Stress management has often been referred to as "crisis management" for good reason. Unfortunately, many of our environmental regulatory agencies routinely operate in this fashion.

You might think that the cumulative effect of all these imperfections in the

that there is a crisis.) We will call the adherents a conservative capitalist, a capitalist environmentalist, a Marxist, a socialist environmentalist, and a Spaceship-Earth ecologist. These labels are as descriptive as possible, but, given the nature of ideology, those who adhere to these ideas would probably object to the terms we use to describe them.

The conservative capitalist believes that the free-market system is the best means to allocate resources. For this individual, the less government interference, the better. The consumer and the producer will, through the mechanism of supply and demand, determine how much of a given resource is used and at what price. Every commodity has a price associated with it, or would have if someone were concerned enough to want to control it. The question, for example, of how much of a forest to cut and how much to leave as wilderness would be answered in terms of the price people are willing to pay to have either lumber or wilderness. If wilderness is indeed a desirable commodity, then a price will be offered for it. If this price is greater than the price bid for the lumber, then wilderness it will be. The intervention of government in preserving wilderness represents a misallocation of resources. According to the conservative

capitalist, there is no environmental crisis. Rather, there is a group of selfish people (environmentalists) who are trying to get something for nothing. They are trying to get the government to force industries to provide them with a commodity (clean water) without their having to pay for it directly. As a result, they are demanding cleaner water than they would really want if they had to pay the cost of pollution control. The crisis is one of nonmarket forces (government) trying to do what the market should be allowed to do. As a result, a few environmentalists are getting what they want at the expense of the majority of the population.

The capitalist environmentalist also recognizes that there are certain resources that simply cannot be traded properly on the open market. Freedom from pollution is a good example. Smoke from a factory's chimney represents a commodity exchanged between the factory owner and those who breathe the air polluted by it. And yet no price is bid for the exchange, either by the factory or the population. Consequently, the population has no way of economically choosing whether to receive that smoke. The exchange represents an externality, or an exchange outside the market system, which must be eliminated. Externalities may

decision-making process would prevent good decisions from ever being made. Some might agree. However, with most decisions of this nature, there is a wide range of opinion on how problems should be approached. In most cases only a portion of the population could be completely satisfied with the result. That is, of course, the nature of the political process. But the important thing to recognize is that the push and pull of politics goes on at many levels of decision-making—not just at election time. The administrator and enforcer are just as susceptible to the forces that sway decisions as is the legislator.

SUMMARY AND CONCLUSIONS

Throughout history there has been continual change in the way people view natural resources and in the demands placed on them. This change has resulted in the development of a complex body of thought, tradition, and legislation regarding natural resources. The actions that have been taken with regard to resources have been as diverse as our views about them. In most cases governmental decisions on natural resource use are forced to combine many different approaches and goals and compromise between various interests to achieve the desired goals.

---

be eliminated in any of several ways discussed in Chapter 2. According to the capitalist environmentalist, the cause of the environmental crisis is the existence of market externalities. Government action is necessary to correct these imperfections of the capitalist system. However, if that action is taken according to the basic capitalist principles, there should be no problem with the pollution—either it is there and people do not mind or it is not there. In a few cases the government may have been a little overzealous in its application of pollution controls. The result has been a cleanup that is more costly than we are willing to pay. Careful benefit–cost analyses of pollution controls in the future will correct this problem.

The Marxist believes that natural resources have no intrinsic value; the value of goods is derived solely from the labor that goes into producing them. Like the conservative capitalist, the Marxist believes there is no environmental crisis. Production decisions are made by the population as a whole, through the state. The desirability of any particular environmental condition (pol-

luted or not polluted; high consumption or low consumption) is culturally defined rather than dictated by any absolute principles. Therefore, if it is decided to extract a certain natural resource or discharge certain pollutants, then that is the wish of the people; there is no problem. If there is an environmental crisis, it is because the state is not a truly socialist one and decisions are made in the interests of a few rather than for the entire population.

The socialist environmentalist believes in collective decision-making but also believes that natural resource decisions must take into consideration the inherent limitations of the environment's ability to supply raw materials and absorb waste. If the population as a whole had more control over the decision-making process, they would certainly choose a cleaner environment. The environmental crisis is a result of the fact that production is controlled by an elite few, who waste resources and pollute the environment without regard for the welfare of the general population. Multinational corporations are particularly to blame; not only are they in control of vast natural resources but they

REFERENCES AND ADDITIONAL READING

Carson, R.L. 1962. *Silent spring.* Boston: Houghton Mifflin Co.

Council on Environmental Quality. 1980. *Environmental quality, 1980. The 11th annual report.* Washington, D.C.: Government Printing Office.

Huth, H. 1957. *Nature and the American: three centuries of changing attitudes.* Berkeley and Los Angeles: University of California Press.

Janis, I.L., and L. Mann. 1977. *Decision-making: a psychological analysis of conflict, choice, and commitment.* New York: The Free Press.

Kasperson, R.E. 1969. Political behavior and the decision-making process in the allocation of water resources between recreational and municipal uses. *Natural Resources Journal* 9:176–211.

Marsh, G.P. 1864. *Man and nature, or physical geography as modified by human action.* New York: Scribner.

Mitchell, B. 1979. *Geography and resource analysis.* London: Longman.

Nash, R. 1982. *Wilderness and the American mind.* rev. ed. New Haven: Yale University Press.

Nicholson, M. 1970. *The environmental revolution: a guide for the new masters of the world.* New York: McGraw-Hill.

O'Riordan, T. 1976. *Environmentalism.* London: Pion.

Sandbach, F. 1980. *Environment, ideology, and policy.* Montclair, New Jersey: Allanheld, Osmun.

Swem, T., and R. Cahn. 1983. The politics of parks in Alaska. *Ambio* 12:14–19.

Udall, S. 1963. *The quiet crisis.* New York: Holt, Rinehart.

are also largely outside governmental regulation. There is virtually no way for the people to influence their activities.

The Spaceship-Earth ecologist feels that, regardless of what economic or decision-making system is used, earth has a limited ability to supply living space, raw materials, and waste disposal. Industrialized societies consume vast amounts of natural resources, and not only are they rapidly running out of nonrenewable resources but renewable ones are being damaged beyond repair. The poorer nations consume nonrenewables at a lower rate than richer ones, but deforestation and soil erosion are rampant in the Third World. Most importantly, worldwide population is growing much more rapidly than technological abilities to produce basic goods for those people. Population growth is most rapid in those countries that have the least ability to accommodate it. Worldwide crisis is around the corner, with famines, plagues, and resource wars. What is immediately necessary is the reduction of population growth to zero-growth levels and the complete restructuring of systems of production of goods and disposal of wastes.

The new production system must mirror nature, using such techniques as solar energy harvesting, mixed cropping systems using organic fertilizer and biological control of pests, and total waste recycling. To the Spaceship-Earth ecologist, the environmental crisis is an acute one. It is a result of a Malthusian imbalance between finite resource availability and exponentially growing population, made worse by a production system that damages the ability of the earth to provide for its inhabitants by overexploitation of resources and pollution of the environment.

To some extent the viewpoints chosen represent extremes, but they are by no means so extreme that they are not espoused in the halls of government or in highly regarded academic journals. They are viewpoints held by many respected and powerful people. It should be recognized, however, that most individuals have opinions that are variations on the ones presented, or more likely combinations of two or more of them. Can you name some individuals who fit any of these descriptions? Do you fit any of them?

TERMS TO KNOW

conservation
Homestead Act
incrementalism
Mining Act
multiple use
NEPA
preservation

Reclamation Act
satisficing
stress management
sustained yield
Taylor Grazing Act
Timber Culture Act

STUDY QUESTIONS

1. What is the significance of Hetch–Hetchy in the preservation-versus-conservation debate?
2. How would you characterize each of the phases in the development of natural-resource policies in the U.S.?
3. How have the following pieces of legislation shaped the natural resource policies in the U.S. over the last century?
   a. NEPA
   b. Homestead Act
   c. Taylor Grazing Act
4. What are the primary differences among the three strategies of decision-making, and under what circumstances is each most applicable?
5. How does the Alaska Lands Bill demonstrate the politics of environmental legislation and the role of special interests in this process?

CHAPTER FOUR

The Ecological Bases of Natural Resources

INTRODUCTION TO THE STUDY OF ECOSYSTEMS

Ecology is a term that has been popularized almost to the point of meaninglessness in the last two decades. We see signs that read, "Don't litter—save the ecology," and we may have a feeling that the word means natural beauty or baby seals or clean air and water. In fact, ecology did not suddenly spring into existence on the first Earth Day created to raise conservationist consciousnesses back in 1970. It has been around for over 100 years and describes a complex field of study.

It is probably no coincidence that the word *ecology* was first used in the second half of the 19th century, at about the same time that naturalists were first beginning to worry about large-scale natural resources depletion. Although the term was probably in use earlier, in 1870 the German biologist Ernst Haeckel defined it as "the study of all the complex interrelations referred to by Darwin as the conditions of the struggle for existence" (Haeckel, 1870, cited in Kormondy, 1969).

More recently, Kormondy has termed ecology as "multidisciplinary and almost boundless in its concern" (Kormondy, 1969). He suggests here that we move into other fields of study when we cease to be interested in the interrelationships between processes but focus instead on any one process. That is, when we look at the interactions between the squirrel and its food supply, we are ecologists. When we turn to the physiology of the squirrel, we have become zoologists.

Thus the heart of the study of ecology is the interrelationships between animals and plants and the living and nonliving components and processes that make up their environment. This is why the study of ecological systems is so basic to the conservation of natural resources. Without an understanding of how natural systems work, we cannot begin to conserve, manage, and protect them.

The Big Picture: Biosphere and Biome

Ecosystems, or collections of interacting organisms and their environments, are useful to the researcher because they are large enough to be a reasonably representative slice of the environment yet not so large as to be unmanageable. Ecosystems are themselves ultimately part of larger systems. At the broadest level is the *biosphere,* the worldwide envelope of organic and inorganic substances within which all life functions. Envision the millions of tiny and large ecosystems that make up the biosphere or try to comprehend the awesome complexity of the interactions and meshing of "gears" that have developed over billions of years, so that this global system can function smoothly.

The concept of a biome helps make sense of the patterns of interaction between plants, animals, and the physical environment. A *biome* is a major ecological region within which plant and animal communities are broadly similar, both in their general characteristics and in their relationship to each other and to the physical environment. Because biomes are defined on the basis of organism–environment interactions, it is within each of the world's major biomes that the researcher can make sense of individual ecosystems.

The World's Major Biomes: A Brief Summary

Figure 4.1 is a map of the major world biomes. Looking first at the equator, the equatorial or tropical rain forest is an exuberant response to a rainfall schedule that is year-round and frequent, with little variation in season or the length of day. The resulting vegetation cover is a complex array of broad-leaved evergreens, trees constantly shedding some leaves but never bare. There is a larger diversity of species in the rainforest than elsewhere. For example, an acre of forest in the northeastern United States might sustain two or three tree species, whereas an acre of tropical rainforest might yield several times that many. In addition, tropical species are often unique to only a very small area of rainforest, unlike their northern counterparts, which are found over a very wide geographic area. Tropical rainforests are found straddling the equator with the largest areas found in the Amazon Basin (Brazil), Indonesia and the Southeast Asian peninsula, and in Africa's Zaire Basin (Figure 4.2).

Moving south and north from the equator, *savanna,* a seasonally drier climate and correspondingly less heavily vegetated biome, is found near latitudes 25 degrees north and south, notably in Africa, South America, and Southeast Asia. Most savanna is located in the tropical wet and dry climate zone, characterized by heavy summer rainfall and a dry winter season. The characteristic vegetation varies from open woodland with grass cover to open grassland with scattered deciduous trees. Researchers generally agree that much of Africa's savanna is derived not from natural processes but from the human use of fire. If this is true, savanna is perhaps the oldest of human-shaped landscapes.

The dry climates that produce the desert biome are found in two locations worldwide: in the subtropic latitudes as the result of high-pressure zones and in the midlatitudes in continental interiors far from ocean moisture. Deserts vary from the cartoon image of bare rock and blowing sand dunes where no rainfall is recorded year after year, to areas vegetated with shrubs and annuals and 100 to 300 mm (4 to 12 in.) of rain a year. *Potential evapotranspiration,* or the amount of water that would be evaporated or transpired if it were available, is much higher, leading to a water deficit. Desert vegetation consists of plants with special structural adaptations that enable them to store moisture, to retain it under waxy leaves, and to search for it via long root systems. These species complete their brief life cycles during the short rainy season.

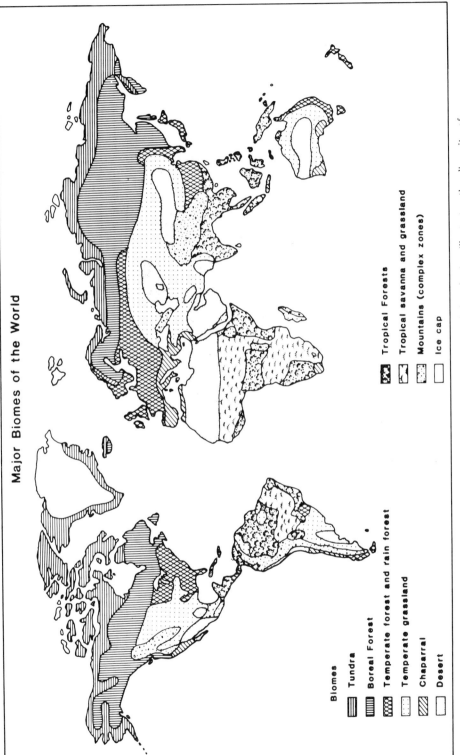

Figure 4.1 The world's major biomes. The broad geographical distribution illustrates the diversity of ecosystems found throughout the world. (Source: From Council on Environmental Quality, 1981)

Figure 4.2   In the United States, the tropical rainforest biome can be seen in Hawaii.

The subtropical deserts are the largest on earth, including the Sahara, which stretches across Africa eastward to join the deserts in Saudi Arabia, Iran, Afghanistan, and Pakistan. Other subtropical deserts are found in the southwestern United States, northern Mexico, Australia, Chile, Peru, and southern Africa (Figure 4.3). Continental deserts are found in the northern hemisphere's continental interiors between the Caspian and Aral Seas in Russia, in the Gobi Desert in Mongolia, and between the Rocky Mountains and the Sierra-Cascade ranges in the U.S.A.

The Mediterranean biome is named after the region that stretches around the Mediterranean Sea, characterized by a cool, moist winter and a hot, dry summer. Typical vegetation consists of a thorny, glossy, and sometimes impenetrable mass of fire-prone species called *chaparral.* Mediterranean climate and chaparral are found in other coastal locations between 30 and 45 degrees latitude north and south of the equator, including coastal Southern California, Chile, South Africa, and parts of southern Australia.

The midlatitude grasslands are found at 30 degrees north and south latitude, in semiarid interior areas. With not quite enough moisture to support trees and shrubs, these fire-prone grasslands once stretched from Texas to Alberta and Saskatchewan in North America, before being put to the plow in the 19th and 20th centuries. The grasslands of South America in Argentina and Uruguay have also been given over to agricultural development. The grassland steppes of the Ukraine in the U.S.S.R. continue east as far as Manchuria in China.

The vast midlatitude or temperate forests (Figure 4.4) stretched from 30 to 50 degrees north and south latitudes across the eastern United States; through much of northwestern Europe, eastern China, and Japan; and in small areas of South America, Australia, and New Zealand. With the colonization and population growth of the last several centuries, much of this deciduous and mixed deciduous/

Figure 4.3 An example of the desert biome in the United States is the Sonoran desert vegetation outside Tucson, Arizona.

Figure 4.4 This example of the temperate forest biome in upstate New York is characterized by second-growth midlatitude deciduous trees.

evergreen woodland cover has been removed. The characteristic climate of this region is cold winters and warm summers, with average annual precipitation generally equal to or greater than potential evapotranspiration.

The *boreal,* or northern coniferous, biome is located between 50 and 60 degrees north latitude (there being no significant land mass at this latitude south of the equator). In contrast to the diversity of the tropical rainforest, the number of species in this biome is smaller. These woodlands stretch in a belt across Alaska, Canada, and as far south as the northern portions of Michigan, New York, and New England. In Europe this belt continues across Scandinavia and Russia. Mean monthly temperatures range from −29°C (−20°F) in the winter to 24°C (75°F) in the brief summer. Precipitation is moderate, but because of the relatively cool temperatures there is usually a moisture surplus for the entire year. The vegetation cover is dominated by fir, spruce, and pine, with thick needles and bark to withstand the cold. In the far north, trees 1 m (3 ft) high may be 100 years old or more.

It is at this tree-line boundary that the *tundra* biome begins, generally poleward of 60 degrees north and south latitude. The average temperature of the growing season does not exceed 10°C (50°F) for more than a few weeks, which prohibits tree growth. Much of this area is underlain by *permafrost,* or permanently frozen ground. With low precipitation, the tundra is often called a frozen desert; in its brief thaw, like the warm deserts, a low and colorful mat of shrubs, mosses, lichens, and grasses temporarily springs up.

This is a highly simplified picture of a complex pattern of biomes. There are numerous exceptions to the general picture caused by microclimate, soil variability, and human impact. The main point to note is that vegetation and climate have interacted over millions of years resulting in adaptive vegetative patterns. We should remember that portions of these biomes have been altered by the work of humanity, and this is the cause of much discussion and dissent among those who would conserve and those who would develop and further alter these biomes.

A Smaller Focus: The Individual Ecosystems

An ecosystem can encompass a large or small geographic area. It usually consists of several organisms whose needs and requirements are complementary, so that the available resources are used in a stable and non-depleting fashion (Figure 4.5). It can become difficult to define the precise boundaries of an ecosystem, since organisms are often participants in more than one. *Ecotones* or broad transitional zones are the more flexible alternative to outlining a sharp boundary (Figure 4.6). Within a single ecosystem, researchers tend to separate the stable plants and animals into *communities.* These are further subdivided into local societies or colonies, each containing a population of one or more species. Finally, the ecologist can examine the individual organism's function in this larger system.

An ecosystem is an open system (see Chapter 1) where matter and energy are exchanged between ecosystems and with the larger environment. The ecosystem receives inputs of energy and material, which are stored, used, or passed through the ecosystem, leaving as outputs. An ecosystem in which inputs and outputs are about equal is in equilibrium. When inputs are larger than

Figure 4.5 A pond in central Ontario, Canada. The water surface, the shoreline, and the deeper water can each be considered a subsystem of the pond ecosystem.

outputs, the ecosystem is in a growth period. When outputs are larger than inputs, the ecosystem is in decay (Figure 4.7).

An ecosystem usually has several feedback loops that make it a more complex entity than the above simple input-output model might suggest. Feedbacks can have both negative and positive effects on the organisms in an ecosystem and on the overall functioning of the system itself. Positive feedback loops, for example, amplify an existing trend, providing additional inputs to the system. Negative feedback loops dampen fluctuations in the system. When negative feedback dominates a system, it will tend toward a steady or equilibrium condition.

Interaction between the physical environment of the Los Angeles basin and the human patterns imposed on it produces a complex picture of inputs and outputs (Figure 4.8). In this urban ecosystem, inputs include raw materials and other imports, immigration of new residents, relatively clean Pacific air, water supplies, and electric power. Within greater Los Angeles, products are created for export, as is air pollution; and emigrants move on in search of other opportunities. This diagram is, of course, a simplification, presenting only a few of the major elements that make up the input–output model of an urban ecosystem. (See Detwyler and Marcus, 1972, for further discussion of the urban ecosystem.)

ENERGY AND MATERIAL CYCLES IN ECOSYSTEMS

Natural resources come from the earth's physical environment. To manage a natural resource for sustained use, we need to understand the workings of the environment. Without this knowledge, it is possible to damage or destroy a

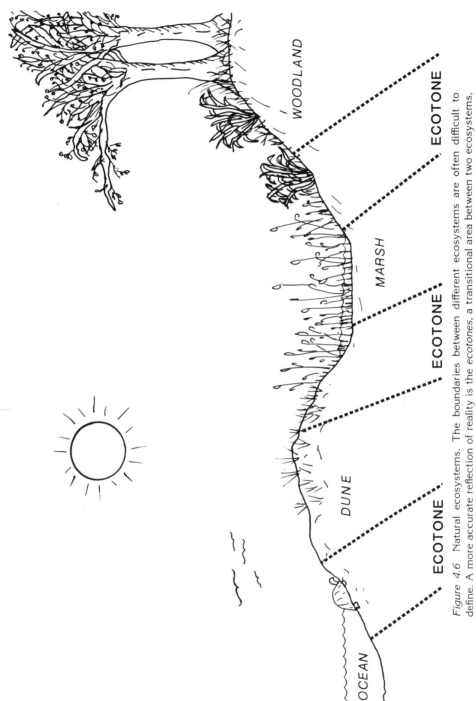

Figure 4.6 Natural ecosystems. The boundaries between different ecosystems are often difficult to define. A more accurate reflection of reality is the ecotones, a transitional area between two ecosystems, with plants and animals from both. An ecotone is more diversified and usually more productive than a simple ecosystem.

OCEAN

ECOTONE

DUNE

ECOTONE

MARSH

ECOTONE

WOODLAND

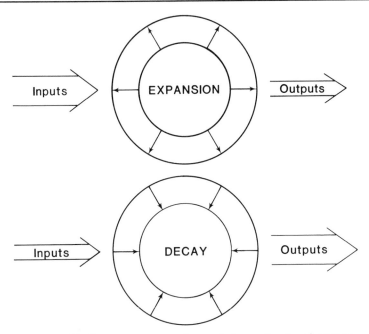

Figure 4.7 Ecosystem expansion and decay. Inputs of energy and materials are stored, are utilized, or flow through the ecosystem, leaving as outputs. When inputs are greater than outputs, the ecosystem is in a growth stage. When outputs exceed inputs, the ecosystem is in a stage of decay.

valuable resource permanently. In such situations, where a resource is used without cognizance of the workings of the environment, damage can spread to other portions of the natural or built world. For example, in the 19th century, farmers moved into the dry lands of Oklahoma and West Texas, with little concern for the fact that they were growing crops in a much drier region than the one from which they had moved. Thus their cropping, tilling, and soil conservation methods were based on the workings of a more humid environment. When low farm prices and a series of dry years struck these semiarid lands in the 1930s, environmental disaster followed. Topsoil was blown to distant regions, and thousands of people were forced to migrate from the Dust Bowl in search of new lives. The soil and water resources were depleted, and interrelated natural systems were adversely affected. It is only since farmers have begun to recognize the limitations and requirements of semiarid lands that we have seen some recovery in this region (see Chapter 6).

Other examples of the damage to resources when they are used without cognizance of environmental systems abound. These include the accelerating contamination of water supplies caused by mismanaged waste disposal and increasing acidification of rainfall resulting in damage to trees and fish. These problems have global implications for the future availability and quality of our most basic resources.

Good resource management depends on understanding the natural processes controlling the availability of natural resources. For resource use decision-making sophisticated scientific knowledge is needed. This is the reason for detailed

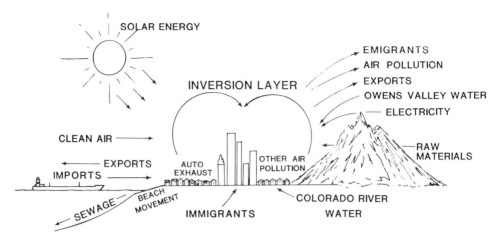

Figure 4.8 An urban ecosystem. This simplified and idealized model of the Los Angeles urban ecosystem shows some of the physical, social, and economic inputs and outputs.

environmental impact assessments and similar studies routinely conducted by resource managers. But at a more general level, it is important to understand some of the basic characteristics of natural systems before analyzing specific resources in more detail. This section deals with the general characteristics of energy and material cycles in the environment and their relation to ecological systems and natural resources.

Energy Transfers

Energy in ecosystems (and human systems) is ultimately derived from the sun. This energy passes through a series of storages via many paths, before finally being returned to space as radiant energy. The first and second laws of thermodynamics are the two fundamental laws governing all energy transfers.

   The *first law of thermodynamics* is the law of conservation of energy, but it also governs conversion of matter into energy. It states that in any energy transfer, the total amount of energy is unchanged; energy is neither created nor destroyed. You cannot get more out than you put in. The *second law of thermodynamics* is a little less obvious than the first. It says that any time energy is converted from one form to another, the conversion is inefficient. Energy is always converted to a less concentrated form, or dissipated as heat. In other words, not only is it impossible to get more out than you put in, but you cannot even break even. Systems tend toward increasing *entropy,* a measure of the degree of organization present. Greater entropy means greater disorganization or randomness. The following two examples may help to illustrate these concepts.

   The first example deals with the conversion of solar energy to food energy by *photosynthesis.* A leaf on a plant is exposed to sunlight, which stimulates a chemical reaction where carbon dioxide and water are converted to carbohydrates. Oxygen is given off as a by-product. In the process, however, the leaf must be heated, and this causes a loss of energy by radiation or convection from the leaf surface. In addition, water is both moved through the leaf stem to deliver nutrients to the leaf and evaporated by the leaf as a cooling mechanism. This water loss involves a conversion of water from liquid to vapor form, which requires energy. Finally, plants must also respire, a process in which food energy is converted to heat energy, which is dissipated. When all these things are weighed against one another in an *energy budget* for a single plant or for an entire plant community, only a very small fraction of the incoming solar energy is converted to food energy or *biomass,* generally about 1 percent or less. The rest of the energy is dispersed by reflection, reradiation, or use in the conversion of liquid water to water vapor.

A coal-fired electric-generating plant provides a second example. Coal, of course, is formed by chemical modification of formerly living matter, mostly plants. The energy released was first stored by plant photosynthesis at some time in the geologic past. When the coal is burned, some heat is lost in the smokestack, but most of the heat is used to convert water to steam. The steam, in turn, drives turbines, which drive generators, which produce electricity. The steam is cooled in the process, but not enough to condense it. It must, however, be returned to the boiler as water. To do this it must be cooled, usually by dissipating the heat in the atmosphere or in the nearest river or other body of water. Heat is also produced by the generator and by friction in moving parts, and this must be dissipated as well. In the end, only about 35 percent of all the heat stored in the coal is finally converted to electric energy. The rest is dissipated as heat, either in the stack gases or in the steam-condensing system. This dissipation of energy is an example of entropy.

Ecosystems consist of all the living organisms in a defined geographic area, together with all the physical entities (e.g., soil, water, dead organic matter) with which they interact. As such, they are exceedingly complex, and the energy and material transfers within them are difficult to quantify. Several important studies of energy transfers within ecosystems have been done, however, and from these some generalizations are possible. As one type of organism in an ecosystem consumes another, a pattern of energy flow through the ecosystem is set up, called a *food chain* (Figure 4.9). Some food chains are simple. Consider, for example, a plant, which is consumed by a rabbit, which is consumed by a fox. Such a simple chain is usually part of a more complex *food web* in which several animals and plants may be dependent on one another. Many organisms eat more than one kind of food and may in turn be consumed by several other species.

Energy is transferred from one *trophic level* to another within the chain or web. Terrestrial green plants are producers, as they convert solar energy to food energy, at the first trophic level. Consumers can, in turn, be classified as primary consumers, which feed on producers at the second trophic level, secondary consumers, which feed on primary consumers at the third trophic level, and so forth. In addition there are decomposers, which feed on dead organic matter and return nutrients to the soil or water where they are available to producers. There may be fourth- or fifth-level consumers. However we rarely find more than five in an ecosystem, since the energy produced at the first level has been mostly consumed at intermediate levels. Human beings are able to take advantage of the food energy at different levels, because we can consume energy both in the form of plants and animals. There is some debate over whether we are wasteful of the world's food energy when our diets are high in animal products, since it is generally more efficient in terms of energy production and consumption to obtain our food directly at the first trophic level (see Chapter 6).

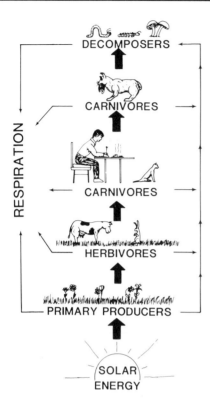

Figure 4.9 Food chain. Herbivores, or primary consumers, eat producers and are then consumed by carnivores. Sometimes a food chain can support additional trophic levels of consumers, before decomposers take their turn.

Figure 4.9 provides an example of a relatively simple food chain. Notice that in each step in the system energy is either stored as biomass (the living and dead organic matter in an ecosystem) or used in respiration. Most of the energy consumed at any given level is used in organism metabolism. Only a small percentage is stored as biomass, available for the next higher level to consume.

Biogeochemical Cycles

Just as energy flows through an ecosystem in a cyclic manner, so do many of the materials necessary for life—carbon, oxygen, nitrogen, potassium, water, and many others. The paths these substances take in the environment are called biogeochemical cycles. Some *biogeochemical cycles* are regulated by large storages in the atmosphere. The nitrogen cycle is a good example of this type. Others are dominated by terrestrial storages, usually in rocks and sediments, such as the phosphorus, potassium, sulfur, and calcium cycles. Although the cycles differ because of the different chemical and biological processes regulating them, the patterns are generally similar. We will discuss only four of the important biogeochemical cycles: the nitrogen, phosphorus, carbon, and hydrologic cycles.

Nitrogen comprises about 80 percent of the earth's atmosphere, and most of the earth's nitrogen is in the atmosphere at any given time (Figure 4.10). Nitrogen is also an essential nutrient, and a fundamental component of many proteins. Nitrogen cannot be directly used by most organisms in its gaseous form. For it to be available to living matter, it must be fixed, or incorporated

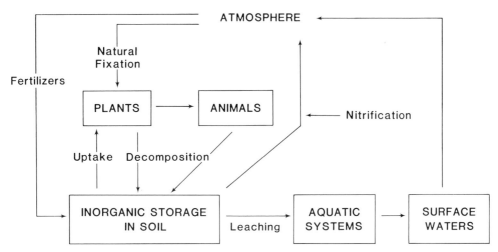

Figure 4.10 The nitrogen cycle. The atmosphere provides the primary storage of nitrogen. Unusable by plants in its gaseous state, nitrogen must first be converted by nitrogen-fixing bacteria before it can be used by plants.

in chemical substances such as ammonia, nitrates, or organic compounds that plants are able to use. Some nitrogen is added directly to the soil as impurities in rainfall, primarily nitric acid. But the much more important mechanism is the action of nitrogen-fixing bacteria, some of which live in association with plant roots. These bacteria are able to extract nitrogen directly from the air. Some plants, such as legumes, have symbiotic or mutually beneficial relationships with particular nitrogen-fixing bacteria. But many other plants also accommodate nitrogen-fixing bacteria, and some nitrogen fixers do not depend on the environment of plant roots at all.

Once nitrogen is incorporated in organic matter, it follows much the same route as energy in the food chain, passing from producer to consumer and ultimately to decomposer. Decomposers return nitrogen to the soil in mineral forms such as ammonia that are again available to plants. In addition, nitrifying bacteria convert nitrogen from ammonia to nitrates and eventually to gaseous forms, N_2O, NO, and N_2, which are returned to the atmosphere. Finally, some nitrogen is leached from the soil or incorporated in runoff and makes its way to groundwater or through rivers and lakes to the sea, from which it can be returned to the atmosphere.

The *phosphorus cycle* (Figure 4.11) is a good example of a biogeochemical cycle dominated by terrestrial, rather than atmospheric storage. Phosphorus, an essential nutrient, is found primarily in rocks and enters the soil as those rocks weather. But many rocks contain little phosphorus, and areas underlain by non-phosphate rocks must derive their phosphorus from trace amounts contained in rainfall. Once in the soil, phosphorus travels through the food chain, ultimately being returned to the soil by decomposers. Considerable amounts of phosphorus are leached or eroded from the soil, however, and this phosphorus eventually accumulates in the sea. There it is concentrated in the bones of fish. As the fish die and their bodies decay, phosphorus is deposited on the ocean floor and eventually incorporated in sedimentary rocks. Since the excrement of fish-eating birds contains large amounts of phosphorus, the rocks and offshore islands where

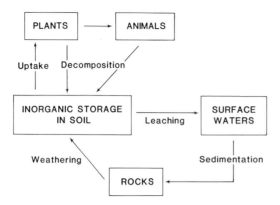

Figure 4.11 The phosphorus cycle. Phosphorus naturally enters the environment through the weathering of rocks. Human uses of phosphorus include phosphate fertilizers and detergents.

seabirds roost are an important source of phosphate fertilizer. Fish bones from processing plants are also used as fertilizer in some parts of the world. In the United States, most of our phosphate fertilizer is derived from mining phosphate-rich rocks.

One of the most important biogeochemical cycles is the *carbon cycle* (Figure 4.12). It includes large storages in the atmosphere, in living organisms, and in rocks. Carbon dioxide in the atmosphere enters plant leaves and through photosynthesis is incorporated in living matter, forming a basic part of starches, sugars, and other foods. As it passes through the food chain, carbon dioxide is returned to the atmosphere by respiration of consumers and decomposers. Significant amounts of organic matter accumulate in soils, marshes, lake bottoms,

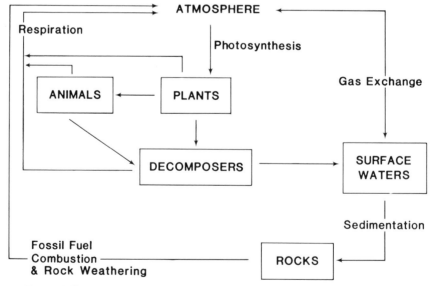

Figure 4.12 The carbon cycle. Carbon is stored in the form of carbon dioxide in the atmosphere, in plants, and in the decayed remains of organic organisms found in rocks and oceans. Fossil-fuel combustion has altered the normal carbon cycle by removing carbon from terrestrial storage, burning it, and returning it to the atmosphere faster than it can be placed into storage.

and the like. This organic matter is, of course, largely carbon. Some of it may be oxidized from time to time, but some is semipermanently stored in sediments. In addition, large amounts of carbon are in the oceans, both in living organisms and as dissolved carbon dioxide. Carbon is continually deposited on the ocean floor in sediments, which over time become sedimentary rocks. Limestone, which is primarily calcium carbonate ($CaCO_3$), is a good example of such a rock (Figure 4.13), as are the fossil fuels in sedimentary rocks. The carbon in rocks reenters the atmosphere as rocks weather and erode and as fossil fuels are burned. In the last few hundred years, humans have removed and burned much more carbon from terrestrial storages of coal, oil, and natural gas than has been returned in that time, and the atmospheric concentration of carbon dioxide has increased accordingly (see Chapter 11). In addition, clearing forests and depleting soil organic matter by poor land management practices have reduced these storages of carbon and contributed to the atmospheric carbon dioxide increase.

Another example of an important environmental cycle is the *hydrologic cycle* (Figure 4.14). It is not a biogeochemical cycle in the same way as the others already discussed; instead, it is a regulator of flows of nutrients and energy. The hydrologic cycle is the set of pathways that water takes as it passes from atmosphere to earth and back (Figure 4.15). It is primarily regulated by climate, but the terrestrial components of the cycle (rivers, lakes, soil, and groundwater) are also regulated by the characteristics of surficial materials and by topography. Analyzing water budgets, which quantify various components of the hydrologic cycle, is essential for water management.

Beginning with the atmosphere, water is delivered to the earth's surface by precipitation. Rain strikes the leaves of plants. Some of the rain remains there

Figure 4.13 Limestone cliffs in England. Large amounts of carbon are stored in rocks, including both organic sedimentary rocks and fossil fuels.

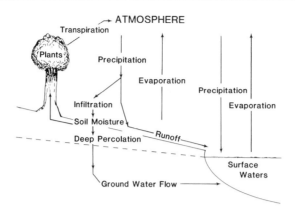

Figure 4.14 The hydrologic cycle. Water flows in the environment play a major role in regulating material and energy cycles.

and is evaporated, but most reaches the soil surface. Once on the soil, the water may either evaporate, soak into the soil, or run off. Several factors determine how much water soaks in and how much runs off, but the primary controls are the rate at which rain falls, or *precipitation intensity,* and the ability of the soil to soak up water, or its *infiltration capacity.* These factors are of critical importance in controlling soil erosion, and they will be discussed further in Chapter 6. Water that runs off the soil surface or through the regolith enters stream channels, becoming surface water. Surface waters flow by gravity to the ocean, via rivers, lakes, swamps, and so forth. Depending on climatic factors such as atmospheric humidity and temperature, varying amounts are lost from surface water by evaporation.

Precipitation may add directly to surface water. Moisture is temporarily stored in the soil, where it is available to plants. As plants use water, it is returned to the atmosphere by evapotranspiration from their leaves. Water that is not used by plants percolates down into the ground, where it eventually reaches a level below which the pores in the rocks are saturated, known as the *water table.* Water in this saturated zone is *groundwater,* and flows by gravity, over long periods of time returning to the surface in valleys and becoming surface water. The rate of flow of ground water is very much less than for surface water, and depending on subsurface characteristics very large amounts of water may be stored there. Groundwater flow is primarily responsible for maintaining river flow during periods between rains. Eventually, most water is returned to the atmosphere by either evapotranspiration by plants or evaporation from surface waters, particularly the oceans. Some water may be stored for such long periods of time in groundwater, ice caps, and isolated deep-water bodies, that it is essentially removed from the cycle.

These environmental cycles are important in regulating natural processes so that the viability of natural resources is affected by them. They provide the major means by which resources are renewed following harvesting. For example, when a forest is logged, the environmental system of the forest is drastically altered. Removing trees reduces evapotranspiration, while it increases water movement both through and over the soil. This increased water movement, together with the decay of plant matter left behind (smaller branches and leaves), contributes to a greatly increased removal of nutrients from the area, both dissolved and as part of soil particles. Were it not for weathering, nitrogen fixation, and other additions of nutrients over time to replace these losses, the soil would be less able to support the regrowth of the forest for future harvest. Similarly, grazing, cultivation, and water-resource development depend on replacement of substances by these natural cycles. Additionally, the timing of these cycles may place significant constraints on human use, in the same way that finite, or stock, resources lead to constraints. This means that "renewable" also has an element of finiteness.

The operation of biogeochemical cycles also has implications for activities that disturb some portion of the cycle, either by removing or introducing substances. Using nitrogen fertilizers in agriculture substantially increases the inorganic nitrogen content of the soil. This increase, of course, benefits crop plants, but it also leads to greater leaching of nitrogen by water and, hence, greater nitrogen concentrations in rivers and lakes draining agricultural areas. This added nitrogen causes serious pollution problems in some areas, since it not only modifies aquatic ecosystems but is also potentially dangerous to humans if consumed in drinking water. By modifying the nitrogen inputs to the soil, we also change conditions farther downstream, often with undesired consequences. A second example relates to the use of pesticides in the environment. An insecticide may be intended to act on only one small component of an ecosystem—the population of some particular insect species—but the food chain can carry both food and unwanted substances to other organisms with unforseen and undesired effects.

Figure 4.15 The hydrologic cycle: a thunderstorm in Colorado. Moisture held in storage in the atmosphere precipitates out as rain, where it is used by plants, runs off into surface waters, or percolates through the soil for storage as ground water.

Thus biogeochemical cycles serve as conduits for substances from one part of the environment to another. They also cause the effects of human activities to extend beyond the immediate area of impact. For these reasons, we have become increasingly aware of the interrelatedness of natural resources, particularly renewable resources, and of the need to understand natural processes more completely for improved resource management.

ECOSYSTEM CARRYING CAPACITY AND POPULATION GROWTH

No matter how complex or simple the ecosystem, its component organisms are always working to reproduce themselves and to find adequate food. Obviously, the number of organisms cannot exceed the amount of food available to them for very long, or the equilibrium of the ecosystem will be threatened. For an ecosystem to maintain equilibrium, population size and food supply must be stable over the long run, although there can be short-term fluctuations. As a result, we find an intricate relationship among the size of populations of the different species in an ecosystem and among their competitive or complementary food needs relative to other populations in that ecosystem. These relationships can change over time, since the ecosystem's population dynamics shift as a result of internal and external changes (Issue 4.1).

It is calculated that with ample food, living space, good health, and no predators, a species population could grow to its *biotic potential*. This is the maximum rate of population growth resulting if all females breed as often as possible, with all individuals surviving past their reproductive period. Obviously, a species breeding at an exponential rate of increase would soon outstrip the available food supply for it and other species in its ecosystem. Just as obviously,

---

ISSUE 4.1: Tamarisk: Unchecked Growth

Species that are introduced to a new environmental setting often experience a population-boom period. They occupy underused portions of one or more ecosystems or else are more aggressive than the native species. Examples abound. Consider the kudzu vine, which was introduced as a ground cover in Florida and has spread throughout the South, or rabbits, which when introduced to Australia caused great environmental damage as they competed with sheep, another introduced species.

The tamarisk, or salt cedar (*Tamarix pentandra*), was introduced to the American Southwest in the 19th or 20th century as a rapid-growing and drought-resistant tree, suitable for windbreaks and shade. It soon escaped from cultivation, taking over river banks and moist areas and crowding out native species.

It is only since the 1930s that tamarisk has come to be seen as a problem. In the mid-1930s, it was still being planted on eroding stream banks in New Mexico and along the property lines of many farms. It spread rapidly and became a problem. In 1936 the mapped vegetation of the Rio Grande River Valley (of Colorado, New Mexico, and Mexico) revealed that tamarisk was present, although not over large areas. In 1947, eleven years later, 24,550 hectares (60,640 acres) were covered (Hay, 1972).

The tamarisk was able to invade in part because the Rio Grande's farming and natural ecosystems had been weakened by sedimentation and resultant salinization from

various types of *environmental resistance,* such as exhaustion of the food supply, adverse weather, and disease, ensure that the population is kept at a level far below its biotic potential. In systems terms, environmental resistance is a good example of negative feedback. For example, as a population grows, its food consumption increases, and food becomes harder to find. As food becomes scarce, however, competition for food intensifies and organisms are less likely to survive to reproductive age. As a result, population growth is reduced.

Although these restrictions to population growth prevent exponential rates of increase, there are several fairly predictable growth patterns for populations within ecosystems (Figure 4.16). One of the most common is the *sigmoidal growth curve,* which describes a population with only a small difference between the rates of growth, due to birth and immigration, and decline, due to disease, predation, uncertain food supply, and other forms of resistance. Over time, however, the population may increase more rapidly as long as there is enough food and other necessities. Eventually, the resources a population demands may exceed those available for its use, and environmental resistance will put a damper on the rate of increase.

The portion of the curve that is almost level suggests a zero growth rate, in which births plus immigrations equal deaths plus emigrations. This is an equilibrium situation in which biotic potential equals environmental resistance. The *carrying capacity* for this species in this ecosystem has been reached. This is the maximum number of organisms in one species that can be supported in the given environmental setting. It is not constant, but varies with changing environmental conditions. Extinction of a species can occur when a population fluctuates dramatically, dropping so low that the species cannot reproduce quickly enough to remain in competition with others for available resources.

---

the badly eroded Rio Puerco (see Chapter 7). The moist, silty banks along the Rio Grande were the perfect environment for the tamarisk. In addition, dam building resulted in more sedimentation, creating shallow deltas that the tamarisk was better prepared to use than were any native species.

Why is the tamarisk a problem? Its dense growth along the banks restricts water flow, which leads to more sediment deposits, waterlogged soils, and more and better tamarisk habitat. Because the tamarisk exudes salt from its glands, it can tolerate saline water, while it pollutes the soil surface, making agriculture impossible. In addition, the tamarisk consumes a great amount of water. In 1947 tamarisk was estimated to be responsible for 45 percent of the total water consumption in the Rio Grande Valley. On an annual basis, 1 hectare (2.5 acres) of tamarisk consumes about 12,200 m^3 of water (10 acre-ft), or a depth of 1.22 m (4 ft) (Hay, 1972).

Chemicals, burning, mowing, plowing the roots, and bulldozing have been used to try to control the tamarisk. Some of these solutions have caused more environmental problems, including chemical contamination of soil and water and increased erosion.

Tamarisk is a species that has been able to take advantage of a weakened ecosystem or systems, and its population size and areal extent have spread beyond all the expectations of those who introduced it. At present, the tamarisk remains prosperous and largely unchecked in the arid West.

Population patterns in ecosystems

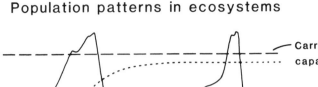
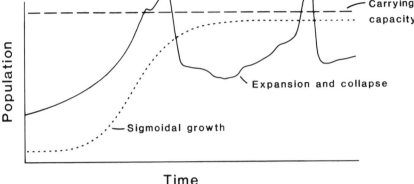

Figure 4.16 Population patterns in ecosystems. Populations can stabilize below carrying capacity. If the carrying capacity is exceeded, however, population collapse and die-back can occur.

Principle of Limiting Factors

One of the most important principles relating populations to ecosystem characteristics is the *principle of limiting factors.* There are usually many factors (e.g., nutrients and physical site characteristics) that are necessary for an organism to exist. The availability of these factors varies from site to site, and some factors are plentiful while others are rare. An organism requires different environmental conditions in varying degrees or in different amounts, and there is no reason to assume that every condition is available in exactly the amount required. Small changes in limiting factors may have profound effects. Similar changes in non-limiting factors may have few or no effects.

Plant nutrients provide a simple example. A particular plant may require sunlight, water, a stable substrate, and a variety of nutrients from the soil. These nutrients may include nitrogen, phosphorus, potassium, magnesium, copper, and zinc. They may all be available in plentiful supply except one, say, phosphorus. The rate of growth of the plant will be restricted by the lack of phosphorus, even though there is more than enough nitrogen, potassium, and other necessary nutrients. In this situation, nitrogen fertilizer applied to the soil will do little to help the plant, but phosphorus fertilizer will be very effective. Phosphorus is the limiting factor in this instance.

Nutrients are not the only condition that can be limiting. Sunlight, carbon dioxide, or any other environmental characteristic that an organism requires may be limiting. If substances are present in quantities that may poison an organism, these can also be considered limiting. Predators are often limiting factors for animal populations. It is usually difficult to determine just what factor or factors are limiting in any given situation. Clearly, however, this information is essential to predicting the effects of environmental changes on ecosystem development and helps illustrate the critical importance of good environmental information for sound resource management.

Ecology, Natural Resource Use, and Conservation

Careful and painstaking research by ecologists provides a strong argument for thoughtful resource management. The complexity of ecosystems is such that we can never assume that an action will only affect the immediate location. Ecological research has shown that the interconnectedness of ecosystems leads to far-reaching and often unexpected effects. If resource managers fail to recognize this, a disruption in natural systems can occur, leading to a disruption of connected systems or possibly to a domino effect in which distantly related systems and organisms may suffer.

We must always keep in mind that the ecological viewpoint is open to political uses, as are all scientific approaches. Ecosystems are both realities and abstractions (Kormondy, 1969). It is the abstract idea of interrelatedness that can be used by individuals or organizations eager to protect some special interest from change or development. For example, if a certain stream is dammed, they may argue that this act will eventually lead to the collapse of civilization, or life on earth, since everything is interrelated. Ecology as a serious field of study makes no such sweeping guarantees or generalities. In the context of resource management it needs to be used in a sober and factually based manner.

REFERENCES AND ADDITIONAL READING

Detwyler, T.R., and M.G. Marcus, eds. 1972. *Urbanization and environment.* Belmont, California: Duxbury Press.

Hay, J. 1972. Salt cedar and salinity on the upper Rio Grande. In *The careless technology: ecology and international development,* ed. M.T. Farvar and J.P. Milton. Garden City, New York: The National History Press.

Kormondy, E.J. 1969. *Concepts of ecology.* Englewood Cliffs, New Jersey: Prentice-Hall.

Simmons, I.G. 1981. *Ecology of natural resources.* 2nd ed. London: Halstead Press.

Turk, J., et al. 1975. *Ecosystems, energy, population.* Philadelphia: W.B. Saunders.

Watts, D. 1971. *Principles of biogeography.* New York: McGraw-Hill.

TERMS TO KNOW

biogeochemical cycles
biome
biosphere
biotic potential
boreal
carbon cycle
carrying capacity
chaparral
communities
ecology
ecosystem
ecotone
energy budget

environmental resistance
first law of thermodynamics
food chain
food web
hydrologic cycle
infiltration capacity
nitrogen cycle
permafrost
phosphorus cycle
photosynthesis
potential evapotranspiration
precipitation intensity
principle of limiting factors

savanna
second law of thermodynamics
sigmoidal growth curve

trophic level
tundra
water table

STUDY QUESTIONS

1. What are the differences among eco-systems, ecotones, and communities?
2. Briefly describe the vegetative and climatic characteristics of each of the world's major biomes.
3. What are some of the adverse effects of disrupting the carbon, nitrogen, and phosphorus cycles?
4. How does environmental resistance provide negative feedback within an ecosystem?
5. Describe the principle of limiting factors and explain the role of this principle in the functioning of ecosystems.

CHAPTER FIVE

Population: The Human System

INTRODUCTION

The world's population is rising. In 1980, global population was estimated at 4.5 billion, and by 1983 it had reached 4.7 billion (Population Reference Bureau, 1983). Over one-fifth of this total or 1.023 billion live in China, the world's most populous country, with another 730 million living in India. As the world's population increases, so does its use of resources. Environmentalists and population theorists such as Paul Ehrlich and Lester Brown have warned of increased population pressures on natural resource consumption. People must be fed, housed, and clothed; the more people there are, the more food resources, housing materials and fibers must be produced. Others, such as economist Julian Simon, are confident that population growth does not mean a drop in standards of living.

Population Growth: Good or Bad?

The population problem, or crisis to some, is not a recent phenomenon. In 1798 the British economist Thomas Malthus foresaw some of the world's current population problems. Malthus wrote that populations increase in size geometrically; that is, they double in size in a fixed time period. Geometric growth is shown by a J-shaped curve (Figure 5.1a). Malthus also wrote that food supplies increase arithmetically, that is they increase by addition of a fixed amount in a given time period. Arithmetic growth is shown as a straight line (Figure 5.1b). Eventually, he said, population growth would outstrip the food resources (assuming, of course, no new resources are developed) with catastrophic consequences—mass starvation, poverty, and the collapse of economic and social systems.

Debates over the relationship between population growth and resource scarcity, which originated during Malthus' time, continue today. Neo-Malthusians take the same perspective as Malthus yet argue for strong birth control measures to postpone or delay population growth to below the limit of resource availability. Using birth control to stabilize population growth, instead of expecting nature to do the job through famine and war, differentiates Neo-Malthusianism from the original form.

An early critic of Malthus, Karl Marx, stressed that there was no single theory of population growth and resource use. Increased population growth did not by itself, as Malthus suggested, result in increased resource use and a lowering of the standard of living of individuals. Marx felt that poverty was caused by the economic system, which exploited labor for the benefit of the elite. The cause of poverty was economic, not increased numbers of people.

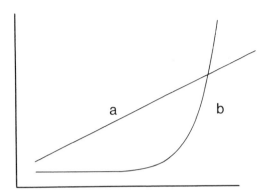

Figure 5.1   Arithmetic versus geometric growth. Arithmetic growth (a) follows a straight line, increasing by addition. Geometric growth (b) follows a curve, increasing by multiplication.

Esther Boserup (1965; 1981) suggests that population growth may be beneficial in providing a stimulus for the improvement of the human condition. Population growth would intensify land use, resulting in increased agricultural production. The end result would be that all individuals would benefit by the increased production and thus would achieve a higher standard of living. She suggests that Malthus was incorrect in his assumption that increased population led to increased poverty, starvation, and war.

Today there are those population experts who anticipate some form of population catastrophe in the near future. There are others, however, who are confident that human needs can be met no matter how large the world's population becomes. The following historical perspective and some of today's population figures may help you decide where you stand on this issue.

A Short History of World Population Growth

Although it is impossible to measure the world's human population accurately in the distant past, demographers and archaeologists, among others, have developed low to high ranges for population size and growth over thousands of years. These estimates change, of course, with new evidence such as the unearthing of ancient communities, new dating methods, and new theories. The world human population at the end of the most recent ice age, about 10,000 years ago, was somewhere between 2 million and 10 million people. It had taken perhaps 1 million to 2 million years for the population to grow to this size. When we consider that population has burgeoned to 4.7 billion in the past 10,000 years—and most of that growth in the last 300 years—it is clear that extraordinary changes have taken place in all aspects of human life, to adjust to this astonishing growth (Figure 5.2).

Between 8000 B.C. and 1 A.D. the population doubled almost six times, to between 200 million and 400 million. The doubling time was more than 1000 years. Of course, this growth was not steady and smooth. A closer look would reveal sudden rises and drops, due to the vagaries of famine, war, and disease over small and large regions. The tendency, however, was toward growth. Between 1 A.D. and 1750 A.D. growth continued at about the same rate, ultimately reaching

750 million by 1750. Though scholars differ, there is no doubt that the technological developments of agriculture and irrigation, in the first few thousand years after the ice retreat, had much to do with this population increase, as did warmer weather worldwide.

Since 1750 A.D. the world's population has begun its modern climb. It took only 150 years, from 1750 to 1900, for the population to double from 750 million to 1.5 billion. The population doubled once again between 1900 and 1965, a doubling time of sixty-five years. *Doubling time* is the number of years it takes a population to double in size. The lower the number of years to double in size, the faster the growth rate. If we assume an annual worldwide growth rate of 1.8 percent, it will take about thirty-nine years for the world's population to double in size from 4.7 to 9.4 billion. Recent projections by the World Bank, however, have suggested that this doubling may take longer, as much as sixty-five years. Present population projections for selected countries are shown in Table 5.1. Mexico, at twenty-seven years, has one of the fastest doubling times, while the U.S. at ninety-five years has one of the slowest. There are many explanations for this extraordinary change over such a short period of humanity's life span. Some of these include a broader worldwide food base due to increased trade; an eventual (after a two-century-long period of fluctuation) rise in overall disease resistance, also due to increased trade and travel; better medical technology and theory, leading to a drop in infant and child mortality rates; and an increased life span for large segments of the world's population (Durand, 1967). Chapter 16 discusses the possibilities and implications of present and future growth rates.

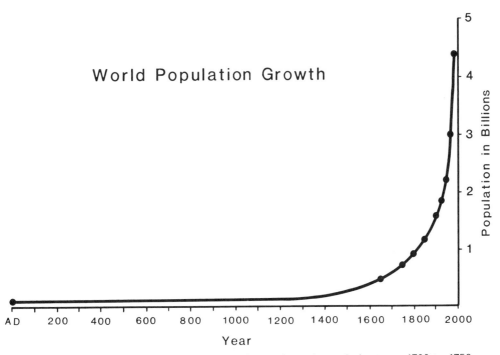

Figure 5.2 World population growth was slow and steady until about A.D. 1700 to 1750. Since then, population has expanded rapidly.

Table 5.1 Population Projections

	Pop. Est. 1983	Pop. Est. 2000	Annual Percentage Increase	Doubling Time (Years)
World	4,722	6,130	1.8	39
More developed	1,158	1,273	0.6	118
Less developed	3,564	4,857	2.1	32
Regions				
Africa	513	851	3.0	23
Asia	2,730	3,564	1.9	36
Latin America	390	564	2.3	30
U.S.S.R. & E. Europe	383	429	0.7	104
Western Europe	378	391	0.3	230
North America	259	302	0.7	94
Oceania	24	29	1.2	57
Selected countries				
Peop. Rep. China	1,023	1,245	1.5	46
India	730	966	2.1	33
Indonesia	156	199	1.7	41
Bangladesh	97	149	3.1	22
Pakistan	96	142	2.8	25
Philippines	53	77	2.7	26
Thailand	51	69	2.0	36
South Korea	41	52	1.7	41
Egypt	46	67	3.1	22
Nigeria	84	148	3.3	21
Brazil	131	188	2.3	30
Mexico	76	115	2.6	27
U.S.A.	234	268	0.7	95
United Kingdom	56	57	0.1	533

Source: Population Reference Bureau, 1983

POPULATION DYNAMICS

There are two helpful tools for examining the human population system. The first is made up of the rate and causes of population growth, termed *population dynamics.* The second is the location of growth, that is, its spatial distribution around the world. Both are essential to our understanding of current and future population trends. In examining population dynamics, a first question is, How and why do populations grow? There are three factors that contribute to population growth. These are rates of natural growth/decline, the age structure of a population, and immigration/emigration.

Natural Growth

Natural growth (sometimes termed natural increase or decrease) is a simple measure of population growth, involving the differences between births (fertility) and deaths (mortality) in a given group. First let us look at the component involving births. The crude birth rate (CBR) is the number of births that occur during a given period, usually a year, divided by the total population as of midyear. CBR is usually expressed as a rate per 1000 population. For example, if 3000 babies were born in a population of 150,000, then the CBR would be 20 per 1000. Similarly, the crude death rate (CDR) is the number of deaths over a period such as a year, also divided by the midyear population and expressed as a rate per 1000 population.

Natural growth rates are expressed as the difference between the two (crude birth rate minus crude death rate). This difference is then converted to a percentage figure. An annual natural growth rate of 0.7 percent, roughly that of the U.S., means that a country is increasing in population by 0.7 percent each year. This translates to about 1.6 million people annually at present, or a doubling in 95 years.

Annual growth rates must be considered in combination with the actual population figure. A small annual growth rate of a small population is significantly different from a comparable annual figure for a much larger population. India and Thailand, for example, have almost identical annual growth rates (2.1 and 2.0 percent, respectively). India, with a base population of 730 million will increase by 15 million annually. Thailand, on the other hand, has a much smaller population base, 51 million people. With an annual growth rate of 2.0 percent, the country will add only 1.0 million people annually (Table 5.1).

Fertility Rates

The simplest measure of fertility is the CBR. Another frequently used measure is the total *fertility rate,* which is a measure of the average number of children a woman has in her reproductive years (ages 15 to 49). One of the most important reasons for a decline in the natural rate of growth in the U.S. has been a steady decrease in the number of children born per family. In 1980, for example, the fertility rate among American women was 1.8. This means that, on the average, every American woman would have 1.8 live births during her lifetime. The total fertility rate in the U.S. has steadily declined since the 1950s (Table 5.2).

On a global scale, the fertility rate was 3.9 in 1983 (Population Reference Bureau, 1983). The rate is significantly higher in the less developed nations (4.5) than in the more developed nations (1.9). There are, however, some regional differences. For example, Africa has a total fertility rate of 6.5 versus 5.2 in south-central Asia and 4.1 in Asia. While fertility rates are high in some regions of the world, this is partially offset by high mortality rates in some of these areas (most notably Africa). High fertility rates, then, do not necessarily imply high annual growth rates. For decades now, debate has continued over whether high-growth nations should work to decrease their fertility rates. The People's Republic of China (fertility rate 2.8), for example, has instituted a one-child limit for all families (Figure 5.3). A second child means the loss of state medical and school aid, ostracism, and official criticism. India has struggled for two decades to reduce birth rates with various economic and social incentives, as well as involuntary measures. Its most recent census revealed, however, that growth rates

Table 5.2 U.S. Fertility Rates

Year	Rate
1950	3.3
1960	3.4
1970	2.5
1980	1.8

Source: Conservation Foundation, 1982

Figure 5.3   A one-child family in China. The Chinese government has encouraged marriage late in life and has imposed economic penalties on families with more than one child. This has resulted in a significant lowering of the fertility rate. (United Nations Photo 152,769/John Isaac)

did not decline significantly between 1970 and 1980. There has been a decline in fertility in some countries primarily as a result of government-sponsored family planning programs. Not all family planning programs have been successful and there are many countries that still have high fertility rates (Figure 5.4). These include Kenya at 8.0, Nigeria at 6.9, Pakistan at 6.3, and Bolivia at 6.6. There are many theories and explanations for continued high growth rates, and we will discuss one of these later in this chapter.

Zero population growth (ZPG) refers to the number of births per family that will replace a population, without further growth. It takes a fertility rate of about 2.1 in developed nations or 2.7 in developing nations to maintain a population at a constant size, assuming a stable age structure and no net migration. The difference is explained by higher mortality rates in the developing nations, which require a higher birth rate to offset losses. A fertility rate of less than 2.1 would eventually lead to population decline, assuming no net immigration. To achieve ZPG globally, a fertility rate of about 2.5 is needed. But a much lower rate (below replacement levels) would be needed in some regions to stabilize population. Even if a ZPG fertility rate were reached, which is highly unlikely in this century, the population would continue to expand due to its age structure.

Age Structure

The second factor that contributes to overall population change is the age structure of a population. The age and sex profiles of populations will help us understand whether a country has an expanding, declining, or stable population.

Fertility Rate*

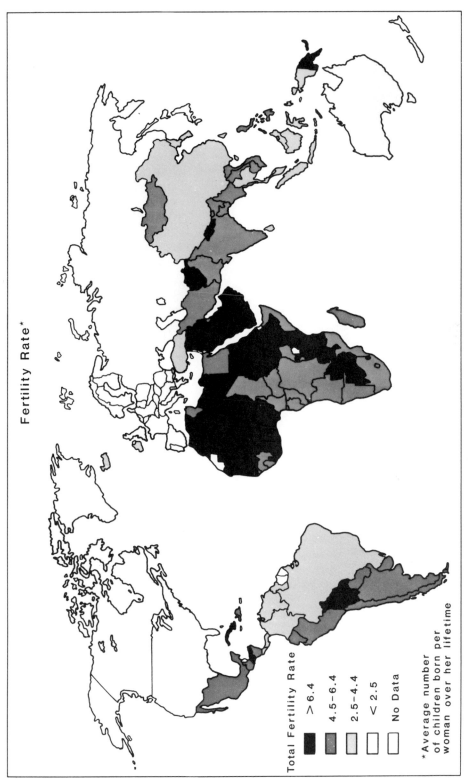

Total Fertility Rate

■ > 6.4

▨ 4.5 – 6.4

▨ 2.5 – 4.4

□ < 2.5

□ No Data

*Average number
of children born per
woman over her lifetime

Figure 5.4 Fertility rates are generally high in less industrialized nations, particularly Africa, and low in the industrialized world. (Source: Data from Population Reference Bureau, 1983)

How is a population's profile drawn? The population pyramid is a visually striking representation of the age and sex structure of a population (Figure 5.5). To make up a pyramid, a population is classified in age groups or *cohorts* by five-year intervals (e.g., 0–4, 5–9, 10–14) and by sex. The actual number of people or the percentage of a population that falls into each of these age categories is then graphed. The percentage of males in specific age groups is shown on the left and the percentage of females on the right. The general shape of the pyramid indicates the relative growth of the population. For example, a rapidly expanding population such as Brazil's (Figure 5.5a) has a very broad base because a large percentage of the population is less than 14 years old. Many of the developing nations have population pyramids of this shape. One hundred years ago, the U.S. population had a similar shape. Stable populations, such as Canada's (Figure 5.5b), have population pyramids with narrower bases. As the population ages, the actual number or percentage in each cohort declines, due to mortality. In stable populations such as those of the U.S., Canada, and the Scandinavian countries, the pyramid maintains a stable shape. A declining population, such as West Germany's (Figure 5.5c), is one where the base of the pyramid is small and bulges in the reproductive and/or postreproductive age categories. East Germany is another good example of a declining population.

In the decade from 1970 to 1980 the U.S. population, as a whole, aged (Figure 5.6). The median age in 1970 was 28, and in 1980 it was 30 (Conservation Foundation, 1982). Since 1970 there has been a gradual decrease in the number of people under age 14. Declining birth rates and the general aging of the *baby boom* cohort of the 1950s coupled with a long life expectancy account for this trend. There are some indications that the early 1980s saw a minor baby "boomlet" since women born in the post-World War II boom are having babies somewhat later in life than did earlier generations.

Population pyramids similar to those of the U.S. can be found throughout the industrialized world. Nearly 65 percent of the population in these countries is in the work-force age groups (ages 15 to 64). The young (under 15) comprise about 25 percent of the total population, and the old (over 65) around 10 percent. In contrast, between 40 and 50 percent of the population in developing nations is under 14 years of age. Another 50 percent of the population is in the working-age groups. Demands for food and education will be quite pronounced in the short run for these youthful populations. As of 1983, there were 1.6 billion people worldwide aged 15 years or less; many of these were in Africa where fertility rates are also high. They will be in the prime of their productive and consumptive years in the year 2000. The work force of less industrialized nations will have increased 40 percent over these twenty years. Based on current trends, it is clear that there will be a shortage of jobs for the majority of them. Today, with most men and a quarter of the women estimated to be job seekers, the total labor force of the less industrialized nations is 1.2 billion. With some countries averaging an unemployment rate of 40 percent, it is estimated that nearly 0.5 billion jobs are needed for today's adults. Where will the jobs be for 1.6 billion more? One of the major causes of this work shortage is the move by many individuals from relatively self-sufficient agricultural livelihoods in rural areas to urban areas in search of wage employment. Some of the possible reasons for this pattern are discussed in the following section.

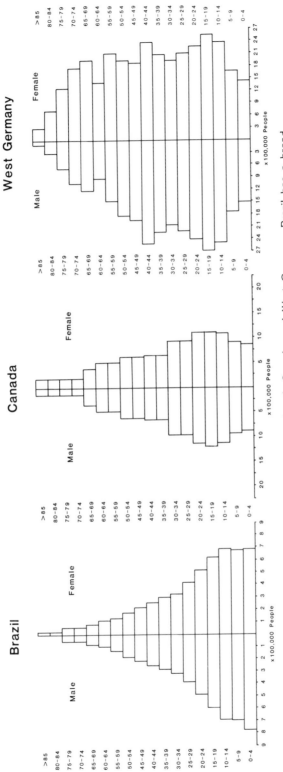

Figure 5.5 Population pyramids, 1979, for Brazil, Canada, and West Germany. Brazil has a broad-based pyramid, indicating large numbers of young people whose child-bearing years are in the future. Canada and West Germany have narrow-based pyramids, typical of more stable populations. (Source: Data from United Nations, 1982)

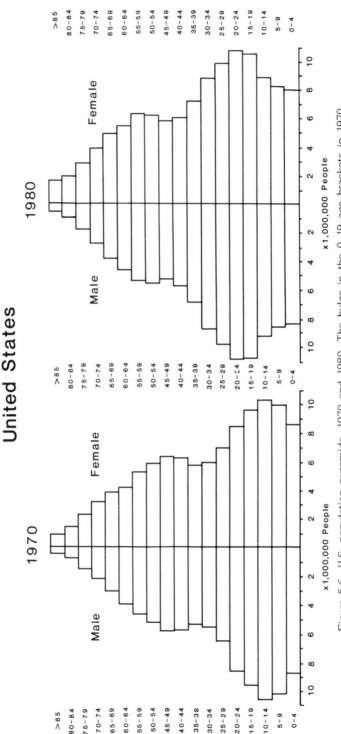

Figure 5.6 U.S. population pyramids, 1970 and 1980. The bulge in the 0–19 age brackets in 1970 has moved up by 1980, and these persons are now in their child-bearing years. They are producing fewer children than their parents did, however, and the base of the pyramid is now narrow. (Source: Data from Bureau of the Census, 1981)

Migration

Migration, which includes immigration and emigration, is the movement of individuals from one location to another. It has no influence on global population projections but does have a significant impact at national, regional, and local levels. Migration flows are caused by economic inequalities and group conflicts between and within nations. These flows can be permanent or temporary. Historically, many large-scale migrations have been from more densely populated to less densely populated areas.

Early migration to North America was of two basic types. Free immigrants came in search of a better life. Forced immigrants, or slaves, helped make life better for others. By the late 19th century, mass migration increased the flow greatly as entire ethnic or regional groups decided collectively to move to the United States and Canada, largely in search of better economic opportunities.

Since World War II, the international migration flow has to a large extent reversed, with the largest percentage of migrants moving from less-industrialized nations to European and North American urban areas. The principal destinations of transnational migrants from 1950 onward have been the U.S., Canada, Australia, and New Zealand, with large numbers moving to Europe and Great Britain as well. All of these countries currently have low birth rates, and the native population is stabilizing or shrinking. These new immigrants account for much of the increase in population in these countries. This trend is accelerated by political unrest; for example, the Vietnamese population in the U.S. has increased since the end of the Vietnam War.

As a result of increasing numbers of migrants to these regions, some of the affected nations have chosen to implement restrictive policies governing immigration. Authorities maintain that the immigrants are stealing wages from native-born citizens. Of course, there is usually a large component of fear and dislike—racism—on the part of natives regarding these new residents. It is often in the best economic interests of a nation, however, to allow entry to large numbers of immigrants on a temporary basis (as with Europe's guest workers) or to encourage illegal immigration so that low-level jobs can be filled at low wages. While a government may go to some lengths to discourage immigration publicly, it may allow private interests to encourage this exploitation.

This situation is only a symptom of a larger problem, that is, population pressure and perceived lack of opportunity in many less industrialized nations. People were once pulled off the land into the cities by the opportunities available. Now they are pushed off the land because their parents cannot subdivide the small farm between siblings any further, and no new land is available. Moving to the regional or capital city brings no satisfaction, since the colonizing countries have made little effort to create stable industrial economies in their colonies. Instead, they have chosen to export resources to the Euro-American centers for processing. Thus the dispossessed rural dwellers follow the jobs to the industrialized nations, where doors are often shut in their faces or they must take up demeaning employment. Clearly, this situation will worsen as populations continue to grow and economic opportunity does not increase in rural areas and ex-colonial cities.

The effect of transnational migration on population growth regionally is well illustrated by the following example. In the U.S., immigration laws set a quota of 270,000 net immigrants per year. The actual amount is significantly more than that due to refugees, families of Americans who enter outside the quota, and illegal immigrants. Over the past five years, legal immigration has accounted for nearly one-fourth of the total U.S. population growth (Conservation Foundation, 1982). Immigration quotas are often relaxed for immigrants from politically troubled areas, and the U.S. has seen an influx of immigrants from Southeast Asia and the Caribbean in recent years.

The case of illegal immigrants is quite different. The U.S. and Mexico share a common border. Better job opportunities in the U.S. act as a magnet for the illegal immigrant. The U.S. Immigration and Naturalization Service has very few statistics that accurately measure the actual number of illegal migrants to this country. The U.S. Bureau of the Census officially states that its count of the Spanish-speaking population of the country is underestimated by at least 10 percent as a result of illegal immigrants.

California is a new focus of immigration for the U.S. Not since the turn of the century when millions of southern and eastern Europeans went to northeastern U.S. cities, have so many alien immigrants traveled to a particular part of the country. These thousands of new arrivals include people from Southeast Asia, Cuba, Ethiopia, the Soviet Union, Taiwan, Samoa, Korea, and Latin America. Between the 1970 and 1980 censuses, Anglos, as a percentage of the population of California, dropped from 89 to 76 percent. Over the same period, Asians and Pacific Islanders population rose 140 percent, Hispanics 92 percent, Blacks 30 percent, and Amerinds 118 percent. This reflects a national trend for growth in the population percentage of these groups. Between 1970 and 1980, the percentage of Americans belonging to these minorities rose from 12.5 to 16.8 percent of the total U.S. population (Lindsey, 1981). Transnational migration thus will be a major factor in determining worldwide population patterns for the forseeable future.

The Temporal Pattern of Population Growth

The general pattern of rapid population growth in recent centuries can be explained by a combination of the changes in fertility and mortality rates (Figure 5.7). Prior to the Industrial Revolution with its attendant social changes and medical advances, most human populations had both high fertility rates and high mortality rates, resulting in relatively stable populations. In the industrialized nations in recent centuries, mortality rates began to decline as a result of increased standards of living and medical care. This decline preceded the decline in fertility. The result was a period of time in which fertility rates were substantially greater than mortality rates, and population increased accordingly.

This period of increase was characterized by a particularly broad-based population pyramid. It was also during the 18th and 19th centuries that the large populations of Europe found an outlet by settling in North America, Australia, and other frontier areas. Later, social changes brought about in part by the Industrial Revolution led to a decline in fertility in the industrialized nations, so that the base of the population pyramids narrowed and populations stabilized. Thus, Europe and the Americas have been through the period of intense population growth. In the less industrialized nations, however, mortality rates have declined substantially, but a decline in fertility is not yet clearly in sight. This is the fundamental reason for the high rates of population growth in the world as a whole and in the less industrialized nations in particular.

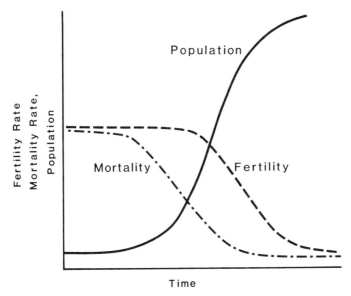

Figure 5.7 The demographic transition. Preindustrial populations generally have or had high birth rates and death
rates. When death rates fall before birth rates, population
rises rapidly.

SPATIAL DISTRIBUTION OF POPULATION

Currently, the most rapid population growth is occurring in the less industrialized
nations. Nearly 92 percent of all the world's growth is there (Council on
Environmental Quality, 1981). In 1950 66 percent of the global population lived
in the less industrialized nations, and in 1975 this rose to 72 percent. By 2000
it is expected to reach 79 percent (Figure 5.8) (Population Reference Bureau,
1983; Council on Environmental Quality, 1981). One recent estimate suggests a
world population of 6.35 billion in 2000 assuming current growth rates, with
nearly 5 billion of these people living in the less industrialized nations.

Much of the growth has been in urban places, in both the industrialized
and less industrialized nations (Figure 5.9). Movement away from rural areas,
where in most instances the population was largely food self-sufficient, has
complicated the population pressures in the less industrialized nations. It certainly
has intensified the pressures on usable resources, including space, water, and
food, and it taxes national abilities to promote social and economic welfare. This
trend toward increasing urbanization is seen as the major problem facing the
less industrialized nations in the future. Even if we assume moderate growth
rates, such urban places as Mexico City will have a population of over 30 million in the year 2000 (Table 5.3). It is estimated that the urban areas of the
less industrialized nations are growing at a rate two and a half times that of
the industrialized nations (Council on Environmental Quality, 1981). In 1950 there
were seventy cities worldwide with 1 million or more inhabitants. By the year
2000, one estimate gives 276 million-plus cities, the majority of these in the
less industrialized nations. In 1900 5 percent of the world's population lived in
large cities. By 2000 between 40 and 70 percent of the world's population will
live in urban areas of 20,000 or more people (Newland, 1980). Within our

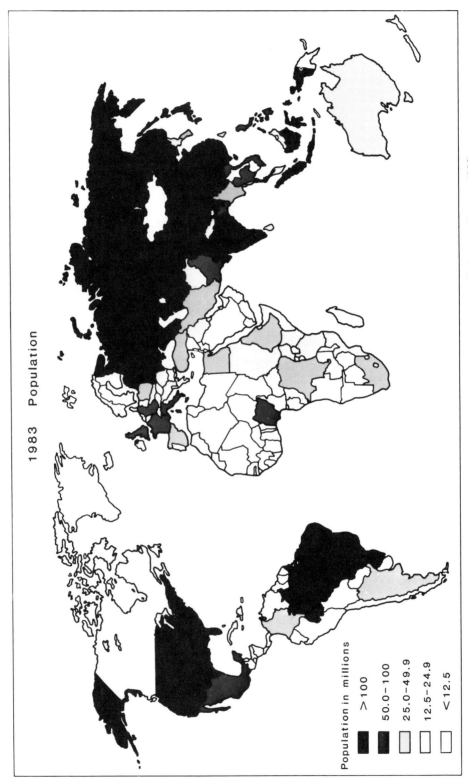

1983   Population

Population in millions

>100
50.0-100
25.0-49.9
12.5-24.9
<12.5

Figure 5.8   World population, 1983. (Source: Data from Population Reference Bureau, 1983)

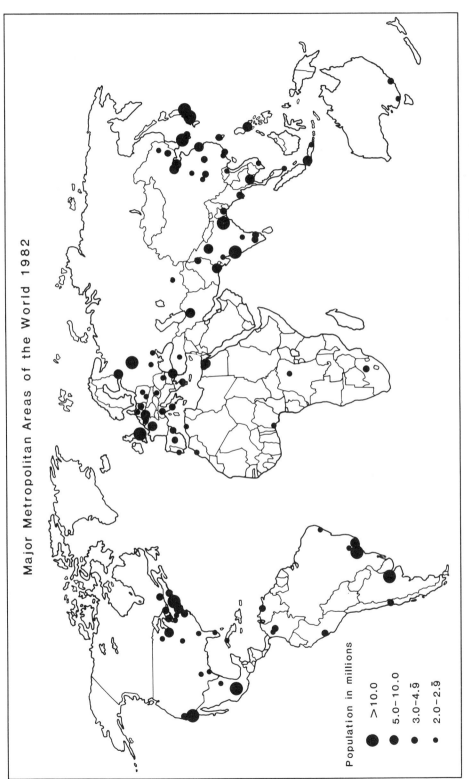

Figure 5.9 Major metropolitan areas of the world, 1982. In most of the world, cities are growing much faster than rural areas. (Source: Data from Rand McNally, 1983)

Table 5.3 Population Projections for Major World Cities

	1960	1970	1975	2000
Calcutta	5.5	6.9	8.1	19.7
Mexico City	4.9	8.6	10.9	31.6
Greater Bombay	4.1	5.8	7.1	19.1
Greater Cairo	3.7	5.7	6.9	16.4
Jakarta	2.7	4.3	5.6	16.9
Seoul	2.4	5.4	7.3	18.7
Delhi	2.3	3.5	4.5	13.2
Manila	2.2	3.5	4.4	12.7
Tehran	1.9	3.4	4.4	13.8
Karachi	1.8	3.3	4.5	15.9
Bogotá	1.7	2.6	3.4	9.5
Lagos	0.8	1.4	2.1	9.4

Source: Council on Environmental Quality, 1981

lifetimes, then, more than half the world's population may find itself living in cities.

Internal migrations are a cause for concern in both the industrialized and less industrialized nations. In the less industrialized nations, internal migrations are causing accelerated urban growth. The movement from rural areas to urban centers is placing severe demands on governments in terms of provision of food, sanitary facilities, jobs, and housing.

This is not just a problem abroad, however. One of the great internal migrations of this century in the U.S. has been that of American blacks and poor whites moving from the rural south to the nation's cities (Ernst and Hugg, 1976). This movement, largely from the 1920s onward, has been large. Cotton acreage was decreased, mechanical pickers took over, and small farmers found their livelihoods increasingly expensive. Thus, these families moved first to southern cities; then, with the pressure of many more behind them, they moved north. By the 1970s, 60 percent of the U.S. black population was in urban areas, in sharp contrast to a largely rural pattern as recently as the 1920s. One of the unfolding tragedies of American urban life is that there are not enough entry-level jobs and training available for these Americans. They remain outside the economic mainstream.

Interestingly, present demographic trends within the U.S. suggest simultaneous urban and rural growth, or perhaps better termed widespread population dispersal. For the first time since the 1820s, the 1980 census showed that rural areas and small towns were growing more rapidly than the nation's metropolitan areas (Table 5.4). The greatest increase, both in rural and urban growth, was in the sunbelt states of the South and West (see Issue 5.1). Thus, we see a simultaneous shift to a new region and to less densely populated areas. These moves have had a profound effect on the debates and decisions regarding resource use nationwide and is explored more fully in following chapters.

POPULATION GROWTH: RESOURCES AND PEOPLE

There is a finite amount of arable land in the world. Many experts suggest that at some future date the carrying capacity of available resources may be reached, and the human population will be plunged into a series of famines and resource wars until the population is reduced to a level within the boundaries of available resources. One alternative to this scenario is to control or limit population growth. While reproduction is a private act between individuals, it does have profound social and economic consequences and, as such, is a social problem. Many planners and resource experts believe that limiting the world's population growth is the only way to a stable and prosperous future.

On the other hand, there are many who resist the concept of control of reproduction. Julian Simon, an American economist, maintains that there is no population problem. Every new human being is a new source of mental creativity, to help solve humanity's problems, invent new resources, and increase the productivity of existing resources so that the earth can support an infinite number of people (Simon, 1981). For religious and moral reasons, formed in an era when there was no fear of a limit to resources, millions of Americans and probably billions worldwide resist the idea of birth control. Recently, the Reagan administration has moved to withhold birth control funds from nations permitting abortions.

For most people in the less industrialized countries, where farming is the key to prosperity, another child has always meant another pair of hands to help out. Until very recently, of course, parents might produce ten offspring, only to have over half of them die before adulthood. Now, better infant health care and, to some extent, improved nutrition enable more children to make it to adulthood. The economic need for having many children is now less pressing, and in its place new reasons for limiting family size are arising. However, ideas are slow to change, often for good reason. There is no guarantee that good times will last, and children are for many the greatest and perhaps only pleasure in a hard life.

Politically, population control is a complex issue. As mentioned earlier, the industrialized nations went through a period of rapid population growth from the mid-18th to the early 20th centuries. This was also the great period of colonization and settlement by those countries. Many people in the less industrialized nations say it is now their turn to do the same. They argue that they have the same rights to reproduction and resource use as the industrialized nations have. Any attempt to control their growth is seen as racism on the part of the older powers,

Table 5.4 U.S. Population Change

Total U.S. Population Growth: 1960–1980

	Growth	Nonmetropolitan Areas	Metropolitan Areas
1960–1970	13%, to 203.3 million	+4.4%	+17.0%
1970–1980	11.4%, to 226.5 million	+15.4%	+9.1%
Regional Population Growth, 1970–1980			
West		+31.8%	+21.2%
South		+17.1%	+20.1%
Middle West		+7.8%	+1.6%
Northeast		+12.4%	−2.0%

Source: U.S. Bureau of the Census, 1980

out of fear that these new centers of population growth will also become new power centers. Whatever the arguments, there is undeniably a strong tendency worldwide toward at least considering population control. This consideration is directly tied to fears over resource depletion.

Family Planning

Family planning programs in the U.S. were first institutionalized in the form of birth control clinics in the 1920s. The first birth control clinics were established in New York City by Margaret Sanger, a leader in the women's rights movement. Sanger was concerned with the suffering of women who had too many children, too close together, and no options for fertility control other than illegal abortions. The first birth control clinics were designed to liberate women from the traditional roles of wife and brood mare. They also allowed them to exercise active control over the number of children they bore and the amount of time between conceptions.

ISSUE 5.1: The U.S. Population Is Moving: South, West, and Out-of-Town

From the first European colonization of the continent to the early 1970s, America's cities grew much more rapidly than did rural areas and small towns. This trend accelerated in the late 19th century, when mass migrations brought hundreds of thousands of eastern and southern Europeans to the Northeast. Impetus was added to this trend by two world wars and the mechanization of agriculture, which drove millions of farmers and farm workers off the land and into the cities in search of industrial employment. Also, between 1920 and 1970, America's cities went through a great period of suburbanization, spreading over vast areas (Figure 5.10).

Between 1970 and 1980, two new trends began to develop, and these emerged from the 1980 Census. First, the Northeast has been losing population to the South and West. Second, rural areas and small towns have been growing faster than urban areas. As a corollary, growth is occurring beyond the suburbs in once-rural areas.

Within the Northeast, metropolitan areas with populations over 50,000 lost 2 percent of their population between 1970 and 1980, whereas nonmetropolitan areas (small towns and rural areas) gained 12.4 percent in the

same period (see Table 5.4). More specifically, in New Jersey, small towns and rural areas grew by 51 percent and metropolitan areas lost 1 percent. Ocean County, once regarded as rural and remote, had a population increase of over 65 percent during this past decade. This pattern was consistent over much of the nation, with nonmetropolitan areas growing substantially faster than metropolitan areas. Only in the South was metropolitan growth faster than rural growth, 20.1 to 17.1 percent. This may be because the rural South is still rebuilding its cities, trying to catch up with the rest of the nation.

At the state level, in the decade 1970–80, northeastern populations grew very slowly or declined. For example, Rhode Island lost 0.3 percent and New York lost 3.8 percent of their populations. Michigan's population grew 4.2 percent, and Ohio's was up by 1.3 percent. In contrast, Georgia's population was up 19.1 percent, Florida's 43.4 percent, Arizona's 53.1 percent, Wyoming's 41.6 percent, and Nevada's 63.5 percent.

Why has this shift occurred? What does it mean? It is in large part economic. Heavy industry, the backbone of the northeastern economy, is going through a long-term de-

These early clinics met with strong resistance, in much the same way that the equal rights movement has met resistance fifty years later. The link, however, between a woman's role in her society and her desire to increase or decrease the size of her family is a strong one. Understanding women's roles in society is a prerequisite for any successful family planning effort.

Family planning programs are generally voluntary. In the less industrialized nations, however, many countries have taken a more radical approach, finding it necessary to implement compulsory programs or incentives to encourage family planning. Prior to 1965, only a handful of less industrialized nations had officially supported family planning programs. The international spread of family planning began after 1965 and quickly gained momentum in the next ten years. By 1975, only three of the thirty-eight less industrialized nations with populations greater than 10 million had no officially adopted family planning programs. These were Burma, Peru, and North Korea. Five years later, all but a few Third-World countries had family planning policies, although some were only on paper (Brown, 1979).

cline. Steel making, automobile production, and related industries and services are no longer profitable in the face of foreign competition and more modern production methods. Thus America's industrial wealth has been moving out of its old locations, seeking new opportunities, modern facilities, and lower labor costs. These can be found in the South and West, as well as in rural areas. In addition, much of the population growth in the West is a result of increased mining, and thus may be temporary.

This massive and profound movement of American capital is accompanied by an

Figure 5.10 During the 1970s, many people in the U.S. moved to rural areas, as in this upstate New York example.

The relationship between effective family planning programs and fertility is quite pronounced. According to projections, those programs that receive good governmental support and economic assistance will be more successful in bringing down the fertility rate. As always, the program must not only include the distribution of contraceptives but also increased education about their use. The bitter reaction by many to India's IUD (intrauterine device) program is a case in point. The IUD was being adopted by many Indian women as a method of contraception. Family planning personnel would visit rural villages and after medical examinations, insert the devices. The doctors failed to warn the women, however, of potential side effects. When these became apparent, rumors spread, causing the program to virtually collapse overnight (Conservation Foundation, 1979).

The success of family planning will be difficult to monitor. What works well in one society may not in another. The tradition of imposing industrialized nations' remedies may not be appropriate elsewhere. The increased support of family planning in less industrialized nations by their governments has been joined by increased financial contributions by the industrialized nations and the international agencies involved in family planning. Some of these, such as the International Planned Parenthood Federation and the U.N. Fund for Population Activities, have all seen significant financial contributions in the last decade.

increased desire on the part of young Americans to live in rural areas. The baby-boom generation has entered its most productive and prosperous years. Urban society, tastes, and spending habits are moving to areas once regarded as "the sticks." One result of this shift is an aging and impoverished population in the Northeast, where the median age is around 32, well above the national 30—and well above Utah's 24.2, Wyoming's 27.1, Colorado's 28.6, and Arizona's 29.2.

Demands for goods and services are also shifting. The Northeast needs an increased tax base to rebuild its cities and industry and to provide community services for the elderly and poor. However, with a loss of population and industry and an unfriendly White House administration, the region's governments have struggled to cope. Political clout has diminished because seventeen seats in the House of Representatives have been lost through reapportionment to the South and West.

In the South and West, as well as in rural areas, growth means a surge in demand for housing, schools, hospitals, stores, jails, service industries, water, sewage treatment, and other social and environmental amenities and necessities. Problems result when roads crumble under increased traffic, water supply is insufficient, and sewage overwhelms even state-of-the-art systems. In addition, housing cannot keep up with demand, housing prices are inflated, and taxation systems are often not able to take advantage of the influx. This results in a lack of basic community services such as street lights, curbs, public emergency vehicles, and aid for increasing numbers of unemployed who have come in search of a future.

It is clear that political power and capital are moving out of the Northeast, accompanied by the ever-mobile American, always in search of an empty frontier and the chance for a better life. The long-term effects of this shift are not at all clear, but preliminary mid-1980s censuses suggest that the trend is slowing (U.S. Bureau of the Census, 1980; Robbins, 1982; Schmidt, 1981; Herbers, 1981).

Non-family Planning

In those nations where standards of living and increased literacy have helped to improve women's status, fertility has declined. There are a number of specific factors that have influenced the decline in fertility. These include increased educational levels of women, increased female employment outside the home, and marriage at a later age. All of these create conditions that motivate women to limit the size of their families (Newland, 1977).

Increased educational levels have opened opportunities other than motherhood to many women. Acquiring more knowledge has not only made these women more aware of family planning and contraceptive information but has also increased their knowledge of the need for family planning. Increased education also influences goals and aspirations so that as a woman receives more education she may seek new alternatives or life-styles and perhaps a career. Finally, educated women realize the value of education and want to have their own children educated as well. To do so effectively and in some instances economically, these women feel the need to limit the size of their families.

Increased female employment outside the home is another factor that has contributed to declining fertility rates. The need for two income earners in North American households is a response to increasing economic pressures. With a large percentage of women now in the labor force, large families are as easily sustained as when women were mainly homemakers. According to the U.S. Bureau of the Census, by the mid-1980s over half of the nation's married women worked outside the home.

Delaying the age of marriage has also contributed to declining fertility. If a woman marries later in her life, late 20s or early 30s, the number of children she can bear will be lower. This practice has been used for years in the People's Republic of China as a method of family planning but has shown mixed results.

FUTURE POPULATION ESTIMATES AND CONCLUSIONS

Population control programs are having an effect on worldwide population growth, according to a 1983 report by the U.N. Fund for Population Activities. The report states that the world's annual population growth rate dropped from 2.4 percent in 1965–70 to 2 percent in 1980–84. The U.N. is predicting a total drop in the rate of population increase of 16 percent between 1965 and 1985. Further, they predict that global population will stabilize at 10.2 billion late in the 21st century. This will be a little more than twice the current 4.7 billion (Nossiter, 1983). While in 1969 only twenty-six of the less industrialized nations had population control programs, fifty-nine had them in 1981. Cuba showed the largest decline in population growth rate, falling by 47 percent between 1965–80. China followed, with a 34 percent decline, and seven other countries had declines of between 15 and 25 percent. Other demographic indicators are not changing as rapidly. According to the report, mortality rates are not dropping as hoped. In 2000 people in the less industrialized nations will have a life expectancy of sixty-three to sixty-four years, or ten years below the U.N.'s target (Gupte, 1982).

Population growth and resource use are intertwined and interdependent. The world is still undergoing a massive population boom that began several hundred years ago, and it is far too soon to know what the end results will be for human beings. In the future we may see privation and suffering due to worldwide resource shortages or inequities in resource distribution. Perhaps there will be a cataclysmic collapse of the human population, with effects akin to those wrought by the European plagues of the late middle ages. On the other hand, we all may get used to living close together and will adapt creatively to the conditions and new resources as the world becomes an urban and crowded place. Certainly, however, the time is past when one group of people can use a resource without concern for the effects of that use on others. We are already a bit too crowded for that kind of behavior, and resource management is a real worldwide necessity, at present in short supply.

REFERENCES AND ADDITIONAL READING

Boserup, E. 1965. *The conditions of agricultural growth.* Chicago: Aldine.

––––––– . 1981. *Population and technological change.* Chicago: University of Chicago Press.

Brown, L.R. 1979. Resource trends and population policy: a time for reassessment. Worldwatch Paper 29. Washington, D.C.: Worldwatch Institute, May.

––––––– , et al. 1984. *State of the world, 1984.* New York: WW Norton & Co.

Conservation Foundation. 1982. *State of the environment, 1982.* Washington, D.C.

Conservation Foundation Letter. 1979. *Keys to birth control still elude experts.* Washington, D.C. March.

Council on Environmental Quality. 1981. *The Global 2000 report to the president.* Washington, D. C.: Government Printing Office.

Durand, J.D. 1967. The modern expansion of world population. *Am. Philosophical Soc. Proc.* vol. 111:136–45.

Ehrlich, P. 1968. *The population bomb.* New York: Ballantine Books.

Ernst, R.T., and L. Hugg. 1976. *Black America: geographic perspectives.* New York: Anchor Press.

Gupte, P.B. 1982. UN lowers estimates of population in 2000. *New York Times* June 13.

Gwatkin, D.R., and S.K. Brandel. 1982. Life expectancy and population growth in the Third World. *Scientific American* 246:5:57–65.

Herbers, J. 1980. Urban centers' population drift creating a countryside harvest. *New York Times* March 23.

––––––– . 1981. Rural areas end trend, surpass cities in growth. *New York Times* March 3.

Holdgate, M.W., M. Kassas, and G.F. White. 1982. World environmental trends between 1972 and 1982. *Environmental Conservation* 9:11–29.

Keeley, C.B. 1982. Illegal migration. *Scientific American* 246:3:41–77.

Lindsey, R. 1981. California becomes melting pot of 1980s. *New York Times* August 23.

Newland, K. 1977. Women and population growth: choice beyond childrearing. Worldwatch Paper 16. Washington, D.C.: Worldwatch Institute, December.

––––––– . 1980. City limits: emerging constraints on urban growth. Worldwatch Paper 38. Washington, D.C.: Worldwatch Institute, August.

Nossiter, B.D. 1983. UN study sees slower growth in population. *New York Times* June 19.

Population Reference Bureau. 1981. *Population dynamics of the world.* Washington, D.C.

––––––– . 1983. 1983 World population data sheet. Washington, D.C.

Rand McNally. 1983. *Commercial atlas and marketing guide.* 114th ed. Chicago.

Robbins, W. 1982. Pennsylvania keeping its old but not its young. *New York Times* June 10.

Schmidt, W.E. 1981. Rockies adjusting to a youth boom. *New York Times* November 12.

Simon, J. 1981. *The ultimate resource.* Princeton: Princeton University Press.

Stokes, B. 1980. Men and family planning. Worldwatch Paper 41. Washington, D.C.: Worldwatch Institute, December.

United Nations. 1982. *Demographic yearbook, 1980.* New York.

U.S. Bureau of the Census. 1980. Population characteristics, series p-20 #374. Washington, D.C.: Government Printing Office.

TERMS TO KNOW

baby boom
Esther Boserup
crude birth rate
crude death rate
demographic transition
doubling time
fertility rate
guest workers
illegal immigration
Thomas Malthus

Karl Marx
migration
Neo-Malthusianism
population dynamics
population pyramid
replacement level
Margaret Sanger
Julian Simon
zero population growth

STUDY QUESTIONS

1. What are the differences between geometric growth and arithmetic growth?
2. When did the period of rapid human population growth begin?
3. What are the major demographic differences between less-developed and more developed nations?
4. Why do people resist birth control measures? What incentives to use them do some nations provide?
5. When did the U.S. population pyramid resemble that of a developing nation?
6. What were the three major migration patterns to the U.S.?
7. What will world population patterns be like in 2000, according to recent projections?
8. What two significant shifts in U.S. population patterns first showed up in the 1980 census?

CHAPTER SIX

Agriculture and the Soil Resource

INTRODUCTION

To Thomas Jefferson, the future of American agriculture was based on the family farm. It provided subsistence to the family that owned and ran it and allowed surplus to be sold to non-farm families, bringing cash income to the farmer. This vision was realized for the first one and a half centuries of American history, when westward expansion and settlement, aided by government land grants to soldiers and homesteaders, facilitated the establishment of family farms in the fertile Midwest. However, over the last century, the introduction of hybrid corn and heavy machinery changed the economics of the farm. No longer was 65 hectares (160 acres) a reasonable size farm for a family to operate. Instead, it was possible, even necessary, to cultivate much larger areas with only a few workers. Changing agricultural technology increased the capital requirements of farming so that land itself was no longer the major requirement for farming; access to large amounts of capital was also necessary. The mid-20th century, then, has seen a shift away from the small family farm toward large farms run as businesses. Many are still family owned but many are owned by corporations. This change in the needs and aspirations of farmers has changed the way farmland is managed.

The world agricultural situation has also changed. Issues of trade, famine, and poverty in much of the world have heightened our awareness of agricultural production as a global resource. American farmers today serve markets around the world, and production is thus affected by world market and trade factors. Even though the American agricultural system is immensely productive so that the U.S. is a major food exporter, it has not yet made a significant contribution to alleviating food shortages in the Third World. To begin this chapter, a brief look at the global agricultural situation will put the U.S. agricultural resource base in economic and environmental perspective.

The World Agricultural-Resource Base

Arable Land

The total land area of the world is about 13.1 billion hectares (32.6 billion acres). Of this, only 10.5 percent (or 1.46 billion hectares [3.61 billion acres]) is presently

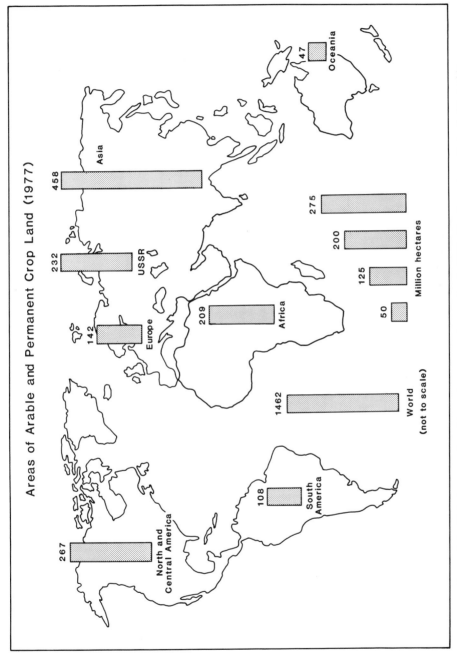

Areas of Arable and Permanent Crop Land (1977)

Figure 6.1 Global areas of arable and permanent crop land, 1977. The largest portion of the arable land in the world is in Asia where the population is also the greatest. (Source: From Crabbe and Lawson, 1981)

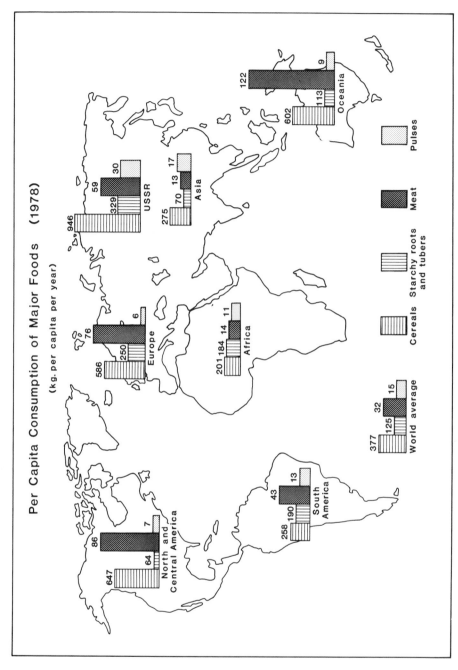

Per Capita Consumption of Major Foods (1978)

(kg. per capita per year)

North and Central America
647, 86, 7, 64

Europe
586, 76, 6, 250

USSR
946, 59, 30, 329

Asia
275, 70, 13, 17

Africa
201, 184, 14, 11

Oceania
602, 122, 9, 113

South America
258, 190, 43, 13

World average
377, 32, 15, 125

Legend:
- Cereals
- Starchy roots and tubers
- Meat
- Pulses

Figure 6.2 Per capita consumption of major food sources, 1978. Rich areas, such as North America and Oceania, consume more food per capita than the poorer areas of the world. (Source: From Crabbe and Lawson, 1981)

arable or suitable for cultivated agriculture (Crabbe and Lawson, 1981). Figure 6.1 is a map showing the distribution of arable land in the world. One Food and Agricultural Organization (FAO) estimate for 1978 suggests that 200 million hectares (494 million acres) must be brought into use by 2000 just to keep pace with population increases. According to the Global 2000 Report (Council on Environmental Quality, 1981a), the potential for increased arable land worldwide is more than double that presently cultivated, but it is unlikely that this land area will ever be placed in production. Rather, more realistic estimates of the potential increase in arable land over the next few decades are on the order of 10 percent. Much of the potentially arable land is semiarid or arid and would require irrigation or has other limitations such as forest cover, poor drainage, or steep slopes. Large increases in agricultural land would require major technological advances in water supply, plant breeding, and cultivation techniques, as well as displacing other land uses such as forestry and grazing. Technological advances and replacement of these other resources require large amounts of capital, which is not likely to be available in the areas in which it is needed most.

Arable land is not uniformly distributed in relation to population. Although Asia has the most arable land, it also has an immense population to feed. On the other hand, North America has much arable land and a relatively small population. When we consider that the American agricultural system generally produces higher yields per hectare (acre) than systems where fertilizers and pesticides are less available, the disparities from one area to another are even greater.

Major Crops

The world's food supply is based on about thirty major crops. The top seven (wheat, rice, maize, potatoes, barley, sweet potatoes, and cassava) have annual harvests of over 100 million tonnes (110 million tons) and account for more than half the harvest of the top thirty crops. In terms of global meat supply, seven animals provided more than 95 percent of all meat production in 1978. Pigs and cattle were first and second, poultry third, followed by much smaller contributions from lamb, goat, buffalo, and horse (Crabbe and Lawson, 1981; Harlan, 1976). Meat supplies about 17 percent of the calories and 35 percent of the protein humans consume.

There are great disparities in the amounts and kinds of food consumed in rich and poor nations, with rich nations not only eating more, but better food (Figure 6.2). Increasingly, in many parts of the world, locally domesticated and harvested plants and animals are being replaced by these relatively few global food sources, either grown locally or imported. This replacement is the result of many complex factors, including increased trade, mechanization, the spread of high-yielding varieties, and cultural change. Some experts decry this loss of food-source flexibility in the belief that a broader base of food crops is safer in case of widespread plant diseases. A broad crop base can also reduce susceptibility to weather fluctuations and climatic change.

Food Production and Population Growth

Agricultural production has been increasing in the Third World as a result of cultivation of new land and improved production on a per-hectare (acre) basis.

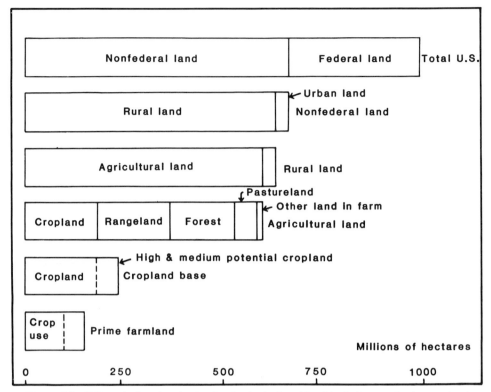

Figure 6.3 U.S. agricultural and other lands. Agricultural land includes cropland, rangeland, forest land on farms, and pastureland. Only 30 percent of U.S. agricultural land is used for growing crops. (Source: From Brewer and Boxley, 1981)

But population is also rising. Over a fifteen-year period to the mid-1970s, ninety-two nations with developing market economies expanded their food production at a rate of 2.6 percent per year, just barely keeping even with population growth.

India is one success story. The agricultural improvements of the last fifteen years have made it possible to produce enough food for self-sufficiency, even after severe droughts. The Indian government and development experts, have achieved this through planning and through expanding the use of fertilizers, irrigation, and high-yielding crop varieties. However, the question of distribution remains basic, as it is estimated that nearly half of India's population eats less than two meals a day (Kaufman, 1980).

In other parts of the world the situation remains critical. In 1982 a drought in southern Africa destroyed hopes for increased self-sufficiency in that region. Botswana, Namibia, Mozambique, Zimbabwe, and South Africa were reduced once again to importing grain. A 1982 FAO survey listed twenty-four countries with "serious food shortages"; nineteen of them were in Africa. Faced with rising costs of fuel oil, conversion to cash crops for sale or export, rising populations, warfare, and uncertain weather, it is a continuing struggle for these and other countries to attain food self-sufficiency.

Figure 6.4 An abandoned farm in Massachusetts. Much of the Northeast was profitably farmed in the 18th and early 19th centuries, but agriculture declined when more fertile western lands came into production.

The U.S. Agricultural Resource Base

About sixty percent of U.S. land is classified as agricultural land (U.S. Department of Agriculture and Council on Environmental Quality, 1981). "Agricultural land" is a broad term, however, and includes cropland, rangeland, forest land, and pastureland (Figure 6.3). Cropland, or land on which crops are presently grown, is only about thirty percent of agricultural land. The cropland area of the U.S. amounts to about 0.6 hectares (1.5 acres) per person, as compared with the global average of 0.32 hectares (0.79 acres) per person.

America has always been a land of agricultural abundance, with a large area of arable land and a relatively small population. Through the first two centuries of European settlement in North America, agriculture was based largely on a fertile soil resource, supplemented in some sectors by slave and indentured labor. In the mid-19th century, the opening of the Great Plains was facilitated in part by the development of the steel plow, one of many major innovations contributing to the growth of U.S. agricultural production (Figure 6.4). Today the United States' agricultural system is among the most technologically advanced in the world. The trend of U.S. agricultural output over time is shown in Figure 6.5.

American agriculture, based on high and continual inputs of capital and replacement of animal power and human labor by machines, has resulted in drastic reductions in numbers of farms and farm workers. This has culminated in an agricultural system that, unlike those in traditional societies, is operated

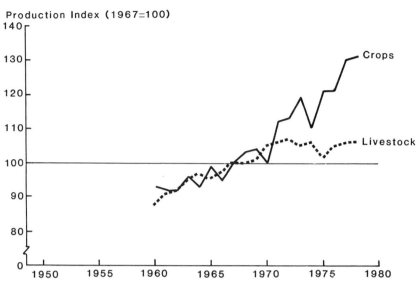

Figure 6.5 Trends in U.S. agricultural production 1960–1978. Crop and livestock production have risen steadily. Much of the increase in crop production has supported a growing export market. (Source: From Council on Environmental Quality, 1981a)

ISSUE 6.1: The Merchants of Grain

The independent, self-sufficient farmer is one of the most enduring images we have of agriculture in the United States. Yet the price our farmers are paid, what they choose to grow, and the eventual use of those farm products are completely beyond their control. Instead, the world's agricultural production is largely controlled by privately-owned trading companies: companies that have at least as much impact on the world's economy as any of the better-known cartels or multinational corporations.

In his book, Merchants of Grain, Dan Morgan explains how five trading companies, privately owned by members of only seven families, control the majority of the world's grain trade and have for the last eighty years. The international grain deals made by these individuals greatly influence the amount of farmland cultivated each year and the price of grain worldwide. Additionally, they operate with only limited govern-

mental control. Also, as privately held companies, they do not have to disclose profits or losses nor justify investments to stockholders. There are none.

Continental, owned by the Fribourg family, is headquartered in New York City. Cargill, one of the largest, is owned by the MacMillan and Cargill families with headquarters in Minneapolis. Cargill and Continental handle half of the grain (including corn and soybeans) exported from the United States, and the U.S. exports half of all of the grain traded in the world each year. The other companies are Louis Dreyfus (owned by the Louis-Dreyfus family) based in Paris, Andre (owned and run by a family of the same name) in Switzerland, and the Bunge Corporation owned by the Born and Hirsch families with operations centered in Brazil and Argentina.

These five companies control the distribution and processing of grain and provide

as a complex of small and large businesses whose primary goal is earning money, rather than producing food for subsistence. This system is known as *agribusiness*.

The U.S. and the World Food Situation

U.S. agriculture dominates food exports in the world economy, with grain exports from the U.S. accounting for over half the world total. By the mid-1970s it was estimated that American agriculture was feeding about 50 million more people than lived in the U.S. and that there was potential for even greater food exports. In addition, the average consumer in the U.S. pays about 20 percent of his or her disposable income for food. Comparable figures for the early 1970s were 65 percent in the developing nations, 30 percent in the U.S.S.R., and about 25 percent in Western Europe (Heady, 1976).

Farming in the U.S. has generally been profitable, but highly competitive. Like many industries, it has its good and bad times. The most recent period of hardship for American farmers began in the early 1980s, primarily because of a period of inflation combined with an economic recession. Bumper harvests in recent years forced prices down, while inflation continued to force costs up. In 1981 farm debts were at $194.5 billion, double the 1975 figure, and by 1983 they were $216 billion (U.S. Bureau of the Census, 1984). Over the same length of time, farm expenses rose from $75.9 billion to $141.5 billion annually, with a 1981 net farm income of $22.9 billion as compared to $24.5 billion in 1975. Prices paid for crops rose 34 percent from 1977 to 1981, while fuel prices were

---

needed technology (including seed) and capital to farmers. They also maintain a worldwide communications network.

In the early 1970s, poor harvests in the Ukraine and Siberian Steppes forced the Soviet Union to import millions of tons of grain. These five companies negotiated the grain sales without the knowledge or approval of the U.S. government. Exports overseas mean less grain available at home, resulting in a rapid rise in wholesale and retail food prices. This action has later been referred to as "The Great Grain Robbery."

The actions of the grain merchants had a significant indirect impact on agriculture in the U.S. as well. It was now possible to make money on what had been marginal farmland. For example, Japanese and Italian investors started "superfarms" by draining freshwater wetlands in North Carolina. Shelter belts and windbreaks planted in the 1930s in Nebraska to control wind-induced erosion

were destroyed to make room for intensive irrigation systems. One result of these secretive grain deals was the increase in soil erosion in the U.S. and the destruction of valuable wildlife habitat.

The United States is considered the "superpower" of the world's grain trade. U.S. grain exports dwarf those of other nations such as Australia and Argentina. For example, the states of Kansas and South Dakota alone produce more grain than all of Australia. Many advocate the use of "food weapon" to further U.S. foreign-policy objectives. Yet the mechanism for export is controlled by grain barons with little allegiance to federal governments. These private merchants of grain, with little responsibility to any nation or stockholder, can directly affect the direction of U.S. agriculture and indirectly increase the environmental impact of current agricultural practices.

up 113 percent (Jaynes, 1982). With grain production 60 percent above that of internal consumption and grain sales not fully recovered from President Carter's 1979 embargo on grain sales to the U.S.S.R., American farmers are faced with an enormous surplus of food, most of which is stored.

For American farming to prosper at its present high level of technological development, consumption must keep pace with rising production capabilities. Crops not sold at home should be marketed abroad, but in recent years American goods, including agricultural commodities, have become expensive to foreign consumers. Eventually, experts suggest American consumers must become willing to pay a higher share of their income for food if farming is to remain profitable. In 1983 President Reagan introduced a new plan that encourages farmers to produce less without the threat of bankruptcy. Very simply, a farmer can agree to not farm a certain number of acres and in return receive a quantity of surplus grain comparable to the production lost, to be disposed of as the farmer sees fit. This payment-in-kind plan attempts to reduce surpluses while enabling farmers to recover from recent losses. As a result of the plan, the total area planted to crops nationwide in 1983 was reduced by 34 million hectares (84 million acres), down thirty percent from 1982. Even so surpluses and low prices continue to plague farmers (King, 1983).

When viewed in the context of global hunger, actions to reduce production seem strange, yet overproduction is a chronic problem in much of the developed world. It is the result of agricultural systems that are so efficient they can produce enormous quantities of food, while domestic purchasing power keeps the price of that food high. In addition, farmers in the U.S., as in many countries, enjoy substantial political power, which helps maintain systems of subsidies for farmers that contribute to this domestic overproduction.

MODERN AMERICAN AGRICULTURAL SYSTEMS

American agriculture today includes both mixed and monocultural cropping systems. *Mixed cropping systems* are agricultural systems that combine several different crops in a single farm unit. They usually include crops for both human consumption and fodder (animal feed). Mixed cropping is used in areas where several different crops can be grown with roughly the same profit per hectare (acre), as well as in dairy farming areas. A typical dairy farm in the Northeastern U.S. might include corn and alfalfa grown for fodder and dairy cattle, whose milk is marketed for cash income. By producing several different animal and vegetable products simultaneously, mixed-farming systems make efficient use of the land resource, while minimizing susceptibility to unfavorable weather or market conditions for any one commodity. Mixed systems benefit from crop rotation, where the crops grown on a given parcel of land are changed from year to year or season to season, reducing depletion of particular soil nutrients. These farmers also may make greater use of plants by feeding otherwise unused parts of plants to animals and by returning some organic matter to the fields in the form of manure.

Monoculture is an agricultural system in which just one crop is cultivated repeatedly over a large area. Other distinctive characteristics of a modern monocultural system include a reliance on technology in the form of machines and specialized plant varieties, fertilizers, and pesticides. This technological agriculture is used in both mixed and monocultural systems in the United States and in most of the wealthy nations of the world. Monoculture takes advantage of the labor-saving benefits of machines. Additional benefits include economies of scale, more efficient marketing, and access to uniform plant varieties. These plants not only produce high yields, but also have similar dimensions and ripening times. If an entire 65-hectare (160-acre) field is to be harvested at one time by machines that harvest many rows at a pass, then clearly all of the plants must mature at the same time. A food production system that is primarily monocultural is a highly specialized one. It must have the capacity to store produce over long time periods, and transport it efficiently from one area to another.

One consequence of the uniformity of plants in monocultural systems is their susceptibility to disease and pest infestation. If a species of insect attacks a particular variety and takes hold, large fields can be devastated quickly. For this reason, substantial inputs of pesticides are normally required. Many of these specialized plant varieties also require large inputs of fertilizer or irrigation water to realize maximum yields. In addition, the machines, fertilizers, and chemicals require large amounts of energy, in the form of fossil fuels and electricity, to operate or produce.

Monoculture under these conditions produces very high yields of uniformly high quality. As a result, the value of crops on a per-hectare (per-acre) basis is very high. However, to achieve this high-value harvest, much capital is needed to purchase such inputs of production as land, machines, seed, and fertilizer. It is a capital- and energy-intensive system rather than a labor-intensive one. This has consequences for the way it uses the land, and its ability to continue to be productive in the future. These consequences will be discussed later in this chapter.

COMPONENTS OF AGRICULTURE

Soil

Soil is the uppermost part of the earth's surface, which has been modified by physical, chemical, and biological processes over time. It is the essential medium for plant growth. It is a complex and dynamic mixture of solid and dissolved mineral matter, living and dead organic matter, water, and air. Soil is formed over long periods of time, usually thousands of years.

Many factors affect soil formation, including climate, parent material, topography, erosion, and biologic activity. Climate affects soil by determining the amount of water that may enter the soil from rainfall and the amount that can be drawn from the surface by evaporation. Climate also determines soil temperatures, which are important in regulating chemical reactions in the soil as well as influencing plant growth. *Parent material* is the mineral matter on which soil is formed. It affects the soil by supplying the mineral matter that forms the bulk of the soil. Parent material has a fundamental influence on *soil texture,* which is the mix of different sizes of particles, and on the chemical characteristics of the soil. Topography influences soil primarily by regulating water movement within and over the soil. On slopes, water moves down and laterally through the soil, providing drainage. In low-lying areas, water accumulates, and soils may become waterlogged. Along stream courses, sediment may accumulate, producing fertile alluvial soils. Topography also affects the rate of erosion. *Erosion* is the removal of soil by running water or wind. It is a natural process that can be greatly accelerated by human influences such as vegetation removal. The rate of erosion relative to the rate of new soil formation is an important determinant of soil characteristics. Finally, biologic activity is what makes soil the distinctive, living, dynamic substance it is, rather than just an accumulation of sterile rock particles. Biologic activity includes the growth and decay of plants and animals in and above the soil. It contributes organic matter to the soil, which constitutes the basic storage of nutrients for most ecosystems. Biologic activity also aids in the physical modification of the mineral soil by contributing organic acids that break down rocks, by exerting physical forces that fracture rocks, and by stirring and aerating the soil so that water and air may penetrate below the surface. Vegetation cover regulates water losses by evapotranspiration and protects the soil from excessive erosion. The type of vegetation is also important in determining soil characteristics. For example, the thick grass cover of a prairie leads to the development of a soft topsoil that is not usually found in forest soils. In short, biologic activity plays a fundmental role in soil formation and helps maintain the ability of soils to support life.

Soil is a four-dimensional medium. It varies vertically, in the two horizontal dimensions, and through time. In the vertical dimension, most soils exhibit several layers, or *horizons,* with different characteristics. Figure 6.6 shows a generalized soil profile for humid midlatitude regions. The uppermost horizon is called the A horizon. This layer contains the most organic matter and is usually a zone from which dissolved materials are removed by downward percolation of water. It includes an upper litter layer (the A0 horizon), a zone of moderately high organic content (A1), a zone of maximum downward movement of clays and dissolved materials (A2), and a zone (A3) that is transitional to the next lower horizon. The B horizon is a layer of accumulation of materials removed from the A horizon. It is usually lower in organic content than the A horizon and is often rich in clay. The C horizon consists of partially weathered parent material. It is much less altered than the upper layers, and some dissolved materials removed from the A and B horizons may accumulate in the C horizon. Unweathered parent material is below the C horizon.

These layers are found in most well-developed soils in humid midlatitude environments, but their characteristics vary from place to place, depending on variations in the soil-forming factors of climate, topography, and so on. In semiarid and arid areas, upward water movement caused by high evaporation rates at the surface may result in the accumulation of dissolved minerals in the A horizon. On hilltops, rapid drainage may cause much removal of minerals, whereas in poorly drained lowlands, saturated conditions can lead to the accumulation of organic matter that is not broken down due to the lack of oxygen.

The way in which individual soil particles group together in aggregates is called *soil structure.* Some common soil structures include platy, prismatic, blocky, and spheroidal. Soil structure is important in determining the water-holding capacity of soil and the speed with which water soaks into and through the soil. Plowing, dessication and depletion from cultivation can sometimes destroy soil structure to the detriment of its water acquisition and holding properties.

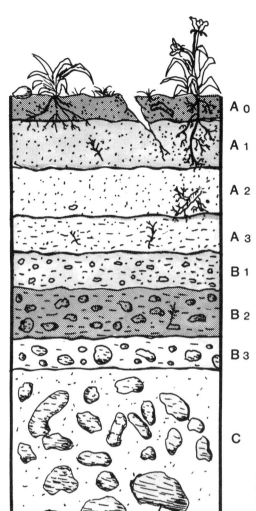

A 0

A 1

A 2

A 3

B 1

B 2

B 3

C

Figure 6.6 A generalized soil profile. The characteristics of the individual soil horizon vary between different soil types (see text for explanation of types).

Soils develop slowly from unweathered bedrock to a complete soil profile. The rate of new soil formation varies from place to place, but as a rule it is very slow in human terms, requiring hundreds to tens of thousands of years. Eventually, soils reach an equilibrium with the prevailing climatic, topographic, and biologic conditions and then retain fairly constant properties. But even in this equilibrium condition, new soil is being formed. Erosion is part of the natural soil system, and soil eroded from the surface must be replaced by formation of new soil from parent material. If the soil erosion rate is high, then the soil may not develop as thickly or as completely as in areas with low erosion rates. Alluvial soils, which continually receive inputs of new material at the top of the profile, also show incomplete development.

Soils vary greatly in their ability to support agricultural production, depending on their fertility, water-holding characteristics, temperature, and other factors.

Soil fertility is defined as the ability of a soil to supply essential nutrients to plants. This depends on both the chemical and textural properties of the soil. Generally soils that have a high proportion of clay and organic matter also have high fertility, since these substances have the ability to store and release nutrients. Sandy soils, on the other hand, generally have lower amounts of nutrients available to plants, although as little as ten to fifteen percent fine particles may be sufficient to supply needed nutrients. The abundance of various elements in the soil, such as phosphorus and calcium, is also important. This is often controlled by the chemical composition of the bedrock and the leaching of these nutrients as water percolates through the soil.

The *water-holding capacity* of a soil is primarily determined by its texture. As a rule, coarse-textured soils have low capacities to store water, whereas clayey soils can hold large volumes of water in the upper parts of the profile. At the same time, however, clay soils may be poorly drained, with the tendency to become waterlogged, preventing air from reaching plant roots. Waterlogging is particularly common in humid areas, on floodplains, or other flat land. In addition, irrigated areas often experience waterlogging if irrigation causes a rise in the local groundwater table.

The productive capabilities of soils are thus of fundamental importance in determining what plants can be grown, what particular management techniques should be used, and what typical yields will be. The U.S. Soil Conservation Service has developed a system, called the *Land Capability Classification System,* for assessing and classifying this productive capacity (Table 6.1). There are eight major capability classes, designated I through VIII, with classes I through IV indicating arable land, and classes V through VIII indicating land useful for grazing or forestry. For both agriculture and other uses, the first category includes land that is nearly ideal for production, with few or no limitations such as fertility or drainage. The next two classes include land with increasing degrees of limitations, including such problems as poor drainage, excessive erosion hazard, and poor water-holding capacity. The fourth class is land that is generally not usable. Note that the land of the U.S. is about equally divided between suitability for agriculture and suitability for forestry or grazing, and that in each of these groups about eighty percent of the land has some limitations for use. This further indicates the great importance of proper land management techniques adapted to the inherent capabilities and limitations of each land unit.

Such capability classifications are just one part of the work of the U.S. Department of Agriculture's Soil Survey, which includes nationwide mapping of soil types, their physical characteristics, and their productive capabilities. These

Table 6.1 Land Capability in the U.S.

Capability Class		% U.S. Nonfederal Land
I	Few limitations on use	3
II	Moderate limitations for agricultural uses	20
III	Severe limitations reducing choice of plants or requiring special conservation practices	20
IV	Very severe limitations for cropping	13
V	Few limitations for pasture or woodland uses	2
VI	Moderate limitations for pasture or woodland uses	19
VII	Very severe limitations for pasture or woodland uses	20
VIII	Generally suitable only for wildlife, recreation, or aesthetic purposes	3

Source: Soil Conservation Service, 1980

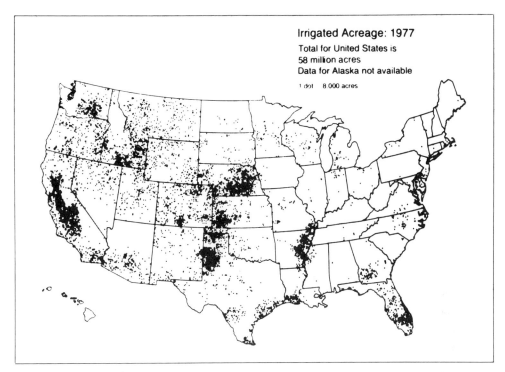

Irrigated Acreage: 1977

Total for United States is
58 million acres
Data for Alaska not available

1 dot   8.000 acres

Figure 6.7 U.S. irrigated acreage, 1977. Most of the irrigated land in the U.S. is in the Great Plains region and California's Central Valley. (Source: Soil Conservation Service, 1980)

maps are useful to farmers and land use planners as they attempt to make the best possible use of the soil resource.

Water

Water is, of course, essential to plant growth. Water is supplied to crops naturally by rainfall and artificially by irrigation. Rainfall farming depends entirely on the weather to provide a sufficient, but not excessive, supply of moisture to plants. If there is not enough, plants wither and die; if there is too much, the soil cannot be worked, crops rot in the field, or roots suffocate from lack of air. The amount and timing of rainfall are major determinants of what can be grown, where, and when. In areas without irrigation, rainfall variability is a major cause of year-to-year variations in yields. Droughts, early rains, and late rains take their tolls in crop failures or low yields in many regions of the world each year. Some climatologists feel that climates will change or become more variable and climate-related yield fluctuations could become an even more severe problem than they are today (Thompson, 1975).

In those parts of the world with sufficient and reasonably dependable rainfall, crops can be grown without irrigation. But about 13 percent of the world's arable lands can be cultivated because water has been artificially made available to plants. Also, much of the land deemed potentially arable will become so only through irrigation. The distribution of irrigated lands in the U.S. is illustrated in Figure 6.7.

a

Figure 6.8 Irrigation systems. (a) Flood irrigation of rice fields in Japan. (b) Furrow irrigation in a desert valley in California.

b

There are four major types of irrigation used in the world today: flood, furrow, sprinkler, and drip. *Flood irrigation* involves inundating entire fields with water or allowing water to flow across entire fields (Figure 6.8a). The most widespread use of flood irrigation is in growing paddy rice, primarily in South and East Asia. Fields are quite flat and bounded by dikes. During the wet season the fields are flooded, and rice seedlings are planted in standing water. Later the fields are drained, and the rice ripens in a relatively dry field. Flood irrigation is also used to irrigate pastures in some areas.

Furrow irrigation (Figure 6.8b) also requires very flat land, but in this case the water flows between rows of plants, which are grown on low ridges. Water is delivered to the furrows by small ditches or in pipes and applied as needed throughout the growing season.

Sprinkler irrigation (Figure 6.9a) requires substantially more equipment than flood or furrow irrigation. In sprinkler irrigation, water is pumped under pressure to nozzles and sprayed over the land. Nozzles may be fixed, or moved across a field manually or automatically. Sprinkler irrigation usually results in much higher evaporative losses than other methods. However, in areas of very permeable soils, seepage losses are major, so that in these cases as well as on sloping land sprinklers are preferred to furrow irrigation.

Drip irrigation is a relatively recent development and is used primarily in orchards and vineyards (Figure 6.9b). Each plant has a small pipe that delivers water at a controlled rate directly to the base of the plant. The water drips out very slowly so that little is lost to evaporation or seepage. It is an expensive system to install, but it is cost effective in areas where water is scarce.

Irrigated agriculture generally produces high yields as long as water is available. This is because the other environmental characteristics of dry lands, plentiful sunshine, and warm temperatures are conducive to crop growth. This high productivity is not without its costs, however, and in many areas of the world waterlogging, salt accumulation, groundwater depletion, and disease are serious side effects of irrigation. In some areas, salinization is severe enough that it is forcing abandonment of formerly productive land. In most of the world's farming regions, water is already being used intensely, and there are relatively few opportunities to increase irrigation on a large scale. Although it will be important in some areas, increased use of irrigation is generally not thought to offer great potential for increasing world food production.

Fertilizers and Pesticides

Average yields of grains worldwide have increased over 50 percent in the last twenty years, and most of this increase has been a result of increases in the use of fertilizers. Fertilizer use has increased over four times in that same twenty-year period. It is generally agreed that fertilizers will continue to play the dominant role in increasing grain yields for some time to come (Scrimshaw and Taylor, 1980). One of the main reasons is the development of high-yielding plant varieties, which require large inputs of fertilizer to realize their potential. In addition, fertilizers may make production possible on otherwise marginal land.

The three most important nutrients required by plants are nitrogen, phosphorus, and potassium. Nitrogen is ultimately derived from the atmosphere, but it is made available to plants by nitrogen-fixing bacteria. It is the nutrient that is most often deficient and that is most widely applied to crops. Additions in amounts of 50 to 100 kg/hectare (45 to 90 lb/acre) may increase yields from one and one-half to three times, depending on the plant variety and inherent soil fertility. Most nitrogen fertilizers are manufactured from natural gas; ammonia (NH_4) and urea ($CO(NH_2)_2$) are the most common. Phosphorus is usually present in small quantities in soils, but it is often found in relatively unusable forms. Phosphorus is particularly important in encouraging good root growth, which is necessary to deliver large amounts of water and nutrients to the above-ground

a

Figure 6.9 Irrigation systems. (a) A center-pivot sprinkler irrigation system in eastern Colorado. (b) Drip irrigation system in the Mondavi Vineyards, Napa Valley, California.

b

portions of plants. It is usually applied as superphosphate or as phosphoric acid, which are manufactured from phosphate rock or from guano (bird dung) deposits found in some coastal areas. In soils, potassium is usually found in larger quantities than phosphorus because it is a more abundant constituent of most rocks. Plants demand large quantities of potassium, and in many areas potassium fertilization is important. In some areas local soil conditions or the particular needs of plants require that other fertilizers be added, with lime (a source of calcium and magnesium as well as a regulator of soil pH) being the most common.

Organic fertilizers (primarily manure) have historically been the most important source of nutrients, especially nitrogen. Organic fertilizers also aid in maintaining good soil structure and water-holding capacity by keeping the organic matter content of the soil high. In the wealthy nations inorganic fertilizers are today more important, but in the developing nations manure is still the most common fertilizer. In most areas manure supplies are limited, and it is more difficult to apply than other forms of fertilizer. Manure is low in nutrient content relative to synthetic fertilizer and is not capable of providing the large inputs of nutrients demanded by high-yielding crop varieties. Increasingly, therefore, inorganic sources of nutrients have been replacing organic sources. This trend can be expected to continue.

A *pesticide* can be any of a number of chemical agents used to control organisms harmful to plants including insects, fungi, and some types of worms. Pesticides include insecticides, rodenticides, and fungicides. Herbicides are used to control weeds. The use of pesticides and herbicides has accounted for a large part of recent increases in crop yields, particularly in the wealthier nations. There are thousands of different kinds of pesticides and herbicides, and the vast majority are complex organic compounds manufactured using petroleum as an important raw material. The more important insecticides are organochlorines, organophosphates, and carbamates.

Some pesticides, including most insecticides, are very general in their effects; that is, they are toxic to almost all species in a large group such as insects. Although there may be just a few species that are a problem for a given crop, it is easier to apply just one or two insecticides to deal with the problem than to develop pesticides that kill only the targeted populations and do not affect others. On the other hand, some pesticides are very specific in that they only affect a few species or types of organisms. Herbicides used in agriculture must be specific so that they kill undesired weeds without harming the crops that are being protected. This need for specificity is one reason why there are so many different kinds of pesticides. Another reason, in the case of insecticides, is that insects have the ability to become resistant to insecticides due to their short life span and high reproductive rate. The organochlorines, such as DDT, aldrin, dieldrin, and chlordane, were the most widely used during the 1950s and 1960s. Recently these have been replaced by organophosphates for most uses, in part because insects began to develop resistance to the effects of organochlorines and in part because organophosphates break down more rapidly and therefore are less likely to accumulate in the environment.

While pesticides have been a boon to modern technological agriculture, they also have harmful side effects. The primary side effects of concern are adverse ecological effects, health effects on the general population through contamination of water and air, and health hazards to agricultural workers using the pesticides. The effects of persistent pesticides on bird populations are well known (see Chapter 10), but unintended changes in insect populations are also important. Not all insects are harmful, but most insecticides are non-specific, so that beneficial species are affected. In most cases the ecological effects of thse changes on food webs and other ecosystem characteristics are at best poorly understood, yet there is potential for serious ecological damage. Health hazards to general human populations are usually the result of pesticide contamination of water supplies. Even though this is discussed in more detail in Chapter 10, it is useful to cite an example here as well.

Long Island, New York, is an area with relatively permeable soils that help it to be an important potato-producing region, while also providing it with plentiful, but shallow, groundwater. Potato farmers have used insecticides for many years to combat the Colorado potato beetle and the golden nematode, pests which reduce potato yields. These pests developed resistance to DDT, malathion, and other pesticides, so that farmers turned to a carbamate called Temik. Temik is water soluble, which facilitates its absorption into plants where it is toxic to the beetles and nematodes. It breaks down relatively quickly, but the high permeability of Long Island soils has allowed it to reach groundwater before decaying, thus contaminating many wells. As a result, wells had to be closed, Temik was banned in the area, and farmers had to search for a new pesticide.

The most severe health hazards associated with pesticides are those associated with occupational exposure of farm workers handling the substances. For example, the non-persistent pesticides that are generally used today do not accumulate in high concentrations in the environment. However, they are highly toxic at the time they are applied; hence, those in contact with pesticides at that time are most at risk (Johnson, 1982).

The combined hazards of pesticide use are great, but so also are the benefits in terms of increased yields. Concern for the problems associated with massive pesticide use has prompted research on alternative methods of pest control, most importantly *integrated pest management.* This approach recognizes that there are several different means to control pests including pesticides, crop rotation and other habitat controls, and biological controls such as predator introduction. No single technique is likely to be completely successful in any given place. However, it should be possible to use a mix of different control techniques tailored to the situation for each particular set of agricultural needs and pest problems. This approach will require considerable research and development before it can be widely used, but it offers the greatest promise in solving pest problems without poisoning humans or the environment.

Seed

Ever since the development of agriculture, farmers have practiced crop improvement through seed selection. After observing the variations in a single crop, farmers saved seed from those plants that possessed the characteristics they preferred and planted these seeds the following year. Over a period of thousands of years, this process led to the development of the world's major modern crops. One of the most spectacular examples of this long-term process is maize, or corn. Since 6000 B.C., corn has been altered from a small grain head to its present size and productivity. The success of hybrid corn varieties was a major factor contributing to a large increase in acres of corn planted in the U.S. over the past few decades. Another example is the kale species *Brassica oleracea,* which has been altered into several distinct vegetables due to selection for different characteristics. These include broccoli, brussels sprouts, and cauliflower.

Since the early 20th century, the application of Mendel's laws of genetics has sped the process of selection. Not only does this allow for the creation of new plant varieties, but hybrid seeds tend to produce more vigorous plants than non-hybrid varieties. Thus, substantial increases in yield have been achieved. More recently, advances in bioengineering are making it possible to manipulate the genetic material directly, so that alterations can be made in a single generation of a plant species. Those farmers who can afford to pay for these sophisticated seeds can choose among a wide array of disease, insect, and drought resistance, and for specific fruit or grain size, flavor, ripening time, and packing and processing qualities, among others.

As a result of selection experiments pioneered by N.E. Borlaug in the 1940s, advanced varieties of wheat, rice, and other staples were first made available to Third-World farmers in the early 1960s as part of a package termed the Green Revolution. These seeds guaranteed much greater productivity as long as the farmer also applied increased amounts of fertilizer, pesticides, and/or water. Of course, these things cost money; so some farmers have profited from the new seeds while others have not. There is no disputing, however, the effects the seeds have had on worldwide crop production. Between 1950 and 1970 per capita grain production increased 30 percent (Brown, 1980).

One example of the great benefits of seed and fertilizer combinations is found in Mexico, in the decades from 1950 to 1970. Wheat production during this period increased from 300,000 to 2.6 million tonnes (330,000 to 2.8 million tons) per year, an eightfold increase. Over the same period, corn output increased 250 percent, the bean crop doubled, and the sorghum crop increased fourteenfold. By the 1970s a leveling trend was seen, and population began to catch up with this vastly increased output. Seeds cannot do the job alone, especially when there is not enough water for irrigation. Much of Mexico's remaining cropland is marginal for agriculture, and inequities in land ownership prevent small holders from earning enough to pay for Green Revolution materials (Wellhausen, 1976). Ten agricultural research and training centers in Africa, Asia, and Latin America are financed by a variety of governmental, public, and private concerns and are designing seeds to fit local conditions.

There is some evidence that, at least in the U.S. and other countries with technologically advanced agriculture, the "miracle seed" productivity is leveling off. This may, in large part, be due to diminishing returns from the addition of more fertilizer. Experts argue, however, that there is still room for greatly increased productivity in the Third World where chemical fertilizers are as yet underused (Wortman, 1976).

In recent years controversy in the seed development industry has been focused on the granting of seed patents to large agribusiness concerns. With the possession of these patents, the companies would criminally prosecute anyone using their seeds without permission. In addition, some countries are attempting to enforce laws declaring old traditional varieties to be illegal. Thus, many crop varieties are threatened with extinction. In a world fraught with periodic and endemic food shortages, there is clearly room for abuse and manipulation as agribusiness concerns gain greater legal and technological control over the basic materials of agriculture (National Academy of Sciences, 1972; Rural Advancement Fund, 1981).

Labor, Machines, and Energy

To grow crops, soil must be tilled, weeds removed, and plants harvested. Until the 19th century in North America, most of this work was done by human and animal labor, using simple tools such as plows and hoes. Today, heavy machinery driven by fossil fuels predominates. In the non-industrialized countries, an impetus toward mechanization was introduced as part of the Green Revolution.

In the U.S., Canada, and other countries dependent on mechanized production, the percentage of the labor force employed as farmers has dropped steadily. In 1850, 64 percent of the U.S. labor force was made up of farmers; this dropped to 3.1 percent by 1982. In the early days of mechanization, these out-of-work farm laborers were absorbed by the availability of industrial jobs in cities. From 1950 to 1980, the number of people on farms and the numbers of farm workers have dropped, respectively, from 23 and 9.9 million to 6 and 3.7 million (Rasmussen, 1982). However in this period the demand for unskilled labor in industry has also dropped precipitously, leaving farm workers with little employment opportunity. In addition, much of the remaining non-mechanized farm work is performed by seasonal and permanent legal and illegal immigrants to the U.S., who are an essential cog in the nation's economy.

The technological developments in agriculture involving farm machinery have had their greatest effects to date in the industrialized, wealthier nations. It is estimated that agricultural production per farm worker increased sevenfold between 1850 and 1980 (Rasmussen, 1982). As an example of the effects of mechanization, in 1793 Eli Whitney's cotton gin provided a practical method for separating seeds from cotton fibers, leading to a boom in the planting and production of cotton, an intensification of the Southern plantation system, and the development of Northern industrial mill towns. Today's cotton harvester strips two rows of plants at a time, cleans the fiber from the bolls, and has a storage capacity of 18 m^3 (636 ft^3) of picked cotton.

Grain production was revolutionized through a series of inventions. The plow evolved from a wooden horse- or ox-drawn implement, to today's gang plow with up to sixteen blades capable of plowing 4 hectares (10 acres) per hour. Reaping and threshing grain were once done with sickles, scythes, and human muscle power. Today the diesel-powered combine both harvests and threshes grain, up to 5 hectares (12 acres) an hour. These machines need a single human operator who rides in an air-conditioned cab. Labor shortages during World War II forced farmers to increase their use of machinery, eliminating the need for large farm crews (Rasmussen, 1982).

The petroleum products required to fuel this mechanical transformation are enormous. Recent studies estimate that 1974 energy use in American agriculture was 2000 trillion BTU, or about 5300 BTU per hectare (2150 BTU per acre) (Council on Environmental Quality, 1981b). Comparable figures for systems using animal power vary depending on how energy is accounted, but fossil-fuel uses per hectare are commonly 10 percent or less of those in wealthy nations. The largest uses in mechanized agriculture are fuels for tilling, planting, harvesting,

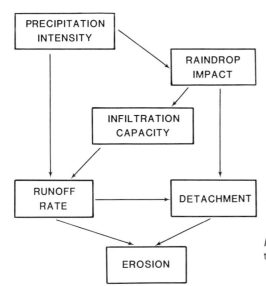

Figure 6.10 The process of soil erosion. See text for explanation of each stage.

transport, and water pumping. In addition heat and light are needed for livestock and poultry production, crop drying, and frost protection. Energy is also used in the form of agricultural chemicals, which amounts to more than a third of total energy used in U.S. agriculture. The *Global 2000* report summarizes recent estimates of potential energy savings and concludes that more efficient practices in such operations as cultivation, crop drying, and transportation could bring savings of 50 percent of the energy used in cultivation and 10 to 20 percent in irrigation (Council on Environmental Quality, 1981a). Substantial savings are also possible through more careful selection and use of fertilizers.

SOIL EROSION: A PROBLEM MANY ARE UNWILLING TO FACE

Physical Processes

Soil erosion on agricultural lands takes place by three major processes: overland flow, wind, and stream-bank erosion. Of these, overland flow erosion is the most widespread and is quantitatively the most important in most agricultural areas. Wind erosion occurs primarily in arid and semiarid areas, where the soil can become dry enough for wind to pick up particles. Stream-bank erosion is limited to fields that border streams, and while locally significant it is not generally a major factor in soil erosion.

Overland Flow Erosion

Accelerated overland flow erosion is primarily the result of intense rainfall striking bare ground. Raindrops striking a bare soil surface physically affect the soil in two major ways (Figure 6.10). First, they break up clumps of soil into individual particles, which are moved by the splash made on raindrop impact. In addition, the soil surface is compacted and sealed so that water is less able to soak in,

Figure 6.11   Rill erosion. Intense rainfall caused this erosion on Long Island, New York.

reducing the *infiltration capacity*, or the maximum rate at which soil will absorb water. When the precipitation intensity exceeds infiltration capacity, water flows across the surface rather than soaking in. Raindrop impact leads to an increase in the volume of runoff and a corresponding decrease in soil-moisture recharge. Overland flow, in turn, may further detach individual soil particles, as well as transport detached particles downslope to streams. When overland flow rates are particularly high, small stream channels may be formed to carry the water away. If these channels are small enough to be obliterated by a plow or by similar frequent movements of the soil, they are called *rills* (Figure 6.11). If they are larger, they are called *gullies.* Rills and gullies tend to grow rapidly, and in so doing they concentrate more overland flow and erode considerable volumes of soil.

Soil erosion resulting from overland flow varies considerably from place to place. Some areas are extremely susceptible to erosion, whereas it is hardly a problem in other areas. Some of the major factors influencing the severity of erosion are topographic factors such as slope steepness, the inherent susceptibility of the soil to erosion, the intensity and frequency of rainfall, and the cropping and management practices of the farmers.

Topographic factors affect overland flow erosion by affecting the volume and velocity of runoff. If the distance from a drainage divide to the bottom of a slope is large, at the bottom of the slope the area contributing overland flow will be large with more water to cause erosion. The ability of overland flow to carry soil depends on water velocity, and the steeper the slope the greater the velocity of overland flow. Thus hilly areas are generally much more susceptible to water erosion than flat land.

The characteristics of the soil itself that influence erosion, or soil erodibility, include infiltration capacity and cohesiveness. Soils with a high infiltration capacity generate less overland flow, and so less erosion occurs. The ability of overland flow to detach and transport particles is affected by the cohesiveness of the soil, or the tendency of particles to stick together. Cohesiveness is determined by many factors, but the organic matter content of the soil is one of the more important factors. Organic matter adds cohesiveness, as well as water- and nutrient-storage capacity, to the soil. Clay minerals are also important in determining soil erodibility, primarily through affecting soil structure and the ease with which aggregates can be broken down.

Rainfall intensity is a major control on soil erosion rates, with intense storms causing more erosion and gentle rains causing very little. In most areas, the major part of erosion is caused by just a few storms in a year, and erosion rates vary greatly by season and year. The ability of a given storm to cause erosion can be measured; Figure 6.12 is a map of the average annual erosivity of rains in the U.S. The part of the country that has the most erosive rain is the Southeast, with somewhat lower values in the North and Midwest. In some areas of the country, particularly the Pacific Northwest, melting snow is also an important cause of erosion.

Finally, and most importantly, farmers' cropping and management practices are very significant to overland flow erosion. Cropping practices include the kinds of crops that are grown and when they are planted. Row crops, such as corn and soybeans, tend to allow more erosion than do continuous cover crops such as wheat or hay. If the field is bare during part of the year, then that will be the time when there is the greatest susceptibility to erosion. As the plants grow and mature, they cover a greater amount of the ground so that erosion susceptibility decreases. In most cases, the time of planting is dictated by plant characteristics and weather; however, there are cases where crops that provide greater cover at times of more erosive rainfall have been chosen. In addition, the decision of whether or when to plow stubble under has effects on erosion susceptibility. This is an example of a management practice. Others include the choice of various conservation techniques such as contour plowing, terracing, or minimum tillage.

The role of weather, soil characteristics, topography, and land management techniques in controlling soil erosion is illustrated by the *Universal Soil Loss Equation* (Wischmeier and Smith, 1965). This equation is a statistical technique for predicting average erosion by rainfall under a variety of climatic, soil, topographic, and management conditions. It is based on many years of U.S. Department of Agriculture research on experimental farms, where field characteristics were controlled and erosion rates measured. It takes the form

$$A = R \times K \times LS \times C \times P$$

where A is the average soil loss in tons per acre per year, R is the rainfall factor, K is soil erodibility, LS is the slope length and steepness factor, C is a crop factor that measures the effect of vegetation cover in reducing erosion, and P is a management practice factor that measures the effects of practices such as contour plowing. The use of the equation is illustrated in Table 6.2. The R factor is based on the intensity and kinetic energy of rainfall at the location considered. The K factor is a number such that when multiplied by R the average erosion rate for a standard plot is obtained. The standard plot is one that is 22 m (72 ft) long, with a 9 percent slope, kept in continuous bare fallow and plowed up and down slope. The LS, C, and P factors are the ratios of erosion rates for

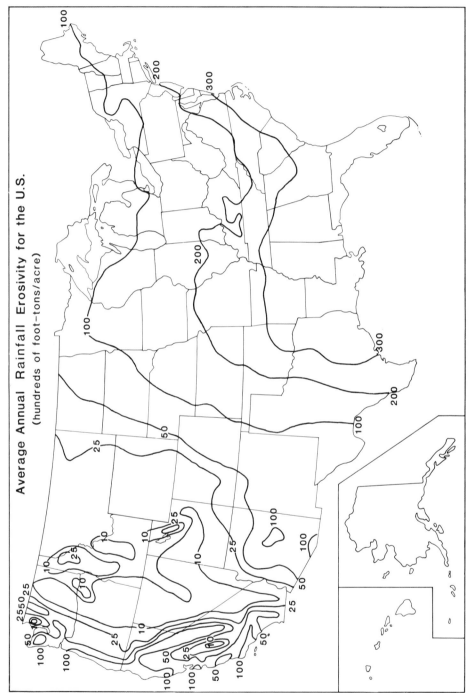

Figure 6.12 Average annual rainfall erosivity for the U.S. The highest rates of rainfall erosion are found in the humid East, particularly the Southeast. (Source: Soil Conservation Service, 1975)

Table 6.2 Examples of Calculation Using Universal Soil Loss Equation

4-year rotation of wheat-with-meadow-seeding, meadow, corn, corn in central Indiana, on 4% slopes 220 feet long, contour plowed
R-factor: 175
K-factor for silt loam soil with fine granular structure and moderate permeability: 0.48
LS factor for 4% slopes 220 feet long: 0.6
C factor for wheat-with-meadow-seeding, meadow, corn, corn: 0.119
P factor for contour plowing on 4% slope: 0.52

Soil loss = A = 175 × .48 × .6 × .119 × .52 = 3.1 tons/acre/year

Soil loss, with conditions same as above but plowing up and down slope instead of on contour: 6.0 tons/acre/year

Soil loss, with conditions same as above, but with contour cultivation of corn continuously instead of rotation: 7.2 tons/acre/year

Source: Based on Wischmeier and Smith, 1965 and Wischmeier, 1974

particular conditions to erosion rates on a standard plot. In the example in Table 6.2, the C factor for continuously planted corn in central Indiana is 0.275, indicating that the vegetation cover provided by the corn reduces erosion to about 28 percent of that on bare ground.

Wind Erosion

Wind erosion occurs when wind velocities at the soil surface are high, in combination with a soil surface that is easily eroded. High wind velocities obviously depend on weather conditions, and some areas are windier than others. Vegetation cover is more important since it controls wind speed at the soil surface. Plants are very effective at reducing surface wind velocities, and wind erosion is essentially negligible under continuous vegetation cover.

The shape of the soil surface is also important in slowing wind velocities and soil erosion. If the ridges and furrows of a plowed field are perpendicular to the wind, the rate of erosion will be much less than if the field is plowed parallel to the prevailing wind direction. Soil texture is also important. Soils that have a high clay content and/or high organic content are generally less susceptible to wind erosion than sandy soils, although there are many exceptions. Soil moisture is also a significant contributor to wind erosion. Moderate levels of soil moisture tend to hold soil particles together, so that as long as the soil surface is moist very little wind erosion will occur. Dry weather can dry out the top few millimeters of a soil even though deeper layers are moist, and thus a bare soil may be susceptible to wind erosion any time of the year.

Figure 6.13 is a map of average annual wind erosion in the Great Plains. The U.S. Department of Agriculture has developed a Wind Erosion Equation similar to the Universal Soil Loss Equation for rainfall erosion. It takes the form,

$$E = f(I,C,K,L,V)$$

where E is the soil loss by wind erosion, I is the erodibility (by wind) of the soil, C is a climate factor, K is a surface roughness factor, L is the length of the field in the prevailing wind direction, and V is a vegetation cover factor. The techniques for computing soil loss differ somewhat from those in the Universal

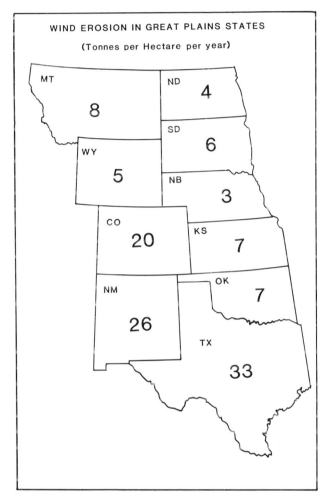

Figure 6.13 Wind erosion in the Great Plains states. Wind erosion is influenced by wind velocity, vegetative cover, soil shape, and soil moisture. Dry weather, in combination with little or no vegetative cover, produces the higher rates of wind erosion found in Texas and New Mexico. (Source: Council on Environmental Quality, 1981)

Soil Loss Equation, but the principles are the same. Both the Universal Soil Loss Equation and the Wind Erosion Equation are effective in estimating average erosion rates under a wide range of conditions and, thus, are a valuable tool in selecting appropriate conservation techniques. Their use as a soil conservation tool is discussed later in this chapter.

Soil Erosion Processes: Summary

Vegetation acts in nearly every aspect of both runoff and wind erosion processes to reduce the rate of erosion. The leaves of plants intercept raindrops, slowing them down and allowing the water to reach the soil slowly instead of with a strong impact. In addition, the stems of plants and the litter of dead leaves on the soil surface slow down overland flow, reducing its ability to transport soil particles. Finally, a good vegetation cover helps to stir the upper parts of the soil profile, keeping it rich in organic matter and permeable so that a high infiltration capacity is maintained. When vegetation is removed, such as by plowing to prepare the soil for crops, the soil is left bare. The increases in raindrop impact, overland flow volumes, and flow velocity that cause accelerated erosion. Similarly, vegetation slows down wind at the soil surface and protects it from intense sunlight or drying winds that could make it more susceptible to wind erosion.

Accelerated erosion has physical effects on the soil, which not only reduce its fertility but may also make it more susceptible to further erosion. Erosion removes the upper portions of the soil profile, which are usually the portions that contain the most stored nutrients and organic matter and are, therefore, most important for soil fertility. These upper layers are often very important in maintaining a high infiltration capacity and in storing soil moisture. Thus when the surface horizons are removed, the lower layers are exposed and the soil may be less able to absorb and store moisture, less fertile, and even more susceptible to erosion.

Extent of the Problem

Accelerated soil erosion is found on virtually all cultivated lands, but the extent of the problem varies greatly from place to place. Recently the U.S. Department of Agriculture completed a survey of sheet and rill erosion on U.S. lands (U.S. Department of Agriculture, 1981); the results are summarized in Figure 6.14. The greatest rates of soil erosion are found in the Southeast and in the Corn Belt states, with average rates ranging from 8 to over 12 tonnes per hectare per year (4 to about 6 tons per acre per year). These rates correspond to a loss of about 0.5 to 1 cm (0.2 to 0.4 in.) from the soil surface in ten years. If we recognize that the top 10 to 30 cm (4 to 12 in.) of most soils hold the greatest proportion of the nutrients and organic matter, then these rates may lead to removal of much of this very fertile layer in just a few decades.

The effect of this erosion on crop production is difficult to assess, primarily because there are relatively few opportunities to measure quantitatively these effects directly or to predict future consequences of erosion. There are so many factors that affect crop yields that it is nearly impossible to determine the effects caused by changes in single factors, such as inherent soil fertility. This is particularly true when the adverse effects of excessive soil erosion accumulate very slowly and are masked by changes in farming techniques, weather, or farm economics.

One criterion commonly used to determine how much erosion is tolerable is the rate of new soil formation. Soil is continually being formed. If the rate of erosion can be kept equal to or less than this rate, then the long term viability of the resource is not jeopardized. The rate of new soil formation is itself difficult to determine, but working estimates have been made for most of the major agricultural soils in the U.S. For the most part, these estimates range from about 1 to 10 tonnes per hectare per year (0.5 to 5 tons per acre per year). In 1977, the most recent year for which data are available, the rainfall erosion rate exceeded

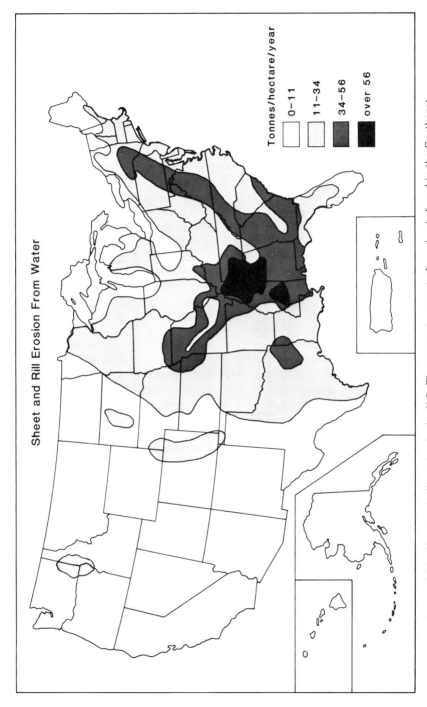

Sheet and Rill Erosion From Water

Tonnes/hectare/year

☐ 0–11

☐ 11–34

▨ 34–56

■ over 56

Figure 6.14 Sheet and rill erosion in the U.S. The greatest amount of erosion is found in the Southeast. (Source: Water Resources Council, 1978)

the tolerable rate on 18.4 million hectares (45.4 million acres) of cropland. This does not include wind erosion, which exceeds rainfall erosion in some of the Great Plains states (Figure 6.13).

A few studies have been conducted on the reductions in crop yields that occur as a result of erosion, other factors held constant. These show that losses can be significant, particularly if erosion over periods of several decades is considered. Larson et al. (1983), for example, conclude that for some soils in the upper Midwest, as much as 15 to 20 percent of the productive capability of the soils may be lost in 50 years of erosion, although in most cases projected losses were less. In the long term, this loss of productive capacity may be significant, particularly when we consider a growing population and likely world food demands. But on a per-year basis, the losses are very small, only a fraction of a percent.

Conservation Techniques

Over the years, many techniques have been developed to control erosion while still allowing efficient agricultural production. Some of these, such as crop rotation, have been known for centuries, while others have been developed fairly recently. Some of the important techniques are discussed below.

Crop rotation is a farming method that is primarily aimed at maintaining soil fertility, but plant growth is also enhanced and erosion is reduced. Crop rotation simply means that over a period of several years the crops grown on a field will change in a systematic pattern. Some crops demand more of some nutrients than others. By changing crops from year to year, excessive depletion of nutrients can be prevented. Typical rotation patterns may include fallow periods or plantings of crops like alfalfa that restore some nutrients to the soil. Often such crops are plowed under rather than harvested, a technique called green manuring. Crop rotation may also allow the ground to be covered a greater percentage of the time, thus reducing erosion. Some rotation patterns may repeat one or more crops, such as a rotation of corn, corn, oats, hay. In the short run, this may require planting less profitable crops in some years, a fact that reduces the ability and willingness of farmers to use this technique.

Contour plowing is another important soil conservation method. It involves plowing across a slope, or on the contour, rather than up and down a slope. Contour plowing reduces erosion by causing water to be trapped in the furrows where it can soak in, rather than running down the furrows and causing erosion. It is thus also a water conservation technique. On hilly land, contours are rarely straight, so that contour plowing requires plowing in curvy lines across a field. Because field boundaries rarely follow the contours, contour plowing usually results in irregularly shaped patches and some unused land, making it more time-consuming and perhaps less profitable for the farmer than plowing in straight rows parallel to the borders of a rectangular field.

Contour plowing is often used in conjunction with *terracing*. Terracing involves constructing ridges or ditches parallel to the contours. These trap runoff and divert it into drainage channels, preventing it from continuing downslope and causing erosion. In some parts of the world, notably Southeast Asia, terraces are constructed with flat surfaces to pond water for rice production. In the U.S. most terraces are subtle ridges on sloping fields. In many cases the farmer plows and plants on them as if they were not there. Contour plowing, terracing, or crop rotation may be combined with *strip cropping,* where crops are planted in parallel strips along the contour or perpendicular to prevailing winds. One strip may be planted with a less protective crop or left fallow, while the adjacent strip has a protective cover. Soil eroded in one area is deposited nearby, and little of the soil is lost.

With regard to wind erosion, the most useful prevention methods are stubble mulching and windbreaks. *Stubble mulching* simply means leaving plant residue on the ground between growing seasons rather than plowing it under immediately after harvest. Windbreaks are lines of trees planted perpendicular to the most erosive winds. Both these techniques act to reduce wind velocity at the soil surface and thus reduce erosion. Some of these methods are illustrated in Figure 6.15.

Another conservation technique that is rapidly growing in acceptance is *minimum tillage.* This technique reduces erosion by minimizing the number of times a plow or other implement is passed through the soil. It reduces erosion because it usually means leaving crop residue on the surface through the winter rather than plowing it under in the fall. In addition, undisturbed soils will maintain a thin crust that is more resistant to erosion than a disturbed soil. Minimum tillage also greatly reduces the fuel costs of operating a tractor, which has been increasingly important in recent years. One of the major drawbacks of minimum tillage is that instead of physically removing weeds by plowing, herbicides are used to a greater extent, risking the harmful side effects of these chemicals.

One of the greatest advances in soil conservation was the development of the Universal Soil Loss Equation, which has been refined so that an extension agent can easily estimate the amount of erosion that will be expected to occur on a specific field, assuming particular practices by the farmer. It is then possible to choose the mix of cropping and management practices that best suits the needs of the farmer and minimizes erosion. The range of alternatives to control erosion is usually large, so that, in theory, most farmers should be able to find a combination of crop types, planting times, and conservation practices that still allows a profitable farm operation. In practice, however, the equation has enjoyed only limited success, largely because of economic constraints on farmers.

The Economics of Erosion

Decisions on how to manage agricultural land are made by individual farmers, who, like any businessmen operating in the short run, are primarily concerned with maximizing their incomes. Farmers are aware of the threat of erosion to the productivity of their lands, which in the long run means destruction of their capital base, and most feel that more should be done to prevent it. The problem is that their management decisions must consider the costs of inputs such as seed, fertilizer, irrigation water, fuel, and pesticides relative to the value of the crops that will be produced. Inputs of fertilizers and pesticides will generally result in substantial increases in crop yields, and so variations in these inputs are much more significant to short-term returns than long-term reductions in inherent soil fertility caused by erosion. Most farmers in the U.S. today are struggling under enormous debts, and farm prices have not been high enough to pay off loans and provide a comfortable profit. This profit is necessary if

Figure 6.15   Erosion control. (a) Windbreaks used to control erosion of alluvial soils in California. (b) Contour plowing and strip cropping in New Jersey. (Source: U.S. Department of Agriculture-Soil Conservation Service photo)

farmers are to restrict planting, invest in erosion control structures, or otherwise constrain their activities.

Government officials concerned with soil conservation have recognized this problem and, since the 1930s, have implemented programs to ease the economic burden of soil conservation. One important method used is payments to the farmer in exchange for planting soil-conserving cover crops such as alfalfa instead of more profitable, but non-protective, crops. Such payments serve a second purpose, reducing farm production so as to increase prices. In addition to these payments, subsidies have been made available from time to time to pay for capital improvements such as construction of terraces or gully control. Finally, Soil Conservation Service extension agents provide technical assistance to farmers, providing information on different erosion control methods and how they can be incorporated into a profitable farm management plan.

In spite of these measures, the erosion problem persists. In the late 1970s, economic difficulties for farmers led them to plant more and more land, rejecting cover crops in favor of more profitable row crops. The large machinery in use today is not well suited to terraced fields, and in many areas terraces have been destroyed. These trends have prompted new warnings on the severity of the erosion problem, but no new government programs have emerged to deal with it. Many experts feel that as long as new agricultural technologies can increase yields at the same time that erosion control reduces either yields or profits, few farmers will do much to control erosion. Although farmers might be will-ing to accept mandatory programs to control erosion, they would only be willing to do so if society as a whole, through the government, compensated farmers for reduced incomes (Seitz and Swanson, 1980).

AGRICULTURAL LAND CONVERSION

As discussed earlier in this chapter, the amount of land on which crops are planted in any given year is only a portion of the available agricultural land. The amount of cropland changes through time, increasing as new land is cleared or irrigation water made available and decreasing as land is converted to other uses or lost from agricultural uses as a result of erosion, salinization, or other degradation processes. The actual amount of land that is in crops at any time is a function of farm economics, available technology, and demand for land for other uses. In any event, the total amount of potentially arable land is finite.

As growing populations seek living space and resources, there are tremendous pressures on the available land base worldwide. These pressures cause land to be more or less permanently allocated to nonagricultural uses, irreversibly limiting potential arable land area. In a world already experiencing problems of food supply, this indicates even greater problems in the future.

Causes

There are many reasons why agricultural land is lost to other uses, and often it is difficult to separate them. Some of the major factors are urban growth, water resource development, changing farm economics, and land degradation. Conversion of cropland to residential, commercial, industrial, and transportation

Figure 6.16 Residential development encroaching on agricultural land in southern Ontario. This is but one of the many causes of loss of agricultural land in North America.

uses is an irreversible change that accompanies urban growth (Figure 6.16). In the U.S. this process consumes about 0.4 million hectares (1 million acres) annually. Most of this occurs at the urban fringe, where new shopping centers, housing developments, highways, and the like are being constructed. The principal reason for the change in land use is simply that the land can return a greater profit to its owner from nonagricultural than agricultural use. Through the price system, society is demanding more urban and residential land and less agricultural land. In this case, however, the change at any given location is irreversible. Houses can be torn down to build highways, and factories can be converted into apartment houses. But once land is paved, sewers installed, and buildings erected, it cannot be returned to agricultural use except at prohibitive cost. What can be done, of course, is to convert other agricultural land into cropland to replace what has been lost.

If we accept that there is a genuine need for urban land, then some cropland must be sacrificed for these uses. An important question is whether the conversion is made efficiently, minimizing the land loss and converting poor quality land rather than the best cropland, to urban uses. There is a tendency for development to take the best cropland, rather than less productive land. This is because the best land for agriculture is flat land, often in accessible areas such as river valleys, which are also the best sites for shopping centers and highways, and the like. It seems that in the U.S. today, the conversion is not being made as efficiently as it might, largely because proximity to cities often makes agriculture difficult.

Near an expanding urban area, several processes contribute to loss of agricultural land. First, demand for land causes land values to rise. If property taxes are based on land value, then the farmers' taxes rise, making farming less profitable. As farmers see land around them being sold to developers, they recognize that they too are likely to sell out in the near future. They are then reluctant to make major investments in farm equipment or improvements that will keep the farms competitive in the long run but take longer to pay for themselves than the expected life of the farm. In addition, the rural economic system begins to be replaced with urban-oriented businesses, so that farm supplies and occasional labor become more difficult to obtain. In many areas farm vandalism and theft perpetrated by urban residents further hinders farming operations. Urban residents also complain about nuisances such as odors, dust, and pesticides. All these things tend to encourage farmers to abandon agriculture and sell out to land speculators, often much sooner than would be the case if these additional pressures were not acting.

Urban demands for land extend well beyond the suburban fringe. Cities need water, and dams that impound water also inundate substantial acreages. In the U.S., about 29 percent of the land lost annually is lost to water uses, mostly reservoirs and catchment areas, and 71 percent of the loss is to urban uses (Schmude, 1977). In many cases, inundated bottomlands were the most fertile lands. In areas where water is in short supply, allocating water for urban uses often precludes other uses such as agricultural irrigation. In Arizona, for example, accumulation of salts in soils and depletion of groundwater have limited productivity to the point where farms are being abandoned. If more water were available, these farms could remain productive, but rapid population growth is causing what water is available to be diverted to cities. Electric power transmission lines and petroleum pipelines also take rural land, sometimes breaking up fields and making farming more difficult.

Extent and Severity

No reliable data are available on a global level, which would indicate how much agricultural land is lost to other uses. Urbanization is a worldwide phenomenon, but losses are presently masked by opening of new lands, so that on a global level arable land is increasing slightly. At the national level, the best data available for the U.S. are for the period 1967–75 (Brewer and Boxley, 1981). During that period, a total of 9.45 million hectares (23.3 million acres) were converted to other uses, or about 1.18 million hectares (2.92 million acres) per year. Of these, about 0.35 million hectares (0.87 million acres) were taken from the cropland base of actual and potential cropland shown in Figure 6.3. The remaining 0.83 million hectares (2.05 million acres) were taken from land that was rangeland, forest land, pastureland, and other agricultural land. The annual loss was about 0.16 percent of our present cropland base. This figure sounds low, but the rate of loss of land appears to have been accelerating in recent decades. In addition, a substantial amount of the land lost was prime farmland—the very best land for farming. In the 1967–75 period, about 0.4 million hectares (1 million acres) per year of prime farmland were lost. Not all prime farmland is presently cropped, and much of what was lost was not in production at the time.

The question of whether these losses constitute a serious problem is open to debate. The primary considerations in such a debate are (1) what the expected and future demands for farmland are and (2) whether these demands can be met by the available land plus new land that may be brought into production. With regard to the first question, we can look to projections made by the Council on Environmental Quality (1981b). On a worldwide basis, future demands for farmland will be large. World population is expected to reach 6.1 billion by 2000, whereas arable land will increase only slightly. The result will be a decline in arable land per capita, from about 0.39 hectares (0.94 acres) in 1971–75 to about 0.25 hectares (0.62 acres) in 2000. This will require substantial increases in yield per hectare (or acre), which can only occur with much greater increases in fertilizer, pesticide, and irrigation water inputs and use of high-yielding varieties of plants. Such increases will probably occur only with large increases in the cost of food and in accelerated erosion. The more land available, the more food can be produced at relatively low cost, with an associated improvement in diet for the poorer nations of the world. In the U.S., population is not rising rapidly and there is no reason to believe that improvements in agricultural technology will not be able to keep pace with demands for higher yields. However, since the U.S. is a major food exporter, we must have as much good quality land as possible to maintain and expand that role in the future. Furthermore, the land that is lost is generally better quality than that which will replace it. This means that more fertilizer will be needed and more soil erosion will result, since poorer lands will be farmed.

The Need for Preservation

Beyond the simple need for food production, there are several other reasons for preserving agricultural land. An agricultural base that is diversified and dispersed, rather than concentrated in a few very productive regions, is less susceptible to disruption by bad weather, crop diseases, and the like. In many areas, agriculture is an important local industry that helps maintain the economic viability of a region. Economic viability depends not only on generating income but also on minimizing outlays, and many people feel that regional self-sufficiency in food production is a worthwhile goal.

Changes in regional economies, such as the growth of urban industrial economies, often are accompanied by the downfall of agriculture in those regions. For example, New Jersey (the Garden State) was once an important exporter of vegetables to the markets of the Northeast. At the turn of the century it supplied virtually all of the tomatoes used by the Campbell Soup Company. Today 82 percent of its food is imported from other states or nations, and Campbell gets its tomatoes from the Southwest (Swackhamer, 1982).

There are also specific regions that have climatic or soil characteristics that make them the only good areas suitable for cultivation of specific crops. The Salinas Valley artichoke region south of San Francisco is an example. If this area were converted to other land uses, artichokes would become unavailable or very expensive in the U.S.

Finally, there are aesthetic and recreational considerations for farmland preservation. Many urban residents desire open space, wildlife habitats, or other attributes of agricultural land. Cities that are compact, rather than sprawling, preserve more open space and some features of a natural landscape. This is an important justification for agricultural land preservation in many areas.

Several institutional measures have been devised to limit the conversion of agricultural land to other uses. The most common of these is property taxes that are based on the use value of land rather than on the market value. Thus, if a parcel of land is in agricultural use, it is taxed at a rate that reflects the relatively low profits that can be made by that use, rather than the higher value of the land if it were sold for development. This eliminates the effect of excessive taxes on farmers in urbanizing areas. A second method that has been used in several areas has been the establishment of agricultural districts. These districts have been designated productive areas that are to remain agricultural, even though other areas around them are allowed to be developed. Landowners within agricultural districts receive tax advantages for maintaining agricultural land use, and various measures are used to restrict or prevent conversion of farmland to other uses. In New Jersey, this concept includes the sale of development rights by farmers in agricultural districts. Development rights are purchased by land developers, who may then build at higher than normal densities in planned growth areas, if they buy an appropriate amount of development rights. These are acquired from farmers within agricultural districts who then gain the profits associated with increased land values without having to give up farming. In other areas, development rights have been acquired directly by local or state governments.

These measures have met with limited success. In some areas, such as New Jersey and Long Island, New York, farmland preservation has strong public support, and innovative laws have been passed to preserve the remaining agricultural areas. Yet conversion continues. To some extent the causes are national in scope, with competition from farmers in one part of the country constraining actions in another part. Under these circumstances it is difficult to prevent farm abandonment. Once land is no longer farmed, it is difficult to prevent a farmer from selling to developers. Unless there is a considerable growth in strong land-use planning efforts on a regional as well as local scale, it seems that the only thing that will stop conversion of farmland to other uses will be large increases in food prices.

CONCLUSIONS

Debate continues regarding the future of world agriculture. There are millions of hungry people in the world today, yet crop production increases are leveling off in the "breadbasket" nations of the world. Self-sufficiency in food production is far from a reality in many nations.

Some ecologists accept the inevitability of large-scale epidemics and die-offs of the human population to return it to a stable size. Alternatively, many food production experts in the wealthier nations encourage further transferral of mechanized agriculture to the less affluent, with the implication that the American system should be adopted worldwide. This would have to be accompanied by a massive industrialization program to employ the billions of farmers and families pushed off their land by mechanization and other economies of scale. There are immense social, environmental, and economic implications of such a transformation.

Another alternative is the continuing effort to encourage agricultural self-sufficiency, both in the United States and abroad. Major regions within the U.S., such as New England, have long been unable to feed themselves. In these areas there is a trend toward a return to farming, but on a different basis than most American agriculture. Farming is done on small parcels, in a small-scale, low-technology, energy-efficient fashion. This contributes to a true self-sufficiency but is presently more of an ideological movement than an economic one. It involves only a tiny fraction of a percent of American farms and cannot contribute significantly to the region's food supply.

Many countries are attempting to stimulate a return to small-scale, subsistence-oriented farming for their rural residents but are fighting a massive flow of people to the cities. It is unlikely that these plans can be effective without a strong guarantee to farmers that they can turn a profit growing food for themselves and others. This is impossible under most present-day land ownership and cash-crop oriented systems.

In the U.S., technological improvements will probably continue to produce increases in crop yields, and the U.S. will continue to be a major food exporter. Concerns for the future of agricultural resource development revolve mainly around the problems of energy efficiency, pesticide use, and soil erosion. In the last few years, rising oil prices have hit farmers particularly hard, because they depend on oil for fuel, fertilizer, and pesticides, three of the most important inputs in American agriculture. Although energy prices fluctuate, it seems clear that in the long run they must continue their upward trend. In addition, there is growing concern over the ecological and health effects of pesticide use. Pesticides are applied in increasing quantities as pests become resistant to them and as farmers turn more to chemical, rather than mechanical, means for controlling weeds. Pesticides contaminate water supplies, poison agricultural workers, and alter ecosystems. They also appear in the foods we eat. Although pesticide content is monitored and regulated by the government, public concern is likely to grow and force tighter restrictions on pesticide use, making farming even more expensive. Finally, soil erosion continues at unacceptable rates in many areas of the U.S. Although it will probably not be an acute problem causing abandonment of land, it will be a chronic problem that will ultimately force farmers to increase inputs of fertilizer and possibly organic matter to replace lost nutrients and to improve deteriorating soil structure. All of these things will further increase the cost of producing food and fiber. Thus, it seems that the U.S. will continue to be an important food provider but that food prices will probably have to rise substantially in the next few decades to allow this production to take place.

REFERENCES AND ADDITIONAL READING

Brewer, M.F., and R.F. Boxley. 1981. Agricultural land: adequacy of acres, concepts, and information. *Am. J. Ag. Econ.* 63:879–87.

Brown, L. 1980. Food or fuel: new competition for the world's cropland. Worldwatch Paper 35. Washington, D.C.: Worldwatch Institute, March.

Buckman, H.O., and N.C. Brady. 1969. *The nature and properties of soils.* 7th ed. New York: Macmillan.

Council on Environmental Quality. 1981a. *Environmental trends.* Washington, D.C.: Government Printing Office.

———. 1981b. *The Global 2000 report to the president.* Washington, D.C.: Government Printing Office.

Crabbe, D., and S. Lawson. 1981. *The world food book.* London: Kogan Page.

Harlan, J.R. 1976. The plants and animals that nourish man. *Scientific American* 235:3:88–98.

Heady, E.O. 1976. The agriculture of the U.S. *Scientific American* 235:3:107–27.

Hulse, J.H. 1982. Food science and nutrition: the gulf between rich and poor. *Science* 216:1291–94.

Jaynes, G. 1982. U.S. farmers said to face worst year since 1930s. *New York Times* March 28.

Johnson, K. 1982. Equity in hazard management. *Environment* 24:9:28–38.

Kaufman, M.T. 1980. No longer a charity case, India fills its own granaries. *New York Times* August 10.

King, S.F. 1983. Big crops likely despite cutbacks. *New York Times* July 5.

Larson, W.E., et al. 1983. The threat of soil erosion to long-term crop production. *Science* 219:458–65.

Morgan, D. 1979. *Merchants of grain.* New York: Viking.

National Academy of Sciences. 1972. *The genetic variability of major crops.* Washington, D.C.

Rasmussen, W.D. 1982. The mechanization of agriculture. *Scientific American* 247:3:77–89.

Rural Advancement Fund. 1981. Agriculture's vanishing heritage. Spring:4–5. Charlotte, North Carolina: Rural Advancement Fund/National Sharecroppers Fund.

Schmude, K.O. 1977. A perspective on prime farmland. *J. Soil & Water Cons.* 35:240–42.

Scrimshaw, N.S., and L. Taylor. 1980. Food. *Scientific American* 243:3:78–88.

Seitz, W.D., and E.R. Swanson, 1980. Economics of soil conservation from the farmer's perspective. *Am. J. Ag. Econ.* 62:1084–88.

Soil Conservation Service, 1975, Procedure for computing sheet and rill erosion on project areas. Technical Release 51. Wash-ington, D.C.: Government Printing Office.

———. 1980. *America's soil and water: condition and trends.* Washington, D.C.: Government Printing Office.

Swackhamer, P. 1982. *The New Jersey food system: cultivating the Garden State.* Emmaus, Pennsylvania: Rodale Press.

Thompson, L. 1975, World weather patterns and food supply. *J. Soil & Water Cons.* 30:44–7.

U.S. Bureau of the Census. 1984. *Statistical abstract of the United States.* Washington, D.C.: Government Printing Office.

U.S. Department of Agriculture. 1981. *RCA appraisal, parts 1 and 2.* Washington, D.C.: Government Printing Office.

U.S. Department of Agriculture and Council on Environmental Quality. 1981. *National agricultural lands study, final report.* Washington, D.C.: Government Printing Office.

Water Resources Council. 1978. *The nation's water resources, 1975–2000.* Washington, D.C.: Government Printing Office.

Wellhausen, E.J. 1976. The agriculture of Mexico. *Scientific American* 235:3:128–53.

Wischmeier, W.H. 1974. New developments in estimating water erosion. *Proc. 29th Annual Meeting, Soil Cons. Soc. Am.,* pp. 179–86.

———, and D.D. Smith. 1965. Predicting rainfall erosion losses from cropland east of the Rocky Mountains—guide for selection of practices for soil and water conservation. USDA Agr. Handbook 282. Washington, D.C.: Government Printing Office.

Wortman, S. 1976. Food and agriculture. *Scientific American* 235:3:30–39.

TERMS TO KNOW

accelerated soil erosion
agribusiness
arable
contour plowing
crop rotation
drip irrigation
erosion
flood irrigation

furrow irrigation
Green Revolution
gully erosion
infiltration capacity
integrated pest management
Land Capability Classification System
minimum tillage
mixed cropping systems

monoculture
parent material
pesticide
rill erosion
soil fertility
soil horizons
soil structure
soil texture

sprinkler irrigation
strip cropping
stubble mulching
terracing
Universal Soil Loss Equation
water-holding capacity
windbreaks

STUDY QUESTIONS

1. Compare and contrast mixed cropping with monocultural agricultural systems. What are the benefits and costs of each?
2. Explain how climate, parent material, topography, erosion, and biological activity affect soil formation.
3. Describe each of the four major types of irrigation systems used in the world today.
4. Discuss the pros and cons of integrated pest management versus sole pesticide application.
5. What factors influence accelerated soil erosion?
6. Compare and contrast the various soil-conservation techniques.
7. Why are economic considerations important in the selection of soil-conservation techniques?
8. What factors have influenced the conversion of agricultural land to other uses, and what can be done to control it?

CHAPTER SEVEN

Rangelands: Food Resources for Animals

INTRODUCTION

Several resource issues are particularly important in predicting and planning for future world supplies of meat, milk, and hides. These issues include the predictability of rainfall patterns in lands already marginal for grazing, overgrazing, competing land uses, ancient cultural traditions, and the efficiency of using meat for food. In this chapter we will look at the quantity and quality of grazing lands, both globally and within the United States. As defined by the U.S. Forest Service, *range* is land that provides or is capable of providing forage for grazing or browsing animals. This includes grass, shrub, and forest lands that can support nutritive plant species, both native and introduced, natural and managed (U.S. Forest Service, 1981).

Human beings and domestic animals have depended upon one another for thousands of years. In fact, one way of defining a *domesticate* or *domesticated species* is its inability to survive without human assistance. As with the plants that are now our major crops, we have carefully chosen our major food animals generation by generation and bred them for those characteristics that we found valuable, such as thick wool, milk and meat, and resistance to disease. As a result, characteristics that enable an animal to survive in the wild, such as intelligence or agility, are often not found in our domesticated animals. Thus they and we are mutually dependent for survival. For optimal production, herders and ranchers must provide livestock with high-quality food, ensuring that the land grazed is not overused.

Most of the world's grazing lands are in semiarid climates, for in these low-rainfall areas the land generally cannot support arable agriculture without irrigation. Palatable grasses and low shrubs are, however, available to livestock (Figure 7.1). Animals are also grazed on other lands that are unsuited for agriculture such as mountainous areas and forests. Through the ages, livestock have been able to make use of land that was otherwise classified as useless for human occupancy. In the United States, cattle grazing was the early backbone of the western states' economy and, in fact, makes up much of the region's folklore. Today raising and selling cattle is part of the nation's agribusiness industry. There are often conflicting demands on the land available for grazing, and a debate ebbs and

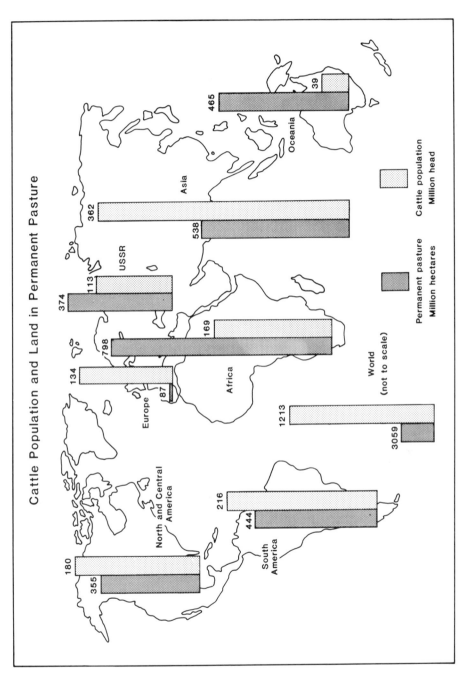

Figure 7.1 Global cattle population and land in permanent pasture. The global average is about one animal for every three hectares. Europe and Asia have large numbers of cattle relative to pasture area, while Africa and Oceania have smaller cattle populations per hectare. Africa has more pastureland than any other continent. (Source: Data from Crabbe and Lawson, 1981)

flows over the comparative value of meat versus grain production for national and global food supplies.

USE AND ABUSE OF RANGELANDS:
A GLOBAL VIEW

Range, or grazing land, provides forage for limited numbers of domestic animals. *Overgrazing* occurs when the numbers of animals on these lands exceed carrying capacities. Several areas of the world, notably the dry lands around the Mediterranean, have been long overgrazed, with resulting problems of devegetation, erosion, and, ultimately, the threat of desertification. *Desertification* is the process of land becoming more desert-like, as a result of devegetation and related soil deterioration aggravated by drought. It occurs in parts of all the major semiarid regions of the world. There are several misconceptions about desertification. One is that global rainfall is decreasing. There is no evidence that modern desertification is the result of climate change, although droughts play a major role in the process. Also, we often hear statements about "advancing deserts"; this is also improper. Deserts do not move—they are created in place by overuse of a sensitive resource.

Livestock Use Patterns

The herding of animals is an ancient system of arid lands resource use. Patterns of life dependent on livestock developed thousands of years ago in Asia and Africa and are still important to a remnant population of at least fifteen million people in the broad band of arid and semiarid lands stretching across the northern third of Africa, much of East Africa, India, and Mongolia (Grigg, 1974). Traditional *pastoral nomads* are not oriented toward the production of large quantities of meat and dairy products for market. These small groups of people and cattle follow the seasons, traveling in search of new pasture. Products of these sheep and goat herds of Asia and cattle herds of Africa are used locally or traded on a small scale. Over the past one hundred years, numbers of these pastoral nomads have declined as they have settled in permanent locations. Governments have been enforcing the process of *sedentarization,* which directs herding groups to villages and controls the crossing of national borders. Additionally, many nomads have left their herds and families for work in urban areas.

In other agricultural systems, livestock are of varying importance. For example, in the wet-rice cultivation regions that provide food for the populations of the Far East, there is little room on cultivated acreage for growing animal feed. Thus meat and dairy products play only a small role in the diet of southern and eastern Asia. This is changing, however, as American-style fast food chains and the high-status appeal of beef make inroads into the traditional eating habits of the region.

With 19th-century settlement of drier areas in the Americas and Australia, it became environmentally and financially feasible to raise and transport large numbers of livestock for transport to distant markets. The vast open stretches of shrub and grassland were well-suited for grazing, since there was and is not today enough rainfall for any other agricultural system except for risky *dry farming.* This approach to agriculture involves planting a crop and hoping for enough rain, a gamble in semiarid areas. There are important differences between the traditional Asian and African pastoralism and cattle-raising in the more recently settled dry lands. One is that livestock raising in the Americas and Australia is oriented toward meat instead of milk consumption. The newer system also depends on a technologically complex set of elements including truck transport, antibiotics, and other food supplements.

Another element of these newer livestock-raising patterns is the grazing land itself, which can be brought more fully under the control of human managers than was technologically possible for Old World nomads. The main tool available to the nomad for range improvement or alteration was fire. The American farmer can alter vast stretches of land with defoliants, irrigation systems, and new seeds; and has helicopters, trucks, and bulldozers as tools. Even with these new developments, however, the problems of overuse, degradation, and erosion loom as large in these modern systems as they have for millennia in the dry lands of Asia and Africa.

Today, overgrazing is having a major effect on the world's rangelands. Figure 7.2 is a world map of the main areas affected by desertification. Many of these areas are in the semiarid regions of west and east Africa, northern China, and southwest Asia. The sharp rise in population in these areas has led to an ever-increasing demand for food. As a result, cattle and sheep populations are also rising. The increase in cattle populations globally from 1955 to 1976 was 38 percent, with most of this occurring in the Near East and Latin America (Council on Environmental Quality, 1981). In the same period sheep population increased worldwide by 20 percent. This increase in animal populations meant a rise in the use of grazing lands and is thus a major cause of recent desertification. For example, in the Republic of the Sudan, located on the southern margins of the Sahara Desert, there is evidence that the line separating scrub from barren lands shifted south 90 to 100 kilometers (56 to 62 miles) between 1958 and 1975 (Eckholm and Brown, 1977). Desertification in the *Sahel* was particularly severe during the 1968–73 drought. In this semiarid region that spans Africa, located south of the Sahara and north of humid regions, much of this damage may not be reparable in the short term, especially if resource management patterns remain unchanged (Council on Environmental Quality, 1981).

The Human Context

According to a study done for the U.N. Conference on Desertification (Kates et al., 1976), an estimated 50 million people worldwide are directly affected by desertification. The 3 million residents of the world's dry lands, who are dependent on traditional and modern animal-based livelihood systems, are disproportionately affected by desertification. The origins of desertification are complex. The condition develops from the interaction between agriculture-based, animal-based, and urban-based livelihood systems in semiarid areas; fluctuations in the natural environment; and changes in human social systems. These changes include the growth and decline of human populations, alterations in and losses of traditional life-styles, and changing governmental directions (Kates et al., 1976).

All of these societal and institutional factors work with natural factors to bring about desertification. For example, changes in carrying capacity are brought

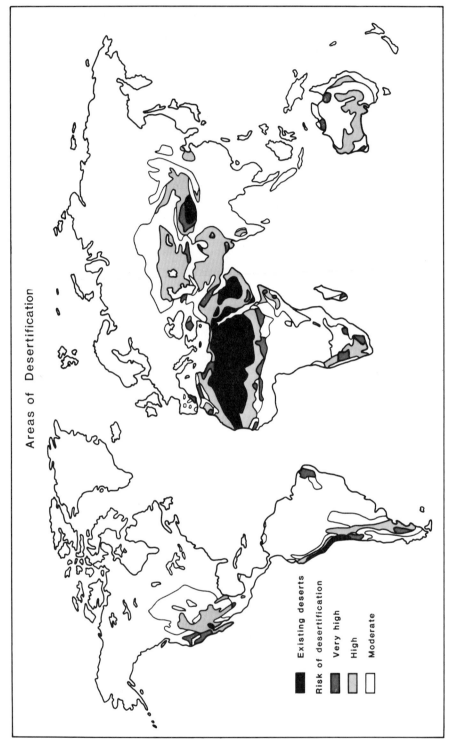

Areas of Desertification

Figure 7.2 World areas affected by desertification. Regions with a high risk of desertification are in the semiarid regions of Africa; northern China and southwest Asia. A primary area of concern is the Sahel region of Africa, located along the southern margin of the Sahara Desert.

Existing deserts

Risk of desertification

Very high

High

Moderate

about by rainfall variations. Pastoralists want to keep as many cattle as their land can tolerate; to keep fewer would mean less income and decreased economic stability.

It takes years to build up a herd by reproduction alone. The herd represents savings, which should be used as slowly as possible if the length of drought is uncertain (Figure 7.3). In times of plentiful rain and good forage, pastoralists increase herd sizes to make use of the expanded resource. During droughts, forage production and carrying capacity are reduced, and overgrazing results. Animals are slaughtered to provide food and income, which reduces grazing pressure, although not before considerable damage is done to vegetation and soil. This pattern is a common one, resulting from the lag time between changes in the forage supply and changes in the affected animal population. Thus in times of increasing carrying capacity the range is understocked, but it is overstocked when carrying capacity is decreasing. The only ways to avoid this problem are either to continually ship animals long distances from areas short in forage to areas with surplus or to keep herd sizes at a constant low level, well below carrying capacity for all but the worst years. For many of the poorer countries of the world, these methods require expensive government regulation and a further reduction in the freedom of the traditional pastoral nomad. It should be noted that especially in Africa national boundaries add another constraint in that they interfere with the traditional migration routes of pastoral nomads.

GRASS FOR ANIMALS; MEAT FOR PEOPLE

Rangeland Ecology

Most of the world's prime grazing lands are natural grasslands, found in semiarid areas. Grasses do well in a semiarid climate for several reasons. When water is in short supply, it takes precedence over sunshine as a limiting factor (see Chapter 4). Trees, which require relatively large amounts of water, do not compete well. Grasses and other plants that can grow and reproduce in a short wet season are better equipped to survive. In addition, aridity increases the likelihood of fire, and this also favors grasses. Trees take longer to regenerate after fire than do grasses, and frequent fires may prevent trees from taking hold. Many of the world's grassland areas exist because of frequent fires, either of natural or human origin.

The ability of grasses to grow rapidly when conditions are favorable combined with the variability of precipitation in semiarid areas leads to seasonal and annual variations in the amount of grass that grows in grassland areas. This means that the number of herbivores that can be supported by the land also varies. Under natural conditions, populations of these grazing animals such as rodents and deer are kept in check by competition for available food. But the population levels of domestic animals are controlled by humans, not by natural conditions. To maximize animal production in the short run, herders often exceed the carrying capacity of the land, resulting in damage to the vegetation.

Grazing affects plants in several ways. Plants are reduced in size by grazing, which usually inhibits their ability to photosynthesize and grow. Animals damage plants by trampling, which is particularly detrimental to young plants. The

Figure 7.3 Pastoralism and overgrazing in Kenya. (Source: United Nations photo 152.440/Ian Steele)

reduction in plant cover caused by grazing leads to a deterioration of soil conditions, which also inhibits plant growth. On the positive side, the seeds of some plant species are spread by grazing animals, either by being attached to fur or by being eaten and excreted. Other plant species may be inhibited from reproducing under grazing pressure, if seeds are digested for example. Finally, grazing may stimulate plant growth by reducing competition among plants for moisture or nutrients, and thus the plants may be able to replace some of the biomass taken by animals.

Range plant species vary in their ability to survive and reproduce under grazing pressure. Some species may be able to quickly regenerate leaves lost to animals, while others cannot. Some are relatively unaffected by trampling, while for others this is fatal. Most importantly, some species are more palatable to grazing animals and thus are eaten first; others are less palatable and are eaten only after the desirable forage is consumed. These differences in susceptibility of plants to grazing impact are the basis of the ecological changes that result from grazing.

Range ecologists classify plant species in a particular area as decreasers, increasers, or invaders. *Decreasers* are plant species that are present in a plant community, but decrease in importance (as measured by numbers of plants or percent of ground covered) in a plant community as a result of grazing. They are generally the most palatable plants, but they may also include species that are negatively affected by animals in other ways, such as trampling. *Increasers* are species that were present prior to grazing and that increase in importance as a result of grazing. They may be less palatable species, or they may increase simply because there is less competition from the decreasers for water or nutrients. *Invaders* are species that were not present prior to grazing but that are able to colonize the area as a result of the change in conditions.

No species can be classified as decreaser, increaser, or invader without reference to a particular site. A species may be an increaser in one area, an invader in another; or it may be a decreaser in one area and an increaser in another. For example, big sagebrush (*Artemisia tridentata*) is present on much of the rangelands of the U.S., and over most of this area it is an increaser (Figure 7.4). Although high in nutrients, it is unpalatable to cattle and sheep except when other forage is unavailable. It is also unaffected by trampling. In some areas of the American West, big sagebrush was insignificant or not present prior to the onset of grazing in the 19th century, but today it is a dominant species. In these areas it is an invader.

Mesquite (*Prosopis juliflora*) is another example of an increaser or invader, which is today perceived as inferior to grass cover as a food source for livestock, even though its fleshy pods were a major food source for the Southwestern American Indians and their livestock (see Chapter 1). Mesquite has taken over large areas of grassland, affecting an estimated 28 million hectares (70 million acres) of range in the American Southwest over the past century. Its spread is directly attributable to overgrazing. In search of food on land with little grass cover, cattle eat mesquite pods and deposit them in their dung on grasslands that have been overgrazed. Subsequently, grasses are unable to compete with the better-adapted mesquite (Vale, 1978; Harris, 1977).

As a final example, some grasslands that supported perennial (permanent) grasses before grazing began, today are covered mainly by annual grasses. The

Figure 7.4   Sagebrush in Owens Valley, California.

annual grasses, by spreading large numbers of seeds each year, can replace themselves even though the plants are eaten or trampled. The perennial grasses, on the other hand, produce fewer seeds; thus, once trampled or eaten they are less able to reproduce.

Overgrazing not only causes changes in plant communities, but it also affects the soil resource. Removal of plant cover and compaction of the soil by trampling reduces infiltration capacities, resulting in greater erosion and reduced soil moisture (see Chapter 6). Thus it becomes more difficult for remaining plants to survive or for new seedlings to take hold. The process is reversible, but this requires significant reduction in grazing pressure and in many cases active range improvement measures.

Accelerated erosion caused by grazing has plagued most of the world's semiarid lands. In the southwestern U.S., for example, vegetation removal has caused significant increases in soil erosion rates over wide areas. This erosion is caused by both wind and water, but water erosion is particularly dramatic. Large gullies called *arroyos* have been cut in valley floors over much of the western U.S. The period 1880–1930 was one of particularly intense arroyo formation. Some attribute this to the effects of cattle, although other factors may also be responsible (Cooke and Reeves, 1976).

The Energy Efficiency of Meat Production

Beef production in the U.S. involves raising cattle on rangelands or farms and transporting them to feedlots where they are fattened with grain so that their meat will be well-marbled. Consumer preferences and grain prices influence forage- versus grain-consumption by cattle. In the 1950s the price of grain was low, enabling U.S. feedlot operations to accept younger cattle. Grain contributed a higher percentage of an animal's finished weight in the 1950s than twenty years later, when high grain prices led meat producers to rely more heavily on grazing.

In the mid-1970s, the high cost of grain led to an alteration in grazing standards for beef set by the U.S. Department of Agriculture (USDA). In 1975, the standards were changed so that a smaller percentage of grain in the diet could still result in the meat being labeled "USDA Choice." In addition to cost, other reasons have emerged for reducing the amount of marbling in beef. Consumer groups have advocated fat reduction in beef by reducing the grain consumed. Their principal reasons include the health benefits of a lowered consumption of cholesterol found in animal fat and the freeing of grains and croplands to feed hungry people instead of cattle (U.S. Forest Service, 1981).

Humans are omnivores, consuming both plant and animal foods. Meat is a high-quality food in that it contains a high proportion of protein and other important nutrients. The efficiency of converting vegetable food energy to animal food energy in the U.S. is about 5 percent (Cook, 1976). That is, twenty calories of food energy as feed (range grasses and grains in the feedlot) are needed to produce one calorie of food energy as meat on the table. A balanced vegetable diet can also provide the same nutrients found in meat.

If the food used to produce meat is grown on land that could be used to grow grain for human consumption, then we are in effect substituting a substantial amount of vegetable food for a small amount of meat, which would seem to be unwise in a world short of food. On the other hand, meat produced by grazing animals on land that is not otherwise usable for food production represents an important increase in available food supplies. Thus, range animals can be an important means of converting otherwise unusable vegetable matter to valuable food, even if the efficiency of conversion is relatively low. It is when livestock are fed high-quality corn and other grains that the questions of efficiency and equity arise. Despite these debates on health and wealth, most Americans still prefer well-marbled beef (U.S. Forest Service, 1981).

U.S. RANGELAND RESOURCES

Historical Development of Rangeland Use

Prior to European colonization, North America's wide open spaces were home to huge herds of elk, buffalo, and pronghorn antelope, with an estimated 23 million to 34 million head (Wagner, 1978). Cattle domestication was unknown until Spanish settlers brought livestock to their New World settlements in the early 16th century. The American Indians had not found any need to harness animal power, since their agriculture was performed with hand tools and their loads were carried or dragged. Wild animals for meat and hides were plentiful and widely available, so there was little need to bring them under human control.

The Spaniards and later colonists brought with them a cattle-based livelihood pattern adapted to European culture and resource availability. These settlers were accustomed to the crowded conditions and overgrazed lands of Europe. In contrast, the apparently limitless grazing opportunities available in North America helped build a cattle-raising industry, which today is land-extensive on the open range and capital-intensive in feedlots. This has enabled Americans to have one of the highest per capita rates of meat consumption in the world.

The range resource was first used in the eastern parts of the continent, and along with settlement moved westward. The colonial settlers sent frontier-fattened cattle to city markets and were the precursors of those who raised stock on a large scale, which developed in Texas and other western states. By the 1840s, Texas cattle drives were delivering cattle to markets in Ohio, Louisiana, and California.

The boom period in both cattle and sheep raising came in the decades between the Civil War and the early 20th century, by which time the once-wild frontier areas were being transformed for farming and urban uses. During the 1870s, expansion accelerated as the Great Plains Indian tribes were subdued and the vast buffalo herds were decimated (see Chapter 13). Between 1870 and 1890 the cattle population in the West rose from between 4 million and 5 million to over 26.5 million. Sheep raising was introduced in several locations, notably along the Eastern seaboard and in New Mexico, Arizona, Texas and California during the 17th and 18th centuries. Between 1850 and 1890 the estimated sheep population in the West rose from 514,000 to over 20 million (Dale, 1930).

The availability of free or low-cost forage on federally owned lands was essential to the profitability of the developing cattle industry. In addition to leasing the water and forage rights on government property, many ranchers obtained title to vast areas of federal land by evading the acreage limitations imposed by the 1862 Homestead Act (see Chapter 3). By the early 20th century, the use of barbed wire had created boundaries to the great American pasture, and the days of open-range cattle and sheep drives wound down. These were replaced by truck and train transport to regional markets, notably Chicago, Minneapolis, Omaha, Dallas, and Denver.

The federal government has imposed several constraints on the traditional independence of the western rancher by establishing the National Forest System (1905), passing the Taylor Grazing Act (1934), and establishing the Bureau of Land Management (BLM) in 1946. Initially, ranchers were not permitted to let animals graze in the national forest reserves, but a nominal fee system later permitted the land to be opened for use. Battles have raged ever since over the government's right to control numbers of cattle and the seasonality of grazing. The Taylor Grazing Act organized federal lands into a system of 144 grazing districts for joint management by the federal government and local stock raisers. Some cattlemen resisted this scheme and attempted to turn management of these lands over to the state governments (Figure 7.5). However, the effects of overgrazing were evident, and the Taylor Grazing Act's range-rehabilitation plans received congressional support. The act was passed but remained underfunded and subject to constant disagreement between federal and local interests (Stegner, 1981a). Today, 22,000 ranchers lease grazing rights from the BLM to graze 4 percent of the nation's beef cattle. A recent estimate suggests that ranchers lease lands at bargain prices. In 1982, for example, the BLM collected $20.9 million in grazing fees. The fair-market value of these grazing rights indicates that $104 million should have been collected (Baker, 1983).

The BLM took over the administration of these and other public lands from the General Land Office and administered them in a similar manner until 1976. In that year Congress passed the Federal Land Policy and Management Act

Figure 7.5   Old ranch house in Florissant, Colorado. Ranchers strongly resisted federal attempts to control western public lands in the early twentieth century.

(FLPMA), which brought together thousands of pieces of legislation related to public land management. It also increased the power of the BLM to manage its 69 million hectares (170 million acres) for the public good, with *multiple use* and *sustained yield* (see Chapter 3) as basic principles. Through the use of inventories, comprehensive plans, and public participation, power over America's public lands began to slip away from the ranching, timber, and energy interests influential at the state level (Stegner, 1981b; Nothdurft, 1981).

Current Rangeland Status

In 1976, there were 357 million hectares (882 million acres) of rangeland, about 39 percent of total U.S. land area. In addition to this rangeland, there are about 130 million hectares (321 million acres) of woodland that can be grazed. Alaska contains 94 million hectares (232 million acres) of the total rangeland. In the lower forty-eight states, 99 percent of the 263 million hectares (650 million acres) of rangeland is found in seventeen western states (Figure 7.6). Only 1 percent is in the thirty-one eastern states, mostly in the South. Any potential for increased grazing in the East depends on more intensive grazing of forests, or removal of forest cover. Almost two-thirds of the available range was grazed in 1976. Of this, about two-thirds was privately owned land. In the six Great Plains states, 98 percent of the range is privately owned, and this area accounts for 25 percent of the range grazed in the lower forty-eight states. Only in the Pacific Northwest does federal land supply more than half the grazed range (U.S. Forest Service, 1981).

There are serious problems of degradation on much of the nation's range, especially in the Southwest. The Forest Service defines range condition as "an estimate of the degree to which the present vegetation and ground cover

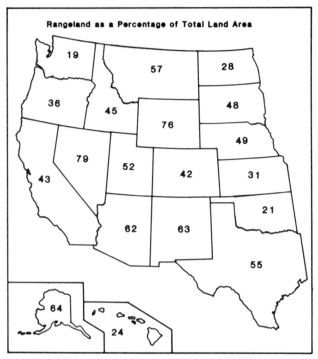

Figure 7.6 Rangeland as a percentage of total land area, western U.S. More than 75 percent of the land area of Nevada and Wyoming is currently classified as range. (Source: United States Forest Service, 1981)

depart from that which is presumed to be the natural potential (or climax) for the site" (U.S. Forest Service, 1981:158). They use a four-class scale to judge range quality: good, fair, poor, very poor (Figure 7.7). In 1976 the U.S. Forest Service found that if Alaska is included 50 percent of the nation's range is in fair to good condition. Of the lower forty-eight, however, only 46 percent is in fair to good condition. There is a gradient in quality running from north to south in the seventeen western states, with the highest quality range in the wetter north and poorer range condition in the drier south. In the arid and semiarid southwestern states including California, Arizona, New Mexico, and Texas, less than 40 percent of the range is in fair to good condition. Most of the remaining western states states have 40 to 60 percent of range in fair to good condition (U.S. Forest Service, 1981). It is calculated that 36.8 percent of North America's arid lands are in a state of "severe" desertification. Within the U.S., perhaps 91 million hectares (225 million acres, or about 25 percent of the rangeland total) are in a state of "severe" or "very severe" desertification (Dregne, 1977; Sheridan, 1981a).

Taking a broader view beyond the health of the region's ecosystems, the grasslands are in slightly better condition than the shrublands (Figure 7.8). The mountain meadows, grasslands, and the Great Plains ecosystems are generally in better condition than the semiarid and arid range of the West and Southwest. This is a function of many factors including a shorter grazing history, different

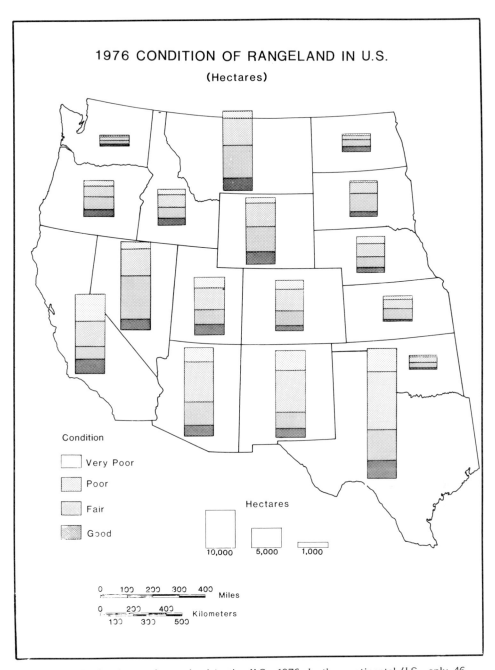

Figure 7.7 Condition of rangeland in the U.S., 1976. In the continental U.S., only 46 percent of the nation's rangelands are classified as either in fair or good condition. (Source: United States Forest Service, 1981)

Figure 7.8 Cattle grazing on privately owned rangeland in California. This land is in poorer condition than most rangelands in the more humid central Plains states.

management practices, and greater moisture availability. All of these enable an area to recover more rapidly when grazing pressures are removed (U.S. Forest Service, 1981).

Rangeland Degradation

Rangeland degradation in the U.S. has many causes. Two case studies will help illustrate that poverty, carelessness, and fluctuating climatic conditions can contribute to the spread of desert-like conditions. In the case of the Navajo Indians of Arizona and New Mexico, very severe rangeland degradation is the result of too many people, with few economic alternatives, being crowded onto too little land. During the past century, the Navajo population has multiplied by a factor of ten, while the land available has only tripled. From the late 1930s, when overgrazing was first tackled by the U.S. government, the Navajo's sheep population has grown from an estimated 1.3 million to 2.17 million in the early 1980s (Sheridan, 1981b). Considering that the U.S. government believes that the 6 million hectare (15 million-acre) Navajo reservation has a carrying capacity of 600,000 sheep, the problem of overgrazing becomes quite clear.

What are the environmental effects of this overgrazing? Why do the Navajo continue it? Most of the land surface of the reservation is badly eroded, and the plant cover that the animals rely on for food is not maintained. Until recently the Navajo have had few alternatives but to continue grazing on these marginal lands. Conflicts between traditional livelihood patterns and high unemployment rates (over 60 percent) forced the Navajo to continue their overgrazing practices.

Since sheep and cattle herding remain the major source of income for many Navajo, they are naturally unwilling to reduce animal-population levels to reach what they see as a U.S. government-generated ideal called carrying capacity when their own security is thus cast in doubt.

In the Rio Puerco basin of New Mexico, the BLM finds itself in a losing battle to reduce overgrazing in what is perhaps the most environmentally degraded western river basin (Sheridan, 1981b). First settled by poor Spanish families in the late 18th century, the Rio Puerco basin was termed the "bread basket of New Mexico" by the late 19th century. During this period there were about 240,000 sheep and 9000 cattle on the 1.5 million hectare (3.7 million acre) range. Villages and farms prospered along the river.

During the 1880s, a period of adverse weather conditions developed from which the Rio Puerco basin and other parts of the dry West have yet to recover. Water tables fell, arroyos grew, and eroded sediment flowed out of the Rio Puerco and into the Rio Grande. It is estimated that between 1885 and 1962, 1 billion to 1.35 billion tonnes (1.1 billion to 1.49 billion tons) of sediment were eroded. Today it is estimated that between 0.8 and 3.2 tonnes per hectare (0.4 and 1.6 tons per acre) are eroded annually (U.S. Bureau of Land Management, 1978).

How did this situation develop and what are some of its effects? There is some question as to whether overgrazing or climatic changes were the major cause of the initial arroyo cutting. Perhaps a minor change in precipitation patterns was sufficient to initiate arroyo cutting, with continued erosion aggravated by overgrazing. At any rate, arroyos, once a minor landscape feature, now dominate the basin. In the 1930s typical arroyos were a little over 30 m (100 ft) wide. On either side of these arroyos were lands still suitable for grazing and irrigated farming. Today, however, that land is being eaten away, with an average arroyo width of 91 m (300 ft). Socially, the effects have been severe, with many former riverside villages ghost towns today.

Grazing continues in the basin, though at reduced levels. The BLM, which manages a quarter of the basin's land, estimated in 1975 that 55 percent of the area's public land was undergoing "moderate to severe" erosion (U.S. Bureau of Land Management, 1978). This will increase, BLM predicts, to 73 percent by the year 2000 if current grazing practices continue. The ranchers who hold grazing permits are being restricted in the number of animals they can graze on public land, and BLM's plans include a schedule of a fallow year for about a third of the land at any given time. Fences, wells, rainwater catchments, water tanks, and reseeding are also options; however, with three-quarters of the basin's land in private hands, the BLM can only restore a small portion of the degraded range. In addition, critics doubt that the most delicate soils can recover in a year's time, and the lack of any plant litter over large areas makes seed germination difficult (Sheridan, 1981b).

Rangeland Management and Improvement Techniques

The U.S. Bureau of Land Management and predecessor agencies have struggled from their inception to reduce overgrazing. Today's grazing allotments (numbers of animals permitted per hectare [acre]) were established according to 1930s estimates of historical rangeland use. It is suggested that the 1930s cattlemen provided the government with inflated figures of past cattle populations. Thus, in agreeing to reduce their allotments, many ranchers may in fact do very little (Sheridan, 1981a).

The best way to manage rangelands is to maintain animal populations at or below carrying capacity. Carrying capacity varies from location to location and from year to year. Range ecologists have developed techniques for estimating carrying capacity based on vegetation type, average precipitation, soil characteristics, and other data. It remains difficult, however, to predict rainfall months in advance, so planning herd sizes to suit range conditions is sometimes a problem. Over the long run, though, it is possible to determine fairly closely just how many animals should be allowed to occupy a given piece of land and under what conditions. For most federally-owned lands, this long-term planning is done by the BLM; for privately-owned lands, it is the responsibility of the land owner.

Rangeland, which is damaged by overgrazing, is not lost forever; it will recover if grazing pressure is reduced. In contrast, there are several more active techniques that are used to improve range quality. These include such mechanical, chemical, and biological controls of undesirable plants as burning, seeding, fertilization, and irrigation (Vallentine, 1971). Mechanical brush control by plowing, bulldozing, or dragging heavy chains across the land is widely used to control sagebrush, mesquite, juniper, and other undesirable species (Figure 7.9). In some cases the slash from such operations is burned; in others it is left to control erosion. In some areas goats are used to control woody species, since they will strip plants of leaves and eat entire seedlings, whereas cattle will not. Care must

ISSUE 7.1: Coping with Coyotes

One of the more controversial issues surrounding grazing in the Western U.S. is the effect of coyotes on grazing animals, particularly sheep. Sheep ranchers claim that coyotes kill substantial numbers of sheep on the open range, and accordingly most ranchers support measures to reduce coyote populations. On the other hand, many wildlife experts maintain that although coyotes do kill sheep, their overall effects on ranching activities may be positive rather than negative. In any case, they maintain that killing coyotes does not solve the problem.

Coyotes (*Canis latrans*) are smaller relatives of wolves, being about 0.5 m (1.6 ft) high and weighing 10 to 15 kg (22 to 33 lb) (Pringle, 1977). They are omnivores, so that in the absence of sheep they eat small rodents (such as mice and rabbits), carrion, and plant materials. They live in small packs, but unlike wolves they do not hunt in packs,

preferring to hunt alone or in pairs. Wolves are their natural enemies. As population expanded through the Western U.S., ranchers killed off most of the wolves that lived there. Removing the wolves allowed the coyote to significantly expand its range; this expansion continues today.

In a landscape composed of ranches, farms, and undeveloped land, coyotes are able to find plenty to eat. In addition to their primary staples of mice, insects, and other small prey, they are able to kill lambs and chickens and occasionally to raid a vegetable garden or farm. Coyotes are not as wary of humans as are wolves, and they even live in suburban areas of Los Angeles, Denver, and other cities, where they can find garbage and other food not found in wilder areas. They are generally regarded as pests, and most states allow unlimited year-round hunting of coyotes.

Figure 7.9 The lighter areas in this view of western Colorado have been cleared of trees by chaining, to open land for the growth of palatable grasses for livestock grazing.

Over the years ranchers and government agencies (particularly the BLM) have tried many techniques to reduce coyote populations, but with little success. They are too numerous and too cautious to be hunted effectively, and so traps of various kinds are frequently used. These have included poisoned bait, traps set with explosive charges, and toxic collars on sheep. These methods have stirred the ire of wildlife groups for several reasons. Among these are that they also kill other predators that may be rare or endangered (such as eagles, bobcats, or badgers) or nontarget animals (such as dogs). Some range ecologists also argue that the coyote may benefit grazing animals by helping to control populations of smaller herbivores (especially rabbits), which compete with large herbivores such as cattle or deer for forage. Sheep, however, and particularly lambs, are small enough to be killed by coyotes.

In spite of efforts to reduce or control coyote populations, they continue to expand their range and are now appearing in the eastern U.S. Coyotes are very adaptable animals and are able to prosper in a wide range of environments. Their populations grow rapidly when food is plentiful, and litters tend to be larger when population densities are low. This adaptability is probably the primary cause of the lack of success of coyote-control programs. Many range managers are now recommending that coyotes be controlled selectively, such as by limiting control to areas where lambs are unprotected. In addition, it may be that the most effective way of reducing losses of sheep to coyotes may be by protecting the sheep with fences and guard dogs, rather than attempting to eradicate the coyotes.

be taken that the goats do not overgraze the range, however, or desirable species will also be lost.

Herbicides are widely used, through aerial and ground applications, sometimes in combination with other control methods. Seeding and fertilization are usually used to stimulate growth of forage plants after brush is removed. Irrigation is a very costly method of range improvement and is only used in special circumstances. These range improvement measures, though expensive, can be very effective in increasing the available forage, sometimes by as much as five to ten times. In some areas, notably Arizona, conversion of shrubs to grassland is justified as a method of increasing water runoff for agricultural and urban uses as well as providing forage for cattle.

Rangeland improvement measures are used on both private and public lands. The federal government, particularly the BLM, plays a major role in attempting to repair some of the damage done by overgrazing in the past. In 1979, the U.S. Bureau of Land Management began a twenty-year program to improve the rangeland it administers, including range improvement on 55 million hectares (139 million acres) and erosion control on 60 million hectares (148 million acres). The goal of the program is to double annual forage production on BLM lands from 5.1 million to 10.2 million tonnes (5.6 million to 11.2 million tons) annually.

An experimental stewardship system has been devised that provides for collective management by ranchers and government agencies of five range areas. A BLM proposal would permit certain ranchers to carry out the range improvements at their own expense in return for lengthened grazing leases (Baker, 1983).

Rangeland Resource Issues

Rangeland management includes many controversial issues. One involves the administrative responsibility for public lands. Another controversial issue is predator control, particularly the coyote, which is seen as a menace to sheep ranching (see Issue 7.1). In response to the passage of the Federal Land Policy and Management Act, Western ranchers formed a loose but well-funded alliance, the *Sagebrush Rebels,* to fight these increased federal controls. The main aim of the group has been to return Western lands to state and local control by removing them from the jurisdiction of the U.S. Bureau of Land Management, the U.S. Forest Service, or any other federal agency. Opponents of the rebels maintain that these lands cannot be returned to the states, since the states never owned them in the first place. That is, the disputed regions were under federal control long before the Western states came into existence and legally were never under state control. This argument has not deterred the rebels, however, who brought suit in Nevada in 1980. The suit maintained that the clauses in Western states' constitutions that relinquish their claims to public lands are invalid.

There is much more at stake here than inexpensive access to grazing lands. Of greater importance is access by private interests to the timber, coal, oil, natural gas, oil shale, and minerals that are located on or under much of the nation's federal lands. The real aim of the Sagebrush Rebels appears not to be the transferral of federal lands to state management, but instead to be a vehicle that would enable the Western states to sell and lease the lands for private use. With the election of President Reagan in 1980, the rebels soon had friends in the White House, the U.S. Department of the Interior, and the U.S. Bureau of

Land Management. As a result, many of the goals of the rebels have been achieved administratively, without the need to wrest control from the federal government.

THE FUTURE OF RANGELAND RESOURCES

At present, the world's rangelands are overgrazed. In drier areas this overuse has led to soil and vegetation loss associated with the spread of desert-like conditions. There is potential for expansion of both the world's rangelands and its deserts. If the best management techniques are brought into use, as developed in both traditional and modern animal-based economies, the world's rangelands can be strengthened and in fact expanded.

For example, the U.S. Forest Service advocates increased but intelligent use of the nation's rangelands. They estimate that in 1976 only a third of the biological potential for grazing was used. In other words, if these resources are managed for their highest productivity, they can withstand three times the amount of grazing without any detrimental effects. The U.S. Forest Service recommendations include shifting grazing to more efficiently productive ecosystems; intensifying the use of management techniques on both private and public rangelands; improving the amount and quality of forage produced; constructing livestock control and handling facilities; reducing loss of forage to fire, insects, and diseases; and reducing livestock losses to disease, parasites, and predators (U.S. Forest Service, 1981). However, these recommendations are frequently intrusive; their implementation would mean changes in the patterns of livelihood of the American rancher. If attempted in other areas of the world, the human impacts would be even more severe. In addition, many of the improvements suggested are extremely costly and might be difficult to justify in terms of the increased value of the animals produced.

At the same time, population pressures on rangelands continue, and there are few opportunities to do the one thing that is virtually guaranteed to improve range quality—reduce the number of animals using the land. In addition, it seems unlikely that rangeland conditions will improve worldwide under present climatic patterns and intensive use. Instead, we will probably see a continuing patchwork of range improvement in some areas, degradation in others, shifting both with the weather and with human fortunes.

REFERENCES AND ADDITIONAL READING

Baker, J. 1983. The frustration of FLPMA. *Living Wilderness* 47:163:12–24.

Cook, E. 1976. *Man, energy, society.* San Francisco: Freeman.

Cooke, R.U., and R. Reeves. 1976. *Arroyos and environmental change in the American southwest.* New York: Oxford University Press.

Council on Environmental Quality. 1981. *The Global 2000 report to the president.* Washington, D.C.: Government Printing Office.

Crabbe, D., and S. Lawson. 1981. *The world food book.* London: Kogan Page.

Dale, E.E. 1930. *The range cattle industry.* Norman, Oklahoma: University of Oklahoma Press.

Dregne, H. 1977. Desertification of the world's arid lands. *Econ. Geogr.* 52:332–46.

Eckholm, E., and L.R. Brown. 1977. Spreading deserts—the hand of man. Worldwatch Paper 13. Washington, D.C.: Worldwatch Institute. August.

Grigg, D.B. 1974. *The agricultural systems of the world, an evolutionary approach.* London: Cambridge University Press.

Harris, D.R. 1971. Recent plant invasions in the arid and semiarid southwest of the U.S. In *Man's impact on environment,* ed. T.R. Detwyler, pp. 459–75. New York: McGraw-Hill.

Kates, R.W., D.L. Johnson, and K. Johnson. 1976. *Population, society, and desertification.* Worcester, Massachusetts: Clark University.

Nothdurft, W.E. 1981. The lands nobody wanted. *Living Wilderness* 45:153:18–21.

Pringle, L. 1977. *The controversial coyote.* New York: Harcourt, Brace, Jovanovich.

Sheridan, D. 1981a. Can the public lands survive the pressures? *Living Wilderness* 45:153:36–39.

_____ . 1981b. Western rangelands: overgrazed and undermanaged. *Environment* 23:4:14.

Stegner, W., 1981a. If the sagebrush rebels win, everybody loses. *Living Wilderness* 45:153:30–35.

_____ . 1981b. Land: America's history teacher. *Living Wilderness* 45:153:5–7.

U.S. Bureau of Land Management. 1978. *Final environmental impact statement—the proposed Rio Puerco livestock grazing management program.* Washington, D.C.: Government Printing Office.

U.S. Forest Service. 1981. An assessment of the forest and rangeland situation in the United States. Forest Res. Rept. no. 22. Washington, D.C.: Government Printing Office.

Vale, T.R. 1978. The sagebrush landscape. *Landscape* 22:2:31–37.

_____ . 1983. *Plants and people: vegetation change in North America.* Washington, D.C.: Association of American Geographers.

Vallentine, J.F. 1971. *Range development and improvements.* Provo, Utah: Brigham Young University Press.

Wagner, F.H. 1978. Livestock grazing and the livestock industry. In *Wildlife and America,* ed. H.P. Brokaw, pp. 121–49. Washington, D.C.: Council on Environmental Quality.

TERMS TO KNOW

arroyos
decreasers
desertification
domesticate
dry farming
Federal Land Policy and Management Act
increasers
invaders

multiple use
overgrazing
pastoral nomads
range
Sagebrush Rebels
Sahel
sedentarization
sustained yield
U.S. Bureau of Land Management

STUDY QUESTIONS

1. What is the relationship between overgrazing and desertification?
2. What is the importance of the Taylor Grazing Act to the management of rangeland resources?
3. How has the Sagebrush Rebellion influenced the management of rangeland resources?
4. What are some of the ways in which plants are affected by grazing?
5. How can rangelands be improved?
6. Is it possible for a plant species to be both an increaser and an invader? Why?
7. Some argue, from an energy-efficiency standpoint, that humans should be herbivores rather than omnivores. Do you agree or disagree? Why?

CHAPTER EIGHT

Forests: A Multiple Use Resource

INTRODUCTION

Forests are among the most widespread, versatile, and easily exploited of the world's natural resources. They are used for fuel, construction materials, paper, wildlife habitat, and erosion control. They are found in virtually all humid and subhumid regions of the world, from the tropics to the margins of the tundra. They occupy areas of poor soil and steep slopes as well as high quality lands. Trees can survive on marginal lands, and thus many forests remain intact even though there is great demand for agricultural land. Forests are not inexhaustible and have been severely depleted in many areas of the world. In some cases, as in most of the wealthy nations, forests have recovered in recent decades and remain important renewable resources. In many poorer countries, rapid population growth has caused great increases in demand for wood, primarily for fuel. In these areas wood is in critically short supply and deforestation is causing accelerated soil erosion and degradation.

In Kenya, for example, current consumption of fuel wood already exceeds production, and this may increase by as much as 80 percent by the year 2000. It is estimated that the equivalent of 2 million hectares (809,000 acres) of forest must be planted by 2000 A.D. to meet this demand (Shakow et al., 1981). In South America, more than 20 percent of the Amazon rainforest of Brazil has been cleared for agricultural and rangeland uses (Moran, 1981; U.N. Educational, Scientific, and Cultural Organization, 1978) (Figure 8.1). Ecologists are concerned about the long-term effects of this clearing on soil resources and species diversity (see Chapters 6 and 13), as well as the social impacts on native human populations.

Globally, the forest resource picture is bleak. In the late 1950s, forests covered one-quarter of the world's land area and by 1980 that had dropped to one-fifth (Council on Environmental Quality, 1981a). Rising demand for fuel and building, as well as a desire to open new lands for farming, suggests that the worldwide forest resource is in jeopardy.

Although the U.S. forest cover has dropped dramatically in the centuries since first European settlement, it is in good shape in comparison to many other nations. In fact, after 300 years of continual and often extravagant logging, the U.S. forest resource is today considered abundant and resilient, according to

Figure 8.1   Tropical deforestation in Vanimo, Papua New Guinea, 1976. (Source: United Nations)

many measures. However, it often seems that there is not enough forest to go around, and the future stability of the resource is regarded by many to be in doubt.

How can a resource be abundant, yet scarce? It is possible because forests and their lands are used for an extraordinarily wide range of activities. It is the diverse users of the nation's forests who disagree so strongly over the amount and stability of the forest resource. For the decision-maker in a paper products company, there is more forest than the nation could ever need, because forests are renewable when properly managed. But for the wilderness preservationist, a second-growth forest is profoundly different from forest that has never been cut, and hence all forested wildlands should be protected from the axe forever. Prospectors and miners, another major interest group, do not care about the trees so much as what lies underneath them. This group and the other two have incompatible management and use goals for forest lands. Most other users, such as the wide array of people who visit forests for leisure activity, are not at such extreme odds.

There is another, less tangible factor that influences American attitudes and policy toward forest lands. Fresh in the memory of many Americans is the forest cover of a century or more ago, so vast and unmeasurable that hundreds of thousands of settlers vanished into it, not emerging until they had cut much of it down. For those to whom the nation's forests retain this mythical appeal, any further loss of forest cover is seen as a tarnishing of American ideals and dreams. For these people, there is a sense of defeat attached to managing the forest resource, because in their minds the forests are still infinite, capable of absorbing all uses without overlap or conflict.

This chapter provides a summary of both the natural and human aspects of the forest resource in the United States. The management of these forests including the actors involved is also discussed.

FOREST ECOSYSTEMS

Characteristics of Forest Ecosystems

Worldwide, forests occupy 2.66 billion hectares (1.08 billion acres), about 20 percent of the world's land area (Council on Environmental Quality, 1981a) (Figure 8.2). They are found primarily in the more humid areas of the world because of greater moisture availability. Where moisture is not a limiting factor, dominant tree species compete for sunlight by growing tall and producing broad canopies that shade out plants below (Spurr and Barnes, 1980).

Trees are more long lived than most other plant types, and their growth rates are relatively low. Primarily because of their size, trees contain an abundance of nutrients stored in living *biomass*. Forests are ecosystems in which most of the available nutrients accumulate in live trees over a long period of time. Relatively small amounts of nutrients are contained in herbs, shrubs, and the soil. In an experimental forest in New Hampshire, it was found that annual uptake rates of nutrients by trees are a small fraction of the total amounts in storage. Restoration of ecosystem nutrients lost in clear cutting may take several decades (Likens et al., 1978). For most tree species the rate of growth (as measured by biomass) is relatively slow when a tree is young, primarily because it is small and does not have a large photosynthetic capacity. Growth rate increases as a tree gains a larger total leaf area and declines as it reaches maturity. In many forests the amount of stored biomass reaches a steady state in which old trees die and their nutrients are taken up by younger ones. For a large portion of the world's forests, cyclic disturbances kill all or nearly all affected trees at the same time. This releases nutrients to begin a new cycle of forest growth. These cyclic disturbances include fire, disease, insect infestation, and windstorms.

The Role of Fire

In the past it was believed that fire was harmful to forests, but today it is recognized that forest fires are a natural and important part of most forest ecosystems (Figure 8.3). Trees are susceptible to fire. As a result, many species are fire-adapted with mechanisms for rapid regeneration after fires. These include sprouting from the root crown and seeds that are released or germinate only after being heated. Some species, on the other hand, resist fire, either by being relatively inflammable or by having particularly thick bark.

Fires cause major, if temporary, disruption of the forest ecosystem. They consume dead and living biomass and, if severe enough, kill most or all of the

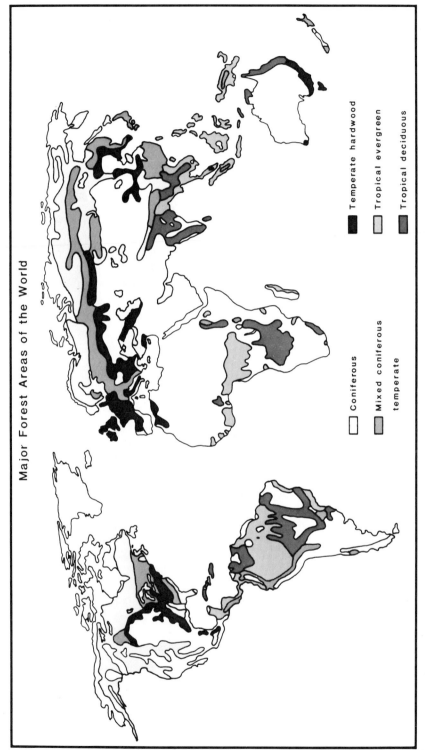

Figure 8.2 Major forest areas of the world. Forests occupy 2.66 billion acres (1.08 billion ha.), 20 percent of the world's land area. (Source: From Rand McNally, 1979)

Figure 8.3 Forest fire in Oregon. Forest fires are a natural component of the forest ecosystem. (Source: Yvonne DeLorenzo)

trees. Evapotranspiration is greatly decreased by the loss of live trees and shrubs, and this results in large increases in runoff. Reduction in vegetation cover may also increase overland flow (see Chapter 6), causing large losses of nutrients from the forest soil. Downstream, eroded soil and nutrients contribute to sediment and dissolved solid load of streams and may cause eutrophication in lakes (see Chapter 10).

Fires also have beneficial effects. They promote the release of nutrients stored in dead biomass, stimulating growth. They remove old stands of timber that are particularly susceptible to insect or disease infestation, and thus inhibit the spread of pests. After the forest canopy is removed, sunlight can reach ground level and promote rapid growth of early successional species, beginning the process of reestablishing the forest. More importantly, though, frequent fires allow accumulated fuel, in the form of downed timber and leaves, to be burned off relatively harmlessly, preventing the severe fires that occur in areas of high-fuel accumulation. In many commercial forests, particularly the loblolly pine forests of the southeastern United States, fires are set from time to time to kill off competitive, unwanted plants and to maintain an even-aged stand. In Maine's Acadia National Park, a recent study has indicated that forest fires are infrequent but quite destructive when they do occur. A parallel study of the fire history in Massachusetts' Cape Cod National Seashore indicates that fires there are frequent but small, not doing much damage (Patterson et al., 1983).

Forest ecosystems vary in their susceptibility to fire, and thus in how frequently fires occur. *Fire frequency* is the average number of years between successive forest fires at a given site. Some forests, such as the chaparral woodlands of southern California, are particularly susceptible to fire and have a natural fire frequency of twenty to sixty years. The pine forests that grow on areas of very sandy soils along the east coast of the U.S. also have very frequent fires. Most forests, however, have natural fire frequencies of 100 to 400 years (Spurr and Barnes, 1980). Fire frequency depends on many factors, including the rate of fuel accumulation, fuel moisture levels, and ignition sources.

There are three basic kinds of forest fires. Ground fires are fires that burn within the organic matter and litter in the soil. They smolder slowly, having little effect on trees. Surface fires burn on the ground surface, consuming litter and also herbaceous and shrubby vegetation of the forest floor. They burn faster than ground fires and may clear all of the low vegetation; nevertheless, they have little effect on large trees. Finally, crown fires burn treetops as well as low vegetation, usually killing all or almost all above-ground vegetation. They are the most destructive to timber, wildlife, and the soil. Fires vary greatly in the temperatures that develop within the canopy and at ground level. Crown fires are much hotter than surface fires, but wind, fuel availability, and moisture levels are important influences on fire temperature. Hotter fires are more destructive than cooler ones, particularly in that they consume greater amounts of organic matter. This results in greater postfire soil erosion and nutrient loss and retards the process of forest regeneration.

In the U.S. Forest Service and other forest management agencies, the long-standing policy of fighting naturally started fires has had a paradoxical effect on forest fires and the damage they cause. The easiest fires to extinguish are those that occur during relatively wet and/or low-wind conditions. Consequently, these low-temperature fires rarely occur. But it is these fires that cause only minor damage to the forest, while performing the valuable function of consuming available fuel. The fires that are the hardest to put out are those that occur during dry, windy conditions, and/or that burn in areas of substantial fuel availability. These fires tend to have relatively high temperatures and are more likely to be crown fires rather than surface or ground fires. By suppressing or extinguishing the less harmful low-temperature fires, managers are increasing the severity of the fires that do occur. Recognition of this fact has recently led to a reevaluation of fire-fighting policies in many areas. In commercial forests, where the timber has considerable value, fires are still put out. In many areas forest managers use prescribed fires, which are deliberately set under controlled conditions to reduce fuel accumulation.

VARIABILITY IN TIMBER SUPPLY

Timber Location and Types

There are about 300 million hectares (740 million acres) of forest land in the United States and 336 million hectares (830 million acres) in Canada. To be classified as forest, 10 percent of the land must be forested and not developed for nonforest use. Most of the U.S. forest resources are concentrated in the Pacific Northwest, Alaska, and the East and Southeast regions (Figure 8.4). In Canada, they are located in the Pacific coast area (British Columbia) and in the central and eastern provinces.

Forest Lands in the United States

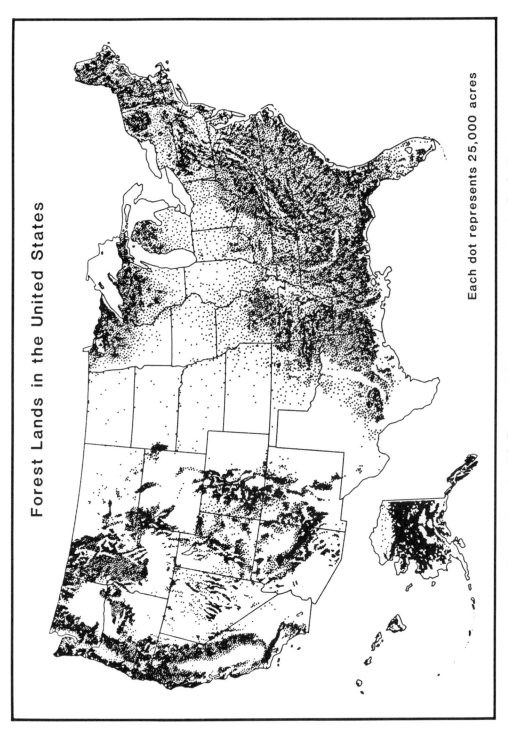

Each dot represents 25,000 acres

Figure 8.4 Forest lands in the U.S. The nation's forests are concentrated in the Pacific Northwest, Alaska, the East and Southeast. (Source: Council on Environmental Quality, 1981)

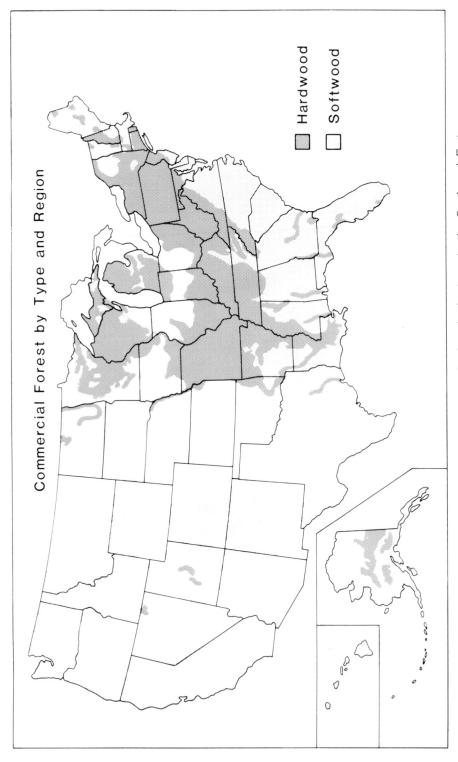

Figure 8.5 Commercial forest, by type and region: hardwoods dominate in the South and East, softwoods in the Southeast, Northeast, West, and Alaska. (Source: Haden-Guest, et al., 1956)

Commercial Forest by Type and Region

Hardwood

Softwood

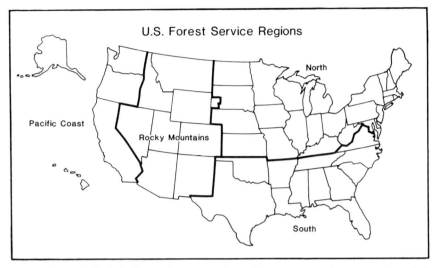

Figure 8.6 U.S. Forest Service regions. For management purposes, the U.S. is divided into four major forest regions: the Pacific Coast, Rocky Mountains, North and South. These are further divided into 16 subregions. (Source: United States Forest Service, 1982)

Nearly two-thirds of the forest lands in the U.S. are rated as commercial forests. This means that the land is capable of growing at least 1.4 m³ of wood per hectare (20 ft³ of wood per acre) in a fully stocked stand on an annual basis (U.S. Forest Service, 1982). The timber produced is, therefore, commercially profitable. The remaining one-third of forest land is classified as noncommercial and is used for parks, wildlife habitat, recreation, and wilderness.

Commercial forest land in North America is differentiated by the type of vegetation or tree species and is divided into hardwoods and softwoods. *Hardwood* forests generally consist of broadleaf and deciduous trees such as oak, maple, and hickory. In the U.S., hardwood forests are located primarily in the northern and southern regions of the eastern half of the country (Figure 8.5). Commercial hardwood stands are largely used for furniture making and flooring. The total acreage of hardwood stands in North America is greater than that of softwoods, but the timber is commercially less valuable because of the difficulty in harvesting.

Hardwood stands occur in mixed species forests. Thus, harvesting the commercially valued species involves selective cutting. This involves greater costs because the trees are not uniform in species, age, or height. Certain cost-effective harvesting techniques such as clear cutting are simply not appropriate for mixed stand forests. As a result, the timber price is increased to cover the costs of the harvesting, and demand drops.

Softwoods are conifers, usually evergreens. The primary North American species of softwoods are spruce, pine, and cedar. The wood is softer and the grain is farther apart than in hardwood species. Softwoods are used primarily for paper products, lumber, and plywood. Softwood forests are located throughout North America but dominate in the Pacific Coast, Rocky Mountain, and Southern National Forest Service regions (Figures 8.5 and 8.6).

The economic value of softwoods is greater than hardwoods as a result of ease in harvesting and rapid growth rates. Softwoods grow in dense single-species stands at a relatively uniform rate and are easily harvested using clear cutting techniques. Because of growth patterns and harvesting techniques, the total volume of wood and the volume of wood per area is greater for softwoods than for hardwoods.

Most of our demand for wood is for softwood, 83 percent of total demand in 1981 (U.S. Bureau of the Census, 1984). Net growth of softwood is presently highest in the South, with lower rates of net growth in the remaining regions. Hardwood is obtained from the North and the South with the South having higher rates of net growth and harvesting. Net growth for the contiguous forty-eight states is presently about 1.3 times the demand for softwoods and about 3.2 times the demand for hardwoods. There are significant variations in supply and demand from region to region. In the West, for example, harvesting of softwoods is slightly greater than net growth, resulting in depletion in that region. In the North and South, softwoods are still being grown at a rate higher than they are cut. In each of the major regions shown in Figure 8.6, growth rates for hardwoods exceed current demands. Much of net growth is in smaller trees. Depletion of standing commercial timber may be greater.

Forest Land Ownership Patterns

In the U.S. six different classes of forest land ownership are normally identified. These include:

(1) national forests owned and managed by the federal government, generally the U.S. Forest Service;

(2) other forests owned by the federal government and managed by other agencies such as the U.S. Bureau of Land Management and National Park Service;

(3) other publicly owned forests managed by state and county agencies;

(4) private forests owned by forest or timber industries and managed by them, such as Boise Cascade, Weyerhaeuser, and Georgia Pacific;

(5) private forests or woods that are part of farms or land holdings of individuals and managed by individual owners; and

(6) other lands that are private forests of mixed lots and ownership categories and cannot be placed in any of the other five groups.

Seventy-two percent of the commercial forest land in the U.S. is privately owned (Table 8.1, Figure 8.7). The major part of this land is owned in small holdings and in farms. Only 14 percent of the private commercial forest land is owned by the large-scale forest industry companies. In contrast, the federal government is the largest forest land owner in the public sector yet accounts for only 20 percent of the total amount of commercial forest land. The U.S. Forest Service, the largest public manager of forest lands, has jurisdiction over only 18 percent of the nation's commercial forests. Nearly 30 percent of the forest land in the U.S. is noncommercial.

When ownership patterns are examined on a regional basis a number of interesting trends emerge. These patterns are also quite influential in determining variations in management policies. As Marion Clawson has pointed out,

Table 8.1 Ownership of U.S. Forest Land, 1977

	Classification	Acres (Million)	Percentage Total Commercial Forest Acreage	Percentage Total Forest Acreage
I	Commercial	488	100	66
	Private:	351	72	47
	Small holdings	166	34	22
	Farms	117	24	16
	Industry	68	14	9
	Public:	137	28	19
	Federal	100	20	14
	FS	89	18	12
	BLM	6	1	0.8
	Other fed.	5	1	0.7
	Other Public:	37	8	5
	State	24	5	3
	Local	7	1	0.9
	Indian tribal	6	1	0.8
II	Noncommercial	228	—	31
III	Other[a]	24	—	3
Total		740	—	100

[a]Other means reserved and deferred: commercial forest land, mostly National Forest land, that is exempted from timber uses.

Source: Council on Environmental Quality, 1981b

There is a substantial correlation between region and ownership which affects public policy on forest issues. The national forests especially those with large timber volumes, are in the West, and are a matter of particular concern for western people and their elected representatives. The small private forests are dominantly in the East, both northern and southern sections, and are of particular concern to people in these regions and to their elected representatives (1975:62).

FOREST EXPLOITATION AND MANAGEMENT IN THE U.S.

A Brief History

At the time of European settlement of North America, forests covered about two-thirds of the U.S. This forest was both a resource and an obstacle to the early settlers. It provided fuel and building materials but, at the same time, stood in the way of land clearance for agriculture. Timber was plentiful in most settled areas in the 17th and 18th centuries, and no one had to go far for wood. By the mid-19th century, though, population pressures and economic growth caused an increase in the demand for wood while local supplies were diminishing. Local or regional shortages developed in the northeastern U.S. as the focus of timber harvesting moved west to the Great Lakes states. In the 1840s the Massachusetts writer Henry David Thoreau complained about the absence of large trees in settled areas of New England. Even on his canoe trips into wilderness areas of Maine, he found that most desirable large trees especially eastern white pine had already been removed by lumberjacks.

Ownership Patterns by Region

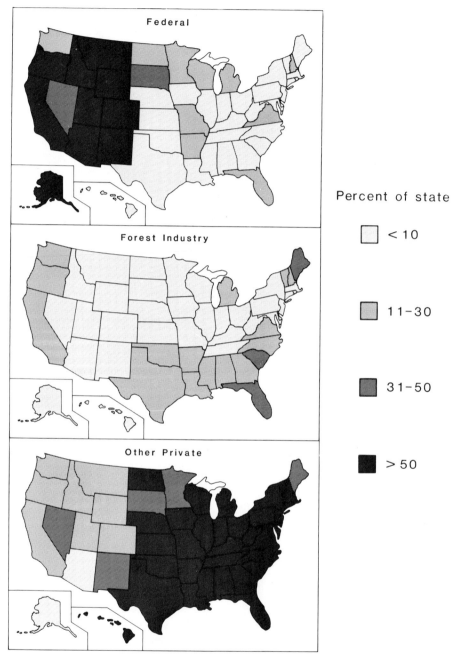

Figure 8.7 Ownership of commercial forest land. Federal ownership is dominant in the West and Alaska. Forest-industry ownership is most evident in the West, South, and Northeast. Other private holdings dominate in the East. "Percent of state" refers to the percentage of forest land in each state by ownership category. (Source: United States Forest Service, 1981)

Land area in forest cover continued to decline in the early 20th century, largely as a result of clearing land for agriculture (Clawson, 1979). By 1920, the clearing of forest land slowed. The more productive agricultural lands of the Midwest had been competing with eastern agriculture for some time. Beginning in the 19th century and continuing into the early 20th century, farmland within and east of the Appalachian Mountains was rapidly being abandoned. This farmland gradually reverted to forest. As a result, forest acreage in the lower forty-eight states has increased about 20 percent in the last sixty years.

Another important trend associated with timber harvesting and cropland abandonment has been a decrease in the average age of timber stands. This has had the effect of greatly increasing the net growth rate for timber because young forests are growing rapidly while an old forest has no net growth. Today then, we are growing much more timber than is being cut, and the standing volume of timber is steadily increasing although problems of overuse still exist.

Statistics show that domestic supplies are adequate for our needs, and we are presently harvesting below the sustained yield level on a national basis. At a regional level, however, the picture is somewhat different. This is a result of (1) the greater demand for softwoods over hardwoods and (2) the location of much of the timber being grown in areas unavailable for harvest today. In the North and South, the majority of forest lands are in relatively small holdings such as farm woodlots, so that it is costly for large timber companies to arrange harvests on a piecemeal basis. In addition, many of the landholders are not particularly interested in selling timber at current prices. In the West, however, forests are much better suited for large-scale commercial harvesting, and there the harvest exceeds growth. The timber companies are running out of wood to harvest on their own lands and are demanding that more federal lands be made available to them. In the future, greatly increased demand must be met by exploitation of hardwoods on private lands. Barriers to harvesting of wood on small, privately owned parcels must be overcome so that these areas can attain their projected importance in timber supply.

Forest Product Technology

To better understand the changing supply and demand for timber, it is necessary to look at the uses to which wood is put. Until the 20th century, wood was used almost exclusively for either fuel or lumber. Fuel was the major use until the mid-19th century, when it was surpassed by growth in lumber use. Gradually fuelwood was replaced by other energy sources, so that this use plummeted after the 1930s (Clawson, 1979). Beginning around 1900, wood came into use for making plywood and pulp paper, and these uses have increased steadily ever since. Today, for example, pulp production and harvest for lumber demand almost equal amounts of wood. In addition, woodchips and sawdust have replaced whole pieces of wood to make boards.

These varying uses require different kinds of wood. For example, just about any kind of wood can be burned, although hardwoods are better than softwoods since they burn more slowly and at a higher temperature. Lumber, on the other hand, requires trees that are straight and as great in diameter as possible—in other words, old trees. Most lumbering requires softwoods, but specialized industries such as furniture construction use hardwoods. Plywood is made from large sheets of veneer, only a few millimeters thick, which are glued together. These sheets are not sawed from logs; they are peeled from a turning log with a large blade that can cut sheets that are hundreds of feet long. Plywood manufacture then does not require logs of large diameter. Much younger trees can be used, provided they are softwoods, relatively straight, and free from knots. Similarly, pulp production does not depend on any particular size of log, and species is more important than age. Particle board and similar products are made using waste from other processes.

For the last several decades, lumber demand has remained fairly constant, while most of the increased demand for building wood has been taken up by plywood. Thus, while we still require many mature, large-diameter trees such as those of the Pacific Northwest, we are increasingly using smaller, younger trees such as those grown in the southeastern U.S. Since 1974, increases in energy prices have once again made fuelwood attractive for home heating, as well as for the generation of electricity in some areas. This has created a demand for the hardwood that has taken over abandoned farmland in the Northeast and may result in a reversal of the recent trend of increasing standing timber volume in much of the country (Issue 8.1).

Current and Projected Supply and Demand

Current supplies and demand for timber in the United States are summarized in Tables 8.2 and 8.3. Annual net growth of timber and demand in 1976 is shown, projected to 2030 (U.S. Forest Service, 1982). Net growth is the total increase by tree growth in volume of wood, less that lost to death, disease,

---

ISSUE 8.1: The Second Deforestation of New England

Today, New England is a region of second-growth forests, some agricultural land, and urban/suburban land. The combination of a large amount of forest in small parcels, a relatively dense population, cold weather, and expensive energy sources make it an ideal area for replacing fossil and nuclear fuels with fuel wood for home heating. In the late 1970s, use of wood for heating in New England grew rapidly, and it appears that this use of the forest may initiate a second phase of partial deforestation in the region.

The first (postglacial) deforestation of New England occurred in the 17th, 18th, and 19th centuries. As discussed earlier, wood not only was the primary fuel of those times but was needed for construction as well. That harvest probably removed in ex-

cess of 60 percent of the forests of New England. Massachusetts is today nearly 60 percent forested (Peters and Bowers, 1977), and the degree of forest cover is even greater for New England as a whole.

Most of the forests of New England are privately owned, particularly in more densely populated southern New England (Connecticut, Massachusetts, and Rhode Island). Individual holdings are relatively small, a few acres to a few tens of acres, reflecting former agricultural land use and present suburban and rural residential ownership patterns. The wood that has grown on these lands has been poorly managed or not managed at all. Thus, much of it has low timber value. Most of the timber is hardwood, and there is a large amount of rough and rotten wood. In Massachusetts some commercial har-

Table 8.2 U.S. Demand for Timber, 1976 and 2030 (Billion Cubic Feet)

	1976	2030
Total Domestic Demand	13.4	25.5
Exports	1.8	1.3
Imports	2.8	3.8
Domestic Supply	12.4	23.0

Source: U.S. Forest Service, 1982

storms, and rot. It is a measure of the amount of available new wood. The amount of standing timber is much higher, but if more wood than net growth is cut, standing timber declines. Demand projections depend on certain assumptions about economic activity, most importantly the price of lumber. If the price is high, demand will be low, and vice versa. The projections shown are based on an assumption of equilibrium market conditions, where supply and demand are equal.

Looking more closely at Table 8.2, total U.S. demand for wood was about 379 million m^3 (13.4 billion ft^3) (U.S. Forest Service, 1982). Imports and exports are diverse, but the major ones include imports of lumber and pulpwood (primarily from Canada) and exports of lumber to Japan and paper to Europe (Clawson, 1975). Net imports supplied about 7 percent of total U.S. demand, and domestic sources, the remainder. By 2030, demand is expected to nearly double to 722 million m^3 (25.5 billion ft^3), with domestic sources meeting all of this increase. Much of the increase in demand is expected to be for hardwoods, partly because softwood supplies will become scarce and also because of the increased use of

vesting does occur, amounting to about 50 percent of annual growth (Leers, 1984).

Presently, most homes are heated primarily with oil. Gas and electricity are also important in some areas, most notably Vermont. When energy prices rose rapidly in 1974–75 and 1978–79, home-heating costs increased substantially for users of fossil fuels and electricity alike. This increase in energy costs stimulated interest in wood for home heating; between 1977 and 1979 the amount of wood consumed for home heating increased 32 percent (Bailey and Wheeling, 1980). This rate of increase has declined somewhat, mainly as a result of a leveling off in energy prices. In 1979, 17 percent of Massachusetts homeowners burned wood in stoves or furnaces.

The amount of wood being burned is large. In Massachusetts, nearly one million cords were burned in 1979. This is a little less than half the sustainable yield of fuelwood for the state (Leers, 1984). If fuelwood use increases at only 10 percent per year, the sustainable yield will be reached very soon. Beyond that, more wood will be cut than grows and the second deforestation will be under way.

Wood cutting by individuals on private land is difficult, if not impossible, to regulate. It is to be hoped that landowners will manage their woodlots carefully to maximize output of wood and minimize environmental damage. Whether this will be done and to what extent New England's forests will become energy farms in the next few decades remain to be seen.

Table 8.3 Projected Regional Net Growth and Harvest (Million Cubic Feet)

	Softwoods				Hardwoods			
	Net Growth		Harvest		Net Growth		Harvest	
	1976	2030	1976	2030	1976	2030	1976	2030
North	1,600	1,374	705	1,088	4,192	3,282	1,953	3,326
South	6,158	6,488	4,471	6,303	4,547	4,120	2,101	5,211
Rocky Mts.	1,589	1,427	842	1,363	100	87	0	1
Pacific Coast	2,872	3,762	3,920	3,625	480	129	121	156
Total	12,219	13,051	9,938	12,379	9,319	7,618	4,175	8,694

Source: U.S. Forest Service, 1982

hardwood for fuel. Wood fuel demand is projected by the U.S. Forest Service to reach about 2 billion cubic feet per year by 2030.

By 2030, the increase in demand is expected to be such that for both hardwood and softwood, harvest will exceed net growth. In the critical western softwood areas (Table 8.3), net annual growth is expected to remain relatively constant, while it will decline in the South. Much of the decline is a result of successional change in softwood to hardwood forests. Only in the North will net softwood growth exceed demand. In the North and South it is estimated that hardwood demand will be nearly three times that of 1976. Hardwood supplies from the West will be low primarily because of the small amount of hardwood available there.

MANAGEMENT OF TIMBER RESOURCES

Prior to the turn of this century, forestry management in the U.S. consisted solely of cutting the timber and moving on. Great stands of mature forests were cut to make way for agriculture and progress. The public, the government, and the lumber companies believed that there was an abundance of trees and no real need to worry about the future supply of wood. In contrast to considerable achievements in forest management in Germany and other European countries, little attention was paid to maintaining the nation's forests. Outcries from academics and preservationists concerning forest deterioration finally reached the White House in the early 1900s and a new forest policy was implemented. This involved the concept of sustained yield, advocated by Gifford Pinchot, the first Chief Forester of the U.S. under President Theodore Roosevelt. As we shall see later in this chapter, this concept was institutionalized as a forestry management technique for public forests in 1960.

The Concept of Sustained Yield

The concept of *sustained yield* describes the management of living or biological resources. Sustained yield is the harvesting of a species at a rate equal to its rate of reproduction or maturation. Thus, the resource is neither overharvested and depleted nor harvested before it is matured. Both the quantity and quality of the resource are preserved.

As an overriding philosophical concept, sustained yield is useful, but it has limitations as an everyday management tool. Most of these involve its application. For example, demand for wood fluctuates with time, particularly as building construction varies with business cycles. It may, therefore, be useful at some times to cut in excess of the sustainable yield, and at other times cut less. Also, in mixed species forests, different species mature at different rates. If the timber is harvested by clear cutting, then for at least some trees the harvest will not occur at the optimal time for maximizing a sustainable yield. Sustained yield management may not be practical for any given parcel of forest land, but on an average regional basis over a period of several years or decades it is certainly feasible.

Harvesting Techniques

There are a variety of harvesting techniques that are used in forestry management. Not all of these can be used interchangeably since they each have specific goals and impacts. The three most important are shelterwood, selective, and clear cutting.

Shelterwood cutting is a two-stage process involving thinning and cutting. First, trees of poor quality are removed both from the forest floor and from the stand itself. This opens up the forest floor to more light, enhancing seedling growth and reducing competition. The remaining trees provide some shelter for the seedlings. When the seedlings take root and become established, some but not all of the mature higher quality trees are removed to reduce competition with the younger trees. Finally, when the younger trees are firmly established, the remaining mature trees are harvested. Shelterwood cutting is a very efficient technique in small plots with relatively homogeneous tree species. It is costly in terms of labor inputs in larger acreages and as such is not widely practiced on commercial forest lands.

Selective cutting is only applicable to forests of mixed-age classes or forests with unequal economic value. The mature trees of the desired species are harvested while the remaining trees are left intact. In an oak–hickory forest, for example, the mature oaks might be selectively cut leaving immature oaks and mature hickories. Selective cutting is primarily used in hardwood forests. When used in mixed-species forests, selective cutting tends to reduce the diversity of species in the forest. Selective cutting is costly and is appropriate only when the value of the harvested trees is high relative to those left. Also, selective cutting keeps the fire potential in a forest low.

Clear cutting is the most controversial harvesting technique in use (Figure 8.8a and b). Currently, over 60 percent of U.S. annual timber production is harvested in this way. The technique involves cutting all the trees regardless of size or species and is appropriate when the trees are relatively uniform in species and age or when it would provide the most desirable form of regeneration. Clear cutting, by leaving large areas bare, has greater potential for causing accelerated soil erosion. It also has a much greater visual impact on the landscape than the other cutting techniques.

a

b

Figure 8.8 (a) and (b) Clear cuts in the Coast Ranges of Oregon, west of Portland.

Ecological Effects of Timber Harvesting

Timber harvesting has many of the same effects as fire on the forest ecosystem. As trees are removed, sunlight reaches ground level and new growth is stimulated. The slash, or limbs and branches that are too small to use, is left on the ground and decays, contributing to nutrient release. Increased runoff causes accelerated erosion and transport of nutrients out of the system, similar to the effect of fire.

There are, however, some important differences. The process of timber harvesting requires that heavy equipment be brought into the forest, including bulldozers, trucks, and yarding gear for moving the logs. Roads must be built to bring the equipment in and carry the logs out. Driving vehicles over the forest soil and dragging logs to truck loading areas cause major damage to the soil surface. These result in a much greater acceleration of erosion than would occur after most fires. This is particularly a problem in mountainous areas such as the Pacific coast of the U.S. and Canada. In these areas, the accelerated erosion includes both surface erosion and landsliding, and resulting large amounts of sediment can move downstream and damage aquatic habitats and fish populations. This accelerated erosion has been the focus of controversy in many areas, especially the forests upstream of Redwood National Park in California. There the effects on streams in the park were so severe that the federal government was forced to curtail commercial logging activites in the upstream areas and to establish corridors where logging was prohibited along streams.

In addition to erosion, logging differs from fire in its effect on the forest in that fire-adapted species may not be stimulated to regenerate as quickly as they would after a fire. Many species require the heat of fire to stimulate germination or sprouting, and others require the massive input of nutrients that results from burning the forest. Slash left after the forest is cut may not release nutrients as rapidly as burned debris, and nutrients are taken out of the area in the form of logs. In general, however, logging has impacts that are quite similar to fire. It is a catastrophic, but temporary, disruption of the ecosystem that removes large amounts of soil, nutrients, and biomass from the system and begins the process of reestablishing the forest cover.

Methods of Reforestation

Reforestation of cutover areas is carried out by natural regeneration, artificial seeding and seedling planting. Natural regeneration simply means letting the forest regrow unaided by human activities, using seedlings that existed before harvest and natural seed sources remaining thereafter. Natural regeneration can be encouraged by harvesting practices that leave seedlings in place or that leave some trees as seed sources.

Artificial seeding is usually done by broadcasting seed from aircraft, as a result of ruggedness or isolation of forest terrain and the large acreages involved. Seeding accounts for only about 4 percent of the land artificially regenerated in the U.S.

Seedling plantings is used more commonly as a reforestation technique primarily because survival rates are higher and tree density can be more closely controlled. Plantings are usually done by hand rather than by machine, especially in rugged terrain.

PRESENT-DAY U.S. FOREST POLICY

Forest policy in the United States is based on an attempt to balance many conflicting needs and desires. Foremost among these are the physical and biological constraints on forest productivity, the need for economic efficiency, the consideration of amenity values, and equity issues (Clawson, 1975). Until the early 20th century, forest policy was largely dictated by considerations of economic efficiency (sufficient supply of timber at the lowest possible price), and private timber interests played a dominant role in the formation of government policy. U.S. Forest Service policies were primarily those developed in the Pinchot era. In the last half century, however, continued depletion of the nation's forests and a growing public awareness of the need for conservation and preservation of wilderness areas have led to the incorporation of a broader range of goals into public forest policy.

Legislative Mandates for Balanced Use

One of the first and most significant pieces of legislation passed regarding forest policy was the Multiple Use Sustained Yield Act of 1960 (MUSYA). Nontimbering interests had registered concern that the national forests were being cut down and that there were other values to a national forest than simply timber production. The passage of this act was significant in two respects. First, the U.S. Forest Service was made to recognize other uses of national forests. Second, the act established a balanced management approach recognizing four primary uses of national forests: timbering, watershed maintenance, wildlife habitat preservation, and recreation. Although conflicting in purpose, each of these uses was to be incorporated into specific management plans for each national forest.

MUSYA was important because it acknowledged the balance between economic and ecological uses of national forest lands. The harvesting of timber, while still important, was to be done under the general principle of sustained yield advocated by Pinchot fifty years earlier.

In 1974, the Forest and Rangeland Renewable Resource Planning Act (FRRPA) was passed. The purpose of this legislation was to clarify legally the management principles initially developed under the MUSYA. The FRRPA required that the U.S. Department of Agriculture make an inventory and assess the quality of national forests every ten years and recommend a comprehensive management program. The management program had to involve each of the four primary uses of forest lands as designated in the MUSYA. The Forest and Rangeland Renewable Resource Planning Act was designed to achieve a balance between economic efficiency, environmental quality, and social values in the management of national forests. It provided more practical guidance on how to do this than did the Multiple Use Sutained Yield Act.

Two years later in 1976, the FRRPA was amended and became known as the National Forest Management Act (NFMA). This act currently provides the operating policy for public forest resources in the U.S. The NFMA provides for integrated management plans for all 126 units of the national forest and national grasslands system. The NFMA also established a number of specific policies involving clear cutting, riparian protection, and the rate of timber harvesting on federal lands.

Under NFMA, the size of clear cuts on federally owned lands is limited. In Douglas fir forests in the Pacific Northwest, for example, the maximum size of a clear cut area is 24 hectares (60 acres). In coastal Alaska, the size is 40 hectares (100 acres) for hemlock and Sitka spruce forests. In the Southeast U.S.

clear cuts of 32 hectares (80 acres) are allowed on public lands with yellow pine forests, and 16 hectares (40 acres) everywhere else.

The second policy was the protection of riparian areas. Management practices that seriously or adversely affect water quality, fish, or freshwater habitat are prohibited. This protection includes a 30.5-m (100-ft) buffer strip between the water body and inland.

The third specific policy developed under the NFMA was regulating the rate of harvest. Biological growth factors combined with physical factors (e.g., soil erosion, slope, and soil types) and economic factors were to be used in determining the rate of harvest. The primary concern was with harvesting immature trees, so the act expressly prohibits commercial harvest until trees reach their peak of rapid growth and maturity.

One of the most significant outgrowths of recent forestry legislation was the establishment of wilderness reviews for all lands under the control of the U.S. Forest Service. Under federal mandate, these lands were to be managed for wilderness as well as timber use. Consequently, the U.S. Forest Service had to develop a program to review potential lands for wilderness status as required by the 1964 Wilderness Act (see Chapter 13). This internal procedure was termed the Roadless Area Review and Evaluation Study (RARE I and RARE II). Major conflicts between the U.S. Forest Service and preservationists arose as a result of this study, and neither side has been happy with the outcome.

To summarize the significance of this forestry legislation, congressional intervention into management was the direct outgrowth of environmentalist concern that the national forests were being harvested by private timber companies with U.S. Forest Service approval. There was also concern that the agency itself did not have the insight to develop a broader outlook in developing policy. Some argue that because the Forest Service is within the U.S. Department of Agriculture, its management guidelines were narrowly defined as managing trees for profit alone, with conservation as a measure to improve the economic viability of the enterprise. If the Forest Service had been under the U.S. Department of the Interior, then perhaps congressional intervention in forestry management would have been less necessary.

The Continuing Debate

There are so many conflicting interests in forest management that debate regarding management of private and public forest lands will always be intense. One of the issues stimulated by Reagan administration policies is privatization. *Privatization* involves the increased purchase of federal timber by the timber industry. To meet expected demand, the industry must increase its own supply of harvestable timber. Most of the private forest land is currently in use or in parcels that are too small to make cutting economical (Clawson, 1982). One of the few ways that the industry can increase supply is to purchase timber on federal lands (Table 8.4). The conflict arises when the timber companies want to increase their purchases and thus increase the amount of timber harvested from these lands. From an economic perspective, this is most advantageous to the timber company because the purchase of federal timber costs less and is of higher quality than comparable timber on small private landholdings. Environmentalists

Table 8.4 Net Growth of Timber in the U.S. by Species Group and Ownership Category, 1976–2030 (Million Cubic Feet)

	1976		2030	
	Soft	Hard	Soft	Hard
Natl. Forest	2,442	651	3,374	397
Other Public	1,076	879	1,218	413
Forest Industry	2,866	1,207	2,328	1,174
Other Private	5,877	6,643	4,890	5,597
Total	12,261	9,380	11,810	7,581

Source: U.S. Forest Service, 1982

are concerned about the already dwindling acreage set aside for recreation, wilderness, and ecosystem protection and thus oppose increased sales of federal timber. They feel that the timber industry is simply "crying wolf" to increase their harvest in the national forests (Conservation Foundation Letter, 1981).

Among other issues that continue to be important are the allocation of forest lands for water supply. Using herbicides and pesticides in forest management is also controversial. Because they are applied from the air, there is considerable potential for water contamination and harm to nontarget species. Where timber is harvested, the methods of harvest are often controversial. There is even division among those who call themselves environmentalists, with some opposing wood harvesting in general because of damage to wildlife or aesthetic values and others promoting it as a renewable source of energy and raw materials. Finally, the national forest lands are increasingly under pressure from business interests because of the vast mineral wealth found in them. The concept of multiple use has been expanded to include mineral and energy development not only on lands under U.S. Forest Service "protection" but on lands adjacent to national forests. Once believed infinite, the U.S. forest resource is today a known quantity with a future very much open to debate.

REFERENCES AND ADDITIONAL READING

Bailey, M., and P. Wheeling. 1980. Comments on the New England fuelwood survey made at a press conference, March 1980. Broomall, Pennsylvania: USDA, Economics, Statistics and Cooperatives Service.

Clawson, M. 1975. *Forests for whom and for what?* Baltimore: Johns Hopkins University Press.

———. 1979. Forests in the long sweep of U.S. history. *Science* 204:1168–74.

———. 1982. Private forests. In *Current issues in natural resource policy,* ed. P.R. Portney, chapter 9, pp. 283–92. Washington, D.C.: Resources for the Future.

Conservation Foundation Letter. 1981. National forest disputants: at loggerheads again. July.

Council on Environmental Quality. 1981a. *The Global 2000 report to the president.* Washington, D.C.: Government Printing Office.

———. 1981b. *Environmental trends.* Washington, D.C.: Government Printing Office.

Haden-Guest, S., et al. 1956. *A world geography of forest resources.* New York: Ronald Press for the American Geographical Society.

Leers, S.M. 1984. Forest resource management and residential woodfuel use in Mas-

sachusetts. Unpublished dissertation proposal, Clark University, Department of
Geography.

Likens, G.E., et al. 1978. Recovery of a
deforested ecosystem. *Science* 199:
492–96.

Moran, E.G. 1981. *Developing the Amazon.*
Bloomington, Indiana: Indiana University
Press.

Nations, J.D., and D.I. Komer. 1983. Rainforests and the hamburger society: can
the cycle be broken? *Environment*
25:3:12–20.

Patterson, W.A., et al. 1983. *Fire regimes
of Cape Cod National Seashore.* Boston:
U.S. Department of the Interior, National
Park Service, North Atlantic Region, Office of Scientific Studies.

Peters, J., and T. Bowers. 1977. Forest sta-
tistics for Massachusetts. USDA Forest
Service Bulletin NE-48. Washington, D.C.:
Government Printing Office.

Rand McNally. 1979. *Our magnificent earth.*
New York.

Shakow, D., et al. 1981. Energy and development: the case of Kenya. *Ambio*
10:206–10.

Spurr, S.H., and B.V. Barnes, 1980. *Forest
ecology.* 3rd ed. New York: Wiley.

UNESCO. 1978. Tropical forest ecosystem:
a state-of-knowledge report. Paris.

U.S. Bureau of the Census. 1984. *Statistical
abstract of the United States.* Washington,
D.C.: Government Printing Office.

U.S. Forest Service. 1982. *An analysis of
the timber situation in the U.S. 1952–2030.*
Forest Service Report no. 23. Washington,
D.C.: Government Printing Office.

TERMS TO KNOW

deforestation
Gifford Pinchot
hardwoods
multiple use
Multiple Use Sustained Yield Act
National Forest Management Act

privatization
RARE I and II
riparian areas
softwoods
sustained yield

STUDY QUESTIONS

1. What is the cycle of forest growth?
2. Do forest fires ever benefit the environment? Why or why not?
3. What are the three basic kinds of forest
   fires, and what are the effects of each?
4. Describe each of the three most important wood-harvesting techniques.
   What are the pros and cons of each
   method?

5. What are three methods for reforestation
   of cutover areas? Which one is most
   appropriate for hardwood forests? For
   softwoods?
6. What are the four primary uses of the
   National Forests, and how do these influence management decisions?

CHAPTER NINE

Water Supply: Natural and Human Aspects

INTRODUCTION

The water system of the earth, the hydrologic cycle, involves huge quantities of water that circulate between the atmosphere, ocean, and land (see Figure 4.5). As Table 9.1 indicates, however, most of the water in the system is unavailable for human use, because it is either saline (almost 98 percent) or locked up in the polar ice caps (2 percent). While there is plenty of water on the earth, less than 1 percent of it is in a form we can use. Table 9.2, a water budget for the U.S., shows the major flows and storages of water in the hydrologic cycle.

The annual flow of fresh water over the land surface and through shallow groundwater systems amounts to about 40,000 km^3 worldwide, or about .003 percent of the total amount of water in the world. This flow is precipitation less *evapotranspiration* on land surfaces; it represents the amount that is theoretically available for human use. In practice, though, much less is available, because water is not uniformly distributed on the earth's surface. A great deal of runoff occurs in areas with low water needs; many other areas with large water demands have but little available. In addition, the flow is variable over time, with both regular seasonal variability and less predictable fluctuations, such as droughts. As a result, much of the world experiences severe water shortages, which are made worse by the many demands we place on the hydrologic cycle and by deterioration in water quality. In the coming years, these shortages can be expected to become more acute, as an increasing population creates an increasing demand for water for irrigation, industrial, and household uses. One estimate suggests that 30 nations worldwide will be faced with water demand in excess of supply by the end of this century and that by 1990 over a billion people will have difficulty or be unable to obtain acceptable drinking water (Ambroggi, 1980).

NATURAL SURFACE AND GROUNDWATER AVAILABILITY

Surface and Groundwater

Water is found on the land in two basic forms: surface water and groundwater. Both of these are important storages in the hydrologic cycle (see Chapter 4).

Table 9.1 World Quantities of Water in the Hydrologic Cycle

Location	Percentage of Total
Surface	0.0171
Fresh-water lakes	0.009
Saline lakes and inland seas	0.008
Stream channels	0.0001
Subsurface	0.625
Soil moisture	0.005
Ground water	0.62
Ice caps and glaciers	2.15
Atmosphere	0.001
Oceans	97.2

Source: Strahler, 1975

Surface water is liquid water and floating ice above the ground surface, found in rivers, swamps, lakes, and other bodies. It is derived from direct precipitation and from subsurface sources. *Groundwater* is water below the surface, filling pore spaces and cracks in rocks or sediments, in a saturated zone below the *water table.* The water table is simply the top of the saturated zone. Soil moisture above the water table is not considered part of groundwater. Groundwater is derived from downward percolation of rainfall through the soil and, in some areas, from seepage from surface water. In addition, there are many areas of the world with substantial "fossil" groundwater storages that are derived from past humid conditions and that are not being significantly replenished today.

Surface and groundwaters flow from high to low elevations. Surface water flows according to the shape of the land, following channels to the sea. But groundwater flows according to the slope of the groundwater table and according to the permeability of the materials through which it moves. *Permeability* means penetrability, and it determines the speed with which water flows through a porous medium, such as rock or sediments. The steeper the slope of the water table and the greater the permeability of the ground, the faster water flows. Usually, the shape of the water table approximately parallels the shape of the land, so that groundwater flows from upland areas toward lowlands, but this is not always the case. For example, variations in the permeability of subsurface materials affect flow rates and directions, sometimes causing groundwater drainage divides to be different from those for surface water. Thus, a detailed knowledge of subsurface structures is necessary to understand how groundwater flows in any particular area. The locations of permeable and impermeable areas of rock

Table 9.2 Water Budget for the U.S. (Billions of Cubic Meters per Day)

Precipitation	15.9
Evaporation from wet surface	10.4
Reservoir net evaporation	0.06
Streamflow to oceans	4.62
Ground water flow to oceans	0.38
Streamflow to Mexico and Canada	0.03
Consumptive Use	0.40

Source: Water Resources Council, 1978

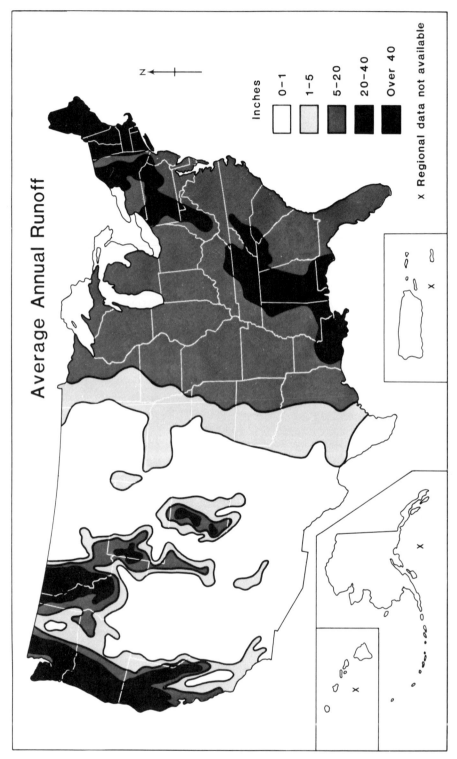

Figure 9.1 Average annual runoff in the U.S. Runoff is greatest in the Pacific Northwest, the Rocky Mountains, the Appalachians, and New England. (Source: Water Resources Council, 1978)

or sediments are important not only for groundwater flow patterns but also for determining where water is stored and available. A porous body of material, such as sand, gravel, or rock, containing groundwater is called an *aquifer.* If the groundwater table is free to rise with additional water, that is, if the overlying layer is permeable, then the aquifer is unconfined. If an impermeable layer overlies the aquifer, it is confined. Such impermeable layers, called *aquicludes,* are particularly important in segregating relatively clean groundwater from brackish or contaminated groundwater. Figure 4.5 (see Chapter 4) shows the relationships between surface and groundwater.

Spatial Variation in Surface Water Supply

Surface water supply is directly determined by precipitation and evapotranspiration rates, with runoff being the difference between the two. In the United States, average annual precipitation is relatively high in the southeastern states, the Appalachians, the Pacific Northwest, the mountainous areas of the West, southern Alaska, and Hawaii. Runoff per area is greatest in the Pacific Northwest, the Rocky Mountains, the Appalachians, and New England (see Figure 9.1). Once this runoff is generated, it flows into rivers and is taken to other areas. Figure 9.2 shows the average discharge for major American rivers. The Mississippi carries the most water, draining about 3.2 million square kilometers (12.4 million square miles) or 35 percent of the U.S. total area carrying an average of about 17,600 cubic meters per second (m³/sec) (620,000 cubic feet per second) to the ocean. The Columbia is next, draining 669,000 square kilometers and discharging an average of 6,650 m³/sec (235,000 cfs). The St. Lawrence drains a larger area than the Columbia but carries less water.

The Colorado, draining 355,000 square kilometers, would discharge only about 480 m³/sec (17,000 cfs) to the sea even if its waters were not withdrawn for human uses. In addition to these, there are many smaller rivers, and immense amounts of water are also stored in freshwater lakes, especially the Great Lakes.

Spatial Variation in Groundwater Supply

There are many different types of aquifers, classified according to the nature of the materials and the source of water in them. Figure 9.3 shows the major aquifers of the U.S. While not every place has substantial available groundwater, these productive aquifers are widespread. The aquifer distribution pattern corresponds to geologic structures. These include the extensive coastal plain deposits of the Southeast, the sedimentary rocks, glacial deposits, and young sand and gravel deposits in the Midwest, and the accumulations of sediments in the West's intermontane valleys. In addition, most of the major river valleys (the Colorado and Columbia are notable exceptions) are underlain by relatively permeable alluvial deposits that are recharged by the stream flow of the rivers that formed them. The areas without productive aquifers generally are mountain areas and much of the arid West, which have either too little or too brackish groundwater. In addition to those shown, across the country there are smaller and less productive aquifers, many of which are important local water supplies.

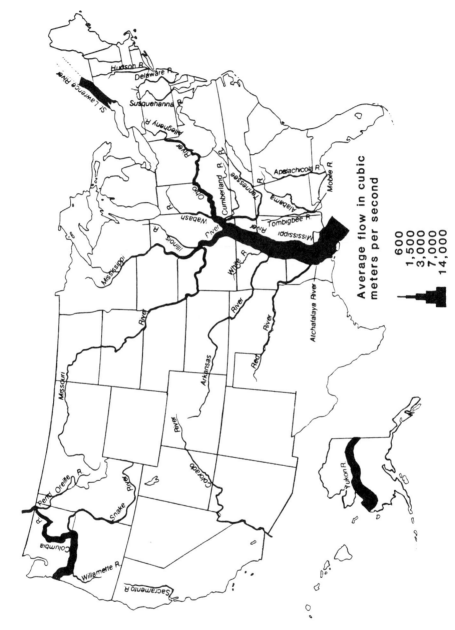

Figure 9.2 Average annual discharge of major U.S. rivers. The Mississippi dominates, with the Yukon, Columbia, and St. Lawrence also major drainage systems. (Source: Council on Environmental Quality, 1981)

Major Aquifers in the U.S.

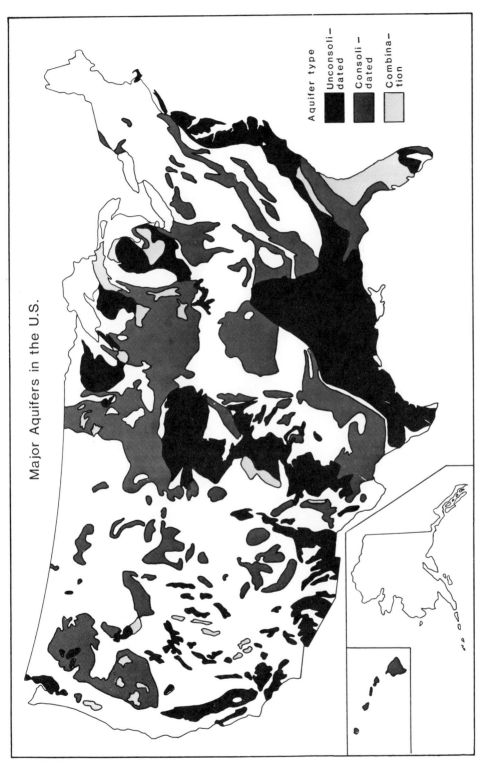

Aquifer type

Unconsoli-
dated

Consoli-
dated

Combina-
tion

Figure 9.3 Major aquifers in the U.S. Unconsolidated aquifers are composed primarily of recent deposits of sands and gravels. Consolidated aquifers consist of older permeable rocks. (Source: Adapted from Water Resources Council, 1978)

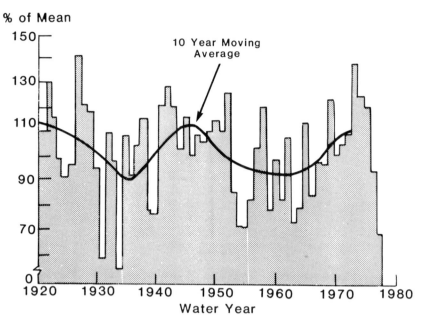

% of Mean

Figure 9.4   Variability of stream flow in the U.S. Ideally, water supplies should be planned to anticipate the low-flow years. (Source: Water Resources Council, 1978)

Temporal Variability in Water Supply

There are two main ways of evaluating water availability: flow and storage. Flow is the rate at which water passes through a system; storage is the volume of water in the system at any given time. The ratio of flow to storage is especially important, as it determines the length of time required to replace stored water if it is depleted or contaminated. If the flow rate is high in relation to storage, then the water can be quickly replenished. Such a system is, however, susceptible to fluctuations in flow resulting from floods and droughts. On the other hand, if storage is high in relation to flow, then there is less short-term variability of flow, but it takes much longer to replenish stored water.

Rivers have very high ratios of flow to storage, and thus short-term fluctuations in discharge greatly limit the amount of water they can supply. Seasonal mean monthly discharges for rivers typically vary by one or even two orders of magnitude, depending on seasonal amounts of precipitation and evapotranspiration. This means that if the average flow in the driest month is 5 m³/sec, the flow in the wettest month may be 50 or 500 m³/sec. In midlatitude climates, the low-flow periods are usually in the summer, because plants are using more water then. Summer is also the time when demand for water is higher, as people water lawns, wash cars, open fire hydrants, and fill swimming pools. As a result, the amount of water we can count on from a river is much less than the total amount that flows in it over the year. In addition, precipitation variations from one year to the next further reduce the amount of water we can depend on from rivers. The short- and medium-term variation in stream flow of U.S. streams is shown in Figure 9.4. Water supplies must be planned for the years with flows well below the mean. If we want the supply to be adequate at least 95 percent of the time, for example, the discharge demanded must be equaled or exceeded by supply in an average of nineteen out of twenty years. For the northeastern U.S., this demand value is generally about 60 percent of the mean discharge, on an annual basis. In the Missouri basin, it is about 40 percent of the mean; for the Rio Grande, it is only 17 percent. This supply problem is compounded by the fact that droughts often last more than one year, so that there may be a succession of three or four dry years in a row, instead of a dry year always being followed by a wet one.

Groundwater supplies, on the other hand, usually have very large storages of water in relation to flow. Aquifers are usually recharged very slowly, and large ones are not significantly affected by seasonal variations in precipitation or even by year-to-year climatic fluctuations. However, smaller aquifers, especially shallower ones, are affected by short-term weather patterns, though less than rivers are.

USES OF WATER: VARIED AND RISING

Water is used for a wide variety of purposes, and these have very different quantity, quality, and timing requirements. The type of use can be evaluated by whether it takes place in the stream or elsewhere and by whether the water is returned to the stream after use. Before proceeding, then, let us define a few terms that describe these aspects of water use. *Withdrawal* is the removal of water from a surface or groundwater source for any of a variety of purposes, such as municipal, industrial, or irrigation use. *Consumption* is the use of that water in such a way that it is not returned to the stream or aquifer; instead, it is returned to the atmosphere by evapotranspiration. *In-stream uses* do not require removal of the water from a river or lake; these include navigation, wildlife habitat, waste disposal, and hydroelectric-power generation.

Water demands fluctuate from year to year, depending on weather patterns. In wet or cool years, demand is usually lower; in dry years, demand is greater. To evaluate long-term trends, it is useful to average the short-term fluctuations. The water-use statistics shown in Table 9.3 are adjusted for these fluctuations and are preferable to yearly data for this purpose (Water Resources Council, 1978).

Domestic and commercial uses for water include those we are familiar with in our everyday lives at home and work. They include washing, cooking, drinking, lawn watering, sanitation, and the like. In 1975, about 83 percent of the U.S. population was served by municipal water supply systems, 15 percent had individual domestic systems (usually wells) and about 2 percent had no piped water supply. By 2000, it is expected that 90 percent will be served by central-ized water supply systems (Water Resources Council, 1978). In centralized systems, the average domestic water use is about 447 liters (118 gallons) per person per day, and commercial uses add another 49 liters (13 gallons). In individual systems, domestic use is about 250 liters, or 66 gallons. The difference is that municipal use also includes pipeline leaks, fire protection, street washing, park maintenance, and similar community functions. This per capita use is not expected to change very much in the next few decades; the total amount of water demanded will increase as population increases. Domestic and commercial uses are not highly

Table 9.3 Total Withdrawals and Consumption, by Functional Use, 1975, 1985, and 2000 (Million Cubic Meters per Day)

	Withdrawals			Consumption		
	1975	1985	2000	1975	1985	2000
I. Fresh water						
A. Domestic						
Central (municipal)	80.11	90.78	105.67	18.83	21.44	25.12
Noncentral (rural)	7.92	8.78	9.08	4.89	5.33	5.44
B. Commercial	20.93	22.89	25.48	4.20	4.60	5.18
C. Manufacturing	193.88	89.66	74.45	22.93	33.70	55.64
D. Agriculture						
Irrigation	600.84	629.26	582.31	326.99	351.32	350.14
Livestock	7.24	8.45	9.66	7.24	8.45	9.66
E. Steam electric	336.55	359.04	300.76	5.37	15.37	39.90
F. Mineral industry	26.70	33.43	42.88	8.31	10.52	13.66
G. Public lands/other	7.06	8.18	9.31	4.68	5.53	6.55
Total fresh water	1281.22	1250.47	1159.61	403.44	456.26	511.28
II Saline water	226.10	345.33	449.71			
Total	1507.33	1595.80	1609.33			

Source: Water Resources Council, 1978

consumptive, since most of the water is returned via individual or community sewage systems. On the average, about 26 percent of these uses is consumed.

Use of fresh water in manufacturing is much greater than domestic and commercial use, averaging about 900 liters per person per day in 1975. The largest manufacturing uses are in the chemical and metal industries, which together account for almost two-thirds of all manufacturing withdrawals (see Figure 9.5). The manufacture of paper and related products, the production of petroleum and coal, and food processing are also important industrial uses of water. Most of the water is used for cooling or washing, and thus is not consumptive. In 1975, only 11 percent of manufacturing withdrawals were consumed. Some industries recirculate water through their plants, cooling it or cleaning it at the plant site. It is hoped that recirculation will become more widespread in the future, largely as a means to reduce water pollution. This would result in a decline in water withdrawals. Consumption, however, is still expected to increase. Mineral extraction use of water is expected to increase in the next few decades, as demand for minerals, especially coal, increases. Mining withdrew 123 liters per capita per day in 1975, and about 31 percent of this was consumed. Another important use of water is as a coolant in electric-power production. Large amounts of water are withdrawn for this purpose, totaling 1,558 liters per capita per day in 1975. Very little of this water is consumed, however. In the future, this use will also increase and more of the water will be consumed, as evaporative cooling systems rather than once-through convective systems become more widespread.

By far the largest use of water in the U.S., in both withdrawal and consumption, is in agriculture. Irrigation is the major component, although livestock watering accounts for about 1 percent of agricultural use. Agricultural use amounted to about 2,773 liters per person per day in 1975, or almost half of total water withdrawals in the U.S. Irrigation is also the most consumptive of all major uses, accounting for 81 percent of the total consumption and 54 percent of all water

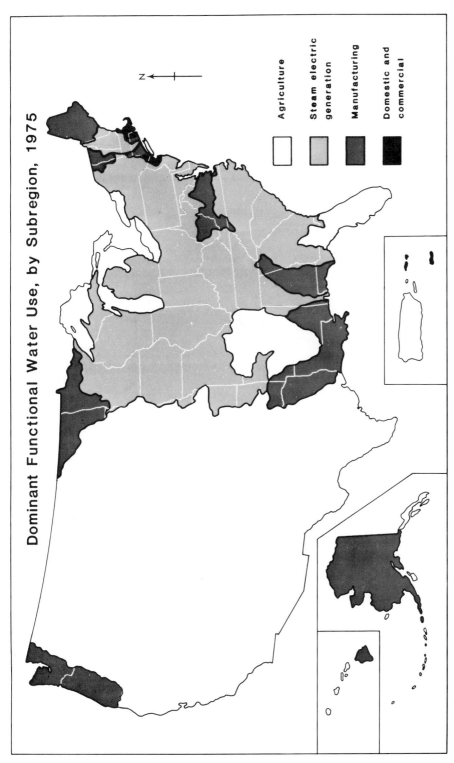

Figure 9.5 Dominant functional water use, by subregion, 1975. Chemical and metal manufacturing industries together account for nearly two-thirds of all manufacturing withdrawals. Nationwide, agriculture is the largest user of water. (Source: Water Resources Council, 1978)

withdrawn. Most of this use takes place in the more arid parts of the country, particularly the western Great Plains, the intermontane basins west of the Rockies, and California (see Figure 9.5). Much of the water for this irrigation is derived from mountain runoff, but groundwater is also a major source. Because of the arid climate of these areas and the large demands for irrigation water, supplies are short and, in many areas, groundwater is used faster than it is replaced. The Water Resources Council (1978) predicts that, as a result of this shortage, agricultural withdrawals will actually decline by 2000, although the efficiency of water use in crop production will increase. This will result from better control of seepage losses and use of water-conserving systems such as drip irrigation (see Chapter 6). Nationwide, however, the amount of water consumed by agriculture is expected to increase, and new sources must be found.

DEVELOPMENT OF WATER SUPPLIES

Methods Used to Increase Available Water

As Figure 9.6 shows, any water supply system must have the following four components: collection system, storage facility, transportation system, and distribution system. Water-supply engineers design and construct water systems in a variety of ways, where possible incorporating natural features in one or more of the above components. In virtually all cases, the collection system is natural: the *drainage basin* of a river, a groundwater aquifer, or some combination of the two. Rivers are particularly efficient concentrators of surface runoff. As a result, usually little is done to modify collection systems, although vegetation conversion to increase water yield or improve water quality has been used in many areas. Aquifers are much more dispersed conveyors of water. Water flows toward low points in the water table, and, when a well is drilled to pump water out, the local water table is lowered. This causes water to flow toward the well, which is exactly what is desired. By drilling wells in particularly porous, permeable underground materials, resource managers tap into aquifers that have a ready supply of available water.

Storage is necessary to smooth out the natural variations in water availability and to save surplus water collected during high rainfall periods for times when water is scarce. Under ideal conditions, a storage facility can allow average withdrawals to equal the long-term average flow and short-term withdrawals to far exceed average flows. In practice, however, average withdrawals are rarely this large. Storages cannot trap all the water during times of flood, and water must be left for in-stream uses. Nonetheless, short-term withdrawals, i.e., for periods of weeks or less, frequently exceed average inflows in large storages.

Surface water storage is accomplished by constructing dams on rivers and impounding the river water in artificial lakes behind the dams. The amount of water that can be stored is a function of the shape of the valley and the height of the dam. The ideal dam site is a relatively narrow and deep valley for the dam, with a broad and deep valley just upstream for the reservoir. In addition, the valley that is to be inundated should be underlain by impermeable rocks and should be relatively unpopulated, and the long-term value of the land should be lower than the value of the reservoir replacing it. There are quite a few locations in the U.S. that fit these criteria, and most of them have dams in them

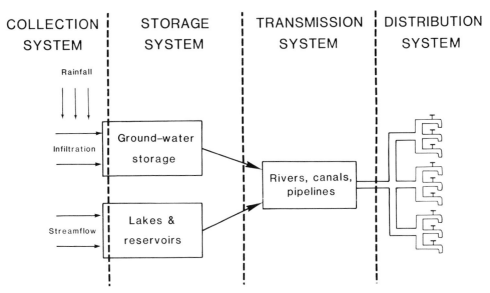

Figure 9.6 Components of a water supply system. The component with the lowest capacity limits the capacity of the entire system.

(see Figure 9.7). In Canada there are many undeveloped dam sites, but most of them are in relatively remote areas, making development costs high. In much of the Third World, numerous dam sites are still available for development.

Transportation and distribution systems are of many types, depending mostly on the distance between the collection site and the use area and on the nature of the final use. In many cases, transportation distances are so short that the entire system is essentially just a distribution system. These facilities include canals, pipelines, and natural river channels, or any combination of these (see Figure 9.8). The choice of type of conduit depends primarily on the terrain, the volumes of water to be carried, the distances involved, and the need to protect against seepage and quality deterioration along the way.

The Role of Weather in Water Resource Development

Due to the variability of water supply and demand, the amount available in any supply system is rarely equal to the demand. Reservoirs smooth out some of the fluctuations, but supply systems are inevitably stressed in time of drought. Thus, the supply provided by any particular system fluctuates between plenty and shortage (see Figure 9.9). As population has increased, the demand for water has steadily risen through time, both on a per capita basis and for regions as a whole. For example, cities have grown both in population and in area, generally tending to develop more centralized water systems to meet the demands of growing populations. If a water supply system is not enlarged to keep pace with growing demand, then the supply will be insufficient at some point. The combination of a fluctuating supply with gradually increasing demand results in periods when supply is insufficient, and local water supply crises result. One example is the recent experience of urban New Jersey.

New Jersey is in an area with plentiful rainfall, approximately 45 inches or

Figure 9.7 Part of the reservoir system of the Colorado River Basin. Currecanti National Recreation Area, Colorado.

115 cm per year. However, twice in the last twenty years, water supply crises have forced state and local governments to require water conservation efforts of both domestic and industrial users. The earlier of these was during the mid-1960s drought on the east coast, in which rainfall was well below normal over a wide area. After that drought, two major reservoirs were constructed in New Jersey, expanding the storage capacity of the state's water supply systems and protecting it against future occurrences of drought like that in the 1960s. However, about fifteen years later, a minor dry spell put the region's water supply systems in danger again.

A dry summer, autumn, and winter in 1980 resulted in lower than normal reservoir levels statewide in January 1981. At that time, the governors of the four states served by the Delaware River (New York, Pennsylvania, New Jersey, and Delaware) imposed a mandatory ban on nonessential water use. This included lawn and garden watering, noncommercial car washing, washing paved surfaces, use of ornamental fountains, nonessential fire-hydrant use, and serving water in restaurants. Golf course greens and tees were excepted from this order, which obviously did not have much of an impact in mid-winter. The ban did, however, prepare the region's citizens for greater shortages in the spring and summer months ahead.

By mid-February, half of New Jersey's 7.3 million people and much of the state's industry were required to cut consumption by 25 percent with per capita limits of 50 gallons (190 liters) a day, down from an average use of 80–100 gallons. Local water companies were to be the enforcers, adding surcharges to the bills of persons exceeding the limit. There was an estimated forty-day supply remaining for the hardest-hit communities, in the Hackensack Meadowlands, in the heavily urbanized northeastern part of the state. Although reservoir levels in other parts of the state also dropped in this period, to 46 percent of capacity on one central New Jersey reservoir, for example, the northeastern reservoirs

Figure 9.8 The California Aqueduct brings water from central and northern California to greater Los Angeles.

dropped to below 30 percent of capacity. Flow in the Raritan River, a major water source, was reduced so that more water could be stored in depleted reservoirs. There were fears that the remaining river flow would contain dangerously higher concentrations of human and industrial pollutants.

Conservation tips publicized by municipal authorities included such ideas as fewer toilet flushes, not washing dishes with running water, not letting the water run while brushing teeth, and the like. But the drought never reached the point for implementing such emergency measures as shipping water in via tankers, evacuating kidney-dialysis patients, closing businesses, and letting buildings burn. February brought some rain, and by November of 1981 reservoirs were once again at acceptable levels, although below normal for that time of year. Water rationing, although remaining in effect in the northeastern cities, was eased with greater rainfall over the followng year (Hanley, 1980a and b).

Conservation of water can help alleviate minor water shortages, but it is rarely a long-term cure for a water shortage. In New Jersey's case, the problem was based on over-selling the reservoir water in the Meadowlands area, which

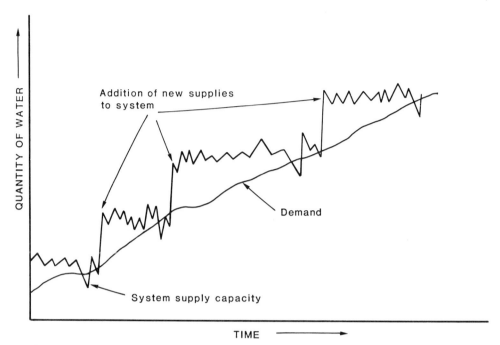

Figure 9.9 Fluctuation in water supply and demand. Demand rises steadily, and crises of supply occur during times of drought. These crises stimulate expansion in the supply system, which lasts a few years, until demand again exceeds supply. (Source: Modified from Russell et al., 1970)

had just gone through a period of tremendous growth. Administrators of the several small reservoirs that served the area had taken on many new customers without expanding the available storage capacity. They depended on the rain to keep falling and allowed their reservoirs to be depleted to risky low levels. After several consecutive dry months, the area was soon in trouble. It is clear that the 1980–81 water shortage was hastened by a minor dry spell, but the real reason for the shortage was that demand was allowed to rise without a concurrent expansion in the capacity of the supply system.

The New Jersey experience is typical of urban and suburban areas everywhere. Droughts are inevitable; when they occur, supply systems are stressed. Governments and the public become aware that new sources of water are needed to avert the next crisis (Ashworth, 1982). This awareness, particularly on the part of the public, is usually necessary before system expansions can be made, because bond issues must be passed by the voters and opposition to projects must be overcome. Within a few months or years, the drought passes, system expansions are completed, and water is again plentiful. Often, this increased supply encourages new development and thus new demands on the water supply. Then, a few years later, the next drought starts the cycle all over again. The important thing to recognize about this process is that water supply crises, such as those in New Jersey and the late 1970s drought in the West, are not aberrations. They are a consequence of demand that exceeds the capability of a particular supply system during occasional periods of low precipitation, which will inevitably occur.

The Extent of Water Resource Development

It should be clear by now that, although water supply is constrained by natural factors, water development in the form of engineering works, such as those described earlier, also determines water availability. The extent of artificial water development can be evaluated only relative to what is naturally available, and that in turn is subject to debate, because there are different definitions of available. One indication of the extent of water use can be gained by comparing withdrawals to natural runoff. In the Mississippi River basin, for example, withdrawals from stream flow are about 21 percent of the runoff. In New England, withdrawals are 6 percent of runoff, in the Middle Atlantic 20 percent, and in California 43 percent. In arid areas, water is used off-stream more than once. In the Colorado River basin, withdrawals from stream flow are 92 percent of runoff, and, if we include withdrawals from groundwater, they amount to 136 percent of natural runoff. In the central Great Basin, freshwater withdrawals are 110 percent of runoff.

Withdrawals can exceed stream flow because not all water withdrawn is consumed; some is returned to the stream. Nonetheless, these withdrawals place a heavy demand on water resources, particularly because they compete with in-stream uses. In the Colorado River basin, for example, a series of power plants at major dams generate about 4 percent of the nation's hydroelectric power, and plants in the Pacific Northwest (mostly in the Columbia River basin) generate almost 50 percent of U.S. hydroelectric power (Water Resources Council, 1978). If water is withdrawn and consumed, rather than returned for this in-stream use, energy production is reduced.

In more densely populated areas of the country, the most important in-stream use is in maintenance of water quality. Sufficient flow must be available to dilute and transport sewage effluents and other pollutants, as well as to provide habitat for aquatic life. The U.S. Fish and Wildlife Service has estimated the flows necessary to support aquatic habitat and recreation. These flows were found to be generally 80 to 90 percent of total stream flow in the eastern US. and 40 to 60 percent of the total flow in most of the western U.S. (Water Resources Council, 1978). Navigation is another important in-stream use that competes with other in- and off-stream uses for the water in our rivers.

Groundwater development is also widespread, and in many areas it is severely overextended. Because groundwater storages are so large in relation to inflows, it is possible to withdraw water at rates far in excess of inflows. This is called *overdraft* or *groundwater mining.* Figure 9.10 is a map of areas of the U.S. with severe problems of groundwater overdraft. The major areas are the western Great Plains, Arizona, California, the lower Mississippi valley, the western Great Lakes states, and the coastal areas from Maine to Florida.

The first effect of groundwater overdraft is declining well levels, often requiring that wells be deepened for withdrawals to continue. In coastal areas, there is usually a boundary between fresh and salt water in the ground. Salt water is denser and so is found underneath the fresh water. A decline in the elevation of the freshwater table causes *saltwater intrusion,* an inland movement

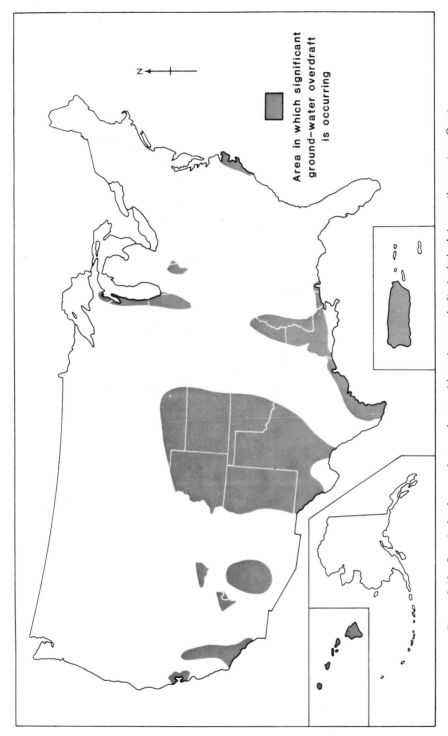

Figure 9.10 Overdraft of groundwater. Areas with major overdrafts include Arizona, the western Great Plains, California, the lower Mississippi Valley, Hawaii, Puerto Rico, the western Great Lakes, and many areas along the East Coast. (Source: Water Resources Council, 1978)

Area in which significant ground-water overdraft is occurring

of the salt/fresh boundary, contaminating wells and making them unusable for drinking water. When this happens, there is usually no recourse but to close the wells and find alternative sources of water, usually wells farther inland. This problem is particularly acute on the coastal plain of the eastern U.S. and in some areas of coastal California. There are also examples of saltwater intrusion into inland aquifers, in areas where saline groundwater underlies fresh. In some areas, notably coastal Texas, southern Arizona, and central California, groundwater overdrafts are causing *subsidence,* or sinking of the land. In Texas this is contributing to coastal flooding, particularly in suburban Houston, and in Arizona large fissues have opened in the ground.

In the western Great Plains, the most important overdraft problem is in the area underlain by the Ogallala aquifer. This aquifer is a thick, porous layer of sand and gravel that underlies an extensive area from Nebraska to Texas. It contains a large amount of water but has an extremely low recharge rate. Most of this area is too dry for rainfall farming, and groundwater-based irrigation has been rapidly expanding since the 1950s. The rate of withdrawal is enormous, exceeding the recharge rate by 100 times in some areas. The Ogallala aquifer allowed the rapid initial development of irrigated agriculture in West Texas. The depletion of the aquifer will eventually end irrigated agriculture in the region and hasten the decline of economic growth. In the Arkansas-White-Red Rivers region, which includes much of the Ogallala aquifer, overdrafts represent over 60 percent of all groundwater withdrawals. Another area of extreme overdraft is the Texas-Gulf region, where overdrafts are 77 percent of groundwater withdrawals. For the nation as a whole, about 25 percent of all groundwater withdrawals are overdrafts (Water Resources Council, 1978).

Environmental Impacts of Water Resource Development

Water resource development has many positive and negative environmental impacts. Some of these occur only in the immediate area of the development; others are felt hundreds of kilometers away. Groundwater withdrawal usually has little impact if overdrafts are not made. An important exception to this is that any groundwater extraction lowers the water table, and in wetlands this may seriously affect vegetation and associated ecological communities. Surface water development, on the other hand, usually has quite dramatic effects. The most common of the positive impacts are flood control and creation of recreational facilities. Among common negative impacts are loss of land, loss of the natural qualities of streams, and increased sedimentation.

Floods cause more property damage in the U.S. than any other natural hazard, with annual damages averaging $3 billion to $4 billion. Many different methods are used to reduce these losses, one of the most important being dam construction. Dams control floods by storing runoff during exceptionally high discharge periods and releasing it when flows are low or when it is needed for water supply. Usually dams are built with multiple purposes in mind, with water supply and flood control foremost. These multiple-purpose schemes are more than just water developments, so flood control is not just a side benefit of water development; it is integral to the planning of a system. Since 1936, the U.S. government has spent about $13 billion on flood-control structures that have prevented an estimated $60 billion in damages. An additional benefit of dam and reservoir construction is increased recreational opportunities. These usually include boating, swimming, and camping. Recreation benefits are seldom the primary reasons for constructing a dam, but they often figure importantly in benefit-cost computations for such projects. Recreational use of our waterways has been increasing in recent decades, and this rise is expected to continue. The Water Resource Council (1978) projects a need for a 6 percent increase in the surface water area available for recreation nationwide by 2000.

Loss of land is probably the most important of the negative impacts of surface water development. Nearly 8 million hectares (19 million acres) of land in the U.S. are covered with ponded water in reservoirs and regulated lakes. Some of this land, of course, was underwater before reservoir development, such as that in the river channel itself. Much of it, however, was fertile alluvial land that was cropland, potential cropland, forest, or wetland before the reservoir was filled, and it is permanently lost to those uses today. In many cases, towns, roads, and other structures once stood on the land. From 1967 to 1975, 2.7 million hectares (6.7 million acres) of land were inundated by water development (Brewer and Boxley, 1981), and a similar pace is likely in the future. Loss of land is often the most controversial element of water development schemes, because land has a tangible value as well as an emotional attachment for those displaced. For others, loss of the natural qualities of a river or associated wetlands is a major concern. For example, the Glen Canyon Dam in Arizona created Lake Powell but inundated a portion of the Colorado River that was almost as spectacular as the Grand Canyon. The famous Tellico Dam in Tennessee was controversial because it modified the habitat of an endangered species of fish (see Chapter 13). But these values are not easily measured, and it is largely a matter of opinion whether a natural river or an engineered reservoir presents a greater environmental amenity. These issues are discussed more fully in Chapter 13.

The effects of reservoirs on sediment movement in streams are another important group of negative impacts. Reservoirs trap sediment carried by streams, so that storage capacity decreases through time. For many reservoirs, this is a major problem, reducing the usable life of a reservoir to a few decades in some cases. At Imperial Dam on the lower Colorado, sediment is of sufficient importance to justify constructing and maintaining a costly system of sediment traps to clean the water before it enters the reservoir. Sediment trapped in the reservoir is not available to the river below the dam, but in most cases the river still has the capacity to transport sediment. Without its natural sediment load, the river is able to erode into its bed. This results in greater channel erosion below the dam. In most cases, this is a relatively minor problem, but it can be significant. For instance, the combined effects of sediment removal and flow regulation at Glen Canyon Dam have caused erosion of sands from the channel banks in the Grand Canyon of the Colorado, restricting areas where boaters can land and camp along the river (Coats, 1984). At the same time, the river is less able to remove large boulders that accumulate in rapids, so that certain rapids have become more difficult to navigate since the erection of Glan Canyon Dam. If left unregulated, river sediment also provides sand for beaches in many coastal areas, particularly on the west coast of the U.S. Removal of sediment from rivers prevents it from reaching the beaches, aggravating problems of beach erosion (California Department of Navigation and Ocean Development, 1977).

In addition to these impacts, many others may occur. These include *eutrophication* (see Chapter 10) of the artificial lakes, changes in water temperatures due to water-temperature stratification in reservoirs, seepage, increased water losses, and increased dissolved solids concentrations due to evaporation. Rivers and water supply systems are so complex and affect so many important natural processes that it is often difficult to predict the many impacts associated with these projects. Such prediction is essential, however, and continues to be an important environmental issue as more and more water projects are proposed.

INCREASING FUTURE WATER AVAILABILITY

Interbasin Diversions of Water

Interbasin diversions are transfers of water from one drainage basin to another. Water problems, such as those in the Southwest, have led to the development of schemes to pipe water enormous distances from areas of surplus to areas of deficit. Already water from Northern California is used to supply Los Angeles (Seckler, 1971), and from time to time proposals are discussed to pump water from the Columbia River basin into California. The lower Mississippi has been discussed as a source of water for West Texas.

One of the largest long-distance water diversion schemes currently under construction in the U.S. is the Central Arizona Project (Hanson, 1982). While not truly an interbasin transfer, the project has the scale and cost typical of such ventures. It was authorized by Congress in 1968 and is scheduled for completion in 1985. Its main purpose is to take water from the lower Colorado and pump it to the booming urban and agricultural area around Phoenix and Tucson. These cities are the heart of one of the fastest growing major urban areas in the country, an area which is very hot and very dry. Mean annual rainfall in the area is only about 175 mm (7 inches), and mean annual lake evaporation is about 1800 mm, or 71 inches. Migrants from the North and East are drawn by the sunny climate but also expect many of the amenities of wetter areas, such as lawns and swimming pools. The agriculture of the region has depended primarily on overdrafts of groundwater, but the aquifers are drying up and new sources of water are needed. Nearly half the groundwater withdrawn in the lower Colorado region is overdrawn.

The Central Arizona Project includes an aqueduct that will convey water from the Colorado at Parker Dam to the Phoenix region. The water must be pumped over 400 kilometers horizontally and 600 meters vertically. It is to be stored in reservoirs built on the Salt and Gila rivers, and from these it will be distributed to the thirsty cities and farms of the area.

One of the striking features of this project is that it will withdraw water that is already allocated elsewhere. Even without the Central Arizona Project, all the water in the Colorado is used in most years, so that, by the time it reaches the Gulf of California, it is barely a trickle. This project means there will be new withdrawals, and so other areas, including Los Angeles, must take less. In a year like 1983, when unusually heavy snows and a rapid melt caught reservoir operators by surprise and caused widespread flooding on the Colorado, this extra withdrawal was feasible. But in average and drought years, there will not be enough to go around.

In most cases, major new long-distance diversions such as these are extremely expensive, and pumping costs alone are often prohibitive. In addition, opposition from residents of exporting areas, along with environmental considerations, are substantial barriers to these projects. Arguments for the projects are usually heard from farmers, landowners, and developers in the areas concerned. As a rule, the water users benefit from large public subsidies of these projects, paying only a fraction of the total cost of the water they use (see Issue 9.1).

Instead of expanding water use in arid areas, it is usually much cheaper, both in economic and in environmental terms, to reduce demand by water conservation, to increase local supplies, or to invest in environmentally sounder means of generating income.

New Techniques to Expand Water Supplies

In addition to the more traditional methods of water supply development by dams, canals, and pumps, several other methods are now being discussed and tested. These include water harvesting, wastewater reclamation, and desalinization.

Water harvesting is not a new idea; it has been practiced for thousands of years. Water harvesting is simply collecting water just as it falls as rain, rather than drawing it from rivers or wells. There are many ways to do this, some of them very simple and some relying on high technology. In dry areas around the world, especially Central America, the Near East, and southern Asia, early

---

ISSUE 9.1: The Peculiar Politics of Water

In the spring of 1982, the front page of the *Washington Post* carried a photograph of a policeman chasing a turkey off the steps of the U.S. Capitol. The turkeys were a "present" for the senators and representatives supporting dams and other water projects in an annual public-works appropriations bill. Opponents claimed that dam proponents were "swilling at the public trough" by supporting "pork barrel" projects that were "turkeys." The poor birds had inadvertently escaped (or was it deliberate?) and caused a considerable ruckus before being captured by police. Was this an example of politics as usual?

The process by which federally supported public-works projects are conceived, funded, and built is often extremely convoluted. This is especially true for dams, water diversions, and other water supply projects built by large federal agencies, such as the Army Corps of Engineers, the Bureau of Land

Management, and the Bureau of Reclamation. These federal agencies periodically conduct regional water supply studies, assessing the demand for and supply availability of water.

Theoretically, these broad regional studies identify potential projects, with specific project proposals prepared for and then examined by Congress. Congressional oversight of public works is divided between its authorizing and appropriation committees. Based upon legislation dating back to the 1930s, authorizing committees supposedly review the need for projects and ensure that they are cost-effective (see Chapter 2). Appropriation committees then determine the funding schedules, balancing the need for public works with other items, such as defense and public health and welfare. On paper, this process looks rational and democratic. Checks and balances are built into the system to assure that projects are truly

civilizations had well developed water-harvesting systems. Techniques included constructing ditches and low berms on hill slopes to catch water and building underground cisterns to store it. Among the modern adaptations of these techniques are corrugated roofs with gutters and ground-catchment areas with compacted soil. Stone, log, or vegetation barriers might be used to direct runoff and trap sediment on slopes. In very dry areas, single plants or trees are placed at the lowest point in small catchments, so they receive more water. More complex technologies involve clearing vegetation from large areas or converting shrub to grasses to increase water yield, covering the soil with impervious materials, such as wax or asphalt, and constructing large lined catchment basins. Because the water is not filtered by the soil, the runoff is often not of high enough quality for human consumption but can be used for watering cattle and for irrigation. Most water-harvesting techniques are best for very local applications, although vegetation conversion is being used on a large scale in parts of Arizona (Johnson and Renwick, 1979).

Wastewater reclamation simply means using dirty water over again instead of returning it to a stream or lake. During the late 1970s' drought in northern California, many people used the "grey water" from baths, dishes, and clothes washing to irrigate gardens and lawns. Most of the impurities are not harmful to plants, and wastewater contains many nutrients that may even be beneficial. Reuse of wastewater can satisfy additional demand for water without requiring additional supplies. Israel is the world leader in wastewater reuse. There, 95

needed and make economic sense. In practice, however, the federal government rarely if ever follows this procedure.

A good example of the peculiar politics of water supply projects is the Garrison Diversion Unit, an irrigation system being built by the Bureau of Reclamation in North Dakota. The project was first authorized by Congress in 1965 to open up new farmland to replace land lost along the Missouri River by an earlier flood-control project. By 1970 the entire rationale for the project had changed, without the expressed consent of Congress. Instead of mitigating farmland losses along the Missouri, the project now transferred water between two major watersheds, shifting water from one side of the state to another. The project included a 118-kilometer (74-mile) canal to irrigate 101,000 hectares (250,000 acres) on 1,300 farms, provide a source of water to 14 communities, and improve fish and wildlife

habitat. To irrigate these 101,000 hectares, 89,000 hectares (220,000 acres) of already productive farmland would be flooded, for a net gain of 12,000 hectares (30,000 acres). The project would also introduce polluted water into two rivers flowing north into Canada, raising trans-boundary pollution issues. Finally, the real costs and benefits of the project are unclear. The total cost is approximately a billion dollars, and the benefit-cost ratio is one to one. Yet the Bureau of Reclamation used an interest rate of 3.225 percent, the cost of borrowing money when the project was authorized in 1965, which reduced costs while inflating benefits.

Congress continued to authorize planning and construction money each year, until a lawsuit halted construction in 1977, with five percent of the project completed. The 1977 court order asked the Bureau to reexamine the project, giving Congress the chance to reauthorize, modify, or deauthorize

percent of the water used in industry and the home is recovered for use in irrigation (Ambroggi, 1980). Water from municipal sewage systems has been used for irrigation in several areas of the U.S., especially Texas and California, with considerable success. It must be partially treated (primary treatment is usually sufficient) to reduce health hazards, and it must not contain substantial amounts of hazardous substances, such as metals and toxic organic compounds. It is technically possible to treat wastewater thoroughly enough to make it suitable for drinking, but as yet this has not become widespread.

The greatest concerns with water reuse in irrigation are public health problems. The use of wastewater on food crops, possible discharges of polluted waters, and concentration of toxic substances, especially metals, in plant tissues are all cause for concern. Another possible problem is pollution of groundwater by percolation of irrigation water high in nitrates. These hazards require careful handling of the water and, in some cases, restrictions on what crops may be grown. For example, wastewater irrigation of crops that concentrate metals in edible portions of the plant should be avoided. However, if carefully managed, wastewater reuse offers considerable potential for providing new supplies of irrigation water in semiarid and arid areas.

Desalinization, or removing salt from seawater or brackish groundwater, is an appealing but costly undertaking. Water must be distilled by evaporating and condensing it, and this requires energy. Large-scale plants are expensive to run and maintain, and output is low compared to most conventional water sources.

---

it. By 1981, no new proposals had been presented, so area senators and representatives sponsored legislation to exempt the project from consideration by both Congress and the courts. The measure easily passed the Senate but was defeated in the House of Representatives. Two months later, an appeals court invalidated the 1977 court decision, throwing the issue back to Congress. The annual battle over the Garrison Diversion continues, with local representatives and senators ignoring the normal authorization and funding process and with the courts periodically adding to the confusion.

The twenty-year conflict over the Garrison Diversion follows a pattern set by other federal water projects, such as the Central Arizona Project, Tocks Island on the Delaware and the Cross-Florida Barge Canal. These projects take on a life of their own:

issues never seem to be resolved, politics not economcs dictate the actions of Congress and the courts, and the federal agencies responsible appear to operate independently. One reason for these long-drawn-out battles is the very nature of the federal government's role in water resource development.

The federal government pays as much as 90–95 percent of construction costs, and local matching funds are usually required only after construction is complete. Prices charged to local users of a project's water are also low. To local politicians, these projects provide tangible evidence of their work in Congress and their bringing jobs and money back to constituents. Reform-minded senators and representatives have therefore proposed legislation requiring cost-sharing and realistic pricing on public-works projects. To date, however, such reforms have failed to become law (Luoma, 1982).

In energy-rich Saudi Arabia, desalinization plants process 150 billion liters (40 billion gallons) of seawater per year (Ambroggi, 1980). However, over the ten years since desalinization was begun, the country's water demands have risen by 900 billion liters (220 billion gallons). It is unlikely that desalinization will make a significant impact on future water supplies, except in very special circumstances. Similarly, there have been some recent attempts to test the feasibility of towing icebergs from the Antarctic to water-poor areas. The amount of water that could be moved practically is very low, and the costs are very high.

Water Conservation

With any natural resource, problems of insufficient supply can be considered as problems of excess demand, and this is certainly true for water. Where water is plentiful and cheap, as it is in most of the U.S., it is used for a great many activities that are considered excessive in areas of short water supply or in time of drought.

The role of high demand in water resource problems is most evident in the dry states of the American West and Southwest. The region is dependent on the Colorado River for domestic and agricultural water, and competition for that source is rising with the Sunbelt population boom. One example is California's arid Coachella Valley, about 200 kilometers east of Los Angeles. A mountain-ringed basin, the valley receives an average of 75 to 125 mm (3 to 5 inches) of rain per year. With water diverted from the surrounding mountains for irrigation, American Indian populations and 19th-century white settlers were able to sustain a comfortable living. The mid-20th century brought tremendous population growth, from an estimated 850 in 1901 to 107,000 in 1978, not counting 60,000 seasonal residents and 1.5 million visitors annually. With this growth has come an immense rise in water use (Renwick, 1984).

The Coachella obtains its water from several sources, including groundwater, some mountain runoff, and water piped in from northern sources and from the Colorado River. These sources provide a reliable supply to the valley, and groundwater supplies are in good shape, according to official estimates.

Thus the residents, visitors, and developers have had no qualms about using water freely. There are over 35 public and private golf courses, which demand huge amounts of water in the summertime heat, with daily highs of around 46°C (115°F). Most of the valley's communities have green lawns and shade trees, which are very thirsty under desert conditions (see Figure 9.11). New developments and subdivisions, feeding on the human desire to see deserts transformed into gardens, include condominiums surrounded by moats and a proposed village in the style of Venice, Italy, with lagoons and canals and travel via gondola. One private estate supports a full-scale golf course dotted with twelve small lakes. The Coachella Valley also has a small but profitable agricultural industry, producing dates, grapes, carrots, and other vegetables and fruits. Although residential water demand is rising more rapidly than farming use, irrigation water must be pumped to every field to take advantage of those months when the heat is tolerable to crops (Renwick, 1984).

The Coachella is perhaps an extreme case of high water use in an arid climate, but it does illustrate the enormous demands placed on water resources

Figure 9.11 The Coachella Valley, California. Once a desert, this valley has been made lush with groundwater and imported water.

by a recreation- and irrigation-oriented society. It also highlights the tremendous potential for eliminating "nonessential" uses, should water supplies dwindle.

Several techniques are available to encourage conservation. One of the earliest to be widely used is metering, with payment for water based on use. Most American cities today meter almost all water, although New York City is a notable exception. Installation of meters has typically resulted in reductions in per-capita demand of 20 to 40 percent (Baumann and Dworkin, 1978). Pricing systems can also reduce demand. Most cities have either uniform or decreasing rates. Uniform rates do not vary with volume used; decreasing rates are highest per unit of water for small users and lower for those who use more. Increasing-rate schedules, in which rates increase with amount used, both encourage conservation and more closely reflect the costs of providing water. Such rates can significantly reduce consumption, depending on what price level is set.

Several structural or mechanical means to reduce water use are also available. Water pressure reduction is one of these. If the pressure in a distribution system is reduced, both flow rates through pipes and leakage rates are reduced. Flow regulators and similar devices can be used in homes and commercial establishments. Some are quite simple, including small discs inserted in faucets and shower heads, to reduce flow, and bricks, water bottles, or spacers used to reduce the amount of water used in each flush of the toilet. These devices can reduce water usage in the home by 30 to 70 percent (Flack, 1978).

Finally, restrictions on use are frequently employed, although these are generally short-term measures, enacted during time of shortage, rather than permanent measures. Some of the common restrictions are prohibition of car washing, restriction or prohibition of lawn watering or swimming-pool filling, and eliminating the automatic service of water at restaurants. Some of these can be quite effective, and in many areas lawn-watering restrictions are permanent. Other areas, such as Tucson, have landscaping restrictions to conserve water. This encourages use of desert plants rather than humid-region species, which need more water. Other methods, such as restricting water service in restaurants, are aimed more at generating public awareness of the problem than actually reducing water use.

CONCLUSIONS

When we consider all of the ways water consumption can be reduced in our daily lives, the potential reduction is great. Most of us could probably be just as comfortable and accomplish all the things we need to, while using half the water we currently use. Water conservation in industry and commercial establishments is not simple, but technological and process changes are possible, given the economic incentive to institute them. The potential for increased efficiency of manufacturing uses is reflected in the Water Resources Council's projections for water use in 2000, discussed earlier. Similarly, there is room for more efficient use of water in agriculture, particularly by installation of drip-irrigation systems. A major conservation method, as yet underused, is the rehabilitation of existing irrigation works, including reservoirs, canals, and drainage systems. The Food and Agricultural Organization recommends this overhauling as much less costly and having greater return on investment than the construction of new irrigation works.

Water is used in such large quantities that, for a water development plan to be feasible, it must provide water at a relatively low unit cost. In general, techniques that involve high technology, very large structures, or extensive public works are expensive. Long-distance pumping is a particularly expensive way to provide water because, in addition to the capital investment, there are substantial energy costs in running pumps. In evaluating the feasibility of water development for irrigation or industrial uses, it can be argued that the goal is really to provide employment and income for people rather than water per se. When the water development being considered is a high-cost project, one should ask whether the money could be better spent in providing jobs that either do not depend on water or are located in an area where water is more plentiful. For these reasons, most increases in water supply are more likely to be derived from more intensive use of surface and groundwaters near their sources, rather than use of icebergs, seawater, or water in remote polar areas.

Groundwater is still a developable resource for some dry regions, although it is not readily replaced once it is depleted. There are many areas of untapped groundwater resources, especially in the Third World. New groundwater supplies cost perhaps a third as much as water obtained by dam building. Surface-water development by dam construction has great potential for increasing supplies, particularly in the Third World. Many potential dam sites have been identified, and these can be developed as long as capital is available and the lost land can be replaced. However, with both costs and population levels rising, increases in supply and better management of demand will both be needed to provide adequate and high-quality water to areas where it is in short supply.

REFERENCES AND ADDITIONAL READING

Ambroggi, R.P. 1980. Water. *Scientific American* September 243:3:101–16.

Ashworth, W. 1982. *Nor any drop to drink.* New York: Summit Books.

Baumann, D.D., and D. Dworkin. 1978. Water resources for our cities. *Am. Assoc. Geogr. Resource Paper 78-2.*

Brewer, M.F., and R.F. Boxley. 1981. Agricultural land: adequacy of acres, concepts, and information. *Am. J. Ag. Econ.* 63:879–87.

California Department of Navigation and Ocean Development. 1977. Study of beach nourishment along the southern California coastline. Sacramento: The Resources Agency.

Coats, R. 1984. The Colorado River: river of controversy. *Environment* 26:2:7.

Council on Environmental Quality. 1981. *Environmental trends.* Washington, D.C.: Government Printing Office.

Flack, J.E. 1978. Management alternatives for reducing demand. In *Municipal water systems,* ed. D. Holtz and S. Sebastian, pp. 200–210. Bloomington, Indiana: Indiana University Press.

Hanley, R. 1980a. Water is franchised trouble in New Jersey. *New York Times* October 5.

———. 1980b. Delaware River water supply cut second time in a month for New York. *New York Times* November 20.

Hanson, D. 1982. The Colorado complex. *Living Wilderness* 45:157:27–35.

Johnson, J.F. 1971. *Renovated waste water: an alternative source of municipal water supply in the U.S.* University of Chicago, Department of Geography, Research Paper no. 135. Chicago.

Johnson, K., and H.L. Renwick. 1979. Rain and storm water harvesting for additional water supply in rural areas. Nairobi, Kenya: Unpublished monograph. U.N. Environment Programme.

Kasperson, R.E. 1969. Political behavior and the decision-making process in the allocation of water resources between recreational and municipal use. *Natural Resources Journal* 9:176–211.

Luoma, J.R. 1982. Water: grass-roots opposition stymies Garrison Diversion. *Audubon* 84(2):114–17.

Matthews, O.P. 1984. Water resources: geography and law. Washington, D.C.: Association of American Geographers.

Renwick, H.L. 1984. The decorated desert: a comparative study of vegetation resource cognition in the Coachella Valley, California. Ph.D. dissertation, Clark University.

Russell, C.S., D.G. Arey, R.W. Kates. 1970. Drought and water supply. Baltimore: Johns Hopkins University Press.

Seckler, D., ed. 1971. *California water: a study in resource management.* Berkeley and Los Angeles: University of California Press.

Sewell, W.R.D. 1976. The changing context of water resources planning: the next twenty-five years. *Natural Resources Journal* 16:791–806.

Strahler, A.N. 1975. Physical geography. 4th ed. New York: Wiley.

Water Resources Council. 1978. The nation's water resources, 1975–2000. Vol. 1. Summary. Vol. 2. Water quantity, quality, and related land considerations. Washington, D.C.: Government Printing Office.

White, G.F. et al. 1961. Papers on flood problems. University of Chicago, Department of Geography, Research Paper no. 70. Chicago: University of Chicago Press.

TERMS TO KNOW

aquiclude
aquifer
consumptive use
drought
desalinization
evapotranspiration

interbasin transfer
nonconsumptive use
overdraft
permeability
wastewater reclamation
water harvesting

STUDY QUESTIONS

1. Is groundwater a renewable resource? How does it travel below the ground surface?
2. What are two major ways to evaluate water availability?
3. What are the four components of water supply systems?
4. What are some negative and positive environmental impacts of water resource development?
5. Name and describe three newly important methods for increasing water supplies.
6. What are some major water conservation methods for industry and for the home?

CHAPTER TEN

Water Quality: Everybody's Problem

INTRODUCTION

Water pollution is perhaps the most universally recognized form of environmental pollution and the one about which people have been concerned the longest. Water is so basic to human health and prosperity that few people in either traditional or industrial societies are unaware of the importance of water quality. Our need for clean water and the importance of natural waterways in waste disposal caused it to be the first form of pollution that received widespread government attention, and it continues to be an important political topic. In many parts of the world, water free from disease or harmful chemicals is a scarce commodity. In the wealthier nations, the most visible forms of contamination are routinely removed from drinking water, but concern about minute quantities of toxic substances is increasing. And in nearly every populated area, the effects of water pollution on aquatic wildlife are significant.

BASIC PROPERTIES OF WATER

Although water is one of the most common substances on the surface of the earth, it has several unusual and remarkable properties. First, it is able to store large amounts of heat. Second, it is an excellent solvent, capable of dissolving large quantities of a wide range of substances. Third, it is relatively inert, able to dissolve substances without reacting with them. Salts, for example, are precipitated as easily as they are dissolved. Water therefore is an ideal transporter of other chemicals. Just as this property makes it the basis of life, it also makes water potentially dangerous, especially when it contains unwanted substances or excessive concentrations of normally harmless substances.

Among the many impurities found in natural and polluted waters are all of the common elements of the earth's crust and also some uncommon ones. While some of these, such as oxygen, are found in elemental form, most are in the form of compounds. Silicon dioxide (SiO_2), common salt ($NaCl$), iron sulfate ($FeSO_4$), and ammonia (NH_4) are among the common *inorganic* impurities. *Organic* (carbon-containing) compounds are usually found at lower dissolved concentrations, because they are generally less soluble than other substances. Carbonate (CO_3) is commonly found at relatively high concentrations, but generally organics are highly varied and include decay products from plant and animal matter, hydrocarbons of natural and human origin, and many other substances. In addition, water contains many living microorganisms, such as bacteria and protozoa, and of course larger organisms, from insects and water lilies to fish and giant kelp.

Just as there is a great range of kinds of impurities, the range of concentrations is also large. Impurities are usually measured in parts per thousand (ppt), parts per million (ppm), or parts per billion (ppb) and numerically range from one to 999. One part per million means that, by weight, for every million units of water, there is one unit of the impurity. One part per million is equivalent to one milligram per liter (mg/l). Seawater contains about 35 ppt of dissolved solids, or 3.5 percent by weight. Some groundwaters and inland lakes in arid regions have natural concentrations of dissolved solids several times greater than this. In humid regions with relatively insoluble bedrock formations, dissolved concentrations in surface waters are generally in the range of 10 to 100 ppm, on the order of 1000 to 100 times less than sea water. In the central part of North America, total dissolved solids are typically a few hundred ppm; some streams in the arid western U.S. reach 1000 to 2000 ppm (1 to 2 ppt) during part of the year. Individual ions, such as copper or silicon, in contrast, are usually found in concentrations of a few parts per million or less, although there are notable exceptions. Finally, relatively uncommon elements and such substances as exotic organic compounds like chloroform or PCBs are generally found only in concentrations of a few parts per billion or even parts per trillion.

These impurities come from many different sources, both natural and human, and it is often difficult to separate the two. When we speak of *pollution* or *pollutants,* we are usually referring to substantial human additions to a stream's or lake's load of impurities. A "polluted" stream is generally defined relative to its condition if unaffected by human activity, rather than in absolute terms. Similarly, acceptability of given levels of contamination depends on what we use the water for. For drinking water, absolute levels are important, so standards for drinking water are established by governmental and other agencies.

Pollutants come from diverse human-made and natural sources. One way to classify pollutant discharges is by point versus non-point sources. A *point source* is a specific location, such as a factory or municipal sewage outfall. A *non-point source* originates, as far as we know, from a large, poorly defined area. Runoff, subsurface flow, and atmospheric sources of water pollution are the primary non-point sources.

Some pollutants, such as iron or suspended particulates, may have very large natural sources, so that human activities only marginally increase concentrations. Other pollutants, such as synthetic pesticides, are produced only by humans. Most common impurities, however, are contributed by both human and natural processes. Therefore, except in extreme cases, human pollution is difficult to define quantitatively. Further, in a complex system such as a drainage basin, a given pollutant may have many different sources, including urban runoff, industrial effluents, municipal sewage, and even atmospheric precipitation, in addition to natural sources. Once in a stream system, pollutants may be removed by deposition, they may be broken down or combined with other impurities to make new substances, or their concentrations may be increased by chemical or biological processes. If a known quantity of a substance is put into a waterway, the amount that leaves may be greater or less, depending on the nature of the substances and the processes acting on it. Under these circumstances, it is virtually impossible to determine accurately the relative contributions of many sources or to predict with confidence future pollution levels. Understanding or managing a polluted water system is like trying to make a good pot of stew when there are half a dozen other cooks, and a few others you don't know about, who slip into the kitchen and add things when you aren't looking. For a government to carry out a rational, successful regulatory program is even more difficult.

MAJOR WATER POLLUTANTS AND THEIR SOURCES

The list of substances of concern in water quality assessments is long and getting longer every year. In part this increase is the result of advances in the analytic capabilities of laboratories and of the growth in available water-quality data. But there are so many substances that could be measured in a water sample and the analyses are so complex and costly, that usually only a few major (or indicator) pollutants are determined. Most analyses summarize pollution levels with such parameters as total dissolved solids (TDS) or biochemical oxygen demand (BOD). The following paragraphs describe, in general terms, the major classes of pollutants and their sources, human-health effects, and impacts on aquatic ecology. These categories are somewhat arbitrary and are intended to indicate the diversity of the pollutants found in our waters. The major pollutants, their sources, and environmental effects are shown in Table 10.1.

Organisms

Of the many living things found in natural or polluted waters, only a small fraction can be regarded as important pollutants from a human standpoint. These are the bacteria, viruses, and parasites that cause disease in humans and livestock. The earliest awareness of water pollution as an important human problem came from the recognition that water, particularly drinking water, transmits many diseases. Among the infectious diseases communicated largely through drinking water are cholera, typhoid fever, hepatitis, and dysentery, but many other less well known diseases are also transmitted in this manner. Most of these are transmitted through human or animal wastes, with sewage pollution as their primary source. Many different types of organisms are potentially dangerous, and even only one individual in a large amount of water may be sufficient to cause infection. The presence of *coliform bacteria* is an indicator of the likelihood of contamination by infectious organisms. Coliform bacteria live in great numbers in human and animal digestive systems, and their presence indicates the possibility that more dangerous organisms also inhabit the water. Chlorination of public water supplies has eliminated these diseases from common occurrence in the developed nations, but disease outbreaks still occur. For example, between 1971 and 1974, 99 outbreaks of waterborne infectious diseases, totaling 16,950 cases, occurred in the U.S. (National Research Council, 1977). Most of these were intestinal diseases, but four outbreaks of typhoid fever occurred. Major outbreaks of waterborne infectious diseases still occur in less developed nations, where public water supplies are not well protected or treated. Many other diseases are transmitted via organisms that live in water, such as snails and insects, schistosomiasis and malaria being well known examples. However, infection results from insect bites, skin contact, and other means, rather than from ingestion, and hence these organisms are not usually considered components of water quality.

Particulate Organic Matter

Suspended organic particles place the greatest burden on a stream or lake as a pollution assimilator. Particulate organics are small bits of living or dead and decaying plant and animal matter. They are broken down in the water by bacteria that use dissolved oxygen in the process. There is no widely used direct measurement for them, but *total suspended particulates* (TSP) and *biochemical oxygen demand* (BOD) are the most often used indicators of the concentration of particulate organics in the water. TSP includes both organic and inorganic matter. BOD indirectly measures organic particulates by measuring the amount of dissolved oxygen that is required to decompose the organic matter. A stream with a high BOD loading will consequently have a low concentration of dissolved oxygen (DO). The depletion of oxygen is primarily responsible for the ecological degradation of rivers and lakes. A second important role of organic particulates is their relation to trace pollutants, both organic and inorganic. Many of these substances travel attached to particles, and so their fate is in part governed by that of particulates.

Organic particulates are derived from surface runoff, internal production by algae and other plants, agricultural wastes, sewage, and various industries—especially food processing and paper pulp. The relative contributions of these sources vary from one area to another, but historically large concentrated sources have been responsible for the most severe cases of organic particulate pollution. These point sources include feed lots, pulp mills, sewage-treatment plants, and other major dischargers. More recently, however, as treatment facilities have been installed and upgraded, these sources have been reduced in importance. Since the 1930s to 1950s, when most states enacted pollution control laws, this most noticeable form of water pollution has been significantly reduced. Today, with the major point sources under regulation, more attention is given to diffuse or non-point sources, such as urban and agricultural runoff.

Inorganic Particulates

By weight, the largest pollutant in our waters is *inorganic particulates,* or sediment. These are measured, along with organic particles, as total suspended particulates in water samples. Sediment consists of particles of soil and rock, eroded from the land and from stream beds. Erosion is a natural process, and the movement of sediment through a river system helps to maintain the ecological integrity of that system. However, accelerated erosion of agricultural lands, erosion associated with urban construction, and similar activities have greatly increased the sediment loads of many streams.

Table 10.1 Major Water Pollutants, Their Sources and Effects

Type of Waste	Wastewater Sources	Water-Quality Measures	Effects on Water Quality	Effects on Aquatic Life	Effects on Recreation
Disease-carrying agents—human feces, warm-blooded animal feces	Municipal discharges, watercraft discharges, urban runoff, agricultural runoff, feedlot wastes, combined sewer overflows, industrial discharges	Fecal coliform, fecal streptococcus, other microbes	Health hazard for human consumption and contact	Inedibility of shellfish for humans	Reduced contact recreation
Oxygen-demanding wastes—high concentrations of biodegradable organic matter	Municipal discharges, industrial discharges, combined sewer overflows, watercraft discharges, urban runoff, agricultural runoff, feedlot wastes, natural sources	Biochemical oxygen demand, dissolved oxygen, volatile solids, sulfides	Deoxygenation, potential for septic conditions	Fish kills	If severe, eliminated recreation
Suspended organic and inorganic material	Mining discharges, municipal discharges, industrial discharges, construction runoff, agricultural runoff, urban runoff, silvicultural runoff, natural sources, combined sewer overflows	Suspended solids, turbidity, biochemical oxygen demand, sulfides	Reduced light penetration, deposition on bottom, benthic deoxygenation	**Reduced photosynthesis,** changed bottom organism population, reduced fish production, reduced sport fish population, increased non-sport fish population	Reduced game fishing, aesthetic appreciation
Inorganic materials, mineral substances—metal, salts, acids, solid matter, other chemicals, oil	Mining discharges, acid mine drainage, industrial discharges, municipal discharges, combined sewer overflows, urban runoff, oil fields, agricultural runoff, irrigation return flow, natural sources, cooling tower blowdown, transportation spills, coal gasification	pH, acidity, alkalinity, dissolved solids, chlorides, sulfates, sodium, specific metals, toxicity bioassay, visual (oil spills)	Acidity, salination, toxicity of heavy metals, floating oils	Reduced biological productivity, reduced flow, fish kills, reduced production, tainted fish	Reduced recreational use, fishing, aesthetic appreciation

Pollutant	Sources	Parameters	Environmental effect	Effects on fish	Effects on use
Synthetic organic chemicals—dissolved organic material, e.g., detergents, household aids, pesticides	Industrial discharges, urban runoff, municipal discharges, combined sewer overflow, agricultural runoff, silvicultural runoff, transportation spills, mining discharges	Cyanides, phenols, toxicity bioassay	Toxicity of natural organics, biodegradable or persistent synthetic organics	Fish kills, tainted fish, reduced reproduction, skeletal development	Reduced fishing, inedible fish for humans
Nutrients—nitrogen, phosphorus	Municipal discharges, agricultural runoff, combined sewer overflows, industrial discharges, urban runoff, natural sources	Nitrogen, phosphorus	Increased algal growth, dissolved oxygen reduction	Increased production, reduced sport fish population, increased non-sport fish population	Tainted drinking water, reduced fishing and aesthetic appreciation
Radioactive materials	Industrial discharges, mining	Radioactivity	Increased radioactivity	Altered natural rate of genetic mutation	Reduced opportunities
Heat	Cooling water discharges, industrial discharges, municipal discharges, cooling tower blowdown	Temperature	Increased temperature, reduced capacity to absorb oxygen	Fish kills, altered species composition	Possible increased sport fishing by extended season for fish which might otherwise migrate

Source: Council on Environmental Quality, 1981

For practical purposes, inorganic sediment is chemically inert and thus has little direct effect on the chemical quality of water. Like organic particulates, fine-textured inorganic sediment plays a role in the transport and deposition of trace substances in water. In this way, it can carry pesticides and nutrients from agricultural fields, as well as a wide range of harmful substances contained in urban runoff. Most sediment is easily filtered from water in drinking water treatment plants, and thus health hazards associated with sediment pollution are probably minimal. In some areas, notably western Lake Superior and some parts of Quebec, mining activities have polluted the water with significant quantities of minute asbestiform particles, suspected of having carcinogenic effects. The major harmful effects of sediment are economic, including damage to turbines and pumps, and reduction in reservoir capacity as sediment is deposited in impoundments. In extreme cases, sediment may also reduce stream channel capacity and contribute to flooding. Excessive sediment loads also modify stream habitats and restrict fish reproduction. Some fish are sensitive to chronic high levels of suspended sediment, which clogs gills, restricts vision, or otherwise interferes with their normal activity. There are also a few rivers, especially in the western U.S., where reduction in sediment loads through reservoir construction has caused detrimental effects downstream, notably erosion in the Grand Canyon and on Pacific beaches.

Plant Nutrients

Although aquatic plants require many different substances for growth, algal production is generally limited to a few key substances, primarily nitrogen and phosphorus. Nitrogen is available to plants in the form of nitrate (NO_3), nitrite (NO_2) and ammonia (NH_4); phosphorus is available mostly as phosphate (PO_3) (McCaull and Crossland, 1974). In natural systems, nitrogen is derived primarily from the decay of plant matter. Phosphorus, on the other hand, is made available by weathering of phosphorus-bearing rocks, entering streams either directly in ground or surface water or through decay of organic matter. Some phosphorus is also contained in precipitation. Nitrogen and phosphorus are found in large quantities in sewage, and they enter waterways both by the decay of organic particulates and dissolved in sewage treatment plant effluent. Runoff from urban and rural areas is also an important source. The close association between intensive agriculture and nitrogen in streams is clearly seen in Figure 10.1. Densely populated areas, such as the mid-Atlantic states, also have concentrations of nitrogen, which is derived from a combination of agricultural and urban sources.

When one or both of these nutrients are the factors limiting algal growth, their introduction stimulates rapid algal growth, called blooms. The algae then die and decay, releasing nutrients anew and adding to BOD. In swift-flowing rivers, this extra BOD loading is a relatively minor problem, but, in sluggish rivers and standing bodies of water, serious problems can result. One of the effects of increased nutrients in surface water is *eutrophication*. This is the process whereby a water body ages over geologic time, with the water becoming progressively shallower and nutrient-rich. Eutrophic lakes typically support species such as carp and catfish, while geologically young *oligotrophic* lakes support pike, sturgeon, whitefish, and other species that require higher oxygen levels,

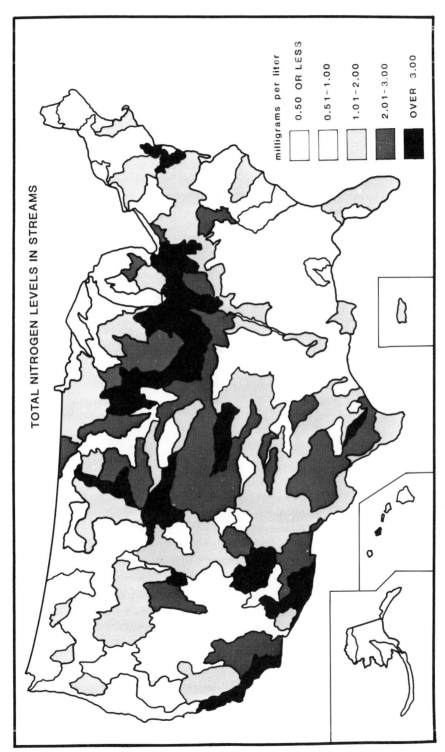

TOTAL NITROGEN LEVELS IN STREAMS

milligrams per liter

0.50 OR LESS
0.51–1.00
1.01–2.00
2.01–3.00
OVER 3.00

Figure 10.1 Total nitrogen levels in U.S. streams. Note the close association between intensive agriculture and nitrogen levels in streams. (Source: Water Resources Council, 1978)

cooler temperatures, or both. In summer, lakes commonly develop a stratification, or layering, that prevents the mixing of bottom and surface waters. If algal blooms occur, the algae settle to deeper waters, where decay depletes oxygen and deep-water fish suffocate. The absence of oxygen can also cause anaerobic decomposition of organic matter on the bottom, which produces unpleasant odors and may make water unsuitable for drinking. In addition, nutrient-rich waters may allow pathogenic organisms to live longer in the water, increasing the hazards of disease transmission to swimmers. Finally, decay of algae may impart unpleasant odors to the water, affecting the aesthetic quality of a river or lake.

In drinking water, phosphorus is not a problem, because it is an essential nutrient that humans require, generally ingested far more in food than in drinking water. Nitrate and nitrite, however, do present health hazards. When ingested in high concentrations, these lead to methemoglobinemia, a condition in which the ability of the blood to carry oxygen is impaired. In addition, ingestion of nitrate or nitrite may lead to the formation of compounds called nitrosamines, some of which have been found to cause cancer in laboratory animals, though the carcinogenic potential in humans is unknown.

Trace Minerals

Dissolved inorganic substances form a major part of the load of most rivers, and they include many different elements and compounds. Most of these are derived from rock weathering and soil leaching; geographic variations in mineral concentrations are often attributable to varying bedrock types. Hardness, which is measured by the presence of $CaCO_3$ and related minerals in water, is one of the most often measured indicators of dissolved minerals. Calcium carbonate, a good example of a substance dominated by natural sources, is primarily derived from marine sedimentary rocks. In areas of limestone bedrock, such as Florida and many areas of the central U.S. and Canada, hardness is commonly several hundred mg/l, but in areas of calcium-poor rocks, such as New England and the Canadian Shield, values of 5 to 25 mg/l are typical. In contrast, silver is relatively rare in the earth's crust but is quite important in a number of industrial processes. Cases of high silver pollution are almost always associated with mining or ore-processing activities, such as smelting, or with industrial sources. For most trace minerals, though, regional variations are attributable to natural factors, while local "hot spots" are almost always human-made.

There are many different inorganic minerals found in water, and it is wrong to make generalizations about their effects on humans or the environment. Many minerals are essential nutrients in trace quantities, but virtually all have detrimental effects at higher concentrations. Table 10.2 lists some of the important substances found in North American rivers. Major substances tend to be found at the ppm level, and minor substances generally in ppb.

Trace Organic Compounds

Organic compounds in the environment are even more diverse than inorganic substances, as are their sources. Some are of natural origin, primarily by-products of algal or bacterial activity. But those of greatest concern are human-made chemicals that enter waterways in industrial and municipal wastewaters and from

Table 10.2 Major and Minor Substances in North American Rivers, with Typical Concentrations

Major Substances		Minor Substances	
Substance	Concentration (ppm)	Substance	Concentration (ppb)
SiO$_2$	1–20	Ag	0–1
Fe	.001–2	Al	10–2500
Mn	.001–2	B	1–50
Ca	5–500	Ba	10–200
Mg	1–50	Co	0–10
Na	1–300	Cr	.5–100
K	1–10	Cu	.5–100
HCO$_3$	1–500	Mn	0–200
SO$_4$	5–1000	Ni	0–100
Cl	1–300	Pb	0–100
F	.01–1	Sr	5–1000
NO$_3$	1–10	V	0–10
CaCO$_3$	5–1000	Zn	0–300

Source: Modified from Durum, 1971

agricultural and urban runoff. They include herbicides, insecticides, and a wide variety of industrial organic chemicals, such as benzene, carbon tetrachloride, polychlorinated biphenols (PCBs), chloroform, and vinyl chloride. Oils and grease can also be included in this category; they are usually found at higher concentrations than the compounds mentioned above.

Trace organics are a major concern because many of them are toxic, carcinogenic, or both. They can be dangerous if present in only a few parts per billion or parts per trillion, particularly if they are accumulated in tissues or concentrated in the food chain. Table 10.3 shows some of the substances that are toxic or are known or suspected carcinogens. Adverse health effects may not be observed until many years after exposure. Consequently there is great uncertainty as to what substances are dangerous, at what levels of exposure. Many more years of intensive research are needed to understand the hazards associated with these substances.

One example of the problem of health hazards of trace organic substances is shown in a study of leukemia in the Boston suburb of Woburn, Massachusetts. The town contains a large toxic waste dump, which is believed to be a source of contamination for wells in the city's water supply. The wells have been closed since 1979. The study found a significant correlation between leukemia rates and consumption of water from contaminated wells. In a fourteen-year period, the leukemia rate in Woburn was 2.4 times the national average. There are also indications of a higher incidence of birth defects and other disorders associated with consumption of the water. However, not enough is known about the mechanisms by which consumption of contaminated water causes disease, to be sure that the wells were at fault or to know exactly what chemicals may be to blame.

In the environment, the greatest problems encountered with organic compounds are associated with *biomagnification* of persistent pesticides, which chemically break down very slowly. Thus, they may be passed up the food chain, becoming more concentrated at each stage, until they reach lethal levels. DDT is the most famous of these, because it was very widely used in the U.S. until it was banned in 1972. Since then concentrations in the biosphere in the U.S.

Table 10.3 Categories of Known or Suspected Organic Chemical Carcinogens Found in Drinking Water

Compound	Highest Observed Concentrations in Finished Water, μg/liter	Upper 95% Confidence Estimate of Lifetime Cancer Risk Per μg/liter
Human carcinogen		
Vinyl chloride	10	4.7×10^{-7}
Suspected human carcinogens		
Benzene	10	I.D.
Benzo (a) pyrene	D.	I.D.
Animal carcinogens		
Dieldrin	8	2.6×10^{-4}
Kepone	N.D.	4.4×10^{-5}
Heptachlor	D.	4.2×10^{-5}
Chlordane	0.1	1.8×10^{-5}
DDT	D.	1.2×10^{-5}
Lindane (γ-BHC)	0.01	9.3×10^{-6}
β-BHC	D.	4.2×10^{-6}
PCB (Aroclor 1260)	3	3.1×10^{-6}
ETU	N.D.	2.2×10^{-6}
Chloroform	366	1.7×10^{-6}
α-BHC	D.	1.5×10^{-6}
PCNB	N.D.	1.4×10^{-7}
Carbontetrachloride	5	1.1×10^{-7}
Trichloroethylene	0.5	1.1×10^{-7}
Diphenylhydrazine	1	I.D.
Aldrin	D	I.D.
Suspected animal carcinogens		
Bis (2-chloroethyl) ether	0.42	1.2×10^{-6}
Endrin	0.08	I.D.
Heptachlor epoxide	D.	I.D.

I.D. = insufficient data to permit a statistical extrapolation of risk; N.D. = not detected; D = Detected but not quantified.

Source: National Research Council, 1977

have generally declined, with a corresponding improvement in sensitive indicators, such as bird reproduction (see Figure 10.2). Nonetheless, it is still present and has been found all over the globe, including Antarctica. Other persistent pesticides banned or restricted in the U.S. since 1972 include chlordane, 2,4,5,T (silvex), and dieldrin.

In surface waters, trace organics are usually diluted, so that they are present only in very low concentrations, generally a few parts per trillion. They are found in higher concentrations in fine-grained sediments in many waterways, with runoff sources being particularly important. In groundwater, dilution is very slow and much higher concentrations have been found than in most surface waters. This is discussed in more detail in a later section of this chapter.

Heat

Electric-power generation, petroleum refining, and many other industrial processes depend on the production and dissipation of large amounts of thermal energy—

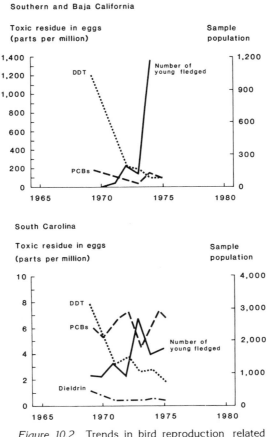

Figure 10.2 Trends in bird reproduction related to DDT, PCB, and Dieldrin pollution. (Source: Council on Environmental Quality, 1981)

heat. For example, typical efficiency levels in electric generation are 32 to 36 percent. This means that about a third of the energy produced at a power plant is converted to electricity, and the other two-thirds must be dissipated as heat, usually in the form of condensing steam. Any industrial process that requires heating and cooling produces waste heat, and water is the most effective means of dissipating that heat. Depending on the amount of heat discharged and the rate at which it is dispersed by the receiving waters, the temperature increase of the water may be as much as 10° to 20°C, though usually it is less. Another cause of *thermal pollution* in streams is removal of vegetation that shades the water. This is particularly severe when an area is deforested. Stream corridors, where shade trees are left along the stream banks, are effective in preventing this.

Heat in water has little direct effect on humans; warm water may be less pleasant to drink, but it is no less safe. The primary detrimental effects of thermal pollution are on fish. Most fish have critical temperature ranges required for survival, and these ranges differ among species (McCaull and Crossland, 1974). Spawning and egg development in lake trout, walleye, and northern pike, for example, are inhibited at temperatures above 9°C. Smallmouth bass and perch will not grow at temperatures above about 29°C; growth of catfish is possible at temperatures as high as 34°C. In some cases, thermal discharges have benefited fisheries by making otherwise cool water suitable for commercial species that require warmer temperatures, but generally the effects are negative. Equally important is the effect of temperature on dissolved oxygen concentrations. The amount of oxygen that can be dissolved in water decreases with temperature; water at 33°C holds only about half the oxygen that water at 0°C will hold. At high temperatures, the rate of bacterial activity increases, putting more demand on oxygen supplies just when saturation concentrations are low. Many fish kills are caused by a combination of high BOD and high temperatures, particularly in summer.

Radioactivity

Radioactivity, or the emission of particles by decay of certain radioactive substances, is a subject of much public concern today. Ionizing radiation, consisting primarily of alpha, beta, and gamma radiation, comes from many natural and human-made sources. The *rem,* or roentgen equivalent man, is a dosage measure of ionizing radiation, in terms of the biolgoical effect it causes. On the average, Americans receive a dosage of about 100 millirems (0.1 rems) per year from natural sources, and another 80 millirems from artificial sources, primarily diagnostic X-rays (National Research Council, 1977). The radiation from natural sources is primarily cosmic radiation from the sun and radiation from terrestrial materials, such as rocks, bricks, and concrete. An average of about 15 to 20 millirems comes from radioactive potassium 40 found in bone tissue.

Radioactive substances in water are primarily derived from rock weathering, particularly by groundwater. The greatest amount of radioactivity in water is from potassium 40, but this source is probably only about a hundredth of the amount derived from food sources. However, some substances tend to become concentrated in bone tissues, particularly strontium 90, radium 226, and radium 228. In certain areas, these isotopes occur in groundwater, and if the concentration is high, an increase in the risk of bone cancer is possible (National Research Council, 1977). In areas of mining or industrial operations that process rocks with a high content of radioactive materials, local radioactive water pollution may occur. In general, however, surface waters dilute these substances to the extent that concentrations are lower than those found in natural groundwaters.

Relative Contributions of Different Pollution Sources

The pollutants discussed in the preceding paragraphs come from many sources, and it is important to examine which sources are quantitatively most important. The relative contributions of point and non-point sources to U.S. waters are illustrated in Figure 10.3 for six important pollutants. Note that point sources contribute 10 percent or less of the total loading for suspended and dissolved solids, nitrogen, and phosphorus. For BOD, point sources are somewhat more important, but non-point sources still dominate. Dissolved heavy metals are derived mostly from point sources. Comparable data are not available for trace organic chemicals, but it is likely that pesticides are derived mostly from non-point sources, such as urban and agricultural runoff. Point sources are probably

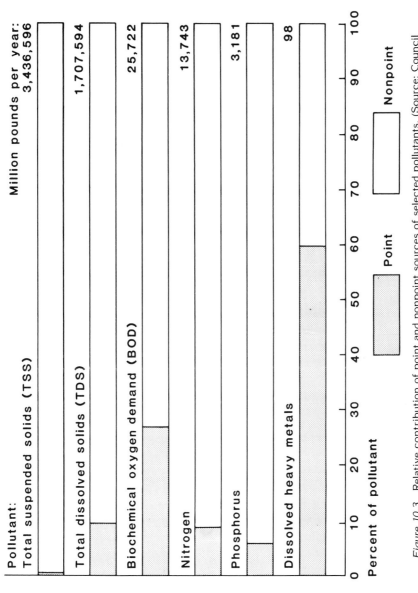

Figure 10.3 Relative contribution of point and nonpoint sources of selected pollutants. (Source: Council on Environmental Quality, 1981)

Table 10.4 Point Sources of Important Pollutants, 1977

Total Suspended Solids		Total Dissolved Solids		Biochemical Oxygen Demand	
Sector	Million Pounds per Year	Sector	Million Pounds per Year	Sector	Million Pounds per Year
Municipal sewage plants	3,850.0	Organic chemicals	36,540.4	Municipal sewage plants	3,800.0
Powerplants	1,165.7	Municipal sewage plants	30,255.2	Pulp & paper mills	530.2
Pulp & paper mills	781.8	Powerplants	18,418.1	Organic chemicals	107.6
Feedlots	422.0	Pulp & paper mills	16,825.8	Feedlots	95.9
Iron & steel mills	254.3	Misc. chemicals	8,176.4	Seafoods	86.9
Organic chemicals	144.0	Misc. food & beverages	7,420.2	Misc. food & beverages	54.8
Misc. food & beverages	91.9	Oil & gas extraction	6,077.0	Cane sugar mills	50.4
Textiles	61.7	Petroleum refining	2,389.8	Iron & steel mills	37.8
Mineral mining	52.7	Coal mining	1,328.7	Misc. chemicals	35.2
Seafoods	50.0	Iron & steel mills	1,324.0	Textiles	24.8
Total, Top 10 Sectors	6,874.1	Total, Top 10 Sectors	128,755.6	Total, Top 10 Sectors	4,823.6
Total, All Sectors	13,746.0	Total, All Sectors	170,759.0	Total, All Sectors	6,944.0
Total, Top 10 as Percent of All Sectors	50%	Total, Top 10 as Percent of All Sectors	75%	Total, Top 10 as Percent of All Sectors	69%

Nitrogen		Phosphorus		Dissolved Heavy Metals	
Sector	Million Pounds per Year	Sector	Million Pounds per Year	Sector	Million Pounds per Year
Municipal sewage plants	813.5	Municipal sewage plants	73.9	Powerplants	24.4
Pharmaceuticals	87.6	Feedlots	21.8	Municipal sewage plants	9.3
Organic chemicals	41.1	Misc. food & beverages	4.7	Iron & steel mills	7.6
Feedlots	39.9	Meat packing	3.4	Petroleum refining	6.0
Meat packing	36.0	Laundries	3.3	Organic chemicals	3.6
Petroleum refining	15.5	Fertilizers	2.6	Ore mining	2.5
Misc. food & beverages	12.3	Petroleum refining	1.5	Electroplating	0.5
Seafoods	9.5	Seafoods	1.4	Machinery	0.5
Pesticides	8.9	Organic chemicals	1.4	Oil & gas extraction	0.4
Leather tanning	7.1	Poultry	1.2	Foundries	0.1
Total, Top 10 Sectors	1,071.4	Total, Top 10 Sectors	115.2	Total, Top 10 Sectors	54.9
Total, All Sectors	1,237.0	Total, All Sectors	191.0	Total, All Sectors	59.0
Top 10 sectors as Percent of All Sectors	87%	Top 10 sectors as Percent of All Sectors	60%	Top 10 sectors as Percent of All Sectors	93%

Source: Council on Environmental Quality, 1981

more important for most industrial chemicals, although these are found frequently in urban runoff. Table 10.4 is a list of the most important point sources for the six pollutants in Figure 10.3.

FATE OF POLLUTANTS IN SURFACE WATER

Once added to rivers and lakes, the concentrations and chemical nature of pollutants change. These changes occur principally through four processes: dilution, biochemical decay, sedimentation, and bioconcentration.

Dilution

Dilution, the simple process of reducing pollutant concentrations by addition of water, is the most important way pollutant concentrations are reduced in the environment. The extent of dilution is a direct function of the volume of water in which the mixing takes place relative to pollution inflow. In a large river with high discharge, relatively small amounts of pollution are quickly reduced to low concentrations. Conversely, large inputs to small streams are diluted much less. In lakes, estuaries, and oceans, dilution is often restricted by stratification of the water body. Such layering, in which cold water underlies warm in lakes or salt water underlies fresh in estuaries, restricts vertical mixing and thus reduces the volume of water available to dilute pollutants.

There are two major problems with depending on dilution to disperse pollutants. First, river flow must not be depleted by dry spells or consumptive uses. A river may be able to assimilate wastes when flow is high, but the capacity to dilute pollutants is reduced at low flow. When a river is also used for public water supply or irrigation, which commonly demand the most water when flow is low, there may be acute problems. In the 1981 drought in New Jersey, discussed in Chapter 9, pollutant concentrations became so high that water treatment plants had to increase chlorination of potable water significantly.

Second, some pollutants may be undesirable regardless of their concentrations. This is true for extremely toxic substances, such as dioxin, and especially true for substances that are bioconcentrated in the environment. Environmentalists have long said: "The solution to pollution is prevention, not dilution," and this is certainly true for many substances. Nonetheless, dilution is effective for most pollutants, and it will probably continue to be the most effective and most used method of pollution reduction.

Biochemical Decay

Organic matter, especially particulate matter, is decomposed by organisms in water, particularly bacteria. This process leads to the release of nutrients, which stimulate growth of aquatic plants, which are in turn decomposed by bacteria. This cycle continues until the nutrients are removed from the system by dilution or sedimentation and are thus no longer available. A typical pattern observed downstream from a point source, such as a sewage outfall, is illustrated in Figure 10.4. This general pattern is essentially the same as the changes observed through time after a sudden influx of organic matter into a standing body of water, such as a lake.

Upstream from the pollution source, DO is relatively high and BOD and dissolved and suspended solids are low. The large increase in BOD causes a rapid decline in DO, and there is a corresponding decline in suspended solids as these are decomposed. Dissolved solids decline less rapidly, and their decline is usually more by dilution than by decomposition, though both may take place. Ammonia and phosphate are primary decay products, and their concentrations increase below the outfall. Further downstream, the concentration of nitrate increases as ammonia is oxidized to become nitrate. Dissolved oxygen recovers gradually, partly through contact with air above the stream, but also as algae, stimulated by the increase in nutrients, grow and add oxygen to the water.

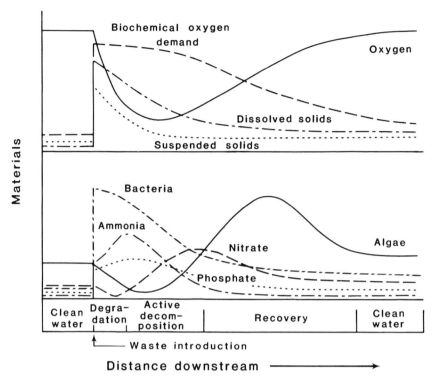

Figure 10.4 Schematic representation of downstream changes in pollution below a sewage outfall. (Source: Hynes, 1978, 6th edition)

Finally, further downstream, the nutrients are reduced in concentration and the stream returns to its original "clean" condition. The Delaware River provides a useful example (see Figure 10.5). A major DO sag occurs near the Philadelphia metropolitan area, but, within about forty miles downstream, DO has returned to about 80 percent saturation.

Two important conclusions can be drawn about biochemical decay. First, rivers have an enormous capacity to absorb common organic wastes and cleanse themselves through natural processes within a relatively short distance or period of time. Second, this assimilation of pollutants takes place at the expense of dissolved oxygen, which is of course essential to a productive aquatic community. If too much BOD is put on a river or if successive outfalls are closely spaced along the valley, the entire river may be damaged for the duration of the pollution input—or longer.

Sedimentation

Sedimentation is the deposition of organic and inorganic particles in water. It is a natural geologic process that occurs in rivers, lakes, and oceans, consisting simply of a settling out of particles in areas where flow velocity is low. Large particles eroded by a stream, such as sand and silt, are usually deposited quite near the stream channel, along the banks or on the floodplain. Smaller particles, such as clays and fine organic particles may be deposited in the channel, but

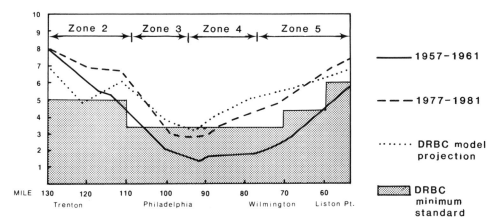

Figure 10.5 Dissolved oxygen patterns on the Delaware River. Dissolved oxygen declines below Trenton and in the vicinity of Philadelphia as a result of BOD discharges. Further downstream, DO levels recover. (Source: Council on Environmental Quality, 1983)

they are more likely to be carried to lakes or estuaries or else left on the floodplain during floods. Some trace substances—inorganic and organic—have a tendency to travel attached to particles rather than being dissolved, and sedimentation may remove substantial amounts of these pollutants from the water. In areas that receive large amounts of urban runoff or industrial discharges, contamination levels in sediments can be quite high. Pollutants then accumulate in the mud at the bottom of lakes and along streams. How permanent this removal from the water is depends on many factors, including the ability of plants and animals to consume the pollutants and reintroduce them to the environment. In some environments, particularly rivers, contaminated sediments may become resuspended and the contaminants reintroduced to the water (Renwick and Ashley, 1984). Concern about this possibility recently forced the dredging of large amounts of sediment contaminated with PCBs in the Hudson River. In most cases, however, sedimentation is an effective, if temporary, method of removing pollutants from the water.

Biomagnification

Biomagnification is the process of increasing the concentration of a substance in animal tissues, step by step through a food chain. As a rule of thumb, it takes about ten kilograms of food to make one kilogram of tissue in the animal or human consumer. If a substance has a tendency to be retained in animal tissues rather than metabolized or excreted, then its concentration in those tissues could be increased by as much as ten times for every step in the food chain. When a food chain has many steps, the ultimate concentration in the top consumer may be quite high.

Many of the persistent pesticides accumulate in the fatty tissues of animals. Although concentrations in most waterways now generally range from none detectable to several parts per billion, fish and bird tissues frequently contain DDT and other pesticides at the level of a few parts per million. U.S. average concentrations of DDT and its metabolic derivatives in human tissues were about

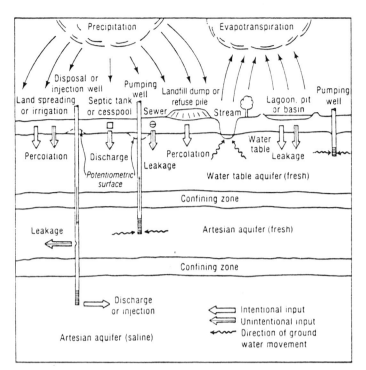

Figure 10.6 Sources of groundwater contamination include septic tanks, landfills, lagoons, and waste disposal wells. (Source: Environmental Protection Agency, 1980)

8 ppm in 1970, but declined to 5 ppm by 1976 (Council on Environmental Quality, 1981). Other hazardous substances that have become bioconcentrated include PCBs and strontium-90, the latter of which tends to become concentrated in bone tissues. Persistent pesticides generally occur in higher concentrations in aquatic sediments than in the water, and it is likely that they will be found in animal and human tissues for a long time.

GROUNDWATER POLLUTION

Groundwater pollution is probably the most serious water-quality problem facing the U.S. today. As shown in Chapter 9, groundwater is an essential source of drinking water. Awareness of the potential magnitude of the problem has come only recently, and there is still much to be learned. In the past, it was generally thought that groundwater was free from contamination by surface sources. But since the late 1970s, concern about toxic chemicals in the environment has prompted much more extensive sampling and analysis of both surface water and groundwater. In many areas, these analyses have shown alarming concentrations of such substances as nitrate, chloride, trichloroethylene, chloroform, benzene, toluene, and carbon tetrachloride. The concentrations are often much greater than those found in surface waters.

Figure 10.7 The Kin-Buc landfill (center), a toxic waste dump adjacent to the Raritan River, New Jersey. In the lower left is an abandoned sanitary landfill.

Vulnerability of Groundwater to Pollution

As discussed in Chapter 9, groundwater represents a large storage of water that is replaced very slowly. Whereas typical flow velocities for rivers are measured in meters per second, groundwater is likely to flow at rates of meters per day or even meters per year. In most cases, flow distances are quite large, and it takes from decades to millennia to replace contaminated water in an underground reservoir, if it can be replaced at all. This has two important consequences. First, once an aquifer is contaminated, it is lost for an indefinite period of time, except for uses not affected by the contaminants. Second, the contamination being discovered in wells today may result from pollutant discharges years in the past, and chemicals dumped today may not show up in well water for years to come. Not only are flow rates low, but the purification processes that remove natural particulates and bacteria are not as effective against human-made chemicals, such as chlorinated hydrocarbons. Such chemicals that seep into an aquifer are likely to remain there with little or no dilution or degradation.

Sources of Contaminants

There are many different sources of groundwater contamination, including municipal and industrial landfills, industrial impoundments, household septic systems, and waste disposal wells. These sources are illustrated in Figure 10.6.

Municipal and industrial landfills are used to dispose of nearly every kind of waste imaginable, most of it relatively harmless but some quite dangerous. Industrial landfills may receive much greater volumes of toxic materials (see Figure 10.7). The Love Canal site near Niagara Falls, New York, the Petro

Figure 10.8 An unlined chemical waste lagoon. This lagoon was built on floodplain alluvium, a few hundred meters from a potable water supply intake.

Processors site in Louisiana, and the Stringfellow Acid Pits in California are some of the more notorious industrial landfills that have contaminated groundwater through improper disposal of hazardous wastes (Brown, 1979). Municipal landfills, of which there are tens of thousands in the U.S., also receive hazardous wastes from household, commercial, and industrial sources, though generally in small quantities. Landfills are often located on whatever land is available, rather than specifically in areas that are geologically suited for waste disposal. Until recently little care was taken to see that *leachate* (liquid seeping out of the base of a landfill) could not percolate to an important aquifer.

Industrial impoundments, such as storage lagoons and tailings ponds, are another important cause of groundwater pollution. Lagoons may be used to store liquid wastes temporarily prior to disposal, reprocessing, or other use (see Figure 10.8). If the impoundments are unlined, as most are, liquid wastes can percolate to groundwater. In still other cases, wastes are intentionally pumped into the ground as a disposal method. In confined, unusable aquifers, this can be a safe practice, but leakage may occur. Tailings ponds, or impoundments used to trap mining debris, sometimes cause severe contamination with acids or metals.

Household septic tanks with leach fields are used for sewage disposal in almost 20 million households in the U.S. Properly designed, constructed, and maintained septic systems are effective water purifiers, returning clean water to the ground and nutrients to the soil. They are generally used where population density is relatively low, such as in rural and outer suburban areas. If they are used in higher density areas than is appropriate for the local soil and water conditions or if they are not properly built and maintained, pollution can result.

Table 10.5 Concentrations of Selected Synthetic Organic Compounds in Raw and Finished Groundwater (Micrograms per Liter = Parts per Billion)

Compound	Number of cities sampled		Percentage with chemical present		Concentration Mean		Concentration Median		Concentration Range	
	Raw	Fin	Raw	Fin	Raw	Fin	Raw	Fin	Raw	Fin
Trichloroethylene	13	25	38.5	36.0	29.72	6.76	1.3	0.31	0.2-125.0	0.11-53.0
Carbon tetrachloride	27	39	7.4	28.2	11.5	3.8	11.5	2.0	3.0- 20.0	0.2 -13.0
Tetrachloroethylene	27	36	18.5	22.0	0.98	2.08	0.6	3.0	0.1- 2.0	0.2 - 3.1
1,1,1-Trichloroethane	13	23	23.1	21.7	4.8	2.13	1.1	2.1	0.3- 13.0	1.3 - 3.0
1,1-Dichloroethane	13	13	23.1	23.1	0.7	0.3	0.8	0.2	0.4- 0.9	0.2 - 0.5
1,2-Dichloroethane	13	25	7.7	4.0	0.2	0.2	NA	NA	0.2- NA	0.2 - NA
Trans-dichloroethylene	13	13	15.4	15.4	1.75	1.05	1.75	1.05	0.2- 3.3	0.2 - 1.9
Cis-dichloroethylene	13	13	38.5	30.8	13.56	9.35	0.1	0.15	0.1- 69.0	0.1 -37.0
1,1-Dichloroethylene	13	13	15.4	7.7	0.5	0.2	0.5	NA	0.5- 0.5	0.2 - NA
Methylene chloride	27	38	3.7	2.6	4.0	7.0	NA	NA	4.0- NA	7.0 - NA
Vinyl chloride	13	25	15.4	4.0	5.8	9.4	5.8	NA	2.2- 9.4	9.4 - NA

NA = Not applicable

Source: U.S. Environmental Protection Agency, Office of Drinking Water, "The Occurrence of Volatile Organics in Drinking Water," briefing paper, March 6, 1980; Council on Environmental Quality, 1980

Figure 10.9 A secondary sewage treatment plant in Seattle, Washington.

This pollution may be either in the form of nutrients and bacteria seeping into surface waters or in the contamination of groundwater, usually with nutrients. Nitrate contamination of groundwater by septic systems is a subject of concern in some areas.

Septic tanks must be cleaned regularly, either by pumping out accumulated sludge or by using a chemical cleaner that dissolves the sludge and allows it to pass through the leach field. These chemical cleaners usually contain trichloroethylene, benzene, or methylene chloride, and in most areas they are readily available and cheaper than a pump-out. Trichloroethylene and benzene are suspected carcinogens. In areas with a high density of houses with septic systems, this can cause widespread groundwater contamination.

The Extent of Groundwater Pollution

Only recently have people begun to realize the nature of groundwater contamination, and thus relatively few data are available. The nationwide studies that have been done in the U.S. suggest great potential for pollution, if not confirming its occurrence. In 1980, the U.S. Environmental Protection Agency (EPA) surveyed 39 cities that use groundwater for drinking, testing untreated and treated water for a variety of organic chemicals (see Table 10.5). They found that a significant percentage of the water supplies tested had these substances in both untreated and treated groundwater, usually at the level of tenths to tens of parts per billion. This is a very small sample of water supplies, however, and conditions may vary locally. Many people feel that there is a great potential for more contamination to occur in the future or for present contamination to be found, and there is

Figure 10.10 Shopping carts: ubiquitous pollutants of urban streams.

reason to be fearful. For example, a 1980 survey (Silka and Brasier, 1980) identified some 25,749 industrial impoundments in the U.S. Of the 8,163 studied, it was found that 50 percent may contain hazardous substances, 70 percent are unlined, and 95 percent have no groundwater monitoring to detect contamination. Clearly, there is widespread potential for pollution. Whether or not this results in actual pollution and whether or not such pollution is hazardous to humans or the environment remain to be determined.

WATER POLLUTION CONTROL

Control Methods

Because of the many different sources and kinds of water pollution, control is a complex and expensive problem. Wastewater discharged by point sources can be treated by a variety of methods, but non-point sources must be controlled through land management. Sewage-treatment methods include primary, secondary, and tertiary techniques. *Primary treatment* (see Figure 10.9) consists of removal of solids by sedimentation, flocculation, screening, and similar methods. Primary treatment may remove about 35 percent of BOD, 10 to 20 percent of plant nutrients, and none of the dissolved solids. *Secondary treatment* removes organic matter and nutrients by biological decomposition, using methods such as aeration, trickling filters, and activated sludge. It became widely used in the U.S. during the 1960s. This treatment removes about 90 percent of BOD, 30 to 50 percent of nutrients, and perhaps 5 percent of dissolved solids. *Tertiary methods* have come into widespread use only in the last decade or so, and today only a small proportion of communities have tertiary treatment. There are many methods under this heading, and they vary considerably in their effectiveness, but generally they remove 50 to 90 percent of nutrients and dissolved solids. Treatment methods for industrial wastewater are usually specific to the type of wastes being considered. Many industries discharge into municipal sewage systems rather than treating wastes on site, although pretreatment is often required.

Non-point sources are the most difficult to control. In rural areas, pollution from non-point sources consists primarily of suspended and dissolved solids, nutrients, and pesticides contained in runoff, either dissolved or in particulate form. In agricultural areas, control of overland flow can do much to limit these sources, because soil eroded by water often contains harmful pollutants, such as pesticides and nutrients. But, as shown in Chapter 6, such management practices are often difficult to establish or enforce. In urban areas, runoff from streets, parking lots, and similar surfaces usually contains large amounts of suspended solids and BOD, as well as many toxic substances (see Figure 10.10). In cities with combined storm and sanitary sewers, runoff is routed through the treatment system, but during storms the treatment plant cannot handle the increased flow, so sewage and runoff are both discharged untreated. The sewage discharge has generally been regarded as the more serious problem, and most cities have converted or are converting to separate sanitary and storm sewer systems. This eliminates the problem of untreated sewage discharges, but does little to solve the problem of urban runoff pollution, as storm water is discharged directly without treatment. In newly developing areas, storage basins can be incorporated into storm water systems to retain runoff temporarily or permanently,

---

ISSUE 10.1: The Manasquan River Basin Project: More Problems than Solutions

Central and southern New Jersey need new water supplies. As people and industry move into once-rural areas and as visitors are drawn by the immense attraction of Atlantic City, the area's surface and groundwater supplies have become inadequate for the demand. To increase water-storage capacity in this region, New Jersey's Water Supply Master Plan has called for reactivation of a reservoir scheme that had, after much earlier research, been set aside as unnecessary.

The Manasquan River drains 210 square kilometers, with headwaters in Freehold Township. It flows through areas of agricultural, residential, and light industrial development, emptying into the Atlantic Ocean. Under the present plan, a small reservoir, a pumping station, and a series of pipes would collect and convey the water from the Manasquan. If developed, the reservoir system would yield 133 million liters (35 million gallons) of potable water per day to coastal and inland communities, helping to rectify a projected water shortfall for the year 2000.

The catch in this apparently simple development lies in the word potable. Since the original proposal to develop a reservoir here was made in the late 1950s, two major toxic-waste dumps have been found within the Manasquan drainage. Thus, there is great concern, especially on the part of local citizens, that the new water supply will be undrinkable from its inception.

How realistic are these fears? The two dumps, Lone Pine Landfill and Bog Creek Farm, are located sixteen and five miles,

and these may be useful in reducing runoff pollution. But in developed areas, control of urban runoff is usually prohibitively expensive.

Government Efforts to Control Pollution

Prior to the early 20th century, little was done to control water pollution in the U.S. Some cities experienced problems of sewage contamination of water supplies, but generally the solution was simply to separate the water intake from the sewage outfall, rather than to treat the sewage. Beginning around 1900 and growing rapidly by the 1940s, wastewater treatment was instituted in the cities. A few states had pollution control laws, and the 1948 Federal Water Pollution Control Act provided impetus for construction of treatment plants. As recently as 1960, however, only about 36 percent of the population served by sewers had wastewater treatment, and this was almost exclusively primary treatment (Council on Environmental Quality, 1981). The remaining 64 percent were served by sewer systems with no treatment at all. In 1961 and 1965, however, new federal laws greatly increased nationwide efforts at pollution control, mostly by providing funds for construction of treatment plants. By 1970, over 85 million Americans, or 52 percent of those with sewer systems, were served by treatment plants (Council on Environmental Quality, 1981). The most ambitious and comprehensive law to date is the Federal Water Pollution Control Act of 1972, with its amendments of 1977 and 1980. Collectively known as the Clean Water Act, they now form the basis of our nationwide pollution control efforts.

The Federal Water Pollution Control Act of 1972 established a federal goal of making all waters clean enough to fish and swim in by 1985. It provides for

respectively, upstream from the planned water supply intakes, at which point river water would be transferred to the reservoir. It is likely that later, if not sooner, contaminants from these two sites will reach the river and enter the water supply. Both dumps are discharging organic pollutants, some of them known or suspected carcinogens and mutagens. Samples taken from the water column, sediment, and fish tissues indicate that there is no present danger from these contaminants. However, groundwater supplies near the two landfills have been affected, though the size of the plumes is unknown. River biota near Lone Pine have been greatly damaged.

Clearly, a problem exists. This area of New Jersey needs new water supplies. The reports, preliminary studies, and land ac-

quisition processes are complete for the project. Everything is in place to rapidly construct and use this much-needed storage facility. However, the water may be unusable. The New Jersey Water Development Authority is going ahead with the next stages of the project, confident that, because a team of water quality experts has been brought in early on, the two toxic waste sites can be cleaned up and their eventual impact minimized by treatment of the water (Division of Water Resources, 1982). It is symptomatic of America's rapidly growing water quality problems that the best choice for a new water supply is already contaminated.

establishment of effluent standards for industries and municipal treatment plants and for comprehensive local planning to reduce both point and non-point pollution. Municipal plants were required to achieve secondary treatment by 1977 and "best practicable" technology by 1983. Similarly, industries were required to use best practicable technology by 1977 and best available technology by 1983. All point dischargers are required to obtain discharge permits under the National Pollutant Discharge Elimination System, which was originally administered by the EPA, though today some states are taking over the permitting process. Permits allow discharges only within limits established by the permitting agency.

The actual conditions for issuance of permits are primarily determined by the permitting agency, and these conditions have changed with changing public opinion and availability of funds. During the 1970s, for example, the Environmental Protection Agency was relatively rigorous in enforcing compliance with effluent standards, although deadlines for compliance were frequently postponed. More recently, however, standards have been relaxed in some areas, where it is argued either that water quality is already high enough or that improved treatment will probably not result in significant improvement of water quality. One example of this administrative modification of the law came in 1982, when the EPA announced that it would no longer require secondary treatment for certain cities, including New York, discharging wastes into coastal waters.

The importance of non-point sources (particularly when major point sources are controlled) is recognized by the Federal Water Pollution Control Act of 1972, which requires the establishment of local- or regional-level planning to reduce non-point pollution. Plans vary from one area to another, depending on the nature of the sources and local needs. Most plans include provisions for runoff and sediment control at construction sites, as well as guidelines for non-point pollution control in new developments. In some urbanized areas, measures such as street sweeping have been instituted. As with the measures for controlling point sources, local plans are subject to modification by the agencies concerned, depending on local needs and desires. As a result, actual implementation of the federal law's guidelines has varied greatly from place to place and from time to time.

In 1977 the Clean Water Act was passed, amending earlier legislation. One of the more important aspects of this act was to focus government regulatory efforts on toxic substances rather than on the more conventional pollutants, such as BOD or nutrients. Under this law, the EPA has established industry-specific effluent limits for many common toxic substances and has developed a system of monitoring certain index contaminants as a means to reduce monitoring costs.

Water Quality Trends

As a result of these and other legislative efforts, water quality has improved in many areas. As of 1978, virtually all sewer systems had treatment methods, most of these with secondary treatment or better. Water quality violation rates for some pollutants have declined markedly in major rivers. The Cuyahoga River, near Cleveland, Ohio, notorious for catching fire repeatedly in the 1950s and 1960s, is no longer flammable. Lake Erie, pronounced "dead" by environmentalists in the 1960s, has shown some signs of improvement. But progress has generally not been as dramatic as was hoped. The regulations were effective in reducing industrial discharges in many areas, and industries made substantial investments in pollution-control equipment. Municipal pollution-control efforts depended on both local revenues and federal assistance, and lack of funds or political disputes often delayed treatment plant construction. For example, a 1980 estimate by the EPA indicated that 63 percent of the major municipal treatment facilities were not yet in compliance with the 1977 deadline for secondary treatment (Council on Environmental Quality, 1980). Difficulties experienced by municipalities in meeting federal requirements have led to some relaxation of the regulations.

Average annual violation rates for fecal coliforms, DO, and total phosphorus have remained relatively constant, at about 35 percent, 5 percent, and 50 percent, respectively. It is also quite clear that many of our major rivers are not going to be suitable for either fishing or swimming for several years at least, if ever.

One reason water quality has not improved nationwide is that, while on a per-capita basis we are discharging less, the nation is still growing. Improvements in some areas are offset by degradation in formerly less developed areas. In addition, the overwhelming importance of non-point sources and the difficulty in controlling them are major barriers to further water quality improvements. Finally, few data are available on pollution by toxic substances. Most of the reductions in discharges have been in substances more easily detected with indicator pollutants such as oil and grease or BOD. There continues to be considerable public concern about toxic substances in the environment, however, and they are the primary focus of most new regulatory initiatives at both the federal and the local levels. Detection and control of toxic substances are difficult, and the effectiveness of present regulations is unknown.

REFERENCES AND ADDITIONAL READING

Brown, M. 1979. *Laying waste.* New York: Pantheon.

Camp, T.R., and R.L. Meserve. 1974, *Water and its impurities.* 2nd ed. Stroudsburg, Pennsylvania: Dowden, Hutchinson & Ross.

Council on Environmental Quality. 1980. *Environmental quality 1980.* Washington, D.C.: Government Printing Office.

———. 1981. *Environmental trends.* Washington, D.C.: Government Printing Office.

———. 1983. 1982 annual report of the council on environmental quality. Washington, D.C.: Government Printing Office.

Division of Water Resources. 1982. The Manasquan Reservoir project: summary and recommendations. Trenton: New Jersey Department of Environmental Protection.

Durum, W.H. 1971. Chemical, physical, and biological characteristics of water resources. In *Water and Water Pollution Handbook, vol. 1,* ed. L.L. Ciaccio, pp. 1–49. New York: Marcel Dekker.

Haynes, H.B.N. 1966. *The biology of polluted waters.* Liverpool: University of Liverpool Press.

McCaull, J., and J. Crossland. 1974. *Water pollution.* New York: Harcourt, Brace, Jovanovich.

National Research Council. 1977. *Drinking water and health.* Washington, D.C.: Government Printing Office.

Renwick, W.H., and G.M. Ashley. 1984. Sources, storages and sinks of fine-grained sediment in a fluvial-estuarine system. *Bull. Geological Soc. of America* 95.

Silka, L.R., and F.M. Brasier. 1980. *The national assessment of the ground water contamination potential of waste impoundments.* Washington, D.C.: U.S. Environmental Protection Agency.

Water Resources Council. 1978. *The nation's water resources, 1975–2000.* Washington, D.C.: Government Printing Office.

Wolman, M.G. 1971. The nation's rivers. *Science* 174:905–18.

TERMS TO KNOW

biochemical decay
biomagnification
BOD
coliform bacteria
DDT
dilution
dissolved oxygen
Federal Water Pollution Control Act
leachate

non-point source
point source
polychlorinated biphenyl
primary treatment
rem
secondary treatment
suspended particulates
2,4,5,T
urban runoff

STUDY QUESTIONS

1. What are the main properties of water?
2. List the eight major classes of water pollutants. What are their sources and health effects?
3. What four major processes alter pollutant concentrations, once pollutants are added to waterways?
4. Why is groundwater pollution a growing problem?
5. What are the major contaminants of groundwater?
6. What do primary, secondary, and tertiary treatment methods consist of?

CHAPTER ELEVEN

Air Quality and Global Impacts

INTRODUCTION

Although air quality may appear as a recent issue to many people, some parts of the U.S. and Europe have been plagued with air pollution problems since the industrial revolution. Air pollution is a significant health hazard, in which acute episodes cause death and lower prolonged levels adversely affect health (National Research Council, 1979; Goldsmith and Friberg, 1977; Lave and Seskin, 1977). Some of the more prolonged air pollution episodes can even be classified as disasters. For example, 20 people died in Donora, Pennsylvania, in 1948, and between 3,000 and 4,000 people lost their lives in London, England, in 1952 due to thick smog. More recently, nearly 6,000 people were treated for "smog poisoning" in Tokyo during a 1970 oxidant and sulfate episode (Goldsmith and Friberg, p. 476). All of these disasters were the result of a combination of meteorological conditions and excessive emissions of sulfur from coal burning. The situation today is not so dramatic, yet in some parts of the country, we find that major pollution episodes require both industry and individuals to curtail their activities on a fairly regular basis.

AIR POLLUTION METEOROLOGY

Composition and Structure of the Atmosphere

The atmosphere is divided into a number of layers, based on temperature and gaseous content. The *homosphere,* or lower atmosphere, extends from sea level to an altitude of 80 km (50 miles) (see Figure 11.1). It is called the homosphere because the gases are perfectly diffused, so that they act as a single gas. These gases include nitrogen (78 percent), oxygen (21 percent), carbon dioxide (0.03 percent), and inert gases, such as argon, neon, helium, and krypton (<1 percent).

The homosphere is further divided into the troposphere, stratosphere, and mesosphere. The *troposphere* is the layer humans live in. It extends from sea level to approximately 13–14 km (8–9 miles). In this layer, temperature steadily decreases with altitude, at an average rate of 6.4°C/km (3.5°F/1000 feet). This rate is called the *environmental lapse rate.*

The next layer is the *stratosphere.* Air temperatures are essentially constant in this layer and then gradually increase with altitude until they reach 0°C (32°F)

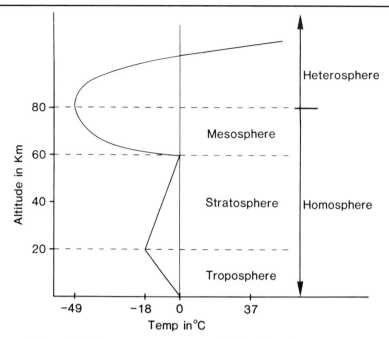

Figure 11.1 Temperature variation with altitude in the atmosphere. Most pollution is found in the troposphere, but some pollutants are carried to the stratosphere.

at an altitude of about 50 km (30 miles). The protective ozone (O_3) layer is located in the stratosphere. This layer serves as a shield, protecting the earth's surface and the troposphere from harmful ultraviolet radiation.

The third layer of the homosphere is the *mesosphere.* Here, temperatures decrease with altitude, reaching a low of $-83°C$ ($-120°F$) at approximately 80 km (50 miles) altitude.

Air pollutants are not confined to the lower parts of the troposphere. Certain concentrations of contaminants may have disastrous effects at higher altitudes, with great impact on global climate changes.

Role of Meteorology and Topography

Air pollution problems are the result of two factors: excessive emissions of pollutants and insufficient atmospheric dispersal. The first factor is the reason most cities have pollution problems and most rural areas do not. The second explains much of the variation in pollution problems from one city to another. It also explains why some very small cities have pollution problems as severe as those in major metropolitan regions.

Atmospheric dispersal of pollutants depends on air motion—both horizontal and vertical. Horizontal movements, or winds, carry pollutants away from cities. On windy days, the air in most cities is generally cleaner, and on calm days it is dirtier. Despite the reputations that some cities have for being windy, average wind speeds do not vary much from place to place, and wind speed is not an

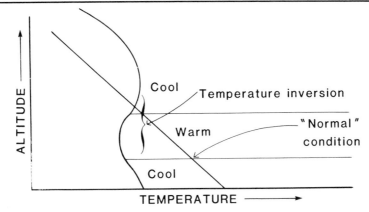

Figure 11.2 Temperature inversion. A temperature inversion consists of a layer in which temperature increases with altitude instead of decreasing. This prevents vertical circulation through the inverted layer.

important factor in explaining spatial variations in pollution. Horizontal movements also contribute to vertical motions, which play a much more important direct role in air pollution.

Vertical movement in the atmosphere results from wind-generated turbulence and convection. Convection is a result of differential heating of the lower layers of the atmosphere by sunlight. The warmer layers become less dense and therefore rise, while cooler layers sink. Regional circulation patterns, characterized by areas of high and low pressure, can be seen as a larger-scale form of convection. The normal temperature pattern—cooler air at higher elevations—prevails when there is sufficient vertical mixing through the lower atmosphere. Sometimes, however, warmer air overlies cooler air. This condition is called a *temperature inversion* (see Figure 11.2). An inversion keeps the atmosphere stable and thus inhibits vertical motions. Such inversions are the major meteorological factor in most air pollution problems.

Temperature inversions are caused by several different processes, including subsidence, radiation, and advection. A *subsidence inversion* develops when an air mass sinks slowly over a large area, as is common in a high pressure cell. The atmosphere is compressed as the air mass sinks, and higher layers are warmed more than lower layers, resulting in an inversion. Subsidence inversions are formed over large areas (hundreds of square kilometers), usually at relatively high altitudes, but can occur as low as 1000 meters above the surface. The weather that produces them (slow-moving high pressure cells) also produces sunny conditions and gentle winds, which contribute to photochemical smog formation and poor dispersal of pollutants. Subsidence inversions are responsible for most of the severe pollution episodes in large cities east of the Rocky Mountains and contribute to problems in mountainous areas.

Radiation inversions also develop in clear, relatively calm weather, but, unlike subsidence inversions, they are a diurnal phenomenon. On clear nights, the ground radiates heat upward, and the absence of clouds allows this radiation to escape to the upper atmosphere and into space. The result is that the ground cools more than the atmosphere, cooling the air near the ground, so that it becomes cooler than higher up. Radiation inversions are fairly thin and usually temporary, but cold air drainage can cause them to thicken and thus slow their dispersal in the morning. In hilly or mountainous areas, the dense, cooler air near the ground flows downhill, accumulating in valleys, producing a large pool of cool air. In hilly areas, most cities are situated on the valley bottoms and thus the inversion traps the cities' pollutants in the valleys. They are prevented from dispersing horizontally by the valley walls, and the inversion keeps them from dispersing vertically. Valley inversions, often reinforced by subsidence inversions, are responsible for pollution problems in many cities in western North America, including Denver, Salt Lake City, Albuquerque, and Mexico City (see Figure 11.3).

The third type of inversion, the *advection inversion,* is a problem primarily on the west coast of the U.S., where local winds in the form of sea breezes blow off the Pacific Ocean. Before reaching land, however, they pass over the cold ocean current along the coast of California. The lower layers of the air are cooled by contact with this water, becoming cooler than the air above. These inversions are usually of moderate thickness, from a few hundred meters to 1500 meters or more. Los Angeles, San Diego, and, to a lesser extent, the San Francisco Bay area are bordered on the east by mountains that prevent pollutants from being dispersed inland. The particularly severe pollution problems of those cities are essentially the result of the presence of the mountains combined with very persistent advection inversions.

In addition to dispersion, two other aspects of weather are important to understanding air pollution problems. These are sunlight and atmospheric humidity. Sunlight contributes to the formation of photochemical smog. Such smog is therefore more severe on sunny days than on cloudy ones, and cities that have a lot of sunshine have more photochemical smog than do those in cloudy areas. High altitude cities, such as Denver and most other cities in the Mountain West, have particularly intense sunlight, because of the thinner atmosphere, and this is an important factor in their pollution problems. In areas of high sulfur oxide emissions, atmospheric humidity is more of a problem, because water and oxygen combine with sulfur oxides to form sulfates and sulfuric acid. In areas of high humidity, high sulfur emissions and foggy days can be more dangerous than dry days.

The various combinations of all these factors make each metropolitan region's problem different. Some cities suffer mostly from photochemical smog, while others have the greatest problems with particulates or carbon monoxide. Some cities have pollution episodes that last only a day or two, and others have much longer episodes. In the Northeast, pollution is usually the most severe in summer and fall, because that is when emissions are highest, as a result of high electrical demand and increased automobile usage, and subsidence inversions most frequent. In the Mountain West, winter is usually the time of the most persistent inversions, and that is when pollution is worst. Within metropolitan regions, local variations in wind direction or speed also contribute to variations in pollution. These regional and local differences in weather conditions are the major factor in explaining differences in pollution problems and the need for local or regional, as well as national, approaches to control.

Figure 11.3 Smog in Mexico City. Mexico City has high rates of emissions, but also lies in a mountain basin. The high altitude causes solar radiation to be intense, contributing to formation of photochemical smog. The topographic basin contributes to the formation of inversions and the lack of dispersal, which make the problem particularly severe. (Source: United Nations/H. Bijur)

MAJOR POLLUTANTS

Air pollutants can come from both natural and non-natural sources, with the latter being the most important in the U.S. Some natural sources of pollutants include smoke from forest fires, hydrocarbons from coniferous trees and shrubs, dust from a variety of sources, volcanic eruptions, and pollen. At the national level, natural sources are quantitatively significant, even dominant. But in areas of severe pollution problems, human-made sources are locally much more important.

Non-natural sources of air pollutants are either stationary or mobile. *Stationary sources* are site specific and include stack emissions from refineries, smelters, electric-power plants, and other manufacturing industries. *Mobile sources* are those that are not site specific. They include automobiles, motorcycles, buses, trucks, airplanes, trains, ships, boats, and off-highway vehicles.

Criteria pollutants are those specific contaminants that adversely affect human health and welfare, for which the U.S. Environmental Protection Agency (EPA) has set air quality standards. *Primary* standards are designed to protect human health, and *secondary* standards are designed to protect human welfare (property, vegetation, etc.).

Carbon Monoxide (CO)

Carbon monoxide is a tasteless, odorless, colorless gas. It combines with hemoglobin in the blood, reducing its oxygen-carrying capacity and damaging some of the functions of the central nervous system. In small doses, CO impairs some mental functions as well, resulting in headaches and dizziness. In large doses, especially in enclosed areas, CO causes death.

Most CO pollution results from the incomplete combustion of carbonaceous materials, including fossil fuels. There are some natural sources of CO, such as forest fires and decomposition of organic matter. In 1981, 83 percent of all non-natural CO emissions were from transportation (mobile) sources, with an additional 15 percent from stationary sources, industrial processes, and fuel combustion (see Table 11.1). CO is the most pervasive of all air pollutants, accounting for over half of the total emissions (see Figure 11.4).

Table 11.1 Air Pollutant Emissions by Type and Source, 1981 (Million Metric Tons)

	CO	SO_2	HC	TSP	NO_x
Transportation	69.5	0.8	7.7	1.4	8.5
Fuel combustion	6.3	17.8	0.9	2.1	10.1
Industrial processes	6.2	3.9	9.8	3.7	0.6
Solid waste disposal	2.1	—[a]	0.6	0.4	0.1
Miscellaneous[b]	6.4	—[a]	2.3	0.9	0.2
Total	90.5	22.5	21.3	8.5	19.5

[a]Less than 50,000 metric tons
[b]Includes forest fires and other uncontrollable burning

Source: Council on Environmental Quality, 1982

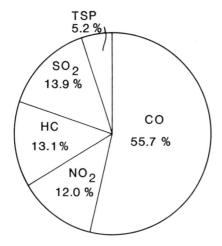

Figure 11.4 Air pollutant emissions in the U.S., 1981. By weight, carbon monoxide is the largest human-made emission. (Source: Data from Council on Environmental Quality, 1982)

Sulfur Dioxide (SO_2)

Sulfur dioxide is a colorless gas with a strong odor. It is highly reactive in the presence of oxygen and moisture, forming sulfuric acid, a corrosive.

SO_2 stings the eyes and burns the throat. More important, SO_2 contributes to respiratory diseases, including bronchitis, emphysema, and asthma; chronic exposures can permanently impair lung functions. SO_2 also corrodes metals, discolors textiles, and speeds the deterioration of building material, especially stone and metals. Perhaps the most significant effect of SO_2 is its role in the formation of acid rain and the resultant damage and decrease in plant growth. This is discussed in detail later in this chapter.

SO_2 emissions are a direct result of burning sulfur-bearing fossil fuels and of the smelting of sulfur-bearing metal ores. In annual emissions, it is the second-largest pollutant. Certain industrial processes, notably petroleum refining, also contribute SO_2 to the atmosphere. The most significant natural source of SO_2 is volcanic eruptions. The majority of SO_2 emissions in 1981 were from electrical utilities (65.8 percent), followed by industrial plants (17 percent), and other stationary fuel-combustion sources (13 percent).

Hydrocarbons (HC)

Hydrocarbons are volatile organic compounds containing only hydrogen and carbon. Methane, propane, ethylene, and acetylene are some of the specific compounds generically termed hydrocarbons. Many hydrocarbons are suspected carcinogens. Aside from their direct health impacts, hydrocarbons are important in the formation of photochemical smog.

Hydrocarbons are released through the incomplete combustion of carbon-containing fuels and through the evaporation of fossil fuels from natural gas pipelines, gas tanks, and gas station pumps (Council on Environmental Quality, 1982). Nearly 50 percent of all non-natural HC emissions are from stationary industrial sources, and 36 percent are from mobile transportation sources. There are some natural sources of HC, such as coniferous forests, but they are relatively insignificant in their contribution to urban pollution problems.

Total Suspended Particulates (TSP)

Total suspended particulates include any solid or liquid particles with diameters from .03 to 100 microns. Examples of TSP include soot, fly ash, dust, pollen, and various chemicals and metals, such as arsenic, cadmium, and lead.

The adverse health effects of suspended particulates include the direct toxicity of some of the metals and chemicals. Other health impacts include aggravation of cardiorespiratory diseases, such as bronchitis and asthma. Suspended particulates also have been linked to lung cancer. Aside from health, some of the negative effects involve the corrosion of metals and the soiling and discoloration of buildings and sculptures. More important, suspended particulates both scatter and absorb sunlight, thus reducing visibility. They also provide nuclei upon which condensation can occur, which increases cloud formation. They can also inhibit photosynthesis in plants.

Suspended particulates are produced primarily by stationary sources, particularly those industries that use coal as a fuel source, such as power plants, steel mills and fertilizer plants. Construction activities and solid waste disposal (burning) also contribute minor percentages of TSP emissions, as shown in Table 11.1. Natural sources of suspended particulates are volcanic eruptions, forest fires, and wind erosion.

ISSUE 11.1: Smog and the Olympics

Smog has been a persistent problem in southern California since Cabrillo first discovered the Bahia de los Fumos (Bay of Smokes) in 1542. By 1877 air pollution, in the form of dust from the streets, was so bad it prompted one citizen to remark, "It does not allow invalids with lung disease to remain here" (Weaver, 1980, p. 197). By 1944 the term smog (smoke and fog) was coined, describing the brown haze that hung over the Los Angeles basin. With post-war urbanization and industrialization, the now-famous Los Angeles smog worsened, and residents began to experience discomfort and adverse health effects. Smog alerts became commonplace, and, as early as the 1950s, people were advised to curtail their outdoor physical activities.

By the 1960s and 1970s, scientists began to document the effects of smog (Goldsmith and Friberg, 1977). While they were unable to determine conclusively that smog caused death, they were able to document an increased susceptibility to lung and other respiratory diseases. For example, in clinical studies involving ozone, normal eye irritation was noticed with minimal exposures. At an exposure rate of 0.3 ppm (slightly higher than a Stage I air pollution alert), the researchers noticed irritating effects just a few minutes after exposure. The lung capacity functions decreased as well, particularly among continuously exercising adults (Avol et al., 1983).

Ozone and carbon dioxide have been linked to reduced lung capacity among individuals, with the degree of reduction influenced by physical activity: the more strenuous the activity, the greater the inhalation rate, and the greater the reduction in lung function. Ozone also effects the performance of athletes at track events (Goldsmith and

Nitrogen Oxides (NO_x)

Nitrogen oxide emissions include nitrogen monoxide (NO), and nitrogen dioxide (NO_2). Nitrogen dioxide is a reddish-brown gas. It aggravates respiratory diseases and increases susceptibility to pneumonia and lung cancer. NO_2 causes paints and dyes to fade. There are, however, two effects of NO and NO_2 that cause NO_x to be considered a criteria pollutant. The first is its crucial role as an ultraviolet light absorber in the formation of photochemical smog. Second, and perhaps more important, NO_x is a factor in the formation of acid rain.

Nitrogen is usually inert, but it combines with O_2 at high temperatures in internal combustion engines and furnaces to form NO_x. Thus, the primary sources of NO_x are motor vehicle exhaust (44 percent) and power plants (52 percent).

Lead (Pb)

Lead is a non-ferrous, heavy metal that occurs naturally. In the atmosphere, lead occurs in the form of vapor, dust, or aerosol. Lead acts as a cumulative poison in the human body, causing general weakness and impaired functioning of the central nervous system. It can lead to severe anemia and even death.

For many years, lead has been added to high-octane gasoline to reduce engine knock. The primary sources of lead in the atmosphere are vehicle exhaust from lead additives in gasoline, lead mining and smelting, and manufacturing of lead products, such as batteries. Volcanic dust, the major natural source of lead,

---

Friberg, 1977). Carbon monoxide has been shown to affect pulmonary functions as well, including the performance of swimmers (Goldsmith and Friberg, 1977).

In 1932, when the tenth modern Olympiad was held in Los Angeles, there was no hint of a smog problem that might affect the performance of athletes. Fifty-two years later, however, smog is very much on the minds of both medical personnel and organizers of the 1984 Olympic games. A public referendum several years earlier prohibited the use of public tax monies to support the 1984 Summer Olympic Games. Funding was therefore largely provided by corporate sponsors and the sale of television rights. The demand for prime-time coverage of key athletic events forced schedule changes and raised the question of the impact of smog. This was particularly true for the long-distance and endurance events, such as the marathon and cycling. Prevailing onshore breezes keep temperatures moderate and smog levels low in the L.A. basin for much of the year. The months of July and August are the exception. Inversions develop, and temperatures soar. As a result, July and August are the smoggiest times of the year in Los Angeles; the 1984 games were held from July 18 to August 12.

Ozone is the air pollutant of particular concern to athletes. The impact of ozone on human health is well documented and the L.A. basin historically has had high ozone levels during summer. At an exposure of 0.2 ppm, a Stage I alert, athletes would experience painful and shallow breathing, with some lung function impairment. Unfortunately, the chance of harm is greatest for the world-class athletes. The better conditioned the athlete, the more oxygen is taken in, increasing the effects of the pol-

contributes less than 1 percent of the total emissions. Another source of lead in the air is cigarette smoke (Council on Environmental Quality, 1980).

Oxidants (O$_x$)

Oxidants are a group of compounds that are the most important component of photochemical smog. The best known of these is ozone (O$_3$). In combination with HC, NO$_x$, and sunlight, oxidants comprise the now-famous Los Angeles-type smog. In simplified form, the process is this: sunlight causes NO$_2$ to break down into NO and monatomic oxygen (O). This O atom combines with O$_2$ to form O$_3$. In addition, HC, O$_2$, NO, and NO$_2$ interact to form both ozone and a class of compounds called peroxyacetyl nitrates (PAN), which, like ozone, are harmful photochemical oxidants.

Photochemical oxidants are eye and respiratory irritants, and prolonged exposures result in aggravation of cardiovascular and respiratory illnesses (Issue 11.1). Other non-health effects include deterioration of rubber, textiles, paints, and reduced visibility and vegetation growth. Leaves and fruit seem the most susceptible to oxidants, the effects of which result not only in injury, but also in leaf drop and premature fruit. Since oxidants are produced in chemical reactions in the atmosphere, there is no direct source of emissions other than the sources for HC and NO$_x$. Naturally occurring atmospheric ozone may sometimes contribute significantly to urban smog.

---

lutants or ozone toxicity (Broughton, 1983).

The Los Angeles Olympics Organizing Committee (LAOOC) was not willing to relocate the marathon and other endurance events out of the Los Angeles basin, although requested to do so by the competing athletes. Because of television coverage during prime time, the LAOOC was also unwilling to reschedule endurance events during low pollution times, such as dawn or around midnight. In addition, the constraints of television coverage prohibited the LAOOC from rescheduling major endurance events at the last minute, if it was too hot or too smoggy. Such constraints were less evident for more obscure events. The LAOOC, for example, was asked to shift the equestrian endurance event to suburban San Diego at the request of Prince Phillip of Great Britain who was concerned about the health of the athlete's horses.

Fate was kind to the Los Angeles Olympic Organizing Committee. Despite several cautionary articles appearing in major medical journals, the Games went on as scheduled. For sixteen days before the start of the Games, the L.A. basin suffered periodic Stage I smog alerts. At the request of the LAOOC, many industries in the area agreed to alter working hours to cut down on rush hour traffic and reduce air emissions. Most important, however, was a break in the weather. While heat was a problem in several events including the men's marathon, a long-term inversion did not develop. Wind and temperature varied enough to keep smog levels average, thus avoiding major health problems for both athletes and spectators.

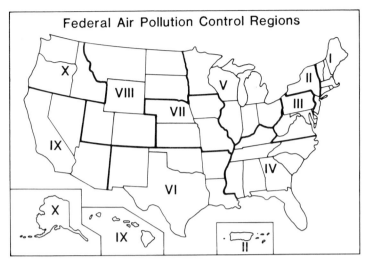

Figure 11.5 Federal Air Pollution Control Regions. (Source: From Environmental Protection Agency, 1980a)

POLLUTION MONITORING AND TRENDS

Legislative Mandates

The original enabling legislation establishing air pollution control was the Clean Air Act passed in 1963. Amendments to that legislation, the Air Quality Act of 1967 and the Clean Air Act Amendments of 1970, provided the framework for air resource decision-making at both the regional and the national levels. The Clean Air Act Amendments of 1970 established standards for ambient air quality for the five major pollutants and also provided timetables for their achievement.

The Clean Air Act Amendments of 1977 further refined the monitoring of air pollutants and clarified previous legislation. The 1963, 1967, 1970, and 1977 acts are collectively known as the *Clean Air Act.* The 1977 amendments required standard monitoring of the criteria pollutants and also standardized reporting methods. Under this legislation, the EPA was to review the standards for criteria pollutants and establish deadlines for compliance with the standards. States were to meet the primary standards for SO_2, NO_x, and TSP by 1981 and the primary standards for O_3 and CO by 1987.

The Clean Air Act expired in 1982. However, all the rules and regulations in effect at that time are still valid. In 1982 Congress passed a continuing resolution that provides appropriations and legal authority to the EPA to continue the air-quality program under the 1977 amendments. In essence this provided for a hold status on the legislation while it was debated in Congress. The Reagan administration wanted to relax standards and also to limit provisions for trans-boundary pollution problems, such as acid rain.

Monitoring Network and Air Quality Standards

Under the 1970 amendments, a national network of air quality control regions (AQCRs) was established, with regional offices (see Figure 11.5). Data from each

Table 11.2 National Ambient Air Quality Standards (NAAQS)

Pollutant	Avg. Time	Primary	Secondary
TSP	annual geometric mean	75 μg/m^3	60 μg/m^3
	24 hrs	260 μg/m^3	150 μg/m^3
SO$_2$	annual arithmetic mean	80 μg/m^3 (0.03 ppm)	—
	24 hrs	365 μg/m^3 (0.14 ppm)	—
	3 hrs	—	1300 μg/m^3 (0.5 ppm)
CO	8 hrs	10 μg/m^3 (9 ppm)	10 μg/m^3 (9 ppm)
	1 hr	40 μg/m^3 (35 ppm)	40 μg/m^3 (35 ppm)
NO$_2$	annual arithmetic mean	100 μg/m^3 (.05 ppm)	100 μg/m^3 (.05 ppm)
O$_3$	1 hr	240 μg/m^3 (.12 ppm)	240 μg/m^3 (.12 ppm)
HC[a]	3 hrs	160 μg/m^3 (.24 ppm)	160 μg/m^3 (.24 ppm)
Pb	3 months	1.5 μg/m^3	1.5 μg/m^3

[a]Not to be exceeded more than once a year

Source: Council on Environmental Quality, 1980

of these regions are stored in a national aerometric data base. Monitoring is actually done on a county level. In 1979, problems with the frequency and accuracy of monitoring data led the EPA to standardize and regulate the monitoring network. State and local monitoring sites were thus incorporated into a national system, with consistent and uniform readings, including frequency, type of pollutant, and placement of monitoring stations (central city versus suburban location).

Primary and secondary standards were established under the Clean Air Act for the seven criteria pollutants (see Table 11.2). As stipulated by the 1977 amendments, these standards were subject to review and revision prior to the 1982 reauthorization. The only standard that was changed was that for ozone.

The Non-Degradation Issue

Interesting quirks in the clear air legislation began to emerge in the mid-1970s; these involved conflicts between economic development and air quality. The intent of the 1970 amendments was to keep clean air clean, while cleaning up dirty air. Primary standards for the criteria pollutants were to have been met by 1975. But there were no provisions or policies for those areas that were already clean in 1970. Industry noticed this and began to relocate into these relatively clean areas. The EPA did not move on this issue, which became known as Prevention of Significant Deterioration (PSD), until the Sierra Club filed a legal suit over the Kaiparowitz energy facility in southern Utah.

In response to a court order, the EPA established its PSD policy, which effectively limits the extent to which clean air can be degraded by managing economic growth in various regions (National Research Council, 1981). The entire U.S. was divided into three classes. Class I areas could not have any increases in TSP or SO$_2$ levels. All National Parks and National Wilderness Areas were designated mandatory Class I areas. Class I status limits industrial growth in the area. Most of the Class I areas are located in the western half of the country (see Figure 11.6).

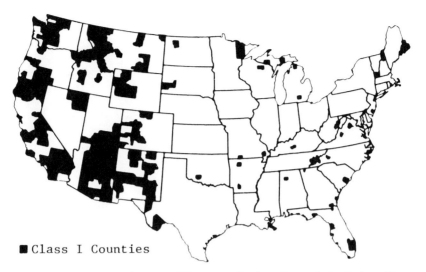

Figure 11.6   Class I Counties. These counties have been designated as Class I areas, to prevent significant deterioration of air quality, because these are areas that have the highest air quality, and new industrial growth in these areas is limited. (Source: Environmental Protection Agency, 1980a)

Class II areas allow for moderate development and industrial growth. All areas of the country that were not mandatory Class I regions were assigned to this group. The states were given the opportunity to change this designation to Class I or Class III. Class III areas allow for significant industrial growth and residential development. Changes into Class III areas, however, require environmental impact statements, public hearings, and EPA approval.

There was and still is considerable debate over the PSD program. These debates are particularly acute in the western half of the country, where issues over energy development, industrialization, and pristine areas are hotly contested. Energy developments in the Golden Circle region of the Southwest (see Figure 11.7) illustrate some of the issues in the clean air versus energy development debate; these issues are discussed in more detail in Chapter 12. Aerial visibility over the Grand Canyon and the general deterioration of air in the other national parks in the region have brought this issue to the public's attention (Rudzitis and Schwartz, 1982).

Trends

Although the U.S. has had air pollution control measures for more than a decade, the quality of the air has only slightly improved during that time. There are 247 AQCRs, with monitoring stations in 3,000 counties in the U.S. (National Commission on Air Quality, 1981). One of the reasons for the lack of significant improvement may be the way in which the data are collected. Emissions data, for example, are actually estimates and illustrate how well the regulations on industrial and vehicular emissions are working. Ambient data, in contrast, are collected from specific monitoring locations and, based on the appropriate health standards, indicate how close we are to achieving clear air.

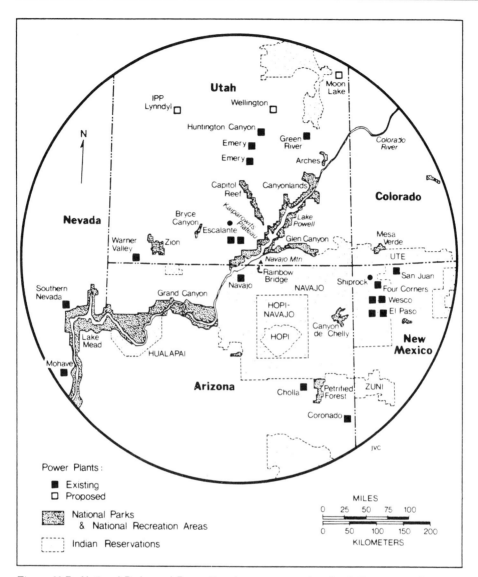

Figure 11.7 National Parks and Recreation Areas, proposed and existing power plants, and Indian Reservations in the Golden Circle area of the U.S. Southwest. This is an area of significant natural beauty and recreational use, but it also has large coal reserves. Power plants have been built there to burn the coal and export electricity to urban areas. The result has been a deterioration of air quality. (Source: Rudzitis and Schwarz, 1982)

TSP

Total suspended particulate emissions have declined by almost 53 percent since 1970 (see Table 11.3). However, as Table 11.4 shows, there has been very little change in ambient levels. While there has been some improvement in emissions from industrial sources, fugitive sources, such as dust from fields, roads, and construction, account for the disparity between emissions and ambient quality.

Table 11.3 National Air Pollutant Emissions, 1970–1981 (Million Metric Tons)

Year	TSP	SO$_2$	NO$_2$	HC	CO
1970	17.9	28.4	17.6	27.2	112.8
1971	16.8	26.9	18.0	26.3	112.4
1972	15.4	27.6	19.1	26.7	111.7
1973	14.4	28.9	19.4	26.3	108.9
1974	12.6	27.1	19.0	24.7	103.8
1975	10.6	25.6	18.6	23.2	100.2
1976	10.0	26.4	19.8	24.2	104.8
1977	9.2	26.0	20.3	24.4	102.5
1978	9.3	24.7	20.5	25.0	101.7
1979	9.1	24.5	20.5	24.4	98.2
1980	8.7	23.4	19.8	23.0	95.0
1981	8.5	22.5	19.5	21.3	90.5
Change, 1970–1981	−53%	−21%	+11%	−22%	−20%

Source: Council on Environmental Quality, 1982

In 1980, 211 counties failed to attain the primary standard for TSP (U.S. Environmental Protection Agency, 1980a). An independent national committee, the National Commission on Air Quality (NCAQ) report predicted in 1980 that 27 metropolitan areas would exceed the primary standard in 1982 (see Figure 11.8). The major reason was the noncompliance of industry, particularly the steel and utilities industries. Regionally, the Northeast, Great Lakes, and South improved through the 1970s, with the western section of the country showing no improvement, largely because of wind and agricultural dust.

SO$_2$

SO$_2$ emissions went down by 21 percent from 1970 to 1981. This was largely a result of the switch from coal and high-sulfur oil to natural gas and low-sulfur oil. Also, the decrease is directly related to the construction of tall stacks by industry to disperse SO$_2$ emissions away from their source. Ambient quality was also improved by 27 percent from 1975 to 1981, with almost all cities meeting the primary standard. According to the NCAQ, four metropolitan regions did not meet standards in 1982, as well as smaller areas near smelters in Idaho, Washington, Arizona, Utah, and New Mexico. These metropolitan regions are Pittsburgh, Indianapolis, Gary, and Chicago (see Figure 11.8).

Table 11.4 National Ambient Air Pollution Concentrations, 1975–1981

Pollutant	Sites	1975	1976	1977	1978	1979	1980	1981
TSP (μg/m^3)	1,972	60.5	61.3	60.8	60.0	60.3	61.6	58.5
SO$_2$ (ppm)	416	.015	.015	.013	.012	.012	.011	.011
CO (ppm)	224	11.3	10.7	10.1	9.6	9.0	8.4	8.4
NO$_x$O$_3$ (ppm)	445	.024	.025	.025	.027	.027	.026	.025
	209	.150	.149	.149	.152	.137	.139	.129
Lead (μg/m^3)	92	.91	.89	.94	.84	.73	.46	.39

Source: Council on Environmental Quality, 1982

Figure 11.8 Cities which have not attained federal air quality standards for: (a) total suspended particulates; (b) sulfur dioxide; (c) ozone; and (d) carbon monoxide. (Source: National Commission on Air Quality, 1981)

NO_x

Emissions of NO_x have increased by 11 percent since 1970, as a result of increased motor vehicle usage and power plant emissions. Ambient quality has also deteriorated, with a 4 percent increase in monitored levels since 1975. The NCAQ study found that seven counties exceeded the NO_x primary standard in 1980. The NCAQ also stated that control methods should be aimed at stricter emissions standards for NO_2 on trucks, as a way to limit emissions and improve ambient quality.

O_x

Since oxidants are by-products of chemical reactions, there are no emissions data for them. However, there are data for one group of the contributing emissions—hydrocarbons. HC emissions were down by nearly 22 percent in the period 1970–81. Ambient quality also improved from 1975 to 1981, but worsened from 1979 to 1980. Figure 11.8 shows that the NCAQ expected 48 regions to exceed primary standards for ozone in 1982. The NCAQ further expects the following four regions to exceed the ozone standard in 1987: Philadelphia-Camden; north-eastern New Jersey-New York City-southwestern Connecticut; southern California; and Houston. Nationally, nearly 94 million people are exposed to unhealthy levels of ozone yearly (Council on Environmental Quality, 1982, p. 26). While stationary sources do contribute to the problem, the EPA efforts and the NCAQ recommendations focus on auto emissions, stressing motor vehicle inspections and maintenance as control methods.

CO

Emissions were down by 20 percent for carbon monoxide from 1970 to 1981, as were ambient levels. But 145 counties still exceeded the primary standard in 1980, and 39 of these had CO levels that were 100 percent above the standard, affecting 75.5 million people (National Commission on Air Quality, 1981, p. 128). The NCAQ predicted that 28 areas would exceed primary standards in 1982, with 13 of these having ambient levels 150 percent above the standard. These 13 regions (see Figure 11.8) are Portland, Los Angeles, Denver, Seattle, Phoenix, San Jose, the New York metropolitan area, Cleveland, Pittsburgh, Atlanta, Chicago, Louisville, and Washington, D.C. The NCAQ report also noted increased ambient CO levels in rapidly growing metropolitan regions with under 200,000 inhabitants. Four of these (Medford, Oregon; Greeley-Ft. Collins, Colorado; Las Vegas, Nevada; and Anchorage, Alaska) exceeded primary standards in 1979 and were predicted to not meet them in 1982. The primary reason was the failure of autos to meet emissions standards, as a result of lax inspection and maintenance on the part of state regulators and owners.

SPATIAL COMPARISONS OF AIR QUALITY

Before 1978, each state relied on its own air quality monitoring and reporting program. Some states' programs were very good; others' were non-existent. As a result, readings were taken at irregular intervals, and reporting was erratic.

Table 11.5 Comparison of PSI Values

PSI Value	TSP[a]	SO$_2$[a]	CO[b]	O$_3$[c]	NO$_2$[c]	Descriptor
400+	875+	2000+	46.0+	1000+	3000+	Very Hazardous
300–399	625–874	1600–1999	34.0–45.9	900–1099	2260–2999	Hazardous
200–299	375–624	800–1599	17.0–33.9	480–899	1130–2259	Very Unhealthful
100–199	260–374	365–799	10.0–16.9	240–479	NR	Unhealthful
50–99	75[d]–259	80[d]–364	5.0– 9.9	120–239	NR	Moderate
0–49	0–74	0–79	0– 4.9	0–119	NR	Good

[a]24-hr μg/m³
[b]8-hr mg/m³
[c]1-hr μg/m³
[d]Annual primary NAAQS

NR No index value reported at concentration levels below those specified by "alert-level" criteria

Source: Council on Environmental Quality, 1980

This made interstate comparisons impossible. There was no mechanism to allow comparison of air quality between New York and Los Angeles, for example. There was no way to tell which region or city had the dirtiest or cleanest air.

Pollution Standards Index (PSI)

In an effort to standardize monitoring efforts nationwide, the EPA adopted a uniform air quality index in 1978. This index, the *Pollution Standards Index,* or PSI, is a health-related comparative measure, based on the short-term NAAQS primary standards for criteria pollutants.

The index translates concentrations of NO$_2$, SO$_2$, CO, O$_3$, and TSP into a single value, which ranges from 0 to 500 (see Table 11.5). When the levels for all five of these pollutants are below NAAQS primary standards, the air is termed good or moderately polluted (PSI values 0–99). When ambient concentrations of any of the criteria pollutants exceed their primary standard, the PSI reading is in the 100–500 range depending on the concentration level. PSI values in the range 100–200 are labeled unhealthful. Values from 200 to 300 are termed very unhealthful; values in excess of 300 are termed hazardous. Similarly, public warnings, corresponding to these PSI levels, are given. Good air corresponds to PSI values of less than 100. An air quality alert is called when PSI values range from 100 to 200: persons with heart or respiratory ailments should reduce physical exertion. An air pollution warning is given when the PSI ranges from 200 to 300. During a warning elderly and other persons with heart and lung diseases should remain indoors. Industry is also asked to curtail emissions temporarily, until the warning is removed. An air pollution emergency is called when PSI readings exceed 300. The general population is advised to refrain from outdoor activities, and persons with heart and lung diseases are advised to remain indoors and minimize their physical activity. Industry and motorists are asked to curb emissions through lower production and less driving, respectively.

Urban Trends in Air Quality

Overall air quality in metropolitan regions is improving. Selected metropolitan regions had an average number of 72 days of unhealthful air (above 100 on the

PSI) in 1978 (Council on Environmental Quality, 1980), down 16 percent from 1972 for the same locations. While overall quality shows signs of improvement, some metropolitan regions, specifically New York and Los Angeles, still have dangerously polluted air. During 1981, Los Angeles had more than 200 days with PSI readings in the 100–200 range and an additional 111 days with readings over 200 (see Table 11.6). Among the 53 metropolitan areas analyzed by the Council on Environmental Quality, Los Angeles has by far the worst air quality in the country, as does southern California in general. Los Angeles is followed by San Bernardino-Riverside-Ontario (part of the greater Los Angeles area), New York, and Anaheim-Santa Ana-Garden Grove (again part of the greater Los Angeles region).

Air quality has worsened since 1978 in both the Los Angeles and San Bernardino-Riverside-Ontario metropolitan areas. In 1978, Los Angeles had 242 days with PSI levels greater than 100, and by 1981 the count rose to 248. Los Angeles had 118 days with PSI levels greater than 200 in 1978; this dropped slightly in 1981 to 111 days. San Bernardino, on the other hand, had 167 days with PSI greater than 100 in 1978, and this rose to 184 days in 1981. The number of days in San Bernardino with PSI readings greater than 200 also rose from 88 in 1978 to 92 in 1981 (Council on Environmental Quality, 1982).

New York and Pittsburgh were the other two metropolitan regions that recorded more than 150 days with PSI levels greater than 100 in 1978. By 1981, New York had dropped from 224 to 106 days with PSI readings greater than 100, going from 51 to only 4 days with very unhealthful (PSI 200–300) air. Pittsburgh showed the most dramatic improvement in air quality during this time. In 1978, the metropolitan region recorded 168 days with PSI levels in the unhealthful range, and by 1981 this had dropped to 28. There was also a drop in the number of days with PSI readings over 200, from 31 to only 1 in 1981.

Nationwide, some of the cleaner urban areas include Buffalo, New York; Tucson, Arizona; and Kansas City, Missouri-Kansas, each with less than ten days per year exceeding 100 on the PSI.

AIR QUALITY CONTROL AND PLANNING

Economic Considerations

In 1981, $60.3 billion was spent in the U.S. in compliance with federal regulations for pollution abatement (U.S. Bureau of the Census, 1984, p. 214). Nearly 50 percent of this, or $29.5 billion, was for air quality control alone. Government (federal, state, and local) expenditures were $1.5 billion for air pollution control for hospitals, military installations, incinerators, and miscellaneous municipal facilities. Nearly $8.1 billion was spent on emissions controls for automobiles and trucks, with another $8.4 billion spent on controls for electrical utilities' emissions. Industry spent nearly $4.3 billion for pollution-control equipment.

Clean air is a costly business. The NCAQ, however, estimates that nearly $6.8 billion would be saved yearly just by achieving current NAAQS goals. These savings would be in reduction in crop losses, materials, soiling, and increased visibility. In addition, between $4.6 to $51.2 billion could be saved annually in health effects related to air pollution (National Commission on Air Quality, 1981,

Table 11.6 PSI Rankings of 56 Metropolitan Areas, 1981 (Number of Days Exceeding Level)

Group	SMSA	PSI > 100	PSI > 200
More than 100 days	Los Angeles	248	111
	San Bernadino-Riverside-Ontario	184	92
	New York	106	4
50–99 days	Anaheim-Santa Ana		
	Garden Grove	98	19
	Phoenix	95	16
	Denver	79	23
	San Diego	69	2
	Baltimore	67	1
	Houston	67	20
	Las Vegas	56	8
25–49 days	Albuquerque	48	17
	Anchorage	47	7
	Fresno	46	1
	Oxnard-Simi Valley	43	2
	El Paso	38	16
	Minneapolis	35	1
	Seattle-Everett	35	1
	Philadelphia	32	1
	Portland	30	4
	Salt Lake City	30	1
	Birmingham	29	4
	Pittsburgh	28	1
	Bridgeport	26	2
	St. Louis	26	3
11–24 days	Detroit	23	0
	Washington, D.C.	21	0
	Louisville	20	1
	Spokane	20	4
	New Haven	19	2
	Baton Rouge	18	0
	Boise	18	0
	Boston	18	0
	Chicago	18	0
	Dallas	18	0
	Cleveland	17	2
	Provo-Orem	17	4
	Indianapolis	16	1
	Providence	16	1
	Charlotte	14	0
	Danbury	14	1
	Nashville	13	0
	Lincoln	12	4
	Nassau-Suffolk	12	0
	Bakersfield	12	1
	Gary-Hammond-E. Chicago	12	1
	Tulsa	12	1
	Milwaukee	11	1
	Akron	11	3
	Atlanta	11	0
	Racine	11	0
< 11 days	Jersey City	10	0
	Reading	10	0
	San Jose	10	0
	Buffalo	7	1
	Tucson	7	0
	Kansas City	4	0

Source: Council on Environmental Quality, 1982

Table 11.7 Exhaust-Emission Standards for Automobiles

Model Year	Standard (gm/m³)			Percentage Reduction from Precontrol Vehicles		
	HC	CO	NO_x	HC	CO	NO_x
Pre-1968	8.2	90.0	3.4	—	—	—
1968–1971	4.1	34.0	NA	50	62	NA
1972–1974	3.0	28.0	3.1	63	69	9
1975–1976	1.5	15.0	3.1	82	83	9
1977–1979	1.5	15.0	2.0	82	83	41
1980	0.41	7.0	2.0	96	92	41
1981	0.41	3.4	1.0	96	96	76

Source: National Commission on Clean Air, 1981

pp. 262, 265). In an era of economic uncertainty, some individuals are still questioning the value of air pollution control programs.

In an attempt to assuage these economic fears, the EPA developed its *bubble approach* to stationary source control. Instead of considering each smokestack as an emitter, which was the previous policy, the EPA now views the entire plant as a point source. Thus, it allows emissions from one smokestack to exceed standards so long as another stack at a different location in the same plant has compensating reductions. As long as the emissions from the entire plant do not exceed the standards, then the plant is not in violation of the Clean Air Act and so is not subject to criminal prosecution. This policy allows the plant to average emissions from all stacks, thus allowing internal decison-making about what is most appropriate for the plant. Production levels and expenditures for control equipment are made by the plant management, so long as the total emissions are below federal limits.

Control Programs

According to the NCAQ, vehicle exhaust emissions offer the greatest potential for decreasing mobile source contributions to non-attainment of NAAQS. Exhaust emissions have been federally regulated since 1968 and have become increasingly stricter (see Table 11.7). The emissions standards apply only to the newer model year cars and trucks. Older models have less stringent controls. One of the problems with emissions control is that many individual car owners tamper with the controls to increase gas mileage. Also, more and more people are keeping their older model cars rather than buying new cars with the more stringent emissions controls.

As states are required to have implementation plans on how they will approach the air pollution problems under their jurisdictions, many have developed inspection and maintenance programs for vehicle emissions. Not all states did this voluntarily, however. The EPA ordered twenty-nine states to develop such programs when it was estimated that, without them, the states would continue to exceed primary NAAQS for ozone and carbon monoxide as late as 1987. As of 1980, only seven of the twenty-nine had yearly inspections of all vehicles licensed within their borders. By 1983, eighteen states had complied. Those states which did not have auto emissions inspection and maintenance programs were

Figure 11.9 Gasoline pump nozzles in some areas of severe hydrocarbon emission problems are being fitted with devices that capture vapors displaced from the fuel tank when it is filled with gasoline. This example is in Los Angeles.

Other methods have been used to control mobile sources. One of these is the catalytic converter now fitted on all gasoline engines (Fleischaker, 1983). The converter oxidizes unburned gases, thus reducing emissions. It requires more expensive unleaded fuel, and as a result, many automobile owners damage the device by using the cheaper leaded fuel. The development of new automotive fuels, such as alcohol and methane, is a potential option, but these fuels are not widely available at this time. The most obvious way to reduce vehicle emissions is to force people to drive less. Admittedly, this is a rather impractical solution to the problem.

Stationary source control involves installing mechanical devices on smokestacks and switching from high-sulfur to low-sulfur fuels. Fitting gasoline pumps with pollution control equipment is another method currently in use to prevent hydrocarbons from escaping at the gas station (see Figure 11.9). There are over 27,000 major stationary sources of air pollution in this country alone. The EPA considers "major" any plant that produces more than 100 tons of pollutants per year. Stack scrubbers, precipitators, and filters are costly capital investments for industry, especially for facilities with old, outdated plants.

As a result, compliance with federal standards is spotty. The EPA estimates

Table 11.8 Compliance Status by Industry, 1980

	Total No. Sources	No. in Compliance	Percentage
Power plants (oil/coal)	700	559	80
Iron and steel (integrated)	60	8	13
Iron and steel (other)	144	102	71
Primary smelters	28	13	46
Pulp and paper	475	417	87
Municipal incinerators	72	60	83
Petroleum refineries	214	170	79
Aluminum reduction	49	37	76
Portland cement	200	176	88
Sulfuric acid	262	246	94
Phosphatic fertilizers	69	62	90
Coal cleaning	409	395	97
Grey iron	433	381	88
Asphalt concrete	2,862	2,752	96
Total	5,977	5,378	90

Source: Council on Environmental Quality, 1981

that nearly 90 percent of a sample of 6,000 major stationary sources were in compliance with federal regulations in 1980 (see Table 11.8). The CEQ notes that these numbers are misleading, however, and should not be used as definitive evidence of widespread compliance. Only 5 percent of the sources were tested for emissions. For the others, compliance was determined by certification or inspection but not by actual measurement of emissions (Council on Environmental Quality, 1980, p. 182). The industries that are the leading non-compliers are iron and steel, with a 13 percent compliance rate, and smelters, with a 46 percent compliance rate.

Reductions in enforcement actions as a result of cuts in federal budgets and decentralization of the federal role in air quality control obviously do not improve air quality. In 1977 the EPA had 662 enforcement actions, which increased to 772 in 1979 (Council on Environmental Quality, 1980, p. 182), and then dropped during the early 1980s. There has also been a concomitant decrease in the federal budget for enforcement and aid to states since 1981. Federal outlays for pollution abatement and control dropped by 9 percent ($678 million) from 1980 to 1982, and federal aid to states for pollution abatement dropped by $677, or 13 percent (U.S. Bureau of the Census, 1984, p. 215). The Fiscal Year 1983 budget was reduced by 20 percent for air quality control programs alone (Conservation Foundation, 1982, p. 390). Air pollution control is expensive and requires federal action. Local and state controls cannot do the job alone.

REGIONAL AND GLOBAL ISSUES

Acid Rain

Acid rain is a general term that refers to the deposition of acids in rainfall, snow, and dust particles falling from the atmosphere. Although normal rainfall is slightly

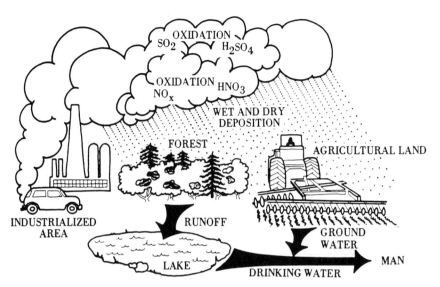

Figure 11.10 Formation and deposition of acid rain. Sulfur and nitrogen oxides emitted from industries, automobiles, and other sources are oxidized in the atmosphere to form nitric and sulfuric acids. These are deposited on the land either in precipitation or in dry dustfall, and affect vegetation, soil, and water quality. (Source: Environmental Protection Agency, 1980b)

acidic, air pollution, particularly emissions of sulfur and nitrogen oxides, have greatly increased the acidity of rainfall over wide areas in the last several decades. It is a regional rather than a local consequence of fossil-fuel combustion, having been identified as a problem in the eastern U.S. and Canada and in northern Europe. Acid rain has broad-ranging environmental effects, including damage to vegetation and structures and reduced surface water quality. It will no doubt continue to be an important environmental issue in industrialized regions of the world for many years.

The Formation and Extent of Acid Rain

Acids are substances that give up a proton (hydrogen nucleus) in a chemical reaction. Acidity of solutions is measured on the pH scale, which gives the negative logarithm of the concentration of hydrogen nuclei in a solution. A pH of 7 is neutral, and numbers less than 7 are increasingly acidic. A pH greater than 7 indicates alkaline conditions. Rainwater is slightly acidic, even under natural conditions. Carbon dioxide dissolves in water to form carbonic acid, a weak acid of about pH 5.6. There are other natural sources of acids in the atmosphere, including sulfur compounds emitted from volcanos and nitric acids created by lightning passing through the atmosphere. The relative contributions of these other sources to the acidity of rainfall is not known, but the pH of natural rainfall is variable, slightly lower than 5.6, perhaps as low as 5.0 (Katzenstein, 1981). Acid precipitation, on the other hand, has much lower pH values, commonly in the low 4s and sometimes in the low 3s, about the same as vinegar. A drop of one unit on the logarithmic pH scale means a tenfold increase in acidity, so these are substantial differences.

Two major pollutants are responsible for the increased acidity of rainfall, sulfur dioxide and nitrogen oxides. Sulfur dioxide (SO_2) combines with oxygen and water in the atmosphere to form sulfuric acid (H_2SO_4). Nitrogen oxides (NO_x) combine with water to form nitric acid (HNO_3). These acids are found in water droplets and on dust particles in the atmosphere, and they are deposited on the ground either in precipitation or in dry dust. The chemical processes that form these acids are not instantaneous; they take from minutes to days to occur, depending on atmospheric conditions (see Figure 11.10).

Sulfur dioxide emissions derive primarily from combustion of impure fossil fuels, such as coal and fuel oil. In the U.S., the areas with the largest sulfur emissions are in the urban industrial areas of the Northeast, particularly the region extending from Illinois to Pennsylvania (see Figure 11.11). Major urban areas along the east coast also have large sulfur emissions. Most of these are from coal-fired power plants, which are heavily concentrated in the region (Environmental Protection Agency, 1980b). These plants burn coal that is much higher in sulfur content than the coal burned in the western U.S. In Canada, smelting is a major contributor of sulfur. The world's largest single source of SO_2 emissions is a nickel smelter at Sudbury, Ontario.

The acidity of precipitation in the northeastern U.S. is mostly attributed to sulfuric acid. The greatest acidity (lowest pH) is found in this area and adjacent areas of Canada, downwind from the major sources of sulfur (see Figure 11.12). In the eastern U.S., nitric acid is generally a smaller component of acid precipitation than is sulfuric acid, but it is a major component of acid precipitation in the western U.S.

Effects of Acid Rain

Acid rain has many effects on the environment, most of which are poorly understood at present. The most severe effects are those involving the hydrologic cycle. Acid neutralizing substances, such as calcium and magnesium compounds, are leached by water as it passes through the ground. In areas of calcium-rich rocks or soil, there are more than enough neutralizing substances to buffer most of the downstream effects of acid precipitation. In areas of more acidic soils or in headwater areas where the water does not pass through much soil or rock before entering streams and lakes, the problem is much more severe (Patrick et al., 1981). In the Adirondacks of New York, for example, several high-altitude lakes have become so acidic that most fish cannot survive in the water. In some areas, lime has been added to lakes in an attempt to buffer the acids, but this has had limited success and is viewed as only a temporary solution to the problem.

In addition to its effects on fish life, acid rain is suspected of contributing to the decline of forests in the U.S. and elsewhere (Postel, 1984). On Camel's Hump Mountain in New Hampshire, spruce trees have been dying for several years (Vogelmann, 1982). A drop in the pH tends to make minerals more soluble and thus increase their uptake by plants. Aluminum is of particular concern because of its toxic effects on plants. Analysis of cores from these trees suggests

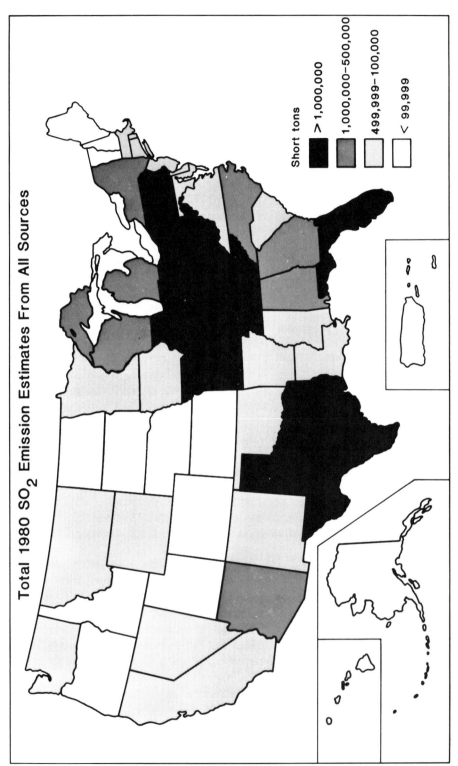

Figure 11.11 Total SO$_2$ emissions, 1980. The major sources are in the industrial states of the Midwest. This is one reason why the Northeast suffers the most from acid rain. Compare with Figure 11.12. (Source: Data provided by Environmental Protection Agency, Region II)

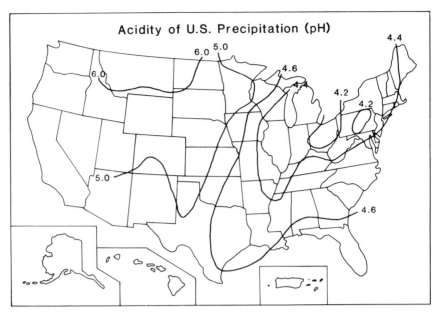

Figure 11.12 Acidity of precipitation in the U.S. The greatest acidity (lowest pH value) is in the northeastern states. Compare with Figure 11.11. (Source: Conservation Foundation, 1982)

markedly increased accumulations of aluminum leached from the soil since 1950. Damage to spruce has also been documented in Vermont and in the Adirondacks. In West Germany, trees have died over 60,000 hectares, and another 100,000 hectares of forests are reported to be severely damaged (Wetstone and Foster, 1983).

There are also concerns about acid rain and its effect on drinking-water supplies and human health. Most metals are relatively insoluble in water at near-neutral pH, but, as pH decreases, their solubility increases. Aluminum in soils, for example, may be leached out by acid rain and increase aluminum concentrations in surface water. Lead, derived from both natural and human sources, is found in lake and stream sediments. As pH decreases, lead concentrations in water may increase. In addition, copper and other metals used in water supply and distribution systems may be dissolved if the water becomes too acidic. Concern with these problems has recently prompted officials in Massachusetts to add lime to Quabbin Reservoir, the major source of water for metropolitan Boston.

Finally, acid rain contributes to corrosion of building stone and exposed metal, including steel rails, unpainted metal surfaces on bridges and buildings, and so forth. The economic costs of these effects are difficult to estimate, but they are believed to be substantial (Scholle, 1983).

Control of Acid Rain

Acid rain can be controlled by the same methods used to control SO_2 and NO_x concentrations in urban areas, including burning low-sulfur fuels, installing sulfur scrubbers, and reducing combustion temperatures. The National Research Council has recently concluded that reductions in emissions will bring proportionate reductions in acid rain (National Research Council, 1983). This is significant, because large reductions in emissions usually bring somewhat smaller reductions in ambient concentrations of most pollutants, due to the continued presence of uncontrolled and natural sources of pollution.

Unfortunately, acid rain is a regional problem, afflicting major industrial regions of North America and Europe. The solutions to the problem must therefore be regional, and this has been one of the primary barriers to reducing acid rain. In the U.S., for example, the Clean Air Act was aimed at urban air pollution problems. Its goal was to reduce pollutant concentrations in those areas. One of the techniques used was tall smokestacks, which dispersed the pollutants over a larger area in lower concentrations. This reduced local pollutant concentrations but also helped to spread sulfur and nitrogen oxides over larger areas, by placing pollutants into stronger upper winds, adding to the acid rain problem at remote locations. If emissions are reduced, acid rain will probably be reduced also, but it is unclear at this time where the benefits will occur.

The U.S. government has been slow to act on the problem (Rhodes and Middleton, 1983). The cost of controlling emissions is estimated to be on the order of billions of dollars per year, depending on how much control is required (Marshall, 1982). These measures have been resisted by a powerful coal and utility lobby, which have argued that the costs would be too burdensome on consumers and would slow the nation's drive for increased energy self-sufficiency. A panel commissioned by President Reagan reported in mid-1983 that acid rain is indeed a serious problem and that controls would be effective in reducing its effects (National Research Council, 1983). The federal government has taken positive steps in recognizing the problem of acid rain, but it has not taken an active role in reducing emissions. Some states, particularly New York, are attempting to urge the federal government to action by enacting sulfur-emission regulations of their own.

International agreements will be necessary to solve this transnational pollution problem. There are some regions that cause the pollution and other regions that suffer its effects. Persuading one country to pay for cleaning up the environment somewhere else may be difficult. Canada, for example, claims that two-thirds of the sulfur deposited in its eastern provinces comes from the U.S. and has argued unsuccessfully that the U.S. should take steps to reduce its emissions. In Europe, more success has been achieved in international negotiations, but there are still unresolved claims by the Scandinavian nations that their lakes are being damaged by pollution from France, Britain, Germany, and the Soviet Union.

Carbon Dioxide

Carbon dioxide (CO_2) constitutes only about 0.03 percent of the earth's atmosphere, yet it plays a vital role in regulating the earth's energy budget, atmospheric circulation, and climate. The global carbon cycle is the biogeochemical cycle that human activity has affected the most. There is reason to believe that this will result in significant climatic changes within the next several decades. If this is true, it will amount to the most profound impact humans have ever had on the global environment and will require substantial adjustment in our use of natural resources.

The Greenhouse Effect

The earth's atmosphere is a partially and differentially transparent medium with respect to energy, regulating flows of energy between space and the earth's surface. It is highly transparent to the wavelengths of most solar radiation, so sunlight passes through the atmosphere relatively unimpeded. The energy returned to space by the earth has much longer wavelengths than sunlight does. The atmosphere is only partly transparent to these wavelengths, and much of the outgoing radiation is temporarily trapped in the atmosphere. This keeps the atmosphere warmer than it would otherwise be. Several atmospheric components are responsible for this action, among them water vapor, ozone, and, most important, CO_2. The ability of CO_2 to pass shortwave solar radiation but absorb long-wave terrestrial radiation, causing atmospheric warming, has been termed the *greenhouse effect.* Glass is transparent to shortwave but opaque to longwave energy, which is why a greenhouse heats up on a sunny day. The same principle applies in the atmosphere, with CO_2 taking the place of the glass, hence the term.

The amount of heat stored in the atmosphere and its distribution within different layers and regions of the atmosphere play an important role in regulating atmospheric circulation and hence climate. The CO_2 content of the atmosphere has changed considerably throughout the history of the earth. A billion or more years ago, it was probably much higher than today. During the Carboniferous era, about 280 to 345 million years ago, much of the land surface of the globe was covered with vast swamp forests. The fossil fuels we burn today are derived from carbon taken from the atmosphere and stored in those forests and other ecosystems in the past. Atmospheric carbon dioxide content also fluctuates on a seasonal basis. In the northern hemisphere, the concentration of CO_2 varies about 5 ppm within a given year. The maximum is in April; as plants photosynthesize and store carbon throughout the summer, the CO_2 content steadily decreases. It reaches a minimum in October, then climbs back up as more plant matter decays than grows. This annual cycle shows the close relation between CO_2 in the atmosphere and processes at the earth's surface.

Sources of Carbon Dioxide

Since the early 19th century, we have steadily increased our extraction and combustion of fossil fuels, returning stored carbon to the atmosphere as CO_2. Not all the CO_2 emitted stays in the atmosphere; a substantial amount enters the oceans, and some is stored in living biomass. Since the 19th century, the atmospheric content has been steadily increasing (see Figure 11.13). The rate of increase is itself steadily increasing, a result of the exponential growth in fossil fuel use worldwide. In 1880 the average concentration was 280 to 300 ppm, and in 1980 it was 340 ppm (Hansen et al., 1981; Environmental Protection Agency, 1983). At present, the annual increase is about 1 ppm, or 0.3 percent.

Not all fuels contribute the same amount of CO_2. Coal emits about 20 percent more CO_2 per unit of energy than oil. Natural gas emits about 75 percent of the CO_2 per unit of energy of oil. In the late 1970s, coal supplied about 29 percent of the world's energy from fossil fuels, but emissions from coal burning were 36 percent of fossil fuel sources. Oil and natural gas supplied about 50

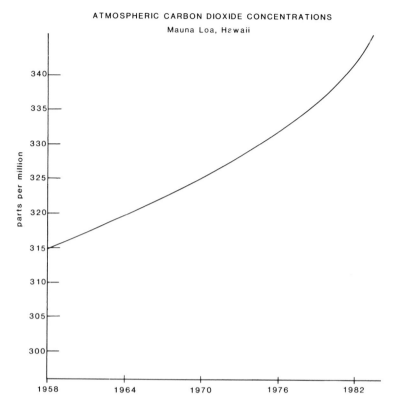

ATMOSPHERIC CARBON DIOXIDE CONCENTRATIONS
Mauna Loa, Hawaii

Figure 11.13   Trend in annual average carbon dioxide concentrations at Mauna Loa Observatory, Hawaii. (Source: Data from U.S. Bureau of the Census, 1984)

percent and 15 percent respectively, of the world's energy from fossil fuels. The undeveloped fuels of heavy oils, tar sands, and oil shale are expected to contribute even more CO_2 than coal does, around 75 percent more than oil per unit of energy (Hansen et al., 1981). Fossil fuel combustion rates have been increasing worldwide, and this trend can be expected to continue in the future.

In addition to fossil fuel sources, more carbon is currently being released from the biota than is absorbed by it (Woodwell et al., 1978). It is estimated that about 28 percent of net CO_2 emissions come from deforestation and the loss of soil carbon due to soil degradation. Deforestation is the largest source, contributing an estimated 22 percent of total net emissions (Wong, 1978). The future concentration of CO_2 is difficult to predict and is of course dependent on future rates of fossil fuel use, which are determined by many economic, political, and technological factors. Most estimates predict a doubling of atmospheric CO_2 sometime in the 21st century.

Effects of Increasing CO_2

Increases in atmospheric CO_2 cause more rapid plant growth. But some plants respond more dramatically than others. For example, soybeans respond much more than corn, and silver maple responds more than sycamore. These differences may lead to significant agricultural and ecological effects of CO_2 (Eckholm, 1984). But the most dramatic environmental impacts will probably result from climatic change.

There has been considerable debate over the nature of the climatic impact of CO_2 emissions. Some have argued that the average temperature of the atmosphere must go up. Others have suggested that there will be an increase in cloudiness and that temperatures will go down as a result. Most predictions of the future effects are based on the use of general circulation models, which are computerized mathematical models of the circulation of the earth's atmosphere. Because of the enormous number of calculations that would be necessary for absolute accuracy, these models make many simplifying assumptions about the atmosphere that affect the results, but in recent years a consensus has emerged (Environmental Protection Agency, 1983). Given a doubling in the CO_2 content of the atmosphere (to about 600 ppm), we can expect an eventual average global temperature increase of a few degrees Celsius, with most estimates falling between 1° and 3°C. The models also agree that the temperature change will be relatively small in the tropics but as much as several degrees in high-latitude areas.

One of the greatest uncertainties in these predictions is the rate at which the temperature increase will take place. This rate depends on many factors, especially the amount of CO_2 emissions and the mixing characteristics of the ocean. Because of the inherent variability of weather, we have not been able to measure long-term climatic changes accurately. Some argue that this lack of detection is evidence that those predicting climate change are wrong. One recent study (Hansen et al., 1981) suggests that the increase in temperature may move out of the range of natural climatic variability and thus become detectable very soon, before the year 2000.

If we conclude that the world will certainly be warmed by the CO_2, then the next question is what the effects on atmospheric circulation and weather will be. This is an even more difficult question to answer because of limitations on our knowledge of atmospheric processes and on computers, the best of which are not powerful enough to model accurately such a complex system. One approach is to look at previous periods of earth history with climates different than today's. About 20,000 years ago, for example, the earth was in the depths of an ice age, with glaciers extending as far south as Long Island, New York, on the east coast of North America, and central Illinois in the Midwest. The circulation and weather patterns that allowed those glaciers to exist were certainly radically different from the present-day climate, yet the average global temperature was only about 5°C cooler than today. The change in temperature predicted for the next century is only slightly less than what occurred during the ice ages, though it is a change to conditions warmer than the present whereas 20,000 years ago the climate was cooler.

The possible consequences of such climatic changes are imaginable, if unpredictable. Circulation changes might cause today's extreme weather to become the norm fifty years from now. Areas now growing wheat might become so dry that only grazing is possible, or they might become wet enough to grow fleshy vegetables. Growing seasons in the mid-latitudes might become several weeks longer—or shorter. Droughts, floods, and similar problems could become commonplace rather than rare. Significant warming in polar areas might cause rapid melting of some ice caps, producing a global rise in sea level of as much as 5 meters. If this occurred, it would inundate 10 percent of New Jersey and 25 percent of Louisiana and Florida (Hansen et al., 1981).

Chlorofluorocarbons

Another global air pollution problem is the accumulation of *chlorofluorocarbons* (CFCs) in the atmosphere (Forziati et al., 1983). CFCs are a class of synthetic substances that were originally developed for use in refrigeration. They also have many other uses, including aerosol propellants and a wide range of industrial applications. The use of CFCs has been increasing exponentially, doubling in five to seven years. The use of CFCs in aerosol sprays was discontinued in the U.S. in 1979, but this is only a fraction of what is used worldwide. In 1981, 1.4 billion pounds were produced (Council on Environmental Quality, 1982, p. 304).

One of the properties of CFCs that makes them so useful in their intended applications is that they are chemically inert and therefore very stable. They remain intact in the atmosphere and accumulate rather than breaking down and being removed. This stability allows them to reach the stratosphere. There they are broken down by intense solar radiation, and their components enter into other chemical reactions. One of these reactions results in the reduction of the amount of ozone in the stratosphere. Ozone intercepts ultraviolet radiation from the sun, and so one of the results of CFCs in the stratosphere is that more ultraviolet radiation reaches the earth's surface. This radiation is responsible for biological damage to plants and animals. From a direct human standpoint, ultraviolet radiation contributes to skin cancers, thus an increase in the amount of ultraviolet radiation would produce an increase in the number of skin cancers worldwide in the coming years.

CFCs also play a role in the troposphere similar to that of CO_2. They absorb longwave radiation and thus enhance the greenhouse effect. Although they are present in much lower concentrations, they are much more effective than CO_2 in raising atmospheric temperatures. As their concentrations in the atmosphere increase, they contribute more and more to the greenhouse effect and may eventually have an impact greater than that of CO_2 (Forziati et al., 1983).

Conclusions

This is of course a highly speculative discussion. No one knows whether any of the predicted climatic changes will occur, let alone when. Most scientists agree that some changes are likely and that major changes are possible within the next several decades. These effects are slow to come, becoming felt only long after their causes have occurred; to prevent them, we would have to act now or, better yet, a few decades ago. For the present, the best that can be done is to become more aware of the problem, to try to predict the future more precisely, and to prepare for the various possible events that are predicted.

SUMMARY

As we have seen, the quality of our air resource has improved in some regions of the country but has worsened in others. Instead of cleaning up pollutants, we often exacerbate the problem, by shifting from one source to another. The long-term consequences of air pollution, the degradation of the air resource, have in some cases already become transnational problems requiring international cooperation in managing this common property resource.

REFERENCES AND ADDITIONAL READING

Avol, E.L., et al. 1983. Acute respiratory effects of Los Angeles smog in continuously exercising adults. *J. Air Pollution Control Assn.* 33:1055–60.

Broughton, D. 1983. Dirty air: the biggest hurdle. *Not Man Apart* 13:6:12–13.

Conservation Foundation. 1982. *State of the environment.* Washington, D.C.

Council on Environmental Quality. 1980. *Environmental quality, 1980. 11th annual report.* Washington, D.C.: Government Printing Office.

————. 1981. *Environmental quality, 1981. 12th annual report.* Washington, D.C.: Government Printing Office.

————. 1982. *Environmental quality, 1982. 13th annual report.* Washington, D.C.: Government Printing Office.

Eckholm, E. 1984. New predictions see rise in CO_2 transforming earth. *New York Times,* August 7.

Fleischaker, M.L. 1983. Converting the converters: tampering with cars and the clean air act. *Environment* 25:8:33–37.

Forziati, H., et al. 1983. The chlorofluorocarbon problem. *Resources* 72:8–9.

Goldsmith, J.R., and L.T. Friberg. 1977. Effects of air pollution on human health. In *The Effects of Air Pollution,* 3rd ed., Arthur C. Stern, ed., chapter 7, pp. 457–610. New York: Academic Press.

Hansen, J., et al. 1981. Climate impact of increasing atmospheric carbon dioxide. *Science* 213:957–66.

Katzenstein, A.W. 1981. *An updated perspective on acid rain.* Washington, D.C.: Edison Electric Institute.

Lave, L.B., and E.P. Seskin. 1977. *Air pollution and human health.* Baltimore: Johns Hopkins Press for Resources for the Future.

Marshall, E. 1982. Air pollution clouds U.S.-Canadian relations. *Science* 217:1118–19.

National Commission on Air Quality. 1981. *To breathe clean air.* Washington, D.C.: Government Printing Office.

National Research Council. 1979. *Airborne particles.* Baltimore: University Park Press.

————. 1981. *On prevention of significant deterioration of air quality.* Washington, D.C.: National Academy Press.

————. 1983. *Acid deposition: atmospheric processes in eastern North America.* Washington, D.C.: National Academy Press.

Patrick, R., et al. 1981. Acid lakes from natural and anthropogenic causes. *Science* 211:446–48.

Postel, S. 1984. *Air pollution, acid rain, and the future of forests.* Worldwatch Paper 58. Washington, D.C.: Worldwatch Institute.

Rhodes, S.L., and P. Middleton. 1983. The complex challenge of controlling acid rain. *Environment* 25:4:6–9.

Rudzitis, G., and J. Schwartz. 1982. The plight of the parklands. *Environment* 24:8:6–11.

Scholle, S.R. 1983. Acid deposition and the materials damage question. *Environment* 25:8:25–32.

U.S. Bureau of the Census. 1984. *Statistical abstract of the United States, 1984.* Washington, D.C.: Government Printing Office.

U.S. Environmental Protection Agency. 1980a. *Environmental outlook.* EPA-600/8-80-003. Washington, D.C.: Government Printing Office.

_____ . 1980b. *Acid rain.* EPA-600-79-036. Washington, D.C.: Government Printing Office.

_____ .1983. *Can we delay a greenhouse warming?* Washington, D.C.: Government Printing Office.

Vogelmann, H.W. 1982. Catastrophe on Camel's Hump. *Natural History* 91: Nov:8–14.

Weaver, J.D. 1980. *Los Angeles: the enormous village 1781–1981.* Santa Barbara: Capra Press.

Wetstone, G.S., and S.A. Foster. 1983. Acid precipitation: what is it doing to our forests? *Environment* 25:4:10–12.

Wong, C.S. 1978. Atmospheric input of carbon dioxide from burning wood. *Science* 200:197–200.

Woodwell, G.M., et al. 1978. The biota and the world carbon budget. *Science* 199:141–46.

TERMS TO KNOW

acid rain
ambient concentration
carbon monoxide
chlorofluorocarbons
Clean Air Act
criteria pollutants
greenhouse effect
hydrocarbons
lead
mobile source
nitrogen oxides

oxidants
photochemical smog
prevention of significant deterioration
primary standard
secondary standard
stationary source
stratosphere
sulfur dioxide
suspended particulates
temperature inversion
troposphere

STUDY QUESTIONS

1. What is an inversion, and how does it affect air pollution?
2. How do sunlight and atmospheric humidity affect air pollution?
3. What are the seven criteria pollutants? For each one, what are the major emission sources?
4. What emissions cause photochemical smog?
5. What has the government done to prevent air quality deterioration in relatively clean areas?

6. Does your city meet all federal air quality guidelines?
7. Summarize the trends in emissions and ambient concentrations for each of the major pollutants over the last several years.
8. What emissions cause acid rain, and where is it a problem?
9. What emissions are expected to cause global climate changes, and when are these changes expected to occur?

CHAPTER TWELVE

Oceans: A Common Property Resource

INTRODUCTION

We tend to think of the earth in terms of land area, yet 71 percent of the earth's surface is covered by water, most of it in the oceans. Virtually all living and non-living resources are somehow influenced by the oceans. We therefore live on a water planet, with much of our food, energy, transportation, and national defense dependent upon marine resources.

The living and non-living resources of the sea have slightly . different characteristics from those found on land. First, they are often unseen and thus unmeasurable and uncountable. It is impossible, for example, for a fisheries biologist to know exactly how many fish there are in a given ocean area. It is also difficult to know the size of an oil field in deep water offshore, as exploration technology used on land does not work in the more resistant marine environment. Second, the oceans are the ultimate diffuser and therefore the ultimate pollution sink. Oceanic oil pollutants, for example, can travel immense distances, confounding attempts to identify and regulate the polluter.

Finally, despite a number of international treaties, the question of who owns the majority of the oceans and the resources within them is still unanswered. On land, governments and individuals claim, occupy, and defend areas, based upon legally binding boundaries, using easily recognized geographic features. Ownership of the oceans is less clear and depends on the current use of the ocean area and on the political, technological, and military powers of a country or private corporation. For example, U.S. companies seeking to mine deep-ocean minerals cannot obtain commercial financing until legal ownership of sections of the deep ocean bottom is established either by international treaty or by unilateral action by the U.S. government. Such disputes are common, and resource managers frequently focus attention on *who* should have access to ocean resources rather than on *how* those resources should be allocated and used.

THE WATER PLANET: PHYSICAL PROPERTIES

Salinity

The physical properties of seawater, the rotation of the earth, and the hydrologic cycle shape the distribution of marine resources and control the ocean's impact on terrestrial ecosystems. Seawater is a solution of minerals and salts of nearly

Table 12.1 Composition of Dissolved Sea Salts in Seawater

Element	Percentage
Chlorine	55.0
Sulfur	7.7
Sodium	30.6
Magnesium	3.7
Potassium	0.7
Calcium	0.7
Minor Elements (Bromine, Carbon, Strontium)	1.6
Total	100.0

Source: Gross, 1971

constant composition throughout the world. Sea salts, a product of billions of years of terrestrial erosion, contain at least traces of most elements found in the earth's crust. Six elements, however, comprise more than 98 percent of all sea salts (see Table 12.1). On the average, a kilogram of seawater contains about 35 grams of salt, or 35 parts per thousand (ppt). These salts are dissolved in variable amounts of water, and slight differences in the *salinity* of seawater can influence the speed and direction of ocean currents and the vertical mixing of surface and bottom waters.

Salinity change also has major impact on the ocean's living resources. It governs, for example, the spawning time of oysters and other shellfish on the east coast of the U.S. and the shrimp migrations in the Gulf of Mexico. Juvenile shrimp can tolerate the wide-ranging salinities (0–25 ppt) found in coastal areas; adult shrimp can survive only in ocean waters of 35 ppt salinity. Thus, the success of the shrimp fishing season is dictated largely by rainfall and freshwater river discharge.

As salinity changes, the density of seawater also changes. Freshwater or low salinity water floats on top of heavier, saltier water, creating *stratified estuaries* in coastal areas and *haloclines* in the open ocean. Such stratification can complicate efforts to protect shellfish beds and to monitor pollutants, and it can even threaten public drinking-water supplies. For example, at the mouth of the Delaware River, near Philadelphia, the movement of the so-called salt wedge is dictated by the volume of freshwater flow in the Delaware River. If river flow is low, salty ocean water creeps up Delaware Bay, threatening the city's drinking water intake. Conversely, seasonal high flows of fresh water lower the salinity in the oyster beds downstream from Wilmington, Delaware, discouraging the spread of oyster parasites and predatory oyster drills. The size and movement of the salt wedge in this partially stratified estuary affects everything from commercial fishing to the drinking-water supplies of over 3 million people.

Heat Exchange

Water temperature and water temperature gradients are other physical aspects of the ocean environment that influence conservation and management of marine resources. The worldwide distribution of the ocean's surface-water temperature depends upon the general supply of heat available from the sun. Surface temperature is highest at the equator and declines northward and southward, toward the poles. Total heat loss from the ocean waters (as opposed to the temperature of the water itself) also declines as one moves away from the equator, but not at the same rate. The difference between a surplus of heat at the equator and relatively little elsewhere results in the global heat-transfer mechanisms (air and water currents) that shape our weather. The oceans, then, can be viewed as a giant weather machine. The major ocean currents in the world are shown in Figure 12.1.

A change in ocean water temperatures can have a worldwide impact. In the late fall of each year, a warm water current, which local fishermen call "El Niño," develops along the coasts of Ecuador and Peru. At irregular intervals, a much larger ocean warming occurs at the same time of year along the same coast but stretching westward along the equator, two-thirds of the way across the Pacific Ocean. This large-scale warming completely reverses the wind and current systems of the Pacific Ocean, influencing worldwide weather patterns and causing rare winter and spring hurricanes, floods, and droughts. In addition, El Niño affects the catch of anchovies off Peru, and a drop in the Pacific coast fish catch has been linked to the 1982–83 El Niño (Rasmusson and Hall, 1983; Brock, 1984).

Dissolved Oxygen

The last important physical feature of the oceans that affects marine conservation and management is *dissolved oxygen,* the total amount of oxygen within a body of liquid, in this case, water. Dissolved oxygen is absolutely essential for aquatic life.

The distribution of dissolved oxygen is controlled by exchanges with the atmosphere, photosynthesis of phytoplankton, and respiration of oxygen-consuming biota. The solubility of a gas such as oxygen is a function of water temperature; the lower the temperature, the more dissolved oxygen. The vertical distribution of dissolved oxygen in the oceans is a function of currents and of photosynthetic activity of phytoplankton in the *euphotic zone,* the upper regions that receive sufficient sunlight for plants. Dissolved oxygen levels, then, generally decline with depth. The deep oceans, however, are rarely anoxic, or devoid of oxygen, as cold, deep water generally contains more oxygen than is consumed by the limited populations of animals in deep water.

Dissolved oxygen is a key variable in determining the distribution of living resources in the sea and gauging the sensitivity of the oceans to pollutants. An example of the complex relationship among dissolved oxygen, weather, currents, and nutrients is the massive fish and shellfish kill that occurred off New Jersey in the summer and autumn of 1976. An early, wet, warm spring in the region resulted in increased river discharge and earlier than normal warming of sea-surface waters. Unusual atmospheric pressure patterns in the late winter and early spring also caused winds to shift to the south earlier than expected. These weather conditions produced a lens of relatively warm, fresh surface water, isolating bottom water and preventing its normal replenishment of dissolved oxygen from the surface. This *stratification* of the waters on the continental

OCEAN CURRENTS

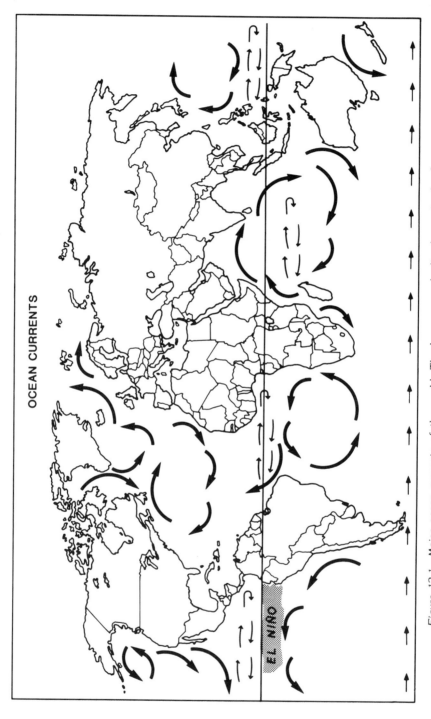

Figure 12.1 Major ocean currents of the world. The large ocean bodies have circular flow patterns, called *gyres*, which are clockwise in the Northern Hemisphere and counterclockwise in the Southern Hemisphere. Superimposed on this pattern are smaller currents such as the equatorial counter-currents. Periodic disruptions of circulation, labeled El Niño, occur in the eastern Pacific.

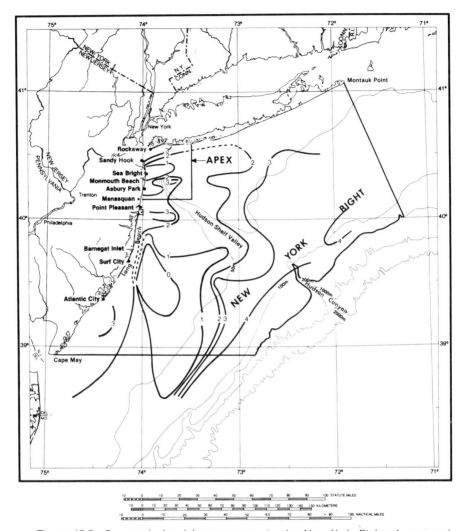

Figure 12.2 Oxygen-depleted bottom water in the New York Bight, August and September, 1976. Dissolved oxygen content is shown in milliliters per liter. This oxygen depletion resulted from weather conditions that altered normal circulation patterns and was aggravated by pollution from the New York metropolitan area. (Source: Swanson and Sindermann, 1979)

shelf resulted in a decline in dissolved oxygen at the bottom (see Figure 12.2). The impact of this anoxic condition was dramatic. One-half of the surf clam population off New Jersey died, lobster catches dropped by 50 percent, and bluefish migrating from southern waters turned around, thus failing to appear at northern spawning areas (Swanson and Sindermann, 1979). Eventually, lower than normal levels of dissolved oxygen were reported over a 8,600 km² area. This anoxic condition was caused by unusual atmospheric and oceanographic events. A key variable, however, may have been the nutrient inputs into the shelf waters from sewage sludge, dredge spoil, atmospheric fallout, municipal and industrial wastewater, and urban runoff.

BIOLOGICAL PRODUCTIVITY AND FOOD

Major Productive Regions

The biological productivity of the oceans is highly variable and is dictated by a combination of bottom topography, salinity, water temperature, sunlight, and currents. We can spatially delimit three major productive regions of the oceans—estuaries, near-shore and continental-shelf waters, and the deep ocean. Each of these has a different level of importance to marine fisheries and food resources.

An *estuary* is an enclosed coastal body of water that has a direct connection to the sea and a measurable dilution of seawater by fresh water from the land. Estuaries are transition zones where fresh and salt water mix in a shallow environment that is also strongly influenced by tidal currents. Estuaries can be classified as ecotones (see Chapter 4) or as transitional areas between two distinct natural systems, terrestrial and marine. Ecotones generally have a greater diversity of species and higher biological productivity than do the natural systems on either side. This edge-effect is especially true in estuaries. The primary productivity of estuaries is twenty times that of the deep oceans and two to three times that of a typical forest (Odum, 1971).

Since phytoplankton and other primary producers serve as the basis for most marine food chains, the majority of fish and shellfish caught for human consumption are dependent upon estuaries during at least a portion of their life cycle. A few species are permanent estuarine residents, but the majority of fish species migrate between estuaries and near-shore and continental shelf waters to spawn or feed. Estuaries are also important nursery areas for immature fish and shellfish. In addition, estuaries play a key role in the migration of *anadromous* and *catadromous* fish, such as Pacific salmon, the American eel, and the striped bass. Fishery biologists estimate that 75–90 percent of all fish and shellfish caught by commercial and recreation fishermen in the U.S. are in one way or another dependent upon estuaries.

Near-shore and continental shelf waters are the second geographic division. They encompass a larger portion of the world's total ocean area (7–8 percent) than estuaries (which occupy 2–3 percent), yet they are less biologically productive. They slope from the shoreline out to a depth of approximately 200 meters and are affected by geologically recent changes in sea level. The continental shelves are the submerged coastal plains that were above water as late as the last ice age, 10,000 years ago. Often low and marshy in prehistoric times, subject to repeated burial and changes in pressure as sea level fluctuated, the continental shelves today are a major source of petroleum reserves.

The waters above the continental shelves are also the site of the majority of the world's fisheries. Close to highly productive estuaries, continental shelves are subject to wind-driven and tidal currents and are shallow enough to permit constant mixing of warm surface waters and cool, nutrient rich bottom waters. The primary productivity of the shelves is approximately double that of the open ocean. One key feature of the continental shelf region is *upwelling*. Upwelling is caused by wind-driven surface currents moving away from the shoreline. Deep, nutrient-rich, water is drawn to the surface, creating exceptionally productive areas (Figure 12.3). Upwelling occurs on a large scale along the western edge of continents and, to a lesser extent, in specific portions of the eastern shelf,

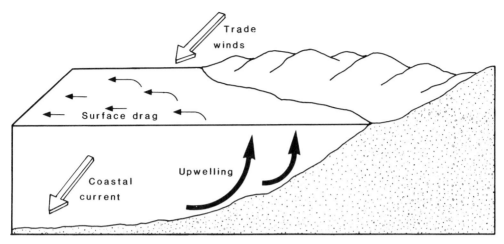

Figure 12.3 Upwelling is caused by wind-driven currents that move away from a coastline. Nutrient-laden water is drawn upward to replace the water moved at the surface. Regions of upwelling are generally areas of very productive fisheries.

such as Georges Bank off the coast of Massachusetts. Nearly 99 percent of all fish production occurs in estuaries and continental shelves, and the majority of continental shelf fisheries are concentrated in upwelling regions (see Issue 12.1).

Compared to the continental shelves, the *deep oceans* are a biological desert, even though they encompass 90 percent of the earth's ocean area. They are only half as productive as continental shelves, with most biological activity concentrated in the euphotic zone, where sunlight penetrates. At present, there are only a few important fisheries found in the deep ocean, and the most valuable of these is tuna. As coastal nations have claimed the fishery resources of their continental shelves, deep ocean fisheries are becoming increasingly important to nations such as Japan and the Soviet Union, which have relatively small continental shelf areas under their direct control.

Food from the Oceans

The importance of the ocean as a potential food resource is increasing. In the 1970s, about 9 percent of the protein consumed by the world's population came from marine fish and shellfish. By the year 2000, this figure may rise as high as 20 percent (Council on Environmental Quality, 1981b). This rising demand for protein and a leveling off of agricultural production in many parts of the world results in a rapid climb in the world's catch of fish (see Figure 12.4). Nearly 70 percent of all fish caught are eaten by people as fresh or frozen fish; the remaining 30 percent of the catch is reduced to fish meals, which are made into fertilizers, animal feed (primarily chicken feed), or oils used in paints and other industrial products (see Table 12.2). Fishery resources are unevenly distributed around the globe in both fresh and salt water, with nearly 90 percent of the total fish catch in marine waters (United Nations Food and Agricultural Organization, 1981). The leading fishing nations in the world are Japan, the U.S.S.R., and the People's Republic of China (see Table 12.3). These nations do not necessarily

MILLION METRIC TONS

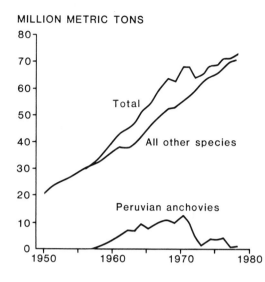

Figure 12.4 World fish catch, 1945–1978. Catch has steadily increased, with the exception of the collapse of the Peruvian anchovy fishery in the early 1970s. (Source: Council on Environmental Quality, 1981)

ISSUE 12.1: Getting a Handle on Cod

A wooden model of a codfish hangs in the Massachusetts statehouse in Boston. It was placed there in recognition of the role this species played in the colonization of New England. Although a part of history, codfish are also a modern-day headache for New England's fishermen, biologists, and politicians.

In 1976 the U.S. Congress unilaterally declared a 200-mile-wide exclusive fishing zone, over the objections of then-President Ford and the State Department. The key sponsor of the legislation was Congressman Gerry Studds, representing Cape Cod and the fishing port of New Bedford. He pleaded for the immediate protection of cod, haddock, and yellowtail flounder stocks from overfishing by the fleets of huge Soviet and Japanese fishing vessels on Georges Bank, 50 miles off the cape. The Fishery Conservation and Management Act was passed, halting virtually all foreign fishing off New England. Fearful of further overfishing, the federal government also imposed catch limits on domestic fishermen, based on complex biological assessments of cod, haddock, and yellowtail flounder populations. Eleven weeks after the quotas were established, fishermen exceeded the entire 1977 *groundfish* quotas.

Chaos followed, with management regulations changing thirty times and quotas increasing five times within a two-and-one-half-year period. Fishermen claimed that there were more cod on Georges Bank than ever before, and biologists admitted that the margin of error in their population estimates was at least as large as the quotas they had proposed.

How did this situation arise? Management of renewable resources has two often-conflicting objectives: (1) maximizing economic return, and (2) preserving the sustainable nature of the resource. To meet these objectives, biologists calculate the surplus production of a species beyond that required to renew itself. This surplus is defined as the *maximum sustainable yield* (MSY). The MSY is the largest average catch that can be harvested indefinitely under existing environmental conditions. It is calculated using various population models, which combine such variables as the recruitment of young fish into the harvestable population, reproductive rates, and natural mortality. The concept of MSY assumes that a wildlife population produces a harvestable surplus when the size of the population is kept at an intermediate level. Growth rates, repro-

catch all of these fish in their own territorial waters. For example, 58 percent of the fish caught in the U.S. Fishery Conservation Zone (3–200 miles offshore) are caught by U.S. fishing vessels. The remaining 42 percent are caught by foreign fishing fleets (see Figure 12.5). Of these, Japan captures 72 percent of the foreign catch in this zone, mostly from Alaska and the Bering Straits region (UNFAO, 1981). Access to fish is therefore a key issue in ocean management, with countries such as the United States using fisheries as a "food weapon" in political controversies, such as the Soviet invasion of Afghanistan (*New York Times,* 1980).

ENERGY FROM THE OCEANS

The United States and other nations are increasingly dependent upon the oceans for energy production. The share of traditional energy sources, such as oil and gas, from offshore areas is growing, and several non-traditional sources of energy from the oceans are under intensive development (see Chapter 15).

duction, and recruitment are theoretically higher when older, slow-growing members are removed and competition for food, space, and other factors is reduced.

The principle of MSY is used in the management of timber, game species such as deer, and most marine fisheries. The concept of MSY has, however, been less than successful in the real world of fisheries management. First, traditional MSY calculations require a species-by-species approach. A "desirable" species is identified and the surplus production calculated, keeping all other variables constant. Thus, predator-prey relationships are ignored, and a value judgment is made about the importance of a particular species. People interested in the preservation or enhancement of an entire ecosystem, as opposed to a specific species, therefore consider the MSY approach dangerously exploitative. Conversely, hunters and fishermen distrust the MSY concept because catch is dictated strictly on biological grounds, ignoring economic considerations.

Second, a MSY calculation assumes that other variables affecting the population remain constant. In the case of New England's cod, haddock, and yellowtail flounder, it was this limitation in the MSY calculation that created chaos in the fishing industry between 1977 and 1980. For example, a comparison between the yearly expected surplus of flounder and water temperature indicates that temperature has more impact on population size than does predicted fishing mortality. In another example, scientists have discovered that it is the flow of the Mississippi River, not the size of the catch, that dictates the number of shrimp available for harvest each year in the Gulf of Mexico.

Scientists and politicians now realize that MSY is an overly simplistic approach to managing renewable resources. Federal laws on fisheries, marine mammals, and timber therefore now require managers to determine the optimum yield of a species, taking into account environmental variables, economic interests, and the biological uncertainties of managing entire ecosystems. While it is a more realistic approach to management, the calculation of optimum yield is a delicate balancing act between competing interests. In the future, fishery biologists may have to be equally adept at political mediation and population biology (Warner, 1982; Warner, Finamore, and Bean, 1981).

Table 12.2 World Fishery Catch

		1977		1981
Total World Catch (Metric Tons)		68,766,700		74,760,400
Human Consumption[b]	70.2		70.4	
Fresh		20.2		19.4
Frozen		21.9		22.5
Curing		14.2		14.5
Canning		13.9		14.0
Other[b]	29.8		29.6	
Reduction[c]		28.3		28.2
Miscellaneous		1.5		1.4
Total	100.0	100.0	100.0	100.0

[a]Excludes whales, seals, mammals, and aquatic plants
[b]Percentage of total world catch
[c]Includes reduction to oils and meals

Source: U.N. Food and Agricultural Organization, 1981

Approximately 30 percent of the earth's exploitable hydrocarbons are found beneath marine waters, with 90 percent of these unexplored. The majority of these explored oil and gas deposits are found on the continental shelf, near land-based oil and gas reserves. The U.S. outer continental shelf, for example, is roughly 4.7 million km² (1.8 million square miles) in size. This is comparable to the 4.4 million km² (1.7 million square miles) of geologically favorable land in the U.S. that currently supports most domestic oil and gas production. There is a good chance, then, that the offshore regions under U.S. control could produce at least as much oil and gas as is currently produced on land (Halbouty, 1982). A similar pattern can be found worldwide.

This rapid growth of offshore oil and gas development depends upon the ability to drill for hydrocarbons in ever deeper water. Early efforts at offshore drilling were simple extensions of land-based techniques in water less than 6 meters (20 feet) deep. Advances in drilling technology, semi-submersible drilling-

Table 12.3 Leading Fishing Nations, 1981

Country	Metric Tons Caught
Fish, Crustaceans, Molluscs	
Japan	10,656,515
USSR	9,545,922
People's Republic of China	4,605,000
U.S.A.	3,767,425
Chile	3,393,399
Seaweed	
People's Republic of China	1,387,398
Japan	648,210
Republic of Korea	444,237
Norway	148,365
Chile	109,631

Source: U.N. Food and Agricultural Organization, 1981

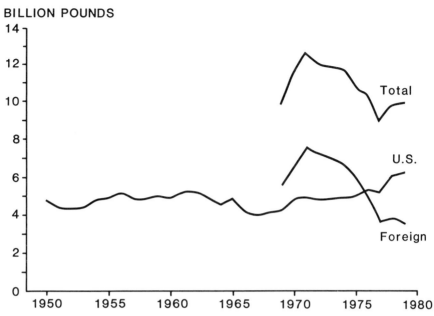

Figure 12.5 Fish catch in the U.S. 200-mile zone, excluding catch in the territorial sea, 1950–1979. U.S. catch has remained fairly constant, increasing slightly in the 1970s. Foreign catch has declined in the 1970s, partly because of the imposition of the 200-mile limit. (Source: Council on Environmental Quality, 1981)

rig designs, offshore pipelines, and other equipment now permit construction of conventional drilling platforms in up to 305 m (1,000 feet) of water (see Figure 12.6). In fact, technology for drilling temporary exploratory offshore oil and gas wells has outstripped the technology for building the permanent platforms needed to bring an area into regular production. Exploratory wells have been drilled in up to 1.5 km (5,000 feet) of water, opening up large areas of the continental slope and even deep ocean areas to eventual development (U.S. Department of the Interior, 1981).

DEEP SEA-BED MINERALS

For hundreds of years, sand, gravel, coal, tin, gold, and diamonds have been mined from the sediments beneath shallow water areas around the world. By the early 1970s, mineral deposits found in the deep ocean had become technically and economically exploitable. Many of these mineral deposits contain strategic minerals such as cobalt, currently imported by industrial nations, including the U.S. (see Chapter 14). Of particular interest to the developed nations are manganese nodules. These potato-sized lumps are common features of the sea floor in water from 4 to 6 kilometers in depth. The nodules are composed of hydrated oxides of iron and manganese, which often form around a nucleus of shell, rock, or other material, just as the pearls oysters create form around a grain of sand. Manganese nodules are found in all of the world's oceans, although the grade

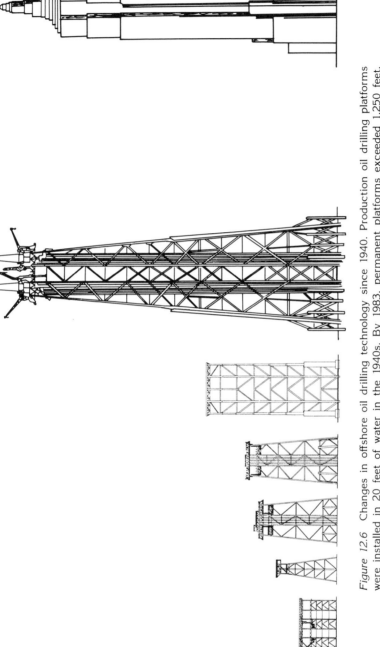

Figure 12.6 Changes in offshore oil drilling technology since 1940. Production oil drilling platforms were installed in 20 feet of water in the 1940s. By 1983, permanent platforms exceeded 1,250 feet, approximately the height of the Empire State Building. (Source: From U.S. Department of the Interior, 1981)

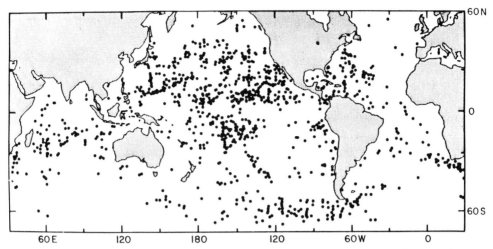

Figure 12.7 Manganese in the oceans. Scientific research vessels have found accumulations of manganese nodules at these locations over the last 100 years. (Source: Heath, 1982)

(percentage of various metals) and coverage (weight and number per area) vary. The eastern Pacific Ocean several hundred miles south of Hawaii appears to contain exceptionally dense nodule deposits, containing minerals in sufficient quantity to permit commercial exploitation (Knecht, 1982). (See Figure 12.7.)

Manganese nodules contain four principal minerals: manganese, nickel, copper, and cobalt. Virtually all the cobalt and manganese and 70 percent of the nickel consumed by U.S. industries each year is imported from South Africa, Zaire, Canada, and the Soviet Union. As a result, U.S., Japanese, and European mining companies are interested in gaining access to the billions of tons of deep sea bed minerals that are expected to become available as the technology improves.

Exploitation of sea-bed minerals would require an investment of many millions of dollars. To protect such an investment, mining companies would undoubtedly demand guaranteed and probably exclusive access to this resource. The exploitable fields of sea-bed nodules, however, are in deep ocean waters, beyond any single nation's jurisdiction. The interest in sea-bed mining has prompted a total reevaluation of the concept of ownership of marine resources, resulting in the negotiation of a complex Law of the Sea Treaty, which is discussed later in this chapter. Thus far, the United States has refused to sign, partly because the treaty limits unrestricted access to manganese nodules.

THE OCEAN AS A POLLUTION SINK

The oceans are so large that we often think of them as a place where we can discard the unwanted by-products of civilization. This attitude runs the gamut from passively allowing pollutants in streams and rivers eventually to make their way to the ocean to actively and deliberately burying wastes in the ocean. We will briefly discuss two of the sources of marine pollution—spills of hazardous materials and ocean dumping.

There have been many major transportation accidents involving oil tankers (see Figure 12.8). The most famous of these include the wrecks of the *Torrey Canyon,* which spilled about 95,200 tonnes (700,000 barrels) of oil off the southern coast of England in 1967; the *Argo Merchant,* which spilled 28,179 tonnes (207,200 barrels) off the coast of Massachusetts near Nantucket Island in 1976; the *Amoco Cadiz,* losing 221,410 tonnes (1,628,000 barrels) off the French Coast in the English Channel in 1978; and, finally, the collision in 1979 of the *Atlantic Empress* and the *Aegean Capitan* in the Caribbean, spilling over 141,071 tonnes (1,034,000 barrels). The resulting pollution of the ocean from these spills, including the land-based effects, was quite extensive (Fairhall and Jordan, 1980; Winslow, 1978).

Although tanker accidents account for specific pollution episodes, oil spills also occur in ports and harbors, from stationary offshore drilling platforms, and through runoff from land-based facilities. In the U.S. alone, there were 10,072 accidents in marine waters in 1981, with 19,638 million gallons (467 million barrels) of oil spilled (U.S. Coast Guard, 1981). The majority of these were in inland waters (see Figure 12.9). Offshore oil exploration and drilling accounts for only 5 percent of the world's total oil pollution of the oceans, although at times the local impacts are quite severe. During 1979–80, nearly 364,000 tonnes (over 2.7 million barrels) of crude oil were spilled in the Gulf of Mexico, as a result of the blowout of IXTOC-1, a Mexican-owned oil well in the Bay of Campeche (Council on Environmental Quality, 1981b). The drifting oil spill caused an international dispute when it washed ashore on beaches in Texas, destroying wildlife and habitat and severely affecting recreational and fishing industries in the region.

Ocean dumping is one of the major contributors to ocean pollution. Ocean dumping includes the disposal of sewage sludge, industrial and solid waste, explosives, demolition debris, radioactive materials, and dredge spoils.

During the 1960s, nearly 8.3 million tonnes (7.4 million tons) of debris were dumped annually into U.S. coastal waters (Council of Environmental Quality, 1982). In addition, 61.5 million tonnes (54.9 million tons) of dredged material were dumped during this time. Dredged material, by weight, is the most significant material currently being dumped in the oceans, accounting for over 90 percent of the waste disposed of in the marine environment. In the U.S., dredged material was traditionally dumped in estuaries and on tidal wetlands. Concern over protecting these productive areas has led to a shift to near-shore and continental shelf dumping of dredged materials. Toxic materials, such as cadmium, lead, copper, and polychlorinated biphenyls (PCBs), found in dredged materials are another problem. Bottom sediments in many ports and rivers contain high levels of toxic pollutants left over from decades of uncontrolled dumping and pollution. These sediments are usually immobile if undisturbed, but, during dredging activities, they become suspended in the water. The cost of disposing of such polluted sediments on land is significantly greater than ocean disposal, yet scientific evidence on the safety of various ocean-disposal techniques is lacking.

In some parts of the world, sewage sludge and industrial wastes are a major source of contaminants in the marine environment. While great efforts have been made to upgrade onshore sewage treatment plants to reduce water pollution, the result has been a higher volume of sewage sludge that needs disposal. In 1972 Congress passed the Marine Protection, Research, and Sanctuaries Act,

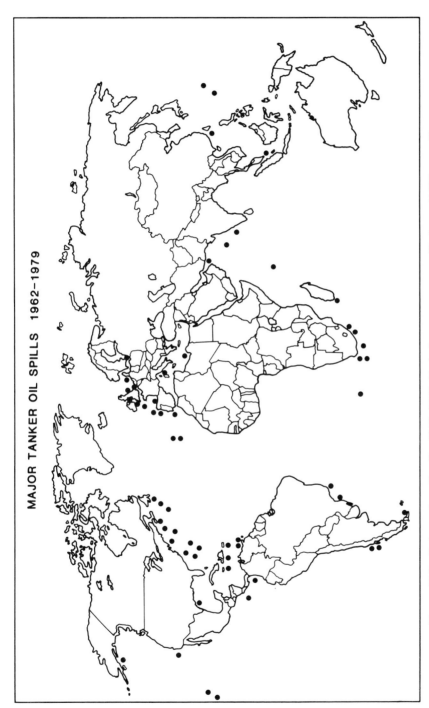

MAJOR TANKER OIL SPILLS 1962–1979

Figure 12.8 Major tanker oil spills, 1962–1979. Each dot represents a spill of over 5,000 tons. (Source: From Winslow, 1978)

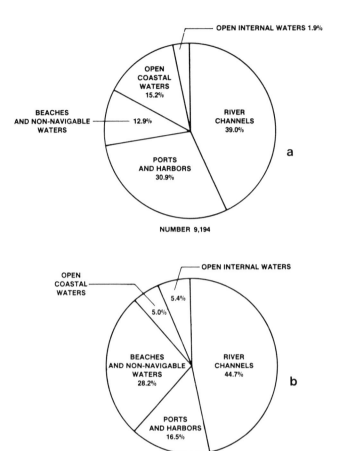

Figure 12.9   Oil spills in U.S. waters. (a) Numbers of spills, by location. River channels and ports and harbors are the most likely locations for spills. (b) Volume of oil spilled, by location. River channels have received the most oil spilled, but beaches and nonnavigable waters have also received large volumes. (Source: U.S. Coast Guard, 1981)

which, among other things, requires a permit for ocean dumping. In 1977 the act was amended to encourage land disposal of sewage sludge after December 31, 1981. Ocean disposal of sewage sludge has therefore declined throughout the U.S., except in the New York Bight (Swanson and Devine, 1982).

New York City, parts of Nassau and Westchester Counties, New York, and parts of New Jersey have been routinely dumping sewage sludge 19 km (12 miles) off Sandy Hook, at the entrance to New York Harbor, for decades. Scientists have identified a 32 km² (20-square-mile) area, locally known as the "dead zone," where there is little or no marine life. A total of 9 billion liters (2.4 billion gallons) of raw and treated sewage and industrial waste are discharged into the New York Bight daily (Carney, 1984). In 1984 the U.S. Environmental Protection Agency ordered New York City and other municipalities to move the dump site 171 km (106 miles) offshore, to deep water beyond the edge of the outer continental shelf.

MANAGEMENT OF MARINE RESOURCES

The Concept of Ownership

No one nation owns the world's oceans or controls the resources found in them. The oceans, then, are a *common property resource.* Common property resources cannot be managed by a single individual, nation, or corporation, because, without some form of governmental or international regulation to allocate resources among users, there is little incentive to preserve or protect resources for future generations (see Chapter 2). Historically, those nations that could exploit the world's marine resources, such as oil, fish, whales, and minerals, simply did so.

A classic example of the problems with managing a common property resource is the international regulation of whaling. The introduction of the harpoon gun and steam-powered whaling vessels in the late 1800s, coupled with the advent of the seagoing factory ship in the early 20th century, revitalized the whaling industry of *Moby Dick* fame. This new technology permitted the exploitation of larger, faster species of whales, such as the blue whale, and the processing of oil, bone, and meat at sea. Several European nations developed fleets of small vessels, called whale catchers, centered around a large factory ship. These fleets caught several different species in both Arctic and Antarctic waters, raising problems of overfishing as early as 1920. The first international whaling treaty, signed in 1931, proved ineffective. The International Whaling Commission (IWC) was therefore established in 1946, ostensibly to protect and ensure species survival. Currently, thirty-nine countries are members of the IWC.

The wording of the preamble to the 1946 International Convention for the Regulation of Whaling, which created the IWC, is a good example of the difficulty of using a scientifically rational management approach on a common property resource such as whales. The treaty directs that the IWC safeguard for future generations the great natural resources represented by the whale while also increasing the size of whale stocks to bring the population to an 'optimal level' to make possible the orderly development of the whaling industry (Bean, 1977, pp. 304–5). Is the objective of the IWC to protect whales, to encourage industry development, or both? Nearly four decades of efforts to manage whales by the IWC indicate that nations generally seek to protect whales only when it is in their national interest to do so.

The 1946 treaty permits member nations to object to and then legally ignore the quotas established by the Commission and its scientific committees. Thus, in 1983, when the IWC formally declared a complete moratorium on all whaling at the urging of the U.S. and other non-whaling member nations, Japan, and the Soviet Union formally objected. These two nations continue whaling, while technically remaining within the limits of international law.

International efforts to protect whales are complicated by the slow reproductive rates of these marine mammals. For example, one of the reasons cited in support of the international whaling conventions was the slow rate of recovery of the Atlantic right whale and the Pacific bowhead whale. The world catch for these species peaked in the mid-1800s, and the IWC's first act was to ban all further commercial harvest. However, right and bowhead whale populations have not recovered, despite forty years of complete protection. It appears that the slow reproductive rate of these species is responsible for the inability of the small, dispersed population to grow rapidly.

Table 12.4 Whale Abundance and Catch

Species	Virgin Population[a]	Current Population	Peak Catch	Year of Peak Catch	1980 Catch
Blue	215,000	13,000	19,079	1930	0
Humpback	50,000	7,000	5,063	1950	16
Fin	448,000	101,000	32,185	1955	472
Sei	200,000	76,000	25,454	1965	102
Sperm	922,000	641,000	25,842	1970	2,091
Gray	11,000	11,000	NA	NA	NA
Minske	361,000	325,000	12,398	1977	11,709

[a]Estimates of population before harvesting began

Source: Council on Environmental Quality, 1982

Given the structure of the IWC, recent whaling follows a pattern of heavy exploitation of one species, leading to a dramatic population decline, and a shift to another species. For example, 11,559 blue whales were caught in 1940, declining to less than 2,000 in 1960 and 613 in 1965. The catch of the slightly smaller fin whale peaked at 32,185 in the mid-1950s and dropped to 5,057 by 1970. The harvest of the still smaller sei whale was minimal until 1960, when it rose and subsequently declined (Council on Environmental Quality, 1982, p. 314). The status of those stocks in 1980 is shown in Table 12.4.

ISSUE 12.2: Flipper versus Charlie the Tuna

Many of us regard tuna fish as a staple of our diet. Buy a can of tuna, and you've almost got a meal. Purchasing a can of tuna meant, until recently, that you were also paying for porpoise carcasses discarded from the tuna catch.

Schools of tuna often swim below porpoises, which travel in groups near the surface. In the early 1960s, fishing vessels operating out of San Diego began setting their seine nets around the porpoises to get at the tuna. When the tuna were hauled in, hundreds of porpoises were suffocated.

A 1972 estimate of these by-product killings was 300,000 annually. The most affected species were the spotted and spinner porpoises and the common dolphin (Scheffer, 1977). Why did this rather clever fishing technique generate so much public outrage?

Porpoises, whales, sea otters, seals, and sea cows are mammals. Porpoises are often called dolphins, which can be confusing, as there is also a fish called a dolphin. To many people, the simple fact that porpoises are mammals sets them above other sea creatures. In addition, scientific research on porpoises suggests that they may be highly intelligent and possess a complex and subtle language. Thus, while tuna fish fill our stomachs, porpoises provide us with other, less tangible benefits. It seemed to many people simply wasteful to kill and discard all those porpoises.

Operators of the tuna seiners were not impressed with these arguments. The development of nylon seining nets had helped put the languishing American tuna industry back into competition with other tuna sources (Orbach, 1977). When the Marine Mammal Protection Act was passed in 1972, it dictated that porpoise killing had to stop, and soon. From 1973 to 1977, the tuna fishers negotiated with the government, environ-

There has been an interesting reaction to the failure of international efforts to regulate whales. In 1976 the United States adopted legislation linking the permitted harvest of fish within U.S. waters by foreign nations to their adherence to IWC quotas. Thus, when Japan refused to abide by the IWC's moratorium in 1983, the U.S. withheld 100,000 metric tons of Japan's 1984 allocation of fish to be caught off Alaska and threatened to limit fishing further if Japan's objections to the IWC were not withdrawn. Several other nations are adopting a similar strategy. In the U.S., all marine mammals (whales, porpoises, seals, manatees, and walruses) are protected by legislation. At the international level, however, an agency such as the IWC has no real enforcement powers and must rely on economic sanctions and on the diplomacy of its member nations. Non-whaling nations, such as the U.S., often cite the need to protect whales as an aesthetic resource. This argument does not carry much weight in whaling nations, such as Japan, Norway, and the Soviet Union, where whales have significant economic value. Thus, international management of such common property resources as whales often depends upon resolving differences over the perceived value of the resource in question (see Chapter 13) (Issue 12.2).

Jurisdiction: Who Controls What?

Given the difficulty in managing a common property resource, such as whales or fish, it is important to understand where control of marine resources by a

---

mentalists, lawyers, and biologists to decide on an allowable annual porpoise quota.

The 1977 quota of 59,050 porpoises was too low for the fishermen, who refused to leave port and threatened to sell their boats to foreign investors. The Carter administration eventually responded by supporting a congressional measure to raise that year's quota to 68,190. The eventual goal was to bring down the quotas, as new techniques and equipment were developed to aid in the reduction of porpoise mortality (Scheffer, 1977). From 1978 to 1980, the quotas were 52,000, 42,000, and 31,000. If the annual quota was exceeded for any of the protected porpoise species, then yellowfin tuna fishing associated with that type of porpoise was at an end for the year.

A study of incidental porpoise mortality since 1977 indicates that the mortality levels have decreased (Lo, 1983). An important technique for reducing porpoise deaths is to lower the net, once the porpoise and tuna are fully encircled, to a level where the porpoise escape but the tuna do not. This requires considerable skill and experience, especially in heavy seas. The tuna industry has a vested interest in porpoise survival, in that porpoise lead them to tuna and are thus worth more alive than dead.

There is some irony in the fact that this sensitive and innovative group of entrepreneurs was accused of cruelty and lack of concern. Since the seine net's introduction, the industry has gone to great lengths to return porpoise to the sea (Orbach, 1977). Whether it was a matter of learning how to use new equipment or of heartlessly destroying a valued mammal, these business people saw the situation in strict economic terms, while the public saw it in aesthetic and environmentalist terms, and the two have been negotiating ever since.

single nation stops and where international control begins. Diplomats and inter-national law experts make a distinction between control of ocean space and control of the use of ocean space. Thus, international treaties recognize a 3- to 12-mile wide territorial sea along a nation's coastline as the exclusive territory of that nation. Both ocean space (including bottom sediments) and the use of that space by fishing vessels, navy ships, and oil companies are controlled by the individual nation. Other types of jurisdiction or "ownership" are less clear. Many coastal nations claim control over all fishing resources within 200 miles of shore. Yet national control over other activities, such as the transit of military vessels of hostile nations, in this 200-mile area is not recognized by international law. In some cases, even particular types of fish, such as tuna, for example, do not fall under the jurisdiction of individual coastal nations. In short, the definitions of jurisdiction and of ownership of marine resources can vary with the distance from shore and the type of marine activity (see Figure 12.10).

There are three general types of jurisdiction over marine resources that are accepted by most of the world's nations. *Internal waters* include bays, estuaries, and rivers and are under the exclusive control of the coastal nation. In the United States, jurisdiction over the resources found in these internal waters is shared between federal and state governments. Most states and some municipalities control fishing and shellfishing, while the states and the federal government share jurisdiction over water pollution, dredging, and other activities.

The *territorial sea,* a band of open ocean adjacent to the coast, is measured from a baseline on the shore out to a set distance. The United States currently claims a 3-mile-wide (4.8 km) territorial sea; however, many nations claim a 12-mile-wide (19 km) zone. Similarly, a coastal nation controls all activities, such as fishing, within its territorial sea—except for the right of "innocent passage" by foreign vessels. A Japanese fishing boat can, for example, pass between the Aleutian Islands, in U.S. territorial waters off Alaska, without permission from the state or federal government, but it cannot drop nets and proceed to fish. A foreign military vessel may also pass through territorial waters unhindered, as long as it remains outside the internal waters of the coastal nation. Curiously, the right of innocent passage through the territorial sea does not include aircraft. Foreign aircraft must seek permission to enter U.S. air space before moving within three miles of shore. In the U.S., the coastal states manage fisheries and oil drilling in the territorial sea, while the federal government patrols and protects it.

The third type of jurisdiction is the 200-mile-wide (322 km) *exclusive economic zone,* created by the Law of the Sea Treaty. The exclusive economic zone (EEZ) is a special use area where such activities as fishing and oil drilling are controlled by the coastal nation, while other activities are not. In 1946 the U.S. claimed exclusive jurisdiction over its outer continental shelf, which extends out to a depth of about 200 meters of water, to control oil and gas development. In 1976 the U.S. created a 200-mile-wide Fishery Conservation Zone, claiming control over all fish and shellfish except the highly migratory tuna. Many other nations adopted this idea and made similar claims. The Law of the Sea Treaty creates a single EEZ that includes fishing and all forms of mineral extraction, no matter what the water depth. Control over other activities in the EEZ is less clear. Some nations (including the U.S.) claim jurisdiction over ocean dumping

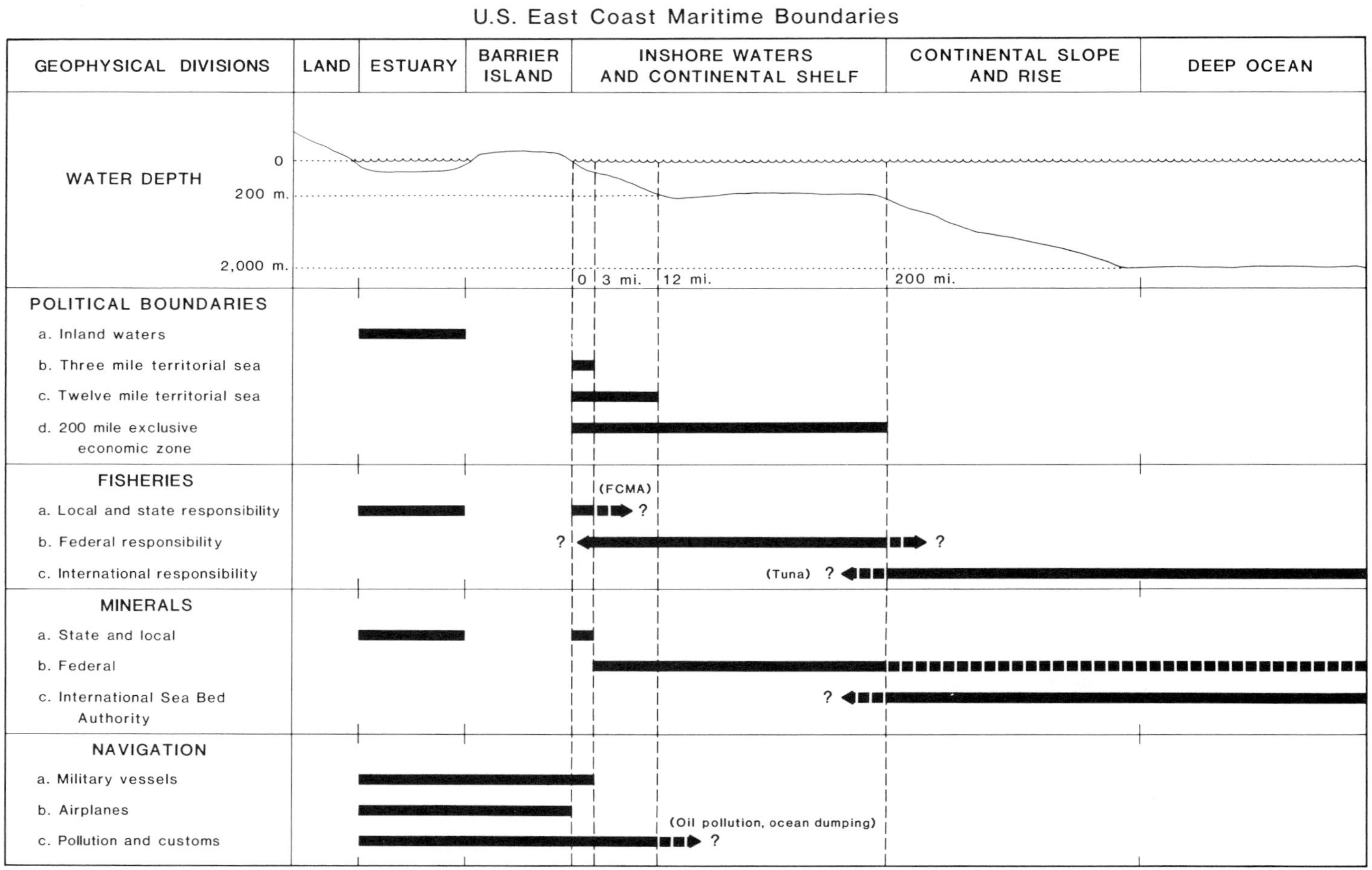

U.S. East Coast Maritime Boundaries

Figure 12.10 U.S. east coast maritime boundaries. The U.S. claims jurisdiction over various portions of the sea for different purposes. Dashed lines indicate shared jurisdictions; question marks indicate disputed or ambiguous boundaries.

and water pollution, and others (excluding the U.S.) claim jurisdiction over the movements of vessels and oil spills in this zone.

Finally, the high seas are those ocean areas that are beyond the jurisdiction of any individual nation. Traditionally, the limits to activities on the high seas are set by international treaties, such as the Law of the Sea Treaty.

The Law of the Sea Treaty

There is a long history of confusion over who owns or controls the oceans. There are hundreds of conflicting territorial claims made by coastal nations, many of which either clash with or ignore the international treaties signed in 1958 on territorial seas and the outer continental shelf. There are over ninety independent nations in the world today that did not exist as such when the 1958 treaties were signed. Many of these nations are landlocked, underdeveloped, or both, and most are former colonies whose boundaries and economy originally were designed to benefit only the colonial power.

The combination of maritime boundary problems, coupled with the desire of many newly independent countries to allocate or reallocate marine resources, led to the negotiations over a new Law of the Sea Treaty. Negotiations started in 1974, with over 160 nations participating, and lasted until 1982, when a final version was approved. Participating nations are now in the process of ratifying the treaty, which should become legally binding sometime in 1987–88. The United States refused to sign the treaty, due to a disagreement over mining rights for deep-sea manganese nodules.

What happens next? The Law of the Sea Treaty is clearly the most far-reaching international agreement ever governing marine resources, yet one of the world's foremost maritime powers has thus far refused to sign or ratify it. The United States claims control over approximately 20 percent of the world's marine fish and shellfish and is one of the world's largest markets for ocean-borne commerce. Can the Law of the Sea Treaty survive without the U.S. as an active participant? Can U.S. economic and national defense interests be preserved without our signing the treaty? A brief overview of the key elements of the treaty illustrates the dilemma and the potential conflicts the U.S. faces by its refusal to sign.

The Law of the Sea Treaty clarifies boundary claims by establishing internationally agreed-upon limits on the territorial sea, continental shelf, and exclusive economic zone. It establishes a universal 200-mile-wide exclusive economic zone, giving the coastal nation exclusive control over exploitable resources, such as fish, oil, and gas. It also preserves the right of free navigation through this zone by foreign ships, airplanes, and submarines.

A universal 12-mile-wide territorial sea would effectively close off 175 straits or narrow passages, through which the majority of shipping travels. The most important of these are the straits of Gibraltar, Dover, Hormuz, and Malacca. The Strait of Gibraltar is 15 km (8 nautical miles) wide and is the major point of access to the Mediterranean Sea. The Dover Strait is the easternmost part of the English Channel and is 32 km (17.5 nautical miles) wide. Virtually all oil imported into northern Europe by ship passes through this narrow portion of the Channel. The Strait of Hormuz, while only 38 km (20.7 nautical miles) wide, is perhaps the most important in the world. It is located between Iran and Oman, in the Persian Gulf. All of the oil that is transported by ship from the Middle East must pass through this vital and strategic strait. The Malacca Strait (16 km or 8.4 nautical miles) lies between the Malay Peninsula and the island of Sumatra. Ship traffic between the Indian and Pacific oceans must use this strait or others in Indonesian waters. All of Japan's imported oil from the Middle East traverses this strait.

The rights of neighboring nations to regulate traffic, including aircraft, through straits has never been clear. At the insistence of the United States and other nations, the Law of the Sea Treaty creates an internationally recognized right of "transit passage" through straits, permitting unimpeded access so long as ships and aircraft comply with minimal navigational rules. This right-of-transit passage is one of the most significant provisions of the treaty. The industrial nations with large navies insisted on this provision, at the expense of less developed countries, which border most of the straits in question.

The treaty also provides for the regulation of pollution and for the conservation of living resources, including increased protection of marine mammals. Finally, the treaty allows for the exploitation of deep sea-bed minerals but states that these resources constitute the common heritage of humankind. Although the developed nations possess the technology and knowledge of deep sea-bed mining, the fruits of this expertise would be shared by all nations. In other words, those developed nations would not have exclusive right to the resources, even though they were the only ones with the technology and knowledge to get to them. The U.S. has refused to sign the treaty because of the deep sea-bed mining provisions, which it feels are contrary to the interests and security of all industrialized nations (Kimball, 1983).

SUMMARY

As a common property resource, the ocean is accessible to all nations. Responsibility for allocation and management of the ocean's vast resources is clouded by lack of clear title of ownership of the resource. International efforts, such as the IWC and the Law of the Sea Treaty, are important steps in recognizing this problem and in confirming the value and wisdom of conserving this resource.

REFERENCES AND ADDITIONAL READING

Bean, M.J. 1977. *The evolution of national wildlife law.* Washington, D.C.: Council on Environmental Quality.

Brock, R.G. 1984. El Niño and world climate: piecing together the puzzle. *Environment* 26:3:14–20.

Carney, L.H. 1984. Ocean dumping: no guidelines. *New York Times,* May 20.

Council on Environmental Quality. 1981a. *Environmental trends.* Washington, D.C.: Government Printing Office.

_____ . 1981b. *The Global 2000 report to the president.* Washington, D.C.: Government Printing Office.

_____ . 1982. *Environmental quality 1982, 13th annual report.* Washington, D.C.: Government Printing Office.

Fairhall, D., and P. Jordan. 1980. *The wreck of the Amoco Cadiz.* New York: Stein and Day.

Gross, M.G. 1971. *Oceanography.* 2nd ed. Columbus, Ohio: Merrill.

Halbouty, M.T. 1982. Petroleum still leader in energy race. *Offshore* 42:7:49–52.

Heath, G.R. 1982. Manganese nodules: unanswered questions. *Oceanus* 25:3:37–41.

Kimball, L. 1983. The law of the sea—on the shoals. *Environment* 25:9:14–20.

Knecht, R.W. 1982. Deep ocean mining. *Oceanus* 25:3:3–11.

Lo, N.C.H. 1983. Sample size for estimating dolphin mortality associated with the tuna fishery. *J. Wildlife Management* 47:413–21.

New York Times. 1980. Text of Ronald Reagan's State of the Union message, January 24.

Odum, E.P. 1971. *Fundamentals of ecology.* Philadelphia: Saunders.

Orbach, M.K. 1977. *Hunters, seamen, and entrepreneurs: the tuna seinermen of San Diego.* Berkeley and Los Angeles: University of California Press.

Rasmusson, E.M., and J.M. Hall. 1983. El Niño: the great equatorial Pacific Ocean warming event of 1982–1983. *Weatherwise* August:166–75.

Scheffer, V.B. 1977. The magnificent mammals: best 13 most. *Environment* 19:7:16–20.

Swanson, R.L., and M. Devine. 1982. Ocean dumping policy. *Environment* 24:5:14–20.

Swanson, R.L., and C.J. Sinderman. 1979. *Oxygen depletion and associated benthic mortalities in New York Bight, 1976.* NOAA Professional Paper 11. Washington, D.C.: U.S. Department of Commerce.

United Nations Food and Agricultural Organization. 1981. *Yearbook of fishery statistics.* Vol. 52 *Catches and landings.* Vol. 53 *Fishery commodities.* Rome: United Nations.

U.S. Coast Guard. 1981. *Polluting incidents in and around U.S. waters 1980 and 1981.* Washington, D.C.: Government Printing Office.

U.S. Department of the Interior, Bureau of Land Management. 1981. *Final supplement to the final environmental statement proposed five-year OCS oil and gas lease sale schedule January 1982–December 1986.* Washington, D.C.: Government Printing Office.

Warner, L.S. 1982. The conservation aspects of the Fishery Conservation and Management Act and the protection of critical marine habitat. *Natural Resources Journal* 23:97–130.

———, B.A. Finamore, and M.J. Bean. 1981. Practical application of the conservation aspects of the Fishery Conservation and Management Act. *Harvard Environmental Law Review* 5:1:30–70.

Winslow, R. 1978. *Hard aground. The story of the Argo Merchant oil spill.* New York: Norton.

TERMS TO KNOW

anadromous fish
catadromous fish
common property resource
dissolved oxygen
El Niño
estuary
exclusive economic zone
high seas
internal waters

International Whaling Commission
Law of the Sea Treaty
maximum sustainable yield
salinity
shelf
stratification
territorial sea
upwelling

STUDY QUESTIONS

1. What is the importance of estuaries to marine fisheries?
2. What are some of the major problems in estimating maximum sustainable yield for a given fishery?
3. Describe some of the important achievements and failures of the International Whaling Commission.
4. Why does the U.S. refuse to sign the Law of the Sea Treaty?
5. What control does a coastal nation commonly exercise over its internal waters, its territorial sea, its exclusive economic zone, and the high seas?
6. What waste materials are commonly dumped in the oceans?

CHAPTER THIRTEEN

Potential and Amenity Resources

INTRODUCTION

As discussed in Chapter 1, the list of available resources is not permanently fixed. On the contrary, what is valued changes with technological, social, and economic conditions. Fads and fashions can alter what we see as useful and therefore valuable. For example, in the 18th century, European tastes for hats made from beaver fur had a profound effect on the value of beaver pelts and thus on the North American beaver population. More recently, both the black and white African rhinoceros populations have declined by 50 percent as a result of poaching. In some parts of the world, rhino horns are regarded as an aphrodisiac and are used as handles for ceremonial daggers given to pubescent males (*New York Times,* 1982a and b).

In this chapter, we examine the shifting makeup of resources, by looking at those portions of the natural world that were not highly valued until very recently. Decisions about the value of many of these new resources are still being debated. How can we set a value for something that has shown no evidence of being useful, beyond the promises made by its promoters? This question is especially pertinent to the preservation of plant and animal species and to evaluating the potential recreational use of urban landfill areas.

Another problem in defining and evaluating resources is the notion of beauty (see Figure 13.1). Questions of aesthetics were once the realm of philosophers, but today costly decisions are made on the basis of *economic* versus *amenity* evaluations of a contested resource. That is, one group of people will evaluate the potential development of a ski resort in a remote area according to its economic value. It might create jobs, stimulate local investment, and improve the life of consumers. Others evaluate the ski resort from an amenities viewpoint, asking if the resort would contribute to the world's beauty, ecological stability, or spiritual happiness.

These qualities obviously are very difficult to quantify, yet pressure on resource use demands realistic, practical evaluations. Thus, as you read about the different ways of calculating the value of an intangible, ask yourself: What is the economic value of habitat and species preservation? How important is a beautiful environment? What kinds of recreation are necessary for the happiness and well-being of the public?

Figure 13.1 Grand Teton National Park, Wyoming, has natural beauty in a landscape with high economic and amenity value.

HABITAT AND SPECIES CONSERVATION

For thousands of years, the human race has been altering animal and plant *species* and the places they inhabit, and some life forms have been obliterated. The European lion was extinct by 80 A.D. Wolves vanished along with the forest cover in Europe. In the United States, the American bison or "buffalo," whose vast herds impeded agricultural settlement and held up trains for hours, was almost wiped out in the second half of the 19th century. Today, the American bison lives in protected refuge areas. The passenger pigeon suffered a more drastic fate. In 1810 the estimated total passenger-pigeon population was about five billion. In most of the 19th century, killing these birds for food or sport was easy, as they could be shot down in the hundreds by aiming into their roosting places at night or by firing into the air at random as they flew overhead. The passenger pigeon was extinct in the wild by 1899, and the last one died in a zoo in 1914 (Dwyer, 1970). The human role is not always one of destruction; often we are responsible for the swift spread of species to new areas. It is estimated, for example, that one-eighth of California's plant species are *exotic species,* that is, imported from other places (Ornduff, 1974). Some suburbs offer a very comfortable habitat for deer, squirrels, and racoons. The whitetail deer population had dropped to 500,000 in 1900; with control over their hunting, their numbers have risen to 13 million, at least as many as when Europeans first arrived (Iker, 1983).

Researchers and naturalists such as Eckholm (1978), Campbell (1980), and Ehrlich and Ehrlich (1981) warn that the destruction and alteration of habitats and species mean the destruction of potential resources with both economic and

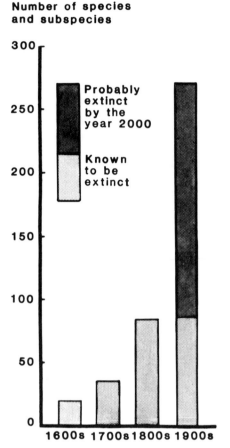

**Number of species
and subspecies**

Figure 13.2 Many vertebrate species and subspecies have become extinct since 1600, and others are predicted to become extinct by 2000. (Source: Council on Environmental Quality, 1981)

amenity value. They maintain that species and habitat destruction have reached epidemic proportions worldwide. At a 1981 conference on genetic diversity, sponsored by the U.S. Department of State and the U.S. Agency for International Development, researchers predicted then that by the year 2000, a million additional species of all types would become extinct (Wolkomir, 1983).

The effects of this biocide, or destruction of species, are several. Ecosystems are undermined when plant and animal species are destroyed or when they move into new areas. The possibility of using as yet untried species for food, fuel, fiber, or medicine disappears when they are eradicated. Human appreciation and understanding of nature are diminished by species and habitat loss. Many question the right of human beings to deny other species the right to exist. Most profoundly, even from a completely "selfish," homocentric point of view, it is feared that removal of even a few species from the *web of life* could cause a chain reaction, leading to widespread ecological disaster. One early warning of this possibility was the introduction of sea lampreys to the Great Lakes when the St. Lawrence Seaway was first opened. The sea lampreys killed off lake trout, the natural predators of alewives. This caused a population boom for alewives. As a result, the alewife population shot beyond available food supplies, and for years dead alewives in the hundreds were washed up on Great Lakes beaches (Ragotzkie, 1974).

Many people in favor of resource development and exploitation feel that the situation is hardly so dire as this suggests. They point out the long record of human destruction and alteration of species and habitats, stressing that this is not a recent phenomenon and implying that the world has yet to suffer much from these losses. It has even been stated that there are so many plant and animal species worldwide (estimates range from 3 to 10 million) that the loss of a few thousand cannot seriously affect potential resource development. In addition, it is felt that the economic benefits derived at the cost of occasional species and habitat destruction outweigh the benefits of their artificial preservation for the enjoyment of a few nature lovers.

These questions and arguments are not easily resolved, because they involve unknown consequences in an unpredictable future. In almost two thousand years, humankind has directly or indirectly brought about the *extinction* of over 200 species and subspecies of vertebrate animals (Dwyer, 1970) (see Figure 13.2). In this century, the pace of human-caused extinctions has quickened. Today it is estimated that one species becomes extinct daily, and that, by the end of the 1980s, the rate of species extinctions will be one per hour. These statistics are especially alarming when we examine historical rates of species extinction. From 1600 to 1900 an average of one species became extinct every one to four years. What has happened to accelerate the rate of species extinctions since 1900, and why should we care?

Biological Diversity

Biological diversity refers to both the genetic variability among individuals of a species, and the number of species and abundance of individuals within a species. Wide variations in genetic traits increase the likelihood that at least some individuals of a given species will survive environmental change. The number of different species and the abundance of individuals in that species are also indicators of biological diversity in a particular ecosystem. The most ecologically diverse environments are the tropical forests, where there is a much greater abundance of plant and animal species than in any other single geographic environment.

Species extinction is a fundamental threat to biological diversity. The death of an individual represents the loss of an organism capable of reproducing the same form as other individuals in the species. The death of individuals is a natural process. By contrast, the death of an entire species is an irreversible process where both the basic form and the reproductive potential are lost. The contribution of the species to the vitality of the planet, is also lost. Species extinctions are also natural. However, humans can accelerate the process.

Human activities often result in the reduction of biological diversity. Two major causes are the destruction and simplification of natural habitats. Urban sprawl increases the amount of asphalt and concrete at the expense of fields,

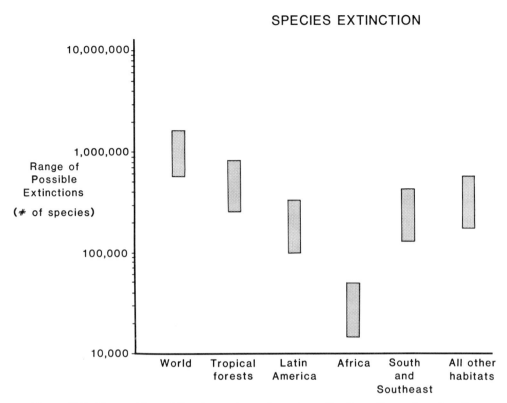

Figure 13.3 Geographic variation in numbers of species extinctions. For each region, the graph shows the estimated numbers of possible extinctions of plants and animals during the next 20 years. Tropical forests, with the greatest number of species, are being rapidly altered, and thus will probably suffer the greatest number of extinctions. (Source: Council on Environmental Quality, 1981)

forests, marshlands, and other valuable habitat. Modern farming and forest cultivation result in single-crop patterns over broad areas, supported by chemicals that destroy unwanted species. These practices endanger the genetic and ecological diversity of plant and animal communities. The global extent of these reductions in biological diversity is quite pronounced (see Figure 13.3).

Ethics and Economics

Should endangered species be preserved or simply allowed to become extinct? At one extreme is the view that it is the fault of human beings that many plant and animal species are on the verge of dying out and that it is thus our responsibility to keep them alive at any cost. Supporters of this position maintain that the aggressive, environmentally destructive nature of technologically advanced societies has led to the extinction and near-extinction of many species. This ethical argument centers on the rights of non-human entities merely to exist, regardless of any usefulness to humans. Ehrenfeld (1981) argues that all living things have a right to coexist on the planet. Humans, possessing the power to destroy and alter plant and animal species, should exercise stewardship in preserving plant and animal species. This non-homocentric view represents only one of the arguments for preserving biological diversity.

An opposite position is the "survival of the fittest" viewpoint: those species that are dying out should be allowed to die, because they have been unable to compete successfully with humans and other species. Furthermore, these critics maintain that we should not feel guilty about species extinction, in that it is a natural process, and that we do not have to keep rare creatures alive at great cost to society.

Certainly, keeping rare plants and animals alive costs a lot and is sometimes of debatable merit. Florida's dusky sparrow is a good illustration. During the 1970s, the U.S. government spent over $2.5 million to buy 6,250 acres on Florida's east coast to create the St. John's River Refuge for the dusky sparrows. By 1981, there were five male sparrows living in a large cage (for their own safety), and a sixth male was believed to be alive in the wild. There were no known females in existence. How did this highly artificial situation develop?

The sparrows' original island habitat had been flooded to control mosquitos around Cape Canaveral. Fires and drainage of marshes had further destroyed the birds' nesting and living area. Scientists proposed that the males be allowed to mate with a close relative, the Scott's seaside sparrow: after five generations, the offspring would be nearly full-blooded dusky sparrows. This suggestion was turned down in 1980, when the U.S. Fish and Wildlife Service decided that this hybrid sparrow would not meet the requirements of the Endangered Species Act. The agency instead gave a "pension" of $9,200 per sparrow to care for them until their death (*New York Times*, 1981). This is an extreme example of preservation, but what are the alternatives? Who can play God, deciding which species should survive and which need not?

Animal Species: Victims of a Crowded World

The claims of animals on food and space conflict with a rapidly expanding human population, and, more often than not, the animal loses (see Figure 13.4). For example, in 1900, there were an estimated 100,000 tigers worldwide. There are only 4,000 to 5,000 today. One subspecies, the Bali tiger, is extinct; the Caspian tiger probably is. There are a few Javan and Chinese tigers in the wild, several hundred Sumatran, 250 Siberian, and perhaps 2,000 each of the Indochinese and Bengal tigers. This extreme drop over such a short period can be attributed to hunting and to loss of habitat to human uses. The ethical argument centers on the animals' rights to their own territory (Shepard, 1978; Regan and Singer, 1976). In Nepal's Royal Chitawan National Park, the Bengal tigers, outfitted with radio collars, are tracked to learn about their habits and requirements. The hope is that the animals can be accommodated and their future made secure and stable. The park is not large, however, and on one occasion a young tiger, evidently wanting his own territory, wandered out of the park into a village and killed a man before being captured and removed to a zoo (Jackson, 1978).

As the human population continues to grow, these interspecies conflicts grow as well. It is most likely that the non-human species will continue to lose, at least in the short run. For example, the black bear was once a resident of New Jersey, but it long ago almost disappeared from the state in the face of hunting pressures and incompatibility with increased human populations. In 1983

Figure 13.4 A moose in Glacier National Park, Montana. Moose populations in much of the U.S. declined substantially in the 19th century, but recently they have recovered. Renewal of moose hunting is now under consideration in some areas.

there were an estimated 80 to 100 bears in northern New Jersey (Carney, 1983). In 1982, the State Department of Environmental Protection's Bureau of Wildlife Management had announced an experimental program to re-introduce the black bear to areas of New Jersey's Pine Barrens. The bureau argued that, if managed carefully, bears could co-exist with human beings in the relatively unpopulated area. Local residents by and large did not agree. They felt that the age of the bear in New Jersey was and should remain history. The struggle for space and food between humans and bears is a part of daily life in the western United States, where bears become too devoted to human garbage and must be removed by helicopter to wilder areas. Unfortunately, even this measure is decreasingly effective, as more and more wilderness hikers penetrate remote bear country in search of solitude.

A 1982 study suggests that the grizzly bear is an endangered species, even within the Yellowstone National Park ecosystem: only 200 bears remain. In their search for food, the animals have moved out of areas classified as preservation lands into multiple-use lands, where the chance of a face-off with human beings is much greater. Although most human-bear meetings are trouble-free, the occasional mauling or killing leads experts to wonder if the grizzly bear can survive long in the Yellowstone (Larmer, 1983).

Currently, over 700 faunal species worldwide are either threatened or endangered (Council on Environmental Quality, 1982). The majority of these are mammals (253) and birds (199). Endangered species of mammals and birds are primarily in danger of extinction in foreign locales rather than in the U.S. (see Table 13.1). There are 144 endangered species of animals in the U.S., mostly birds, fishes, and clams. Among the better known of these are the bald eagle, eastern timber wolf, peregrine falcon, American alligator, Florida manatee, and the gila trout.

Aside from the ethical arguments for animal species preservation, a number of economic arguments can also be made. First, there are direct human medical benefits from animal products for such medical purposes as anticancer agents and antibiotics. Bee venom, for example, has been used to relieve arthritis. The venom of the Malayan pit viper is used as an anticoagulant to prevent blood clots and to lessen the danger of heart attack (Ehrlich and Ehrlich, 1981, p. 70). Cytarabine, or cytosine arabinoside, which is derived from a sponge, has antiviral properties that make it useful in the treatment of leukemia and against herpes infections (Ruggieri, 1976). Second, animals have long been used for drug testing and experimentation in medical research. Their contributions to the advancement of medicine cannot be overlooked. Third, animals have economic importance as a source of protein for human populations.

Even when a species is protected from extinction, zoologists worry about the consequences of inbreeding among the relatively few surviving members. A small group of animals is not enough for a breeding population. Within a few generations of interbreeding, negative recessive traits may become prevalent, and the species can even die out, a victim of its own genetic weaknesses. For example, some of California's rare Tule elk have short lower jaws, which makes eating difficult. This may be the result of interbreeding within the small group of animals that biologists used to establish the herd. Therefore, researchers advocate a more sophisticated use of genetics when attempting to re-establish species. Today, for example, "embryo banks" preserve, frozen, the genes of some vanishing species. Another solution, of course, is to use more animals for the initial breeding population. However, there is just not enough room in wildlife refuges to maintain larger populations. Fewer than five percent of the world's preserves have the space for a genetically diverse breeding population of large wild mammals. It is probable that, in a crowded world, species survival will depend on human genetic technology (Wolkomir, 1983).

Plant Species: Short-Term Decisions Can Mean Long-Term Losses

The world's plant species are disappearing at an increasing rate. The loss of this diversity and richness has become a major environmental issue, affecting the world's food supply, health, and scientific research. Newly discovered species are an important potential resource; but, once extinct, they are lost to scientific and other uses. In Africa, an average of more than 200 new plant species are collected by scientists annually. South America is even less well known to western science; a 1970s expedition to the Panama-Colombia border found that one in every five of the species collected was previously unknown to science (Eckholm, 1978). However, many more species than are discovered have already been destroyed. Forty percent of the earth's tropical moist forest have been cut down since 1945, and this figure rises annually. It has been estimated that between 40 and 50 percent of all species on the planet occur in tropical rain forests, which occupy only 6 percent of the earth's land surface. Yet these areas are being destroyed at an annual rate of 5 million hectares (13 million acres) per year—an area about the size of West Virginia (Ehrlich and Ehrlich, 1981, pp. 191–193). These

Table 13.1 Endangered and Threatened Species, 1983

	Endangered		Threatened	
	U.S.	Foreign	U.S.	Foreign
Mammals	15	223	3	22
Birds	52	144	3	—
Reptiles	8	55	8	—
Amphibians	5	8	3	—
Fishes	29	11	12	—
Snails	3	1	5	—
Clams	23	2	—	—
Crustaceans	2	—	1	—
Insects	7	—	4	—
Plants	55	—	9	2
Total	199	444	48	24

Source: U.S. Bureau of the Census, 1984

complex ecosystems are destroyed to obtain timber and to make way for cities and agriculture, with little consideration of the potential aesthetic or economic value of the species being eliminated. The Threatened Plants Committee of the International Union for Conservation of Nature and Natural Resources states that 20,000 to 30,000 plant species, a tenth of the estimated total, are endangered, rare, threatened, or in an uncertain state (Campbell, 1980).

Once again, short-term human uses come first. The main causes of plant species extinction are agriculture, urbanization, air and water pollution, strip mining, industry, and overcollection by hobbyists and commercial interests (see Issue 13.1). Fifty species of native American plants have become extinct in

---

ISSUE 13.1: A Prickly Problem: Desert Plant Depletion

The popularity of desert plants has led to problems of desert species depletion, especially for distinctive and strange cacti. John Hubbard, supervisor of New Mexico's Fish and Game Department's endangered species program, says that people are like stamp collectors when it comes to cacti—they want one of every kind. Some rare small cacti sell for $40 to $50 each, and the giant saguaro goes for $30 to $40 a foot. The saguaro, organ pipe, prickly pear, and agave are the main targets of rustlers in Organ Pipe National Monument. Cacti are thus threatened by their own popularity. Desert landscaping is increasingly chic, and, with water prices rising steadily, green grass lawns will become more expensive to maintain.

The southwestern states have a variety

of laws to control cacti removal. Arizona's Native Plant Act, dating from 1929, imposes fines of $1,000 and one-and-one-half-year jail sentences. To legally remove cacti from the desert for sale, one must obtain permits and tag each cactus for permanent identification. California, on the other hand, has been slow on this, enacting a tag law only in 1979. "We watched them drag our desert away," says Hank Warren, California's chief plant protection agent (Gordon, 1980). Very recently Nevada created a tag law; New Mexico has a law but no tagging system, while Utah has no plant protection laws at all.

In 1979, the U.S. Fish and Wildlife Service listed 21 types of cacti as endangered or threatened. The Smithsonian Institution recommended adding another 30 species to

recent years, among them the Arizona hedgehog cactus, Harper's beauty lily, and the Furbish lousewort, a member of the snapdragon family (U.S. Fish and Wildlife Service, 1982). In 1978 the Smithsonian Institution considered nearly 10 percent of the 22,200 plants native to the continental U.S. to be endangered or threatened. As of January 1982, only 61 of these were protected by the Endangered Species Act.

Why does the protection of plant species matter? For one thing, plant extinctions can be ever more disruptive to ecosystems than animal extinctions are. When a plant species is eliminated, either locally or globally, the species that directly or indirectly rely on it, including insects, higher animals, and other plants, can be adversely affected. For example, a now-extinct shrub may have been a source of food for a browsing animal, a source of shelter for birds and insects, and protective cover for smaller plant species. Also, for the sake of human scientific knowledge alone, biologists feel that plant species should be preserved and protected. More pragmatically, many disappearing plant species could well be of considerable economic and social value.

In recent years, researchers have looked at the possibility that previously unused or even despised plant species could be used for food, fiber, and medicine. Out of the total of about a third of a million higher plant species estimated to exist, only 300–400, or 0.1 percent have ever been used as crop plants by humans. Mesquite, a weedy nuisance on western cattle ranges, is promoted by researchers as a potential world food source. It produces abundant annual crops of a highly nutritious bean, once a staple for the American Indians in the region. Recently, mesquite wood has become popular as a fuel in gourmet cooking, commanding a high price in some urban markets. Another recent discovery—recent to modern science, at least—is the buffalo gourd, used for at least 9,000

---

the list. Overcollection was cited as a major threat for all of these species. There was some hesitation about placing these plants on the list, for fear this would add to their attraction and so boost their value.

These protection efforts may not be enough. One estimate claims that $500,000 worth of rare cacti were lost in 1980; another places the loss at $1.8 million. As cacti are removed, naturalists warn of the loss of a thin topsoil and habitat for animals and birds. The saguaro of Arizona is the desert's most frequently stolen plant. When it is seventy-five years old, it may be about twelve feet in height and begin to push out its famous "arms." It is a very slow-growing cactus and not easily replaced. Four thousand saguaro were removed in a single

operation from the southern Arizona desert in 1979.

Interestingly, nurseries are not overly excited about growing cacti, as they are so slow in development and thus take up land better suited for faster growing plants, with a higher economic return. There are no incentives to grow cacti. Who wants to wait fifty years for a crop? The lack of interest may extend to desert species in general. Cacti might be grown by nurseries if there were more demand, but, due to their slow growth rate, no one is willing to take the risk. The only solution to the problem is to protect cactus habitat from development and exploitation, and that is a tall order in today's Southwest (Campbell, 1980; Gordon, 1980).

years by the American Indians. This widespread wild plant provides vegetable oil, protein, and starch of high quality, thriving on very little water (Kazarian, 1981). Since humans depend on a narrow range of crop species for food, the discovery of new food resources is very important. The Central American amaranthus produces seeds that contain a high-quality protein that could be used in protein-deficient societies in the tropics. Eelgrasses, grown in salt water, offer a potential substitute for grains in some heavily populated seacoast areas.

Historically, Indian tribes in what is now the southwestern U.S. and northern Mexico made use of some 450 wild plants. Anthropologists Felger and Nabhan (1978) suggest that many of these desert-adapted species could be of value to modern society. Guayule is a shrub grown in northern Mexico and Texas. Before 1910 it supplied 10 percent of the world's rubber (Ehrlich and Ehrlich 1981, p. 86). The latex in the guayule shrub is very similar to that in the hevea or rubber tree. Jojoba, a shrub related to boxwood, has seeds that contain a liquid wax. This wax, which makes up as much as 60 percent of the jojoba bean's weight, can be used for lubricating metal parts and other purposes once served by sperm whale oil, now outlawed. The jojoba, like the guayule, can be grown on marginal arid lands. Another seemingly unlikely possibility for development is the all-American goldenrod, whose leaves contain up to 12 percent natural rubber. It is easy to grow, can be mowed and baled, and resprouts without annual sowing. Euphorbia lathyus, a desert shrub, might yield 10–20 barrels of crude oil per acre, if cultivated (Wilford, 1980; Johnson and Hinman, 1980; Broad, 1978). Clearly, these are just a few of the thousands of potential useful plant species, making a strong economic argument for preserving not only rare but also abundant species.

After food, medicine is the most important economic use of plants. Vincristine, discovered in the mid-1950s, is an alkaloid found in the Madagascar periwinkle. The chemical, which causes a decrease in white-blood-cell counts, has been used to fight cancer and cancer-like diseases. Quinine, an alkaloid in Cinchona bark, was used to treat malaria until synthetic quinine was developed in the 1930s. Digitalis, from foxglove, is widely used to treat chronic heart failure by stimulating the heart to pump more blood and use less energy. A number of well known pain killers, including morphine and codeine, are derivatives of the opium poppy. In 1980 alone, the value of plant-derived medicines in the U.S. was put at $6 billion (Ehrlich and Ehrlich 1981, p. 69).

Humans depend on only a few dozen plant species for food. A substantial loss of any one of these crops in a given year would almost certainly lead to widespread human starvation. How might such a loss occur? Modern agricultural technology has led to greater uniformity in the world's crops. The seed sown in a field is genetically uniform, minimizing irregularities in the mature crop and making the plants easy to harvest by machine. Unfortunately, a genetically uniform crop also means that the individual plants are equally vulnerable to attack from pests and diseases. If such a crop is exclusively planted over a wide geographic area, the food supply of an entire region could be drastically reduced in a very short period of time.

Crop species are also endangered by a decrease in their genetic diversity and by the disappearance of wild relatives. It is therefore seen as necessary to maintain germ-plasm banks of the wild relatives of our principal crops. Agricultural experts can interbreed the positive characteristics of these wild plants, such as resistance to particular diseases, with the high productivity of the crop plants. In the event of an ecological disaster that eradicated an entire crop, we would have a well preserved, genetically less vulnerable replacement to fall back on. The likelihood of such a large-scale disaster is exceedingly small, however, because experts have learned to provide seed with greater built-in genetic diversity, following a nearly disastrous failure of the American corn crop in the early 1970s (National Academy of Sciences, 1972). Crop plants are very sophisticated genetic packages.

Germ-plasm banks are also a refuge of last resort for threatened plant species. Even if the plant dies out, its genetic makeup is preserved for the need to revive the species. Unfortunately, this is impossible for the great numbers of species eradicated in the clearing of tropical rain forests, without being catalogued or noted by the scientific community, much less collected and preserved.

A clearinghouse for germ-plasm collection and research is the National Plant Germplasm System, managed by the U.S. Department of Agriculture. It has over 400,000 accessions, and new ones are being added at a rate of 7,000 to 15,000 a year. The NPGS collects, preserves, evaluates, and distributes U.S. and international plant germ-plasm resources.

Protection of Species: Recent Legislation

The United States has taken an active role in the protection of species. The most comprehensive piece of legislation, regulating protection of all species of flora and fauna, is the Endangered Species Act (ESA), passed in 1973. The act had four main provisions:

1. The Department of the Interior is responsible for identifying non-marine species that are in imminent danger of extinction and for naming these *endangered species.* The Department of the Interior should actively pursue the preservation of these species. Those species with rapidly declining populations but that are not in imminent danger of extinction are classified as *threatened species* and are provided with the protection necessary to prevent further decline in numbers. The National Marine Fisheries Service (NMFS) of the Department of Commerce is responsible for marine species.
2. The act makes it illegal to capture, kill, sell, transport, buy, possess, import, or export any species on the endangered or threatened list.
3. The act also requires the Department of the Interior and Commerce to delineate the habitats of endangered and threatened species and to map these critical habitats, a requisite for species survival.
4. The act forbids any private, state, or federal concern from destroying critical habitats as a result of dam building, highway construction, housing developments, or other projects supported in whole or part by federal monies.

The Endangered Species Act was amended in 1978, after the snail darter controversy threatened completion of the Tellico Dam in Tennessee (see Issue 13.2). The amendments required closer consultation between the Office of Endangered Species, Fish and Wildlife Service, U.S. Department of Interior, National Oceanic and Atmospheric Administration, and sponsors of capital improvements projects, to avoid long and costly disputes over the fates of both the endangered species and the construction project. The amendments also allowed some exceptions to comprehensive species protection. Specifically, a major project can go ahead if it can be shown clearly that the benefits of the project outweigh and overshadow the species preservation issue. Exceptions to the ESA can be granted by six high-ranking (cabinet and sub-cabinet) officials and one representative of the state affected. Environmentalists have dubbed this group the God Committee.

Coming into office in 1981, the Reagan Administration was not kind to the Endangered Species legislation. The Secretary of the Interior resisted the inclusion of new species on the endangered and threatened lists, even though the Fish and Wildlife Service had identified 2,000 species eligible for listing. Amendments to the ESA in October 1982 stated that the Department of the Interior would consider only biological factors, not habitat destruction, in evaluating a species for listing. This resulted in a precipitous drop in the number of species considered for protection (Bean, 1983).

Just as terrestrial species are protected by the ESA, the Marine Mammals Protection Act covers marine species. It was passed in 1972, partly in response to pressures from environmentalists and resource managers. The MMPA preempted state authority over marine mammals offshore. It also called for a moratorium on hunting marine mammals in U.S. territorial waters and on importing such

---

ISSUE 13.2: The God Committee: The Story of the Snail Darter and Tellico Dam

Once upon a time there was a three-inch fish known as the snail darter, which became geographically isolated as the last glacial period ended. This species (*Percinia tanasi*), a member of the perch family, found itself a home in what became the Little Tennessee River, in what is now Tennessee. The snail darter was not much to look at, had no real redeeming social value, was not edible, and had no economic potential. It simply existed.

The Tennessee Valley Authority (TVA) had been constructing dams in the entire Tennessee River valley for decades, and the Tellico Dam project was simply another contribution to their hydroelectric network. The project was initiated in the late 1960s, ostensibly as a combined power, water supply, and irrigation project.

Local residents were against the dam from the very first. They felt the dam would destroy as much farmland as it would bring into production downstream. They also claimed that much of the land to be in-

undated by the reservoir was sacred Cherokee land and had archaeological significance. With the aid of a Washington, D.C. group, the Environmental Defense Fund, the residents filed the first legal action to halt construction of the dam in 1968. The initial lawsuit failed, and many others followed, none of them successful.

In 1973 ichthyologist David Etnier discovered the three-inch fish and named it the snail darter, as it fed exclusively on snails. Due to its small population and its apparent geographic isolation from others of its species, efforts were made to get the snail darter designated as an endangered species under the newly passed Endangered Species Act. The U.S. Fish and Wildlife Service listed the snail darter as endangered in 1974, after a lengthy review and comment period. The TVA fought hard against the listing, while simultaneously accelerating work on the project. The local residents filed suit to halt construction, arguing that

catches to the U.S. The act was needed for protection of various species of marine mammals, but even more important is its protection of individual population stocks (Bean, 1977).

Internationally, efforts are also being made to protect species. Early attempts at regulating commercial whaling in the face of declining stocks led to the formation of the International Whaling Commission (IWC) in 1946. The IWC was to promote the conservation of whales by establishing quotas on the amount of commercial whale catch. As discussed in Chapter 12, although the idea is a good one, there are no enforcement mechanisms other than persuasion. Because of this lax enforcement, whalers and some whaling nations, notably Japan and the Soviet Union, routinely ignore the biological harvest quotas set by the IWC.

The Convention on International Trade in Endangered Species of Wild Fauna and Flora, or CITES, regulates and controls commerce in endangered species and other species threatened by overharvest. The treaty negotiations began in 1973, with representatives from 80 countries. It had been ratified by 75 countries, including the U.S., as of June 1982 (Council on Environmental Quality, 1982). CITES prohibits international trade in the 600 most endangered species and their products and requires export licenses for another 200 species and their products. Enforcement is left up to the individual nations that signed the treaty. Enforcement varies according to national motivation, economics, and ability. As a result, trade in endangered species has increased, despite the efforts of CITES.

---

completion of the dam and the filling of the reservoir would completely destroy the habitat of the snail darter. The district court agreed that the snail darter was threatened by the dam but declined to halt the project, which was now 80 percent completed. In early 1977, the district court decision was overturned by a circuit court of appeals, and the case went to the U.S. Supreme Court. The Supreme Court decided in favor of the snail darter (*Hill* vs. *TVA,* 1978) but, in its written opinion, asked Congress to modify or amend the Endangered Species Act of 1973 to allow exemptions. The Court felt that the act did not allow any flexibility within the Executive branch nor did it allow broad judicial review on such matters; it was too clear-cut.

The story does not end here. By 1978 the Endangered Species Act was up for reauthorization by the Congress. With the Supreme Court opinion in mind, members of Congress put forth a number of proposals,

ranging from completely doing away with it, to clarifying some of the terms used, to the establishment of a committee to review possible exemptions. This group, dubbed the God Committee, would rule on whether or not a specific species could be extinguished. It would receive counsel from an endangered species review board, which would first review the specific issues and technical aspects, to ascertain whether the Fish and Wildlife Service had done a proper job of listing the species as threatened or endangered in the first place. This information would be passed on to the God Committee, which would ultimately decide the fate of the species under scrutiny.

One of the first cases reviewed by the committee was the Tellico project. The committee found that continued agricultural production without the dam would be twice what was expected after the completion of the project. Furthermore, statistical analyses of the dam's predicted electricity output

Most of the traded species originate in developing countries and are imported to markets in developed nations. The illegal wildlife trade is often as lucrative as illegal drug trafficking, but without the risks. Products made of ivory and rhino horn and furs from South American ocelots and jaguars and from North American lynxes, bobcats, otters, and wolves are all protected under CITES, but the trade continues. Collectors of rare birds and animals, such as the South American macaw or the Asian cockatoo, pay up to $8,000 for one of these endangered species, thus providing a market for the illegal trade (Ehrlich and Ehrlich, 1981). Do you have handbags, shoes, or coats made from the hides of any of these animals? Unless you obtained them prior to the passage of the 1973 legislation, you are in violation not only of the CITES treaty but also of the Endangered Species Act, and you are therefore subject to criminal prosecution.

In Europe, a treaty for the protection of wildlife has been signed by twenty nations and by the European Economic Community. This treaty, the Convention on the Conservation of European Wildlife and Natural Habitats, became binding on its members in June of 1982 (Council of Europe, 1983).

Habitat Protection

Another method of protecting species is to protect their habitats, those areas best suited to species' needs. Habitat protection has a long history in the United States. Theodore Roosevelt was the first President to propose the establishment

---

showed it would be produced at a deficit. The committee could not condone such an unnecessary and inefficient project and thus ruled in favor of the snail darter. The Tellico project was finished—or was it?

The halting of this $120-million pork-barrel project did not go over well with the dam's proponents, particularly congressmen and senators from Tennessee. After numerous legislative attempts to exempt the project from the Endangered Species Act had failed, proponents attached an amendment to a $10-billion water projects appropriations bill. The amendment exempted the Tellico project from any and all laws that would prevent its successful completion. President Carter could not veto the bill without subjecting many people in the country to harm and placing the welfare of the country in jeopardy. Minutes after the bill was signed, the reservoir began filling up.

Before the dam gates closed, however, some of the snail darters were transplanted to a new home. Unfortunately, the Fish and Wildlife Service accidentally killed between 20 and 30 percent of the population in the relocation process, by using pesticide-contaminated nets. The survivors reproduced, however, and in 1983 the snail darter's status was downgraded from an endangered species to a threatened species, and by 1984 it was no longer threatened.

The significance of the snail darter lies not in its ecological contributions to science but rather in its raising fundamental questions regarding the rights of species to simply exist. As noted biologists Paul and Anne Ehrlich state,

> A Tellico dam will eventually be found for every population and species of nonhuman organism, and there will always be developers, politicians, and just plain people to argue that short-range economic values must take precedence over other value. For they do not understand that their own fates are intertwined with the Snail Darters of our planet. They are unaware of how much they would indeed miss these little fishes (1981, p. 13).

of national wildlife refuges. During his Presidency, the first National Wildlife Refuge was established in 1903 at Pelican Island, Florida, for herons and egrets. This was the beginning of the National Wildlife Refuge System, which is currently managed by the Fish and Wildlife Service of the U.S. Department of the Interior. The system provides sanctuaries for endangered and threatened species of plants and animals. Figure 13.5 shows its geographical extent, with a total area of 89 million acres.

The federal government is not the only agency involved in the protection of wildlife habitat in this country. There are many wildlife refuges, in the form of state game preserves. There are also many private and public-interest organizations, such as the Nature Conservancy, the Trust for Public Lands, and the Izaak Walton League, which purchase critical habitat lands and preserve them from encroachment.

An estimated 2 percent of the world's land surface is under some form of protection from development. To amplify and broaden protection internationally, UNESCO has developed the Biosphere Programme. Biosphere reserves have been established since the early 1970s, with the main objectives of conserving diverse and complete biotic communities, to safeguard genetic diversity for evolutionary and economic purposes; educating the public and training people in conservation; and providing areas for ecological and environmental research. In 1982 there were 214 biosphere reserves in 58 countries. To qualify as a biosphere reserve, an area must have outstanding, unusual, and complete ecosystems, with accompanying harmonious traditional human land uses. A reserve consists of a largely undisturbed core area surrounded by one or more buffer zones of human occupance. Scientific research and training are carried on between the core and buffer zones, and local communities are encouraged to involve themselves in this approach to the preservation of older human and natural ecosystems. At present, certain biomes such as mountains are well represented in the reserve system, whereas others, including tropical, subtropical, warm-arid, and intermediate areas, have very little protection (Batisse, 1982).

A recently established Biosphere Reserve in the United States is the Pinelands National Reserve (PNR) of New Jersey, which was designated a U.S. National Reserve in 1978 and joined the international network in 1983. The PNR is also part of the U.S. Experimental Ecological Reserve network. What makes the Pinelands so ecologically valuable?

Often known as the Pine Barrens, this distinctive area covers about 400,000 hectares of sandy soils on the coast and inland in south-central New Jersey (see Figure 13.6). Threatened on all sides and from within by accelerated development, the Pine Barrens supports a wide variety of plant and animal life in upland, aquatic, and wetland environments, including 39 species of mammals, 59 species of reptiles and amphibians, 91 species of fish, 299 species of birds, and over 800 different kinds of vascular plants. Of the 580 native plant species, 71 are in jeopardy. Over a hundred of these plants are at the northern or southern limits of their geographical range, creating a unique and irreplaceable mix (Good and Good, 1984). The area has long been used by Amerindian tribes. Human population in the area remained low until recent decades. However, pressure has grown to develop the Pine Barrens for residential, retirement, recreational, military, and commercial purposes. The layers of national and international protection will do a lot to ensure the continued integrity of this largely intact natural area.

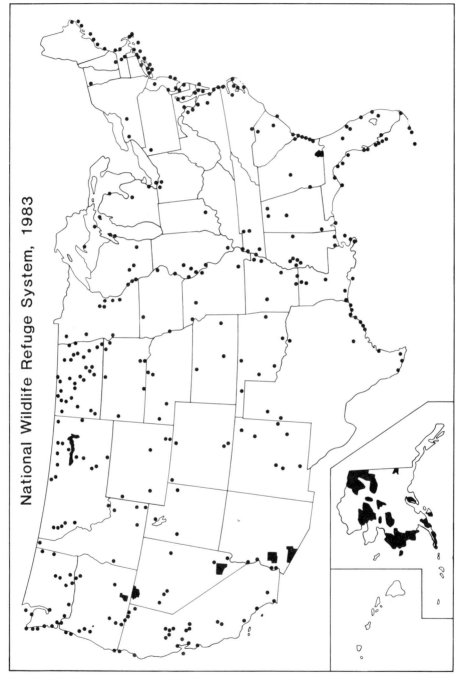

National Wildlife Refuge System, 1983

Figure 13.5 National Wildlife Refuge System. The greatest acreages are in Alaska, but units of the system are found in all but two states. (Source: From Council on Environmental Quality, 1981)

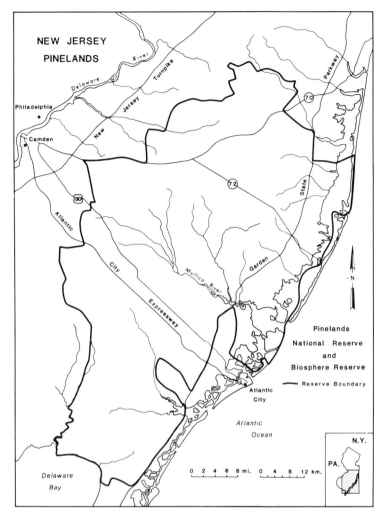

Figure 13.6 The Pinelands National Reserve in New Jersey, a part of the International Biosphere Reserve Programme. (Source: Roman and Good, 1984)

Habitat and Species Preservation: Critical Issues

Species extinction is, of course, a natural process. Over a span of millions of years, a species may develop, flourish, then slowly die out. Human beings, for example, will one day become extinct. The question is whether our own demise will be sudden, in the aftermath of war or some other human-made cataclysm, or a gradual and long-drawn-out process, taking millions of years. It may be that our decline as a species has already begun. A non-human archaeologist may one day piece together the strange history of *Homo sapiens.*

One of the most serious problems with present-day species extinctions is that so many of them are not natural or gradual. Plant and animal species that seemed to be in stable equilibrium have been wiped out in a hundred years or

Figure 13.7 The American recreational dream. This mural on the wall of a bait and camping supply shop in central Maine combines several features that attract people to the outdoors.

less because human beings tampered with their habitats and other necessities of life. The United States could one day be symbolized by an extinct species. The bald eagle has come very close to extinction, though recent reports suggest a modest comeback, over the ten years since the pesticide DDT was banned (*National Wildlife,* 1983). We have discussed the opposing view that, if a species becomes extinct under human pressure, this is merely a matter of "survival of the fittest": the species was not "meant" to survive.

In keeping with the systems theme that underlies this book, there is another point to be made. As species become extinct, they make way for possible new species that could take advantage of changing environmental conditions. Thus, much as we worry about the eradication of present-day species, so should we be keeping an eye on the conditions we are creating for the development of new ones. It is probable that new species can take advantage of the lands that now lie waste. If only a few species, however, can utilize barren soil, toxic wastes, and dirty water, the richness of the world's ecosystems will be diminished. Such an impoverished biota can set the stage for severe environmental disturbances and the world would be a much less interesting place.

RECREATION RESOURCES

Humans are recreators—we love to play. Over the past several decades, the U.S. has seen increases in both the time and money available for both indoor and outdoor recreation. This trend shows no sign of slowing down; some futurists suggest that, with increased automation, North Americans will have more time for play than for work (see Figure 13.7).

Table 13.2 Acreages of U.S. City Parks

City	Number of Parks/ Playgrounds	Acreage
Atlanta GA	20	3,000
Boston MA	NA	2,276
Chicago IL	580	NA
Dallas TX	272	23,434
Denver CO(City Parks)	155	3,600
(Mtn. Parks)	40	13,448
Los Angeles CA	296	14,489
New Orleans LA	69	21,000
New York NY	1,588	37,372
Phoenix AZ	130	25,841
San Francisco CA	120	NA

Source: Dolmatch, 1982

As our capacity to play grows, so do the pressures on available outdoor recreational resources. There is a continuing, growing demand for the development of new recreational activities and areas. Places that were of little recreational value in the past, such as the western deserts, are increasingly crowded with people working hard at play. Recreation is simultaneously an economic and an amenity resource. Those who administer and develop a recreational activity or area earn profits from it, and those who pay to use the resource enjoy the amenities associated with it. Unfortunately, there is often conflict between consumers as to how best to use a recreational resource.

Recreation covers such a wide range of activities that it would be impossible to discuss all of them adequately. Instead, we will limit ourselves to outdoor recreation in naturalistic settings. Recreational use of land has expanded many-fold since the first European settlements in North America, and it now constitutes a major economic part of American land use.

Bringing the Outdoors to the City: Urban Parks

Even the earliest and hardest working European settlers found time for outdoor recreation. They traveled to mineral spas in search of waters to cure illness and maintain good health. It was not until the mid-19th century, however, that the resort or playground gained popularity, with the development of coastal resorts in the East and West. What we today regard as outdoor recreation did not really become popular until the 19th century, when the populations of large U.S. cities began to expand with newly arrived European immigrants. In the mid-19th century, New York City had only 47 hectares (117 acres) of developed open green space, but the countryside was just a few miles distant. In the period between 1850 and 1880, several of the city's greatest parks were built, in the spirit of democracy: parks for all the people, rich and poor alike. Central Park, designed by Frederick Law Olmstead, is one of the most carefully designed "natural" landscapes in the world. It was a place of rubbish heaps, gullies, and squatter settlements in the 1840s; twenty years later, it had been made into 830 acres of vistas, paths, lakes, and pastoral open space. The parks of New York

City were generally not intended for heavy use. Central Park was intended to re-create the country in the city, as a place for contemplation and quiet relaxation. In direct opposition to this ideal, the "Playground Movement" of the same era advocated strenuous play for children and adults, as a way of removing the stresses of urban life. Many parks were built for both types of use. By the early 20th century, the acreage of American urban parks had increased enormously. Cleveland had 38 hectares in 1880 and 600 hectares by 1905; Los Angeles, 2.4 hectares in 1880 and 1500 hectares in 1905; New York City, the pioneer, had 1,500 acres in 1880 and 10,000 hectares by 1926 (Schmitt, 1969; Huth, 1957; Quinlan, 1980). Today, our fifty largest cities have a total of over 137,000 hectares (338,000 acres) of parks. New York's Central Park and San Francisco's Golden Gate Park are among the best known (see Table 13.2).

The National Parks Movement

America's cities became congested in the late 19th century, and many urban dwellers looked westward for solace and solitude. The first National Park, the 800,000 hectare (2-million-acre) Yellowstone National Park in Wyoming, was established in 1872. In 1916, Stephen Mather, a Sierra Club member and borax magnate, was named the first director of the U.S. National Park Service (NPS), under the Department of the Interior. Mather and his assistant, lawyer Horace Albright, brought a tough pragmatism to the job, enabling the NPS to expand in the face of anti-conservationist economic interests.

The NPS was created with a twofold purpose: to preserve nature and to make nature accessible to the American public. As interest in outdoor recreation has grown over the past decades, a conflict has developed between these two purposes.

The first areas were selected for inclusion in the National Parks program for their adherence to traditional European landscape values and for their guaranteed economic worthlessness. After Yellowstone, the Yosemite, Sequoia, and General Grant national parks were established by Congress beginning in 1890. They possessed beautiful valleys, tumbling waterfalls, awesome trees, and other spectacles. Members of Congress were very cautious in agreeing to the demands for parks by John Muir, a wilderness advocate, and other preservationists. They had to be given ample proof that these parks could not be used for some economic purpose; indeed, Congress usually retained the rights to mineral prospecting and timbering when establishing a park's existence.

In 1906 Congressman John F. Lacey of Iowa introduced legislation, which later became the American Antiquities Act, for the preservation of objects of cultural and historical interest on government lands. Lacey had famous historical buildings in mind, and today a wide array of national historic sites and battlefields are included as National Monuments and Parks. In addition, President Theodore Roosevelt used Lacey's act to speed up the preservation of spectacular scenic areas. Empowered as the President to make all National Monument choices, Roosevelt in 1906 made national monuments of Devil's Tower, in Wyoming, Petrified Forest and Montezuma Castle, both in Arizona, and El Morro (Inscription Rock), in New Mexico. Most dramatically, he stretched the definition of *National Monument* to include 325,000 hectares (800,000 acres) around the Grand Canyon in Arizona and 240,000 hectares (600,000 acres) around Mount Olympus in Washington.

Tourism in the national parks was at first largely for wealthier people who could afford long, leisurely trips by train and the accommodations in romantic park lodges and hotels. The Yosemite Valley railroad was opened in 1907. By 1915 about 30,000 visitors arrived annually by car and by train. The widespread use of the automobile very quickly took the lead. One auto visited Yellowstone in 1915; by 1919 about 10,000 cars had brought people to Yellowstone. Auto camping was popular with middle-class Americans from the 1920s onward.

National Park visitations rose from 3 million in 1929 to 12 million in 1940. By the 1950s, population pressures on the parks caused conservationists to wonder whether the protection of nature could long continue to co-exist with the recreational demand. Starting in 1955, a ten-year expansion plan for the parks brought widened roads, more visitor centers, and increased overnight accommodations. Visitation more than tripled between 1955 and 1974, from 14 million to 46 million in the parks alone. Visitors to National Monuments rose from 5 million to 17 million during the same period.

Today, the National Park System is a complex mixture of tiny and huge, rural and urban, historical and primeval units (see Figure 13.8). As American attitudes toward nature and recreation have changed, so has the NPS moved to accommodate the new trends as best it could in the face of an often hostile Congress and President (Runte, 1979).

For example, the 1960s and 1970s saw the creation of a number of National Seashore and National Recreational Areas (NRAs) for urban populations to enjoy. By preserving these areas, the NPS was able to provide recreational opportunities for people who could not travel to more remote national parks. At the same time, the NPS hoped to take some recreational pressure off the overwhelmed ecosystems of Yosemite and other popular parks. The first two NRAs were Golden Gate NRA, in San Francisco, and Gateway NRA, along the coastal margins of metropolitan New York. Later additions included Point Reyes National Seashore, in northern California, Cuyahoga Valley NRA, in Cleveland, and Lowell National Historical Park, in Massachusetts (see Figure 13.9).

Since 1960 more than 130 units have been added to the National Park System. To be eligible for inclusion, an area must have national significance. Areas can be added to the NPS system only by an Act of Congress or by an Executive Order. In 1978 nearly 18 million hectares (45 million acres) were added to the National Park System, almost doubling its size. Most of these additions were Alaskan lands involving changes from National Monument to National Park status. Since 1979 there have been few additions to the system (Council on Environmental Quality, 1982).

Today, the NPS administers over 30 million hectares (74 million acres) in 334 different units. These units range from national parks to seashores to trails to urban parks to historic parks (see Table 13.3).

Small as the rate of new additions to the system has been since 1980, there has been a continuing rise in visitors to units of the National Park System. In 1960, for example, 79.2 million people visited 176 units (Council on Environmental Quality, 1982). By 1970 this had increased to 172 million people, visiting 235 units, and by 1980 the figure was 300 million people, visiting 277

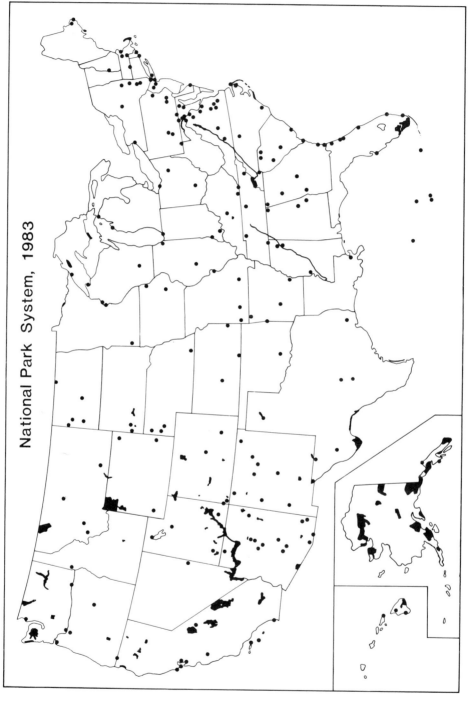

National Park System, 1983

Figure 13.8 National Park System, 1983. There are over 330 units in the system.

Figure 13.9 Ranger station, Lowell National Historic Park, Lowell, Massachusetts. National parks come to the cities.

units (Council on Environmental Quality 1982, p. 259). In one year alone, 1980–81, visitations to the national parks rose by 29.6 million (see Figure 13.10).

The increased demand has made some units overcrowded, polluted, and severely degraded. The 15 most popular national parks (see Table 13.4) bear the brunt of the assault. Because of its dual mission—conserving resources and making them available for public use and enjoyment—the NPS often finds itself in the center of controversy concerning its management plans. One particular issue involves the impact of very heavy use. The challenge for the future is for the NPS to provide recreational opportunities for those who visit the parks while minimizing environmental degradation due to the visitors themselves.

Multiple-Use and Special-Purpose Lands

Wild and Scenic Rivers

In 1968 Congress established the National Wild and Scenic Rivers System, to preserve free-flowing rivers as a balance to future dam and reservoir development. The system is designed to protect recreational river-use at three different levels of development. *Wild rivers* are inaccessible by motorized vehicles and have undeveloped shorelines. *Scenic rivers* are accessible by motorized traffic at certain points and sustain some development along their shorelines. *Recreational rivers* are easily reached and are usually well developed and heavily used. The formal rationale for inclusion in the system is that a river or river segment have one or more outstanding scenic, recreational, geologic, fish and wildlife, historic, cultural, or other similar values. The Secretary of the Interior, in consultation with state governors and others, has the power to designate rivers or river segments as wild and scenic. Originally, the Wild and Scenic Rivers System

Table 13.3 National Park Service Units, 1982

Type of Area	Number	Acreage
National Parks	48	45,414,348
National Historical Parks	26	99,138
National Monuments	78	4,445,874
National Military Parks	10	33,526
National Battlefields	10	8,240
National Battlefield Parks	3	6,675
National Battlefield Sites	1	1
National Historic Sites	63	16,122
National Memorials	23	7,988
National Seashores	10	456,670
Parkways	4	156,886
National Lakeshores	4	126,242
National Rivers	11	222,092
National Capital Parks	1	6,469
Parks, Other	10	30,824
National Recreation Areas	17	3,312,589
National Trail	1	47,939
National Preserves	12	20,399,164
National Mall	1	146
White House	1	18
Total National Park System	334	74,790,951

Source: U.S. Bureau of the Census, 1984

consisted of 8 river segments in 7 states, for a total of about 1280 km (800 miles). As of late 1983, there were 61 rivers and river segments in 23 states, for a total of almost 11,200 km (7,000 miles) (Council on Environmental Quality 1982). Fifteen percent of this total is in doubt due to lawsuits. These cases challenge the designations of 5 northern California rivers during the waning hours of the Carter administration. Almost half of the total river mileage is in Alaska, with 26 rivers in the system. The longest river in the WSR System is a 640 km (400 mile) stretch of the upper Mississippi in Minnesota, with Alaska's Fortymile River second, at 634 km (396 miles).

A variety of state and federal agencies, among the latter the Departments of the Interior and of Agriculture, administer the separate segments in the lower 48 states (see Figure 13.11). Management plans have been individually tailored to retain each river or segment in its present condition.

Although the WSR System tripled since 1968, its expansion almost halted during the early 1980s. Of the 88 river and river segments put forward for possible inclusion, 14 have been added to the system. Four have been declared ineligible, and the rest await study or legislative action (Huser, 1983). The Wild and Scenic Rivers System clearly has not been a high-priority area since 1980, although the sites themselves have increased in popularity among recreationists.

Wilderness

Wilderness has always been special to North Americans (Nash, 1982). Although the meaning of the term *wilderness* has changed over the centuries, it still connotes a sense of wildness, a sense of humans against nature. Many wilderness advocates, such as John Muir, Aldo Leopold, Robert Marshall, and Howard

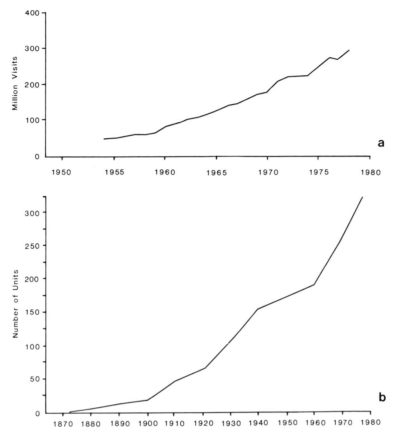

Figure 13.10 Growth in the national parks. (a) Trend in visitation of parks. (b) Trend in numbers of parks in the National Park System.

Zahniser, argued long and hard for the permanent establishment of wilderness areas that would be protected from all encroachment of civilization. Preservation of wilderness was a concern as early as 1840, but it was not until 1964 that the concept was formalized by the passage of the Wilderness Act.

The purpose of the Wilderness Act was to secure lands for protection and preservation and to administer these lands for use and enjoyment as wilderness. Management of these lands was to include strategies to leave them unimpaired for future use, that is, they were to be managed as wilderness areas. Within the legislation is a definition of wilderness that specifies that lands can be considered for inclusion under the Wilderness Act. The definition includes the following:

1) the area should be affected by the forces of nature only, and human impact should be unnoticeable;
2) the area should possess outstanding opportunities for solitude and primitive recreation;
3) the area should have at least 5,000 acres of land or be of sufficient size to make preservation practicable; and
4) the area should contain ecological, geological, or other features of scientific, educational, scenic, or historical value.

Table 13.4 Fifteen Most Visited National Parks

Name	Number of Visitors ($\times$ 1000)
Acadia	2,779.7
Glacier	1,474.6
Grand Canyon	2,305.0
Grand Teton	2,555.6
Great Smoky Mountains	8,441.0
Hawaii Volcanoes	1,692.3
Hot Springs	1,160.6
Mammoth Cave	1,495.8
Mt. Rainier	1,268.3
Olympic	2,032.4
Rocky Mountain	2,641.9
Shenandoah	1,699.2
Yellowstone	2,000.3
Yosemite	2,490.3
Zion	1,123.8

Source: U.S. Department of the Interior, 1981

Under the Wilderness Act, those federal agencies that managed public lands (the Forest Service, the National Park Service, the Fish and Wildlife Service, and the Bureau of Land Management) were asked to review lands under their jurisdiction for possible inclusion in the system. Immediately after the passage of the Wilderness Act, 54 areas, encompassing 9.14 million acres, were preserved (Council on Environmental Quality 1982). Most of these lands were in the western states, under the jurisdiction of the U.S. Forest Service. As part of the Wilderness Act, all federal land managers were also asked to undertake periodic reviews of lands for potential inclusion, and the NPS and the FWS were specifically asked to review lands over a ten-year period.

The definition in the Wilderness Act automatically excluded eastern wild lands that had shown some evidence of human impact (early forestry by settlers, remnant roads, and so on) and that were smaller than the 5,000-acre limit. In response to this, the Eastern Wilderness Act was passed in 1974, adding 16 new areas to the system. Under this legislation, the Forest Service was required to undertake a five-year review of its lands for potential inclusion.

By 1980 nearly 79.83 million acres had been preserved in wilderness status in 257 areas. Little has been added since 1980. The vast majority of the new additions from 1974 to 1980 were Alaskan lands. Nine out of the ten largest wilderness areas, ranging from 2.1 to 8.7 million acres, are in Alaska. The NPS administers the largest acreage of wilderness areas, or 44 percent, the Forest Service administers 31 percent of total acreage, the FWS 24 percent, and the BLM 0.1 percent. The largest number of units, 158, are under Forest Service jurisdiction.

Most of the controversy surrounding wilderness areas has been over the administrative review process. Without legislative prodding, the approval of wilderness or protected status for new areas has been slow. Once lands are included, the concept of multiple use is inapplicable, hence the reluctance of some federal agencies to designate new study lands.

Most of the wilderness areas include alpine and arctic environments; in

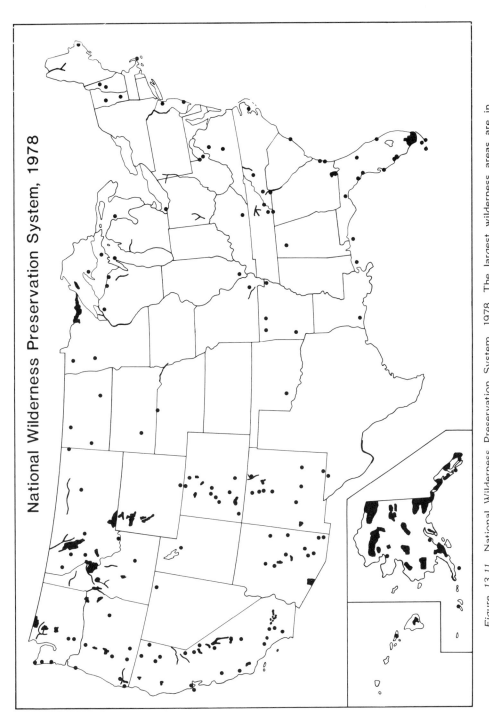

Figure 13.11 National Wilderness Preservation System, 1978. The largest wilderness areas are in Alaska and the northern Rocky Mountains. Wild and scenic rivers are also shown on this map. (Source: Council on Environmental Quality, 1981)

response to this, pressure was put on the Bureau of Land Management to accelerate its review process of desert and semi-desert lands. The Federal Land Policy and Management Act, passed in 1976, codified the role of the BLM and directed the agency to inventory lands for potential inclusion. The BLM review process has been controversial, and a number of legal challenges have been made. In December 1982, 173 areas that had been improperly identified as suitable for wilderness study were deleted from the list of possibilities. The reasons included a failure to meet the legal requirement of 5,000 acres and, in some of the areas, the fact that the federal government did not own the surface mineral rights and thus could not control mining in these areas (Council on Environmental Quality 1982, p. 152).

The Wilderness Preservation System in the U.S. has added many new areas in the last two decades. Environmentalists continue to push for more areas and argue for the need to preserve America's wilderness heritage.

Conflicts over Recreational Resources

Because we are individuals, our definition of recreation varies from one person to another. As a result of these differences, conflicts often arise between individuals or groups of individuals who want to use the same area for different recreational purposes. For years there has been conflict between people who want to sail on small recreational lakes and those who want to use their power boats. In trying to accommodate these different recreational demands, some state agencies have gone so far as to segregate sailing from power boats, either by specifying different uses on different lakes in a region or by specifying different uses on the same lake on alternate days, e.g., Mondays for sailing, Tuesdays for power boats.

Another example is the rivalry between off-road vehicle (ORV) enthusiasts and non-motorized recreational users on Massachusetts's Cape Cod (Godfrey et al., 1980). In the West, the annual Barstow-to-Las Vegas desert motorcycle race is another focus of conflict between these recreational groups. Motorcyclists claim there is nothing wrong in the several-day race by thousands of bikes across the open desert. Non-motorized users maintain that desert areas should be preserved intact, as a place for hiking and camping, undisturbed by noise and dirt-bike trails (see Figure 13.12).

The tension between users is often localized, but the mediation of these competing demands often falls to the state or governmental agency that manages the land. In some cases, BLM managers and NPS personnel, in addition to their other responsibilities, must enforce the laws and police these recreational areas. Recreational disputes will no doubt continue to be a problem, particularly in the face of declining recreational space and increasing demand. The management of recreational resources includes not only resource management but people management as well.

VISUAL RESOURCES

Human beings, if given a choice, would no doubt prefer to live in a beautiful environment rather than an ugly one. They would prefer to gaze upon beautiful landscapes. Beautiful can be defined in many ways, and this fact can lead to

Figure 13.12 Off-road vehicles (ORVs) in a desert canyon, eastern Utah. ORVs are a major point of conflict between different recreational groups in many areas.

conflict over the appearance of our environment. One hundred or more years ago, the suburbanization of the North American landscape had not yet begun; the continent was made up of vast rural expanses and relatively small and discrete urban places. The past century's expansion of populations outward from the cities has produced a new landscape that is a hodge-podge of rural and urban elements. Rapid changes in technology, the development of an automobile-oriented life style, changing tastes, and increased pressures to develop rural areas have all contributed to changes in our appreciation of landscapes. There is therefore greater disagreement today than in the past over what constitutes an attractive visual environment.

Until recently, small towns automatically welcomed growth. Beauty, to the merchant on Main Street, was synonymous with growth. A new building, a new housing subdivision, a new factory all meant progress and profits, and that was beautiful. In many places today, however, small town inhabitants want to preserve their traditional and distinctive ways of life. People in cities, too, are debating the appearance of urban areas. They ask whether the glass canyons produced by vast skyscrapers are conducive to human happiness—or should we work to maintain a human scale within the urban landscape?

Defining Visual Quality

One of the biggest problems in discussing visual resources is the determination and definition of beauty. What is a beautiful landscape? Visual evaluations are based on aesthetic standards, which in turn are a function of the social, moral, and ecological values of the group making the evaluation. These judgments are

Figure 13.13 Visual blight in America. Many Americans regard roads cluttered with neon signs, parking lots, and billboards to be visually offensive. This photo was taken in Mojave, California, but the scene is replicated throughout the country.

then applied to the environment, be it a landscape, city, or town. There is no uniform definition or measure of beauty or, conversely, ugliness. To ruin the visual aspects of a landscape is to create *blight.* Blight varies by culture, region, individual personality, experience, and type of land, town, city, or seascape. What is acceptable to one individual may be blight to another. Beauty is still in the eye of the beholder today.

Lewis, Lowenthal, and Tuan discuss visual blight in America in their 1973 essay. These three geographers, concerned with the plight of America's landscape, sought to discuss the meaning, history, and causes of visual blight. They found that visual blight went beyond such easily defined examples as litter and billboards along roadways. It was found everywhere in the U.S. It was worst in cities where most people lived, along roads where most people traveled, and along approaches to resorts where most people recreated (Lewis, Lowenthal, and Tuan, 1973).

Causes of Visual Blight

How and why do landscapes become blighted? There are a great number of reasons, and we will mention just a few. First, we degrade the visual quality of landscapes out of habit. We grow accustomed to environmental ugliness, and yet we are often surprised and indignant when it is called to our attention (see Figure 13.13). Have you ever thought about why neon, plastic, and a quarter acre of blacktop are needed to sell gasoline, fried chicken, and quarter-pound hamburgers?

Another contributory factor in blight is economic. That is, blight is financially profitable. There are many industries, such as land developing, outdoor advertising, and other roadside industries that create blight in the process of making money.

These industries are spinoffs from the automobile subculture, which has greatly influenced the transformation of the landscape. The development and promulgation of franchise architecture has helped diffuse blight across American landscapes (Rubin, 1979).

Landscapes are blighted because our political institutions rarely provide reliable mechanisms to prevent it. This laissez-faire attitude toward landscapes has let blight become so prevalent that it becomes unnoticeable. Zoning or legislating against blight often leads to court challenges in support of individuals' and communities' rights.

Conserving Visual Quality

Strategies to conserve visual quality include legal action that prohibits the intrusion of unsightly businesses, the preservation of historic places, the restoration of places, and the protection of unspoiled environments, such as wilderness. To take action to conserve visual resources, however, we must first be willing to agree on a definition of beauty. This involves some legal and ethical questions about the determination and regulation of aesthetics. Some recent court cases have decided that the state or federal government has no business making ethical judgments about beauty and that this burden should be placed squarely on the local community. It is the community's responsibility to regulate aesthetic standards within its jurisdiction.

Communities such as Williamsburg, Virginia, and Annapolis, Maryland, have architectural standards aimed at preserving their historical character. Other communities, California's Carmel-by-the-Sea and South Carolina's Hilton Head, for example, require that any new development conform to local building styles and construction materials. The zoning process enables these areas to preserve their character.

Conflicts are bound to arise, especially when there is not a consensus within the local community about what is visually acceptable. Aesthetic standards often divide communities and occasionally result in legal challenges to local zoning ordinances. How has this problem been resolved?

Regulating Roadside Blight in America

One of the most well known attempts at regulating visual quality involves outdoor advertising along America's highways and byways. Outdoor advertising includes on-premise signs that advertise services or commodities available on that parcel of private property (see Figure 13.14). Off-premise advertising includes outdoor displays on land that is leased, owned, or controlled by an advertising service expressly for that purpose. Billboards are the most common form of off-premise outdoor advertising.

There are obvious advantages to outdoor advertising. Since the majority of Americans spend considerable portions of their day in their cars, a merchant can reach a large audience quickly with some well placed billboards. The consumers go past the message at up to 55 mph. The messages are designed to be general, to be read quickly (in less than a 6-second exposure), and to make ample use of trade and logos (see Figure 13.15). The billboards must compete with vehicular traffic, traffic signals, and other outdoor advertising for each individual's attention.

Figure 13.14 On-premises advertising is often a prominent feature of the visual landscape.

Illinois, Indiana, Kentucky, Maryland, Michigan, Missouri, Nevada, Pennsylvania, Tennessee, Texas, and Wisconsin.

Opponents of outdoor advertising point out safety problems caused by motorists' paying more attention to billboards than to other cars and traffic signals.

Billboards have been around as long as there has been automobile traffic. In the late 1950s, roadside America became so unsightly that a number of national legislative attempts were made to get the nation to clean up along the highways. The Federal Aid Highway Act of 1958 established a national policy regulating placement and maintenance of outdoor advertising displays within 600 feet of the right-of-way of the U.S. Interstate Highway System. Displays had to conform to uniform standards of size, number, and location. There was no provision in the legislation, however, for active enforcement of the policy.

Partly as a result of Lady Bird Johnson's attempts to beautify America, a strong outdoor advertising regulation bill was passed. The Federal Highway Beautification Act of 1965 was designed to control advertising within 1,000 feet of the nearest edge of the pavement along the Interstate System and along federally aided primary roads. No federal aid for highway construction or maintenance would be given to states that did not control outdoor advertising. The only billboards permissible along the roadway were directional in nature or

Figure 13.15   The new, officially constructed and officially sanctioned billboard.

for traffic control. The act also required that all non-conforming billboards be removed by July 1, 1970, and that 75 percent of the costs of the removal be borne by the federal government and 25 percent by the states (Houck, 1969).

How successful has this program been? The funding for billboard removal, $75.5 million in 1967, dropped to only $10 million in 1971. From 1965 to 1979, 88,000 billboards were removed, but an estimated 450,000 remain (Romero, 1979). Given the funding level of 1979, it would take 110 years to tear down all the billboards in this country. On a 1981 transect along Interstate 40 from Bakersfield, California, to New Jersey, the authors counted 2,731 billboards on one side of the highway, or one every .88 road miles! The largest percentage of billboards were navigational guides—how far to the next exit, gas station, food, motel—but quite a few advertised communities and towns—"Come Visit Albuquerque." It is no wonder that the Federal Highway Beautification Act is often referred to as the environmental movement's greatest failure (Floyd and Shedd, 1979). A number of states have passed anti-billboard ordinances, so advertisers use a system of standardized small signs adjacent to the roadway, similar to official highway signs (see Figure 13.15).

Litter is another problem that has impaired the visual quality of American roadscapes. Gum wrappers, pull-tabs, and plastic containers can be found along most American roadways. One million tons of litter are picked up each year along our highways. Aside from individual responsibility and action to control bad habits, the most effective strategies are educational and punitive. Fines up to $500 for littering are not uncommon. Campaigns, such as those sponsored by Keep America Beautiful, Inc., constantly remind us that litter has its place (in the trash can). Smokey the Bear reminds us that "Every litter bit hurts," and Woodsy the Owl cries, "Give a hoot, don't pollute."

As a partial solution to the pervasive litter problem, some states have banned detachable pull-tabs on beverage containers. "Bottle bills," or legislative attempts to control litter, have also been effective in cleaning up roadsides. Oregon became the first state to pass beverage-container-deposit legislation in 1972. The law, whose primary purpose was to decrease litter along the state's roadways, placed a five-cent deposit on all beverage containers. Since the passage of the bottle bill, Oregon has decreased roadside litter by 65 percent, to the point that it can now claim to be one of the most litter-free states in the country. Oregon's bottle bill has now been copied by many states, including Connecticut, Vermont, New York, and Michigan.

Amenity versus Economic Value

Fortunately, the United States is rich in natural beauty. In the western states especially, there are many thousands of acres virtually untouched by human activity. Admired by hikers and other visitors, these areas are examples of a resource with a high visual value. They are, however, increasingly important for their economic values as well. Conflict inevitably arises over which is more important, a beautiful view or the mineral resources available underground. Unfortunately, these two resource uses can seldom co-exist. For many Americans, the natural beauty of a scene is destroyed with any hint of human use. If that use includes mining, large buildings, and air pollution, the amenity value of the resource disappears completely.

For energy developers, building power plants in the Southwest's coal fields makes economic sense. It cuts transport costs for the coal, hence lowering the price, and keeps the resulting air pollution in areas distant from the cities where the power is used. Environmentalists are appalled by the idea, feeling this approach threatens the beauty and untouched natural perfection of some of the Southwest's most striking vistas. The Golden Circle is one such area.

The Golden Circle (refer to Figure 11.7) is an area in southeastern Utah and northern Arizona that has the densest concentration of national parks and recreation lands in the U.S. In 1963 energy developers planned the Kaiparowits Project, a 3,000-megawatt power complex, to be built atop a mesa overlooking Utah's Glen Canyon National Recreational Area. Continuous opposition from local and national environmental groups proved so successful that, 13 years later, the major sponsor, Southern California Edison, finally gave up its plan (Josephy, 1976).

In 1977, the Golden Circle was again threatened, this time by a proposal to build the 3,000-megawatt Intermountain Power Project, 13 km from Utah's Capitol Reef National Park. This plan was defeated by Secretary of the Interior Cecil D. Andrus, who refused to grant the project an exemption from the Clean Air Acts. Again, the amenity value of an unspoiled view won out over the dollars and cents. More recently, debate has raged over the proposed Allen-Warner Valley Energy System. This project would place one of the world's largest strip coal mines, two power plants, a pipeline, and a power-transmission system all within view of Bryce Canyon, Zion, and Grand Canyon National Parks (Rudzitis and Swartz, 1982). Environmentalists question the need for this additional power production, pointing out that, in addition to the unsightly mining and construction, visual air quality models indicate that air pollution would significantly reduce the sharpness of these desert vistas. On smoggy days, one would not be able to see across the Grand Canyon.

In these situations, local residents are often divided between the obvious employment and other economic benefits to be gained and the fear that their way of life and independence, as well as their land and water quality, may be damaged beyond repair. During the 1970s, the amenity of beautiful views was generally seen as more valuable than the economic benefits to be derived from new power sources. More recently, the federal government has reversed that trend, moving toward relaxation of environmental regulations, including air quality standards.

SUMMARY

It is possible that today's landfills will be tomorrow's valued fuel sources. Stranger things have happened, as resources have shifted in value over the centuries. We have made no attempt to examine the entire range of potential resources, because that is impossible. How can we discuss the value of substances as yet unrecognized as having value? We can be totally unaware of an object's potential until shown it by an outsider. For example, for most of us a plastic sandwich bag is something that is used once and then discarded. But imagine that if you lived in a part of the world where plastic was still unusual and food was stored in clay jars and woven baskets. Can you imagine the stir a plastic bag would create? It would be used repeatedly and treated with care, so that it would not wear out. One should try to remain open to this awareness of potential and alternative ways of seeing and using the world.

Certainly, the question of what is beauty in the out-of-doors has changed considerably over past centuries. Once only cities were considered beautiful, and now, for millions of Americans, only wilderness is beautiful. Once billboards were indicators of progress and prosperity, like the city; now they are seen by many simply as blocking the view. Once wolves were reviled as monsters; now they are symbols of an unspoiled, golden past.

This chapter has shown that new resources are constantly coming into existence, within the dictates of politics, economics, and cultural background. The resource base is neither static nor unresponsive. In fact, over your lifetime, you will undoubtedly see a shift to a very different mix of resources than we have today.

REFERENCES AND ADDITIONAL READING

Baker, H.G. 1984. *The future of plants and vegetation under human influence.* Special Publication #2. San Francisco: Pacific Division, American Association for the Advancement of Science.

Batisse, M. 1982. The biosphere reserve: a tool for environmental conservation and management. *Environmental Conservation* 9:2:101–11.

Bean, M.J. 1977. *The evolution of natural wildlife law.* Washington, D.C.: Council on Environmental Quality.

————. 1983. Endangered species: the illusion of stewardship. *National Parks* July/August:20–21.

Broad, W.J. 1978. Boon or boondoggle: bygone U.S. rubber shrub is bouncing back. *Science* 202:410–11.

Campbell, F.T. 1980. Conserving our wild plant heritage. *Environment* 22:9:14–20.

Carney, L. 1983. New Jersey environment. *New York Times* January 30.

Council of Europe. 1983. Wildlife protection: ensuring observance through the Council of Europe. *Environmental Conservation* 10:2:167–68.

Council on Environmental Quality. 1982. *Environmental Quality, 1982. 13th annual report.* Washington, D.C.: Government Printing Office.

Dolmatch, T.B., ed. 1982. *Information Please Almanac.* 36th ed. New York: Simon and Schuster.

Dwyer, T. 1970. Americans wipe out 40 animal species. *Environmental Action* June 11:6–7.

Eckholm, E. 1978. *Disappearing species: the social challenge.* Worldwatch Paper 22. Washington, D.C.: The Worldwatch Institute.

Ehrenfeld, D.W. 1981. *The arrogance of humanism.* Oxford: Oxford University Press.

Ehrlich, P., and A. Ehrlich. 1981. *Extinction: the causes and consequences of the disappearance of species.* New York: Ballantine.

Felger, R.S., and G. Nabhan, 1978. Agroecosystem diversity: a model from the Sonoran Desert in *Social and technological management in dry lands—past and present, indigenous and imposed,* ed. N. Gonzalez, AAAS Selected Symposium 10. Boulder: Westview Press.

Foreman, D. 1979. ORVs threaten a wild canyon. *Living Wilderness* 43:146:14–18.

Floyd, C.F., and P.J. Shedd. 1979. *Highway beautification: the environmental movement's greatest failure.* Boulder: Westview Press.

Godfrey, P.J., et al. 1980. ORVs and barrier beach degradation. *Parks* 5:2:5–10.

Good, R.E., and N.F. Good. 1984. The Pinelands National Reserve: an ecosystem approach to management. *Bioscience* 34:169–73.

Goodwin, M. 1980a. Parks plagued by a shortage of good help. *New York Times* October 14.

———. 1980b. City hoping for private operation of parks. *New York Times* October 15.

Gordon, B.B. 1980. Cactus rustling. *Science 80* July/August:53–59.

Houck, J.W., ed. 1969. *Outdoor advertising: history and regulation.* Notre Dame, Indiana: Notre Dame University Press.

Huser, V. 1983. Riding the current—our wild and scenic rivers system. *National Parks* 57:11/12:20–25.

Huth, H. 1957. *Nature and the American.* Berkeley: University of Nebraska Press.

Iker, S. 1983. Swamped with deer. *National Wildlife* October/November:5–11.

Jackson, P. 1978. Scientists hunt the Bengal tiger—but only in order to trace and save it. *Smithsonian* 9:5:28–37.

Johnson, J.D., and C.W. Hinman. 1980. Oils and rubber from arid land plants. *Science* 208:460–64.

Josephy, A.K. Jr. 1976. Kaiparowits: the ultimate obscenity. Audubon 78:2:64–90.

Kazarian, R. 1981. Plant scientists get closer to developing Buffalo Gourd as a commercial food-source. *Environmental Conservation* 8:1:66.

Larmer, P. 1983. Yellowstone grizzlies—losing ground to people. *National Parks* 57:1/2:38–39.

Lewis, P.F., D. Lowenthal, and Y. Tuan. 1973. *Visual blight in America.* Resource Paper no. 23. Washington, D.C.: Association of American Geographers.

Nash, R. 1982. *Wilderness and the American mind.* Rev. ed. New Haven: Yale University Press.

National Academy of Sciences. 1982. *Genetic vulnerability of major crops.* Washington, D.C.

National Wildlife. 1983. Reproduction rates of the bald eagle. *National Wildlife* 21:2:31.

New York Times. 1981. Efforts in Florida provide little hope to save the dusky sparrow. January 19.

———. 1982a. Yemen acts to stem trade in rhino horn. October 31.

———. 1982b. Poachers put Indian rhino at great risk. November 29.

Noyes, J.H., and E.H. Zube, eds. 1977. *Coastal recreation resources in an urbanizing environment.* Amherst: Massachusetts Cooperative Extension Service and Institute for Man and the Environment.

Ornduff, R. 1974. *Introduction to California plant life.* Berkeley and Los Angeles: University of California Press.

Quinlan, A. 1980. New York City park system stands as a battered remnant of its past. *New York Times* October 13.

Ragotzkie, R.A. 1974. The Great Lakes rediscovered. *American Scientist* 62:July/August:454–64.

Regan, T., and P. Singer. 1976. *Animal rights and human obligations.* Englewood Cliffs, New Jersey: Prentice-Hall.

Roman, C.T., and R.E. Good. 1983. *Wetlands of the New Jersey pinelands: values, functions, impacts, and a proposed buffer delineation model.* New Brunswick, New Jersey: Center for Coastal and Environmental Studies, Rutgers University.

Romero, F.B. 1979. The state and federal quandary over billboard controls. *Natural Resources Journal* 19:3:711–19.

Rubin, B. 1979. Aesthetic ideology and urban design. *Annals, Association of American Geographers* 69:3:339–61.

Rudzitis, G., and J. Swartz. 1982. The plight of the parklands. *Environment* 24:8:6–11.

Ruggieri, G.D. 1976. Drugs from the sea. *Science* 194:491–97.

Runte, A. 1979. *National parks—the American experience.* Lincoln: University of Nebraska Press.

Schmitt, P.J. 1969. *Back to nature, the Arcadian myth in urban America.* New York: Oxford University Press.

Shepard, P. 1978. *Thinking animals.* New York: Viking.

U.S. Bureau of the Census. 1984. *Statistical abstract of the United States.* Washington, D.C.: Government Printing Office.

U.S. Department of the Interior. 1981. *National Parks Service statistical abstract.* Washington, D.C.: Government Printing Office.

U.S. Fish and Wildlife Service. 1982. *Endangered and threatened wildlife and plants.* Washington, D.C.: Government Printing Office.

Wilford, J.N. 1980. Agriculture meets the desert on its own terms. *New York Times* January 15.

Wolkomir, R. 1983. Draining the gene pool. *National Wildlife* 21:6:25–28.

TERMS TO KNOW

biological diversity
Biosphere Reserve Programme
conflicts among recreational uses
endangered species
Endangered Species Act
genetic resources
habitat preservation

National Park System
National Wild and Scenic River System
National Wilderness Preservation System
potential resource
threatened species
visual blight
wilderness

STUDY QUESTIONS

1. What is a potential resource?
2. What is the value of plants that are related to crop species but are not themselves cultivated?
3. If a rare species, such as the dusky sparrow or the snail darter, becomes extinct, what are the negative effects?
4. Can you think of a way in which a proxy value (see Chapter 2) for an endangered species might be determined?
5. What are some present economic uses of plants and animals other than for food and fiber?
6. The National Park Service has a dual mission, to preserve natural areas and to provide recreational opportunities. In what ways are these goals compatible, and in what ways do they conflict? How has the Park Service responded to the conflicts?
7. What is wilderness?
8. Describe the growth of federally designated recreational areas over the last few decades.
9. Describe government efforts to reduce visual blight in the U.S.

CHAPTER FOURTEEN

Minerals: Finite or Infinite?

INTRODUCTION

In Chapter 1 we suggested that resources are defined by their use and that they fluctuate in response to changing human evaluations of commodities as resources and our abilities to use them. This is particularly true for minerals. Experts may have knowledge about and the ability to use a given deposit, but more is needed before the substance can be extracted and marketed. Economics and politics cause the status and availability of minerals to fluctuate widely, often much more than that of other natural resources.

Minerals are defined differently in different contexts. For the purposes of this book, minerals are substances that come from the earth, either from solid rocks or from soils and other deposits. Minerals include fossil fuels, such as coal, oil, and natural gas, but these are discussed separately in Chapter 15. The non-fuel minerals include metal ores, phosphate rock, asbestos, salt, precious stones, clay, gravel, building stone, and similar materials. Minerals are valued for their physical properties, such as strength, malleability, corrosion resistance, electrical conductivity, and insulating or sealing capacity, and they are fundamental to any industrial system.

RESERVES AND RESOURCES

Reserves is an important term used to describe the availability of minerals to a production system. Reserves of a mineral are the quantities available for use at the present time. Their location and physical characteristics are known, and they can be extracted using present technology and under prevailing economic conditions. Reserves are a subset of *resources,* which also include deposits that are unavailable for use at present, because of poor geologic knowledge or unfavorable economic or technological conditions, but which might become available in the future. *Unidentified* resources are those that have not yet been discovered; *subeconomic* resources are those that may have been discovered but cannot be extracted at a profit at current prices.

The distinction between reserves and resources is illustrated in Figure 14.1.

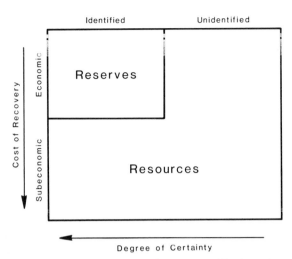

Figure 14.1 Reserves and resources. The boundary between reserves and resources is not fixed. It shifts with new discoveries, price changes, and other technological and socioeconomic factors. (Source: Modified from Brobst and Pratt, 1973)

This diagram was created by Vincent McKelvey, a director of the U.S. Geological Survey during the 1970s (McKelvey, 1972). The horizontal axis of the diagram represents varying degrees of certainty about the existence or nature of deposits of a particular mineral. The vertical axis represents differing economic values of the deposits, that is, the varying economic profitability of extraction. All the occurrences of a given mineral are symbolically contained within the boundaries of the diagram.

The boundaries between reserves and other resources in Figure 14.1 shift over time. Shifts in these boundaries result primarily from three factors: (1) economic conditions; (2) technology of extraction and use; and (3) geologic information. The economic profitability of extraction varies considerably, depending primarily on the price of the commodity. As the price goes up, more and more deposits, of lower grade, higher cost of extraction, or both, become profitable to extract. Similarly, if the price falls, only high-quality or cheaply extracted deposits can be mined at a profit, and the quantity of reserves shrinks. Prices for minerals often fluctuate widely, as discussed in Chapter 2. Fluctuations in the level of production in the economy as a whole affect demand and price for raw materials; competition between substitutable materials can also cause price variations.

Technology is another factor that is of importance, mainly as it affects the costs of mineral extraction and processing. For example, during the 19th and early 20th centuries, high-quality iron ore was shipped in essentially raw form from Lake Superior ports to steel mills on the lower Great Lakes. In time the high-grade ores were depleted, and transportation costs per unit of steel became prohibitive. The development of a means for concentrating a lower grade ore, called taconite, into enriched pellets at the mining site reduced transportation costs and allowed renewed mining activities. This technological development made lower grade ores economically extractable, which they had not been in the past. Technological changes can also cause increases in the costs of extraction. Recently environmental regulations have required changes in mining techniques to minimize environmental disruption. These changes have often resulted in increased expenditures in mining and have increased the cost of extraction, thus decreasing reserves. Underground coal mining is one such example: federal safety standards for miners have significantly increased the costs of mining coal.

Geologic exploration does not directly affect the profitability of extracting minerals but instead brings new deposits to light. If these are extractable at current prices and with current technology, they become reserves. Changes in geologic information are generally more important in long-term trends in reserves rather than in the short term. For most minerals, there are identified deposits that will last at least a few years, and price fluctuations cause much more variation in reserves than do increases in information. It takes time to acquire new geologic information. No longer can an investor send a prospector out to the wilderness and expect to find large deposits at the surface. Instead, geologic structures and rock types must be carefully mapped, possible mineral associations checked by geochemical surveys, gravity surveys conducted, and so forth. When a potential deposit is located, it is usually necessary to drill test boreholes and analyze many rock samples before there is any certainty of the nature and extent of the deposit. Very few valuable deposits exist at the surface. The sophisticated exploration techniques available today help us to see the subsurface in more detail more than they significantly speed the process of exploration.

AVAILABILITY OF MAJOR MINERALS

Geology of Mineral Deposits

There are so many different minerals of importance and the geology of their deposits is so varied, that it is impossible here to describe the specific conditions of all mineral occurrences. However, it is useful to discuss some general principles, providing examples of some major types of mineral deposits.

Minerals differ greatly in their crustal abundance, i.e., in the percentage of the earth's crust that is composed of particular minerals. Iron, for example, composes about 5 percent of the earth's crust, and aluminum about 8 percent (Putnam and Bassett, 1971). Gold, on the other hand, is only about one billionth of the earth's crust, and copper and zinc are each about one ten-thousandth. These fractions obviously affect the frequency with which we find usable deposits of these elements. Many minerals are valuable specifically because of the particular chemical or molecular structure they are found in, and the frequency of such occurrences may be high or low. Carbon is a relatively plentiful element, for example, but diamonds, a crystalline form of carbon, are quite rare.

Many minerals, especially metal ores, tend to be formed by similar geologic processes. For example, if rocks are heavily fractured by stresses in the earth's crust, at high temperatures, then *hydrothermal mineralization* can take place. In this process various elements dissolved in subsurface water flow below the surface, within the crust. If the chemical composition and the temperature of water change in certain ways, then certain minerals are deposited in the surrounding rocks, creating concentrations of those minerals. Many valuable ores are created this way, tending to be found near each other in mineralized districts. Mountain building often includes hydrothermal activity, and as a result many of our important mineralized districts are in mountainous areas.

Shields are areas of very old igneous and metamorphic rocks that form the ancient cores of continents. They are another geologic environment that has yielded large amounts of valuable minerals. In most of the world, they are buried under other rocks, but large surface shield areas occur in Canada, Africa, Australia, and elsewhere. Because of their age, these areas contain different mineral assemblages than do most younger rocks, and many shield areas are very rich in metal ores. Important deposits of iron, nickel, copper, zinc, and other metals are found in the Canadian shield in Ontario, for example.

While concentrated metal ores are usually found in metamorphic rocks, there are also many areas of sedimentary rocks that yield important minerals. Lead, zinc, and uranium are sometimes found in commercially extractable quantities in sedimentary rocks, for example. Some substances, most notably gold and diamonds, are found in *placer deposits.* These are deposits of sand or gravel in which denser particles have been concentrated by the action of running water. Mining usually requires excavating large volumes of sediment to recover small quantities of the minerals.

Another process that concentrates minerals at the earth's surface is weathering, the gradual breakdown of rocks by mechanical and chemical processes. Weathering can selectively remove some elements while leaving others in the soil. Bauxite, the most important ore of aluminum, is formed in this way in humid tropical environments.

These few examples help to show the range of environments in which mineral deposits are found. Some minerals show up in several different types of deposits, but many are located only in restricted geologic circumstances. The common minerals, such as iron, are found all over the globe, and there is great variability in the quality of those deposits. As a rule, very high-grade deposits are relatively rare, but if industry is willing to accept slightly lower grade deposits, there is always more available. This is certainly true for very common elements, such as iron and aluminum. The U.S. has very little high-quality aluminum ore, and most of our best iron ore has been used. As a result, the U.S. imports most of its iron and aluminum ore from other countries. But should those foreign sources become unavailable or expensive or should the price increase dramatically, then substantial domestic low-grade deposits are available. Rarer minerals, such as chromium, platinum, molybdenum, and vanadium, are found in commercial concentrations in fairly restricted conditions. Only a few countries dominate world production and marketing for those minerals, and in some cases, domestic low-grade deposits are unavailable.

Variations in Reserves and Resources

Minerals are stock resources, in that the amount available in rocks is finite. In that sense, it is possible to examine how much is in the ground relative to present and projected future demand. For non-fuel minerals, this is not as easy as it might seem, for the following reasons. First, the amounts of minerals in the ground are extremely large, relative to demand, and the real question is how large reserves are, relative to demand. The amount of a mineral reserve available, however, is very much dependent on price. A doubling in price, for example, may produce a 10- or 100-fold increase in reserves. Price increases also stimulate exploration, which may further increase reserves through new discoveries. In this way, minerals act as flow resources rather than stock resources. Second, an increasing number of minerals are recycled and thus are becoming, from the point of view of human production systems, renewable resources. About one-fourth of U.S. iron and steel supplies are derived from recycled material, and nearly half the nation's lead is produced from recycled sources. When the price of minerals rises, so does the economic attraction of recycling, and the contribution of recycled materials will undoubtedly increase in the future. Third, there is a high degree of substitutability for most minerals. If we run short of steel, we can often use aluminum. If we run short of aluminum, we can use magnesium or synthetic materials. Substitution may not be possible for all uses of a material, but partial substitution usually alleviates supply problems and keeps the material available for necessary uses. This substitutability causes demand for minerals to be highly elastic, changing significantly with changes in price.

Taken together, these factors mean that future demands for minerals are difficult to predict and are vulnerable to small changes in prices and technologies. In addition, a distinction must be made between short- and long-term availability. In the long run, we will never "run out" of any minerals. We may find that a particular mineral has become too expensive to justify using it, and, in that sense, it may become unavailable. For groups of minerals, it may be that worldwide demand will cause a long-term trend of increasing prices, which would likely reduce demand for those minerals (Brooks and Andrews, 1974). In the short run, however, perhaps over periods of less than five to ten years, sharp fluctuations in mineral prices are common. These fluctuations reflect or cause variations in supply or demand, presenting very real problems when they occur. We often misunderstand the nature of these crises, however. They are not the result of the world running out of a mineral; they are a consequence of the vagaries of the world economic and political system.

Domestic Reserves and Resources

With the variability of reserves and resources in mind, we can compare present rates of demand with available reserves, to provide an indication of which minerals are likely to continue to be plentiful and so probably much used and which are likely to be in short supply and thereby fall into disuse. A comparison of present demand with domestic reserves and unidentified or subeconomic resources is presented in Table 14.1.

In the first category of Table 14.1 are those minerals for which present reserves are adequate well beyond the year 2000. Magnesium is an important metal in this category; it is lightweight and can be substituted for other metals in a wide range of uses. Molybdenum, titanium, and boron are ferroalloys, materials used with iron to make specialized metals. In 1982 72 percent of U.S. titanium was imported. This is partly because the nation's industry needs a special form of titanium dioxide, called rutile, that is not cheaply available here, but it probably also reflects the fact that titanium can be produced cheaper

Table 14.1 U.S. Domestic Resources of Selected Minerals Relative to Projected Demand

I Reserves in Quantities Adequate Well Beyond 2000

Boron	Molybdenum
Bromine	Phosphorus
Calcium	Potash
Chlorine	Rare earths
Clays	Sand and gravel
Gypsum	Silicon
Helium	Soda
Lithium	Stone
Magnesium	Titanium (except Rutile)

II Identified Subeconomic Resources Adequate Beyond 2000 and Significantly Greater Than Unidentified Resources

Aluminum	Vanadium
Manganese	Zircon
Nickel	

III Undiscovered Resources Adequate Beyond 2000 and Significantly Greater Than Identified Subeconomic Resources

Beryllium	Lead
Bismuth	Niobium
Cadmium	Platinum
Cobalt	Selenium
Copper	Silver
Fluorine	Sulfur
Gold	Tungsten
Iron	Zinc

IV None of the Above

Antimony	Mercury
Asbestos	Tantalum
Chromium	Tin

Source: U.S. Geological Survey, 1975

elsewhere. The remaining minerals in this category have uses ranging from construction to fertlizers to high-technology applications.

The second category includes minerals that do not fit in the first, but for which identified subeconomic resources seem adequate. For these minerals, a moderate increase in price will be sufficient to produce adequate domestic supplies. Note that aluminum is in this category, as are four important ferroalloys. At present prices, most domestic aluminum ores are uneconomic, and therefore most U.S. needs are supplied by imports. The U.S. has substantial domestic resources of non-bauxite aluminum but does not as yet have the capacity to process this. Similarly, at present most of our nickel, manganese, vanadium, and zircon is imported, but if prices were to rise, identified domestic deposits exist in large quantity to provide our needs.

In the third category are minerals for which the U.S. does not have either large reserves or subeconomic resources, but for which there are likely to be substantial undiscovered resources. What is needed in these cases is more geologic exploration. As yet this exploration has not been justified economically, because sufficient quantities are available on the world market. Again, a significant price rise may stimulate an increase in exploration, and such exploration for these minerals would probably be fruitful.

The fourth category includes minerals that do not fit in any of the other

Table 14.2 U.S. Imports of Selected Minerals

Mineral	1982 Imports as Percentage of Apparent Consumption	Major U.S. Suppliers
Aluminum	4	Australia, Jamaica, Surinam
Antimony	45	Bolivia, Mexico, Guatemala
Asbestos	74	Canada, South Africa
Bauxite	97	Jamaica, Guinea, Brazil
Cadmium	69	Canada, Australia, South Korea
Chromium	88	South Africa, Philippines, U.S.S.R.
Cobalt	91	Zaire, Canada, Japan
Columbium	100	Thailand, Canada, Brazil
Copper	7	Chile, Canada, Peru, Zambia
Iron Ore	36	Canada, Venezuela, Brazil, Liberia
Manganese	99	South Africa, Gabon, Brazil
Nickel	75	Canada, Norway, Australia
Platinum Group	85	South Africa, U.S.S.R., U.K.
Potassium	71	Canada, Israel
Silver	59	Canada, Peru, Mexico
Tin	72	Malaysia, Thailand, Bolivia
Titanium	72	Federal Republic of Germany, France, Canada
Tungsten	48	China, Bolivia, Canada
Zinc	53	Canada, Belgium, Federal Republic of Germany

Source: U.S. Bureau of the Census, 1984

three; these are substances for which domestic resources are truly inadequate. These are commodities that the U.S. will probably always have to obtain through imports, and thus their availability will be primarily determined by world rather than domestic supply and demand.

Table 14.2 is a listing of U.S. imports of selected minerals. Net imports are expressed as a percentage of apparent consumption, which is U.S. primary production plus secondary production (recycling) plus net imports. It should be recognized that imports fluctuate greatly from year to year, and so the figures in Table 14.2 may not accurately reflect long-term trends.

World Reserves and Resources

Most nations' dependence on the world minerals market makes an examination of global reserves and resources important. Just as at the national level, there are some minerals that are available in large quantities worldwide, and there are others that are not. In the short run, fluctuations in mineral availability are caused by variations in economic activity and, to a lesser extent, by political actions, wars, and so on. In the long run, mineral availability is determined by level of economic activity, technological changes, and geological considerations. While these things cannot be predicted with certainty, it is possible to project changes in demand and technology, based on recent trends (see Chapter 16). An attempt to predict future mineral availability is illustrated in Table 14.3.

The first column of numbers contains the ratios of 1977 world reserves to 1977 world production. These ratios are the number of years the reserves would last if the prices, technology, and production levels that prevailed in 1977 continued indefinitely. This is of course an absurd assumption, but it serves as a basis for

Table 14.3 World Reserves and Resources Relative to Demand for Minerals

Mineral	1977 Reserves/ 1977 Production (years)	Global 2000 Projected Life-expectancy of reserves (years from 1974)
Aluminum	306	94
Chromium	260	68
Copper	57	35
Fluorine	36	37
Iron	188	68
Lead	31	29
Manganese	220	69
Mercury	25	21
Nickel	77	44
Phosphorus	243	88
Platinum Group	100	43
Potassium	453	84
Silver	20	14
Sulfur	33	26
Tin	50	31
Tungsten	45	28
Zinc	27	21

Source: Council on Environmental Quality, 1981

comparison. The second column is the Global 2000 Report's projected life expectancies of 1974 reserves, assuming growth in demand, which is more likely than no growth (Council on Environmental Quality, 1981). In general, these numbers are lower than those of the first column. This is reasonable, because 1977 reserves were probably greater than 1974 reserves in some cases, and the growth in demand assumed in column two would mean that they would be exhausted sooner. Let us compare these figures with projected resource depletion dates from Goeller and Zucker (1984). In many cases, Goeller and Zucker's projections differ greatly from those of the Global 2000 Report. For most of the minerals listed in this table, they predict greater than 100 percent depletion by the year 2100. They do, however, predict that many other minerals not listed in this table will not be exhausted in that time period. They also feel that 115 years is ample time for development of new technologies to convert resources that are undiscovered at present to reserves, provided that sufficient and early research and development efforts are made.

Of the minerals listed in Table 14.3, potassium, aluminum, iron, phosphorus, and chromium appear to be among those in reasonably good supply, though Goeller and Zucker disagree in the case of chromium. Those in less plentiful supply include silver, lead, zinc, tungsten, nickel, mercury, and fluorine.

An important aspect of the global mineral market is that minerals are not uniformly distributed around the globe. For certain minerals, it is not uncommon for only a few countries to control most of the world's production. For example, four countries control about 75 percent of the world's bauxite production, six countries produce 90 percent of all manganese, platinum group metals are 95-percent-controlled by two countries, and 80 percent of phosphate rock comes from three countries (Netschert, 1981). This means that there is the potential for the development of cartels that could artificially control supplies of minerals.

The cartels that have been formed, notably those in tin, copper, and bauxite, have been unsuccessful in manipulating world markets. Their lack of success has been due to several factors. In some cases, important producers have refused to join because of political differences with other producers or have refused to cooperate with other cartel members. In addition, many countries have large stockpiles of metals that were accumulated for military uses in times of war, which have been used to manipulate supplies and prices. Probably most important, however, most minerals are simply not in short enough supply or critical enough to world economies to allow a group of producers to put significant pressure on consuming countries (Netschert, 1981). The result has been a continuation of a relatively unregulated world market. For those Third World nations that are mineral-rich and derive substantial foreign exchange from mineral exports (Zaire, Gabon, Zimbabwe, Malaysia, and Mexico are examples), this situation has thwarted many plans to substantially increase national income through market manipulation.

Strategic Minerals and Stockpiling

Although effective mineral cartels or other political organizations have yet to restrict supplies of minerals significantly, the possibility of such restriction is a subject of some concern to the U.S. government. This is particularly true in the case of minerals that are important to military and industrial production and are imported from nations with unstable or unfriendly governments.

This dependency has been recognized for many years. The U.S. government has therefore defined certain minerals as of strategic or critical importance to the welfare of the country and has developed policies to prevent shortages. *Strategic minerals* are those essential for defense purposes and for which the U.S. is totally dependent on foreign sources. Examples of strategic minerals are cobalt, chromium, manganese, and platinum. *Critical minerals* are also necessary for national defense, but the U.S. can meet some of its demand for these from domestic sources and supplies from friendly nations. Examples of critical minerals are copper, nickel, and vanadium. It is an interesting quirk of geology that much of the supply of strategic minerals to the U.S. comes from two nations: the Republic of South Africa and the U.S.S.R.

Over thirty minerals have been identified as having strategic or critical importance to the U.S. (see Table 14.4). The following are examples of that importance.

Chromium is used to harden steel and make it resistant to corrosion. It is an essential component of stainless steel and is used in ball bearings, surgical equipment, mufflers, and tailpipes. It is used in the defense industry in armor plating and weapons and for many parts of piston and jet engines. The leading producers of chromium are South Africa, the U.S.S.R., Albania, Zimbabwe, and the Philippines. The U.S. imports about 90 percent of its chromium, mainly from South Africa, the Philippines, and the U.S.S.R.

Cobalt is a metal used in the aerospace industry. It is a high-temperature alloy important to the manufacture of jet engines, cutting tools, magnets, and drill bits. It is also used in electronics equipment, especially in computers, television receivers, and transmitters. The primary producers of cobalt are Zaire, Zambia, Canada, and the U.S.S.R. Zaire alone has 65 percent of the non-communist

Table 14.4 Strategic and Critical Minerals

Mineral	Uses
Alumina	construction, automobiles, airplanes, high-tension power lines
Antimony	alloy to harden lead, car batteries, bullets
Bauxite	construction, automobiles, airplanes, high-tension power lines
Beryllium	electronics, nuclear engineering, missles, aerospace, high-strength tools, springs, tubes
Cadmium	coating and plating, batteries, paints, pigments, plastic and synthetic products
Chromium	hardening steel, stainless steel, surgical instruments, chemical processing equipment, mufflers, tailpipes
Cobalt	hardening steel, heat-resistant parts for jet aircraft, cutting tools, electric and electronic equipment, paints, chemicals, computers, communications, machinery
Columbium	hardening and strengthening steel, oil and gas pipelines, construction, cars and trucks, blades for aircraft, rocket assemblies
Copper	electrical wiring, roofing, plumbing, household utensils, jewelry, coinage
Gallium	photoelectrical applications, illuminating elements in electronic appliances, (calculators, radios, TV, stereos), fiber optics, solid-state electronics
Germanium	transistors, lasers, infrared optics, weaponry, missile-guidance systems
Indium	solder and sealers, watch dials, electronic instruments
Lead	batteries, auto industry, shield against radiation
Lithium	lubricants, nonrechargeable batteries in pace-makers, cameras
Manganese	removing oxygen and sulfur from steel to harden, cast iron
Molybdenum	alloy for steel, armaments, tubing, heat exchanges, pipelines, energy and aerospace applications, electronics
Nickel	corrosion-resistant steels, jet aircraft
Platinum group	catalyzing chemical reactions, catalytic converters, producing nitrogen fertilizer, upgrading octane rating, electronics, glass manufacturing, synthetic fibers
Rhenium	low-lead and lead-free high-octane gasoline, heating elements, temperature controls, X-ray equipment, semiconductors
Selenium	electronics, photoelectrics, photocopy machines, improving casting of stainless steel
Silver	photography, sterling, electrical contacts, batteries, defense, jewelry, dental, medical
Tantalum	aircraft, missiles, radio communications, machine tools, nuclear engineering, aerospace, electronics
Tin	engine bearings, electrical gears, containers
Titanium	pigments, paint, paper, plastics, aircraft, jet engines, guided missiles, spacecraft, ordnances
Tungsten	machine tools, drill bits, core for armor-piercing projectiles
Vanadium	high-speed tools, gears, crankshafts
Zinc	protecting iron and steel from corrosion, brass, galvanizing construction, rubber manufacturing
Zirconium and Hafnium	nuclear engineering, ceramics, abrasives, control rods for nuclear reactors

Source: Sinclair and Parker, 1983

world's reserves (Sinclair and Parker, 1983). The U.S. is heavily reliant on imported cobalt, mostly from Zaire.

Among the strategic minerals are the metals of the platinum group, which includes six different minerals with similar properties. These metals—platinum, iridium, palladium, osmium, rhodium, and ruthenium—are resistant to corrosion and are used as catalysts in chemical reactions. Other applications include catalytic converters in automobiles, petroleum refining, electroplating, electronics, and fertilizer manufacture. The major producers of platinum-group metals are the U.S.S.R., South Africa, Canada, and Japan. The U.S. imports 87 percent of its platinum, primarily from South Africa (57 percent), the U.S.S.R. (13 percent), and the U.K. (10 percent).

Manganese is essential in steel manufacture and thus has many industrial and military applications. It is added to molten steel to remove oxygen and sulfur, thus hardening the steel. The U.S.S.R., South Africa, Brazil, China, and Indonesia are the world's major producers. The U.S.S.R. and South Africa alone supply about 60 percent of the world's manganese (Sinclair and Parker, 1983). The U.S. imports most of its manganese from South Africa, Gabon, and Brazil. The presence of large quantities of currently subeconomic manganese on deep ocean beds was important to U.S. refusal to sign the Law of the Sea Treaty (see Chapter 12).

Stockpiling, or maintaining large storages of commodities, is one method the U.S. has chosen to protect itself from restrictions in supplies of strategic minerals. The danger of minerals dependency has been recognized since the turn of the century, but actual stockpiling did not begin until shortly before World War II. In 1949 the U.S. Strategic Stockpile was created to avert shortages of minerals during wartime. The intent was to purchase and store materials in sufficient quantities to meet defense and national security needs for a three-year period, which is presumably a long enough period of time for alternative supplies to be developed in the event of a cutoff of supply from other nations. Ninety-three substances, not all of them minerals, were on the list. Congress did not appropriate funds for procurement, however, and the stockpile was well below the official goals for many years. Recently procurement has increased, and the stockpile is at or over 100 percent for many materials (see Figure 14.2). The government occasionally sells some of the material in the stockpile to meet domestic supply needs or to generate revenue to buy more urgently needed materials.

Stockpiling is an important policy, because it protects a nation from the short-term interruptions of supply and rises in price that minerals are susceptible to. Stockpiling in the U.S. implies preparedness for war. Of course, it is unlikely that limited regional wars would cut off supplies from all major mineral suppliers, and, in the case of an all-out world war, it is improbable that the U.S. could make use of a three-year supply of industrial minerals. Nonetheless, the strategic stockpiles are very good guarantees against short-term reductions in supplies caused by an industrial collapse or prohibition of trade in one or two countries. From the standpoint of national economic health, it makes sense to guard against such events.

In summary, the market for many minerals is a world market, in which a relatively small number of suppliers sell to a large number of customers. In the long term, availability of some minerals is essentially infinite, but for others there will be substantial increases in price, which will lead to conservation, recycling, development of substitute materials, and other means for reducing demand for expensive materials. In the short term, prices fluctuate widely, stimulating changes in sources and uses of minerals and creating some economic distress in sensitive industries. Even though the production of many minerals is concentrated in a small number of countries, these nations' lack of political agreement and dependence on exports for foreign exchange, the substitutability of materials, and other factors make the formation of effective cartels unlikely. The volatility of mineral prices makes stockpiling useful for insulating national production

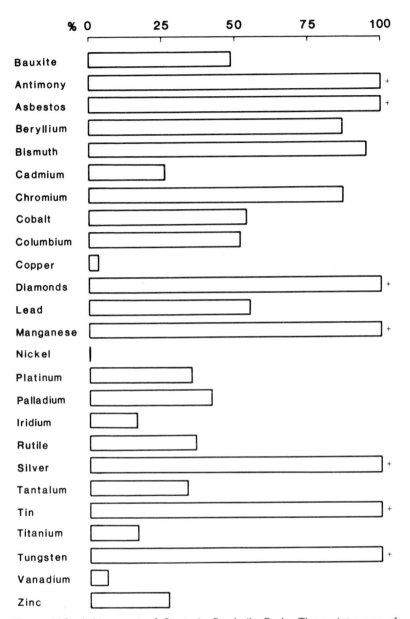

Figure 14.2 Achievement of Strategic Stockpile Goals. The maintenance of stockpiles for minerals and other substances protects the U.S. in times of trade disruption. (Source: Stockpile Report to the Congress, Federal Emergency Management Administration, April–September 1981)

systems from catastrophic changes in the world market. Taken together, these things suggest that the fears of supply cutoffs caused by cartels or unfriendly nations or as a result of political instability in the Third World or South Africa are unfounded. The argument that, for purposes of maintaining mineral supplies, the U.S. must maintain good relations with South Africa or with other governments with which we may have differences seems rather hollow.

Figure 14.3 Open-pit Kennecott copper mine outside Salt Lake City, Utah.

ENVIRONMENTAL AND SOCIAL CONSIDERATIONS OF MINING

Mineral extraction has highly concentrated environmental and social effects. Individual mines are often very large, as economies of scale are important in maintaining profitability. Few mineral ores are more than 30 percent pure, and some less than 1 percent. Large quantities of ore must therefore be processed to obtain relatively small amounts of the finished product. If the mine is at the surface, such as the open-pit mine shown in Figure 14.3, the area disrupted can be quite large. In addition, it is often necessary to remove large amounts of undesired rock to get at an ore body, further increasing the area disturbed. Unused rock and the waste from processing operations must be disposed of (see Figure 14.4). These materials, called *tailings,* are processed with large amounts of water and deposited in tailings ponds. These ponds are often themselves quite large. Water pumped from mines to facilitate extraction or for other use in ore processing is usually of low quality. In many cases, it is highly acidic, and it usually is contaminated with the minerals being mined. The resultant pollution of receiving waters is often severe. The huge volume of ore-bearing rock to be processed requires that processing take place near the mine. Thus, many mine

Figure 14.4 An abandoned gold mine in the Front Range, Colorado. A huge amount of tailings results from a process that yields a very small amount of gold.

sites are also locations for smelting or other methods of purifying minerals. Most of these processes produce large emissions of air pollutants, particularly sulfur dioxide and metals. These emissions may be of such quantity as to severely damage vegetation and soils in the surrounding area. Sudbury and Wawa, Ontario; Palmerton, Pennsylvania; and Ducktown, Tennessee are examples of areas where vegetation destruction is so severe as to be clearly visible on satellite photographs.

Mine sites are generally dictated by the presence of ore, not by the environmental suitability of the location for a large-scale industrial operation. Many of the mines in the Rockies and Sierra Nevada are in areas of considerable natural beauty, in or near important resort areas. Although long-abandoned mines and ghost towns may be appealing to tourists, modern mines and associated residential areas generally are not.

An example of the conflict between mining and recreational interests is Crested Butte, Colorado, an isolated town of about 1,000 people in the San Juan Mountains. Crested Butte is an idyllic mountain resort. Tourism is its major industry, led by a nearby ski area. AMAX, Inc., a large mining concern, is planning to open an enormous molybdenum mine on federal land just outside of town, within Mount Emmons. Under the 1872 Mining Act, mining companies are allowed access to minerals on federal lands. If AMAX does open the mine, it will employ 1,300 people during production and more than 2,000 during the construction phase (Williams, 1979). With accompanying family members and increased services, this would result in a doubling of Gunnison County's population of about 11,000. In addition to these sudden socioeconomic changes the environmental impacts would also be impressive. Over 95 percent of the rock removed from the mountain would be deposited in a huge tailings pond, covering about 1,200 hectares (3,000 acres). Even if the mine were built in the most environmentally sensitive ways, it would be difficult to hide a 1,200-hectare tailings pond. Furthermore, the economy and atmosphere of the town would be completely transformed, and its appeal as a tourist attraction would probably be much reduced.

In addition to its environmental impact, mining has many important social and economic effects in the areas where it occurs. Most mining towns are isolated, away from major urban centers, frequently in mountains (see Figure 14.5). The populations of mining towns are almost entirely dependent on the mines for employment and income. When the mine is operating, they prosper, but when it is not, they are impoverished. Mine operations are governed by the prices of the materials mined, which, as we have shown, tend to fluctuate widely (see Figure 14.6). When demand for a mineral drops, causing a reduction in price, production is usually reduced by closing whole mines rather than by reducing production a little at all mines. This is because economies of scale are important in mining, and it is often more economical to close a mine entirely than to run it at a reduced level. Mining towns thus continually go through boom-and-bust cycles, alternating between full employment and extreme unemployment (see Figure 14.7). The toll this takes on the lives of the mine workers and other residents is understandably severe (see Issue 14.1).

REUSE, RECOVERY, AND RECYCLING

A significant amount of material can be recovered during the manufacture, use, and disposal of goods, enough to decrease our need for raw ores (see Table 14.5). This includes a variety of measures, such as reuse, recycling, and recovery.

Reuse is simply the second (or *n*th) use of a product without any modifications to it. An example of a commodity that is reused is returnable glass beverage containers. By reusing these, we decrease the number of new bottles that have to be manufactured and save the raw materials and energy that would be used in such manufacture. The opportunity for reuse depends on the product. Obviously only very durable materials that are not significantly altered by each use can be reused.

Recycling is the process whereby a material is recovered from the consumer product and then becomes a raw material in the production of a similar or different product. Aluminum recycling is a good example. Aluminum cans that are returned to redemption centers are melted down and used in the manufacture of new aluminum cans and other products. In 1981, 32 percent of the aluminum consumed was produced from recycled aluminum, and over half of all aluminum beverage containers were recycled (Chandler, 1983).

The ease with which minerals can be recycled depends on several factors, including the technology of conversion to a desired product, the ease of accumulation of sufficient used material, and the costs of manufacture of a product from recycled as opposed to raw materials. This last factor is itself partly affected by differences in quality between products made from raw materials and those made from recycled materials. For most minerals, the cost of converting an ore to pure form is significantly greater than the cost of remanufacture from recycled material, not considering the cost of mining ore and the cost of accumulating recycled materials. Not only is this true in monetary terms, but it also applies to energy use and environmental pollution. For example, to manufacture a given amount of aluminum from recycled scrap uses 90 to 95

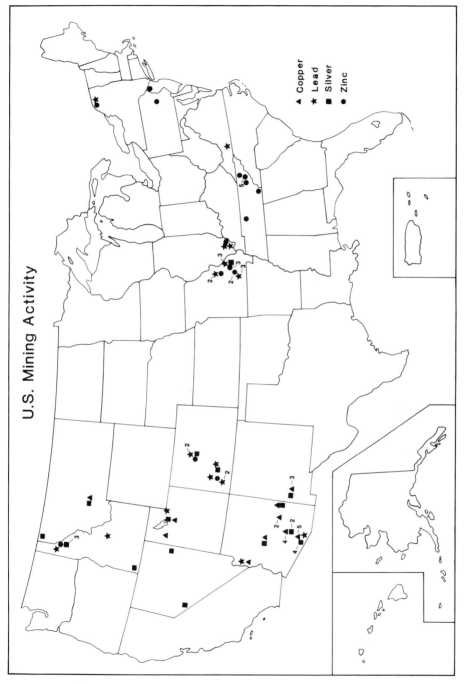

Figure 14.5 U.S. mining activity. Mining is often located in rugged, isolated terrain, resulting in socioeconomic and environmental challenges to the affected communities. Numbers refer to more than one mine. (Source: U.S. Bureau of Mines, 1983)

Value of Nonfuel Mineral Production

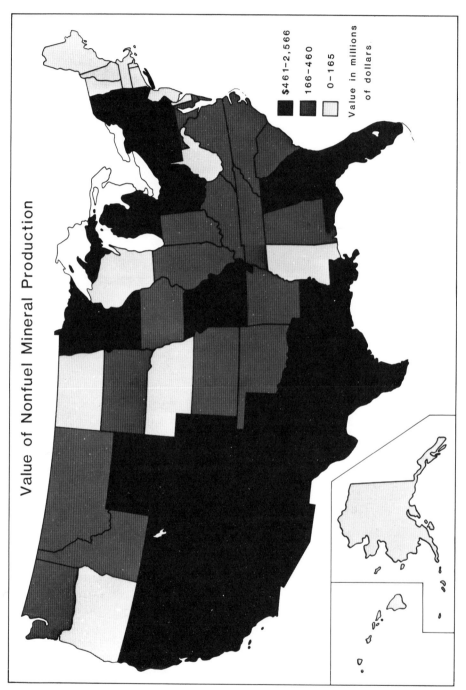

$461–2,566

166–460

0–165

Value in millions
of dollars.

Figure 14.6 Value of nonfuel mineral production. Mining is especially important economically in the West and Great Lakes states, with pockets in other areas. (Source: U.S. Bureau of Mines, 1983)

Figure 14.7 An open-pit iron mine at Hibbing, Minnesota. The mine is closed at present.

percent less energy and generates 95 percent less pollution than does refining aluminum from bauxite (Chandler, 1983).

Accumulating sufficient material to recycle is the biggest problem. This depends to a great extent on the original use of the material. One of the biggest uses of lead, for example, is in storage batteries, such as those in automobiles. Old batteries are found at specific locations, primarily automobile junkyards and auto-repair shops. The lead in them is valuable enough to warrant recycling, as is much of the lead used in other ways. As a result, 35 percent of the lead consumed in the U.S. is made from recycled materials. Titanium, on the other hand, is primarily used in very dispersed forms. About 90 percent of titanium is used in pigments for paints, and thus it winds up on the walls of houses, buildings, and so forth (Barton, 1979). It would be very difficult to collect used paint in quantities sufficient to recycle the titanium it contains. Titanium recycling is therefore insignificant.

Accumulation of material for recycling is easiest in industry, where large amounts of material tend to be found in a few locations. Scrap is generated as part of many manufacturing processes, and this is very easily recovered. For example, steel that does not meet specifications is recovered at the steel plant and immediately returned to the production process as a raw material. This recycling of industrial waste is really just a way of making the manufacturing process more efficient.

Recycling of household waste is more difficult. This is primarily because household waste contains small quantities of many things, instead of large quantities of a few things. Municipal solid waste, for example, is about 33.5 percent paper, 34.5 percent food and yard waste, 9.9 percent glass, 12.9 percent miscellaneous materials, and only 9.2 percent metals. The costs of separating

Table 14.5 Mineral Recycling

Mineral	Recycled Obsolete Scrap as Percentage of Total Consumption, 1981
Antimony	61
Lead	35
Gold	30
Iron	28
Platinum group	25
Copper	24
Nickel	21
Silver	21
Mercury	21
Tin	19
Chromium	18
Tantalum	16
Zinc	5
Aluminum	4

Source: U.S. Bureau of the Census, 1984

ISSUE 14.1: Living with Boom and Bust

Boom and bust, cycles of rapid growth and catastrophic decline, occur wherever mining dominates a local or regional economy. When national or world production of minerals drops slightly, mines that are only marginally profitable close operation, while those with larger profit margins stay open. When prices are high and production increases, new mines open and old ones are reopened. If a mine is located in a remote area, as is often the case, the communities around it depend on the mine for nearly all their income. Nearly everyone works for the mine, for businesses that serve the mine, or for businesses that serve the people who work in the mine. As the mine goes, so goes the community.

Both boom and bust are stressful. During boom times, there is usually an increase in population, a shortage of housing, a rise in rents and property values, and a shortage of public services. When they come in large numbers, immigrants bring problems to small towns. Everyday life for the permanent residents is disrupted. Shops are more crowded, housing costs rise, and streets are blocked by construction. Unemployment and crime may also be problems, if more immigrants arrive than are hired.

Boom times are certainly not all bad, though, as nearly everyone has a job, and business is good. The new money in town brings in new businesses, perhaps a second barbershop, a few gas stations, a discount department store, a bigger supermarket, a few restaurants, and several bars. Those lucky enough to own property or get into business at the right time do very well, amassing small fortunes. Those who came in when the boom was already underway meet stiff competition and high costs, but they still manage to earn a living.

Then comes the bust. Competition from cheaper imports may be too rough, the higher grade ore may be mined out, or the world price may have fallen because of a recession. Maybe new materials are replacing the ore in a few critical industries, or perhaps environmental requirements are making the mine less profitable than one in another state or another country. The actual cause

the recyclable components of municipal solid waste are too high to be justified for that purpose alone. Recently, however, *resource recovery* from municipal solid waste has become feasible in many areas. This feasibility is largely a result of two factors: the high cost of solid waste disposal and the high cost of energy.

Most municipal solid waste in the U.S. is buried in landfills. Once a relatively cheap method of disposal, this has become increasingly expensive, because suitable land within a short distance of an urban area has become scarce. This scarcity is in part a result of land development for other uses and in part a result of environmental regulations, which limit destruction of wetlands and restrict disposal in areas where water contamination is possible. In addition, energy price increases make the heat that can be generated from burning garbage more valuable, helping to offset the cost of such burning.

In 1978 there were 17 resource recovery plants in operation and 12 more under construction in the U.S. (Office of Technology Assessment, 1979). Most of them burn the waste to produce steam, which is then used in industrial processes or space heating. Garbage haulers or municipalities must pay to take their garbage to these plants, but the price can be lower than the corresponding cost of operating a landfill, so the process is economical.

Many communities also have instituted recycling programs that rely on the individual to separate waste into different types; this is called *source separation*.

---

doesn't really matter to those affected, because, whatever the cause, it is beyond their control. At any rate, the mine is shut down, and 40 percent of the town's work force is laid off with two weeks' notice and two months' severance pay. A few stay on for an extra three months to help with removing the machinery that can be used elsewhere.

Some people leave town immediately, particularly those who had arrived most recently and hadn't established themselves there yet. Unemployment compensation and savings keep others going for the better part of a year, but eventually that runs out, so most of them leave, too. Those with large debts go bankrupt. Many of the rest can't sell their houses for as much as they owe on the mortgage, and they also go bankrupt after the mortgage is foreclosed.

Two years after the mine is closed, the town's population has dropped 50 percent. Before the boom, there was one barbershop, three gas stations, and one supermarket, all doing well. Now there are two barbershops,

both having trouble making rent payments, one supermarket open and one closed, a closed department store, and six gas stations, only one of which is doing well. Most of the bars that opened during the boom are still there, but now they get more business during the day than at night.

Although the specific town above is fictional, these things have happened in many mine towns in the U.S., and more than once in most of them. Today, concern about the social impacts of mining is increasing, and many states have taken steps to lessen the blows. Severance taxes, charged to the mining companies when minerals are removed, are often used to pay for improvements in town services and infrastructure during growth times and for relocation or job training afterwards. Mining companies are becoming more willing to contribute to these expenses, in their attempts to maintain public goodwill. These changes will ease the ups and downs to some extent, but the cycle will still occur and recur.

Although these programs are often highly visible, with prominent recycling centers where waste can be deposited, they have not significantly increased household recycling of materials in comparison to industrial recycling.

CONCLUSIONS

Although we often think of minerals as non-renewable resources, we are not going to run out of any of them. Variations in price are far too important in generating new supplies and in controlling demand for geological considerations alone to determine use. Demand fluctuations occur primarily through substitution, but increased efficiency of use is also important. In the future, recycling will become increasingly important, as higher mineral prices make this source of materials economically more feasible.

REFERENCES AND ADDITIONAL READING

Barton, A.F.M. 1979. *Resource recovery and recycling.* New York: Wiley.

Brobst, P.A., and W.P. Pratt, eds. 1973. United States mineral resources. USGS Professional Paper 820. Washington, D.C.: Government Printing Office.

Brooks, D.B., and P.W. Andrews. 1974. Mineral resources, economic growth, and world population. *Science* 185:13–19.

Chandler, W.U. 1983. Materials recycling: the virtue of necessity. Worldwatch Paper 56. Washington, D.C.: Worldwatch Institute.

Council on Environmental Quality. 1981. *The Global 2000 report to the president.* Washington, D.C.: Government Printing Office.

DeVore, C. 1981. Strategic minerals: a present danger. *Signal* January, pp. 63–68.

Goeller, H.E., and A. Zucker. 1984. Infinite resources: the ultimate strategy. *Science* 223:456–62.

McKelvey, V.E. 1972. Mineral resource estimates and public policy. *American Scientist* 60:32–40.

Netschert, B.C. 1981. Dependence on imported nonfuel minerals: the threat of mini-OPECs? *Journal of Metals,* March, pp. 31–38.

Office of Technology Assessment. 1979. Materials and energy from municipal waste. Washington, D.C.: Government Printing Office.

Putnam, W.C., and A.B. Bassett. 1971. *Geology.* 2nd ed. New York: Oxford University Press.

Sinclair, J.E., and R. Parker. 1983. *The strategic minerals war.* New York: Arlington House.

U.S. Bureau of the Census. 1984. *Statistical abstract of the United States.* Washington, D.C.: Government Printing Office.

U.S. Bureau of Mines. 1983. *Minerals yearbook.* Washington, D.C.: Government Printing Office.

U.S. Geological Survey. 1975. Mineral resource perspectives, 1975. U.S. Geol. Survey Prof. Paper 940. Washington, D.C.: Government Printing Office.

Williams, R.N. 1979. A tiny town battles a mining giant. *New York Times Magazine* March 4.

TERMS TO KNOW

cartel
mineralization
recycling
resource recovery
speculative resource
stockpiling

subeconomic resource
substitutability
tailings
unidentified resource
weathering

STUDY QUESTIONS

1. What are three reasons for the shifting of the boundary between reserves and other resources?
2. What are the environments in which minerals tend to be located?
3. How is it that minerals are both stock and flow resources?
4. Have mining cartels been successful in controlling access to their products? Why or why not?

5. President Carter stated that the support of human rights was more important than obtaining strategic minerals. President Reagan's position might be considered the direct opposite of President Carter's. What does each position imply for foreign and domestic policy?
6. How do conflicts arise between mining and other uses of the same land? Name some environmental impacts of mining.

CHAPTER FIFTEEN

Energy: The Universal Resource

INTRODUCTION

The Arab oil embargo of 1973–74 left Americans acutely aware of the end of low oil and gasoline prices. No longer would they be paying 25 cents or even 50 cents for a gallon of gasoline. The economic, social, political, and technological implications of past energy use patterns and energy policies are now becoming clear. Energy is fundamental to economic and physical health, and past energy use patterns cannot be continued indefinitely. This suggests a need for a reevaluation of our energy thinking and its role in contemporary society. Alternative energy futures have been proposed based on "soft" energy paths, i.e., decentralized renewable sources (Lovins, 1977), and on movements away from fossil fuels toward solar energy and conservation (Stobaugh and Yergin, 1979).

Energy exists in many different forms and is used for many purposes. Energy includes the kinetic energy of a speeding train or of the wind, the radiant energy of the sun or of a warm surface, the potential energy in a reservoir above a hydroelectric plant, and the chemical energy stored in fossil fuels. This chapter discusses the forms of energy that are used in producing the goods and services that are the basis of our national and world economies. It examines the complex nature of energy: where it comes from, how it is used, and why it is such a significant subject in our lives, when such a short time ago it was taken for granted.

ENERGY IN THE MODERN WORLD

Efficiency

Efficiency of energy use can be measured in economic gain per unit of energy expended. Throughout much of recent U.S. history, energy has been so plentiful that we did not consider efficiency of energy use in most of our economic decisions. Today, however, we are very conscious of contrasting patterns of energy use and efficiency, especially between different nations and different types of economic systems.

Traditional agricultural economies produce goods and services at a relatively

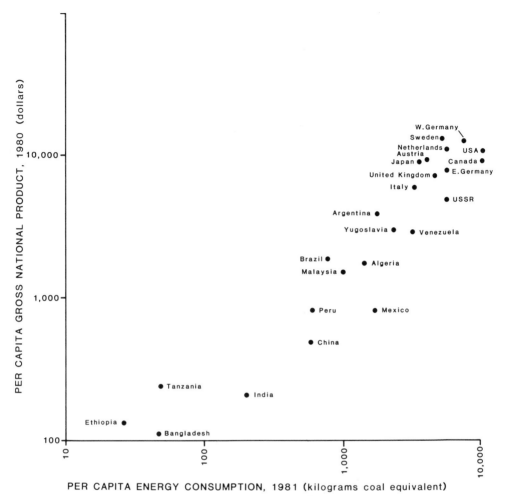

Figure 15.1 Per capita GNP and energy consumption. This comparison is the best indicator of energy efficiency at the national level. In general, the higher the GNP per capita (as in countries like the U.S., Canada, and West Germany), the higher their consumption of energy. (Source: Data from U.S. Bureau of the Census, 1984)

low level, using virtually no energy except that provided by the sun through heat and photosynthesis. In contrast, mechanized agriculture uses large amounts of fossil fuel in every step of the production system, from building the tractor and other equipment to manufacturing the fertilizer to fueling the farm machinery. This system produces much more food per unit of human labor—but much less per unit of industrial energy input. A good discussion of energy contrasts between traditional and industrial societies can be found in Cook (1978).

The best indicator of national energy efficiency is a comparison of per-capita gross national product (GNP) with per-capita energy consumption (see Figure 15.1). As a rule, the higher the GNP per capita, the higher the energy consumption, and vice versa. A nation with a higher income can spend more money on machines and raw materials to increase production and produce a higher standard of living. This in turn leads to more energy consumption, which,

Table 15.1 U.S. Energy Consumption 1951–82

Year	Total Energy Consumed (Quads[a])	Change from Previous Year Pecentage
1951	36.1	7.4
1955	39.2	7.8
1960	44.1	11.1
1965	53.0	16.8
1970	66.8	20.7
1975	70.7	5.5
1980	76.0	6.8
1981	73.9	−2.7
1982	70.9	−3.0

[a]A *Quad* equals one quadrillion BTU. A BTU (British Thermal Unit) is the amount of energy required to raise the temperature of one pound of water one degree Fahrenheit at or near 39.2 degrees Fahrenheit.

Source: Council on Environmental Quality, 1982, Table A-33 Energy, pp. 273–74; Energy Information Administration, 1982, p. 7; U.S. Bureau of the Census, 1984, p. 572

if expended in production, leads to more income. The highly industrialized nations consume much more energy per capita than do the less industrialized nations. The U.S., for example, has 6 percent of the world's population and consumes 35 percent of the world's energy; China, with 21 percent of the world's population, consumes only 6 percent of the world's energy. There are also great variations in energy efficiency between industrialized nations. Most of the western European nations, for example, use less energy per unit of economic return than does the U.S. This is because energy prices have been much higher there for a longer time, and Europeans have adjusted by using public transportation, driving smaller cars, driving shorter distances, and heating buildings to lower temperatures.

First and Second Laws of Thermodynamics Revisited

In Chapter 4, we reviewed the laws of thermodynamics. Those laws are just as important in discussing energy resources as in describing energy transfers in ecosystems. We know that energy cannot be lost, but merely possessing it does little good. Energy is only valuable because of its ability to do work or generate power. Thermodynamic principles can be important considerations when selecting energy sources and allocating them to various uses (Commoner, 1977). For example, if low-intensity energy is used for purposes to which it is best suited, then thermodynamically more costly energy can be spared for uses that need it most. An instance of this would be using solar energy for space heating, which frees up electricity for such uses as air conditioning or driving motors. Similarly, methods of capturing waste energy from some processes and using it for other purposes, e.g., capturing waste heat from electricity generation to heat buildings, are considerably more efficient than allowing that waste heat to escape unused. Increased aggregate efficiency depends on techniques such as these, on the small scale.

TRENDS IN U.S. CONSUMPTION

Beginning in 1950, U.S. consumption of energy steadily increased at the rate of about 3.5 percent annually until 1973 (Council on Environmental Quality, 1981). In 1973 this pattern changed, largely as the result of high energy prices, relative scarcities of oil, a slowing economy, and changes in consumers' attitudes. In 1974 and 1975, for example, total U.S. consumption of energy was down by 6 percent from the previous two years. Immediately following this decline and the end of the oil embargo, energy consumption began to rise again, although more slowly. The U.S. consumed 74.51 *quads* (quadrillion BTUs) in 1976, and this rose to 78.97 quads in 1979. Energy consumption has declined since 1979, and it appears that this downward trend will continue. Total U.S. consumption of all types of energy was 70.9 quads in 1982, down from 79.0 quads four years earlier, and below the 1973 consumption figure of 74.6 quads (see Table 15.1). We are using less energy than we were, largely due to increased prices, shifts in the national economy, and a change in consumer attitudes regarding energy conservation.

Shifts in Fuel Type

In addition to changes in overall consumption, there have been some dramatic changes in the sources of energy consumed. For example, in 1950 the leading sources of energy were petroleum (14.43 quads) and coal (13.20 quads). Ten years later, petroleum consumption was still first, but natural gas had replaced coal as the second most consumed source. This pattern continued until 1972, when natural-gas consumption reached its peak of 22.70 quads. Since then, natural-gas consumption has declined by 11 percent to 19.93 quads in 1981 (see Figure 15.2). Consumption of coal, currently third, has been increasing since 1960. Just from 1970 to 1981, the use of coal has increased by 21 percent. This pattern shows no sign of changing in the immediate future.

Perhaps the most dramatic change in consumption patterns has been with petroleum. There was a steady increase in U.S. oil consumption during the 1960s and 1970s, with the exception of the 1974–75 oil embargo years. The peak in U.S. consumption of oil occurred in 1978, with 37.97 quads. Since 1980, annual petroleum consumption has declined to 32.00 quads, 16 percent below the 1978 peak levels.

The use of nuclear power rose steadily through the 1960s and 1970s but has stabilized since 1979. The production of hydropower peaked in 1974, with 3.31 quads, and its share of the total has been decreasing ever since, as most of the best hydroelectric generating sites have been taken.

One of the most worrisome aspects of fuel consumption patterns is our increasing reliance on imported energy sources. Prior to 1953 the U.S. was self-sufficient in meeting its energy needs. Twenty years later, nearly 17 percent of the nation's energy needs came from imported petroleum (Council on Environmental Quality, 1981, p. 178). Oil imports declined during 1974–75 but rose to peak levels in 1977 (18.76 quads). Since 1977 U.S. reliance on imported oil has declined.

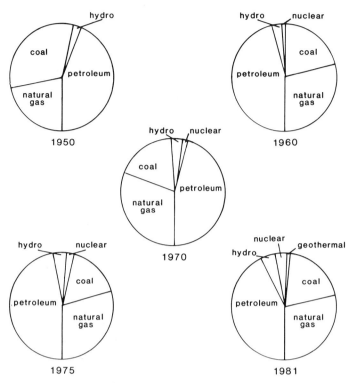

Figure 15.2 U.S. energy consumption by source. Changing source patterns highlight the increased use of coal and the decreased use of natural gas from 1975 to 1981. (Source: Data from Council on Environmental Quality, 1981, 1982; U.S. Bureau of the Census, 1984)

Consumption by Sector

The use of primary energy sources (petroleum, natural gas, coal, nuclear, hydro, geothermal) to generate electricity (a secondary energy source) has increased sharply since 1950. In 1951, for example, electric utilities consumed less energy than any other sector. By 1982 these same electric utilities consumed 34 percent of all energy, followed by the industrial, the transportation, and the residential and commercial sectors (see Figure 15.3).

The largest use of energy in the residential and commercial sector is for space heating. In 1950 coal was the primary home heating fuel, but since 1970 natural gas has been the leader. Nearly six out of every ten households in the U.S. use natural gas to heat their homes (Council on Environmental Quality, 1981, p. 184). Some recent changes that have occurred at the local or regional level do not appear in the national statistics. One of these is the increasing use of wood for home heating (see Chapter 8). In the industrial sector, the major use of energy is to produce steam and heat for industrial processes. The largest user of energy in the transportation sector is the automobile, followed by commercial trucks.

In the following sections, we will discuss each of the major energy sources that are available today and likely to be available in the near future. In the final

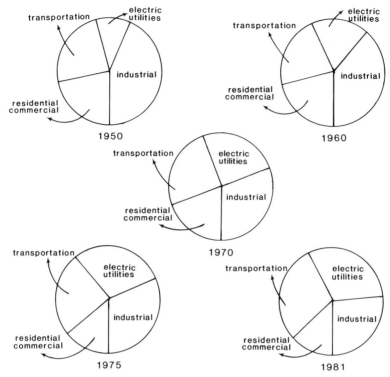

Figure 15.3 U.S. energy consumption by sector. Energy use in the transportation sector has steadily increased since 1950, as has energy consumed by electric utilities. (Source: Data from Council on Environmental Quality, 1981, 1982; U.S. Bureau of the Census, 1984)

part of this chapter, we will examine some of the alternatives available to the U.S. and to the rest of the world, as an expanding population struggles to sustain economic growth while not exceeding the available supplies of energy.

OIL AND NATURAL GAS

Oil and natural gas are the most versatile energy sources in use today. They are used in every sector of the economy, at both the national and international levels. Fluctuations in their availability and price have far-reaching effects on much of the world's economic activity. Oil is a major factor in international politics, and concern about domestic oil production has had significant impacts on other natural resources in the U.S. The complex issues affecting oil availability and price are often clouded with ideology and partisan politics.

Geology

Oil and natural gas are produced by the accumulation of organic matter in sedimentary rocks and the later alteration of that organic matter by the pressure and heat of burial in the earth's crust. Oil and gas are both composed of hydrocarbons, but they differ in their boiling temperatures. Oil is liquid in the ground, but gas is not. Oil and gas usually occur together, but they sometimes can become separated if gas migrates through rock that is not permeable to oil. Crude oil may contain natural gas in solution, and gas sometimes contains liquid petroleum. Because they occur together and are readily substitutable for each other in most end uses, they are discussed together.

Sediments rich in organic matter are relatively common, but the geologic circumstances necessary to accumulate oil or gas in commercially viable quantities are not. For this much oil to accumulate, there must be a reservoir rock permeable enough for oil to flow through it. Oil is less dense than water, and it is forced upward by density differences as well as by pressures in the earth's crust. Another requirement is a trap, in which a reservoir rock is overlain by an impermeable rock, which prevents the oil from escaping to the surface. Many different kinds of traps exist, and exploration geologists usually look for such structures in their initial searches for oil. Accumulations of oil, called fields, vary considerably in size, with the numbers of fields inversely related to their size. There are very few giant fields. The largest known (about 75 billion barrels) is the Ghawar, in Saudi Arabia, although there are indications of a field approaching this size in Mexico. Oil also comes in many different forms, and the quality of crude oil depends on the proportions of the different hydrocarbons in the oil. Crude oil with a high proportion of high-boiling-point hydrocarbons is called heavy oil. Tar and asphalt are the major components of heavy oil. Light oil is rich in hydrocarbons with low boiling points, such as naphtha and kerosene. The proportions of these and other hydrocarbons affect both the ease of extraction and the price of the crude oil. Natural gas is made up of several different gases, including methane, propane, and butane.

Location of Known Reserves

Oil-bearing formations are found all over the world, but the largest deposits are concentrated in a few areas (see Figure 15.4). In 1980 the nations with the greatest proved reserves of crude oil, in descending order, were Saudi Arabia (25 percent of the world total), Kuwait (10.1 percent), the U.S.S.R. (9.4 percent), Iran (8.5 percent), Mexico (8.5 percent), the United Arab Emirates (4.8 percent), the U.S. (4.4 percent), Iraq (4.4 percent), Libya (3.4 percent), Venezuela (3 percent), and China (3 percent). The remaining nations of the world have only about 15 percent of all known crude oil reserves. The U.S.S.R. leads in natural-gas reserves (39.8 percent), followed by Iran (16.6 percent), the U.S. (6.8 percent), Algeria (4.5 percent), Saudi Arabia (4.1 percent), Canada (3.1 percent), Mexico (2.6 percent), Qatar (2.1 percent), the Netherlands (1.9 percent); all others have 18.5 percent. It should be recognized that much of the world is poorly explored, and new discoveries in these areas can probably be expected in the future, but well-explored areas, such as the U.S., are not expected to increase their reserves. Within the U.S., the most important producing regions are the Gulf Coast, West Texas, Alaska, the Great Plains, the Colorado Plateau, and California.

History of Exploitation

The first commercial oil well in the U.S. was drilled in 1859, but rapid growth in oil production and consumption did not come until the early 20th century.

Figure 15.4 Natural gas and petroleum fields. Considerable supplies of oil and natural gas are located in the outer-continental shelf waters of the Atlantic Ocean, the Gulf of Mexico, and coastal California. (Source: From Council on Environmental Quality, 1981)

Natural gas and petroleum fields

At that time, the principal oil fields of Texas, Oklahoma, and California were developed. Simultaneously, the automobile caught on as a means of transportation. The use of oil grew exponentially until the middle of the 20th century, as more oil was discovered and produced, refining and distribution capacity increased, and more uses were found for it. There were shortages during World War I, and gasoline was rationed during World War II. Throughout this period, the real price of oil in the U.S. (adjusted for inflation) steadily declined, reaching a low in the late 1960s.

By the mid-1950s, domestic oil became harder to find, and exploration in other regions of the world increased. Domestic exploration, as measured only by the numbers of wells drilled, peaked in 1956 and has not reached these levels since. Domestic exploration was higher in 1981 than ever before, however, when other indicators, such as exploration expenditures, are included. In the 1950s and 1960s, American oil companies placed more emphasis on overseas exploration, particularly in South America and the Middle East, where large untapped fields could be developed more profitably than could the smaller fields in the U.S. As a result, the U.S. found itself a major importer of oil in the early 1970s, with these imports accounting for 25 percent of its consumption.

Domestic oil production peaked in 1970, and natural-gas production peaked in 1974. Domestic demand continued to climb, and this increase was met by imports. In 1981, 53 percent of our oil consumption was supplied by domestic production and 47 percent by imports. In the late 1970s, domestic production was spurred by high prices, and supply increased. Similar trends occurred in other countries, and a worldwide surplus developed, with oil inventories at high levels and the demand low. This increase in relative supply caused a 15 to 25 percent drop in prices between 1980 and 1983. Our current consumption of oil in the U.S. is about 6 billion barrels per year, and world consumption is around 24 billion barrels per year. U.S. natural gas consumption is 20 trillion cubic feet, and world consumption is about 52 trillion cubic feet.

End Uses

Petroleum and natural gas replaced coal as the primary heating fuel in the middle of this century. Today, oil supplies about 43 percent of the U.S. energy demand, and natural gas another 27 percent (see Figure 15.2). Most of the oil, 58 percent, is consumed in the transportation sector, in the form of gasoline for automobiles. The industrial sector accounts for 25 percent of the oil consumed nationally. Industry consumes oil not only for heating, but also for manufacturing petroleum-based products, such as synthetic fibers, pesticides, and fertilizers. Seven percent of the oil is consumed by electric utilities, while the remaining 10 percent is used in residential and commercial space heating (Energy Information Administration, 1982). Natural gas is used primarily as a home heating fuel and as a cooking fuel. Nearly 53 percent of American households heat with natural gas, and 40 percent use natural gas to cook with (Council on Environmental Quality, 1982, p. 276).

How Much Is Left?

The shortages of the 1970s, like those of earlier years, generated a great deal of discussion about how much oil is available and how long it will be before we

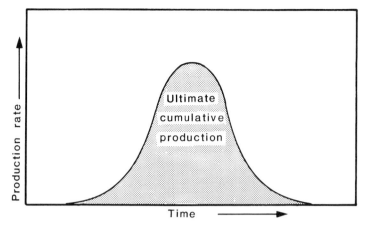

Figure 15.5 Performance-based estimates of oil recoverability. In oil production, a pattern of exponential growth first occurs. Production levels off when the amount used approaches the amount naturally found in the earth. This is followed by an exponential decline in production and use. (Source: From Hubbert, 1969)

run out. First, it should be recognized that, as with nonfuel minerals, we will never completely run out of oil. Rather, it will become so expensive that we will either replace it with other sources or reduce our demand for it. Nonetheless, it is worthwhile to investigate just when oil and natural gas are going to become so hard to find and recover that the price must rise substantially. At that time, we will effectively cease to use these fuels for all but the most essential purposes.

There are two approaches to calculating how much oil we are likely to produce in the future: the geological estimate and the performance-based estimate. The *geological estimate* examines how much oil is in the ground in technically recoverable quantities, without regard to the larger economic forces affecting exploration and production. Most geological estimates classify sedimentary basins with regard to petroleum-producing potential, using the well known basins to extrapolate the quantities likely to exist in less well known areas. The estimates do not reflect whether we have the desire or ability (other than technical) to get the oil and gas out.

Performance-based estimates examine the pattern of exploration and production over time, considering all the economic forces that determine whether an oil company supplies oil and whether a consumer buys it. This technique was pioneered by M.K. Hubbert, who argued that, for any stock resource, there is a pattern of exponential growth in the use of that resource, until the amount used approaches a significant portion of the total amount in the earth (Hubbert, 1969). Then production levels off and declines exponentially (see Figure 15.5). The decline is related as much to the fact that substitute commodities are found and adopted as it is to actual difficulty in obtaining supplies. Hubbert used this method to calculate the total amount of oil likely to be produced in the U.S.

Table 15.2 is a list of oil reserves, and Table 15.3 gives various estimates of the ultimately recoverable petroleum resources in the U.S. and the world. The world estimates are generally in the range of 2000 to 5000 billion barrels, with most of them clustered at the lower end of that range. About 525 billion barrels

Table 15.2 Ultimately Recoverable World Crude Oil Resources

	Known	Additional Recovery in Known Fields	Additional Recovery and New Discoveries	Ultimately Recoverable Estimate	Cumulative Production through 1975	Remaining Resource[a]
North America	179.8	43–95	100–200	280–380	122	160–260
South America	68.4	20–40	52–92	120–160	41	80–120
Western Europe	24.6	5–10	25–45	50–70	3	50–70
Eastern Europe/Soviet Union	102.4	20–40	63–123	165–225	51	110–170
Africa	75.6	15–30	45–94	120–170	21	100–150
Middle East	509.9	250–400	350–630	860–1140	85	780–1060
Asia/Oceanic	50.8	15–25	54–104	105–155	13	90–140
Unspecified	—	50–90	—	—	—	—
Total[a]	1000	420–730	700–1300	1700–2300	336	1360–1960

[a]May not add due to rounding.

Source: U.S. Office of Technology Assessment, 1980: 25

of this had already been used as of 1983. If there are 1500 billion barrels remaining, these will last about 60 years, at current rates of consumption. If there are 4500 billion barrels remaining, we have 180 years to go. The world consumption rate is rising, however, and the total life of the resource is likely to be somewhat shorter. Estimates of ultimately recoverable oil in the U.S. range from about 200 to 600 billion barrels, of which 140 billion had been used and 30 billion were proved reserves in 1982 (Exxon, 1982). Geological estimates are generally higher than performance-based estimates.

Recently a refinement of Hubbert's performance-based method was used to estimate when we will stop finding oil in the U.S. (Hall and Cleveland, 1981). This method is based on the yield of oil per unit of effort expended in looking for it. Both yield and effort are expressed in barrels of oil per foot of exploratory well drilled. It is argued that we will stop looking for oil when it costs as much (in oil) to explore and produce as we are likely to find. As oil gets harder and harder to find, the yield per foot of well drilled decreases. This yield fluctuates with changing conditions in the industry, but generally it has declined steadily. Hall and Cleveland estimate that, for the existing oil regions in the U.S., we will stop finding oil sometime around the turn of the century or shortly thereafter. Unexplored areas, such as some deep-water offshore areas, may extend exploration and production a few years. Estimates for gas are similar to those for oil, with gas lasting a few years longer.

Thus the performance-based estimates, which seem to reflect the true behavior of the U.S. oil industry more accurately than the rather abstract geological estimates do, suggest that we have only twenty to thirty years before we stop finding domestic oil. After that we may have a few years to draw down existing reserves, but not many. It seems very likely, therefore, that the U.S. will cease to be a significant producer of oil and gas in the first few decades of the next century. There are too many uncertainties to allow effective performance-based estimates of remaining world supplies of oil. Many areas of the world are poorly explored, particularly offshore areas. The future of the world oil resource depends more on how rapidly consumption rises than on how much is found.

Environmental Considerations

The most significant environmental concerns involve the transportation, refining, and burning of petroleum and natural gas. Due to the geographic locations of the major world producers and consumers, crude oil must be shipped by ship (supertanker, tanker, barge), pipeline, tank truck, or tank car. The most traffic occurs on the high seas, with shipments of oil from the producing nations in the Middle East to European and North American markets (see Figure 15.6). As a result of shipping these massive amounts so frequently, accidents are likely to happen—and they do. Pollution of the oceans from tanker accidents has both local and global impacts (see Chapter 12).

Another environmental concern is the refining and burning of petroleum. This was discussed in Chapter 11, in the discussions of pollution and the global impacts of burning fossil fuels.

Finally, a number of land-based problems are involved in petroleum production and natural gas storage. The withdrawal of both oil and natural gas has caused ground subsidence in such places as Long Beach, California, and Houston, Texas.

Table 15.3 Estimate of Ultimately Recoverable World Crude Oil Resources

Author	Organization	Date of Estimate	Quantity in Billion Barrels
H. R. Warman	British Petroleum Ltd.	1973	1915
J. D. Moody and R. W. Esser	Mobil Oil Corporation	1974	2000
M. King Hubbert	U.S. Geological Survey	1974	2000
B. Grossling	U.S. Geological Survey	1974	2600–6500
Delphi Approach	World Energy Conference	1977	2230 (average of 28 est.)
R. Nehring	Rand Corporation	1978	1700–2300
R. Nehring	Rand Corporation	1979	1600–2000

Source: U.S. Office of Technology Assessment, 1980

One of the newest problems involves the transportation of liquid natural gas (LNG) by tanker and its storage and support at land-based facilities. Large volumes of volatile gas are vulnerable to fires of disastrous proportions. As yet, the fires that have occurred have been less devastating than has been feared, but the possibility of monumental conflagrations has caused concern over the location of LNG facilities near urban areas.

COAL

Coal is the most abundant fossil fuel in the world, with reserves far exceeding those of oil or natural gas. The U.S. is particularly well supplied with coal, with about a quarter of the world's reserves. Coal is a dirty fuel, and the environmental impacts associated with its extraction and combustion are a matter of considerable concern.

Geology

Coal is the partially decomposed and consolidated remains of plants that were deposited in ancient swamps and lagoons. The original material was modified by heat and the weight of overlying materials into a substance that is harder, drier, and chemically different. The degree to which coal has been modified varies greatly from one deposit to another, so that there are several different kinds or *ranks* of coal (see Table 15.4). The least modified form is *peat,* which has a very high moisture content and is still being deposited in many areas today. In order, the remaining ranks of coal are *lignite, sub-bituminous, bituminous* (soft coal), and finally *anthracite* (hard coal), which is the most completely converted rank. Typical moisture contents vary from over 40 percent for lignite to less than 10 percent for anthracite. As moisture content is reduced and hydrogen is lost, the heat content per unit weight increases. In addition to rank, the ash and sulfur content are important to the value of coal deposits. Ash is derived primarily from mineral sediments deposited along with the plants. In some areas, ash content may be very high; generally, coal with ash greater than 15 percent is uneconomic. Sulfur accumulates in most sediments deposited in

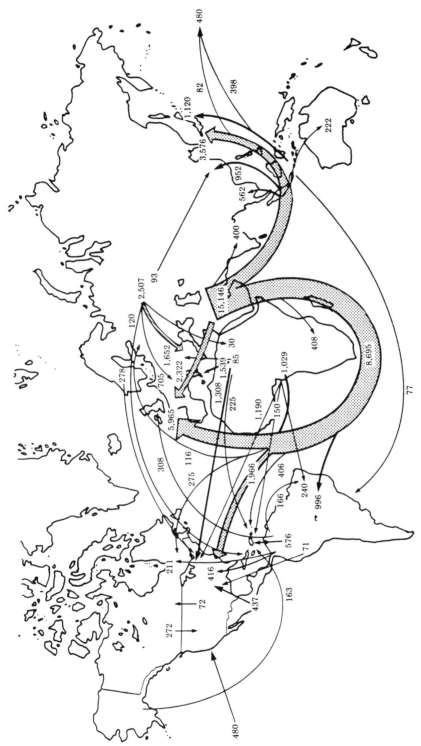

Figure 15.6 International flow of crude oil, 1979. Most of the oil, derived from sources in the Middle East, is transported to distant markets in western Europe, Japan, and the United States. Flows are given in thousands of barrels per day. (Source: From Energy Information Administration, 1982)

Table 15.4 Sulfur Content of U.S. Coal Reserves and Resources (Percentages)

Rank	Low (0–1%)	Sulfur Content Medium (1–3%)	High (> 3%)
Anthracite	97	3	—
Bituminous	30	27	43
Subbituminous	100	—	—
Lignite	91	9	—
All	65	15	20

Source: Brobst and Pratt, 1973

swampy conditions, and in coal, sulfur contents typically vary from less than 1 percent to more than 3 percent.

Location of Reserves

Bituminous coal is the most abundant type of coal found in the U.S. The largest bituminous regions are found in the Appalachian Mountains in the eastern U.S., and in sections of the Midwest, particularly Illinois, Iowa, and Missouri (see Figure 15.7). There are also bituminous deposits throughout the Rocky Mountains and in northern Alaska. Anthracite deposits are quite localized, found in eastern Pennsylvania and in the Appalachian regions of West Virginia and Virginia. Subbituminous deposits are found throughout the Rocky Mountain region. Lignite deposits are found in North and South Dakota and Montana. Although coal is found virtually everywhere in the U.S., the ease and the economics of its extraction vary, as we shall see in the next section.

Extraction

Coal is mined in three ways: underground, strip, and augur. In the 19th and early 20th centuries, most coal mining took place in the eastern U.S., where the coal seams are in hilly areas, many steeply inclined to the surface. In such situations, most of the coal is well below the surface, and underground mining is necessary. *Underground mining* involves drilling, blasting, or otherwise excavating tunnels and chambers underground, from which the coal is then removed and transported to the surface. Much of the coal must be left behind to support the overlying rocks, and generally no more than 50 percent of the coal is removed. Underground mining is the most dangerous form of mining; in fact, it is one of the more hazardous occupations in the world. The greatest dangers are from explosions of methane gas, which is an important component of many coal deposits, and from rock bursts, which result from removal of pressure on rocks deep underground.

Strip mining, or surface mining, is conducted in areas where the coal is within about 30 meters of the surface. The *overburden,* i.e., the rock and soil overlying the coal, is first mined, and then the coal is removed. In areas of relatively flat terrain, where the coal seams are horizontal, strip mining can remove about 90 percent of the coal from a large area and is thus much more efficient than underground mining (see Figure 15.8). In hilly areas, coal outcrops

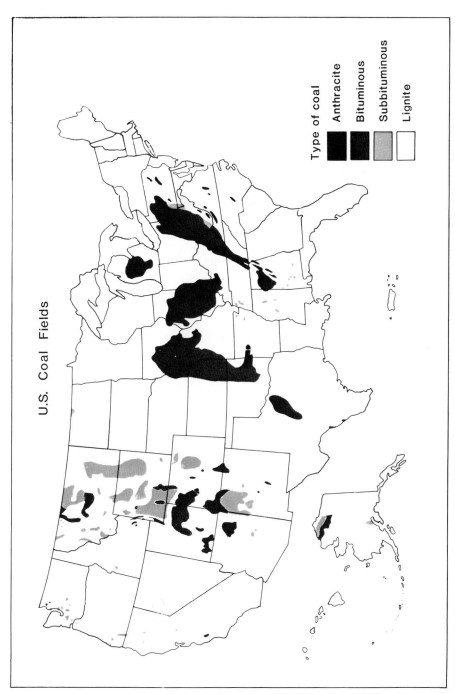

U.S. Coal Fields

Type of coal

■ Anthracite
■ Bituminous
▨ Subbituminous
□ Lignite

Figure 15.7 Coal resources in the U.S. Anthracite deposits are found in eastern Pennsylvania and the Appalachian region of Virginia and West Virginia. Bituminous deposits are found throughout the U.S. Lignite deposits are largely confined to the western half of the country. (Source: From Council on Environmental Quality, 1981)

Figure 15.8 Strip mine in eastern Pennsylvania. The overburden layer (light in color) is removed to mine the deeper coal layer (darker colored strata).

along hillsides are sometimes mined by stripping, leaving deeper coal unmined. Alternatively, surface coal in such areas may be mined by *auguring*, in which a large augur (drill) is bored into a coal seam.

Until recently, most coal in the U.S. was mined underground, particularly in the eastern states. In the last two decades, strip mining has grown substantially, especially in the western coal fields. In 1974 surface mining surpassed underground mining, and as of 1981, over 60 percent of U.S. coal was surface mined (Energy Information Administration, 1982).

End Uses

The rapid expansion of coal use came with the Industrial Revolution, in the 18th and 19th centuries, when it was the primary energy source for industrial production and rail transportation. In the urban areas of Europe and eastern North America, it was also a major fuel for home heating in the 19th and into the 20th centuries. In the early 20th century, however, oil production grew rapidly, and coal began to be displaced as a primary fuel. Those areas that had used coal for home heating began to shift to oil to avoid the smoke and odors of coal use. After World War II, most American railroads replaced steam locomotives with diesel, and coal use continued to decline. The decline ended in the 1960s, when rapid growth in electricity usage increased the demand for new power plants. Coal is an excellent fuel for these high-bulk uses, such as in boilers, and it produces over 50 percent of the electricity generated in the U.S.

Very little coal is used for home heating today, but it still is used in industry, primarily iron and steel. In steelmaking, coal is first converted to coke by driving off water and volatile matter through destructive distillation, and then it is burned in blast furnaces. Industrial use currently amounts to about 17 percent of total

Table 15.5 U.S. Coal Reserves, 1980 (Billions of Short Tons)

Rank	West of Mississippi	East of Mississippi	Total
Anthracite	0.1	7.2	7.3
Bituminous	217.9	203.4	421.3
Lignite	43.0	1.1	44.1
Potential Mining Method			
Surface	115.2	41.6	166.8
Underground	145.8	170.1	315.9
Total	261.0	211.7	472.7

Source: Energy Information Administration, 1983

U.S. coal use, with electric utilities using over 80 percent (Energy Information Administration, 1982).

How Much Is There?

Coal is so abundant in the U.S. that normally we discuss only reserves, without considering undiscovered or subeconomic resources. Most of the economically recoverable deposits have probably already been discovered. This is because the cost of coal recovery is primarily determined by its depth below the surface, with the shallow deposits most easily recovered. Most of the shallow bedrock in the U.S. is well explored, and there is little point in looking for deeper coal. As of 1980, the U.S. had a demonstrated reserve base of 425 billion tonnes (473 billion short tons). This is about 600 times our current annual production. The amounts of this reserve in the various ranks of coal east and west of the Mississippi are given in Table 15.5. Not all of this coal is recoverable, with recoverability for individual deposits ranging from 40 to 90 percent. The total recoverable reserves in the U.S. are about 225 billion tonnes (250 billion tons).

Recoverable world reserves are about 880 billion tonnes (975 billion tons), well over 200 times the annual world production of 3.6 billion tonnes (4 billion tons). Most of the reserves are in only a few nations, such as the U.S., the U.S.S.R., Poland, and the People's Republic of China, which therefore dominate world production. Thus, both on a national and an international basis, there is plenty of coal to meet our demands for many decades. This is true even if we consider the increasing per-capita energy consumption and conversion to coal from oil and natural gas for some uses. The major concern with coal is not supply, but rather the environmental impact of greatly expanded coal use (Perry, 1983).

Environmental Considerations

Coal mining and combustion are the most destructive methods for obtaining energy in use today. The environmental impacts are numerous and far-reaching. Mining impacts include water pollution and the destruction of land underlain by coal. Combustion impacts include urban air pollutants, acid precipitation, and increasing atmospheric carbon dioxide (see Chapter 11).

Underground mining has two major environmental effects: acid drainage and subsidence. *Acid drainage* results when air and water come into contact with sulfur-bearing rocks and coal. The sulfur is oxidized to form sulfuric acid, which groundwater flow carries to streams. This is a particularly severe problem in mining regions of the Appalachians, where some streams have become too acidic to support fish life.

Subsidence is the sinking of the land as underground voids created by mining collapse. It causes structural damage to buildings overlying mined areas, and it is widespread in Pennsylvania and other areas of underground mining.

Strip mining is generally much more disruptive of the land than is underground mining. The overburden must be removed, and as a result, the soil and topography of the area are completely altered. While the mine is in operation and until the land is reclaimed, the overburden is exposed to air and rain, resulting in accelerated runoff and the oxidation of newly exposed rocks. Runoff from spoils piles increases the sediment loads of streams. Oxidation of sulfur-rich rocks leads to formation of sulfuric acid and acidic runoff. These problems are particularly severe in areas of steep slopes, where runoff and erosion are more rapid. In addition, steeply sloping spoils piles are prone to landsliding.

In 1977 Congress passed the Surface Mining Reclamation and Control Act, which requires reclamation of surface-mined lands. Since passage of that act, surface miners are required to remove the topsoil separately from the lower overburden layers and to store it during mining. After mining is completed, the overburden is replaced, with the topsoil over it, and the land is graded to its approximate original contour. Finally, the land must be replanted with vegetation similar to that present before mining. The act also places a tax on surface-mining activities, which is used to pay for reclamation of areas mined and abandoned before 1977. As of 1965, about 1.29 billion hectares had been disturbed by strip mining in the U.S. (U.S. Department of the Interior, 1976). Of these, 41 percent were coal-mine areas, and another 26 percent were sand and gravel quarries. In 1965 only 34 percent of these disturbed lands had been reclaimed, many of these reclaimed by nature. Today, 47.4 percent of all disturbed lands—75 percent of bituminous regions and 14.4 percent of anthracite and peat regions—are reclaimed.

In addition to these problems, coal combustion is a major cause of acid precipitation. Of U.S. coal reserves, about 20 percent is high-sulfur coal, 15 percent is medium-sulfur, and 65 percent is low-sulfur (see Table 15.4). Eastern coal is generally higher in sulfur than that west of the Mississippi, which is unfortunate, because the East is generally more susceptible to problems of acid precipitation than is the West (see Chapter 11). Sulfur can be removed from coal before or during combustion, or it can be removed from flue gases after combustion. Costly as they are, these methods offer the possibility of maintaining or increasing coal use while reducing sulfur emissions and consequently acid precipitation.

Carbon dioxide emissions, on the other hand, are not controllable. CO_2 is produced as the end product of efficient combustion, and there is no known way to prevent this. As stated in Chapter 11, coal produces proportionately more CO_2 than oil and natural gas; if coal combustion is increased, then CO_2 emissions also increase. The environmental impact of these emissions is still open to question, but if we intend to prevent CO_2 buildup in the atmosphere, then there is no alternative but to reduce coal combustion.

SYNFUELS

Synfuels (*syn*thetic *fuels*) are liquid or gaseous fossil fuels that are manufactured from other fuels that are not usable as found in the earth. There are many different kinds, but the most promising ones are gasified coal, tar sands, and shale oil. In some cases, the technology to convert these substances to usable fuels has been available for several decades; in other cases, it has yet to be commercially developed. All synfuels are of interest, because they rely on raw materials that are much more plentiful than the oil or gas they replace.

Geology, Technology, and Location

Coal gasification or liquefication is the conversion of coal to a gas or liquid, which is then transported via pipeline and burned like a conventional fuel. Coal is of course plentiful, and the major barriers to its expanded use are its high cost of transport and its inappropriateness for internal combustion engines or cooking stoves. Several different coal gasification techniques are available, but most involve adding hydrogen to the carbon already in coal, to make hydrocarbons. In some processes, the volatile hydrocarbons in coal are used as a source of hydrogen; in others, water in the form of steam is used. The most common gasification processes make a gas that has a lower heat content than conventional fuels, though it can be further processed into high-quality gas and liquid fuels. Coal gasification is most easily carried out in above-ground facilities, but there is potential for the development of underground, in-situ technologies. The technologies of coal gasification and liquefication are fairly well known, but as yet they are not economically competitive with conventional oil and gas.

Tar sands are deposits of sand high in heavy oil, or tar, content. As it is found, this tar is too viscous to be pumped from the ground like oil, but, if heated, it liquefies and can then be pumped and refined like heavy crude oil. The sands are generally mined from the ground and then heated, using steam to extract the oil. Most of the tar-sand deposits in the U.S. are either inaccessible due to depth or occur in seams too thin to mine. In Alberta, Canada, though, extensive areas of tar sands near or at the surface are being commercially mined today. Tar sands currently supply more than 8 percent of Canada's oil, and by 1990 this share is expected to reach 20 percent (Energy Information Administration, 1982).

Shale oil is not true oil; it is a waxy hydrocarbon called *kerogen*. It is found in oil shale, a fine-textured sedimentary rock. Shale oil is extracted, or retorted, by crushing and then heating the rock. This liquefies the kerogen, which seeps out of the rock and can then be removed. Kerogen can be refined into most of the fuels that are produced from conventional crude oil. Shale oil has been produced intermittently on an experimental basis for several decades, but as yet there has been no full-scale commercial production. Most of the experiments have been conducted in above-ground facilities, but in-situ methods are also available. In either above-ground or in situ retorting, the crushed shale is heated by igniting it. Some of the kerogen in the shale burns, but some is released. Recovery is fairly low, ranging from about 20 to 50 percent in most cases.

Most of our high-quality oil shale is located in a few areas in the western states of Colorado, Wyoming, and Utah (see Figure 15.9). There are also some lower grade deposits in the East, particularly in Tennessee and Michigan. The western oil shale region is a sparsely populated, semiarid rangeland. The richest layers of the shale are located from a few hundred to a few thousand meters below the surface, except along deep river valleys, where the rocks are exposed in the valley walls. For the kerogen to be extracted, either very large areas must be strip-mined or a substantial portion of the retorting must be done underground.

How Much Is There?

One of the most attractive aspects of synfuels is that the raw materials are available in vast quantities. At present rates of extraction, the U.S. has an ample supply of coal, so clearly we could expand use of coal for other purposes without jeopardizing its availability in the near future. In addition, if in-situ methods of coal gasification or liquefication prove economic, then deep deposits of coal could become exploitable. The U.S. has somewhat fewer tar sand resources, which contain 30 to 40 billion barrels of oil (Canby and Blair, 1981). In Canada, tar sand resources are much greater, perhaps 1,000 billion barrels, mostly in Alberta. U.S. domestic oil shale resources are enormous, in excess of 2,000 billion barrels (Brobst and Pratt, 1973). Just considering the shale with the high oil content, resources are about 600 billion barrels, or enough to supply our entire present domestic oil consumption for nearly 100 years.

Environmental and Economic Aspects

None of these synfuels can be extracted without significant environmental impacts. All the impacts associated with mining coal also apply to coal gasification— unless the conversion is made underground. If liquid or gaseous coal fuels are to replace oil, then our use of coal must increase, and so must the area affected by mining. The processing also requires large amounts of water, and this is a scarce commodity in many western coal regions. Gasified or liquefied coal could be cleaned of most sulfur in processing, so sulfur emissions are not likely to be a major barrier to use of these fuels. Use of coal in any form, however, particularly one for which energy is lost in conversion, means that there will be substantial emissions of carbon dioxide.

There are several environmental problems associated with extraction of shale oil. First, to obtain a substantial amount of oil, large areas must be mined. If strip mining is used, then all the problems associated with strip mining of other minerals must be considered. Even with in-situ retorting, about 25 percent of the volume of the rock must be removed and then disposed of at the surface to make room for retorting.

Second, retorting involves burning kerogen under conditions unconducive to clean combustion. This combustion produces emissions of hydrocarbons, carbon monoxide, and particulates. Retorting would take place in areas of good air quality and would almost certainly cause some deterioration.

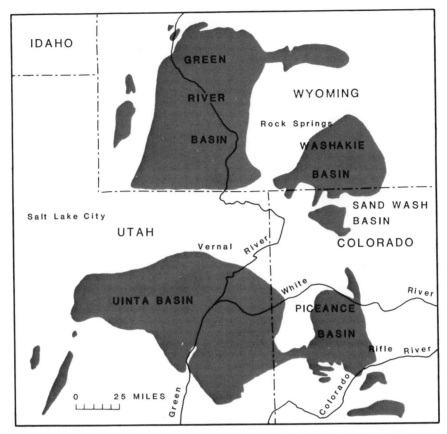

Figure 15.9 Major deposits of shale oil in the U.S. (Source: From U.S. Office of Technology Assessment, 1980)

Third, retorting will use substantial amounts of water where it is already in short supply. Paradoxically, mining will also produce large amounts of brackish water, pumped from the ground to drain the mines. This water is high in dissolved solids, and its disposal may prove difficult.

Finally, the social impacts of development are significant. Large numbers of workers will be needed to construct and operate these facilities, and most of these will migrate into the region. The populations of towns near the planned mining developments will soar, with associated stresses on infrastructure and native populations. After construction is completed, employment will drop, causing a decline in local economic conditions. This boom-and-bust cycle is well known to most mining areas, and the disruption it causes is an important part of the impact of energy development (see Chapter 14).

Economic conditions are also a barrier to extraction of shale oil. Commercial interest developed during oil shortages in the 1920s, but to date there has been no successful commercial scale extraction. This is due to the relatively low price of conventional fuels, uncertainties about the extraction technology, and, more recently, environmental concerns. The first major attempt at stimulating synfuel development was made during the 1960s, when the government offered leases, but no private concerns were then willing to attempt development. Then new leases were offered in 1969, and this time four of six tracts offered were successfully bid. Two of these were later abandoned, and development work began in the early 1970s on two tracts in northwestern Colorado. At first, the plans were to strip mine these lands and retort the shale above ground, but later the companies involved switched to in-situ methods. During the 1970s, environmental studies were conducted, raising the question of whether the proposed plants could meet air-quality regulations. These questions were eventually resolved when the state of Colroado agreed to downgrade its air quality classification for the region, and development proceeded rapidly between 1978 and 1980. Tests of the retorting technology were not as successful as hoped, and, when world oil prices dropped in 1981 and 1982, the projects were suspended. Throughout this history, there have been times when the industry thought that extraction was commercially feasible, only to find, a few years later, that substantially higher oil prices were necessary for profitability. When or whether extraction will become economic remains to be seen.

Tar sands are perhaps the least environmentally destructive synfuels. They are chemically similar to oil and can be refined in much the same way oil is refined. The major negative environmental impact is associated with strip mining; in that sense, tar sands are no worse than coal. Because they are refined and thus burn cleaner than coal, their impact on air pollution is not as severe.

NUCLEAR POWER

The first self-sustaining nuclear reaction occurred in December 1942 at the University of Chicago. Although the first applications of nuclear energy were in weapons, atomic power was also used for peaceful purposes after World War II. While the dichotomy between weapons applications and energy production still exists today, we will discuss only the commercial aspects of nuclear energy.

The first commercial use of nuclear power was to generate electricity in 1957 in Shippingport, Pennsylvania. Westinghouse Electric, in conjunction with the Atomic Energy Commission (now the Nuclear Regulatory Commission and Department of Energy), opened the first full-scale nuclear electrical power plant to be operated by a public utility (Duquesne Light Company). At 60 megawatts, the plant was small by today's standards.

In just twenty-five years, nuclear technology has progressed and has been improved, so that 76 licensed reactors are now operating, with an additional 64 currently under construction (Council on Environmental Quality, 1982, p. 261). How did that initial chain reaction become an alternative source of energy four decades later? A review of the nuclear fuel cycle and of nuclear power in general should provide some answers.

Nuclear Fuel Cycle

Nuclear power is based on the *fission* process, in which the nuclei of heavy atoms of enriched uranium 235 or plutonium 239 (the latter a by-product of the fission process) are split into lighter elements, thereby releasing energy in a chain reaction. The energy thus released is used to heat water into steam. The steam is then used to drive a turbine, which turns an electric generator.

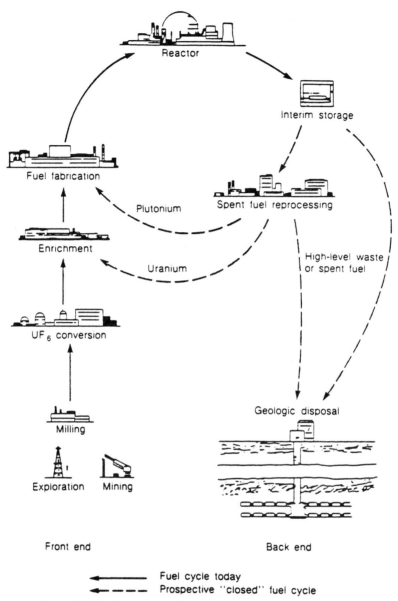

Reactor

Interim storage

Fuel fabrication

Plutonium

Spent fuel reprocessing

Enrichment

Uranium

High-level waste
or spent fuel

UF$_6$ conversion

Milling

Geologic disposal

Exploration   Mining

Front end   Back end

Fuel cycle today
Prospective "closed" fuel cycle

Figure 15.10 The nuclear fuel cycle. At each stage in the cycle,
nuclear material is transported varying distances from mining regions
to conversion and enrichment facilities, fabrication plants and nuclear
reactors. After use, spent fuel is reprocessed and/or disposed of.
(Source: From Council on Environmental Quality, 1981)

The nuclear fuel cycle consists of eight stages (see Figure 15.10). Unlike
some of the more conventional fuel sources, which can be used in situ, nuclear
power requires transportation linkages between all stages in its fuel cycle. Uranium
is the primary fuel for nuclear power plants. Most U.S. uranium resources are
found in the Rocky Mountain states and are mined by both open-pit and
underground techniques. Nearly two-thirds of the uranium is mined in New Mexico

and Wyoming (see Figure 15.11) (Issue 15.1). Of the naturally occurring uranium, which is a mixture of the isotopes U^{235} and U^{238}, less than one percent—that is, only the U^{235}—is highly fissionable. Thus, most of the uranium ore must be enriched and/or converted to make it sustain the fission process. Once mined, the uranium ore is milled, to produce a purer concentrate, called yellowcake. Yellowcake is about 85 percent natural uranium oxide (U_3O_8). The milling process requires about five hundred tons of ore to get one ton of U_3O_8.

The third stage in the fuel cycle is the chemical purification and conversion of the yellowcake to uranium hexafluoride (UF_6). The conversion is carried out at facilities in Metropolis, Illinois; Sequoyah, Oklahoma; Apollo, Pennsylvania; and Barnwell, South Carolina. The conversion process prepares the uranium for *enrichment*, the next stage in the fuel cycle.

At the enrichment plant the concentration of U^{235} is increased from 0.7 percent to about 4 percent, to meet the requirements of the reactors. All of the enrichment facilities in the U.S. are government-owned and are located in only three areas—Oak Ridge, Tennessee; Paducah, Kentucky; and Portsmouth, Ohio. Once the UF_6 has been enriched, it is ready to be made into fuel rods. The UF_6 is converted into uranium dioxide (UO_2), which is then formed into small pellets and placed in alloy tubes. These tubes are then made into fuel rods and assembled into bundles, called fuel rod assemblies. The fuel fabrication process

---

ISSUE 15.1: Winning and Losing on Indian Lands

A century or more ago, the United States government placed the western American Indian tribes on reservations. The government could afford to be generous with acreage, because these dry and dusty lands were useless by all standards of that day. Over the intervening years, the fortunes of most of these tribes did not rise noticeably. Not, that is, until after World War II, when the federal government began seeking sources of uranium ore for use in bombs and nuclear power plants. Much of this ore turned out to be located on Indian land. By 1978, almost half of the U.S.-produced uranium was mined in west-central New Mexico, in Indian country. In addition, strategic minerals and other energy sources, including oil, gas, and coal, are plentiful on these western Indian lands.

As a result of these discoveries, by the mid-1970s, Indian tribes were the world's fifth-largest uranium owners and fourth-largest producers. In 1980 three tribes, the Navajo, Spokane, and Laguna Pueblo, accounted for almost a quarter of the U.S. uranium production and 12 percent globally.

It is estimated that ten tribes own between 15 and 40 percent of all U.S. uranium. What are the benefits and costs of the development associated with this mining activity?

On the positive side, mining has brought wages, jobs, industrial job-training, and contact with mainstream American culture to the reservation. These have traditionally been in short supply, as on-reservation unemployment rates continue at levels ten times that of the national average, and per-capita income is about one-sixth that of all Americans. The Laguna Reservation is the home of Jackpile Mine, the largest uranium mine in the world. In 1980 reservation unemployment was about 25 percent, half of most reservations. Eight hundred people were employed at Jackpile, from its opening in 1952 to its closing thirty years later. Job salaries ranged from $15,000 to $50,000 annually, and tribal royalties were several million dollars a year. Other benefits include higher levels of education and modern housing, complete with plumbing.

What are the costs of these changes? In

is carried out at only five locations in the U.S. The fuel rod assemblies are shipped to individual reactors, where they are used to produce electricity.

Spent fuel is removed from the reactor core and stored on site for several months to permit the levels of radioactivity to decline. Optimally, the spent fuel is then shipped to a reprocessing plant, where the unused portions of uranium and plutonium are separated from the fission wastes. The unused uranium is recycled back to the enrichment plant, and the unused plutonium is refabricated into new fuel pellets. There are currently no fuel reprocessing plants in the U.S.; as a result, spent fuel is stored at the reactor site.

The last stage in the nuclear fuel cycle is disposal of the radioactive waste. *Low-level wastes* (only half of which are generated by nuclear power plants) are buried in metal or concrete containers at 22 sites around the country (see Figure 15.12). In 1981, 145,461 cubic meters of low-level wastes were buried. Since the start of the commercial reactor program, nearly 2.4 million cubic meters of low-level radioactive waste has been buried (Council on Environmental Quality, 1982, p. 297). *High-level wastes* separated at reprocessing plants must be disposed of or permanently stored. Currently, there is no waste disposal facility for high-level wastes. All high-level waste is either stored on site (at the nuclear power plant) or at three temporary locations—Richland, Washington; Idaho Falls, Idaho; and Aiken, South Carolina. Permanent disposal options are currently under govern-

many cases, tribal contracts signed with energy companies were not especially favorable to tribal interests. Often, government mediators saw to it that the financial compensation was low and that the Indians had little or no say over the alterations made to their lands. In recent decades, Indian leaders took these negotiations into their own hands, working to improve the situation.

Another negative effect is the inevitable loss of traditional Indian culture and life ways. The industrial work day has altered family patterns, and the influence of money and outsiders has created a host of new demands that have superseded older, more traditional ways.

Health worries and environmental degradation accompanied energy development. A list of EPA-documented problems in west-central New Mexico suggests the severity and extent of concern. There is widespread contamination of the region's surface water. In addition, the EPA study found groundwater contamination from mill tailing ponds and mine drainage, erosion of uranium and se-

lenium-rich minerals into a major agricultural river, and a complete lack of monitoring of the effects of mining on groundwater. Also, uranium-rich dust from the mining operations is constantly blown into every nook and cranny in the areas adjacent to mines.

The Laguna tribe developed several strategies for survival in the wake of the Jackpile closing, which occurred at least in part because of depressed uranium prices and a poor outlook for the future of commercial nuclear power. These strategies, aimed at offsetting the effects of the 513 layoffs, include an Anaconda-sponsored effort to attract new businesses to the reservation, a job-relocation center, and formation of a tribally owned and operated uranium company. It is clear that not all of today's American Indians remain victims of past policies. Some of them are becoming shapers of future policies (Bregman, 1982).

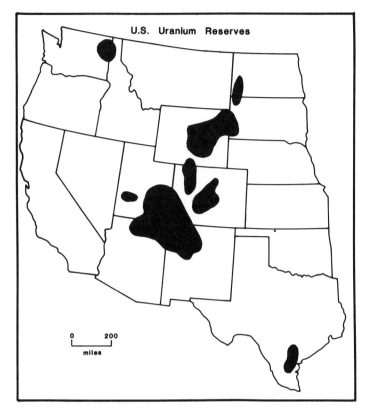

Figure 15.11   U.S. uranium reserves. Large deposits are located in the Four Corners region and Wyoming.

mental review. The most frequently discussed alternative is waste burial in geologically stable formations, such as rock salt or metamorphic rock. The states most frequently mentioned for potential sites are Oklahoma, Texas, and New Mexico.

Power Plants

At present, there are 76 reactors licensed to operate in the U.S., with another 64 in some phase of construction. The total number of reactors under construction or planned has been steadily decreasing since 1976 (see Figure 15.13). This decline is a result of many factors, including reduced demand, increased costs, financial problems, and safety concerns. It should be noted that the decline in the number of reactors ordered started well before the accident at Three Mile Island, Pennsylvania.

There are four basic types of reactors now in use worldwide, but most of the reactors in the U.S. are classified as *light-water reactors* (see Figure 15.14). This means that ordinary water is used as the cooling agent. In one type of light-water reactor, the boiling-water reactor, water is circulated through the reactor vessel, which contains the fuel rods, where the water boils and produces steam, which is then piped to the turbine. In a pressurized-water reactor, another type

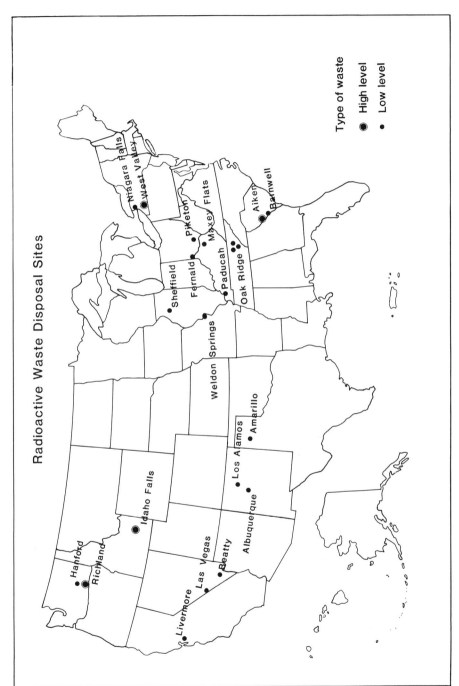

Radioactive Waste Disposal Sites

Type of waste
● High level
• Low level

Niagara Falls
West Valley
Piketon
Maxey Flats
Aiken
Barnwell
Sheffield
Fernald
Paducah
Oak Ridge
Weldon Springs
Amarillo
Los Alamos
Idaho Falls
Albuquerque
Hanford
Richland
Las Vegas
Beatty
Livermore

Figure 15.12 Radioactive waste disposal sites. High-level wastes were formerly disposed of in four locations, but West Valley, New York, has been closed since the early 1980s.

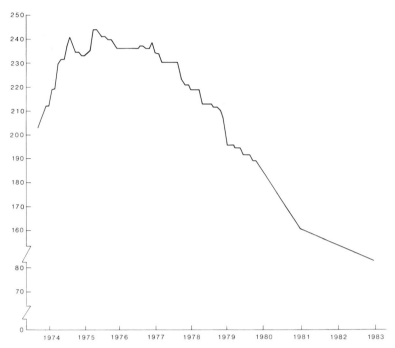

Figure 15.13 Nuclear reactors built, being built, or planned. Construction of and new orders for nuclear reactors have been steadily declining since 1977. Economic considerations and safety concerns have precipitated this decline. (Source: From Council on Environmental Quality, 1981)

of light-water reactor, water is kept at high pressure, to prevent it from boiling in the reactor vessel. The high-pressure water is then pumped through the core, and the superheated water exchanges heat in a secondary water/steam loop.

The second basic type of reactor is the *high-temperature gas-cooled reactor.* Helium gas is used as the coolant, transferring the heat from the core to the steam generator. There is only one reactor of this type in the U.S.—the Fort. St. Vrain plant, just outside of Denver, Colorado.

The third type of reactor is the *heavy-water reactor.* This system uses heavy water (water containing a higher than usual proportion of deuterium) as the moderator of the fission process. Regular water passes through the core and carries heat to the secondary water/steam loop. Heavy-water reactors are not used in the U.S., but they dominate the Canadian reactor program (the CANDU system). Canada is also a large exporter of the the CANDU technology and of the heavy water that is manufactured at the Bruce Nuclear Generating Station, along the shores of Lake Huron.

The fourth type of reactor is the *liquid-metal fast-breeder reactor.* Fissionable material is surrounded by nonfissionable material (U^{238}) in the core. Sodium is used as the moderating substance and heat exchanger. During the fission process, some of the nonfissionable material is converted to fissionable Pu^{239}. The reactor produces more fuel than it consumes, hence the name breeder reactor. The technology is still at the experimental stage in the U.S., although fast breeders have been used in other countries for some time. There are no current plans to develop the technology for commercial applications in the U.S.

Energy: The Universal Resource   385

Figure 15.14 Examples of light water reactors. (a) Boiling water reactor, Nine-Mile Point Unit 1, Scriba, New York. (b) Pressurized-water reactor, Three Mile Island Units I and II, Goldsboro, Pennsylvania.

Nuclear power is used only to generate electricity. In 1982 it produced 12.6 percent of the total U.S. generation of electricity, about 283 billion kilowatt hours (Council on Environmental Quality, 1982, p. 279). Production of electricity is increasing, though the number of reactors coming on line is decreasing. This is largely due to the start-up of larger reactors that are capable of producing more electricity. It is anticipated that nuclear energy will account for 21.2 percent of electrical demand by 1995 (Energy Information Administration, 1982, p. 46).

The overall contribution of nuclear energy to national electrical needs is small. If we examine the use of nuclear energy on a regional or state level, it becomes significant to certain regions. Ten states (see Table 15.6) rely on nuclear energy to generate more than 25 percent of their electrical power needs (Energy Information Administration, 1981). In two of these, Vermont and Connecticut, nuclear energy contributes over half of the electricity produced.

Beginning in the late 1970s, increasing concern about reactor safety, combined with demand below projections, caused problems for the nuclear power industry. Even with rising fuel costs for oil- and coal-fired plants, nuclear power has become much more expensive than conventional fuel use. The accident at Three Mile Island and uncertainties about safety at several other plants forced a careful examination of safety provisions at existing and planned plants. Operating licenses were even denied at some. This caused delays in construction, increases in construction costs, and uncertainty about the economic viability of nuclear power in general. Nuclear plants are expensive to begin with, and, when capital is tied up for long periods, interest costs become very large. Several nuclear plants under construction or on order have been cancelled, and at least one nearly completed plant will probably be converted to burn coal. It thus seems virtually certain that nuclear power will not provide as great a proportion of U.S. electric production as projected in the mid-1970s, and probably not even as great as projected in 1983.

How Much Uranium Is Left?

The U.S. is self-sufficient in uranium, and there are no short-term problems with its availability. If the breeder technology is improved and safety problems resolved, then nuclear energy could be used almost indefinitely. The problems with increased use of nuclear energy to generate electricity are not the availability of uranium but rather the economic, environmental, and safety issues.

Environmental and Health Aspects

The primary concern about the use of nuclear energy is the potential for human exposures to radioactivity, resulting in *somatic* and *genetic damage.* Accidental releases of radioactivity occur at all stages in the fuel cycle, from the mining of uranium, which produces radon gas, to occupational exposures in fabricating fuel rods, to accidental releases at nuclear power plants. Releases of radioactivity can also occur as a result of sabotage and simple mishandling of materials. There is considerable debate on the effects of low levels of exposure to ionizing radiation.

There are also other environmental considerations at each of the stages in the fuel cycle. Land disturbance and radioactive mine tailings are the primary impacts of mining and milling. In the production of power, waste heat is produced, causing thermal pollution. This occurs, of course, with any type of steam-powered electricity plant. The most important environmental aspects of nuclear power production involve the accidental release of airborne or waterborne radioactivity. These safety issues cause great public concern about the use of nuclear energy on a large scale. The technology is hazardous, and the future extent of nuclear energy production will be a function of the risks society is willing to tolerate in exchange for additional electric power.

Table 15.6 Reliance on Nuclear Power, by State

State	Percentage Electricity Generated by Nuclear Sources
Alabama	29
Alaska	0
Arizona	0
Arkansas	23
California	6
Colorado	7
Connecticut	52
Delaware	0
Florida	16
Georgia	10
Hawaii	0
Idaho	0
Illinois	26
Indiana	0
Iowa	13
Kansas	0
Kentucky	0
Louisiana	0
Maine	41
Maryland	29
Massachusetts	18
Michigan	19
Minnesota	34
Mississippi	0
Missouri	0
Montana	0
Nebraska	48
Nevada	0
New Hampshire	0
New Jersey	25
New Mexico	0
New York	15
North Carolina	11
North Dakota	0
Ohio	3
Oklahoma	0
Oregon	13
Pennsylvania	15
Rhode Island	0
South Carolina	44
South Dakota	0
Tennessee	0
Texas	0
Utah	0
Vermont	75
Virginia	20
Washington	4
West Virginia	0
Wisconsin	27
Wyoming	0
U.S. Total	11

Source: Energy Information Administration, 1981

CENTRALIZED RENEWABLES

There are several renewable sources of energy available today, and many more will probably become available in the future. *Renewable energy sources* either are continuously available or are replaced relatively rapidly and therefore can be only temporarily depleted. Renewable energy sources are quite varied, ranging from radiant energy (the sun), chemical energy (biomass), potential energy (water stored in reservoirs), and kinetic energy (wind). Some forms, such as wood fuel and the wind, have been used for thousands of years; some are relatively recent developments (hydroelectric generation); and some are likely to be used in the future (ocean thermal energy conversion, or OTEC). For this discussion, we have grouped renewable energy sources into two main categories: centralized and decentralized.

Centralized renewables are energy sources that are used in large, concentrated facilities, such as electric generating stations. A single facility requires large capital investments, and most such plants generate electricity that is fed into the same grids that transport energy generated from fossil fuels or nuclear power. The primary centralized renewable energy sources in use today are hydroelectric generation, geothermal energy, tidal power, and biomass. The most promising technologies for future centralized renewable power include OTEC and large-scale solar power facilities.

Decentralized renewables will probably be of greatest importance in small facilities not connected to large-scale energy systems. The most important of these is solar thermal energy, for space or water heating. Other important decentralized energy sources for the future include photovoltaics and wind.

Hydroelectric Power

In both economic and environmental considerations, hydroelectric power is the best source of electricity available to us today. Hydroelectric power is generated by impounding water in a location where a substantial vertical drop is available, such as in a lake near a waterfall or in a steeply sloping portion of a river valley, and then passing the water through turbines that drive generators. Water power has, of course, been used for several centuries to drive various industrial facilities, but only in the last hundred years or so has it been used to generate electricity. In that time, many large dams have been built, and today about 9 percent of U.S. electricity is supplied by hydro sources. Some of the major generating facilities in North America include those at Niagara Falls, in the Tennessee Valley, in the Colorado River basin, in the Columbia River basin, and on several rivers in Ontario and Quebec, draining north into Hudson's Bay.

These facilities are all located where there is the greatest potential for hydroelectric generation, with large volumes of water available, good dam sites, and, in some cases, low population density. The cost of generating electricity at these sites is quite low in comparison to other methods. There is, of course, a rather large capital cost in dam construction and land acquisition, but the operating costs are extremely low once this is paid. Most of the large dams in North America have been built either by governments or with large governmental subsidies, and this has contributed to the low cost of hydroelectric power to consumers in many areas. In the northwestern U.S., for example, electricity prices are substantially lower than in the rest of the country, due to the large contribution of hydroelectric power generated at federally built dams along the Columbia and its tributaries.

Unfortunately, there is relatively little potential for expansion of hydroelectric generation in this country. Most of the best dam sites are already in use; potential new sites are generally unavailable because of commitments of the river valleys to other uses, such as agriculture or wilderness preservation. There may be some opportunity for increasing hydroelectric generation at smaller dams, and a few existing dams had been unused until recently, when higher energy prices made small-scale hydroelectric power generation feasible. But the amount of power generated is usually small, and the aggregate impact of small-scale hydro will probably be minor.

In Canada, there is considerable potential for increased hydroelectric generation. Canada already exports substantial amounts of electricity to the U.S., primarily from Quebec to New York. This trade is facilitated partly because the peak demand for electricity in Quebec is for heating in winter, and the peak demand in most of the U.S. is for cooling in summer. Several additional dam sites are available in northern Quebec, to increase this production, although capital costs, transmission distances, and opposition from native populations are significant barriers.

Although hydroelectric generation is probably the cleanest source of electricity we have, it is not without its environmental problems, such as the loss of the land and aquatic habitat that is submerged when a reservoir is filled. The construction of dams and the subsequent regulation of flow may also have adverse effects on stream channels and aquatic life downstream. There have been problems of erosion in the Grand Canyon, for example, as a result of the construction of Glen Canyon Dam upstream. In arid areas, such as the Colorado basin, reservoirs contribute to evaporative water loss by increasing water-surface area. Many valleys contain fertile agricultural land, and reservoir development has been a significant contributor to agricultural land losses (see Chapter 6). Impoundment also affects water quality, as nutrient-laden water stimulates algal blooms and leads to problems of eutrophication (see Chapter 10). Despite these effects, our existing hydroelectric facilities are important energy sources. Construction of new facilities at the cost of some other valued resource, however, is a much more contentious issue.

Geothermal

Geothermal energy is derived from the internal heat of the earth. The core of the earth is hot, and this heat is convected and conducted outward, toward the surface. In many parts of the earth's crust, sufficiently large amounts of heat are delivered to the surface to make its use feasible. Geothermal energy is used in many parts of the world today for space and water heating, for industrial processing, and for electricity generation.

There are three major types of geothermal resources: hydrothermal, geo-pressurized, and hot dry rock. Hydrothermal resources occur where the source of heat is close to the surface and the overlying rocks are fractured and so allow water to circulate. In addition, the water is trapped in the ground, heat is prevented from escaping rapidly to the surface. This results in the formation of hot springs and geysers. If this steam or hot water can be tapped, it can be used to generate electricity or heat buildings. Geopressurized resources are deeper pockets of water, trapped in sedimentary formations, in much the way oil and gas are trapped. Hot dry rock is simply rock in areas of high heat flow, but without large quantities of water in the rock. To tap this heat, the rocks must be fractured and wells drilled, so that water can be injected into the rocks to draw the heat out. At present, geopressurized and hot dry rock resources are not in use, but hot dry rock offers considerable potential for development in the future.

There is currently only one U.S. facility generating electricity from geothermal energy: The Geysers, in California. It presently produces about 1000 megawatts at peak output, or about the same as a large conventional power plant. The output from this plant amounts to only about 0.2 percent of total U.S. electricity generation. In the future, however, there is potential for significant expansion of geothermal energy production. One possibility is the development of hot dry rock facilities. In numerous areas of the U.S., particularly in the West, subsurface temperatures are high enough to offer potential for geothermal power. One such site in New Mexico has recently been tested for geothermal energy production, and the results are promising (Heiken et al., 1981). The economics of such ventures are still uncertain, however, and it is unlikely that geothermal energy will make large contributions to total electric generation in the near future.

Other Centralized Renewables

In addition to hydroelectric and geothermal power, there are a few technologies that offer limited potential for future development. One of these is the combustion of municipal solid waste, to produce steam for turbine-powered generators. Resource recovery involves the burning of mixed waste to produce energy, as well as the recovery of methane gas from waste decomposing in landfills. At present, there are 26 waste-to-steam plants in the U.S., but these plants are processing less than 1 percent of the municipal solid waste generated in the country. The amount of energy produced is also rather insignificant (Environmental Protection Agency, 1980).

The major incentive for developing centralized resource recovery systems is the increasing cost of solid waste disposal. Many municipalities are faced with increasing costs of disposal, making these centralized resource-recovery systems economically viable. Expensive as these facilities are, the costs can be offset by energy recovery and the sale of methane gas. Most of the barriers to large-scale usage of centralized resource recovery are political and economic in nature rather than technological (Cutter, 1984).

Another centralized renewable energy source is tidal power. Tidal fluctuations produce strong currents in coastal embayments, and these currents can be harnessed to produce electricity. A large tidal range is required, and a dam must be constructed across the bay to create the hydraulic head necessary to drive turbines. Power can be generated only during a portion of the tidal cycle, and diurnal or semidiurnal tidal fluctuations do not always correspond to the fluctuations in demand. Thus, tidal power can be viewed only as a supplement to other sources of energy. At present, there is one tidal power plant in operation in

France, and another is under construction in Nova Scotia. Proposals to build large tidal generating facilities in Passamaquoddy Bay, on the Maine-New Brunswick border and in the Bay of Fundy have been discussed over the last several years, but environmental and economic considerations will probably prevent these from becoming reality in the near future.

Large-scale solar collectors, plants that harness wave energy, and large-scale wind-powered generating facilities have also been proposed. These are in the earliest phases of design and development today, and their potential significant contribution to energy production in the near future seems very small. Centralized renewables in general will probably continue to provide only relatively small proportions of our total energy supply, with only hydroelectric generation making a large contribution to total electricity production. New power generation from all centralized renewables together will probably not significantly contribute to U.S. energy production for a few decades.

DECENTRALIZED RENEWABLES

Solar Energy

Solar energy offers enormous potential for heating buildings and water, for which it could replace more conventional energy sources, such as fossil fuels and electricity. Solar energy is plentiful, though not uniformly available in space and time. The technology is reasonably well developed, and it is economically feasible in most of the U.S. The major barriers to its use are institutional.

Solar energy reaches the earth's surface in the form of radiant energy and is converted to heat by the absorption of sunlight by an exposed surface. The amount of radiant energy received varies with the time of day, season, weather conditions, and location on the earth. There is no sunlight at night, for example. During cloudy weather, sunlight is less intense, though it is still present. Seasonality influences the length of day, so that there are fewer hours of daylight in the winter than in the summer. Also, the angle of the sun changes during the year, reducing the intensity of solar radiation per unit of horizontal surface area in the winter. Because of these large fluctuations in solar energy availability, only a few places in the U.S. can rely on solar energy as a single consistent source (see Figure 15.15). In other regions, backup energy systems are required.

Space Heating and Cooling

Solar energy is often discussed in terms of the passive and active technologies. *Passive solar* heating and cooling involves neither mechanical devices nor the production and storage of electricity. Passive solar employs proper design of structures, building materials that insulate or store energy, correct orientation of structures, and careful landscaping to provide heating and cooling. A house with many windows on the southern exposure allows for maximum sun during the winter. Planting deciduous trees on the south side of the house protects it from the hot summer sun's rays, yet allows the sunlight to penetrate during the winter months, when the trees have dropped their leaves. The use of adobe as a building material and the design of houses with shaded arcades and small windows, such

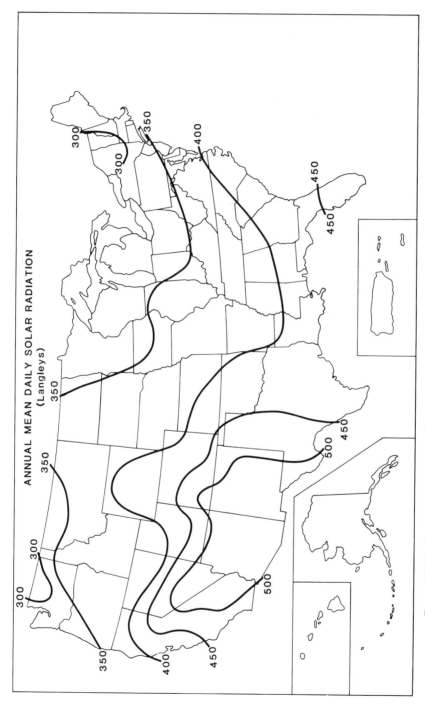

Figure 15.15 Annual mean daily solar radiation. Areas such as the Southwest receive an average of over 500 langleys of solar radiation daily, providing a stable source of solar energy for heating and cooling. The Northeast and Southeast must have backup energy systems because of fluctuations in mean levels of solar radiation. (Source: From U.S. Weather Service, 1965)

Figure 15.16 Adobe construction, Mission Santa Inez, California. This is an example of passive solar heating and cooling.

as those of "Spanish-style" haciendas in the Southwest, are other examples of passive approaches to solar heating and cooling (see Figure 15.16).

Active solar systems use mechanical devices to collect and store solar radiation for heating and cooling. The solar collector is the basic unit of the solar space heating concept. It can vary greatly in size and complexity and is presently available for purchase and use by individual homeowners, larger institutions, and—experimentally—as part of larger-scale power grids.

The simplest type of collector consists of a flat plate, painted black for maximum absorption, encased in an insulated, glass-covered box. The plate absorbs light, while the glass impedes energy loss, so that temperatures rise to about 93°C (200°F). This heat is then used to warm rooms and water, as air moves across the black plate or water circulates through a pipe attached to the plate. Higher temperatures (up to 538°C) or 1000°F are obtained by concentrating the light with one or more curved mirrors, which rotate along with the sun's movement across the sky. Temperatures of up to 2,205°C (4000°F) can be attained by focusing a bank of mirrors on a central point, such as a tower containing a water boiler for operating a steam turbine.

The amount of solar energy received by a collector varies with the time of day, season, and weather. These variations, plus obstructions by trees and buildings, still allow for the use of solar energy for space heating. The heating and hot-water needs of a one- or two-story building can be met by using available roof surfaces, southern walls, and other areas for the installation of collectors (see Figure 15.17).

The use of solar collectors nationwide has risen steadily over the last few years (see Table 15.7). Low-temperature collectors are used almost exclusively for swimming pool heating. Medium-temperature collectors are used both for space heating and cooling and for domestic water heating. In 1980 there were

Figure 15.17   Active solar collectors on a home near Princeton, Massachusetts.

245 manufacturers nationwide, up from 39 just six years earlier (Energy Information Administration, 1981, p. 183). Regionally, there are more collectors in use in the western, high-sunshine states than in the Northeast, but advocates maintain that solar collectors are capable of a quick return on investment, even in cloudier climates.

Electrical Production

One of the main challenges in solar-energy technology is the development of storage devices for use at night, on cloudy days, and in cooler seasons. One advancement in that direction is the *photovoltaic cell.* This is a layered silicon wafer that produces electricity in response to light. At present relatively large surface areas and intense sunlight are necessary to generate usable quantities of power, and thus photovoltaics are still too expensive to gain widespread use. The average cost per watt is now about 10 dollars, which is too costly to be competitive for most applications (Flavin, 1983). Further price reductions may greatly expand the future usefulness of photovoltaic cells, and it is possible that they could be used for some domestic purposes in the next decade or two.

One of the major problems with solar-generated electricity is storage for periods of little or no sunlight. Fuel cells offer some promise for alleviating this problem. Fuel cells operate by passing electricity through a salty solution, splitting water into hydrogen and oxygen. These can later be recombined to produce electricity. One of the important advantages of fuel cells is their high efficiency, but at present they are too expensive for ordinary applications.

While many reports claim that solar is the way of the future, predicting that it will account for 15–33 percent of energy needs by 2000, many obstacles will have to be overcome before such levels are reached (CONAES, 1978). The economic barriers to residential heating and cooling include high capital costs,

Table 15.7 Solar Collector Manufacturers

	Low-Temperature[a]		Medium-Temperature[b]	
	Number	Quantity[c]	Number	Quantity[c]
1974	6	1.14	39	0.14
1975	13	3.03	118	0.72
1976	19	3.88	203	1.92
1977	52	4.74	297	5.57
1978	81	5.87	180	4.99
1979	74	8.39	250	5.86
1980	72	12.23	245	7.16

[a]Low-temperature collectors are used almost exclusively for swimming pool heating.
[b]Medium temperature collectors are used primarily for space-heating and domestic water heating.
[c]quantity of collectors manufactured in million square feet.

Source: Council on Environmental Quality, 1982:267

potential mortgage restrictions, high interest rates on solar equipment, and potential property-tax increases due to the improvements. Institutional barriers include restrictive zoning and building codes, lack of legal protection for solar access or "sun rights," electric-utility rate structures, lack of solar equipment standards and testing, and, last, a dearth of installers. Although these obstacles are great, they will have to be resolved if we are to have a solar future.

Wind Power

Windmills have been used worldwide since ancient times. We perhaps know them best in the United States as a symbol of the 19th-century farm, where wind energy was converted to mechanical energy to pump water from the farm well. Although windmills have largely been replaced with other pumping devices, the windmill is once again being considered, now as a method for generating electricity. The industry is small but increasingly significant. Growth in this area was encouraged by a 1978 federal law requiring public utilities to purchase electric power offered to them by small generating companies. The price is determined by the avoidance costs of producing equivalent amounts of electricity by conventional sources. The prices range from 5.4 cents to 7.17 cents per kilowatt hour.

The first utility company to incorporate windmill-generated power into its power grid was Southern California Edison Company, in 1980. A privately financed 200-foot-tall wind-turbine generator was installed in the desert near Palm Springs, California. The turbine is capable of generating enough electricity for about a thousand homes. The blades are driven by reliable winds, which average 17 mph, with gusts up to 40 mph. The minimum wind speed for efficient operation of windmills is 10 mph. The amount of electricity generated by this turbine is equivalent to an annual saving of about 10,000 barrels of low-sulfur crude oil.

A more recent example is the Wind Farm project, operated by Pacific Gas and Electric, in northern California. It is in the Altamont Pass area, with 407 windmills, each turning out 50 kilowatts (see Figure 15.18). The investment was close to $65 million, and the company expects to reach a capacity of 30,000 kilowatts. According to a PG&E spokesman, with 84,000 kilowatts of wind

Figure 15.18 Wind farm near Altamont Pass, in northern California. Nearly 407 windmills turn out 50 kilowatts each of electricity daily.

generation throughout the region, the company would consume 135 fewer barrels of oil per hour while the wind blows (Turner, 1983).

The U.S. Department of Energy has put millions of dollars into developing prototype machines, rated from 200 to 2500 kilowatts at peak power output. The largest of these has a bladespan of 300 feet. Early 1980 estimates placed wind-generated energy costs equivalent to or better than those of conventional sources by 1986. By the year 2000, wind-generated electricity may account for 2 to 4 percent of electrical needs (Smith, 1980).

Generally, wind power is perceived as the first renewable energy source since hydroelectricity to move beyond government sponsorship and into control by traditional public utilities. Its application to large-scale electricity generation holds fewer uncertainties than does solar energy. It is also more easily integrated into existing utility power grids, making it appealing to investors interested in maintaining the economic status quo.

ENERGY CONSERVATION

It is surprising to many people that energy conservation is our largest single "new source" of energy. In the face of higher energy costs, Americans have cut their consumption dramatically. The potential for energy saving is indicated by U.S. energy-demand projections for the year 2000, which range from 60 to 130 quads. The 70-quad range of the estimate is the amount of energy that could be saved through conservation.

Since the energy crisis of 1973, the U.S. energy situation has improved significantly, much of this due to conservation. *Conservation* in this sense simply means using less or using what you have with more efficiency. As we have seen earlier in this chapter, energy consumption peaked at 79 quads in 1979 and declined by 1982 to less than 71 quads, less than was consumed in 1973. To look at it another way, every year since 1973, it has taken less energy to produce a dollar's worth of goods and services (Landesberg, 1982). Slow economic growth and consumer response to higher prices are both contributors to the decline in consumption.

Energy conservation has many interpretations. According to the Committee on Nuclear and Alternative Energy Systems (CONAES) (1978), it "includes technological and procedural changes that allow us to reduce demand for energy (or specific scarce fuels) without corresponding reductions in the goods or services we enjoy" (p. 143). Energy conservation develops in three stages. In the first stage, less fuel does less work: for example, people drive more slowly and reduce heat and light use. In the second stage, less fuel is used to do the same amount of work. This requires design and investment decisions, such as installing more insulation, storm windows, radial tires, and fluorescent lighting. In the third and final stage, less fuel is used to do more work. This stage provides the greatest savings, yet it requires investment in applied research efforts to be effective. This applied research requires technological innovations that are beyond the grasp of individuals. Some new developments are moving from the experimental stage to the applied level. These include the new supercritical-airfoil airplane-wing design, which has had a significant impact on aircraft fuel consumption, and new auto designs that aerodynamically reduce drag (Grey et al., 1978).

A low-energy future may mean a high-technology future. Newer computer systems and communications components do better work and use less energy than earlier models. There are, however, roadblocks to better energy use and increased fuel savings. Utility companies are not at all eager to reduce supply, as increased supply continues to bring a greater profit than do increased prices. Time itself is a factor. The turnover time for energy-inefficient equipment ranges from a decade for an auto to half a century for industrial equipment. Finally, standards and regulations put in place when energy was cheap and plentiful are slow to change. Price controls, freight-transport regulations, building codes, procurement procedures, and tax policies must all be overhauled at all levels of government, for energy conservation to become truly effective.

ENERGY ALTERNATIVES

There is a high degree of substitutability among the various sources of energy, and there is a wide range of alternatives for aggregate energy supply and demand in the future. The choices of which sources of energy to emphasize, which to use for heating, or which to use for electricity are important policy decisions, each with far-reaching impacts. At the present time, the U.S. government is relying primarily on market forces to determine our national energy policy. During the early 1980s, the result of this policy was an era of plentiful oil and slow economic growth. Energy use patterns have been relatively static. If we should return to energy shortages and rapidly rising energy prices, as in the 1970s, we would probably suffer the same fate as then: severe economic shock. The shortages that occurred were small in comparison to the potential changes in energy supply and demand that could happen in a decade or two. The gasoline

Table 15.8 Projected Energy Use in 2010, by Use Sector

Scenario	Energy price ratio, 2010/1975[a]	Energy conservation policy	Energy in 2010 (quads)					
			Buildings	Industry	Transport	Total	Losses	Primary consumption
I	4	Very aggressive, deliberately arrived at reduced demand requiring some life-style changes	6	26	10	42	16	58
II	4	Aggressive; aimed at maximum efficiency plus minor life-style changes	10	28	14	52	22	74
III	2	Slowly incorporates more measures to increase efficiency	13	33	20	66	28	94
IV	1	Unchanged from present policies	20	39	26	85	51	136
1975			16	21	17	54	17	71

[a]Overall average; assumptions by specific fuel type were made reflecting parity and supply; price increases were assumed to occur linearly over time. The price was assumed to be either that actually charged at the final point of demand or the shadow price reflecting a policy. [b]Losses include those due to extraction, refining, conversion, transmission, and distribution. Electricity is converted at 10,500 BTu/k[Wh,] coal is converted to synthetic liquids and gases at 68 percent efficiency. [c]These totals include only marketed energy. Active solar systems provide additional energy to the buildings and industrial sectors in each scenario. Total energy consumption values are 63, 77, 96, and 137 quads in scenarios I, II, III, and IV, respectively.

Source: Committee on Nuclear and Alternative Energy Sources (J. Gibbons). Copyright 1978 by the American Association for the Advancement of Science.

Table 15.9 Projected Energy Use in 2010, by Energy Type

Fuel type	Total primary energy consumption (quads) Scenario				
	I	II	III	IV	1975
Liquid fuels[a]	24	29	38	50	30
Gaseous fuels[b]	8	9	11	26	17
Coal (direct use)[c]	10	11	13	10	4
Electric inputs[d]	17	26	32	50	26
Total purchased fuels[e]	58	74	94	136	71
Active solar[f]	5	3	2	1	Negligible
Totals	63	77	96	137	71

[a]Liquid fuels include petroleum, shale oil, and synthetic liquids derived from coal. [b]Gaseous fuels include natural gas and gasified coal. [c]Figures do not include coal used for liquid and gaseous fuels (necessary in most of the scenarios) or for electricity production. [d]Includes coal, nuclear, hydro, geothermal, and oil (for peak demand only). [e]Because of rounding off, totals may not equal the sums for fuel sectors. [f]Estimated use of active solar units in buildings and industry.

Total primary energy consumption in 2010 by fuel type. Each set of numbers represents only one of a wide variety of energy resources that could be used to meet energy demands. Because energy resources are largely interchangeable over the long run, the actual mix in 2010 can be influenced by changes in price, technology, and policy.

Source: Committee on Nuclear and Alternative Energy Sources (J. Gibbons). Copyright 1978 by the American Association for the Advancement of Science.

Table 15.10 Energy Use Forecasts

Year of forecast	Beyond the pale	Heresy	Conventional wisdom	Superstition
1972	125 (Lovins)	140 (Sierra)	160 (AEC)	190 (FPC)
1974	100 (Ford zeg)	124 (Ford tf)	140 (ERDA)	160 (EEI)
1976	75 (Lovins)	89–95 (Von Hippel)	124 (ERDA)	140 (EEI)
1977–78	33 (Steinhart)	67–77 (NAS I, II)	96–101 (NAS III, AW)	124 (Lapp)

Abbreviations: Sierra, Sierra Club; AEC, Atomic Energy Commission; FPC, Federal Power Commission, Ford zeg, Ford Foundation zero energy growth scenario; Ford tf, Ford Foundation technical fix scenario; Von Hiippel, Frank Von Hippel and Robert Williams of the Princeton Center for Environmental Studies; ERDA, the Energy Research and Development Administration; EEI, Edison Electric Institute; Steinhart, 2050 forecast by John Steinhart of the University of Wisconsin; NAS I, II, III, the spread of the National Academy of Sciences Committee on Nuclear and Alternative Energy Systems (CONAES); AW, Alvin Weinberg study done at the Institute for Energy Analysis, Oak Ridge; Lapp, energy consultant Ralph Lapp.

Amory Lovins put together this table showing the downward drift in forecasts. Figures represent total U.S. energy demand in year 2000 or 2010.

Source: Marshall, 1980. Copyright 1980 by the American Association for the Advancement of Science.

lines of the 1970s were precipitated by shortages of as little as 5 percent. Yet we can foresee variations in supply and demand of oil and other energy sources of 20 percent or more by the year 2000. Clearly, then, we should be ready to adapt our energy production and consumption patterns to changing times.

Several recent studies have projected energy supplies available to the U.S. in the year 2000 and beyond; the ranges of available alternatives are instructive. For example, the National Research Council in 1978 made a series of projections of energy supply and demand for the year 2010 (CONAES, 1978). They constructed a series of four scenarios regarding government policy, which ranged from vigorously encouraging conservation, at one extreme, to no policy change from the present, at the other. Some of the results of the study are shown in Tables 15.8 and 15.9. In some sectors, such as energy use in buildings, conservation offers considerable potential. In other sectors, such as industry, even under the most aggressive conservation policies, energy use is expected to rise. When we look at the types of fuels used to produce energy, it is interesting to note that, in all cases, there is a substantial increase in the use of coal, primarily for heating and industrial processes, but the scenarios vary greatly in the use of oil, natural gas, and electricity. In the less conservation-oriented scenarios, increases in oil and gas use are supported primarily by imports and secondarily by synfuels. Increases in electricity use are made possible by large increases in both coal and nuclear generation. But the most important feature of the projections is that, for virtually all uses and fuels, the range in energy-consumption figures for 2010 is large in proportion to our present consumption. This range indicates that we have considerable flexibility in our choice of energy futures. The CONAES projections are not significantly different from other projections (Stobaugh and Yergin, 1979).

In the last decade, the energy use projections for the U.S. have steadily

16

declined. In the early 1970s, Americans thought they would need to use more and more energy, but, by the late 1970s, they were beginning to realize that it was possible to prosper at roughly the present energy consumption levels (see Table 15.10). The wide range in possible energy futures presents us with an important set of choices. Given that we can satisfy our needs in any number of ways, it becomes possible to consider other factors than just economic health in choosing future paths. It becomes possible, for example, to consider the environmental consequences of the energy sources we use. From the standpoint of environmental pollution and safety, conservation is clearly the most desirable source of energy for the future.

REFERENCES AND ADDITIONAL READING

Bregman, S.E. 1982. Uranium mining on Indian Lands—Blessing or Curse? *Environment* 24:7:6.

Brobst, P.A., and W.P. Pratt, eds. 1973. *United States mineral resources.* USGS Professional Paper 820. Washington, D.C.: Government Printing Office.

Calzonetti, F.J., and M.S. Eckert. 1981. *Finding a place for energy.* Washington, D.C.: Association of American Geographers Resource Publication.

Canby, T.Y., and J. Blair. 1981. Synfuels: fill 'er up! With what? *National Geographic Special Report,* pp. 74–95.

Commoner, B. 1977. *The poverty of power.* New York: Bantam.

CONAES. 1978. U.S. energy demand: some low energy futures. *Science* 200:142–52.

Cook, E. 1978. *Energy: the ultimate resource.* Washington, D.C.: Association of American Geographers Resource Paper.

Council on Environmental Quality. 1981. *Environmental trends.* Washington, D.C.: Government Printing Office.

———. 1982. *Environmental quality, 1982. 13th annual report.* Washington, D.C.: Government Printing Office.

Cutter, S. 1984. Resource recovery: an overview. In *Solid Wastes,* ed. G.S. Tolley, J. Havlicek Jr., and R. Fabian, Chapter 8, pp. 169–90. Vol. IV of *Environmental Quality.* Cambridge, Massachusetts: Ballinger.

Energy Information Administration. 1981. *State energy report: statistical tables and technical documentation 1960–1979.* Washington, D.C.: Government Printing Office.

———. 1982. *1981 annual report to Con-*

gress. Vol. 1 and vol. 2. Washington, D.C.: Government Printing Office.

———. 1983. *1982 annual energy review.* Washington, D.C.: Government Printing Office.

Environmental Protection Agency. 1980. *Environmental outlook, 1980.* EPA-600/8-80-003. Washington, D.C.: Government Printing Office.

Exxon. 1982. How much oil and gas? Houston: Exxon Corp.

Flavin, C. 1983. Photovoltaics: international competition for the sun. *Environment* 25:3:7.

Grey, J., G.W. Sutton, and M. Zlotnick. 1978. Fuel conservation and applied research. *Science* 200:135–42.

Hall, C.A.S., and C.J. Cleveland. 1981. Petroleum drilling and production in the United States: yield per effort and net energy analysis. *Science* 211:576–79.

Heiken, G., et al. 1981. Hot dry rock geothermal energy. *American Scientist* 69:400–407.

Hubbert, M.K. 1969. Energy resources. In *Resources and man.* Committee on Resources and Man, National Academy of Sciences, Chapter 8, pp. 157–242. San Francisco: W.H. Freeman.

Landesberg, H.H. 1982. Relaxed energy outlook masks continuing uncertainties. *Science* 218:973–74.

Lovins, A.B. 1977. *Soft energy paths.* New York: Harper Colophon Books.

Marshall, E. 1980. Energy forecasts, sinking to new lows. *Science* 208:1353–56.

Office of Technology Assessment. 1980a. *An assessment of oil shale technologies.* Vol. II. *A history and analysis of the federal prototype oil shale leasing program.* OTA-M-119. Washington, D.C.: Government Printing Office.

———. 1980b. *World petroleum availability 1980–2000.* OTA-TM-E-5. Washington, D.C.: Government Printing Office.

Perry, H. 1983. Coal in the United States: a status report. *Science* 222:377–84.

Pryde, P.R. 1983. *Nonconventional energy sources.* New York: Wiley.

Smith, B.P. 1978. Power from yesterday's dams. *Environment* 20:9:16–20.

Smith, J.R. 1980. Wind power excites utility interest. *Science* 207:739–42.

Stobaugh, R., and D. Yergin, eds. 1979. *Energy future: report of the energy project at the Harvard Business School.* New York: Ballantine Books.

Turner, W. 1983. Small investors selling wind power to utilities. *New York Times* February 14.

U.S. Bureau of the Census. 1984. *Statistical abstract of the United States.* Washington, D.C.: Government Printing Office.

U.S. Department of the Interior. 1976. Surface mining, its nature, extent, and significance. In *Focus on environmental geology,* R.W. Tank, 2nd ed., pp. 328–50. New York: Oxford University Press.

U.S. Weather Service. 1965. *Climatic atlas of the United States.* Washington, D.C.: Government Printing Office.

TERMS TO KNOW

acid drainage
active solar
anthracite coal
auguring
bituminous coal
BTU
centralized renewables
coal gasification
coal ranks
conservation
decentralized renewables
fission
geological estimates of recoverable oil
geothermal resources
heavy crude oil
heavy water reactor
high temperature gas cooled reactor
kerogen
light crude oil
light water reactor
lignite

liquid metal fast breeder reactor
LNG
passive solar
peat
performance based estimates of recoverable oil
photovoltaic cell
primary energy source
quad
resource recovery
secondary energy source
shale oil
strip mining
sub-bituminous coal
subsidence
Surface Mining Reclamation and Control Act
synfuels
tar sands
underground mining
uranium

STUDY QUESTIONS

1. What is the significance of the changing patterns of energy use, by fuel type and economic sector?
2. Describe the different methods of calculating how much oil is left. Will we ever run out? Why or why not?
3. Name some of the environmental concerns about the use of oil and natural gas, coal, nuclear power, and synfuels.
4. What are the pros and cons of underground versus strip mining of coal?
5. Briefly explain how synfuels are developed.
6. Describe the stages and linkages in the nuclear-fuel cycle.
7. What is the difference between decentralized and centralized renewable energy sources? Which one will be relied on more in the future?
8. Why isn't solar energy the way of the future?

CHAPTER SIXTEEN

Predicting the Future: Global Modeling

INTRODUCTION

Humankind has always wanted to know what the future would bring. For thousands of years, people have visited sages, seers, and oracles, seeking information about what would happen in one year or in one hundred. Generals needed to know the outcome of the next day's battle, an investor was interested in the fate of a sum of money, and farmers worried over what the weather would be like that season. Today we have predictive tools, based on mathematical and scientific principles, that we like to believe are more accurate than dreams, visions, and tea leaves.

In this chapter, we will examine several global models that predict the future of the world's environment, population growth, agriculture, energy supplies, and

---

ISSUE 16.1: Science Fiction as Forecast

Global models of the future are not solely limited to computer modeling of statistical data; rather, they have a long tradition within the literary world, in the form of science fiction. A separate but related genre is environmental fiction, based on environmental sciences and using current environmental problems as the basis for stories. Normally, environmental fiction novels are set in the near future (A.D. 2000 or earlier), as opposed to science fiction, which is often based in the far-distant future. As environmental concerns became more pervasive in the 1970s and 1980s, so did the number of fiction works on conservation or natural-resources topics.

A few examples of environmental fiction show that these novels forecast future environmental trends just as well as do the global models. Even before Ehrlich's nonfiction *The Population Bomb* was published in 1970, overpopulation was a topic popular with science-fiction writers. Anthony Burgess's 1962 *The Wanting Seed* (Norton) describes the problems of overpopulation. The story is set in England and describes a "Malthusian comedy," where prevailing population policies favor homosexuality. Zoe Fairbairns's 1979 *Benefits* (Avon) describes the consequences of population control in a society that is plagued by an anti-feminist backlash. The government begins paying benefits to women to lure them into the traditional roles of mothers and housewives, but social engineers then exploit the program by restricting reproduction to the most desirable women.

The disruption of ecosystems by humans

socioeconomic patterns. The strengths, weaknesses, and limitations of global modeling will be discussed. Much of the following material is based on a report prepared by the U.S. Office of Technology Assessment (1982).

FROM FORECASTING TO MODELING: A BRIEF HISTORY

The United States government began to use formal forecasting in 1929, when President Herbert Hoover created a Presidential Research Committee on Social Trends. Formal forecasting has since become an invaluable tool in business and governmental planning. Based on the collection and objective analysis of current social and economic data, forecasting predicts the future by extrapolating or extending known and measured trends to some future date (see Issue 16.1).

Not all forecasts claim the same ability to describe the future. Each of the four basic types of forecast has its own strengths and limitations (see Figure 16.1). *Unconditional* forecasts state that certain events or trends will occur. *Conditional* forecasts state that certain events or trends will occur, assuming the presence or absence of particular conditions and policies. *Exploratory* forecasts look at the different directions trends may go under a variety of conditions. *Prescriptive* or *normative* forecasts prove a point, describing trends that should or should not occur, suggesting ways to avoid or ensure particular developments.

In the decades after World War II, the increasing sophistication of computers and programming made increasingly complex forecasts possible. Planners could

---

is another theme often found in environmental fiction. Attempts to control nature backfire, with the inevitable disastrous effects. In *Cachalot* (1980, Ballantine), Alan Dean Foster uses the pollution of the terrestrial ecosystem as the backdrop for a battle for species survival. In this case, the species that survives is the whale, which eventually rules the world. Frank Herbert's *The Green Brain* (1966, Ace Books) tells the tale of rapid tropical deforestation. Insect populations suffer and eventually revolt against the human despoilers, driving them out of the tropics. Kate Wilhelm's *Where Late the Sweet Birds Sang* (1976, Harper & Row) is a classic story of the effects of ecosystem disruption, mixed with human cloning.

Natural resource extraction and allocation

is another theme of environmental fiction. The allocation of water resources shapes the politics of survival in John Nichols' 1974 *The Milagro Beanfield War* (Ballantine). David Hagberg's *Heartland* (1983, Tor Books) centers on American grain and Soviet attempts to control the world grain market by purchasing surplus grains from Canada, Argentina, and the United States. The novel's theme is that control of the world's grain equals control of the world. Finally, Marilyn Harris's *The Portent* (1981, Jove Books) tells the story of nature fighting back in retaliation for exploitation of mineral resources. A new molybdenum mine has opened in western Colorado, and nature—personified—is angered by this assault, striking back through earthquakes, avalanches, floods, and even blizzards in August.

easily extrapolate a dozen trends instead of laboriously plotting out just two or three. Computer programming also made it possible to examine quantitatively the interactions among different trends. Eventually, forecasters were able to calculate the effects that trends and situations have on one another under a variety of conditions. Thus, researchers could present different versions of the future, based on different starting assumptions and operating conditions (see Figure 16.1).

These comprehensive, broad-based forecasts, called *models,* have come into particular favor since the early 1970s. Researchers and planners in most fields of study during this period have favored a systems-dynamics view, which emphasizes the interrelatedness or interdependence of most aspects of our existence. This viewpoint has been integrated with computerized model building, to produce global models of the future that extrapolate the results of intricate interactions among human choices, population growth, climate change, food supply, natural environment, and energy consumption.

Some of these predictive models have been optimistic, such as the model presented in Herman Kahn and Anthony Wiener's *The Year 2000* (1967). This book predicted general economic and political stability, based on an admittedly optimistic assumption that nothing dramatic would happen to alter society. The human race would, with the necessary effort, overcome any problems. On the other hand, Paul Ehrlich's *The Population Bomb* (1968) and his and Anne Ehrlich's *Population, Resources, and Environment* (1970) were both pessimistic about the future. They predicted worldwide collapse and degradation of the human condition if nothing is done to control population growth trends.

Perhaps those works of environmental fiction that are closest to global models are those involving survival of societies in the future. As early as 1949, George R. Stewart, in *Earth Abides* (Random House), wrote about the survival of society in northern California after epidemics virtually wipe out the U.S. population. The most apocalyptic of these future-societies novels are Ernest Callenbach's *Ecotopia* and *Ecotopia Emerging,* written in 1975 and 1981 (Bantam). *Ecotopia* describes the isolated nation state of Ecotopia (western California, Oregon, and Washington), which seceded from the United States in the near future. The novel, which takes place in 1999, is narrated by a reporter from the U.S. who is sent to observe this new society. The reporter's findings sound familiar to those aware of E.F. Schumacher's "small is beautiful" concept. Ecotopia has omy to a decentralized, renewable resource weaned itself from a petroleum-based economy. Bicycles are the main form of transportation, urban places are decentralized and livable, recycling is continuous, and the society has a healthy respect for nature. In *Ecotopia Emerging,* Callenbach describes how Ecotopia came to be. By the 1980s, the United States was moving toward economic and ecological suicide, with the military-industrial complex holding power, backed by the ultra conservative right. Governmental protection of the environment and the workplace had been destroyed. In 1986 residents of the Pacific Northwest and northern California opposing this trend began to revolt. They created a new nation, Ecotopia, which was determined to shape its own evolutionary destiny.

Finally, dozens of science fiction novels

MODEL BUILDING: STRENGTHS AND WEAKNESSES

The word *model* usually implies a simplified version of an object, such as a train or car. A global model is an attempt to re-create the entire earth system, including its physical, social, and technological subsystems. Because of the immensity and complexity of the task, these subsystems and relationships are often simplified into general assumptions and equations suitable for computer programming. Critics of global modeling point out that these simplifications may render a model's prediction useless. Thus, a basic question for modelers is how close to reality a model has to be to produce useful results. Let us look at this in more detail.

How Realistic Is a Global Model?

One of the main appeals of global modeling, compared to the simpler forecasting, is the model's apparent resemblance to "real life." A model can incorporate greater complexities, thanks to the computer's ability to juggle huge numbers of variables, conditions, and equations. Thus, model makers struggle toward a closer and closer approximation of actual conditions, as they refine and improve their tools. This requires accurate data and an understanding of how the world works, both of which are perhaps ultimately unattainable, in an absolute sense. This understanding must furthermore be stated in statistical and mathematical terms, if it is to be part of the computer model's data base.

---

and stories have speculated on the state of the world following nuclear war. At one end of the spectrum are tales in which only small and specific areas are damaged, as in Eugene Burdick and Harvey Wheeler's 1962 *Fail Safe* (McGraw-Hill), in which Moscow and New York are destroyed. Moving toward a picture of total devastation is John Wyndham's *The Chrysalids* (1955, Penguin). He depicts farming communities in temperate-zone Labrador, one to two thousand years after war's end. South of Labrador, are the fearsome Fringes and Badlands, the territory of mutants. What was once the northeastern U.S. is known only as the Black Coasts, and South America is reputedly a "sinful" place, where mutants are allowed to live beyond birth. The societal role of mutants is also the main theme of Walter M. Miller's *A Canticle for Leibowitz* (1959,

Lippincott) and of Aldous Huxley's *Ape and Essence* (1948, Harper and Brothers). One example of future resource availability is provided by Steve Wilson in his 1976 *The Lost Traveller* (St. Martins), in which the U.S. west coast, spared from much nuclear damage, is run by Hell's Angels and university professors. The feudal southern states produce oil, essential to the Angels' motorcycle-based economy.

Does any of this sound familiar? Who is to say whether the computer-generated models of the global future are any better or any worse than these fictionalized accounts? Environmental fiction and science fiction give us another glimpse at what the future may bring, based on current trends. Only time will tell which approach is the most insightful.

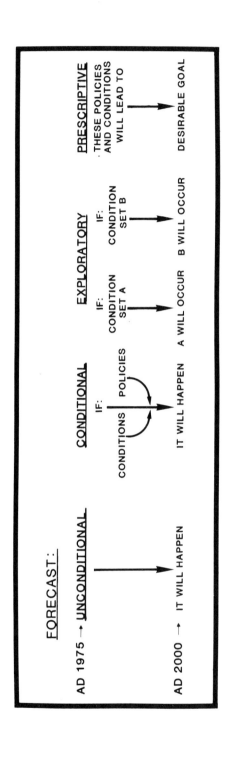

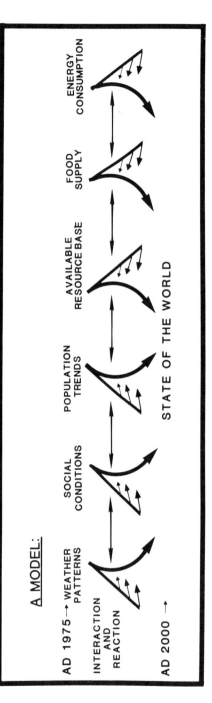

Figure 16.1 Forecasts and models. (a) A forecast is a prediction based on past and present trends. It may include certain conditions, such as government policies. (b) A model is an integrated representation of many different aspects of a system, which can be used to predict the future.

Some aspects of the world's resource base are relatively easy to quantify: for example, the amount of corn harvested on fifty hectares, under a certain set of climatic and technological conditions. Resource-use issues related to human behavior and changes in public attitude are much more difficult to measure. For example, twenty-five years ago, energy-use forecasts predicted that U.S. energy supplies would eventually come mainly from nuclear power plants. This prediction has not come true, because of subsequent developments, including rising costs of construction due to federal safety regulations instituted after the accident at Three Mile Island, due to increased efficiency of energy use in automobiles, appliances, and so forth, and lastly due to falling demand. People are simply using less as the costs increase. None of these factors was predicted by forecasters a quarter of a century go, who saw a glowing future for nuclear energy.

Modelers with an understanding of ecosystems behavior have worked to incorporate cycles and other normal ecosystem changes into models. The applicability of these natural-systems components to predictive models of human affairs has yet to be seen, as a longer time span is needed to test their value. The model of a single simple ecosystem may incorporate enough input, output, and feedback data to approximate reality. A model of all of the world's millions of ecosystems and all the interactions among them is doomed to failure, because of the limited capacity of computers and huge gaps in our knowledge about world patterns. Models are thus reduced to simplification and approximation, which may severely limit their precision as predictive and decision-making tools.

The Value and Uses of Global Models

The question then becomes how useful such a partial approximation of reality can be. No matter whether a model's predictions come true, they at least provide guidelines for future human endeavors. For example, if a model's projections suggest that there will be a worldwide decline in the consumption of wheat, farmers may decide to plant less. The resulting drop in supply leads to a forced decline in consumption, which may not be at all what the modelers were suggesting would take place, yet the farmers may see the projection as having been very helpful. Suppose, on the other hand, that a global model predicted a drop in the price of wheat. Farmers might decide to plant some other, more profitable crop, leading to a drop in wheat supplies and a rise in prices, making the projection false.

Models, then, give us something to hold on to, as indicators and guides for social and economic choices. The use we make of a model's projections, however, may alter the conditions under which the projection was initially made, rendering it incorrect or inaccurate. This does not stop people from finding models and their projections useful.

Despite these constraints and limitations, models of global, national, and regional futures are used for many different purposes. For example, the operations of U.S.-based multinational corporations have grown so complex and are so deeply intertwined with political and economic trends that these companies utilize modeling for planning. Several nations other than the United States provide support for modeling programs, as do a variety of international organizations interested in economic and environmental issues. The U.S. government uses modeling in many of its agencies, particularly the Departments of Agriculture and Energy, the Bureau of Mines, the Central Intelligence Agency, the Agency for International Development, and the Environmental Protection Agency.

Regional and sectoral models are used as planning aids, and congressional members and committees utilize econometric models developed by economists and the Congressional Budget Office. Perhaps the most intriguing (and least public) modeling is done for the Joint Chiefs of Staff, the top U.S. military decision-makers. With the aid of high-capacity supercomputers, the World Integrated Model (discussed later in this chapter) develops long-range defense strategies, based on four future world scenarios.

Users of these models do not rely on them for precise and to-the-penny indicators of what will be but instead use them as tools for estimates of likelihood and probability. Short-term models are also valuable to test the validity of assumptions and outcomes. Models provide "ball-park" figures on various economic, resource-base, and human trends that have proved reliable enough in past tests to be of continued usefulness (U.S. Office of Technology Assessment, 1982, pp. 5, 23).

MAJOR GLOBAL MODELS

Forecasts and models up to the late 1960s, e.g., Kahn and Wiener's *The Year 2000*, were usually optimistic in their predictions. The environmental and resource bases were often regarded as eternal and infinite, not needing to be taken into account in models that consisted largely of econometric measures, predictions of industrial output, GNP per capita, and the like. Early hints of resource scarcity and the worldwide energy crisis that developed in 1973 (see Chapter 15) forced many people to reassess the earth's economic and environmental stability. Fears developed that the human race was beginning its swift descent toward eco-disaster. This crisis brought about major changes in global modeling. Models developed over the past decade have usually been designed to take environmental and ecological factors into greater account. What follows is an overview of the major models developed since 1970. We will explore the purpose, findings, strengths, and weaknesses of each.

The Limits to Growth

Reflecting increased worry over the earth's apparently serious environmental situation, the Club of Rome developed a Project on the Predicament of Mankind in the late 1960s. Made up of civil servants, businesspeople, and academics, the Club of Rome listed a series of escalating problems that human beings seemed unable to understand, much less solve. These included: poverty in the midst of plenty, environmental degradation, loss of faith in institutions, uncontrolled urban spread, insecurity of employment, the alienation of youth, the rejection of traditional values, inflation, and other economic and fiscal problems.

The Club of Rome suggested that these were not local or national problems but were instead global in scope. With the objective of understanding the workings of a worldwide interlocking system, the Club commissioned Jay Forrester, Dennis Meadows, and others of the Massachusetts Institute of Technology to develop several computerized global models (Meadows et al., 1972).

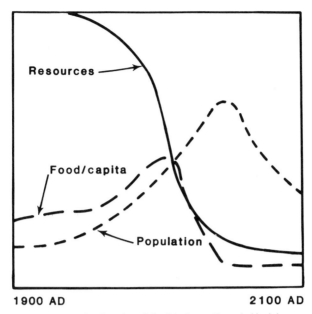

Figure 16.2 Results of the Limits to Growth Model. These curves are based on simple extrapolation of present trends into the future. See the text for further explanation. (Source: U.S. Office of Technology Assessment, 1982)

   Their Limits to Growth (LTG) model introduced two major concepts, *feedback* and *carrying capacity*. In this model, the global system is made up of five interacting subsystems: population, natural resources, capital, agriculture, and pollution. Note that this construction neatly sidesteps the complexities of human culture and behavior by leaving them out. Extrapolating the trends of these five subsystems from 1900 into the future (see Figure 16.2), the Limits to Growth modelers warned of a general systems collapse, because of rapid population growth, increased industrial output, and a vanishing resource base. Even with more optimistic assumptions as part of the data base, the model still predicts that no technological innovations can hold off ecocatastrophe beyond the year 2100.

   To determine how humankind could survive, the LTG modelers worked backwards from their definition of an equilibrium state (see Figure 16.3) and came up with recommendations that, if put into effect within twenty-five years, should save us from ourselves. These recommendations include: restricting population growth by making "perfect" birth-control methods universally available and by controlling family size to no more than two children, restricting growth of capital by maintaining industrial output at 1975 levels and not permitting investment above depreciation rates, reducing resource consumption and pollution to one-quarter of 1970 levels, diverting capital to food production to feed all, even if this is "uneconomic," preventing soil depletion and erosion by using this diverted capital for improvement, and extending the lifetime of industrial hardware and other capital stock, to reduce obsolescence and to free money and resources for other uses.

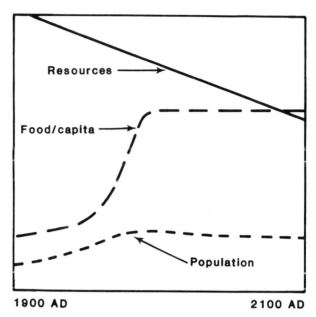

Figure 16.3   Results of the Limits to Growth Model. The curves here are based on early achievement of stability in population and resource use. See the text for further explanation. (Source: U.S. Office of Technology Assessment, 1982)

The Limits to Growth modelers provide two major conclusions to ponder. First, if we follow present trends, we will exceed the earth's carrying capacity within one hundred years, resulting in catastrophic drops in population levels and industrial output. Second, this disaster can be avoided if we move toward an equilibrium state. These conclusions, while striking and perhaps terrifying, are very general, reflecting the limitations of the model that generated them. The LTG model is vague about the workings of its five subsystems, and it is thus unsuitable for exacting, localized decision-making. It draws a broad picture of a possible future, providing overall recommendations on how to achieve or avoid that future. Clearly, it is a stark and uncompromising message, with strong medicine the cure. As the model does not take human variables into account, the task of deciding how best to achieve an equilibrium state is quite properly left up to individuals and their governments.

The World Integrated Model

Because of the controversies surrounding the assumptions in the LTG model, the Club of Rome commissioned a new model in 1974. Mihajlo Mesarovic at Case Western Reserve University in Cleveland, Ohio, and Eduard Pestel of the Technical University in Hannover, West Germany, were the authors (Mesarovic and Pestel, 1974). They attempted to come up with a model that was more flexible, was capable of generating greater detail, and better incorporated socio-cultural variables than had the previous Club of Rome effort.

Released to the public in 1974, the World Integrated Model (WIM) was constructed using five interrelated planes, each representing one of the globe's systems. These correspond to—but are somewhat different in content from— the LTG's five subsystems. The planes or strata in the WIM are environmental, combining the geophysical and ecological factors; technological, including activities that utilize mass and energy transfer; demographic-economic, combining human population and industrial capital; sociopolitical, including institutions, policies, and decisions; and individual, incorporating personal attitudes and values. These last two can be altered to fit the scenario ordered by the model's user. Mesarovic's "multilevel hierarchical systems theory" maintains that these levels generally operate independently of one another but become interactive during a crisis.

Another major change from the earlier LTG model is a more detailed and flexible world map. That is, instead of assuming that the world is a single political entity, as did the LTG model, WIM divides the earth into ten regions, enabling model users to examine future problems within and between regions. As each region is further subdivided into such categories as industrial capital, energy capacity, and agricultural capital, a level of detail and complexity is possible far beyond that of the LTG. While that model contained 200 equations, the WIM modelers claimed 100,000 for theirs.

A user of WIM can insert different scenarios and data bases in so many different places that there is no one set of results WIM is known for. In fact, the WIM can be thought of as a far less fatalistic model than the LTG, as it suggests that the future is not yet determined and that there are many possible routes to travel. Two of WIM's scenarios are the "historical" and the "isolationist" scenarios. The "historical" scenario extrapolates present trends into the future. It predicts higher food costs worldwide and a rise in the death rate in South Asia because of starvation. The "isolationist" scenario restricts U.S. food exports to keep domestic prices down, resulting in quicker and more widespread starvation in Asia. These are but two of the many patterns the WIM model has generated.

The general conclusions of WIM's modelers are fairly similar to those of the LTG group: we are entering an era of scarcity, as indicated by various resource crises. We must approach any solution to these problems in a spirit of international cooperation, and we must do so very quickly. With oil, its substitutes, and agricultural land the commodities most in jeopardy, WIM recommends worldwide diversification of industry and the buildup of economic and export stability for the poorest nations. Additionally, the modelers recommend food aid to the poorest nations, in the form of *appropriate technology*, and massive socioeconomic reforms. The modelers see an excellent prognosis for the future, *if* these steps are taken.

The Latin American World Model

The Latin American World Model was developed in the mid-1970s as a response to the developed-nation orientation of LTG and WIM. Developed at the Fundacion Bariloche in Argentina and first presented in 1974, the Latin American World Model (LAWM) is an explicitly *prescriptive* model (Herrera, 1974; Herrera et al., 1976). That is, it moves away from WIM's and LTG's extrapolations of the present into the future and instead focuses on creating a future in which the earth is freed from underdevelopment.

LAWM was the product of dissatisfaction on the part of people from the world's less wealthy nations, who felt that the crises generated for the future by other models were already at hand in their countries. They also feared that a trend toward a global equilibrium, as defined by the U.S. and other well-off nations, would prevent industrialization in less developed areas, widening technological and income gaps worldwide. Thus, in the viewpoint of the LAWM modelers, the rights and needs of people come first, with resources and the environment as tools to decrease human misery. For Third World planners, LAWM is preferable to other models and is central to the work of the United Nations Educational, Scientific, and Cultural Organization (UNESCO) and of other UN agencies.

The LAWM includes no provision to measure degradation of the environment or of a decrease in the world's resource base. Its developers believe that the "environment and its natural resources will not impose barriers of absolute physical limits on the attainment of an ideal society" (Herrera et al., 1976, p. 8). This is in great contrast to the environmental concerns of both LTG and WIM. In the LAWM, the world is divided into regions, and cooperation is assumed to exist between nations. Further economic alterations have been made. Each region is capable of satisfying basic needs through the development and use of local resources, which are assumed to be unlimited in quantity and unchanging in price. Consumption of resources and income distribution are equal between and within regions.

With all of these changes in place, LAWM's projections of the resulting trends suggest that the basic needs of all regions except Asia can be met within thirty years. Developed nations would have to grow economically at a much lower rate than they do now, for other nations to catch up. Under these conditions, Latin America would meet its basic needs by 1990, Africa by 2008. Asia, on the other hand, does not attain a basic-needs level even under these idealized conditions, due to the inability of food production to keep up with population growth (see Figure 16.4). To minimize the inevitable disaster facing Asia, the modelers recommend population control and the development of unconventional food sources.

The LAWM presents one scenario in which this ideal of egalitarian redistribution is replaced with a pattern resembling that of the present. The result is that, for poorer nations, attainment of basic-needs goals would be delayed by two or three generations, requiring three to five times more resources. This may in fact be the most telling and realistic product of the LAWM, as it is clear that the world's nations are not falling over each other in their rush to embrace the recommended worldwide economic equity. The LAWM modelers conclude that their goals can be achieved by reducing consumption of resources and other commodities, increasing investment, instituting rational land use, justly distributing the basics of life, and eliminating international trade deficits (U.S. Office of Technology Assessment, 1982, p. 29).

The United Nations Input-Output World Model

Designed along the same ideological lines as the LAWM, the United Nations Input-Output World Model (UN Model) aims at narrowing the income gap between wealthy and poorer nations. Natural resources and environmental pollution are larger factors in this formulation than in the LAWM. The overall conclusions

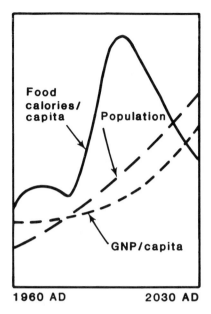

Food calories/capita   **Population**

GNP/capita

1960 AD   **2030 AD**

Figure 16.4 Results of the Latin American World Model. This is a prescriptive model aimed at improving the economic status of Third World nations. See the text for further explanation. (Source: U.S. Office of Technology Assessment, 1982)

drawn from this model's projections are generally more pessimistic than the models previously discussed.

The UN Model was developed by Wassily Leontief for the UN's Centre for Development Planning, Projections, and Politics (Leontief et al., 1977). Its purpose was to determine whether or not resource availability and environmental limits are among the significant factors preventing a more equitable worldwide income distribution. In other words, the modelers wanted to know if income and development disparities are environmentally determined. Leontief and his co-workers viewed the world as a system made up of interdependent processes, in which each process produces outputs and absorbs inputs. For example, an output might be exports or pollutants, and an input could be capital or raw materials (see Chapter 1).

The UN Model divides the world into three categories: developed nations, less developed resource-rich nations, and resource-poor nations. For each region, forty-five sectors of economic activity are programmable. An environmental sector contains eight pollutants and five methods for reducing them, but there is no real interest in or measurement of the impact of human activity on natural systems. As with the LAWM, the environment and resource base are seen as merely a means of obtaining a better socioeconomic future and are not in themselves worth worrying about.

Not surprisingly, the UN modelers concluded that there are no major environmental barriers or unmanageable pollution problems in the way of economic development. For the study's other aim, to produce scenarios for socioeconomic change that would, if implemented, lead to a reduction in the income ratio between rich and poor nations, the conclusions are far less optimistic. A scenario based on current growth rates in per-capita GNP depicts a bleak future for the less developed countries. Even the scenario based on modest economic growth rates in poor nations suggests that income gaps will remain the same so long as population growth rates soar, wiping out gains in GNP per capita. Scenarios depicting a significant closing of the income gap require unrealistically high gains in GNP growth rates for these nations.

Overall, the various scenarios projected by the UN Model make it clear that the future for resource-poor nations will remain bleak as long as present socioeconomic patterns continue. For a better future, change must be sweeping, both within nations and globally. Politics and economics, not the natural resource base, are seen as the major barriers to greater economic equity.

The Global 2000 Report

Within the United States government, many sectoral models have been adopted by federal agencies and other organizations for planning. Realizing that these organizations may function at cross-purposes to one another, President Carter in 1977 directed the Council on Environmental Quality (CEQ) and the Department of State to conduct a study of these submodel projections, to be called the Global 2000 report. The main product of the study would be the compilation, in one single place, of these models and forecasts, with a critique of their success or failure in working together as a cohesive systems-oriented whole.

Taking all of the resulting gaps and shortcomings into consideration, Global 2000 provided the first comprehensive look at the U.S. government's planning strategies, illustrating clearly where improvements can be made. The built-in weaknesses and lack of data agreement between different agencies, however, ensures that the Global 2000 projections will not be used for detailed recommendations and planning.

The Global 2000 report provides projections of changes in the world's population, natural resources, and environment, as determined by the government's many submodels (Council on Environmental Quality, 1981). As these submodels were developed in isolation from and perhaps, in some cases, in opposition to each other, there are conflicts in the data bases and projections. In fact, these conflicts are so significant that a major conclusion of the Global 2000 study is that executive agencies of the U.S. government are not presently capable of developing internally consistent projections of world trends to the year 2000. The CEQ does suggest that their findings are at least qualitatively correct, in basic agreement with other projections and with the more dynamic global models.

The general conclusions of the Global 2000 report are that the year 2000 will be more crowded, hungrier, more polluted, and more vulnerable to environmental and political disruption than is the present, unless the world's nations move to alter current trends. More specifically, Global 2000 analysts state that global population will increase by 55 percent, to 6.35 billion, income gaps between nations will widen, food production will keep ahead of population growth in some areas but not others, and oil consumption will be increasingly replaced by other energy sources and by conservation. Additionally, the environment will be subject to major strains and deterioration, with subsequent negative impacts on human systems, and large numbers of species extinctions (U.S. Office of Technology Assessment, 1982).

THE FUTURE: GENERALLY AND QUALITATIVELY

Although the five models are very different in their approaches, assumptions, methodologies, data bases, and goals, some common themes are visible ((U.S.

Table 16.1 Socioeconomic System Projections

Model	Population	Longer Term Projections
LTG	6.0	Standard run: population increases to 7.0 billion by 2025, then decreases to 4.0 by 2100 Equilibrium run: population stabilizes at 6.0 billion by 2050
WIM	6.4	Population stabilizes at just under 7.0 billion by 2015; death rates due to starvation are high in South Asia
LAWM	6.4	Population reaches 11.0 billion by 2040 and is still growing at 1.1%/year; death rates due to starvation rising rapidly in Asia
UN	5.9–6.5	Population reaches 8.0 to 12.0 billion by 2050, stabilizes at 8.0 to 14.0 billion by 2150
Global 2000	5.8–6.5	Not available

Source: U.S. Office of Technology Assessment, 1982

Office of Technology Assessment, 1982; Meadows et al., 1982). For one, all these projections suggest that population and material capital cannot grow indefinitely on our planet and that we have only partial and often incorrect information available to help us improve the situation. It is not lack of resources that causes such a gap between rich and poor but rather inequities in global distribution of resources, based on political and economic patterns. If extended into the future, these patterns will tend to exacerbate present problems. One implication of the several projections is that, in the next several decades, the world's socioeconomic system will be shifting toward a new state, as yet undetermined, but certainly a product of decisions and changes occurring at present (see Table 16.1).

Another area where the models agree is that changes should be made sooner, not later, as it will probably be more difficult to alter the situation once it has worsened. Technological change is useful and essential but will not be enough without accompanying alterations in worldwide social, political, and economic patterns. Nations are increasingly interdependent, and thus decisions should be as wide-ranging as possible. Small-scale, short-term decisions can reverberate in unexpected and often negative ways, so international cooperation is needed (U.S. Office of Technology Assessment, 1982; Meadows et al., 1982).

As mentioned at the beginning of this chapter, an early and optimistic world view of the future was presented in Kahn and Wiener's 1967 book, *The Year 2000*. In an effort to refute the largely pessimistic models developed over the decade and a half that followed that book's publication, Herman Kahn (now deceased) coedited *The Resourceful Earth* with economist Julian Simon (Kahn and Simon, 1984). Although utilizing much of the same data as did the Global 2000 researchers, the authors in this volume come up with strikingly different conclusions. For example, Kahn and Simon state that, with the continuation of present trends, the world in 2000 will be less crowded and less polluted and will have greater ecological stability and lowered vulnerability to resource-supply disruption. They further predict lower prices, increased wealth, and declining scarcity.

In the chapter on food and agriculture, author D. Gale Johnson states that the annual rise in food production in the poorer nations will be more than the minimum needed to provide people with better diets. Fertilizer prices are not tied to petroleum, and thus will not rise. Further, some food prices may decline, and malnutrition is on the wane. This contrasts with the Global 2000 projections, which warn that food production will rise at a lower rate and will be accompanied by a 95 percent increase in food prices, due to higher costs of fertilizer and the other basics of agriculture. Malnutrition, according to Global 2000, will rise rapidly, with increased prices, and more of the world's resources will be needed to meet demands for food. Kahn and Simon thus provide a profoundly different assessment of the future from those of Global 2000 and of the other models we have looked at in this chapter (Holden, 1983).

In a 1983 interview, Simon provided an explanation for this discrepancy. For one thing, he and Kahn distrust global modeling. "We are hostile to big models. . . . any attempt to have a global model to integrate everything becomes uncontrollable" (Holden, 1983, p. 342). This viewpoint is appealing to economists interested in encouraging the unfettered growth of capitalism. Is it, however, a correct or responsible way of dealing with the environment, which operates according to different laws from those of free enterprise?

In fact, editors Kahn and Simon are not very interested in the environment. It is not mentioned in either the agriculture or energy chapters of their book. According to Kahn, nature is provided for the benefit of human beings, and a global or holistic viewpoint reflects an un-American belief in the right to existence of all living creatures (Holden, 1983). What do you think? Is global modeling in conflict with American ideals and goals?

CONCLUSIONS

As you may have realized from the above summaries, many terms and concepts from these models have become common phrases in the scholarly and popular media and within our everyday lives. Scenario, feedback, carrying capacity, and interrelatedness pepper the conversations of individuals concerned about the future. It is well to ask, however, how precisely we "know" anything about the future as a result of these elaborate modeling projects. We can say very little with precision. Generally, it is clear that environmental and socioeconomic conditions will worsen, though perhaps not catastrophically.

One thing is certain about the future and that is the inescapable presence of resource-use modeling. Just how useful the models are remains to be seen. It may be that, in the long run, models are somewhat right and somewhat wrong, just as with seers and oracles of old. As long as the models' projections are correct often enough and as long as they provide us with much-needed guidance, researchers will continue to develop, refine, and use them.

REFERENCES AND ADDITIONAL READING

Cole, H.S.D., ed. 1973. *Models of doom: a critique of the limits to growth.* New York: Universe Books.

Council on Environmental Quality. 1981. *The Global 2000 report to the president.* New York: Viking Penguin.

Ehrlich, P. 1968. *The population bomb.* New York: Ballantine.

Ehrlich, A., and P. Ehrlich. 1970. *Population, resources, and environment: issues in human ecology.* San Francisco: Freeman.

Herrera, A.O. 1974. *Proceedings of the 2nd IIASA global modeling conference.* Berlin: International Institute of Applied Systems Analysis.

————, et al. 1976. *Catastrophe or new society? a Latin American world model.* Ottawa: International Development Research Center.

Holden, C. 1983. Simon and Kahn versus Global 2000. *Science* 221:341–43.

Kahn, H., and J. Simon, eds. 1984. *The resourceful earth.* New York: Basil Blackwell.

Kahn, H., and A. Wiener. 1967. *The year 2000: a framework for speculation on the next thirty-three years.* New York: Morrow.

Leontief, W., A. Carter, and P. Petri. 1977. *The future of the world economy: a United Nations study.* New York: Oxford University Press.

Meadows, D., et al. 1972. *The limits to growth.* New York: Universe Books.

Meadows, D.H., et al. 1982. *Groping in the dark: the first decade of global modeling.* New York: Wiley Interscience.

Mesarovic, M., and E. Pestel. 1974. *Mankind at the turning point.* New York: Dutton.

Spengler, J. 1974. *Population change, modernization and welfare.* Englewood Cliffs, New Jersey: Prentice-Hall.

U.S. Office of Technology Assessment. 1982. *Global models, world futures, and public policy: a critique.* Washington, D.C.: Government Printing Office.

TERMS TO KNOW

Club of Rome
extrapolation
forecast
Global 2000 Report
Kahn and Simon's *The Resourceful Earth*
Latin American World Model

Limits to Growth Model
model
prescriptive forecast or model
United Nations Model
World Integrated Model

STUDY QUESTIONS

1. What is the difference between a forecast and a model?
2. Can you think of some recent trends that have made forecasts meaningless?
3. How do Simon and Kahn differ from the Global 2000 modelers in their view of the relation between population and wealth?
4. Rank the models discussed in this chapter from most to least optimistic in their predictions of the future.
5. Do you think that global models are better than crystal balls at predicting the future?

Epilogue

Final chapters in textbooks are often not read by the student and not assigned by the teacher. Why? They contain an overview and summary of the entire book's contents, in an attempt to condense within a few pages the scope and complexity of an entire field of study. The result is sometimes meaningless and often not very interesting. Instead of this approach, the three authors of this book have decided to remove their "objective" hats and present you with an epilogue contaning three personal pieces about the conservation of natural resources. After all, resource use and development is a matter of opinion as much as it is a matter of fact.

WHAT ARE THE MOST PRESSING ENVIRONMENTAL PROBLEMS FACING US TODAY?

Before answering this question, it is important to put environmental problems in perspective. Presumably, the ultimate goal of environmentalists is the betterment of the human condition, through proper management of environmental resources. But as we stated in the introduction to this book, resources are created and defined by both human and environmental factors. To better the human material condition, it is necessary to consider both the physical characteristics of natural resources and the ways in which we convert these raw materials into food, clothing, shelter, and the various other physical requirements of a comfortable existence.

It is my view that, although certain aspects of the natural environment are very important to the ultimate well-being of humanity, the social or cultural aspects of our resource use systems are most important in determining the quality of life. These social and cultural aspects include the creation and selection of various technologies for converting the raw materials of natural resources into things usable by humans and the social and economic systems used to allocate and distribute resources and goods to people. I believe this because most of the major cases of large-scale human suffering are primarily (if not entirely) attributable to human causes and because the hardships caused by many environmental problems we have discussed are minor, even trivial, by comparison.

A few examples will help illustrate the relative insignificance of environmental problems. First, most major modern and historical episodes of widespread death or disease are directly attributable to the aggression of one group against another, either explicit, as in the case of most wars, or implicit as in the case of the eradication of native populations in the New World. Certainly, there have been periods of severe population reductions by non-human agents, most notably the plagues in Europe during the Middle Ages. The causes of these tragedies were certainly complex, including environmental factors, such as fluctuations in host animal populations. But few modern diseases cause human suffering on the scale of direct human action.

The present occurrence of famine in much of the Third World is attributable essentially to economic and political causes. Yes, famine occurs as a result of crop failures triggered by unfavorable weather and other environmental factors, and, yes, rapidly rising populations have put stress on the ability of the environment to supply food and water. But many experts on Third World food problems agree that, if domestic and international political and economic conditions were different, these famines would not occur. Some argue that more agricultural technology must be transferred from rich nations to poor ones, while others argue that the colonial status of the poor nations, today or in the past, is the cause of their economic problems. Only a few would argue that the physical limits of the environment's productivity have been reached.

The other side of the issue is the severity of natural resource problems relative to other human problems facing us today. As examples, I will mention urban and industrial pollution, soil erosion, and declining reserves of minerals and fossil fuels. Pollution today is certainly a problem, and we all regret the fouling of water and air, which is most acute in major urban areas. But in most of the industrialized world, large-scale polluting has been going on for a long time—150 years or more. In addition, humans and animals have been fouling their drinking water for thousands of years. The major source of water pollution, contamination of potable water supplies with disease-causing organisms, has been all but eliminated in the industrialized world through a combination of effluent treatment and chlorination. The most visible and acute forms of air pollution that caused severe health problems in major Western cities in past decades have also been reduced. We are concerned about toxic substances in water and the health effects of low concentrations of various substances, but there is little evidence at the present time that health problems from these sources are significant in comparison to those caused by poor diet, smoking, or other habits of individuals.

Soil erosion is a problem. There are many areas of the world where soil erosion has occurred at high rates for decades or even centuries. When economic conditions have allowed substituting other inputs to agriculture, such as fertilizers and improved seeds, yields have increased dramatically, obscuring the effects of soil erosion on production. It is unclear whether we will suffer decreased yields in the future due to soil erosion, but it seems probable.

Finally, in spite of the many dire predictions to the contrary, we are not in danger of running out of oil or any other geologic resources. These will become more expensive, to be sure but the experience of the U.S. in the 1970s showed that the nation is quite capable of reducing its consumption of oil and of finding replacement energy sources, even after a relatively minor increase in price. The effects of that price rise on the lives of most Americans are minor when compared to the effects of fluctuations in business cycles or dramatic shifts in government policy.

Thus, the major environmental problems discussed most today are either being substantially reduced or are ambiguous with regard to their true severity. There is no ambiguity in my mind about the severity of poverty, malnutrition, or war.

Having said all of this, I want to recognize that there are some environmental problems that rival socially induced problems in their impact on human welfare in the next few decades. Most important of these are the factors influencing world agricultural production, particularly climate change and land degradation. Most climatologists now agree that a climatic change caused by CO_2 and other atmospheric pollutants is inevitable in the next few decades. It remains to be seen how large this change will be and how rapidly it will come about. It is probable that the change will cause weather conditions that farmers are unprepared for. It therefore seems likely that the world agricultural system will be increasingly affected by adverse weather, be it too dry, too wet, or too whatever. Land degradation by soil erosion, depletion of nutrients, and conversion to other uses will also add stresses to the food production system. Any one of these stresses can theoretically be overcome in a given location, but, taken as a group, they are so widespread that reversing them globally seems unlikely. They are chronic rather than acute problems, and this too will tend to prevent attention from being focused on them. As long as farmers tend to be poor rather than rich, there is little hope that they will be able to make the investments necessary to overcome poor soil fertility and adverse weather conditions.

In addition to these agricultural problems, it is likely that water supply, water quality, and energy availability will probably become much more significant problems in the next few decades than they have been in the recent past. They will continue to be among the major factors keeping poor nations poor, aggravating problems of health and welfare in the Third World and international tension in general.

Even though these are environmental problems, their solutions are political and economic, rather than requiring some direct technological approach to water management or energy conservation. Given sufficient capital, poor land can be made to produce high yields, clean water can be made available, energy can be supplied or conserved, all without a significant decline in the standard of living. This has been clearly demonstrated in the wealthy nations. What is needed in the Third World are the economic resources and political freedom to make the necessary investments, along with the return of the proceeds of those investments to the land and people that need it most. Only when economic and political changes come about to make this possible will significant progress be made in solving the really important environmental problems. The most pressing environmental problems facing us today are not truly environmental problems. They are economic and political problems.

William H. Renwick

RESOURCE SCARCITY: LEAN YEARS, MEAN YEARS

Throughout this text, we have stressed that the conservation and use of natural resources is a political and economic issue. The access to and allocation of resources is thus controlled by economic and political considerations. Resource scarcity, then, can be viewed as the lack of access to resources. Resource scarcity arises from inequities in the supply of a particular resource, usually as a consequence of some natural or human calamity that temporarily decreases the supply or affects the distribution. These calamities can be natural hazards, such as frost or drought, or they can be human hazards, such as armed conflicts, all of which are capable of disrupting the supply of a particular resource for short or long periods of time. The four-year-old war between Iran and Iraq in the Persian Gulf is one example of the effect of armed conflict on global resource dependencies. Over half of the noncommunist world's oil comes from the Persian Gulf region, and more than 50 percent of Japan's and 30 percent of western Europe's oil supply is from that region. The armed conflict between Iran and Iraq has taken on a new dimension, as daily raids on oil tankers in the Gulf and threats to close the vital Straits of Hormuz have dramatically increased the price of oil (largely as a result of huge insurance premiums) coming from the region. How did we place ourselves in such a precarious position?

Wars are fought for both important and unimportant reasons—boredom, revenge, intolerance of cultural differences. We also fight over territory and the resources in those territories. Most of the important armed conflicts in human history have been fought under the guise of nationalism, but a closer look reveals that access to natural resources (one of the themes of this text) is at least as important as nationalism. With increasing inequities between the less developed resource-rich and the developed resource-poor nations, the number of potential armed conflicts increases. Not all of these will be directly related to natural resources, but many may indirectly affect or limit the international community's access to those vital resources.

A number of historical examples illustrate this theme. Geopolitics, defined by the German philosopher Karl Haushofer, refers to the "geographical conscience" of a nation state and includes its right to protect and defend its living space. This includes not only the land and resources within its borders but also those outside its borders that are critical to the well-being of the nation. This viewpoint has been used to justify the territorial expansion of nations. During the period of westward expansion in the United States, for example, the term Manifest Destiny was used to justify the armed expulsion of native Americans to gain control over western resources. Geopolitical pressures were also behind the actions of Nazi Germany that triggered World War II. In general, historians and political scientists have been able to document the social, economic, and cultural aspects of Haushofer's "geographical conscience." What is not so evident from the history books, however, is the crucial role that natural resources play in maintaining political control.

As resource scarcities develop, will we see an increase in the use of military power to protect or gain access to natural resources? I worry that current inequities in the distribution and use of resources will lead to the addition of "resource determinism" to nations' foreign policies.

We are faced with two types of warfare today: a war between superpowers using nuclear weapons, and smaller wars fought with conventional weapons. From 1945 to 1982, more than 300 small, conventional wars were fought in 70 countries. Each is a potential spark for a worldwide nuclear war. Many of these have been fought over natural resources or have been financed by natural resource wealth. For example, Iran's war efforts have been totally financed by oil revenues since the early 1980s. If no one buys Iranian oil, then the country has few finances to purchase arms. In 1981 Argentina invaded the Malvinas (Falkland Islands). Britain responded, and an armed conflict followed. Many blame this war on the nationalistic pride of both participants, not on access to natural resources. Is it coincidence, then, that both Britain and Argentina have overlapping territorial claims to nearby Antarctica, including its vast mineral wealth, and that their access to those claims could only be enhanced by clear title to the Malvinas? Is it also coincidental that the 200-mile-wide Exclusive Economic Zone around the islands contains currently exploitable fish, oil, and gas resources?

Is the foreign policy of the U.S. dictated by this resource determinism? Is U.S. support for governments with poor human-rights records, such as South Africa, tied to access to oil or strategic minerals? Is the Soviet Union's foreign policy controlled by similar pressures? Answers to such questions are clearly speculative, but two developments lead me to believe that "resource wars" will be more frequent and more dangerous in the future. These two developments are the global patterns of arms sales, and the actions of multinational corporations.

Increasingly sophisticated military technology permits many smaller nations to amass weaponry and other tools of destruction to protect "national" interests. Nearly 75 percent of the Third World countries import sophisticated weapons, to maintain domestic political control or to wage war on their neighbors. Nearly 80 percent of the imports are provided by the U.S. and the Soviet Union. A closer look at arms sales by the two superpowers shows a direct symbiotic relationship between the location of raw resources in the Third World countries, their use in manufacturing in the industrialized nations, and the export of finished weapons and weapons systems to the Third World. These weapons, fashioned from the very resources of the Third World itself, are being used in the many small conventional wars around the world, often with the tacit approval of one or more of the superpowers.

There are many examples of how the actions of multinational corporations and resource cartels influence domestic and international politics, as in the merchants of grain discussion in Chapter 6. Increasingly, decisions on the rate of exploitation of natural resources are being made not by governments but instead by corporations operating under very different political and economic constraints. Loss of control over production leads to a lower return on investment. This is one reason multinational corporations are vehemently opposed to nationalization of resources. The U.S.-aided overthrow of the Allende government in Chile in the early 1970s has been linked to the protection of multinational copper interests, largely based in the U.S. American capitalists' fear that the Marxist regime would have nationalized the copper mines and forced the multinationals out, thus denying access to resources and loss of revenues.

The power of the multinationals, coupled with the arming of resource-rich, politically important Third World nations, makes the prospect of resource wars very real. If the resource cartels and multinationals band together to protect their interests, we may see a new map of the world. Instead of Canada and the U.S., we may see North America, a political entity controlled by Exxon, Cargill, and Weyerheuser. We may see a new nation called OPEC or De Beers, exercising control over strategic resources, such as oil, platinum, and diamonds, and selling them to the highest bidder. While this may seem a little far-fetched, some would argue that this future vision is already present. What do you think?

Susan L. Cutter

WILL IT BE LIKE THIS?

Eileen had always been a happy woman, but lately she suspected that Mother Nature was out to get her. Today was New Year's Eve, 1999, but she didn't feel like celebrating. Her memories of childhood in the 1970s made the new century pale by comparison.

She gazed out the back door of her home at the once-beautiful ocean-front view. Nowadays the sight simply filled her with fear. She had placed a meter stick in the shallow water that covered what was once her backyard, and she was pretty sure the water had risen a millimeter over the past week. Her friends said she was imagining things, but she took the eventual consequences a lot more seriously than they did: the submergence of the beautiful New Jersey shore cottage she'd been given by her grandparents. Her parents had taken early retirement when they reached fifty and had moved north with her grandparents to the Canadian Warmbelt some years previously. The weather was still uneven along the St. Lawrence, but Mom and Dad's videocalls were full of excitement when yet another warming trend month was announced. They had made a bet on the global warming and had won.

Eileen, on the other hand, had let sentiment overrule sense when she'd chosen to make a year-round home out of the site of so many childhood memories. The sea-level problem had begun to intrude itself about two years ago, when her husband Tom noticed that their dock was nearly submerged at high tide. Its being so gradual, she hadn't noticed, but Tom's eyes were those of a visitor. He was on home leave from the United Business Ventures space station, where he was business manager of the Planetary Prospecting Project. So they'd raised the dock, but the water had kept pace, and Eileen hadn't had the energy to get the dock raised again this past summer. Now seawater slapped across its surface and was beginning to seep into their septic system. Eileen's six-year-old daughter said the drinking water was salty. Eileen didn't want to know. Nowadays she felt safe only when she and the two kids boarded the 7 A.M. strato-bullet to Outer Halifax, where she worked in the World Waste Watch monitoring center, after dropping the kids off at the regional International School. It was a two-hour commute each way, but, considering where her husband worked, she didn't complain.

Eileen's job in the Information Flow Subcenter was so interesting that she had little time to be depressed about the implications of her research. Her team was working on the synthesis and interpretation of the pioneering collection work of the late 1980s to mid-1990s. This massive project collected all known information on the location and character of the earth's toxic waste dumps, spills, accidents, and storage areas, both on land and in the sea. Eileen's research group had developed a global model to help in predicting localized and large-scale effects of this waste on the biosphere. One of their frequent tasks was to announce their predictions as to the poisoning of water supplies, fishing areas, and agricultural acreage, as the long-buried wastes worked their way through the ground and along the ocean's currents.

Occasionally Eileen found herself being interviewed for the Global News Service, trying to give a low-key answer to a reporter asking if a toxic waste was to blame for the latest outbreak of Industrial Disease Syndrome in southern Africa. She was thankful that she didn't work for the Precipitation Watch research group. They had a lot to explain, what with the failure of crops worldwide, year after year. They had no simple answers to give, either. They had to talk to the general world public in terms of both acid precipitation and CO_2 buildup, not to mention the climatic backlash caused by the melting ice caps. Global Newsviewers were uncomfortable with complicated answers. They wanted food on the table, and they wanted an end to the massive forced migrations of starved people. The world's cities were sprawling, wretched places, and all the trade and immigration barriers that a series of conservative United States administrations had erected were not enough to keep the unhappy flow at bay. Global Newsviewers wanted solutions, not scientific explanations.

As well paid as Eileen and her husband were, she still had found it a struggle to get a nice feast together for tonight's New Year's Eve party. There had been no flour for sale for two weeks, while the government developed an emergency rationing plan. Nonstop rain the previous summer had wiped out the wheat crop nationwide, after a two-year recovery from the '94 to '96 Climatic Disaster years. So the table was a little light on pastries. Good thing she'd taken the grape shortage seriously last summer and put up two cases of dandelion and elderberry wine. It would be a merry party, the first since the beer and liquor industries had laid off hundreds of thousands of workers when governments worldwide seized their grain stocks for food.

Through her work, Eileen had been able to order some meat for the holiday season, so that she and the kids had had a hamburger stew for Christmas dinner. She'd saved a kilo for tonight, however, and with the discreet addition of soybean concentrate, she'd produced a handsome pot of meatballs. She hoped her generosity would not be interpreted as showing off. Friends were bringing other goodies, homemade from locally collected wild crops. There had been a big newspaper article last week on Holiday Meals from Your Roadside Larder.

Tony and Tara ran in from the front yard, for once not needing to be reminded that their ultraviolet exposure time was up. It was a system that needed getting used to, but they dutifully watched the ozone-depletion readings every morning on the news and followed the guidelines. At least Eileen had managed to locate a reliable water-supply company, Alaskan Pure. She suspected that the water was actually from the Appalachians, but as long as it was well above the minimum on the toxicity standards, she didn't complain. The water tank needed cleaning, though. But she'd think about that in the New Year.

Could this be your life in 1999? Well paid, an interesting job, but somehow things just aren't what they used to be, and the necessities of life hard to come by?

Hilary Lambert Renwick

Glossary

Note: Numbers in parentheses following definitions refer to chapters.

Absolute scarcity
A condition in which there is not enough of a resource in existence to satisfy demand for it. (1)

Acid rain
The deposition of acids, either in precipitation or through dry dust fall, on the land surface. (11)

Advection inversion
A temperature inversion caused by passage of warm air over a cool surface. (11)

Age structure
The relative proportions of a population in different age classes. (5)

Agribusiness
Large-scale, organized production of food, farm machinery, and supplies, as well as the storage, sale, and distribution of farm commodities, for profit. (6)

Amenity value
The non-monetary, intangible value of a good or service. (13)

Anadromous fish
Fish that breed in fresh water but spend most of their adult lives in salt water. Examples are salmon and striped bass. (12)

Anoxic
Water without dissolved oxygen. (12)

Appropriate technology
Technology that is within the social, economic, and material means of those using it. (16)

Aquiclude
An impermeable layer that confines an aquifer, preventing the water in it from moving upward or downward into adjacent strata. Shale and some igneous rocks often form aquicludes. (9)

Aquifer
A geologic unit containing groundwater; an underground reservoir made up of porous material capable of holding usable quantities of water. (9)

Arable land
Land that is capable of being cultivated and supporting agricultural production. (6)

Arroyo
A deep, steep-sided gully found in semiarid areas, particularly in the southwestern U.S. (7)

Benefit-cost analysis
A process of quantitatively evaluating all the positive and negative aspects of a particular action, to reach a rational decision regarding that action. (2)

Biochemical oxygen demand
The amount of oxygen used in oxidation of substances in a given water sample, measured in milligrams per liter, over a specific time period. (10)

Biogeochemical cycle
A general term used to describe the storage and flow of materials within the earth's system. Examples are hydrologic, carbon, and phosphorus cycles.

Biological diversity
The range or number of species or subspecies found in a particular area. (4)

Biomagnification
The process whereby pesticides or other pollutants become increasingly concentrated in living organisms as the pollutants are passed up a food chain. (10)

Biomass
The total amount of living or formerly living matter in a given area, measured as dry weight. (4)

Biome
A major ecological region within which plant and animal communities are similar in general characteristics and in their relations to the physical environment. (4)

Biosphere
The worldwide system within which all life functions; composed of smaller systems, including the atmosphere, hydrosphere, and lithosphere. (4)

Biotic potential
The maximum rate of population growth that would result if all females in a population bred as often as possible and all individuals survived past their reproductive periods. (4)

Blight
Visually undesirable modification of a landscape. (13)

British Thermal Unit (BTU)
The amount of energy required to raise the temperature of one pound of water one degree Fahrenheit at or near 39.2 degrees Fahrenheit. (15)

Bubble approach
An approach to air pollution emissions control that allows a plant to consider emissions from several sources as combined emissions from the plant. (11)

Carcinogen
A substance that causes cancer. (10)

Carrying capacity
The maximum number of organisms of one species that can be supported in a particular environmental setting. (4)

Cartel
A consortium of producers who agree to control production so as to keep the price of the product high or otherwise enhance profits. OPEC is an example of a natural resource cartel. (2)

Catadromous fish
Fish that breed in salt water but live most of their adult lives in fresh water. The American eel is an example.

Chaparral
A subtropical drought-resistant and fire-prone shrubby vegetation, associated with Mediterranean-type climates. (4)

Chlorofluorocarbons
A group of substances that are compounds of chlorine, fluorine, and carbon. They are widely used in refrigeration and many industrial processes and may contribute to deterioration of stratospheric ozone. (11)

Coal gasification
A chemical process converting coal to a gas that can be used in place of natural gas. (15)

Cohort
A group of individuals of similar age, social class, or other characteristic. (5)

Coliform bacteria
Bacteria of the species *Escherichia coli,* commonly occurring in the digestive tracts of animals. An indicator of the potential for disease-causing organisms in water. (10)

Common property resource
A resource, such as air, oceans, sunshine, or public land that in theory is owned by everyone but which may be utilized by only a few. (2)

Community
A collection of organisms occupying a specific geographic area. (4)

Conservation
The wise use or careful management of resources, so as to attain the maximum possible social benefits from them. (3)

Consumptive use
Water use that results in water being lost by evaporation or transpiration, rather than returned to surface or groundwater, after use. (9)

Continental shelf
Area of the sea floor, averaging less than 200 meters (60 feet) deep, which generally was exposed at past times of lower sea level. (12)

Contour plowing
A soil conservation technique of plowing parallel to land contours, across a slope rather than up and down it. (6)

Cost-effectiveness analysis
An analysis of all the costs of taking a specified action, to determine the most efficient way to carry out the chosen action. (2)

Critical mineral
As defined by the U.S. government, a mineral necessary for national defense, available partly domestically and partly from friendly nations. (14)

Crop rotation
The soil conservation technique of changing the crops grown on a given parcel of land from year to year. Crop rotations may include fallow periods. (6)

Decreaser
A plant species in a range community that declines in importance as a result of grazing pressure. Usually decreasers are the plants that are most palatable to the grazing animals. (7)

Deep ocean
Ocean areas seaward of the continental shelf. (12)

Desertification
The process of land's becoming more desert-like, as a result of human-induced devegetation and related soil deterioration, sometimes aggravated by drought. (7)

Diversification
The trend in many large corporations toward owning a wide array of companies, producing unrelated goods and services. (2)

Domesticated species
A species that has been bred for specific characteristics that humans value, thereby rendering the species dependent on humans for its continued survival. (7)

Doubling time
The length of time needed for a population to double in size. It is a function of the growth rate. (5)

Drainage basin
An area bounded by drainage divides, defined with respect to a point along a stream. All the runoff generated within the area passes the point along the stream; runoff generated outside the basin does not pass that point. (9)

Drip irrigation
An irrigation method in which small pipes are placed at the base of plants, delivering water slowly to the plant roots. (6)

Dry farming
Agricultural production in climatically marginal lands without the use of irrigation. (6)

Dynamic
In reference to a system, exhibiting the tendency to change in response to changing conditions. (1)

Ecology
The study of the interrelationships between living organisms and the living and nonliving components and processes that make up the environment. (4)

Economic value
The value of a good or service as determined by the price it would fetch in the marketplace. (13)

Ecosystem
The collection of all living organisms in a geographic area, together with all living and nonliving things they interact with. (1, 4)

Ecotone
A transitional zone between two ecosystems. (4)

Endangered species
A species in imminent danger of extinction. (13)

Energy budget
An accounting of all energy inputs and outputs for a system. (4)

Entropy
A measure of disorder in a system. According to the second law of thermodynamics, systems tend toward increasing entropy. (4)

Environmental cognition
The mental process of making sense of the world we inhabit. (1)

Environmental lapse rate
The average rate at which temperature declines with increasing altitude in the troposphere. (11)

Environmental resistance
Such factors as food supply, weather, disease, and predators that keep a population below its biotic potential. (4)

Erosion
Removal of soil by running water or wind. (6)

Estuary
A semienclosed water body, open to the sea, in which sea water is significantly diluted by fresh water from the land. (12)

Euphotic zone
The upper portion of the sea, in which sunlight is intense enough to allow plant growth. (12)

Eutrophication
The process by which lakes become increasingly nutrient-rich and shallow. It is a natural process that is accelerated by water pollution. (10)

Evapotranspiration
The process, including water use by plants, by which liquid water is conveyed to the atmosphere as water vapor. (9)

Exclusive economic zone
A zone of the oceans over which a particular nation has or claims exclusive control of certain economic activities, such as fishing. (12)

Exotic species
A species found in but not native to a particular area. (13)

Externality
A cost outside of the production and marketing that produces it. (2)

Extinction
The process by which a species ceases to exist. (13)

Feedback
Information transmission that produces a circular flow of information in a system. (1, 16)

Fertility rate
The average number of children that women in a given population bear during their reproductive years. (5)

Fire frequency
The average number of fires per unit time at a given location. (8)

First law of thermodynamics
The law of conservation of energy, which states that energy is neither created nor destroyed but merely transformed from one state to another or converted to or from matter. (4)

Fission
The splitting of heavy atomic nuclei, e.g., uranium or plutonium, into nuclei of lighter elements, thereby releasing energy in the process. (15)

Fixed costs
Costs of operating a business that do not vary with the rate of output of goods and services. (2)

Flood irrigation
A means of irrigation whereby entire fields are occasionally inundated. (6)

Flow resource
A resource that is simultaneously used and replaced. Perpetual and renewable resources are flow resources. (1, 14)

Food chain
A linear path that food energy takes in passing from producer to consumers to decomposers in an ecosystem. (4)

Food web
A complex, interlocking set of paths that food energy takes in passing from producer to consumers to decomposers in an ecosystem. (4)

Forecast
A prediction of the future based on actual or assumed past, present, or future conditions. Forecasts may be unconditional, conditional, exploratory, or prescriptive. (16)

Furrow irrigation
A type of irrigation, in which water is allowed to flow along the furrows (troughs) between rows of crops. (6)

Genetic damage
Damage to individual cell tissues, resulting in changes in chromosomes that are passed along to offspring. (15)

Greenhouse effect
The result of the fact that the atmosphere is relatively transparent to shortwave solar radiation but opaque to longwave terrestrial radiation, causing a warming of the atmosphere. (11)

Ground fish
Bottom-dwelling fish that feed on plants and animals of the seabed. (12)

Groundwater
Water below the ground surface, derived from the percolation of rainfall and seepage from surface water. (9)

Halocline
A marked change in salinity at a particular depth in the ocean or an estuary, signaling the boundary between two layers of water. (12)

High seas
Areas of the oceans beyond the legal control of any nation. (12)

Homosphere
The lower portion of the earth's atmosphere, characterized by relatively uniform gaseous composition. It consists of the troposphere, the stratosphere, and the mesosphere. (11)

Incommensurables
Effects of a given action that do not normally have monetary value, but can, with some effort, be assigned such value. (2)

Increaser
A range plant species that is present in a range ecosystem prior to grazing and increases in numbers or coverage as a result of grazing. (7)

Incrementalism
A type of decision-making strategy that reacts to short-term imperfections in existing policies rather than establishing long-term future goals. Decisions are made on a sequential, step-by-step basis and do not radically depart from existing policy. (3)

Infiltration capacity
The maximum rate at which a soil can absorb water. (4, 6)

Inorganic
Not containing carbon; used of chemical substances. (10)

Input
Energy, matter, or information entering a system. (1)

In-stream uses
Uses of water that do not require it to be removed from a stream or lake. These include such things as shipping, swimming, and waste disposal. (9)

Intangible
A good, service, or effect of an action that cannot be assigned monetary value. (2)

Integrated pest management
A pest-control technique that relies on combinations of crop rotation, biological controls, and pesticides. (6)

Internal waters
Waters under the exclusive control of a coastal nation, including bays, estuaries, and rivers. (12)

Invader
A range plant species not present in a given area before grazing, but entering the area as a result of the ecological changes caused by grazing. (7)

Kerogen
A waxy hydrocarbon found in oil shale. (15)

Land capability classification system
A scheme used by the U.S. Soil Conservation Service for assessing and classifying productivity of land units. (6)

Light-water reactor
A type of nuclear power plant that uses ordinary water as the cooling medium. (15)

Maximum sustainable yield
The largest average harvest of a species that can be indefinitely sustained under existing environmental conditions. (12)

Mesosphere
Layer of the atmosphere between 50 and 80 kilometers in altitude, characterized by decreasing temperatures with increasing altitude. (11)

Minimum tillage
A soil and water conservation technique that leaves the crop residue or stubble on the surface rather than plowing it under, to minimize the number of times the field is tilled. Weeds are controlled by use of herbicides. (6)

Mobile sources
Sources of air pollution that move, such as automobiles, boats, trains, and aircraft. (11)

Model
A representation of the real world that can be used to help understand or predict the operation of that world. (16)

Monoculture
An agricultural system in which a sole crop is grown repeatedly over a large area. (6)

Monopoly
Exclusive control of access to a good or service. (2)

Multiple use
The use of lands for as many different purposes as possible, to gain maximum benefit from them. (3)

Mutagen
A substance that produces genetic mutations. (15)

Non-point source
A pollution source that is diffuse, such as urban runoff. (10)

Non-renewable or stock resources
Resources that exist in finite quantity and are not replaced in nature. (1)

Oligopolistic competition
A process in which a small group controls access to a good or service by agreeing on a single price or by permitting limited access to these commodities by other buyers and sellers. (2)

Oligotrophic
Of lakes, relatively deep and nutrient-poor. Opposite of eutrophic. (10)

Organic
Substance originally derived from living matter. (10)

Output
Energy, matter, or information leaving a system. (1)

Overburden
Rock and soil that lie above coal or other mineral deposits and must be removed to strip-mine the coal. (15)

Overdraft or groundwater mining
Withdrawal of groundwater in excess of its replacement rate over a long period of time. (9)

Overgrazing
Grazing by a number of animals exceeding the carrying capacity of a given parcel of land. (7)

Oxidants
A group of air pollutants that are strong oxidizing agents. Ozone and peroxy-acetylnitrate are among the more important oxidants. (11)

Parent material
The mineral matter from which soil is formed. (6)

Pastoralist
A person whose livelihood is based on grazing animals. (7)

Pastoral nomad
A person who herds animals from place to place, with no permanent settlement. (7)

Permafrost
Permanently frozen layer of ground below the surface. (4)

Perpetual resources
Resources that exist in "perpetual" supply, no matter how much they are used. Solar energy is an example. (1)

Pesticide
A chemical used to control harmful organisms, such as insects, fungi, rodents, worms, and bacteria. Insecticides, fungicides, and rodenticides are kinds of pesticides. (6)

Photosynthesis
The formation of carbohydrates from carbon dioxide and water by chlorophyll-containing plants, utilizing light as energy. (4)

Placer deposit
A deposit of a mineral formed by concentration of heavy minerals in flowing water, such as by a stream or waves. (14)

Point source
A pollution source that has a precise, identifiable location, such as a pipe or smokestack. (12)

Polluter pays principle, or residuals tax
A means of shifting the cost of pollution from the community to the polluter, usually in the form of a tax. (2)

Pollution
Human additions of undesirable substances to the environment. (10)

Pollution standards index
A composite index of air quality that reports pollution levels in health-related terms. (11)

Potable water
Water suitable for human consumption. (9)

Potential evapotranspiration
The amount of water that could be evaporated or transpired if it were available. (4)

Potential resource
A portion of the natural or human environment that is not today considered of value but that one day may gain value as a result of technological, cognitive, or economic developments. (1)

Preservation
The nonuse of resources. Limited resource development for the purpose of saving resources for the future. (3)

Primary standards
Air pollution standards designed to protect human health. (11)

Primary treatment
Sewage treatment consisting of removal of solids by sedimentation, flocculation, screening, or similar methods. (10)

Principle of limiting factors
The principle that whatever factor (nutrient, water, sunlight, etc.) is in shortest supply limits the growth and development of an organism or a community. (4)

Proxy value
A price applied to a commodity that has no established market value. (2)

Quad
A measure of energy use, equal to one quadrillion (1,000,000,000,000,000) British Thermal Units (BTUs). (15)

Radioactivity
The emission of particles by the decay of the atoms of certain substances. (10, 15)

Radiation inversion
A temperature inversion caused by radiational cooling of air close to the ground. (11)

Range
Land that provides or is capable of providing forage for grazing animals. (7)

Recreational river
A designation applied by the U.S. Department of the Interior to rivers that are easily reached, usually developed, and heavily used. (13)

Recycling
Reprocessing of a used product for use in a similar or different form. (14)

Relative scarcity
Short supply of a resource in one or more areas due to inadequate or disrupted distribution. (1)

Renewable resource
A resource that can be depleted but can be replenished by natural processes. Forests and fisheries are examples. (1)

Replacement cost
The cost of replacing a resource that is used. (2)

Reserve
Of mineral resources, a deposit of known location and quality that is economically extractable at present. (14)

Resource recovery
Separation of garbage and trash into recyclable components, such as metal, glass, and heat from incineration. (14)

Respiration
Oxidation of food by living organisms, releasing oxygen, water, and energy which is dissipated in the biosphere. (4)

Reuse
Repeated use of a product without reprocessing or remanufacture. (14)

Salinity
The concentration of mineral salts in water. The average salinity of the oceans is about 35 parts per thousand. (12)

Saltwater intrusion
Movement of salt water into aquifers formerly occupied by fresh water, as a result of groundwater withdrawal in coastal areas. (9)

Satisficing
A decision-making strategy that seeks a course of action that is good enough but not necessarily perfect. A few alternatives are compared, and the best course of action is chosen from this limited range of options. (3)

Savanna
Tropical or subtropical semiarid grassland with scattered trees. (4)

Scenic river
A designation applied by the U.S. Department of the Interior to rivers with strong amenity value that are accessible at certain points by motor vehicles and sustain some development along their shorelines. (13)

Secondary standard
An air quality standard designed to protect human welfare (property, vegetation, etc.), as opposed to primary standards, which protect health. (11)

Secondary treatment
Sewage treatment that removes organic matter and nutrients by biological decomposition, using methods such as trickling filters, aeration, and activated sludge. (10)

Sedentarization
Permanent settlement of once-nomadic people. (7)

Sedimentation
Deposition of solid particles in a water body by settling. (10)

Separate impacts
Effects of a system's activity that can be measured separately. (1)

Social cost
The cost of producing a good or service, plus its cost to humans in pollution and other negative socioenvironmental effects. (2)

Soil fertility
The ability of a soil to supply essential nutrients to plants. (6)

Soil texture
The mix of different sizes of particles in a soil. (6)

Somatic damage
Nonhereditary damage to individual cell tissues from radiation. (15)

Source separation
The sorting of waste materials into recyclable components at the place of waste generation. (14)

Species
A group of organisms with similar genetic and morphologic characteristics, capable of interbreeding. (13)

Spent fuel
Nuclear material that is no longer capable of sustaining the fission process. (15)

Sprinkler irrigation
Irrigation by pumping water under pressure through nozzles and spraying it over the land. (6)

Static
Exhibiting an absence of change; of a system, having the tendency not to respond to changing conditions. (1)

Stationary source
A pollution source that does not move, such as a smokestack. (11)

Steady state system
A system in which the amount of energy and matter flowing in is equal to that flowing out. (1)

Stockpiling
Amassing supplies of some substance well beyond present need, in anticipation of a shortage of that substance. (14)

Strategic mineral
A mineral essential to national defense, for which the U.S. is totally dependent on foreign sources. (14)

Stratification
The layering of a water body, because of differences in water density, commonly caused by temperature or salinity differences. (10, 12)

Stratosphere
Layer of the atmosphere between 15 and 50 kilometers in altitude, characterized by increasing temperature with altitude. (11)

Stress management
A decision-making strategy that is reactive in nature. Once a resource issue becomes critical, then policy is determined to cope with the immediate problem, without any consideration of the long-term implications of such a policy. (3)

Strip cropping
A soil conservation technique in which parallel strips of land are planted in different crops. (6)

Subeconomic resource
A resource that is unavailable for use at present because of the high cost of its extraction. (14)

Subsidence
Sinking of the land surface, caused by removal of water, oil, or minerals from beneath the surface. (9)

Subsidence inversion
A temperature inversion caused by differential warming of a sinking air mass. Upper portions of the mass are warmed more than lower portions, causing the inversion. (11)

Surface water
Water and ice found in rivers, lakes, swamps, and other above-ground water bodies. (9)

Suspended particulates
In air, solid or liquid particles with diameters from .03 to 100 microns. In water, solid particles transported in suspension.

Sustained yield
Management of renewable resources in such a way as to allow a constant rate of harvest indefinitely. (3)

Synergistic impacts
Effects of a system's activity that are different from the individual effects of component parts of the system. (1)

Synfuel
A contraction of *synthetic fuel.* Liquid or gaseous fossil fuel manufactured from other fuels that are less useful as found in nature. (15)

System
An entity consisting of a set of parts that work together, forming a whole. The human body, a transportation network, and the earth are all systems. (1)

Tar sand
Sandy deposits containing heavy oil or tar, which can be extracted by heating the sand. (15)

Temperature inversion
A condition in the atmosphere in which warm air overlies cool air. Inversions restrict vertical air circulation. (11)

Terracing
A soil and water conservation technique in which ridges are built on the contour, or level areas constructed on a slope. (6)

Territorial sea
A band of open ocean adjacent to the coast, over which the coastal nation has control. It is generally either three or twelve miles wide. (12)

Tertiary treatment
Any of a wide range of advanced sewage-treatment processes aimed at removing substances not removed by primary or secondary treatment. (10)

Thermal pollution
Heat added by humans to a water body or to the air. (10)

Threatened species
A species that is not endangered but has a rapidly declining population. (13)

Throughput tax or disposal charge
A fee paid by a producer on materials that go into the production of polluting products. The fee reflects the social cost of the pollution. (2)

Trophic level
One of the steps in a food chain where all organisms are the same number of steps away from primary producers. (4)

Troposphere
The lowest layer of the atmosphere, below about 15 kilometers altitude, characterized by decreasing temperature with increasing altitude. (11)

Tundra
A biome found in arctic and subarctic regions, consisting of a dense growth of lichens, mosses, and herbs. (4)

Universal Soil Loss Equation
A statistical technique developed by the U.S. Department of Agriculture for predicting the average erosion rate by rainfall under a variety of climatic, soil, topographic, and management conditions. (6)

Upwelling
An upward movement of seawater that usually occurs near the margins of oceans. (12)

Utility
Value placed on a good or service, expressed as a price. (2)

Variable costs
Costs of production that vary with the rate of output. (2)

Water holding capacity
The ability of the soil to retain or store water. (6)

Water table
The upper limit of groundwater or of the saturated zone.

Wild river
A designation applied by the U.S. Department of the Interior to rivers with strong amenity value that are inaccessible by motorized vehicles and have undeveloped shorelines. (13)

Willingness to pay
A method of determining the proxy value of a resource by asking how much users of that resource would be willing to pay to use or not use it. (2)

Withdrawal

The removal of water from a surface or groundwater body. (9)

Zero population growth

A condition in which the fertility rate equals the death rate, leading to stable population size. (5)

Index

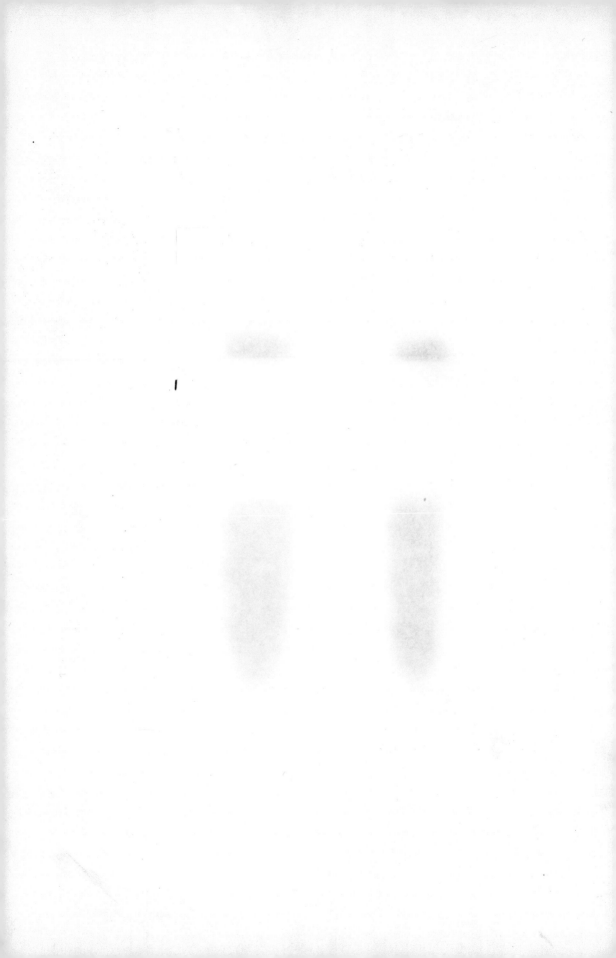